GLOBAL STUDIES

LATIN AMERICA

THIRTEENTH EDITION

Dr. Paul B. Goodwin Jr.
University of Connecticut, Storrs

OTHER BOOKS IN THE GLOBAL STUDIES SERIES
- Africa
- China
- Europe
- India and South Asia
- Islam and the Muslim World
- Japan and the Pacific Rim
- Russia, the Eurasian Republics, and Central/Eastern Europe
- The Middle East
- The World at a Glance

 **Higher Education**

Boston   Burr Ridge, IL   Dubuque, IA   New York   San Francisco   St. Louis
Bangkok   Bogotá   Caracas   Kuala Lumpur   Lisbon   London   Madrid   Mexico City
Milan   Montreal   New Delhi   Santiago   Seoul   Singapore   Sydney   Taipei   Toronto

Higher Education

GLOBAL STUDIES: LATIN AMERICA, THIRTEENTH EDITION

Published by McGraw-Hill, a business unit of The McGraw-Hill Companies, Inc., 1221 Avenue of the Americas, New York, NY 10020.

Some ancillaries, including electronic and print components, may not be available to customers outside the United States.

Global Studies® is a registered trademark of the McGraw-Hill Companies, Inc.
Global Studies is published by the **Contemporary Learning Series** group within the McGraw-Hill Higher Education division.

1 2 3 4 5 6 7 8 9 0 QPD/QPD 0 9 8

ISBN 978–0–07–337982–1
MHID 0–07–337982–4
ISSN 1061–2831

Managing Editor: *Larry Loeppke*
Senior Managing Editor: *Faye Schilling*
Developmental Editor: *Jade Benedict*
Editorial Coordinator: *Mary Foust*
Editorial Assistant: *Nancy Meissner*
Production Service Assistant: *Rita Hingtgen*
Permissions Coordinator: *Leonard J. Behnke*
Senior Marketing Manager: *Julie Keck*
Marketing Communications Specialist: *Mary Klein*
Marketing Coordinator: *Alice Link*
Senior Project Manager: *Jane Mohr*
Design Specialist: *Tara McDermott*
Cover Graphics: *Kristine Jubeck*

Compositor: Laserwords
Cover Image: Courtesy of Paul B. Goodwin

Library in Congress Cataloging-in-Publication Data
Main entry under title: Global Studies: Latin America, 13th ed.
     1. Latin America—History. 2. Central America—History. 3. South America—History.
I. Title: Latin America. II. Goodwin, Paul, Jrl., *comp.*
658'.05

www.mhhe.com

LATIN AMERICA

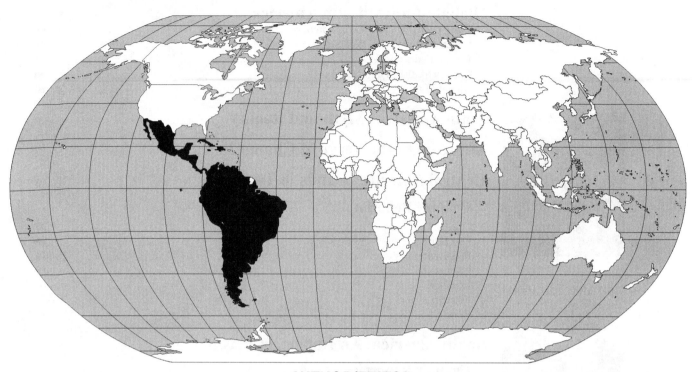

AUTHOR/EDITOR

Dr. Paul B. Goodwin Jr.

The author/editor for *Global Studies: Latin America* is a professor emeritus of Latin American history at the University of Connecticut, Storrs. Dr. Goodwin has written, reviewed, and lectured extensively at universities in the United States and many other countries. His particular areas of interest are modern Argentina and Anglo–Latin American relations. Dr. Goodwin has lectured frequently for the Smithsonian Institution, and he has authored or edited three books and numerous articles.

SERIES CONSULTANT

H. Thomas Collins
PROJECT LINKS
George Washington University

Contents

Articles from the World Press

Regional Articles

Mexico Articles

Central America Articles

South America Articles

Caribbean Aricles

Using Global Studies: Latin America

THE GLOBAL STUDIES SERIES

The Global Studies series was created to help readers acquire a basic knowledge and understanding of the regions and countries in the world. Each volume provides a foundation of information—geographic, cultural, economic, political, historical, artistic, and religious—that will allow readers to better assess the current and future problems within these countries and regions and to comprehend how events there might affect their own well-being. In short, these volumes present the background information necessary to respond to the realities of our global age.

Each of the volumes in the Global Studies series is crafted under the careful direction of an author/editor—an expert in the area under study. The author/editors teach and conduct research and have traveled extensively through the regions about which they are writing.

In *Global Studies: Latin America,* the author/editor has written several regional essays and country reports for each of the countries included.

MAJOR FEATURES OF THE GLOBAL STUDIES SERIES

The Global Studies volumes are organized to provide concise information on the regions and countries within those areas under study. The major sections and features of the books are described here.

Regional Essays

For *Global Studies: Latin America,* the author/editor has written several essays focusing on the religious, cultural, sociopolitical, and economic differences and similarities of the countries and peoples in the various subregions of the Latin America. Regional maps accompany the essays.

Country Reports

Concise reports are written for each of the countries within the region under study. These reports are the heart of each Global Studies volume. *Global Studies: Latin America, Thirteenth Edition,* contains 33 country reports, including 1 Mexico report, 7 reports for Central America, 12 for South America, and 13 for the Caribbean. The reports cover each *independent country* in Latin America.

The country reports are composed of five standard elements. Each report contains a detailed map visually positioning the country among its neighboring states; a summary of statistical information; a current essay providing important historical, geographical, political, cultural, and economic information; a historical timeline, offering a convenient visual survey of a few key historical events; and four "graphic indicators," with summary statements about the country in terms of development, freedom, health/welfare, and achievements.

A Note on the Statistical Reports

The statistical information provided for each country has been drawn from a wide range of sources. (The most frequently referenced are listed on page ii.) Every effort has been made to provide the most current and accurate information available. However, sometimes the information cited by these sources differs to some extent; and, all too often, the most current information available for some countries is somewhat dated. Aside from these occasional difficulties, the statistical summary of each country is generally quite complete and up to date. Care should be taken, however, in using these statistics (or, for that matter, any published statistics) in making hard comparisons among countries. We have also provided comparable statistics for the United States and Canada, which can be found on pages x and xi.

World Press Articles

Within each Global Studies volume is reprinted a number of articles carefully selected by our editorial staff and the author/editor from a broad range of international periodicals and newspapers. The articles have been chosen for currency, interest, and their differing perspectives on the subject countries. There are 21 articles in *Global Studies: Latin America, Thirteenth Edition.*

WWW Sites

An extensive annotated list of selected World Wide Web sites can be found on the next page (viii) in this edition of *Global Studies: Latin America.* In addition, the URL addresses for country-specific Web sites are provided on the statistics page of most countries. All of the Web site addresses were correct and operational at press time. Instructors and students alike are urged to refer to those sites often to enhance their understanding of the region and to keep up with current events.

Glossary, Bibliography, Index

At the back of each Global Studies volume, readers will find a glossary of terms and abbreviations, which provides a quick reference to the specialized vocabulary of the area under study and to the standard abbreviations used throughout the volume.

Following the glossary is a bibliography that lists general works, national histories, and current-events publications and periodicals that provide regular coverage on Latin America.

The index at the end of the volume is an accurate reference to the contents of the volume. Readers seeking specific information and citations should consult this standard index.

Currency and Usefulness

Global Studies: Latin America, like the other Global Studies volumes, is intended to provide the most current and useful information available necessary to understand the events that are shaping the cultures of the region today.

This volume is revised on a regular basis. The statistics are updated, regional essays and country reports revised, and world press articles replaced. In order to accomplish this task, we turn to our author/editor, our advisory boards, and—hopefully—to you, the users of this volume. Your comments are more than welcome. If you have an idea that you think will make the next edition more useful, an article or bit of information that will make it more current, or a general comment on its organization, content, or features that you would like to share with us, please send it in for serious consideration.

Selected World Wide Web Sites for Global Studies: Latin America

**Some Web sites are continually changing their structure and content,
so the information listed may not always be available.**

GENERAL SITES

CNN Online Page
http://www.cnn.com

U.S. 24-hour video news channel. News is updated every few hours.

C-SPAN Online
http://www.c-span.org

See especially C-SPAN International on the Web for International Programming Highlights and archived C-SPAN programs.

GlobalEdge
http://globaledge.msu.edu/ibrd/ibrd.asp

Connect to several international business links from this site. Included are links to a glossary of international trade terms, exporting data, international trade, current laws, and data on GATT, NAFTA, and MERCOSUR.

International Information Systems (University of Texas)
http://inic.utexas.edu

Gateway has pointers to international sites, including all Latin American countries.

Library of Congress Country Studies
http://lcweb2.loc.gov/frd/cs/cshome.html#toc

An invaluable resource for facts and analysis of 100 countries' political, economic, social, and national-security systems and installations.

Political Science Resources
http://www.psr.keele.ac.uk

Dynamic gateway to sources available via European addresses. Listed by country name, this site includes official government pages, official documents, speeches, election information, and political events.

ReliefWeb
http://www.reliefweb.int

UN's Department of Humanitarian Affairs clearinghouse for international humanitarian emergencies. It has daily updates, including Reuters and VOA, and PANA.

Social Science Information Gateway (SOSIG)
http://soig.esrc.bris.ac.uk/

Project of the Economic and Social Research Council (ESRC). It catalogs 22 subjects and lists developing countries' URL addresses.

United Nations System
http://www.sosig.ac.ulc/

The official Web site for the United Nations system of organizations. Everything is listed alphabetically, and data on UNICC and Food and Agriculture Organization are available.

UN Development Programme (UNDP)
http://www.undp.org

Publications and current information on world poverty, Mission Statement, UN Development Fund for Women, and much more. Be sure to see the Poverty Clock.

UN Environmental Programme (UNEP)
http://www.unep.org

Official site of UNEP with information on UN environmental programs, products, services, events, and a search engine.

U.S. Agency for International Development (USAID)
http://www.info.usaid.gov

Graphically presented U.S. trade statistics with Latin America and the Caribbean.

U.S. Central Intelligence Agency Home Page
http://www.odci.gov/cia/publications/factbook/index.htm

This site includes publications of the CIA, such as the World Factbook, Factbook on Intelligence, Handbook of International Economic Statistics, CIA Maps and Publications, and much more.

U.S. Department of State Home Page
http://www.state.gov/www/ind.html

Organized alphabetically (i.e., Country Reports, Human Rights, International Organizations, and more).

World Bank Group
http://www.worldbank.org

News (press releases, summary of new projects, speeches), publications, topics in development, and countries and regions. Links to other financial organizations are available.

World Health Organization (WHO)
http://www.who.ch

Maintained by WHO's headquarters in Geneva, Switzerland, the site uses Excite search engine to conduct keyword searches.

World Trade Organization
http://www.wto.org

Topics include foundation of world trade systems, data on textiles, intellectual property rights, legal frameworks, trade and environmental policies, and recent agreements.

MEXICO

The Mexican Government
http://world.presidencia.gob.mx

This site offers a brief overview of the organization of the Mexican Republic, including the Executive, Legislative, and Judicial Branches of the federal government.

Documents on Mexican Politics
http://www.cs.unb.ca/~alopez-o/polind.html

An archive of a large number of articles on Mexican democracy, freedom of the press, political parties, NAFTA, the economy, Chiapas, and so forth can be found on this Web site.

CENTRAL AMERICA

Central America News/Planeta
http://www.planeta.com/ecotravel/period/pubcent.html

Access to data that includes individual country reports, politics, economic news, travel, media coverage, and links to other sites are available here.

Latin World
http://www.latinworld.com

Connecting links to data on the economy and finance, businesses, culture, government, and other areas of interest are available on this site.

SOUTH AMERICA

South America Daily

http://www.southamericadaily.com

Everything you want to know about South America is available from this site—from arts and culture, to government data, to environment issues, to individual countries.

CARIBBEAN

Caribbean Studies

http://www.hist.unt.edu/09w-blk4.htm

A complete site for information about the Caribbean. Topics include general information, Caribbean religions, English Caribbean Islands, Dutch Caribbean Islands, French Caribbean Islands, Hispanic Caribbean Islands, and the U.S. Virgin Islands.

Library of Congress Report on the Islands of the Commonwealth Caribbean

http://lcweb2.loc.gov/frd/cs/extoc.html

An extended study of the Caribbean is possible from this site.

We highly recommend that you review our Web site for expanded information and our other product lines. We are continually updating and adding links to our Web site in order to offer you the most usable and useful information that will support and expand the value of your book. You can reach us at: *http://www.mhcls.com*.

The United States (United States of America)

GEOGRAPHY

Area in Square Miles (Kilometers):
3,717,792 (9,629,091) (about 1/2 the size of Russia)

Capital (Population): Washington, D.C. (3,997,000)

Environmental Concerns: air and water pollution; limited freshwater resources, desertification; loss of habitat; waste disposal; acid rain

Geographical Features: vast central plain, mountains in the west, hills and low mountains in the east; rugged mountains and broad river valleys in Alaska; volcanic topography in Hawaii

Climate: mostly temperate, but ranging from tropical to arctic

PEOPLE
Population

Total: 293,000,000

Annual Growth Rate: 0.89%

Rural/Urban Population Ratio: 24/76

Major Languages: predominantly English; a sizable Spanish-speaking minority; many others

Ethnic Makeup: 77% white; 13% black; 4% Asian; 6% Amerindian and others

Religions: 56% Protestant; 28% Roman Catholic; 2% Jewish; 4% others; 10% none or unaffiliated

Health

Life Expectancy at Birth: 74 years (male); 80 years (female)

Infant Mortality: 6.69/1,000 live births

Physicians Available: 1/365 people

HIV/AIDS Rate in Adults: 0.61%

Education

Adult Literacy Rate: 97% (official)

Compulsory (Ages): 7–16; free

COMMUNICATION

Telephones: 194,000,000 main lines

Daily Newspaper Circulation: 238/1,000 people

Televisions: 776/1,000 people

Internet Users: 165,750,000 (2002)

TRANSPORTATION

Highways in Miles (Kilometers): 3,906,960 (6,261,154)

Railroads in Miles (Kilometers): 149,161 (240,000)

Usable Airfields: 14,695

Motor Vehicles in Use: 206,000,000

GOVERNMENT

Type: federal republic

Independence Date: July 4, 1776

Head of State/Government: President George W. Bush is both head of state and head of government

Political Parties: Democratic Party; Republican Party; others of relatively minor political significance

Suffrage: universal at 18

MILITARY

Military Expenditures (% of GDP): 3.2%

Current Disputes: various boundary and territorial disputes; "war on terrorism"

ECONOMY

Per Capita Income/GDP: $37,800/$10.98 trillion

GDP Growth Rate: 4%

Inflation Rate: 2.2%

Unemployment Rate: 6.2%

Population Below Poverty Line: 13%

Natural Resources: many minerals and metals; petroleum; natural gas; timber; arable land

Agriculture: food grains; feed crops; fruits and vegetables; oil-bearing crops; livestock; dairy products

Industry: diversified in both capital and consumer-goods industries

Exports: $723 billion (primary partners Canada, Mexico, Japan)

Imports: $1.148 trillion (primary partners Canada, Mexico, Japan)

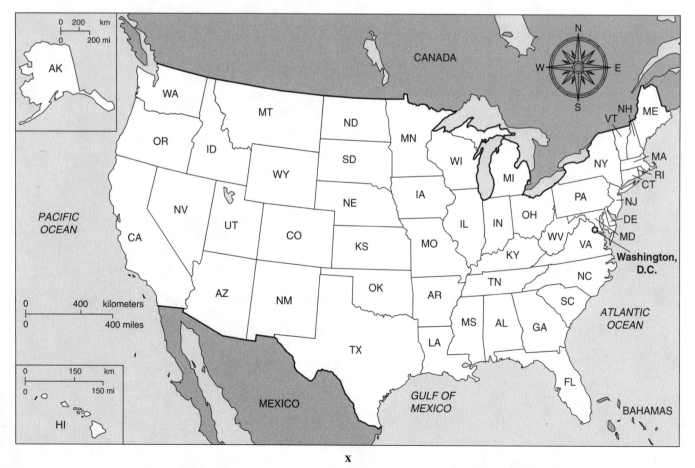

Canada

GEOGRAPHY
Area in Square Miles (Kilometers):
3,850,790 (9,976,140) (slightly larger than the United States)
Capital (Population): Ottawa (1,094,000)
Environmental Concerns: air and water pollution; acid rain; industrial damage to agriculture and forest productivity
Geographical Features: permafrost in the north; mountains in the west; central plains; lowlands in the southeast
Climate: varies from temperate to arctic

PEOPLE
Population
Total: 31,903,000
Annual Growth Rate: 0.96%
Rural/Urban Population Ratio: 23/77
Major Languages: both English and French are official
Ethnic Makeup: 28% British Isles origin; 23% French origin; 15% other European; 6% others; 2% indigenous; 26% mixed
Religions: 46% Roman Catholic; 36% Protestant; 18% others

Health
Life Expectancy at Birth: 76 years (male); 83 years (female)
Infant Mortality: 4.95/1,000 live births
Physicians Available: 1/534 people

HIV/AIDS Rate in Adults: 0.3%

Education
Adult Literacy Rate: 97%
Compulsory (Ages): primary school

COMMUNICATION
Telephones: 20,803,000 main lines
Daily Newspaper Circulation: 215/1,000 people
Televisions: 647/1,000 people
Internet Users: 16,840,000 (2002)

TRANSPORTATION
Highways in Miles (Kilometers): 559,240 (902,000)
Railroads in Miles (Kilometers): 22,320 (36,000)
Usable Airfields: 1,419
Motor Vehicles in Use: 16,800,000

GOVERNMENT
Type: confederation with parliamentary democracy
Independence Date: July 1, 1867
Head of State/Government: Queen Elizabeth II; Prime Minister Stephen Harper
Political Parties: Progressive Conservative Party; Liberal Party; New Democratic Party; Bloc Québécois; Canadian Alliance
Suffrage: universal at 18

MILITARY
Military Expenditures (% of GDP): 1.1%
Current Disputes: maritime boundary disputes with the United States

ECONOMY
Currency ($U.S. equivalent): 1.46 Canadian dollars = $1
Per Capita Income/GDP: $27,700/$875 billion
GDP Growth Rate: 2%
Inflation Rate: 3%
Unemployment Rate: 7%
Labor Force by Occupation: 74% services; 15% manufacturing; 6% agriculture and others
Natural Resources: petroleum; natural gas; fish; minerals; cement; forestry products; wildlife; hydropower
Agriculture: grains; livestock; dairy products; potatoes; hogs; poultry and eggs; tobacco; fruits and vegetables
Industry: oil production and refining; natural-gas development; fish products; wood and paper products; chemicals; transportation equipment
Exports: $273.8 billion (primary partners United States, Japan, United Kingdom)
Imports: $238.3 billion (primary partners United States, European Union, Japan)

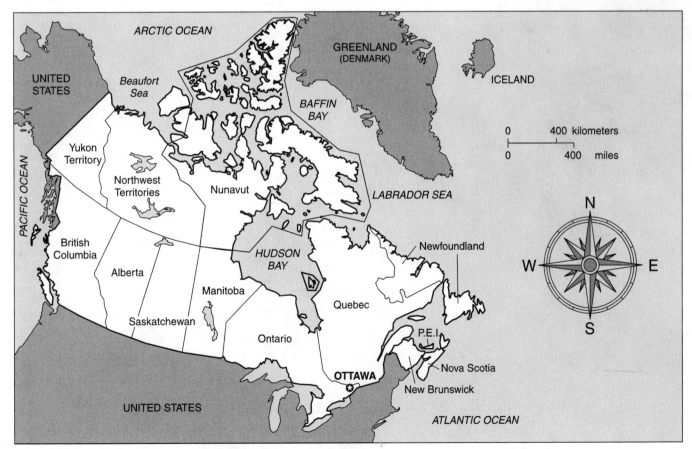

GLOBAL ● STUDIES

This map is provided to give you a graphic picture of where the countries of the world are located, the relationship they have with their region and neighbors, and their positions relative to major powers and power blocs. We have focused on certain areas to illustrate these crowded regions more clearly.

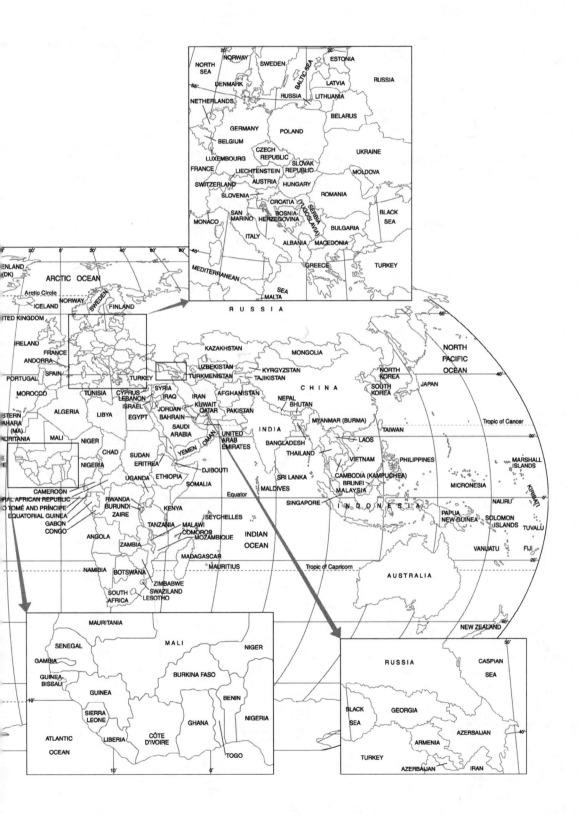

Latin America

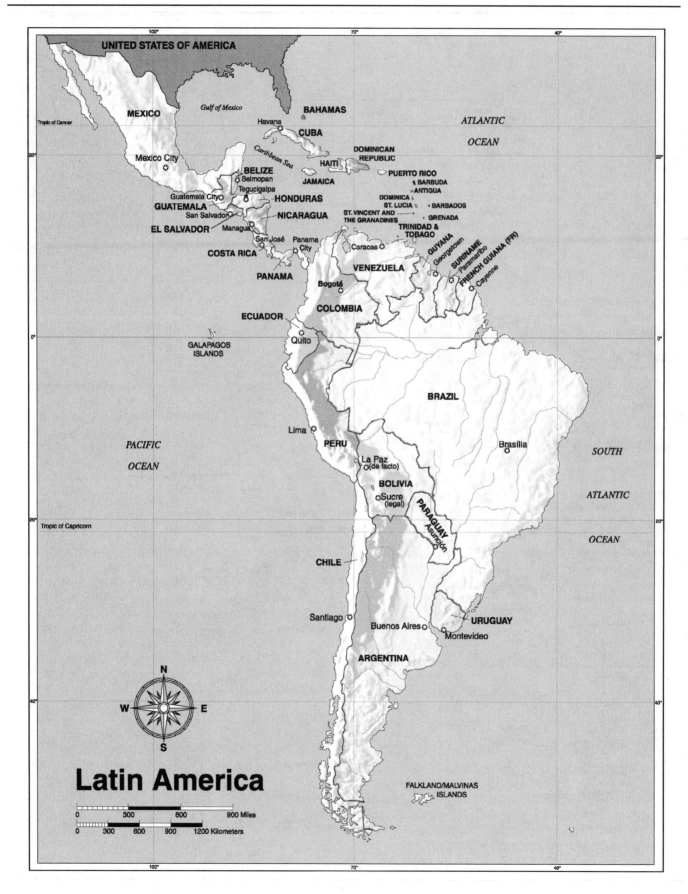

Latin America   Myth and Reality

Much of the world still tends to view Latin Americans in terms of stereotypes. Latin American leaders are in many cases still perceived as dictators or demagogues, either from the left or the right sides of the political spectrum with scant attention paid to their actual goals and policies. The popular image of the mustachioed bandit sporting a large sombrero and draped with cartridge belts has been replaced by the figure of the modern-day guerrilla or drug lord, but the same essential image, of lawlessness and violence, persists. Another common stereotype is that of the lazy Latin American who constantly puts things off until *mañana* ("tomorrow"). The implied message here is that Latin Americans lack industry and do not know how to make the best use of their time. A third widespread image is that of the Latin lover and the cult of *machismo* (manliness).

Many of those outside the culture find it difficult to conceive of Latin America as a mixture of peoples and cultures, each one distinct from the others. Indeed, it was not so long ago that then–U.S. president Ronald Reagan, after a tour of the region, remarked with some surprise that all of the countries were "different." Stereotypes spring from ignorance and bias; images are not necessarily a reflection of reality. In the words of Spanish philosopher José Ortega y Gasset: "In politics and history, if one takes accepted statements at face value, one will be sadly misled."

THE LATIN AMERICAN REALITY

The reality of Latin America's multiplicity of cultures is, in a word, complexity. Europeans, Africans, Asians, and the indigenous peoples of Latin America have all contributed substantially to these cultures. If one sets aside non-Hispanic influences for a moment, is it possible to argue, as does historian Claudio Veliz, that "the Iberian [Spanish and Portuguese] inheritance is an essential part of our lives and customs; Brazil and Spanish America [i.e., Spanish-speaking] have derived their personality from Iberia"?

Many scholars would disagree. For example, political scientist Lawrence S. Graham argues that "what is clear is that generalizations about Latin American cultural unity are no longer tenable." And that "one of the effects of nationalism has been to . . . lead growing numbers of individuals within the region to identify with their own nation-state before they think in terms of a more amorphous land mass called Latin America."

Granted, Argentines speak of their Argentinity and Mexicans of their *Mejicanidad*. It is true that there are profound differences that separate the nations of the region. But there exists a cultural bedrock that ties Latin America to Spain and Portugal, and beyond—to the Roman Empire and the great cultures of the Mediterranean world. African influence, too, is substantial in many parts of the region. Latin America's Indians, of course, trace their roots to indigenous sources. In countries such as Bolivia, however, where indigenous peoples are in the majority,

(World Bank/Foto Anckerman/WB042806GTBW)
In Latin America, the family is an important element in the cultural context. A woman is holding her baby at the Community Center of Basic Health in Chimaltenango, Guatemala.

in recent years there has emerged a strong movement that exalts indigenous cultures over those derived from the West.

To understand the nature of Latin American culture, one must remember that there exist many exceptions to the generalizations; the cultural mold is not rigid. Much of what has happened in Latin America, including the evolution of its cultures, is the result of a fortunate—and sometimes an unfortunate—combination of various factors.

THE FAMILY

Let us first consider the Latin American family. The family unit has, for the most part, survived Latin America's uneven economic development and the pressures of modernization. Family ties are strong and dominant. These bonds are confined not only to the nuclear family of father, mother, children, and grandparents but also present in the extended family (a network of second cousins, godparents, and close friends of blood relatives). In times of difficulty the family can usually be counted on to help. Ideally it is a fortress against the misery and uncertainty of the outside world; it is the repository of dignity, honor, and respect.

Sadly, violence, drugs, gangs, extreme poverty, emigration, and the need to flee have compromised the ideal world in many parts of the region. Guerrilla warfare in Central America and Colombia, for example, has shattered families and forced thousands to become refugees. Drug gangs in the impoverished *favelas* of Brazil's major cities have torn apart neighborhoods and families. Extreme poverty and lack of opportunity have caused additional thousands of people to flee their countries in

(Royalty-Free/CORBIS)

The role of the indigenous woman in Latin America has been defined by centuries of tradition. This woman is carrying a bundle of firewood, just as her ancestors did.

makeshift boats or to emigrate north to the United States and Canada. This, too, often divides families.

AN URBAN CIVILIZATION

In a region where the interaction of networks of families is the rule and where frequent human contact is sought out, it is not surprising to find that Latin Americans are, above all, an urban people. There are more cities of over half a million people in Latin America than in the United States.

Latin America's high percentage of urban dwellers is unusual, for urbanization is usually associated with industrialization. In Latin America, urban culture was not created by industrial growth; it actually predated it. As soon as the opportunity presented itself, the Spanish conquerors of the New World, in Veliz's words, "founded cities in which to take refuge from the barbaric, harsh, uncivilized, and rural world outside. . . . For those men civilization was strictly and uniquely a function of well-ordered city life."

The city, from the Spanish conquest until the present, has dominated the social and cultural horizon of Latin America. Opportunity is found in the city, not in the countryside. This cultural fact of life, in addition to economic motives, accounts for the continuing flow of population from rural to urban areas in Latin America.

A WORLD OF APPEARANCES

Because in their urban environment Latin Americans are in close contact with many people, appearances are important to them. There is a constant quest for prestige, dignity, status, and honor. People are forever trying to impress one another with their public worth. Hence, it is not unusual to see a blue-collar worker traveling to work dressed in a suit, briefcase in hand. It is not uncommon to see jungles of television antennas over shantytowns, although many are not connected to anything.

It is a society that, in the opinion of writer Octavio Paz, hides behind masks. Latin Americans convey an impression of importance, no matter how menial their position. Glen Dealy, a political scientist, writes: "And those of the lower class who must wait on tables, wash cars, and do gardening for a living can help to gain back a measure of self-respect by having their shoes shined by someone else, buying a drink for a friend . . . , or concealing their occupation by wearing a tie to and from work."

MACHISMO

Closely related to appearances is *machismo.* The term is usually understood solely, and mistakenly, in terms of virility—the image of the Latin lover, for example. But machismo also connotes generosity, dignity, and honor. In many respects, macho behavior is indulged in because of social convention; it is expected of men. Machismo is also a cultural trait that cuts through class lines, for the macho is admired regardless of his social position.

THE ROLE OF WOMEN

If the complex nature of machismo is misunderstood by those outside the culture, so too is the role of women. The commonly held stereotype is that Latin American women are submissive and that the culture is dominated by males. Again, appearances mask a far more complex reality, for Latin American cultures actually allow for strong female roles. Political scientist Evelyn Stevens, for example, has found that *marianismo*—the female counterpart of machismo—permeates all strata of Latin American society. Marianismo is the cult of feminine spiritual superiority that "teaches that women are semi-divine, morally superior to and spiritually stronger than men."

When Mexico's war for independence broke out in 1810, a religious symbol—the Virgin of Guadalupe—was identified with the rebels and became a rallying point for the first stirrings of Mexican nationalism. It was not uncommon in Argentine textbooks to portray Eva Perón (1919–1952), President Juan Perón's wife, in the image of the Virgin Mary, complete with a blue veil and halo. In less religious terms, one of Latin America's most popular novels, *Doña Barbara,* by Rómulo Gallegos, is the story of a female *caudillo* ("man on horseback") on the plains of Venezuela. One need not look to fiction, for in 2006 Chile elected a woman as president. Importantly, she won on her own merits; equally important, she was careful to cultivate an image of a caring mother. More recently Argentina elected its first woman president. Substantial numbers of women may now be counted as members of congress in several countries.

The Latin American woman dominates the family because of a deep-seated respect for motherhood. Personal identity is less of a problem for her because she retains her family name upon marriage and passes it on to her children. Women who work outside the home are also supposed to retain respect for their motherhood, which is sacred. In any conflict between a woman's job and the needs of her family, the employer, by custom, must grant her a leave to tend to the family's needs. Recent historical scholarship has also revealed that Latin American women have long enjoyed rights denied to women in other, more "advanced"

(United NationsPhoto/UN160755)

Agriculture is the backbone of much of Latin America's cultures and economies. These workers are harvesting sugarcane on a plantation in the state of Pernambuco, Brazil.

parts of the world. For example, Latin American women were allowed to own property and to sign for mortgages in their own names even in colonial days. In the 1920s, they won the right to vote in local elections in Yucatán, Mexico, and in San Juan, Argentina.

Here again, though, appearances can be deceiving. Many Latin American constitutions guarantee equality of treatment, but reality is burdensome for women in many parts of the region. They do not have the same kinds of access to jobs that men enjoy; they seldom receive equal pay for equal work; and family life, at times, can be brutalizing.

WORK AND LEISURE

Work, leisure, and concepts of time in Latin America correspond to an entirely different cultural mindset than exists in Northern Europe and North America. The essential difference was demonstrated in a North American television commercial for a wine, in which two starry-eyed people were portrayed giving the Spanish toast *Salud, amor, y pesetas* ("Health, love, and money"). For a North American audience, the message was appropriate. But the full Spanish toast includes the tag line *y el tiempo para gozarlos* ("and the time to enjoy them").

In Latin America, leisure is viewed as a perfectly rational goal. It has nothing to do with being lazy or indolent. Indeed, in *Ariel,* by writer José Enrique Rodó , leisure is described within the context of the culture: "To think, to dream, to admire—these are the ministrants that haunt my cell. The ancients ranked them under the word *otium,* well-employed leisure, which they deemed the highest use of being truly rational, liberty of thought emancipated of all ignoble chains. Such leisure meant that use of time which they opposed to mere economic activity as the expression of a higher life. Their concept of dignity was linked closely to this lofty conception of leisure." Work, by contrast, is often perceived as a necessary evil.

CONCEPTS OF TIME

Latin American attitudes toward time also reveal the inner workings of the culture. Exasperated North American businesspeople have for years complained about the *mañana, mañana* attitude of Latin Americans. People often are late for appointments; sometimes little *appears* to get done.

For the North American who believes that time is money, such behavior appears senseless. However, Glen Dealy, in his perceptive book *The Public Man,* argues that such behavior is perfectly rational. A Latin American man who spends hours over lunch or over coffee in a café is not wasting time. For here, with his friends and relatives, he is with the source of his power. Indeed, networks of friends and families are the glue of Latin American society. "Without spending time in this fashion he would, in fact, soon have fewer friends. Additionally, he knows that to leave a café precipitously for an 'appointment' would signify to all that he must not keep someone else waiting—which further indicates his lack of importance. If he had power and position the other person would wait upon his arrival. It is the powerless who wait." Therefore, friends and power relationships are more important than rushing to keep an appointment. The North American who wants the business deal will wait. In a sense, then, the North American is the client and the Latin American is the *patrón* (the "patron," or wielder of power).

Perceptions of time in Latin America also have a broader meaning. North American students who have been exposed to Latin American literature are almost always confused by the absence of a "logical," chronological development of the story. Time, for Latin Americans, tends to be circular rather than linear. That is, the past and the present are perceived as equally relevant—both are points on a circle. The past is as important as the present.

MYTH AND REALITY MERGE

The past that is exposed in works of Latin American literature as well as scholarly writings reflects wholly different attitudes toward what people from other cultures identify as reality. For example, in Nobel Prize–winning writer Gabriél García Márquez's classic novel *One Hundred Years of Solitude*—a fictional history of the town of Macondo and its leading family—fantasy and tall tales abound. But García Márquez drew his inspiration from stories he heard at his grandmother's knee about Aracataca, Colombia, the real town in which he grew up. The point here is that the fanciful story of the town's origins constitutes that town's memory of its past. The stories give the town a common heritage and memory.

From a North American or Northern European perspective, the historical memory is faulty. From the Latin American perspective, however, it is the perception of the past that is important, regardless of its factual accuracy. Myth and reality, appearances and substance, merge.

POLITICAL CULTURE

The generalizations drawn here about Latin American society apply also to its political culture, which is essentially authoritarian and oriented toward power and power relationships. Ideology—be it liberalism, conservatism, or communism—is little more than window dressing. It is the means by which contenders for power can be separated. As Claudio Veliz has noted, regardless of the aims of revolutionary leaders, the great upheavals in Latin America in the twentieth century, without exception, ended up by strengthening the political center, which is essentially authoritarian. This was true of the Mexican Revolution (1910), the Bolivian Revolution (1952), the Cuban Revolution (1958), and the Nicaraguan Revolution (1979). At this moment populist movements in Venezuela, Bolivia, and Ecuador have all strengthened executive power. Indeed, the apparent "moral superiority" of political leaders is used to justify constitutional changes to allow presidents to serve extended terms. Ecuador's current president campaigned with a slogan proclaiming that he was "God's envoy."

Ideology has never been a decisive factor in the historical and social reality of Latin America. But charisma and the ability to lead are crucial ingredients. José Velasco Ibarra, five times the president of Ecuador in the twentieth century, once boasted: "Give me a balcony and I will be president!" He saw his personality, not his ideology, as the key to power.

In the realm of national and international relations, Latin America often appears to those outside the culture to be in a constant state of turmoil and chaos. It seems that every day there are reports that a prominent politician has fallen from power, border clashes have intensified, or guerrillas have taken over another section of a country. But the conclusion that chaos reigns in Latin America is most often based on the visible political and social violence, not on the general nature of a country. Political violence is often local in nature, and the social fabric of the country is bound together by the enduring social stability of the family. Again, there is the dualism of what *appears to be* and what *is*.

Much of this upheaval can be attributed to the division in Latin America between the people of Mediterranean background and the indigenous Indian populations. There may be several hundred minority groups within a single country. The problems that may arise from such intense internal differences, however, are not always necessarily detrimental, because they contribute to the texture and color of Latin American culture.

SEEING BEHIND THE MASK

In order to grasp the essence of Latin America, one must ignore the stereotypes, appreciate appearances for what they are, and attempt to see behind the mask. Although Latin America must be appreciated as an amalgam of cultures, it is largely dominated by behavior that is essentially a derivative of Mediterranean Western models.

A Latin American world view tends to be dualistic. The family constitutes the basic unit; here one finds generosity, warmth, honor, and love. Beyond the walls of the home, in the world of business and politics, Latin Americans don their masks and enter "combat." It is a world of power relationships, of macho bravado, and of appearances. This dualism is deep-seated; scholars such as Richard Morse and Glen Dealy have traced its roots to the Middle Ages. For Latin Americans, one's activities are compartmentalized into those fit for the City of God, which corresponds to religion, the home, and one's intimate circle of friends; and those appropriate for the City of Man, which is secular and often ruthless and corrupt. North Americans, who tend to measure both their public and private lives by the same yardstick, often interpret Latin American dualism as hypocrisy. Nothing could be further from the truth.

For the Latin American, life exists on several planes, has purpose, and is perfectly rational. Indeed, one is tempted to suggest that many Latin American institutions—particularly the supportive network of families and friends—are more in tune with a world that can alienate and isolate than are our own. As you will see in the following reports, the social structure and cultural diversity of Latin America add greatly to its character and, paradoxically, to its stability.

Mexico (United Mexican States)

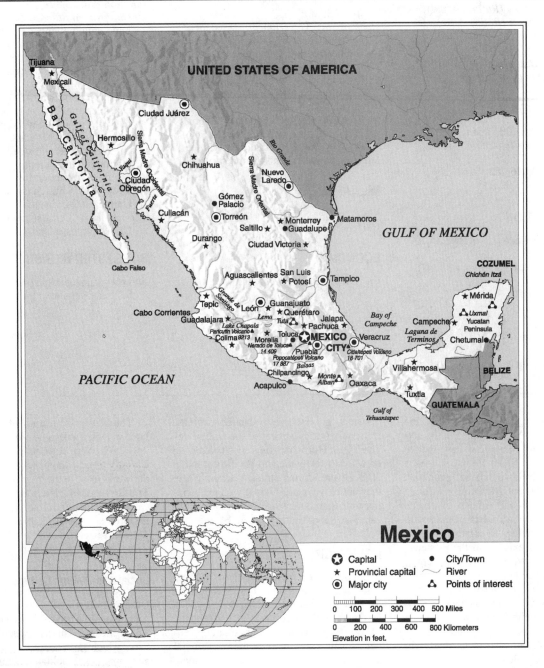

Mexico Statistics

GEOGRAPHY

Area in Square Miles (Kilometers):
764,000 (1,978,000) (about 3 times the size of Texas)
Capital (Population): Mexico City (8,720,916)
Environmental Concerns: Scarce freshwater resources; water pollution; deforestation; soil erosion; serious air pollution

Geographical Features: high, rugged mountains; low coastal plains; high plateaus; desert
Climate: varies from tropical to desert

PEOPLE

Population

Total: 108,700,891 (2007 est.)
Annual Growth Rate: 1.15%

Rural/Urban Population Ratio: 26/74
Major Languages: Spanish; various Maya, Nahuatl, and other regional indigenous languages
Ethnic Makeup: 60% Mestizo; 30% Amerindian; 9% white; 1% others
Religions: 76.5% Roman Catholic; 6.3% Protestant; 13.8% unspecified or none

Health

Life Expectancy at Birth: 73 years (male);
   78 years (female)
Infant Mortality Rate (Ratio): 19.63/1,000
Physicians Available (Ratio): 1/613

Education

Adult Literacy Rate: 91%
Compulsory (Ages): 6–12; free

COMMUNICATION

Telephones: 19,861,000 main lines
Daily Newspaper Circulation: 115 per
   1,000 people
Cell Phones: 57,016,000
Internet Users: 22,000,000

TRANSPORTATION

Roadways in Kilometers (miles): 235,760
   (146,439)
Railroads in Kilometers (miles): 17,665
   (10,977)
Usable Airfields: 1,834

GOVERNMENT

Type: federal republic
Independence Date: September 16, 1810
   (from Spain)
Head of State/Government: President
   Felipe Calderón is both head of state
   and head of government
Political Parties: Institutional
   Revolutionary Party; National Action
   Party; Party of the Democratic
   Revolution; Workers Party;
   Convergence for Democracy; Labor
   Party; Mexican Green Ecological
   Party; Social Democratic Party; others.
Suffrage: universal and compulsory at 18

MILITARY

Military Expenditures (% of GDP): 0.5%
Current Disputes: none

ECONOMY

Currency ($U.S. Equivalent): 10.79
   pesos = $1

Per Capita Income/GDP: $12,500/$1.353
   trillion
GDP Real Growth Rate: 3%
Inflation Rate: 3.8%
Unemployment Rate: 3.7%;
   underemployment: +/− 25%
Labor Force: 41.5 million
Natural Resources: petroleum; silver;
   copper; gold; lead; zinc; natural gas;
   timber
Agriculture: corn; wheat; soybeans; rice;
   beans; cotton; coffee; fruit; tomatoes;
   livestock products; wood products
Industry: food and beverages; tobacco;
   chemicals; iron and steel; petroleum;
   mining; textiles; clothing; motor
   vehicles; consumer durables; tourism
Exports: $267.5 billion (primary partners
   United States, Canada)
Imports: $279.3 billion (primary partners
   United States, Japan, China)

SUGGESTED WEB SITE

http://www.cia.gov/cia/publications/
   factbook/geos/mx.html#geo

Mexico Country Report

There is a story that Hernán Cortéz, the conqueror of the Aztec Empire in the sixteenth century, when asked to describe the landscape of New Spain (Mexico), took a piece of paper in his hands and crumpled it. The analogy is apt. Mexico is a tortured land of mountains and valleys, of deserts in the north and rain forests in the south. Geography has helped to create an intense regionalism in Mexico, and the existence of hundreds of *patrias chicas* ("little countries") has hindered national integration.

Much of Mexico's territory is vulnerable to earthquakes and volcanic activity. In 1943, for example, a cornfield in one of Mexico's richest agricultural zones sprouted a volcano instead of maize. In 1982, a severe volcanic eruption in the south took several hundred lives, destroyed thousands of head of livestock, and buried crops under tons of ash. Thousands of people died when a series of earthquakes struck Mexico City in 1985.

Mexico is a nation of climatic extremes. Much-needed rains often fall so hard that most of the water runs off before it can be absorbed by the soil. When rains fail to materialize, crops die in the fields. The harsh face of the land, the unavailability of water, and erosion limit the agricultural potential of Mexico. Only 10 to 15 percent of Mexico's land can be planted with crops; but because of unpredictable weather or natural

disasters, good harvests can be expected from only 6 to 8 percent of the land in any given year. Hurricanes have also taken a toll on Mexico's Atlantic and Pacific coasts. In 2005 severe storms struck Cancun where they not only wreaked havoc with the lucrative tourism industry but also caused significant losses in farming areas in the south.

MEXICO CITY

Mexico's central region has the best cropland. It was here that the Aztecs built their capital city, the foundations of which lie beneath the current Mexican capital, Mexico City. Given their agricultural potential as well as its focus as the commercial and administrative center of the nation, Mexico City and the surrounding region have always supported a large population. For decades, Mexico City has acted as a magnet for rural poor who have given up attempts to eke out a living from the soil. In the 1940s and 1950s, the city experienced a great population surge. In that era, however, it had the capacity to absorb the tens of thousands of migrants, and so a myth of plentiful money and employment was created. Even today, that myth exercises a strong influence in the countryside; it partially accounts for the tremendous growth of the city and its greater metropolitan area, now home to approximately 18 million people.

The size and location of Mexico City have spawned awesome problems. Because it lies in a valley surrounded by mountains, air pollution is trapped. Mexico City has the worst smog in the Western Hemisphere. Traffic congestion is among the worst in the world. And essential services—including the provision of drinkable water, electricity, and sewers—have failed to keep pace with the city's growth in population.

Social and Cultural Changes

Dramatic social and cultural changes have accompanied Mexico's population growth. These are particularly evident in Mexico City, which daily becomes less Mexican and more cosmopolitan and international.

As Mexico City has become more worldly, English words have become more common in everyday vocabulary. "Okay," "coffee break," and "happy hour" are some examples of English idioms that have slipped into popular usage. In urban centers, quick lunches and coffee breaks have replaced the traditional large meal that was once served at noon. For most people, the afternoon siesta ("nap") is a fondly remembered custom of bygone days.

Mass communication has had an incalculable impact on culture. Television commercials primarily use models who are ethnically European in appearance—preferably white, blue-eyed, and blonde. As if in defiance of the overwhelmingly Mestizo (mixed Indian and white) character of the population, Mexican newspapers and magazines carry advertisements for products guaranteed to lighten one's skin. Success has become associated with light skin.

Another symbol of success is ownership of a television. Antennas cover rooftops even in the poorest urban slums. Acute observers might note, however, that many of the antennas are not connected to anything; the residents of many hovels merely want to convey the impression that they can afford one.

Television, however, has helped to educate the illiterate. Some Mexican soap operas, for instance, incorporate educational materials. On a given day, a show's characters may attend an adult-education class that stresses basic reading and writing skills. Both the television characters and the home-viewing audience sit in on the class. Literacy is portrayed as being essential to one's success and well-being. Mexican *telenovelas*, or "soaps," have a special focus on teenagers and problems common to adolescents. Solutions are advanced within a traditional cultural context and reaffirm the central role of the family.

Cultural Survival: Compadrazgo

Despite these obvious signs of change, distinct Mexican traditions and customs have not only survived Mexico's transformation but have also flourished because of it. The chaos of city life, the hundreds of thousands of migrants uprooted from rural settings, and the sense of isolation and alienation common to city dwellers the world over are in part eased by the Hispanic institution of *compadrazgo* ("cogodparenthood" or "sponsorship").

DEVELOPMENT

Mexico's state-owned oil company, PEMEX, is badly in need of money both to invest in upgrades to an ageing infrastructure and to explore for new oil fields to replace those that are nearly played out. Mexicans, however, are loath to invite the participation of foreign oil companies in an industry that many view as a "sacred" symbol of their sovereignty.

Compadrazgo is found at all levels of Mexican society and in both rural and urban areas. It is a device for building economic and social alliances that are more enduring than simple friendship. Furthermore, it has a religious dimension as well as a secular, or everyday, application. In addition to basic religious occasions (such as baptism, confirmation, first communion, and marriage), Mexicans seek sponsors for minor religious occasions, such as the blessing of a business, and for events as common as a graduation or a boy's first haircut.

Anthropologist Robert V. Kemper observes that the institution of compadrazgo reaches across class lines and knits the various strands of Mexican society into a whole cloth. Compadrazgo performs many functions, including providing assistance from the more powerful to the less powerful and, reciprocally, providing homage from the less powerful to the more powerful. The most common choices for *compadres* are neighbors, relatives, fellow migrants, coworkers, and employers. A remarkably flexible institution, compadrazgo is perfectly compatible with the tensions and anxieties of urban life.

Yet even compadrazgo—a form of patron/client relationship—has its limitations. As Mexico City has sprawled ever wider across the landscape, multitudes of new neighborhoods have been created. Many are the result of well-planned land

(AP photo/Jose Luis Magana)

A man from the state of Puebla asks for money outside a jewelry store in Mexico City, hoping to raise enough funds to supply the peasants of his community with the water and electricity that the government has been unable to provide.

seizures, orchestrated by groups of people attracted by the promise of the city. Technically, such land seizures are illegal; and a primary goal of the *colonos* (inhabitants of these low-income communities) is legitimization and consequent community participation.

Beginning in the 1970s, colonos forcefully pursued their demands for legitimization through protest movements and demonstrations, some of which revealed a surprising degree of radicalism. In response, the Mexican government adopted a two-track policy: It selectively repressed the best-organized and most radical groups of colonos, and it tried to co-opt the remainder through negotiation. In the early 1980s, the government created "Citizen Representation" bodies, official channels within Mexico City through which colonos could participate, within the system, in the articulation of their demands.

From the perspective of the colonos, the establishment of the citizen organizations afforded them an additional means to advance their demands for garbage collection, street paving, provision of potable water, sewage removal, and, most critically, the regularization of land tenure—that is, legitimization. In the government's view, representation for the colonos served to win supporters for the Mexican political structure, particularly the authority of the official ruling party, at a time of outspoken challenge from other political sectors.

Citizens are encouraged to work within the system; potential dissidents are transformed through the process of co-optation into collaborators. In today's Mexico City, then, patronage and clientage have two faces: the traditional one of compadrazgo, the other a form of state paternalism that promotes community participation.

THE BORDER

In the past few decades, driven by poverty, unemployment, and underemployment, many Mexicans have chosen not Mexico City but the United States as the place to improve their lives. Mexican workers in the United States are not a new phenomenon. During World War II, the presidents of both nations agreed to allow Mexican workers, called *braceros,* to enter the United States as agricultural workers. They were strictly regulated. In contrast, the new wave of migrants is largely unregulated. Each year, hundreds of thousands of undocumented Mexicans illegally cross the border in search of work. It has been estimated that at any given time, between 4 million and 6 million Mexicans pursue an existence as illegal aliens in the United States.

Thousands of Mexicans are able to support families with the fruits of their labors,

but, as undocumented workers, they are not protected by the law. Many are callously exploited by those who smuggle them across the border as well as by employers in the United States. For the Mexican government, however, such mass emigration has been a blessing in disguise. It has served as a kind of sociopolitical safety valve, and it has resulted in an inflow of dollars sent home by the workers.

In recent years, U.S. companies and the governments of Mexican states along the border have profited from the creation of assembly plants known as *maquiladoras.* Low wages and a docile labor force are attractive to employers, while the Mexican government reaps the benefits of employment and tax dollars. Despite the appearance of prosperity along the border, it must be emphasized that chronic unemployment in other parts of Mexico ensures the misery of millions of people. The North American Free Trade Agreement (NAFTA) hoped to alter these harsh realities, but after more than a decade real wages are lower, the distribution of income has become more unequal, and Mexicans still cross the U.S. border in large numbers. U.S. immigration policy has only served, from the Mexican perspective, to exacerbate the problem. Increased patrols, the construction of a high wall along the border, and the increased deportation of undocumented workers from the United States has worsened Mexico's problem with an excess labor supply.

THE INDIAN "PROBLEM"

During the 1900s, urbanization and racial mixing changed the demographic face of Mexico. A government official once commented: "A country predominately Mestizo, where Indian and white are now minorities, Mexico preserves the festivity and ceremonialism of the Indian civilizations and the religiosity and legalism of the Spanish Empire." The quotation is revealing, for it clearly identifies the Indian as a marginal member of society, as an object of curiosity.

FREEDOM

In February 2006 Subcomandante Marcos, leader of the Zapatista rebel group, emerged from the state of Chiapas and began a six-month tour of Mexico to promote a new, nonviolent political movement. The government, which considers Marcos a rebel and an outlaw, has not moved to arrest him. In the event of his incarceration, Marcos directed his followers not to resist but to "Run away and spread the word … and bring me tobacco."

In Mexico, as is the case with indigenous peoples in most of Latin America, Indians in many quarters are viewed as obstacles to national integration and economic progress. There exist in Mexico more than 200 distinct Indian tribes or ethnic groups, who speak more than 50 languages or dialects. In the view of "progressive" Mexicans, the "sociocultural fragmentation" caused by the diversity of languages fosters political misunderstanding, insecurity, and regional incomprehension. Indians suffer from widespread discrimination. Language is not the only barrier to their economic progress. They have long endured the unequal practices of a ruling white and Mestizo elite. Indians may discover, for example, that they cannot expand a small industry, such as a furniture-making enterprise, because few financial institutions will lend a large amount of money to an Indian.

NATIONAL IDENTITY

Mexico's Mestizo face has had a profound impact on the attempts of intellectuals to understand the meaning of the term "Mexican." The question of national identity has always been an important theme in Mexican history; it became a particularly burning issue in the aftermath of the Revolution of 1910. Octavio Paz believes that most Mexicans have denied their origins: They do not want to be either Indian or Spaniard, but they also refuse to see themselves as a mixture of both. One result of this essential denial of one's ethnic roots is a collective inferiority complex. The Mexican, Paz writes, is insecure. To hide that insecurity, which stems from his sense of "inferiority," the Mexican wears a "mask." Machismo (the cult of manliness) is one example of such a mask. In Paz's estimation, aggressive behavior at a sporting event, while driving a car, or in relationships with women reflects a deep-seated identity crisis.

Perhaps an analogy can be drawn from Mexican domestic architecture. Traditional Mexican homes are surrounded by high, solid walls, often topped with shards of glass and devoid of windows looking out onto the street. From the outside, these abodes appear cold and inhospitable. Once inside (once behind the mask), however, the Mexican home is warm and comfortable. Here, appearances are set aside and individuals can relax and be themselves. By contrast, many homes in the United States have vast expanses of glass that allow every passerby to see within. That whole style of open architecture, at least for homes, is jolting for many Mexicans (as well as other Latin Americans).

THE FAILURE OF THE 1910 REVOLUTION

In addition to the elusive search for Mexican identity, one of Mexican intellectuals' favorite themes is the Revolution of 1910 and what they perceive as its shortcomings. That momentous struggle (1910–1917) cost more than 1 million lives, but it offered Mexico the promise of a new society, free from the abuses of past centuries. It began with a search for truth and honesty in government; it ended with an assertion of the dignity and equality of all men and women.

The goals of the 1910 Revolution were set forth in the Constitution of 1917, a remarkable document—not only in its own era, but also today. *Article 123,* for example, which concerns labor, includes the following provisions: an eight-hour workday, a general minimum wage, and a six-week leave with pay for pregnant women before the approximate birth date plus a six-week leave with pay following the birth. During the nursing period, the mother must be given extra rest periods each day for nursing the baby. Equal wages must be paid for equal work, regardless of sex or nationality. Workers are entitled to a participation in the profits of an enterprise (i.e., profit sharing). Overtime work must carry double pay. Employers are responsible for and must pay appropriate compensation for injuries received by workers in the performance of their duties or for occupational diseases. In 1917, such provisions were viewed as astounding and revolutionary.

Unfulfilled Promises

Unfortunately, many of the goals of 1917 have yet to be achieved. A number of writers, frustrated by the slow pace of change, concluded long ago that the Mexican Revolution was dead. Leading thinkers and writers, such as Carlos Fuentes, have bitterly criticized the failure of the Revolution to shape a more equitable society. Corruption, abuse of power, and self-serving opportunism characterize Mexico today.

One of the failed goals of the Revolution, in the eyes of critics, was an agrarian-reform program that fell short of achieving a wholesale change of land ownership or even of raising the standard of living in rural areas. Over the years, however, small-scale agriculture has sown the seeds of its own destruction. Plots of land that are barely adequate for subsistence farming have been further divided by peasant farmers anxious to satisfy the inheritance rights of their sons. More recently, government price controls on grain and corn have driven many marginal producers out of the market and off their lands.

(Courtesy of Heather Haddon/haddon01)

Mexican women won the right to vote in 1955. This woman demonstrates her political consciousness in response to an especially disputed gubernatorial election in the state of Oaxaca in August 2004.

Land Reform: One Story

Juan Rulfo, a major figure in the history of postrevolutionary literature, captured the frustration of peasants who have "benefited" from agrarian reform. "But sir," the peasant complained to the government official overseeing the land reform, "the earth is all washed away and hard. We don't think the plow will cut into the earth . . . that's like a rock quarry. You'd have to make with a pick-axe to plant the seed, and even then you can't be sure that anything will come up. . . ." The official, cold and indifferent, responded: "You can state that in writing. And now you can go. You should be attacking the large-estate owners and not the government that is giving you the land."

More frequently, landowners have attacked peasants. During the past several years in Mexico, insistent peasant demands for a new allocation of lands have been the occasion of a number of human-rights abuses—some of a very serious character. Some impatient peasants who have occupied lands in defiance of the law have been killed or have "disappeared." In one notorious case in 1982, 26 peasants were murdered in a dispute over land in the state of Puebla. The peasants, who claimed legal title to the land, were killed by mounted gunmen, reportedly hired by local ranchers. Political parties reacted to the massacre in characteristic fashion—all attempted to manipulate the event to their own advantage

rather than to address the problem of land reform. Yet years later, paramilitary bands and local police controlled by political bosses or landowners still routinely threatened and/or killed peasant activists. Indeed, access to the land was a major factor in the Maya uprising in the southern state of Chiapas that began in 1994 and, in 2008, remains unresolved.

The Promise of the Revolution

While critics of the 1910 Revolution are correct in identifying its failures, the Constitution of 1917 represents more than dashed hopes. The radical nature of the document allows governments (should they desire) to pursue aggressive egalitarian policies and still be within the law. For example, when addressing citizens, Mexican public officials often invoke the Constitution—issues tend to become less controversial if they are placed within the broad context of 1917. When President Adolfo López Mateos declared in 1960 that his government would be "extremely leftist," he quickly added that his position would be "within the Constitution." But some authorities argue that constitutional strictures can inhibit needed change. For example, the notoriously inefficient state petroleum monopoly (PEMEX) has been critically short of investment capital for years. To allow private companies to invest in the oil industry would require a constitutional change that many Mexicans equate to a form of *vendepatria* (selling out the country). Indeed, in 2003–2004 Congress routinely rejected discussions of even limited private participation in a national industry.

Women's Rights

Although the Constitution made reference to the equality of women in Mexican society, it was not until World War II that the women's-rights movement gathered strength. Women won the right to vote in Mexico in 1955; by the 1970s, they had challenged laws and social customs that were prejudicial to women. Some women have served on presidential cabinets, and one became governor of the state of Colima. The most important victory for women occurred in 1974, however, when the Mexican Congress passed legislation that, in effect, asked men to grant women full equality in society—including jobs, salaries, and legal standing. Some improvement has occurred in terms of the percentage of women who have been elected to congress. In 2008, in Mexico's lower house 22.6% of the seats are held by women (the corresponding figure for the United States is 16.3%).

But attitudes are difficult to change with legislation, and much social behavior in Mexico still is sexist. The editor of the Mexican newspaper *Noroeste* asserted that the most important challenge that confronted former president Vicente Fox was to "break the paternalistic culture." For the most part, that has not happened and, according to the *World Economic Forum,* women fall behind men "in key measures of social well-being," such as education, health, and economic participation.

Many Mexican men feel that there are male and female roles in society, regardless of law. Government, public corporations, private businesses, the Roman Catholic Church, and the armed forces represent important areas of male activity. The home, private religious rituals, and secondary service roles represent areas of female activity. One is clearly dominant, the other subordinate.

The Role of the Church

Under the Constitution of 1917, no religious organization is allowed to administer or teach in Mexico's primary, secondary, or normal (higher education) schools; nor may clergy participate in the education of workers or peasants. Yet between 1940 and 1979, private schools expanded to the point where they enrolled 1.5 million of the country's 17 million pupils. Significantly, more than half of the private-school population attended Roman Catholic schools. Because they exist despite the fact that they are prohibited by law, the Catholic schools demonstrate the kinds of accommodation and flexibility that are possible in Mexico. It is in the best interests of the ruling party to satisfy as many interest groups as is possible.

From the perspective of politicians, the Roman Catholic Church has increasingly tilted the balance in the direction of social justice in recent years. Some Mexican bishops have been particularly outspoken on the issue; but when liberal or radical elements in the Church embrace social change, they may cross into the jurisdiction of the state. Under the Constitution, the state is responsible for improving the welfare of its people. Some committed clergy, however, believe that religion must play an active role in the transformation of society; it must not only have compassion for the poor but must also act to relieve poverty and eliminate injustice.

In 1991, Mexican bishops openly expressed their concern about the torture and mistreatment of prisoners, political persecution, corruption, discrimination against indigenous peoples, mistreatment of Central American refugees, and electoral fraud. In

previous years, the government would have reacted sharply against such charges emanating from the Church. But, in this case, there had been a significant rapprochement between the Catholic Church and the state in Mexico. The new relationship culminated with the exchange of diplomatic representatives and Pope John Paul II's successful and popular visit to Mexico in 1990. Despite better relations at the highest level, in 1999 the bishop of Chiapas vigorously criticized the government for backing away from a 1996 accord between the state and leaders of a guerrilla insurgency and returning to a policy of violent repression.

MEXICO'S STABILITY

The stability of the Mexican state, as has been suggested, depends on the ability of the ruling elite to maintain a state of relative equilibrium among the multiplicity of interests and demands in the nation. The whole political process is characterized by bargaining among elites with various views on politics, social injustice, economic policy, and the conduct of foreign relations.

It was the Institutional Revolutionary Party (PRI), which held the presidency from 1929 until 2000, that set policy and decided what was possible or desirable. All change was generated from above, from the president and his advisers. Although the Constitution provides for a federal system, power was effectively centralized. In the words of one authority, Mexico, with its one-party rule, was not a democracy but, rather, "qualified authoritarianism." In the PRI era, Peruvian author Mario Vargas Llosa referred to Mexico as a "perfect dictatorship." Indeed, the main role of the PRI in the political system was political domination, not power sharing. Paternalistic and all-powerful, the state controlled the bureaucracies that directed the labor unions, peasant organizations, student groups, and virtually every other dimension of organized society. Even though the PRI lost the presidency in 2000, its adherents remain influential in Mexico's power centers.

HEALTH/WELFARE

Violence against women in Mexico first became an issue of public policy when legislation was introduced in 1990 to amend the penal code with respect to sexual crimes. Among the provisions were specialized medical and social assistance for rape victims and penalties for sexual harassment.

Historically, politicians have tended to be more interested in building their careers

than in responding to the demands of their constituents. According to political scientist Peter Smith, Mexican politicians are forever bargaining with one another, seeking favors from their superiors, and communicating in a language of "exaggerated deference." They have learned how to maximize power and success within the existing political structure. By following the "rules of the game," they move ahead. The net result is a consensus at the upper echelons of power.

In the past few decades, that consensus has been undermined. One of the great successes of the Revolution of 1910 was the rise to middle-class status of millions of people. But recent economic crises alienated that upwardly mobile sector from the PRI. People registered their dissatisfaction at the polls; in 1988, in fact, the official party finished second in Mexico City and other urban centers. In 1989, the PRI's unbroken winning streak of 60 years, facilitated by widespread electoral corruption, was broken in the state of Baja California del Norte, where the right-wing National Action Party (PAN) won the governorship. A decade of worrisome political losses prompted the PRI to consider long overdue reforms. That concern did not prevent the PRI from flagrant electoral fraud in 1988 that handed the presidency to Carlos Salinas Gortari. When it seemed apparent that the PRI would lose, the vote count was interrupted because of "computer failures." In the words of the recent autobiography of former president Miguel de la Madrid, who presided over the fraud, he was told by the PRI president: "You must proclaim the triumph of the PRI. It is a tradition that we cannot break without alarming the citizens." That "tradition" was about to end. Clearly, the PRI had lost touch with critical constituencies who were interested in fundamental change rather than party slogans and were fed up with the rampant corruption of PRI functionaries. Opposition parties continued to win elections.

In the summer of 1997, the left-of-center Party of the Democratic Revolution (PRD) scored stunning victories in legislative, gubernatorial, and municipal elections. For the first time, the PRI lost its stranglehold on the Chamber of Deputies, the lower house of Congress. Significantly, Cuauhtemoc Cardenas of the PRD was swept into power as mayor of Mexico City in the first direct vote for that position since 1928. In gubernatorial contests, the PAN won two elections and controlled an impressive seven of Mexico's 31 governorships.

Within the PRI, a new generation of leaders now perceived the need for political and economic change. President Ernesto Zedillo, worried about his party's prospects in the general elections of 2000, over the objections of old-line conservatives pushed a series of reforms in the PRI. For the first time, the party used state primaries and a national convention to choose the PRI's presidential candidate. This democratization of the party had its reflection in Zedillo's stated commitment to transform Mexican politics by giving the opposition a fair playing field. Voting was now more resistant to tampering and, as a consequence, the three major parties had to campaign for the support of the voters.

In July 2000, Vicente Fox headed a coalition of parties that adopted the name Alliance for Change and promised Mexico's electorate a "Revolution of Hope." It was a formula for success, as the PRI was swept from power. Although Fox was labeled a conservative, his platform indicated that he was above all a pragmatic politician who realized that his appeal and policies had to resonate with a wide range of sectors. Mexican voters saw in Fox someone who identified with human rights, social activism, indigenous rights, women, and the poor. He promised to be a "citizen president." Pundits described his election as a shift from an "imperial presidency" to an "entrepreneurial presidency." Indeed, Fox's economic policies, if implemented, would have promoted an annual growth rate of 7 percent, lowered inflation, balanced the budget, raised tax revenues, and improved the standard of living for Mexico's poor (who number 40 million). The private sector, in his vision, would drive the economy; and strategic sectors of the economy, notably electricity generation and petrochemicals, would be opened to private capital. Labor reforms would be initiated that would link salaries to productivity.

President Fox also promised a renewed dialogue with rebels in the southern state of Chiapas. There, beginning in 1994, Maya insurgents had rebelled against a government that habitually supported landowners against indigenous peoples, essentially marginalizing the latter. Led by Subcomandante Marcos, a shrewd and articulate activist who quickly became a hero not only in Chiapas but also in much of the rest of Mexico, the rebels symbolized widespread dissatisfaction with the promises of the PRI. A series of negotiations with the government from time to time interrupted the climate of violence and culminated in 1996 with the Agreements of San Andres. The government assured the Maya of their independence over issues of local governance. But lack of implementation of the agreements, in combination with attacks by the military on the Maya, doomed the accord from the outset.

The inability of President Fox to implement fully his programs, Mexico's far-from-satisfactory economic performance (actual GDP growth in 2007 was only 3%), and a general trend in Latin America that has put populist regimes in power, set the stage for an interesting and contentious general election in July 2006. The election, which was likely the cleanest in Mexican history, was also the closest, with PAN candidate Felipe Calderón apparently winning by half a percent of the votes. Calderón, who did well in the north and among middle and upper-class voters, favors a free-market approach to the economy and wants to allow the participation of private investment in the state-controlled energy markets. His economic priorities also include job creation and the reduction of poverty, and in 2007 he won congressional support for fiscal and pension reforms. Runner-up Andrés Manuel López Obrador, a populist, favors the involvement of the state in public works projects to stimulate construction and ease unemployment. He also advocates broad-ranging social programs to address the plight of millions of impoverished Mexicans. The PRI finished a distant third. Regardless of the final outcome, it is clear that the election revealed a polarized nation, divided geographically between the north and the south, and between the rich and the poor. The ultimate winner does not have a mandate and must work with the other party to address Mexico's many problems.

ORGANIZED LABOR

Organized labor provides an excellent example of the ways in which power is wielded in Mexico and how social change occurs. Mexican trade unions have the right to organize, negotiate, and strike. Most unions historically have not been independent of the government. The major portion of the labor movement is still affiliated with the PRI through an umbrella organization known as the Confederation of Mexican Workers (CTM). The Confederation, with a membership of 3.5 million, is one of the PRI's most ardent supporters. Union bosses truck in large crowds for campaign rallies, help PRI candidates at election time, and secure from union members approval of government policies. Union bosses have been well rewarded by the system they have helped to support. Most have become moderately wealthy and acquired status and prestige. Fully one third of Mexico's senators and congressional representatives, as well as an occasional governor, come from the ranks of union leadership.

Such a relationship must be reciprocal if it is to function properly. The CTM has used an impressive array of left-wing slogans for years to win gains for its members. It has projected an aura of radicalism when, in fact, it is not. The image is important to union members, however, for it gives them the feeling of independence from the government, and it gives a role to the true radicals in the movement. In the 1980s, cracks began to appear in the foundation of union support for the government. The economic crisis of that decade resulted in sharp cutbacks in government spending. Benefits and wage increases fell far behind the pace of inflation; layoffs and unemployment led many union members to question the value of their special relationship with the PRI. Indeed, during the 1988 elections, the Mexican newspaper *El Norte* reported that Joaquín Hernández Galicia, the powerful leader of the Oil Workers' Union, was so upset with trends within the PRI that he directed his membership to vote for opposition candidates. Not surprisingly, then, President Salinas responded by naming a new leader to the Oil Workers' Union.

Independent unions outside the Confederation of Mexican Workers capitalized on the crisis and increased their memberships. For the first time, these independent unions possessed sufficient power to challenge PRI policies. To negate the challenge from the independents, the CTM invited them to join the larger organization. Incorporation of the dissidents into the system is seen as the only way in which the system's credibility can be maintained. It illustrates the state's power to neutralize opposing forces by absorbing them into its system. The demands of labor today are strong, which will present a significant challenge to the Calderón government. If labor is to win benefits, it will have to collaborate, but the government must also be prepared for a reciprocal relationship.

ECONOMIC CRISIS

As has been suggested, a primary threat to the consensus politics of the PRI came from the economic crisis that began to build in Mexico and other Latin American countries (notably Brazil, Venezuela, and Argentina) in the early 1980s. In the 1970s, Mexico undertook economic policies designed to foster rapid and sustained industrial growth. Credit was readily available from international lending agencies and banks at low rates of interest. Initially, the development plan seemed to work, and Mexico achieved impressive economic growth rates, in the range of 8 percent per year. The government, confident in its ability to pay back its debts from revenues generated by the vast deposits of petroleum beneath Mexico, recklessly expanded its economic infrastructure.

A glut on the petroleum market in late 1981 and 1982 led to falling prices for Mexican oil. Suddenly, there was not enough money available to pay the interest on loans that were coming due, and the government had to borrow more money—at very high interest rates—to cover the unexpected shortfall. By the end of 1982, between 35 and 45 percent of Mexico's export earnings were devoured in interest payments on a debt of $80 billion. Before additional loans could be secured, foreign banks and lending organizations, such as the International Monetary Fund, demanded that the Mexican government drastically reduce state spending. This demand translated into layoffs, inadequate funding for social-welfare programs, and a general austerity that devastated the poor and undermined the high standard of living of the middle class.

Although political reform was important to then-president Salinas, he clearly recognized that economic reform was of more compelling concern. Under Salinas, the foreign debt was renegotiated and substantially reduced.

It was hoped that the North American Free Trade Agreement (NAFTA) among Mexico, the United States, and Canada would shore up the Mexican economy and generate jobs. After a decade there is a wide range of disagreement over NAFTA's success. The Carnegie Endowment of International Peace concluded in November 2003 that the agreement failed to generate significant job growth and actually hurt hundreds of thousands of subsistence farmers who could not compete with "highly efficient and heavily subsidized American farmers." A World Bank report argued that NAFTA had "brought significant economic and social benefits to the Mexican economy," and that Mexico would have been worse off without the pact. Part of the problem lies with the globalization of the economy. Mexico has lost thousands of jobs to China as well as El Salvador, where labor is 20 percent cheaper and less strictly regulated. Five hundred of Mexico's 3,700 *maquiladoras* have closed their doors since

2001. Opposition politicians, nationalists, and those concerned with the more negative aspects of capitalism have generally fought all free-trade agreements, which they see as detrimental to Mexico's sovereignty and independence of action. Perhaps the most interesting development is not economic, but political. Analysts have noted that NAFTA has contributed to a trend toward more representative government in Mexico and that globalization of the economy undercut the state-centered regime of the PRI. Despite advances in some areas, there are still far too many Mexicans whose standard of living is below the poverty level. Of the 40 million poor, 18 million are characterized as living in "extreme poverty." Income distribution is skewed, with the richest 20 percent of the population in control of 58 percent of the nation's wealth, while the poorest 20 percent control only 4 percent.

Many of those unemployed workers, now estimated at 150,000 per year, will continue to make their way to the U.S. border, which remains accessible despite the passage of immigration-reform legislation and more rigorous patrolling of the border. Others will be absorbed by the so-called informal sector, or underground economy. When walking in the streets of Mexico City, one quickly becomes aware that there exists an economy that is not recognized, licensed, regulated, or "protected" by the government. Yet in the 1980s, this informal sector of the economy produced 25 to 35 percent of Mexico's gross domestic product and served as a shield for millions of Mexicans who might otherwise have been reduced to destitution. According to George Grayson, "Extended families, which often have several members working and others hawking lottery tickets or shining shoes, establish a safety net for upward of one third of the workforce in a country where social security coverage is limited and unemployment compensation is nonexistent."

FOREIGN POLICY

The problems created by Mexico's economic policy have been balanced by a visibly successful foreign policy. Historically, Mexican foreign policy, which is noted for following an independent course of action, has been used by the government for domestic purposes. In the 1980s, President Miguel de la Madrid identified revolutionary nationalism as the historical synthesis, or melding, of the Mexican people. History, he argued, taught Mexicans to be nationalist in order to resist external aggression, and history made Mexico revolutionary in order to enable it to transform unequal social and economic structures. These beliefs, when tied to the formulation of foreign policy,

Timeline: PAST

1519
Hernán Cortés lands at Vera Cruz

1521
Destruction of the Aztec Empire

1810
Mexico proclaims its independence from Spain

1846–1848
War with the United States; Mexico loses four-fifths of its territory

1862–1867
The French take over the Mexican throne and install Emperor Maximillian

1876–1910
Era of dictator Porfirio Díaz: modernization

1910–1917
The Mexican Revolution

1934–1940
Land distribution under President Cárdenas

1938
Nationalization of foreign petroleum companies

1955
Women win the right to vote

1968
The Olympic Games are held in Mexico City; riots and violence

1980s
Severe economic crisis; the peso is devalued; inflation soars; the foreign-debt crisis escalates; Maya insurgency in the state of Chiapas

1990s
NAFTA is passed: the PRI loses ground in legislative, gubernatorial, and municipal elections

PRESENT

2000s
The PRI is ousted from power President Felipe Calderón wins the presidency by less than one-half of one percent of the vote

have fashioned policies with a definite leftist bias. The country has often been sympathetic to social change and has identified, at least in principle, with revolutionary causes all over the globe. The Mexican government opposed the economic and political isolation of Cuba that was so heartily endorsed by the United States. It supported the Marxist regime of Salvador Allende in Chile at a time when the United States was attempting to destabilize his government. Mexico was one of the first nations to break relations with President Anastasio Somoza of Nicaragua and to recognize the legitimacy of the struggle of the Sandinista guerrillas. In 1981, Mexico joined with France in recognizing the opposition front and guerrilla coalition in El Salvador. In the 1990s Mexico, together with several other Latin American countries, urged a negotiated solution to the armed conflict in Central America. Even though the populist candidate did not win the presidential election in 2006, it might be expected that the Calderón government will not distance itself from other populist regimes in Latin America. Indeed, past Mexican policy would seem to dictate a close relationship.

Mexico's traditional leftist foreign policy balances conservative domestic policies. A foreign policy identified with change and social justice has the effect of softening the impact of leftist demands in Mexico for land reform or political change. Mexicans, if displeased with government domestic policies, were soothed by a vigorous foreign policy that placed Mexico in a leadership role, often in opposition to the United States. In economic matters, Mexico's foreign policy will tend more toward centrism, especially with regard to the negotiation of free-trade agreements. Indeed, in 2008, Mexico has in place 12 free-trade agreements with 40 countries.

HARD TIMES

Mexico's future is fraught with uncertainty. In December 1994, the economy collapsed after the government could no longer sustain an overvalued peso. In just a few months, the peso fell in value by half, while the stock market, in terms of the peso, suffered a 38 percent drop. The crash was particularly acute because the Salinas government had not invested foreign aid in factories and job creation, but had instead put most of the money into Mexico's volatile stock market. It then proceeded to spend Mexico's reserves to prop up the peso when the decline gathered momentum. Salinas's successor, President Ernesto Zedillo, had to cut public spending, sell some state-owned industries, and place strict limits on wage and price increases.

To further confound the economic crisis, the Maya insurgency in Chiapas succeeded in generating much antigovernment support in the rest of Mexico. President Zedillo claimed that the rebels, who call themselves

the Zapatista Army of National Liberation (EZLN, named for Emiliano Zapata, one of the peasant leaders of the Mexican Revolution), were "neither popular, nor indigenous, nor from Chiapas." Nobel Laureate Octavio Paz condemned the uprising as an "interruption of Mexico's ongoing political and economic liberalization." The interests of the EZLN leadership, he said, were those of intellectuals rather than those of the peasantry. In other words, what happened in Chiapas was an old story of peasant Indians being used by urban intellectuals—in this instance, to challenge the PRI. Indeed, the real identity of "Subcomandante Marcos" was revealed as Rafael Sebastian Guillen Vicente, a former professor from a rich provincial family who had worked with Tzotzil and Tzeltal Maya Indians since 1984.

George Collier, however, argues that the rebellion is a response to changing governmental policies, agricultural modernization, and cultural and economic isolation. While the peasants of central Chiapas profited from PRI policies, those in the eastern part of the state were ignored. Thus, the rebellion, in essence, was a demand to be included in the largesse of the state. The demands of the EZLN were instructive: democratic reform by the state, limited autonomy for indigenous communities, an antidiscrimination law, teachers, clinics, doctors, electricity, better housing, childcare centers, and a radio station for indigenous peoples. Only vague statements were made about subdivision of large ranches.

During the presidential campaign of 2000, Fox promised to address the complaints raised by the EZLN. Legislation introduced in Congress in the spring of 2001 was designed to safeguard and promote the rights of indigenous peoples. To call attention to the debate, the Zapatistas, with government protection, embarked on a two-week-long march to Mexico City. Significantly, the marchers carried not only the flag of the EZLN but also that of Mexico. But Congress felt that the legislation could damage the nation's unity and harm the interests of local landlords in the south. When a watered-down version of the legislation was passed, Subcomandante Marcos vowed to continue the rebellion. President

Fox urged that the talks continue and publicly complained about the congressional action. This was an astute move, because the EZLN could lose an important ally if it adopted an intransigent position.

On the other hand, the Zapatistas were in danger of fading into the background if they lost the ability to attract the attention of the media. Indeed, the government has essentially ignored them in recent years and much Zapatista support in Mexico has shifted to the populism of the PRD. It is no surprise that Subcomandante Marcos emerged from the jungle and embarked on a nationwide tour in 2006, not only to prevent his movement from becoming irrelevant in the minds of Mexicans, but also to attack the PRD presidential candidate as a "traitor" who would betray Mexico's indigenous peoples.

In summary, the insurgency can be seen to have several roots and to serve many purposes. It is far more complex than a "simple" uprising of an oppressed people.

THE FUTURE

Journalist Igor Fuser, writing in the Brazilian newsweekly *Veja,* observed: "For pessimists, the implosion of the PRI is the final ingredient needed to set off an apocalyptic bomb composed of economic recession, guerrilla war, and the desperation of millions of Mexicans facing poverty. For optimists, the unrest is a necessary evil needed to unmask the most carefully camouflaged dictatorship on the planet."

The elections of 2000 and 2006 tore away that mask, but persistent problems remain. Corruption, endemic drug-related violence, poverty, unemployment and underemployment, high debt, and inflation are daunting. President Fox admitted in his state of the nation address in September 2003 that he had failed to implement the "historic transformations our times demand." Congress blocked many of his initiatives, the unrest in Chiapas continues, and jobs are being lost to the globalization of the economy. President Calderón has inherited a difficult set of problems and a polarized electorate. Change is critical but the policies of transformation render it problematic.

Central America

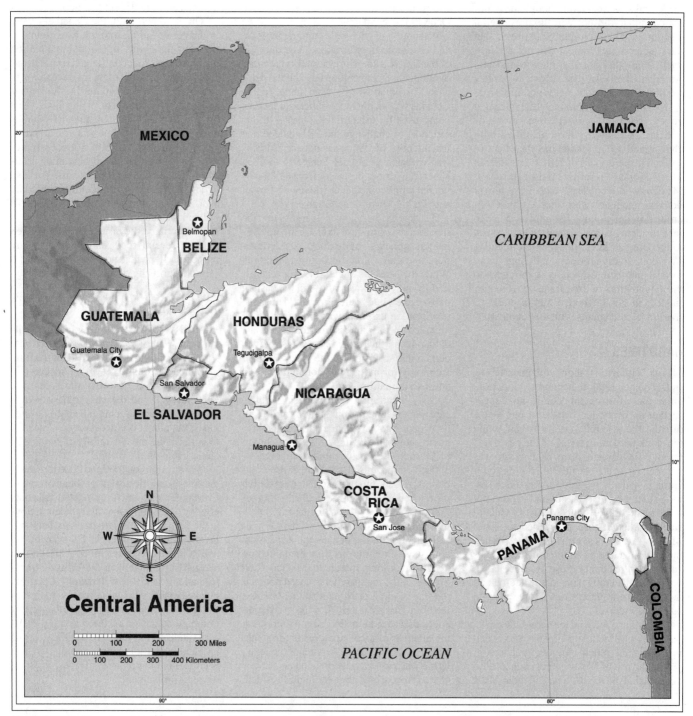

Much of Central America shares important historical milestones. In 1821, the states of Guatemala, Honduras, El Salvador, Costa Rica, and Nicaragua declared themselves independent of Spain. In 1822, they joined the Empire of Mexico; in 1823, they formed the United Provinces of Central America. This union lasted until 1838, when each member state severed its relations with the federation and went its own way. Since 1838, there have been more than 25 attempts to restore the union—but to no avail.

Central America   Lands in Turmoil

LIFE IN THE MOUTH OF THE VOLCANO

Sons of the Shaking Earth, a well-known study of Middle America by anthropologist Eric Wolf, captures in its title the critical interplay between people and the land in Central America. It asserts that the land is violent and that the inhabitants of the region live in an environment that is often shaken by natural disaster.

The dominant geographical feature of Central America is the impressive and forbidding range of volcanic mountains that runs from Mexico to Panama. These mountains have always been obstacles to communication, to the cultivation of the land, and to the national integration of the countries in which they lie. The volcanoes rest atop major fault lines; some are dormant, others are active, and new ones have appeared periodically. Over the centuries, eruptions and earthquakes have destroyed thousands of villages. Some have recovered, but others remain buried beneath lava and ash. Nearly every Central American city has been destroyed at one time or another; and some, such as Managua, Nicaragua, have suffered repeated devastation.

An ancient Indian philosophy speaks of five great periods of time, each doomed to end in disaster. The fifth period, which is the time in which we now live, is said to terminate with a world-destroying earthquake. "Thus," writes Wolf, "the people of Middle [Central] America live in the mouth of the volcano. Middle America . . . is one of the proving grounds of humanity."

Earthquakes and eruptions are not the only natural disasters that plague the region. Rains fall heavily between May and October each year, and devastating floods are common. On the Caribbean coast, hurricanes often strike in the late summer and early autumn, threatening coastal cities and leveling crops.

The constant threat of natural disaster has had a deep impact on Central Americans' views of life and development. Death and tragedy have conditioned their attitudes toward the present and the future.

GEOGRAPHY

The region is not only violent but also diverse. In political terms, Central America consists of seven independent nations: Belize, Costa Rica, El Salvador, Guatemala, Honduras, Nicaragua, and Panama. With the exception of Costa Rica and Panama, where national borders coincide with geographical and human frontiers, political boundaries are artificial and were marked out in defiance of both the lay of the land and the cultural groupings of the region's peoples.

Geographically, Central America can be divided into four broad zones: Petén–Belize; the Caribbean coasts of Guatemala, Honduras, and Nicaragua; the Pacific volcanic region; and Costa Rica–Panama.

The northern Guatemalan territory of Petén and all of Belize are an extension of Mexico's Yucatán Peninsula. The region is heavily forested with stands of mahogany, cedar, and pine, whose products are a major source of revenue for Belize.

The Caribbean lowlands, steamy and disease-ridden, are sparsely settled. The inhabitants of the Caribbean coast in Nicaragua include Miskito Indians and the descendants of English-speaking blacks who first settled the area in the seventeenth century. The Hispanic population there was small until recently. Coastal Honduras is more heavily populated and marginally more prosperous than the rest of the country because of the banana industry. Coffee also is a significant source of revenue. But the coast is vulnerable to hurricanes and "blow-downs" of the banana trees is a frequent occurrence. Honduras, overall, is a very poor country.

The Pacific volcanic highlands are the cultural heartland of Central America. Here, in highland valleys noted for their spring like climate, live more than 80 percent of the population of Central America; here are the largest cities. In cultural terms, the highlands are home to the whites, mixed bloods, Hispanicized Indians known as Ladinos, and pure-blooded Indians who are descended from the Maya. These highland groups form a striking ethnic contrast to the Indians (such as the Miskito), mulattos, and blacks of the coastlands. The entire country of El Salvador falls within this geographical zone. Unlike its neighbors, there is a uniformity to the land and people of El Salvador.

The fourth region, divided between the nations of Costa Rica and Panama, constitutes a single geographical unit. Mountains form the spine of the isthmus. In Costa Rica, the Central Mesa has attracted 70 percent of the nation's population, because of its agreeable climate.

CLIMATE AND CULTURE

The geographic and biological diversity of Central America—with its cool highlands and steaming lowlands, its incredible variety of microclimates and environments, its seemingly infinite types of flora and fauna, and its mineral wealth—has been a major factor in setting the course of the cultural history of Central America. Before the Spanish conquest, the environmental diversity favored the cultural cohesion of peoples. The products of one environmental niche could easily be exchanged for the products of another. In a sense, valley people and those living higher up in the mountains depended on one another. Here was one of the bases for the establishment of the advanced culture of the Maya.

The cultural history of Central America has focused on the densely populated highlands and Pacific plains—those areas most favorable for human occupation. Spaniards settled in the same regions, and centers of national life are located there today. But if geography has been a factor in bringing peoples together on a local level, it has also contributed to the formation of regional differences, loyalties, interests, and jealousies. Neither Maya rulers nor Spanish bureaucrats could triumph over

Central American Indians are firmly tied to their traditional beliefs and have strongly resisted the influence of European culture, as evidenced by this Cuna woman.

the natural obstacles presented by the region's harsh geography. The mountains and rain forests have mocked numerous attempts to create a single Central American state.

CULTURES IN CONFLICT

Although physical geography has interacted with culture, the contact between Indians and Spaniards since the sixteenth century has profoundly shaped the cultural face of today's Central America. According to historian Ralph Woodward, the religious traditions of the indigenous peoples, with Christianity imperfectly superimposed over them, "together with the violence of the Conquest and the centuries of slavery or serfdom which followed, left clear impressions on the personality and mentality of the Central American Indian."

To outsiders, the Indians often appear docile and obedient to authority, but beneath this mask may lie intense emotions, including distrust and bitterness. The Indians' vision is usually local and oriented toward the village and family; they do not identify themselves as Guatemalan or Nicaraguan. When

challenged, Indians have fought to defend their rights, and a long succession of rebellions from colonial days until the present attests to their sense of what is just and what is not. The Indians, firmly tied to their traditional beliefs and values, have tried to resist modernization, despite government programs and policies designed to counter what urbanized whites perceive as backwardness and superstition.

Population growth, rather than government programs and policies, has had a great impact on the region's Indian peoples and has already resulted in the recasting of cultural traditions. Peasant villages in much of Central America have traditionally organized their ritual life around the principle of *mayordomía,* or sponsorship. Waldemar Smith, an anthropologist who has explored the relationship between the *fiesta* (ceremony) system and economic change, has shown the impact of changing circumstances on traditional systems. In any Central American community in any given year, certain families are appointed *mayordomos,* or stewards, of the village saints; they are responsible for organizing and paying for the celebrations in their names. This responsibility ordinarily lasts for a year. One of the outstanding features of the fiesta system is the phenomenal costs that the designated family must bear. An individual might have to expend the equivalent of a year's earnings or more to act as a sponsor in a community fiesta. Psychological and social burdens must also be borne by the mayordomos, for they represent their community before its saints. Mayordomos, who in essence are priests for a year, are commonly expected to refrain from sexual activity for long periods as well as to devote much time to ritual forms.

The office, while highly prestigious, can also be dangerous. Maya Indians, for example, believe that the saints use the weather as a weapon to punish transgressions, and extreme weather is often traced to ritual error or sins on the part of the mayordomo, who might on such occasions actually be jailed.

Since the late 1960s, the socioeconomic structure of much of the area heavily populated by Indians has changed, forcing changes in traditional cultural forms, including the fiesta system. Expansion of markets and educational opportunity, the absorption of much of the workforce in seasonal plantation labor, more efficient transportation systems, and population growth have precipitated change. Traditional festivals in honor of a community's saints have significantly diminished in importance in a number of towns. Costs have been reduced or several families have been made responsible for fiesta sponsorship. This reflects not only modernization but also crisis. Some communities have become too poor to support themselves—and the expensive fiestas have, naturally, suffered.

This increasing poverty is driven in part by population growth, which has exerted tremendous pressure on people's access to land. Families that cannot be sustained on traditional lands must now seek seasonal wage labor on sugarcane, coffee, or cotton plantations. Others emigrate. The net result is a culture under siege. Thus, while the fiestas may not vanish, they are surely in the process of change.

The Ladino World

The word *Ladino* can be traced back to the Roman occupation of Spain. It referred to someone who had been "Latinized" and was therefore wise in the ways of the world. The word has several meanings in Central America. In Guatemala, it refers to a person integration and modernization. Businesspeople and bureaucrats, absentee landlords, and the professional class of doctors, lawyers, and engineers constitute an urban elite who are cosmopolitan and sophisticated. Wealth, status, and "good blood" are the keys to elite membership.

The Disadvantaged

The cities have also attracted disadvantaged people who have migrated from poverty-stricken rural regions in search of economic opportunity. Many are self-employed as peddlers, small-scale traders, or independent craftspeople. Others seek low-paying, unskilled positions in industry, construction work, and transportation. Most live on the edge of poverty and are the first to suffer in times of economic recession. But there exist Hispanic institutions in this harsh world that help people of all classes to adjust. In each of the capital cities of Central America, lower-sector people seek help and sustenance from the more advantaged elements in society. They form economic and social alliances that are mutually beneficial. For example, a tradesman might approach a well-to-do merchant and seek advice or a small loan. In return, he can offer guaranteed service, a steady supply of crafts for the wholesaler, and a price that is right. It is a world built on mutual exchanges.

These networks, when they function, bind societies together and ease the alienation and isolation of the less advantaged inhabitants. Of course, networks that cut through class lines can effectively limit class action in pursuit of reforms; and, in many instances, the networks do not exist or are exploitive.

POPULATION MOVEMENT

For many years, Central Americans have been peoples in motion. Migrants who have moved from rural areas into the cities have often been driven from lands they once owned, either because of the expansion of landed estates at the expense of the smaller landholdings, population pressure, or division of the land into plots so small that subsistence farming is no longer possible. Others have moved to the cities in search of a better life.

Population pressure on the land is most intense in El Salvador. No other Latin American state utilizes the whole of its territory to the extent that El Salvador does. Most of the land is still privately owned and is devoted to cattle farming or to raising cotton and coffee for the export market. There is not enough land to provide crops for a population that has grown at one of the most rapid rates in the Western Hemisphere. There are no unpopulated lands left to occupy. Agrarian reform, even if successful, will still leave hundreds of thousands of peasants without land.

Many Salvadorans have moved to the capital city of San Salvador in search of employment. Others have crossed into neighboring countries. In the 1960s, thousands moved to Honduras, where they settled on the land or were attracted to commerce and industry. By the end of that decade, more than 75 percent of all foreigners living in Honduras had crossed the border from El Salvador. Hondurans, increasingly concerned by the growing presence of Salvadorans, acted to stem the flow and passed restrictive and discriminatory legislation against the immigrants. The tension, an ill-defined border, and festering animosity ultimately brought about a brief war between Honduras and El Salvador in 1969.

(Courtesy of Omar Sahyoun)

An estimated 40 million children throughout Latin America between three and 18 are living and working on the streets. Children, as pictured above, sell trinkets to supplement the family income where parents earn well below a living wage.

of mixed blood, or *Mestizo*. In most of the rest of Central America, however, it refers to an Indian who has adopted white culture.

The Ladinos are caught between two cultures, both of which initially rejected them. The Ladinos attempted to compensate for their lack of cultural roots and cultural identity by aggressively carving out a place in Central American society. Often acutely status-conscious, Ladinos typically contrast sharply with the Indians they physically resemble. Ladinos congregate in the larger towns and cities, speak Spanish, and seek a livelihood as shopkeepers or landowners. They compose the local elite in Guatemala, Nicaragua, Honduras, and El Salvador (the latter country was almost entirely Ladinoized by the end of the nineteenth century), and they usually control regional politics. They are often the most aggressive members of the community, driven by the desire for self-advancement. Their vision is frequently much broader than that of the Indian; they have a perspective that includes the capital city and the nation. The vast majority of the population speak Spanish; few villages retain the use of their original, native tongues.

The Elite

For the elite, who are culturally "white," the city dominates their social and cultural horizons. For them, the world of the Indian is unimportant—save for the difficult questions of social

The migration of poor rural people to Central American urban centers has caused large numbers of squatters to take up residence in slums.

Honduras, with a low population density (about 139 persons per square mile, as compared to El Salvador's 721), has attracted population not only from neighboring countries but also from the Caribbean. Black migrants from the "West Indian" Caribbean islands known as the Antilles have been particularly attracted to Honduras's north coast, where they have been able to find employment on banana plantations or in the light industry that has increasingly been established in the area. The presence of these Caribbean peoples in moderate numbers has more sharply focused regional differences in Honduras. The coast, in many respects, is Caribbean in its peoples' identity and outlook; while peoples of the highlands of the interior identify with the capital city of Tegucigalpa, which is Hispanic in culture.

THE REFUGEE PROBLEM

Recent turmoil in Central America created yet another group of people on the move—refugees from the fighting in their own countries or from the persecution by extremists of the political left and right. For example, thousands of Salvadorans crowded into Honduras's western province. In the south, Miskito Indians, fleeing from Nicaragua's Sandinista government, crossed the Río Coco in large numbers. Additional thousands of armed Nicaraguan counterrevolutionaries camped along the border. Only in 1990–1991 did significant numbers of Salvadorans move back to their homeland. With the declared truce between Sandinistas and Contras and the election victory of Violeta Chamorro, Nicaraguan refugees were gradually repatriated. Guatemalan Indians sought refuge in southern Mexico, and Central Americans of all nationalities resettled in Costa Rica and Belize.

El Salvadorans, who began to emigrate to the United States in the 1960s, did so in much greater numbers with the onset of the El Salvadoran Civil War, which killed approximately 70,000 people and displaced about 25 percent of the nation's population. The Urban Institute, a Washington, D.C.–based research group, estimated in 1986 that there were then about ¾ million El Salvadorans—of a total population of just over 5 million—living in the United States. Those emigrants became a major source of dollars for El Salvador; it is estimated that they now send home about $500 million a year.

While that money has undoubtedly helped to keep the nation's economy above water, it has also generated, paradoxically, a good deal of anti–U.S. sentiment in El Salvador. Lindsey Gruson, a reporter for *The New York Times,* studied the impact of expatriate dollars in Intipuca, a town 100 miles southwest of the capital, and concluded that they had a profound impact on Intipuqueño culture. The influx of money was an incentive not to work, and townspeople said that the "free" dollars "perverted cherished values" and were "breaking up many families."

THE ROOTS OF VIOLENCE

Central America still feels the effects of civil war and violence. Armies, guerrillas, and terrorists of the political left and right have exacted a high toll on human lives and property. The civil wars and guerrilla movements that spread violence to the region sprang from each of the societies in question.

A critical societal factor was (and remains) the emergence of a middle class in Central America. In some respects, people of the middle class resemble the Mestizos or Ladinos, in that their wealth and position have placed them above the masses. But, like the Mestizos and Ladinos, they have been denied access to the upper reaches of power, which is the special preserve of the elite. Since World War II, it has been members of the middle class who have called for reform and a more equitable distribution of the national wealth. They have also attempted to forge alliances of opportunity with workers and peasants.

Nationalistic, assertive, restless, ambitious, and, to an extent, ruthless, people of the middle class (professionals, intellectuals, junior officers in the armed forces, office workers, businesspeople, teachers, students, and skilled workers) demand a greater voice in the political world. They want governments that are responsive to their interests and needs; and, when governments have proven unresponsive or hostile, elements of the middle class have chosen confrontation.

In the civil war that removed the Somoza family from power in Nicaragua in 1979, for example, the middle class played a critical leadership role. Guerrilla leaders in El Salvador were middle class in terms of their social origins, and there was significant middle-class participation in the unrest in Guatemala.

Indeed, Central America's middle class is among the most revolutionary groups in the region. Although middle-class people are well represented in antigovernment forces, they also resist changes that would tend to elevate those below them on the social scale. They are also significantly represented among right-wing groups, whose reputation for conservative views is accompanied by systematic terror.

Other societal factors also figure prominently in the violence in Central America. The rapid growth of population since the 1960s has severely strained each nation's resources. Many rural areas have become overpopulated, poor agricultural practices have caused extensive soil erosion, the amount of land available to subsistence farmers is inadequate, and poverty and misery are pervasive. These problems have combined to compel rural peoples to migrate to the cities or to whatever frontier lands are still available. In Guatemala, government policy drove Indians from ancestral villages in the highlands to "resettlement" villages in the low-lying, forested Petén to the north. Indians displaced in this manner often—not surprisingly—joined guerrilla movements. They were not attracted to insurgency by the allure of socialist or communist ideology; they simply responded to violence and the loss of their lands with violence against the governments that pursued such policies.

The conflict in this region does not always pit landless, impoverished peasants against an unyielding elite. Some members of the elite see the need for change. Most peasants have not taken up arms, and the vast majority wish to be left in peace. Others who desire change may be found in the ranks of the military or within the hierarchy of the Roman Catholic Church. Reformers are drawn from all sectors of society. It is thus more appropriate to view the conflict in Central America as a civil war rather than a class struggle, as civil wars cut through the entire fabric of a nation.

Much of today's criminal violence in urban areas of Central America, and particularly in El Salvador and Honduras, is a direct consequence of the years of civil war. Young children of refugees, who relocated to large United States cities as adolescents, often imitated the gang culture to which they were exposed. When they returned to Central America and encountered a society that they did not recognize, they could not find jobs and the gang culture was replicated. Indeed, violent crime, most of which was attributed to youth gangs, was a central issue in presidential elections in Honduras in 2005.

ECONOMIC PROBLEMS

Central American economies, always fragile, have in recent years been plagued by a combination of vexing problems. Foreign debt, inflation, currency devaluations, recession, and, in some instances, outside interference have had deleterious effects on the standard of living in all the countries. Civil war, insurgency, corruption and mismanagement, and population growth have added fuel to the crisis—not only in the region's economies but also in their societies. Nature, too, has played an important contributory role in the region's economic and social malaise. Hurricane Mitch, which struck Central American in 1998, killed thousands, destroyed crops and property, and disrupted the infrastructure of roads and bridges in Honduras, Nicaragua, Guatemala, and El Salvador.

Civil war in El Salvador brought unprecedented death and destruction and was largely responsible for economic deterioration and a decline of well over one-third of per capita income from 1980 to 1992. Today (2008) the official unemployment rate is nearly 7% but underemployment is a much more significant factor in the economy. The struggle of the Sandinista government of Nicaragua against U.S.–sponsored rebels routinely consumed 60 percent of government spending; even with peace, much of the budget was earmarked for economic recovery. In Guatemala, a savage civil war lasted more than a generation; took more than 140,000 lives; strained the economy; depressed wages; and left unaddressed pressing social problems in education, housing, and welfare. Although the violence has subsided, the lingering fears conditioned by that violence have not. U.S. efforts to force the ouster of Panamanian strongman Manuel Antonio Noriega through the application of economic sanctions probably harmed middle-class businesspeople in Panama more than Noriega.

Against this backdrop of economic malaise there have been some creative attempts to solve, or at least to confront, pressing problems. In 1987, the Costa Rican government proposed a series of debt-for-nature swaps to international conservation groups, such as the Nature Conservancy. The first of the transactions took place in 1988, when several organizations purchased more than $3 million of Costa Rica's foreign debt at 17 percent of face value. The plan called for the government to exchange with the organizations part of Costa Rica's external debt for government bonds; the conservation groups would then invest the earnings of the bonds in the management and protection of

Costa Rican national parks. According to the National Wildlife Federation, while debt-for-nature swaps are not a cure-all for the Latin American debt crisis, at least the swaps can go some distance toward protecting natural resources and encouraging ecologically sound, long-term economic development.

INTERNAL AND EXTERNAL DIMENSIONS OF CONFLICT

The continuing violence in much of Central America suggests that internal dynamics are perhaps more important than the overweening roles formerly ascribed to Havana, Moscow, and Washington. The removal of foreign "actors" from the stage lays bare the real reasons for violence in the region: injustice, power, greed, revenge, and racial and ethnic discrimination. Havana, Moscow, and Washington, among others, merely used Central American violence in pursuit of larger policy goals. And Central American governments and guerrilla groups were equally adept at using foreign powers to advance their own interests, be they revolutionary or reactionary.

Panama offers an interesting scenario in this regard. It, like the rest of Central America, is a poor nation comprised of sub-sistence farmers, rural laborers, urban workers, and unemployed and underemployed people dwelling in the shantytowns ringing the larger cities. For years, the pressures for reform in Panama were skillfully rechanneled by the ruling elite toward the issue of the Panama Canal. Frustration and anger were deflected from the government, and an outdated social structure was attributed to the presence of a foreign power—the United States—in what Panamanians regarded as their territory.

Central America, in summary, is a region of diverse geography and is home to peoples of many cultures. It is a region of strong local loyalties; its problems are profound and perplexing. The violence of the land is matched by the violence of its peoples as they fight for something as noble as justice or human rights, or as ignoble as political power or self-promotion.

Belize

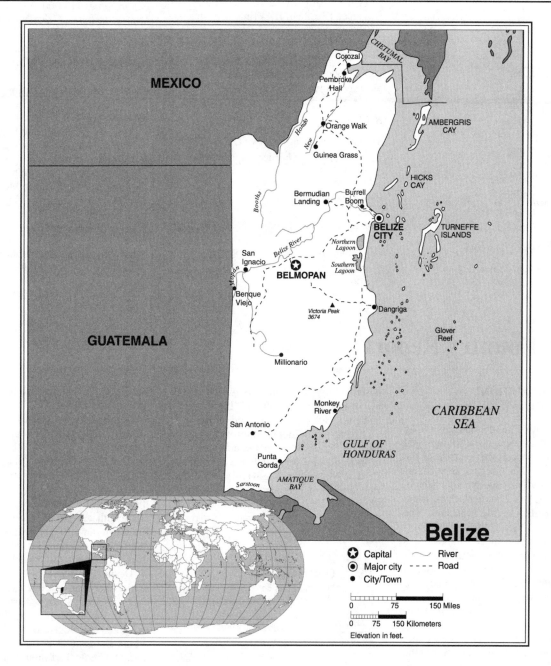

Belize Statistics

GEOGRAPHY

Area in Square Miles (Kilometers):
8,866 (22,963) (about the size of
Massachusetts)
Capital (Population): Belmopan (7,100)
Environmental Concerns: deforestation;
water pollution
Geographical Features: flat, swampy
coastal plain; low mountains in south
Climate: tropical; very hot and humid

PEOPLE

Population

Total: 294,385 (2007 est.)
Annual Growth Rate: 2.6%
Rural/Urban Population Ratio:
54/46
Ethnic Makeup: 48.7% Mestizo; 24.9%
Creole; 10.6% Maya; 6.1% Garifuna;
9.7% others

Major Languages: Spanish 46%; Creole
32.9%; Maya dialects 8.9%; English
3.9% (official)
Religions: 49.6% Roman Catholic;
27% Protestant; 14% others;
9.4% unaffiliated

Health

Life Expectancy at Birth: 66 years (male);
70 years (female)

GLOBAL STUDIES

Infant Mortality Rate (Ratio):
  24.38/1,000
Physicians Available (Ratio): 1/1,546

Education

Adult Literacy Rate: 77%
Compulsory (Ages): 5–14

COMMUNICATION

Telephones: 33,900 main lines
Cell Phones: 118,300
Internet Users: 30,000

TRANSPORTATION

Highways in Miles (Kilometers): 1,723
  (2,872)
Railroads in Miles (Kilometers): none
Usable Airfields: 44

GOVERNMENT

Type: parliamentary democracy

Independence Date: September 21, 1981
  (from the United Kingdom)
Head of State/Government: Governor
  General Sir Colville Young (represents
  Queen Elizabeth II); Prime Minister
  Dean Barrow
Political Parties: People's United Party;
  United Democratic Party; National
  Alliance for Belizean Rights
Suffrage: universal at 18

MILITARY

Military Expenditures (% of GDP): 1.4%
Current Disputes: border dispute with
  Guatemala

ECONOMY

Currency ($U.S. Equivalent): 2.00 Belize
  dollars = $1
Per Capita Income/GDP: $7,800/$1.138
  billion

GDP Growth Rate: 2.3%
Inflation Rate: 2.8%
Unemployment Rate: 9.4%
Labor Force: 113,000
Natural Resources: arable land; timber;
  fish; hydropower
Agriculture: bananas; cocoa; citrus fruits;
  sugarcane; lumber; fish; cultured
  shrimp
Industry: garment production;
  food processing; tourism;
  construction
Exports: $437 million (f.o.b.) (primary
  partners Mexico, United States,
  European Union)
Imports: $670 million (f.o.b.) (primary
  partners United States, Mexico, United
  Kingdom)

SUGGESTED WEB SITE

http://www.cia.gov/cia/publications/
  factbook/geos/bh.html#Geo

Belize Country Report

THE "HISPANICIZATION" OF A COUNTRY

Belize was settled in the late 1630s by English woodcutters who also indulged in occasional piracy at the expense of the Spanish crown. The loggers were interested primarily in dye-woods, which, in the days before chemical dyes, were essential to British textile industries. The country's name is derived from Peter Wallace, a notorious buccaneer who, from his base there, haunted the coast in search of Spanish shipping. The natives shortened and mispronounced Wallace's name until he became known as "Belize."

As a British colony (called British Honduras), Belize enjoyed relative prosperity as an important entrepôt, or storage depot for merchandise, until the completion of the Panama Railway in 1855. With the opening of a rail route to the Pacific, commerce shifted south, away from Caribbean ports. Belize entered an economic tailspin (from which it has never entirely recovered). Colonial governments attempted to diversify the colony's agricultural base and to attract foreign immigration to develop the land. But, except for some Mexican settlers and a few former Confederate soldiers who came to the colony after the U.S. Civil War, the immigration policy failed. Economically depressed, its population exposed to the ravages of yellow fever, malaria, and dengue (a tropical fever), Belize was once

described by British novelist Aldous Huxley in the following terms: "If the world had ends, Belize would be one of them."

Living conditions improved markedly by the 1950s, and the colony began to move toward independence from Great Britain. Although self-governing by 1964, Belize did not become fully independent until 1981, because of Guatemalan threats to invade what it considered a lost province, stolen by the British.

DEVELOPMENT

Belize has combined its tourism and environmental-protection offices into one ministry, which holds great promise for ecotourism. Large tracts of land have been set aside to protect jaguars and other endangered species. But there is also pressure on the land from rapid population growth.

For most of its history Belize has been culturally British with Caribbean overtones. English common law is practiced in the courts, and politics are patterned on the English parliamentary system. A large percent of the people are Protestants. The Belizeans are primarily working-class poor and middle-class shopkeepers and merchants. There is no great difference between the well-to-do and the poor in

Belize, and few people fall below the absolute poverty line.

Nearly fifty percent of the population are classified as *mestizo* and twenty-five percent are Creole (black and English mixture). The Garifuna (black and Indian mixture) who comprise about 6 percent of the population, originally inhabited the Caribbean island of St. Vincent. In the eighteenth century, they joined with native Indians in an uprising against the English authorities. As punishment, virtually all the Garifuna were deported to Belize.

Despite a pervasive myth of racial democracy in Belize, discrimination exists. Belize is not a harmonious, multiethnic island in a sea of violence. For example, sociologist Bruce Ergood notes that in Belize it "is not uncommon to hear a light Creole bad-mouth 'blacks,' even though both are considered Creole. This reflects a vestige of English colonial attitude summed up in the saying, 'Best to be white, less good to be mulatto, worst to be black. . . .'"

FREEDOM

Legislation was passed in October 2000 that calls on trade unions and employers to negotiate over unionization of the workplace if that is the desire of the majority of workers.

24

A shift in population occurred in the 1980s because of the turmoil in neighboring Central American states. For years, well-educated, English-speaking Creoles had been leaving Belize in search of better economic opportunities in other countries; but this was more than made up for by the inflow of perhaps as many as 40,000 Latin American refugees fleeing the fighting in the region. Spanish is now the primary language of a significant percentage of the population, and some Belizeans are concerned about the "Hispanicization" of the country.

HEALTH/WELFARE

In a speech to the Christian Workers Union, former Prime Minister Said Musa noted: "Higher wages will not mean much if families cannot obtain quality and affordable health care services. What good are higher wages if there are not enough classrooms in which to place the children? What good are higher wages if we are forced to live in fear of the criminal elements in society? A workers' movement must . . . concern itself not only with wages but also with the overall quality of life of its members."

Women in Belize suffer discrimination that is deeply rooted in the cultural, social, and economic structures of the society, even though the government promotes their participation in the nation's politics and development process. Great emphasis is placed on education and health care. Tropical diseases, once the primary cause of death in Belize, were brought under control by a government program of insect spraying. Better health and nutritional awareness are emphasized in campaigns to encourage breastfeeding and the selection and preparation of meals using local produce.

ACHIEVEMENTS

Recent digging by archaeologists has uncovered several Maya sites that have convinced scholars that the indigenous civilization in the region was more extensive and refined than experts had previously believed.

With the new millennium, Belize has increasingly turned its attention to the impact of globalization. Concern was expressed by the government about job security and the need for education and training in the skills necessary to compete in a global marketplace. National Trade Union Congress president Dorene Quiros noted that "global institutions are not meeting the basic needs of people," and promises by international organizations to do better have produced only modest results. Worrying, too, is the rising incidence of violent urban crime and growing involvement in the South American drug trade.

In 2006 petroleum was discovered in the western part of the country close to the border with Guatemala. With expectations that the oil field could yield about 50,000 barrels of oil per day, exports could provide a modest boost to the economy. But the discovery could lead to friction with Guatemala.

Timeline: PAST

1638
Belize is settled by English Logwood cutters

1884
Belize is declared an independent Crown colony

1972
Guatemala threatens to invade

1981
Independence from Great Britain

1990s
Belize becomes an ecotourism destination

Said Musa is elected prime minister

PRESENT

2000s
Guatemala continues territorial claims to Belize

Negotiations with Guatemala over border issues continue

Although Guatemala recognized the independence of Belize in 1992, the oil was found in a disputed border area.

Potential oil revenues are still in the future. In the meantime, tourism forms the backbone of the economy. Ongoing problems include a large foreign debt, high levels of poverty and a growing incidence of urban crime. Belize has also become an increasingly significant transit point for South America's drug trade (primarily cocaine).

Costa Rica (Republic of Costa Rica)

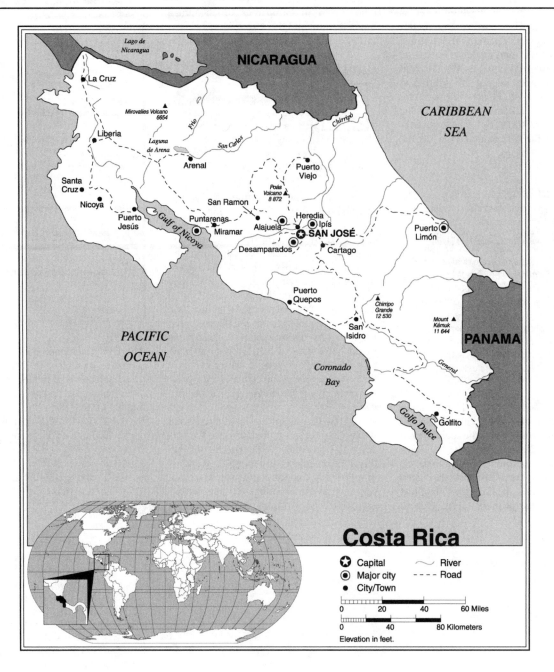

Costa Rica Statistics

GEOGRAPHY

Area in Square Miles (Kilometers):
19,700 (51,022) (about the size of West Virginia)
Capital (Population): San José (346,779)
Environmental Concerns: deforestation; soil erosion
Geographical Features: coastal plains separated by rugged mountains

PEOPLE

Population

Total: 4,133,884 (2007 est.)
Annual Growth Rate: 1.4%
Rural/Urban Population Ratio: 50/50
Major Language: Spanish
Ethnic Makeup: 96% white (including a few Mestizos); 2% black; 1% Indian; 1% Chinese

Religions: 76.3% Roman Catholic; 13.7% Evangelical; 5% others

Health

Life Expectancy at birth: 75 years (Male); 80 years (female)
Infant Mortality Rate (Ratio): 9.45/1,000
Physicians Available (Ratio): 1/763

Education

Adult Literacy Rate: 96%
Compulsory (Ages): 6–15; free

COMMUNICATION

Telephones: 1,351,000 main lines
Daily Newspaper Circulation: 102 per
    1,000 people
Cell Phones: 1,444,000
Internet Users: 1,214,000

TRANSPORTATION

Roadways in Kilometers (miles): 10,886
    (6,764)
Railroads in Kilometers (miles): 278
    (173) None in use
Usable Airfields: 151

GOVERNMENT

Type: democratic republic

Independence Date: September 15, 1821
    (from Spain)
Head of State/Government: President
    Oscar Arias is both head of state and
    head of government
Political Parties: Social Christian Unity
    Party; National Liberation Party;
    National Integration Party; Democratic
    Force Party; National Independent
    Party; others
Suffrage: universal and compulsory at 18

MILITARY

*Military Expenditures (% of Central
    Government Expenditures):* 0.4%
Current Hostilities: none

ECONOMY

Currency ($U.S. Equivalent): 517.7
    colons = $1
Per Capita Income/GDP: $13,500/$23.29
    billion

GDP Growth Rate: 6.13%
Inflation Rate: 9.3%
Unemployment Rate: 5.5%
Labor Force: 1,946,000
Natural Resources: hydropower
Agriculture: coffee; bananas;
    sugar; corn; rice; beans; potatoes;
    beef; timber
Industry: microprocessors; food
    processing; textiles and clothing;
    construction materials; fertilizer;
    plastic products; tourism
Exports: $6.4 billion (primary partners
    United States, European Union,
    Central America)
Imports: $11.84 billion (primary
    partners United States, Japan,
    Mexico)

SUGGESTED WEB SITE

http://www.cia.gov/cia/publications/
    factbook/geos/cs.html

Costa Rica Country Report

COSTA RICA: A DIFFERENT TRADITION?

Costa Rica has often been singled out as politically and socially unique in Latin America. It is true that the nation's historical development has not been as directly influenced by Spain as its neighbors' have, but this must not obscure the essential Hispanic character of the Costa Rican people and their institutions. Historian Ralph Woodward observes that historically, Costa Rica's "uniqueness was the product of her relative remoteness from the remainder of Central America, her slight economic importance to Spain, and her lack of a non-white subservient class and corresponding lack of a class of large land-holders to exploit its labors." Indeed, in 1900, Costa Rica had a higher percentage of farmers with small- and medium-range operations than any other Latin American country.

The nature of Costa Rica's economy allowed a wider participation in politics and fostered the development of political institutions dedicated to the equality of all people, which existed only in theory in other Latin American countries. Costa Rican politicians, since the late nineteenth century, have endorsed programs that have been largely middle class in content. The government has consistently demonstrated a commitment to the social welfare of its citizens.

AN INTEGRATED SOCIETY

Despite the recent atmosphere of crisis and disintegration in Central America, Costa Rica's durable democracy has avoided the twin evils of oppressive authoritarianism and class warfare. But what might be construed as good luck is actually a reflection of Costa Rica's history. In social, racial, linguistic, and educational terms, Costa Rica is an integrated country without the fractures and cleavages that typify the rest of the region.

Despite its apparent uniqueness, Costa Rica is culturally an integral part of Latin America and embodies what is most positive about Hispanic political culture. The government has long played the role of benevolent patron to the majority of its citizens. Opposition and antagonism have historically been defused by a process of accommodation, mutual cooperation, and participation. In the early 1940s, for example, modernizers who wanted to create a dynamic capitalist economy took care to pacify the emerging labor movement with appropriate social legislation and benefits. Moreover, to assure that development did not sacrifice social welfare, the state assumed a traditional role with respect to the economy—that is, it took an active role in the production and distribution of income. After much discussion, in 1993, the Costa Rican Congress authorized the privatization of the state-owned cement and

fertilizer companies. In both cases, according to *Latin American Regional Reports,* "a 30% stake [would] be reserved for employees, 20% [would] be offered to private investors, and the remainder [would] be shared out between trade unions . . . and cooperatives." Tight controls were retained on banking, insurance, oil refining, and public utilities.

DEVELOPMENT

In recent years the country has moved away from its traditional dependence on exports of coffee, bananas, and beef. Tourism is now Costa Rica's main source of revenue. In the late 1990s a large computer chip plants promised further diversification of the economy and high-tech jobs. But fluctuating world demand for microchips has been the cause of some concern.

Women, who were granted the right to vote in the 1940s, have participated freely in Costa Rica's elections. Women have served as a vice president, minister of foreign commerce, and president of the Legislative Assembly. In 2007 more than 38 percent of the seats in the Legislative Assembly were held by women. Although in broader terms the role of women is primarily domestic, they are legally unrestricted. Equal work, in general, is rewarded by equal pay for

(Courtesy of Don Evelio Tarrazu Farm/)

Modern growing and distribution techniques are making more and better coffee available, both for export and for the domestic market. Here two workers are pouring coffee cherries down the measuring machine on a plantation in Costa Rica.

men and women. But women also hold, as a rule, lower-paying jobs.

POLITICS OF CONSENSUS

Costa Rica's political stability is assured by the politics of consensus. Deals and compacts are the order of the day among various competing elites. Political competition is open, and participation by labor and peasants is expanding. Election campaigns provide a forum to air differing viewpoints, to educate the voting public, and to keep politicians in touch with the population at large.

Costa Rica frequently has had strong, charismatic leaders who have been committed to social democracy and have rejected a brand of politics grounded in class differences. The country's democracy has always reflected the paternalism and personalities of its presidents.

FREEDOM

Despite Costa Rica's generally enviable human-rights record, there is some de facto discrimination against blacks, Indians, and women (domestic violence against women is a serious problem). The press is free. A stringent libel law, however, makes the media cautious in reporting of personalities.

This tradition was again endorsed when José María Figueres Olsen won the presidential election on February 6, 1994. Figueres was the son of the founder of the modern Costa Rican democracy, and he promised to return to a reduced version of the welfare state. But, by 1996, in the face of a sluggish economy, the populist champion adopted policies that were markedly pro-business. As a result, opinion polls rapidly turned against him. In the 1998 presidential election, an unprecedented 13 political parties ran candidates, which indicated to the three leading parties that citizens no longer believed in them and that political reforms were in order.

A low voter turnout of 65 percent in presidential elections in 2006 signaled further dissatisfaction with the nation's traditional parties. In 2004 evidence of high-level corruption resulted in the jailing of two former presidents on charges of graft. Although former president (1986–1990) and Nobel Prize–winner Oscar Arias was expected to win easily, the vote was evenly split. Only after a manual recount and a series of legal challenges did Otton Solis concede defeat.

Other oft-given reasons for Costa Rica's stability are the high levels of tolerance exhibited by its people and the absence of a military establishment. Costa Rica has had

no military establishment since a brief civil war in 1948. Government officials have long boasted that they rule over a country that has more teachers than soldiers. There is also a strong public tradition that favors demilitarization. Costa Rica's auxiliary forces, however, could form the nucleus of an army in a time of emergency.

The Costa Rican press is among the most unrestricted in Latin America, and differing opinions are openly expressed. Human-rights abuses are virtually nonexistent in the country, but there is a general suspicion of Communists in this overwhelmingly middle-class, white society. And some citizens are concerned about the antidemocratic ideas expressed by ultra-conservatives.

The aftermath of Central America's civil wars is still being felt. Although thousands of refugees returned to Nicaragua with the advent of peace, many thousands more remained in Costa Rica. Economic malaise in Nicaragua combined with the devastation of Hurricane Mitch in 1998 sent thousands of economic migrants across the border into Costa Rica. "Ticos" are worried by the additional strain placed on government resources in a country where more than 80 percent of the population are covered by social-security programs, and approximately 60 percent are provided with pensions and medical benefits.

HEALTH/WELFARE

Costa Ricans enjoy the highest standard of living in Central America. But Costa Rica's indigenous peoples, in part because of their remote location, have inadequate schools, health care, and access to potable water. Fully 20 percent of the population live in poverty.

The economy has been under stress since 1994, and President Figueres was forced to reconsider many of his statist policies. While the export sector remained healthy, domestic industry languished and the internal debt ballooned. The Costa Rican–American Chamber of Commerce observed that "Costa Rica, with its tiny $8.6 billion GDP and 3.5 million people, can not afford a government that consistently overspends its budget by 5 percent or more and then sells short-term bonds, mostly to state institutions, to finance the deficit." In 1997, there was a vigorous debate over the possible privatization of many state entities in an effort to reduce the debt quickly. But opponents of privatization noted that state institutions were important contributors to the high standard of living in the country.

Acknowledging that the world had entered a new phase of development, President Miguel Angel Rodríguez introduced a new economic program in January 2001. Called *Impulso* ("Impulse"), the plan, as reported in *The Tico Times,* noted that for Costa Rica to compete in the new global economy, "knowledge, technology, quality of human resources and the development of telecommunication and transportation infrastructures are fundamental determinants of national prosperity." The old model of economic development, which, according to the president, was characterized by "a diversification of exports, liberalized markets and high levels of foreign investment," must be replaced with a fresh approach "rooted in advanced technological development, a highly qualified labor force, and exports of greater value." President Abel Pacheco, elected in April 2002, embraced a similar approach to economic development. But he was unable to fulfill his promises in part because of falling commodity prices and continued trade and fiscal deficits and in part because of political opposition to tax reforms, privatization of some sectors of the economy, and his free trade philosophy. President Arias is also committed to free-trade. Costa Rica, in October 2007, narrowly voted to join the Central American Free Trade Agreement with the United States. This close vote, together with President Arias' razor thin victory in the presidential elections of 2006, signal the need for compromise and flexibility in the country's economic policy.

THE ENVIRONMENT

At a time when tropical rain forests globally are under assault by developers, cattle barons, and land-hungry peasants, Costa Rica has taken concrete action to protect its environment. Minister of Natural Resources Álvaro Umana was one of those responsible for engineering an imaginative debt-for-nature swap. In his words: "We would like to see debt relief support conservation . . . a policy that everybody agrees is good." Since 1986, the Costa Rican government has authorized the conversion of $75 million in commercial debt into bonds. Interest generated by those bonds has supported a variety of projects, such as the enlargement and protection of La Amistad, a 1.7 million-acre reserve of tropical rain forest.

ACHIEVEMENTS

In a region torn by civil war and political chaos, Costa Rica's years of free and democratic elections stand as a remarkable achievement in political stability and civil rights. President Óscar Arias was awarded the Nobel Peace Prize in 1987; he remains a respected world leader.

About 13 percent of Costa Rica's land is protected currently in a number of national parks. It is hoped that very soon about 25 percent of the country will be designated as national parkland in order to protect tropical rain forests as well as the even more endangered tropical dry forests.

Much of the assault on the forests typically has been dictated by economic necessity and/or greed. In one all-too-common scenario, a small- or middle-size cacao grower discovers that his crop has been decimated by a blight. Confronted by disaster, he will usually farm the forest surrounding his property for timber and then torch the remainder. Ultimately, he will likely sell his land to a cattle rancher, who will transform what had once been rain forest or dry forest into pasture.

In an effort to break this devastating pattern, at least one Costa Rican environmental organization has devised a workable plan to save the forests. Farmers are introduced to a variety of cash crops so that they will not be totally dependent on a single crop. Also, in the case of cacao, for example, the farmer will be provided with a disease- or blight-resistant strain to lessen further the chances of crop losses and subsequent conversion of land to cattle pasture.

Scientists in Costa Rica are concerned that tropical forests are being destroyed before their usefulness to humankind can be fully appreciated. Such forests contain a treasure-trove of medicinal herbs. In Costa Rica, for example, there is at least one plant common to the rain forests that might be beneficial in the struggle against AIDS.

Timeline: PAST

1522
Spain establishes its first settlements in Costa Rica

1821
Independence from Spain

1823
Costa Rica is part of the United Provinces of Central America

1838
Costa Rica Becomes independent as a separate state

1948
Civil war; reforms; abolition of the army

1980s
Costa Rica takes steps to protect its tropical rain forests and dry forests

1990s
Ecotourism to Costa Rica increases

PRESENT

2000s
Two former presidents jailed on corruption charges

Oscar Arias elected president in 2006

El Salvador (Republic of El Salvador)

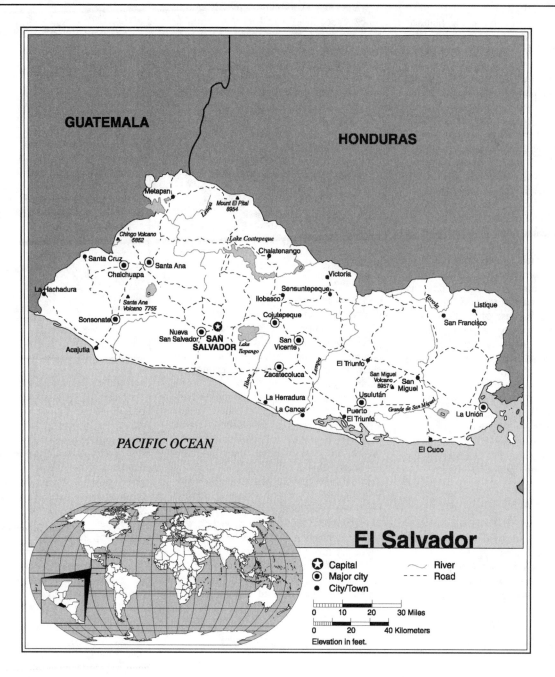

El Salvador Statistics

GEOGRAPHY

Area in Square Miles (Kilometers):
8,292 (21,476) (about the size of
Massachusetts)
Capital (Population): San Salvador
2,224,223 (metro)
Environmental Concerns: deforestation;
soil erosion; water pollution; soil
contamination
Geographical Features: a hot coastal plain
in south rises to a cooler plateau and
valley region; mountainous in north,
including many volcanoes
Climate: tropical; distinct wet and dry
seasons

PEOPLE

Population

Total: 6,948,073 (2007 est.)
Annual Growth Rate: 1.7%
Rural/Urban Population Ratio: 55/45

Ethnic Makeup: 90% Mestizo;
Amerindian 1% white; 9%
Major Language: Spanish
Religions: 83% Roman Catholic; 25%
Protestant groups

Health

Life Expectancy at Birth: 68 years (male);
75 years (female)
Infant Mortality Rate (Ratio): 22.88/1,000
Physicians Available (Ratio): 1/1,219

30

Education

Adult Literacy Rate: 80.2%
Compulsory (Ages): 7–16; free

COMMUNICATION

Telephones: 1,037,000 main lines
Daily Newspaper Circulation: 53 per
   1,000 people
Cell Phones: 3,852,000
Internet Users: 637,000

TRANSPORTATION

Roadways in Kilometers (miles): 10,886
   (6764)
Railroads in Kilometers (miles): 562
   (349) None in use since 2005
Usable Airfields: 65

GOVERNMENT

Type: republic
Independence Date: September 15, 1821
   (from Spain)

Head of State/Government: President
   Elias Saca is both head of state and
   head of government
Political Parties: Farabundo Martí
   National Liberation Front; National
   Republican Alliance; National
   Conciliation Party; Christian
   Democratic Party; Democratic
   Convergence; others
Suffrage: universal at 18

MILITARY

Military Expenditures (% of GDP): 5%
Current Disputes: border disputes

ECONOMY

Currency ($U.S. Equivalent): 8.75
   colons = $1
Per Capita Income/GDP: $5,200/$16.06
   billion
GDP Growth Rate: 3.4%
Inflation Rate: 4.3%

Unemployment Rate: 6.2%
   Underemployment: Significant
   underemployment
Labor Force: 2,913,000
Natural Resources: hydropower;
   geothermal power; petroleum; arable
   land
Agriculture: coffee; sugarcane; corn; rice;
   beans; oilseed; cotton; sorghum; beef;
   dairy products; shrimp
Industry: food processing; beverages;
   petroleum; chemicals; fertilizer;
   textiles; furniture; light metals
Exports: $3.96 billion (primary
   partners United States, Guatemala,
   Germany)
Imports: $8.099 billion (primary
   partners United States, Guatemala,
   Mexico)

SUGGESTED WEB SITE

http://cia.gov/cia/publications/factbook/
   index.html

El Salvador Country Report

EL SALVADOR: A TROUBLED LAND

El Salvador, the smallest country in Central America, was engaged until 1992 in a civil war that cut through class lines, divided the military and the Roman Catholic Church, and severely damaged the social and economic fabric of the nation. It was the latest in a long series of violent sociopolitical eruptions that have plagued the country since its independence in 1821.

In the last quarter of the nineteenth century, large plantation owners—spurred by the sharp increase in the world demand for coffee and other products of tropical agriculture—expanded their lands and estates. Most of the new land was purchased or taken from Indians and Mestizos (those of mixed white and Indian blood), who, on five occasions between 1872 and 1898, took up arms in futile attempts to preserve their land. The once-independent Indians and Mestizos were reduced to becoming tenant farmers, sharecroppers, day laborers, or peons on the large estates. Indians, when deprived of their lands, also lost much of their cultural and ethnic distinctiveness. Today, El Salvador is an overwhelmingly Mestizo society.

The uprooted peasantry was controlled in a variety of ways. Some landowners played the role of *patrón* and assured workers the basic necessities of life in return for their labor. Laws against "vagabonds" (those who, when stopped by rural police, did not have a certain amount of money

in their pockets) assured plantation owners a workforce and discouraged peasant mobility.

To enforce order further, a series of security organizations—the National Guard, the National Police, and the Treasury Police—were created by the central government. Many of these security personnel actually lived on the plantations and estates and followed the orders of the owner. Although protection of the economic system was their primary function, over time elements of these organizations became private armies.

DEVELOPMENT

Since 2004, the government has pursued a policy of economic diversification, especially in the areas of textile production, international port services, and tourism. Formerly state-controlled enterprises, such as telecommunications, the distribution of electric power, banking, and pension funds are in the process of privatization. El Salvador was the first regional nation to ratify the Central American Free Trade Agreement.

This phenomenon lay at the heart of much of the "unofficial" violence in El Salvador in recent years. In Salvadoran society, personal loyalties to relatives or local strongmen competed with and often

superseded loyalty to government officials. Because of this, the government was unable to control some elements within its security forces.

In an analysis of the Salvadoran Civil War, it is tempting to place the rich, right-wing landowners and their military allies on one side; and the poor, the peasantry, and the guerrillas on the other. Such a division is artificial, however, and fails to reflect the complexities of the conflict. Granted, the military and landowners had enjoyed a mutually beneficial partnership since 1945. But there were liberal and conservative factions within the armed forces, and, since the 1940s, there had been some movement toward needed social and economic reforms. It was a military regime in 1949 that put into effect the country's first social-security legislation. In 1950, a Constitution was established that provided for public-health programs, women's suffrage, and extended social-security coverage. The reformist impulse continued in the 1960s, when it became legal to organize opposition political parties.

A TIME FOR CHANGE

Food production increased in the 1970s by 44 percent, a growth that was second in Latin America only to Brazil's. Although much of the food grown was exported to world markets, some of the revenue generated was used for social programs in El Salvador. Life expectancy increased, the

© Photodisc/PunchStock

Civil strife disrupted much of El Salvador's agrarian production, and a lack of fishery planning necessitated importing from other parts of the world. With a new and efficient program to take advantage of fish in domestic waters, El Salvador has been able to develop an effective food industry from the sea.

death rate fell, illiteracy declined, and the percentage of government expenditures on public health, housing, and education was among the highest in Latin America.

The programs and reforms, in classic Hispanic form, were generated by the upper classes. The elite believed that state-sponsored changes could be controlled in such a way that traditional balances in society would remain intact and elite domination of the government would be assured.

The origin of El Salvador's civil war may be traced to 1972, when the Christian Democratic candidate for president, José Napoleón Duarte, is believed to have won the popular vote but was deprived of his victory when the army declared the results false and handed the victory to its own candidate. Impatient and frustrated, middle-class politicians and student leaders from the opposition began to consider more forceful ways to oust the ruling class.

By 1979, guerrilla groups had become well established in rural El Salvador, and some younger army officers grew concerned that a successful left-wing popular revolt was a distinct possibility. Rather than wait for revolution from below, which might result in the destruction of the military as an institution, the officers chose to seize power in a coup and manipulate change from above. Once in power, this *junta,* or ruling body, moved quickly to transform the structure of Salvadoran society. A land-reform program, originally developed by civilian reformers and

Roman Catholic clergy, was adopted by the military. It would give the campesinos ("peasants") not only land but also status, dignity, and respect.

FREEDOM

The end of the civil war brought an overall improvement in human rights in El Salvador. News from across the political spectrum, often critical of the government, is reported in El Salvador, although foreign journalists seem to be the target of an unusually high level of muggings, robberies, and burglaries. Violence against women is widespread. Judges often dismiss rape cases on the pretext that the victim provoked the crime.

In its first year, 1980, the land-reform program had a tremendous impact on the landowning elite—37 percent of the lands producing cotton and 34 percent of the coffee-growing lands were confiscated by the government and redistributed. The junta also nationalized the banks and assumed control of the sale of coffee and sugar. Within months, however, several peasant members of the new cooperatives and the government agricultural advisers sent to help them were gunned down. The violence spread. Some of the killings were attributed to government security men in the pay of dispossessed landowners, but

most of the killings may have been committed by the army.

In the opinion of a land-reform program official, the army was corrupt and had returned to the cooperatives that it had helped to establish in order to demand money for protection and bribes. When the peasants refused, elements within the army initiated a reign of terror against them.

In 1989, further deterioration of the land-reform program was brought about by Supreme Court decisions and by policies adopted by the newly elected right-wing government of President Alfredo Cristiani. Former landowners who had property taken for redistribution to peasants successfully argued that seizures under the land reform were illegal. Subsequently, five successive land-reform cases were decided by the Supreme Court in favor of former property owners.

Cristiani, whose right-wing National Republican Alliance Party (ARENA) fought hard against land reform, would not directly attack the land-reform program—only because such a move would further alienate rural peasants and drive them into the arms of left-wing guerrillas. Instead, Cristiani favored the reconstitution of collective farms as private plots. Such a move, according to the government, would improve productivity and put an end to what authorities perceived as a form of U.S.–imposed "socialism." Critics of the government's policy charged that the privatization plan would ultimately result in the demise of land reform altogether.

Yet another problem was that many of the collectives established under the reform were (and remain) badly in debt. A 1986 study by the U.S. Agency for International Development reported that 95 percent of the cooperatives could not pay interest on the debt they were forced to acquire to compensate the landlords. *New York Times* reporter Lindsey Gruson noted that the world surplus of agricultural products as well as mismanagement by peasants who suddenly found themselves in the unfamiliar role of owners were a large part of the reason for the failures. But the government did not help. Technical assistance was not provided, and the tremendous debt gave the cooperatives a poor credit rating, which made it difficult for them to secure needed fertilizer and pesticides.

Declining yields and, for many families, lives of increasing desperation have been the result. Some peasants must leave the land and sell their plots to the highest bidder. This will ultimately bring about a reconcentration of land in the hands of former landlords.

HEALTH/WELFARE

Many Salvadorans suffer from parasites and malnutrition. El Salvador has one of the highest infant mortality rates in the Western Hemisphere, largely because of polluted water. Potable water is readily available to only 10 percent of the population.

Other prime farmland lay untended because of the civil war. Violence drove many peasants from the land to the slums of the larger cities. And free-fire zones established by the military (in an effort to destroy the guerrillas' popular base) and guerrilla attacks against cooperatives (in an effort to sabotage the economy and further destabilize the country) had a common victim: the peasantry.

Some cooperatives and individual families failed to bring the land to flower because of the poor quality of the soil they inherited. Reporter Gruson told the story of one family, which was, unfortunately, all too common:

> José . . . received 1.7 acres on a rockpocked slope an hour's walk from his small shack. José . . . used to sell some of his beans and rice to raise a little cash. But year after year his yields have declined. Since he cannot afford fertilizers or insecticides, the corn that survives the torrential rainy season produces pest-infested ears the size of a baby's foot. Now, he has trouble feeding his wife and seven children.
>
> "The land is no good," he said. "I've been working it for 12 years and my life has gotten worse every year. I don't have anywhere to go, but I'll have to leave soon."

After the coup, several governments came and went. The original reformers retired, went into exile, or went over to the guerrillas. The civil war continued into 1992, when a United Nations–mediated cease-fire took effect.

HUMAN-RIGHTS ISSUES

Twelve years of war had cost 70,000 lives and given El Salvador the reputation of a bloody and abusive country. Tens of thousands of El Salvadorans were uprooted by the violence and many made their way to the United States. Despite the declared truce, the extreme right and left continued to utilize assassination to eliminate or terrorize both each other and the voices of moderation who dared to speak out.

Through 1992, human-rights abuses still occurred on a wide scale in El Salvador. Public order was constantly disrupted by military operations, guerrilla raids, factional hatreds, acts of revenge, personal grudges, pervasive fear, and a sense of uncertainty about the future. State-of-siege decrees suspended all constitutional rights to freedom of speech and press. However, self-censorship, both in the media and by individuals, out of fear of violent reprisals, was the leading constraint on free expression in El Salvador.

Eventually, as *Boston Globe* correspondent Pamela Constable reported, "a combination of war-weariness and growing pragmatism among leaders of all persuasions suggests that once-bitter adversaries have begun to develop a modus vivendi."

Release of the report in 1993 by the UN's "Truth Commission," a special body entrusted with the investigation of human-rights violations in El Salvador, prompted the right wing–dominated Congress to approve an amnesty for those named. But progress has been made in other areas. The National Police have been separated from the Defense Ministry; and the National Guard, Civil Defense forces, and the notorious Treasury Police have been abolished. A new National Civilian Police, comprised of 20 percent of National Police, 20 percent former Farabundo Martí National Liberation Front (FMLN) guerrillas, and 60 percent with no involvement on either side in the civil war, was instituted in 1994.

President Cristiani reduced the strength of the army from 63,000 to 31,500 by February 1993, earlier than provided for by the agreement; and the class of officers known as the *tondona*, who had long dominated the military and were likely responsible for human-rights abuses, were forcibly retired by the president on June 30, 1993. Land, judicial, and electoral reforms followed. Despite perhaps inevitable setbacks because of the legacy of violence and bitterness, editor Juan Comas wrote that "most analysts are inclined to believe that El Salvador's hour of madness has passed and the country is now on the road to hope."

In El Salvador, as elsewhere in Latin America, the Roman Catholic Church was divided. The majority of Church officials backed government policy and supported the United States' contention that the violence in El Salvador was due to Cuban-backed subversion. Other clergy strongly disagreed and argued convincingly that the violence was deeply rooted in historical social injustice.

ACHIEVEMENTS

Despite the violence of war, political power has been transferred via elections at both the municipal and national levels. Elections have helped to establish the legitimacy of civilian leaders in a region usually dominated by military regimes.

Another endemic problem that confronts postwar El Salvador is widespread corruption. It is a human-rights issue because corruption and its attendant misuse of scarce resources contribute to persistent or increased poverty and undermine the credibility and stability of government at all levels. According to the nonprofit watchdog group *Probidad*, "El Salvador has a long history of corruption. . . . Before the first of many devastating earthquakes on January 13, 2001, El Salvador was the third poorest country in Latin America. . . . Influence peddling between construction companies and their friends and families in government and other corrupt practices resulted in many unnecessary deaths, infrastructure damage, and irregularities in humanitarian assistance distribution."

ECONOMIC ISSUES

In 1998, President Armando Calderón Sol surprised both supporters and opponents when he launched a bold program of reforms. The first three years of his administration had been characterized by indecision. Political scientist Tommie Sue Montgomery noted that his "reputation for espousing as policy the last viewpoint he has heard has produced in civil society both heartburn and black humor." But a combination of factors created new opportunities for Calderón. The former guerrillas of the FMLN were divided and failed to take advantage of ARENA's apparent weak leadership; a UN–sponsored program of reconstruction and reconciliation was short of funds and, by 1995, had lost momentum; and presidential elections were looming in 1999. A dozen years of war had left the economic infrastructure in disarray. The economy had, at best, remained static, and while the war raged, there had been no attempt to modernize. During his final year in office, Calderón developed reform policies of modernization, privatization, and free-market competition. Interestingly, his reforms generated opposition from former guerrillas, who are now represented in the Legislature by the FMLN, as well as from some members of the traditional conservative economic elite.

Perhaps one result of Calderón's reforms was the decisive victory of ARENA at the polls in 1999, and again in 2004. The FMLN, on the other hand, won municipal and legislative elections in 2003, which gave them the largest voting bloc in congress.

OUT-MIGRATION

El Salvador's civil war set into motion some profound changes in the nation. As noted, thousands of people fled to other countries, and especially to the United States. Once established, other family members tended to follow. Indeed, one of every nine people born in El Salvador will migrate to the United States. Salvadoran sociologist Raymundo Calderón, as reported in the *Los Angeles Times,* stated: "Most of the Salvadorans who have migrated . . . are not well educated. But when they get to the U.S., they have access to better housing and better pay. Their view of the world changes, and they communicate this to their families in El Salvador." So many have departed that there is a labor shortage in the agricultural sector that has had to be filled by workers from Honduras and Nicaragua. In November 2005 the nation's minister of agriculture announced that 15,000 foreign workers would be needed to cut sugarcane and harvest the cotton and coffee crops.

The labor shortage is directly related to a more serious issue. *Los Angeles Times* correspondent Hector Tobar notes concerns that Salvadorans are losing their "industrious self-image, a vision celebrated by poets such as Roque Dalton, whose 'Love Poem' recounted the exploits of Salvadoran laborers up and down the Americas." Remittances from the United States to El Salvador prompted one harvest supervisor for a large sugar refinery to say that money from families in the United States has made Salvadorans "comfortable, and they don't want to work cutting cane." This lament was echoed by the minister of the interior in his comments to a local newspaper: "Today people are telling us that their family remittances are sufficient [to live on]. It's not possible that we are abandoning our own fields and we have to bring in labor from abroad." What the minister finds impossible is that El Salvadoran rural workers, because of a labor surplus, had traditionally sought work in neighboring Honduras. Now the flow of labor is in the other direction. War, natural disasters, and out-migration have changed the very culture of the nation.

Finally, an unwelcome consequence of out-migration is that many youths, exposed to and emulating the gang cultures in several United States cities, have become a serious criminal problem for not only United States authorities, but also for those in El Salvador as gangs have made their appearance in urban areas. A BBC report notes: "Poverty, civil war, natural disaster, and consequent dislocations have left their mark on . . . society, which is among the most violent and crime ridden in the Americas."

Timeline: PAST

1524
Present-day El Salvador is occupied by Spanish settlers from Mexico

1821
Independence from Spain is declared

1822
El Salvador is part of the United Provinces of Central America

1838
El Salvador becomes independent as a separate state

1969
A brief war between El Salvador and Honduras

1970
Guerrilla warfare in El Salvador

1979
Army officers seize power in a coup; civil war

1990s
A cease-fire takes effect on February 1, 1992, officially ending the civil war

PRESENT

2000s
Earthquakes devastate towns and cities, with a heavy loss of life and extensive infrastructure damage

Anthony Saca wins 2004 presidential election

Guatemala (Republic of Guatemala)

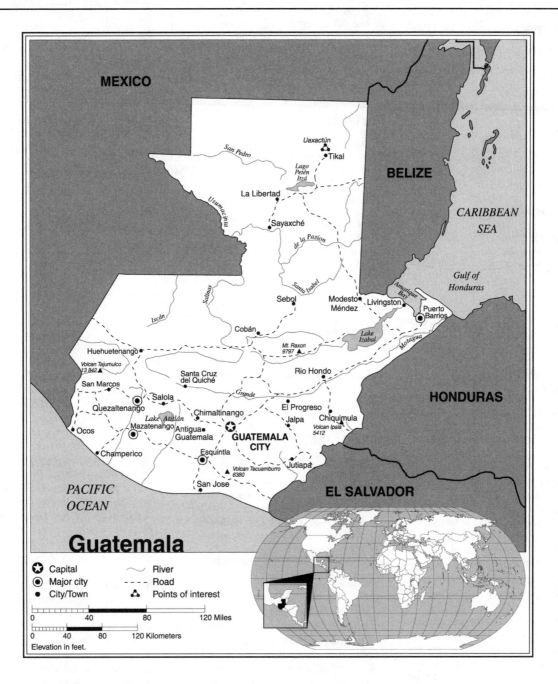

Guatemala Statistics

GEOGRAPHY

Area in Square Miles (Kilometers): 42,000 (108,780) (about the size of Tennessee)

Capital (Population): Guatemala City (2,205,000)

Environmental Concerns: deforestation; soil erosion; water pollution

Geographical Features: mostly mountains, with narrow coastal plains and a rolling limestone plateau (Peten)

Climate: temperate in highlands; tropical on coasts

PEOPLE

Population

Total: 12,728,111 (2007 est.)

Annual Growth Rate: 2.1%

Rural/Urban Population Ratio: 61/39%

Ethnic Makeup: Ladino and white 56%; 44% Amerindian

Major Languages: Spanish; Maya languages

Religions: predominantly Roman Catholic; Protestant and Maya

Health

Life Expectancy at Birth: Male: 68 years Female: 71

Infant Mortality Rate (Ratio): 29.77/1,000

Physicians Available (Ratio): 1/2,356

Education

Adult Literacy Rate: 69%
Compulsory (Ages): 7–14; free

COMMUNICATION

Telephones: 1,355,000 main lines
Daily Newspaper Circulation: 29 per
    1,000 people
Cell Phones: 7,179,000
Internet Users: 1,320,000

TRANSPORTATION

Roadways in Kilometers (miles): 14,095
    (8,758)
Railroads in (Kilometers) (miles): 552
    (343)
Usable Airfields: 402

GOVERNMENT

Type: Constitutional democratic republic

Independence Date: September 15, 1821
    (from Spain)
Head of State/Government: President
    Alvaro Colom is both head of state and
    head of government
Political Parties: National Unity for Hope;
    Grand National Alliance; Patriot Party;
    Unionist Party; Center of Social Action,
    others. Guatemalan Republican Front;
Suffrage: universal at 18

MILITARY

Military Expenditures (% of GDP): 0.4%
Current Disputes: border dispute with
    Belize

ECONOMY

Currency ($U.S. Equivalent): 7.72
    quetzals = $1
Per Capita Income/GDP: $5,400/$31.35
    billion

GDP Growth Rate: 5.6%
Inflation Rate: 6.6%
Unemployment Rate: 3.2%
Labor Force: 3,958,000
Natural Resources: petroleum;
    nickel; rare woods; fish; chicle;
    hydropower
Agriculture: sugarcane; corn;
    bananas; coffee; beans; cardamom;
    livestock
Industry: sugar; textiles and
    clothing; furniture; chemicals;
    petroleum; metals; rubber;
    tourism
Exports: $7.468 billion (f.o.b.)
Imports: $12.67 billion (f.o.b.)

SUGGESTED WEB SITE

http://www.cia.gov/cia/publications/
    factbook/index.html

Guatemala Country Report

GUATEMALA: PEOPLES IN CONFLICT

Ethnic relations between the descendants of Maya Indians, who comprise 44 percent of Guatemala's population, and whites and Ladinos (Hispanicized Indians) have always been unfriendly and have contributed significantly to the nation's turbulent history. During the colonial period and since independence, Spaniards, Creoles (in Guatemala, whites born in the New World—as opposed to in Nicaragua, where Creoles are defined as native-born blacks), and Ladinos have repeatedly sought to dominate the Guatemalan Indian population, largely contained in the highlands, by controlling the Indians' land and their labor.

The process of domination was accelerated between 1870 and 1920, as Guatemala's entry into world markets hungry for tropical produce such as coffee resulted in the purchase or extensive seizures of land from Indians. Denied sufficient lands of their own, Indians were forced onto the expanding plantations as debt peons. Others were forced to labor as seasonal workers on coastal plantations; many died there because of the sharp climatic differences.

THE INDIAN AND INTEGRATION

Assaulted by the Ladino world, highland Indians withdrew into their own culture and built social barriers between themselves and the changing world outside their villages. Those barriers have persisted until the present.

DEVELOPMENT

Although the Peace Accords of 1996 called for distributing land to peasant farmers, more land, in fact, has been concentrated in fewer hands. International institutions such as the World Bank favor export models that endorse "economies of scale," which result in larger agricultural yields. One result is the increasing out-migration of rural families to urban areas or even to the United States.

For the Guatemalan governments that have thought in terms of economic progress and national unity, the Indians have always presented a problem. A 2003 presidential candidate stated: "Indigenous groups do not speak of a 'political system'; they speak of community consensus, and their conception of community is very local. . . . How do you have a functioning nation state, one where indigenous groups participate actively in protecting their political interests, and yet still respect the cultural practices of other indigenous groups for whom participation in Western political institutions is deemed undesirable?"

According to anthropologist Leslie Dow, Jr., Guatemalan governments too easily explain the Indian's lack of material prosperity in terms of the "deficiencies" of Indian culture. Indian "backwardness" is better explained by elite policies calculated to keep Indians subordinate. Social, political, and economic deprivations have consistently and consciously been utilized by governments anxious to maintain the Indian in an inferior status.

Between 1945 and 1954, however, there was a period of remarkable social reform in Guatemala. Before the reforms were cut short by the resistance of landowners, factions within the military, and a U.S. Central Intelligence Agency–sponsored invasion, Guatemalan governments made a concerted effort to integrate the Indian into national life. Some Indians who lived in close proximity to large urban centers such as the capital, Guatemala City, learned that their vote had the power to effect changes to their benefit. They also realized that they were unequal not because of their illiteracy, "backwardness," poverty, or inability to converse in Spanish, but because of governments that refused to reform their political, social, and economic structures.

In theory, indigenous peoples in Guatemala enjoy equal legal rights under the Constitution. In fact, however, they remain largely outside the national culture, do not speak Spanish, and are not integrated into the national economy. Indian males are far more likely to be impressed into the army or guerrilla units. Indigenous peoples in Guatemala have suffered most of the combat-related casualties and repeated abuses of their basic human rights. There remains a

(World Bank Photo/Foto Anckerman/)

In recent years, Indians in Guatemala have pursued their rights by exercising their voting power. Here members of the Defense Fund for Indigenous Women are entering a mobile court in Jocotenango, Guatemala. The Fund provides psychological and social support to victims of violence and abuse.

pervasive discrimination against Indians in white society. Indians have on occasion challenged state policies that they have considered inequitable and repressive. But if they become too insistent on change, threaten violence or societal upheaval, or support and/or join guerrilla groups, government repression is usually swift and merciless.

GUERRILLA WARFARE

A civil war, which was to last for 36 years, developed in 1960. Guatemala was plagued by violence, attributed both to left-wing insurgencies in rural areas and to armed forces' counterinsurgency operations. Led by youthful middle-class rebels, guerrillas gained strength because of several factors: the radical beliefs of some Roman Catholic priests in rural areas; the ability of the guerrillas to mobilize Indians for the first time; and the "demonstration effect" of events elsewhere in Central America. Some of the success is explained by the guerrilla leaders' ability to converse in Indian languages. Radical clergy increased the recruitment of Indians into the guerrilla forces by suggesting that revolution was an acceptable path to

social justice. The excesses of the armed forces in their search for subversives drove other Indians into the arms of the guerrillas. In some parts of the highlands, the loss of ancestral lands to speculators or army officers was sufficient to inspire the Indians to join the radical cause.

According to the *Latin American Regional Report* for Mexico and Central America, government massacres of guerrillas and their actual or suspected supporters were frequent and "characterized by clinical savagery." At times, the killing was selective, with community leaders and their families singled out. In other instances, entire villages were destroyed and all the inhabitants slaughtered. "Everything depends on the army's perception of the local level of support for the guerrillas," according to the report.

To counterbalance the violence, once guerrillas were cleared from an area, the government implemented an "Aid Program to Areas in Conflict." Credit was offered to small farmers to boost food production in order to meet local demand, and displaced and jobless people were enrolled in food-for-work units to build roads or other public projects.

FREEDOM

Former president Ramiro de León Carpio warned those who would violate human rights, saying that the law would punish those guilty of abuses, "whether or not they are civilians or members of the armed forces." The moment has come, he continued, "to change things and improve the image of the army and of Guatemala."

By the mid-1980s, most of the guerrillas' military organizations had been destroyed. This was the result not only of successful counterinsurgency tactics by the Guatemalan military but also of serious errors of judgment by guerrilla leaders. Impatient and anxious for change, the guerrillas had overestimated the willingness of the Guatemalan people to rebel. They also had underestimated the power of the military establishment. Surviving guerrilla units maintained an essentially defensive posture for the remainder of the decade. In 1989, however, the guerrillas regrouped. The subsequent intensification of human-rights abuses and the climate of violence were indicative of the military's response.

There was some hope for improvement in 1993, in the wake of the ouster of President Jorge Serrano, whose attempt to emulate the "self-coup" of Peru's Alberto Fujimori failed. Guatemala's next president, Ramiro de León Carpio, was a human-rights activist who was sharply critical of security forces in their war against the guerrillas of the Guatemalan National Revolutionary Unity (URNG). Peace talks between the government and guerrillas had been pursued with the Roman Catholic Church as intermediary for several years, with sparks of promise but no real change. In July 1993, de León announced a new set of proposals to bring to an end the decades of bloodshed that had resulted in 140,000 deaths. Those proposals were the basis for the realization of a peace agreement worked out under the auspices of the United Nations in December 1996.

But the underlying causes of the violence still must be addressed. Colin Woodard, writing in *The Chronicle of Higher Education,* reported that the peace accords promised to "reshape Guatemala as a democratic, multicultural society." But an estimated 70 percent of the Maya Indians still live in poverty, and more than 80 percent are illiterate. Estuardo Zapeta, Guatemala's first Maya newspaper columnist, writes: "This is a multicultural, multilingual society. . . . As long as we leave the Maya illiterate, we're condemning them to being peasants. And if that happens, their need to acquire farmland will lead us to another civil war." This, however, is only one facet of a multifaceted set of issues. The very complexity of Guatemalan society, according to political scientist Rachel McCleary, "make[s] it extremely difficult to attain a consensus at the national level on the nature of the problems confronting society." But the new ability of leaders from many sectors of society to work together to shape a meaningful peace is a hopeful sign.

Although the fighting has ended, fear persists. Journalist Woodard wrote in July 1997: "In many neighborhoods [in Guatemala City] private property is protected by razor wire and patrolled by guards with pump-action shotguns." One professor at the University of San Carlos observed, "It is good that the war is over, but I am pessimistic about the peace. . . . There is intellectual freedom now, but we are very unsure of the permanence of that freedom. It makes us very cautious."

URBAN VIOLENCE

Although most of the violence occurred in rural areas, urban Guatemala did not escape the horrors of the civil war. The following characterization of Guatemalan politics, written by an English traveler in 1839, is still relevant today: "There is but one side to the politics in Guatemala. Both parties have a beautiful way of producing unanimity of opinion, by driving out of the country all who do not agree with them."

HEALTH/WELFARE

 While constitutional bars on child labor in the industrial sector are not difficult to enforce, in the informal and agricultural sectors such labor is common. It is estimated that 5,000 Guatemalan children live on the streets and survive as best they can. They are often targeted for elimination by police and death squads.

During the civil war, right-wing killers murdered dozens of leaders of the moderate political left to prevent them from organizing viable political parties that might challenge the ruling elite. These killers also assassinated labor leaders if their unions were considered leftist or antigovernment. Leaders among university students and professors "disappeared" because the national university had a reputation as a center of leftist subversion. Media people were gunned down if they were critical of the government or the right wing. Left-wing extremists also assassinated political leaders associated with "repressive" policies, civil servants (whose only "crime" was government employment), military personnel and police, foreign diplomats, peasant informers, and businesspeople and industrialists associated with the government.

Common crime rose to epidemic proportions in Guatemala City (as well as in the capitals of other Central American republics). Many of the weapons that once armed the Nicaraguan militias and El Salvador's civil-defense patrols found their way onto the black market, where, according to the Managua newspaper *Pensamiento Propio,* they were purchased by the Guatemalan Army, the guerrillas of the URNG, and criminals.

The fear of official or unofficial violence has always inhibited freedom of the press in Guatemala. Early in the 1980s, the Conference on Hemispheric Affairs noted that restrictions on the print media and the indiscriminate brutality of the death squads "turned Guatemala into a virtual no-man's land for journalists." Lingering fears and memories of past violence tend to limit the exercise of press freedoms guaranteed by the Constitution. The U.S. State Department's Country Reports notes that "the media continues to exercise a degree of self-censorship on certain topics. . . . The lack of aggressive

Timeline: PAST

1523
Guatemala is conquered by Spanish forces from Mexico

1821
Independence

1822–1838
Guatemala is part of the United Provinces of Central America

1838
Guatemala becomes independent as a separate state

1944
Revolution; many reforms

1954
A CIA-sponsored coup deposes the reformist government

1976
An earthquake leaves 22,000 dead

1977
Human-rights abuses lead to the termination of U.S. aid

1990s
Talks between the government and guerrillas end 36 years of violence

PRESENT

2000s
Economic problems multiply

Alvaro Colom elected president in November 2007

Murder rate in 2007 topped 5,000

Rural and urban violence kills thousands

investigative reporting dealing with the military and human rights violations apparently is due to self-censorship."

HEALTH CARE AND NUTRITION

In rural Guatemala, half the people have a diet that is well below the minimum daily caloric intake established by the Food and Agricultural Organization. Growth in the staple food crops (corn, rice, beans, wheat) has failed to keep pace with population growth. Marginal malnutrition is endemic.

Health services vary, depending on location, but are uniformly poor in rural Guatemala. The government has begun pilot programs in three departments to provide basic primary health care on a wide scale. But some of these well-intentioned policies have failed because of a lack of sensitivity to cultural differences. Anthropologist Linda Greenberg has observed that the Ministry of Health, as part of its campaign to bring basic health-care services to the hinterlands, introduced midwives who were ignorant of Indian traditions. For Guatemalan Indians, pregnancy is considered an illness that demands specific care, calling for certain foods, herbs, body positions, and interpersonal relations between expectant mother and Indian midwife. In Maya culture, traditional medicine has spiritual, psychological, physical, social, and symbolic dimensions. Ministry of Health workers too often dismiss traditional practices as superstitious and unscientific. Their insensitivity and ignorance create ineffectual health-care programs.

THE FUTURE

In February 1999, a UN–sponsored Commission for Historical Clarification, in a harsh nine-volume report, blamed the Guatemalan government for acts of genocide against the Maya during the long civil war. The purpose of the report was not to set the stage for criminal prosecutions but to examine the root causes of the civil war and explain how the conflict developed over time. It was hoped that the report signaled the first steps toward national reconciliation and the addressing of human-rights issues, long ignored by those in power.

But the high command of the military and its civilian allies, accused of planning

and executing a broad range of atrocities against the Maya, may perceive the report as a threat to their position and their future. In fact, the government has done little to implement the recommendations called for in the 1996 peace accords that ended the civil war. Former President Efraín Rios Montt, who engineered the assault against the Maya during the civil war, lost his congressional seat—and his immunity to prosecution—in 2004.

Not surprisingly, the poor and disadvantaged are increasingly frustrated. Illiteracy, infant mortality and malnutrition are among the highest in Central America while life expectancy is among the lowest. Two-thirds of Guatemala's children live in poverty. Violence remains endemic. Presidential elections in 2007 produced a number of unexpected results that captured in microcosm many of Guatemala's problems

and idiosyncrasies. One of the candidates was former Nobel Prize winner Rigoberta Menchú who promised to be an advocate for Guatemala's Maya. Yet she finished sixth in a field of fourteen candidates with only three percent of the vote. Many Maya voted for other candidates simply because Menchú is a Quiche Maya from the highlands, distinct in terms of language and dress from the 19 other Maya groups. As one Tz'utujil Maya noted: "She's one of us, but she's not." The candidates who participated in a run-off election pitted two men, a former army general and a businessman, with radically different platforms. The general, Otto Pérez Molina, promised to rule with a "mano duro" (iron fist) to eliminate the nation's drug traffickers, gang members, and organized crime. The other candidate and eventual winner was Alvaro Colom, described by a *New York Times* reporter as "a gawky policy wonk and businessman who made fighting poverty his campaign's centerpiece." Guatemalans rejected the general in large part because of the past misdeeds and corruption of the military during the years of civil war. President Colom noted that "we had a firm hand for 50 years and it caused more than 250,000 victims in a dirty war." Colom is pledged to confront the widespread poverty among Guatemala's indigenous peoples.

Honduras (Republic of Honduras)

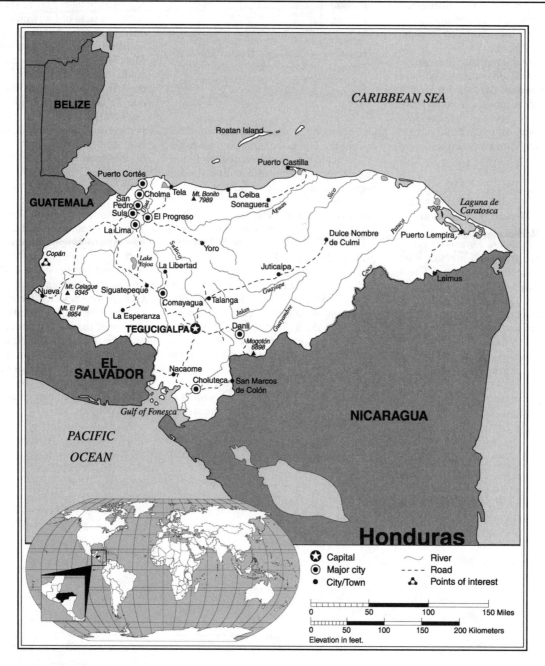

Honduras Statistics

GEOGRAPHY

Area in Square Miles (Kilometers):
43,267 (112,090) (slightly larger than
Tennessee)

Capital (Population): Tegucigalpa
(1,500,000)

Environmental Concerns:
urbanization; deforestation; land
degradation and soil erosion; mining
pollution

Geographical Features: mostly
mountainous in the interior; narrow
coastal plains

Climate: subtropical, but varies with
elevation (temperate highlands)

PEOPLE*

Population

Total: 7,483,763 (2007 est.)
Annual Growth Rate: 2.1%

Rural/Urban Population Ratio: 56/44
Ethnic Makeup: 90% Mestizo (European
and Indian mix); 7% Indian; 2% African;
1% European, Arab, and Asian
Major Language: Spanish .
Religions: 97% Roman Catholic; a small
Protestant minority

Health

Life Expectancy at Birth: Male: 68 years
Female: 71

40

Infant Mortality Rate (Ratio): 22.21/1,000
Physicians Available (Ratio): 1/1,586

Education

Adult Literacy Rate: 80%
Compulsory (Ages): 7–13; free

COMMUNICATION

Telephones: 708,000 main lines
Daily Newspaper Circulation: 45 per 1,000 people
Cell Phones: 2,241,000
Internet Users: 337,300

TRANSPORTATION

Roadways in Kilometers (miles): 13,603 (8453)
Railroads in Kilometers (miles): 699 (434)
Usable Airfields: 112
Motor Vehicles in Use: 185,000

GOVERNMENT

Type: democratic constitutional republic

Independence Date: September 15, 1821 (from Spain)
Head of State/Government: President Manuel Zelaya is both head of state and head of government
Political Parties: Liberal Party; National Party of Honduras; National Innovation and Unity Party–Social Democratic Party; Christian Democratic Party; Democratic Unification Party others
Suffrage: universal and compulsory at 18

MILITARY

Military Expenditures (% of GDP): 0.6%
Current Disputes: boundary disputes with El Salvador and Nicaragua

ECONOMY

Currency ($U.S. Equivalent): 18.9 lempiras = $1
Per Capita Income/GDP: $3,300/$9.2 billion
GDP Real Growth Rate: 6%

Inflation Rate: 6.4%
Unemployment Rate: 27.8%
Labor Force: 2,812,000
Natural Resources: timber; gold; silver; copper; lead; zinc; iron ore; antimony; coal; fish; hydropower
Agriculture: bananas; coffee; citrus fruits; beef; timber; shrimp
Industry: sugar; coffee; textiles and clothing; wood products
Exports: $3.924 billion (f.o.b.) (primary partners United States, Japan, Germany)
Imports: $6.798 billion (f.o.b.) (primary partners United States, Guatemala, Netherland Antilles)

SUGGESTED WEB SITE

http://www.cia.gov/cia/publications/
factbook/geos/ho.html

*Note: Estimates for Honduras explicitly take into account the effects of excess mortality due to AIDS.

Honduras Country Report

HONDURAS: THE CONTAGION OF VIOLENCE

In political terms, Honduras resembles much of the rest of Central America. Frequent changes of government, numerous constitutions, authoritarian leaders, widespread corruption, and an inability to solve basic problems are common to Honduras and to the region. A historian of Honduras once wrote that his country's history could be "written in a tear."

DEVELOPMENT

The Central American Free Trade Zone, of which Honduras is a member, will reduce tariffs by 5 percent to 20 percent on more than 5,000 products traded within the region. In the coming years, more products will be included and tariffs will be progressively lowered.

In terms of social policy, however, Honduras stands somewhat apart from its neighbors. It was slower to modernize, there were no great extremes of wealth between landowners and the rest of the population, and society appeared more paternalistic and less exploitive than was the case in other Central American states. "Ironically," notes journalist Loren

Jenkins, "the land's precarious existence as a poor and unstable backwater has proven almost as much a blessing as a curse." Honduras lacks the sharp social divisions that helped to plunge Nicaragua, El Salvador, and Guatemala into rebellion and civil war. And Honduran governments have seemed somewhat more responsive to demands for change. Still, Honduras is a poor country. Its people have serious problems—widespread illiteracy, malnutrition, and inadequate health care and housing. The government itself reported an unemployment rate of 30 percent in 2005 and that 70 percent of the nation's population lived in poverty. Those figures had not substantially changed in 2007.

A WILLINGNESS TO CHANGE

In 1962 and 1975, agrarian-reform laws were passed and put into effect with relative success. The Honduran government, with the aid of peasant organizations and organized labor, was able to resettle 30,000 families on their own land. Today, two-thirds of the people who use the land either own it or have the legal right to its use. Labor legislation and social-security laws were enacted in the early 1960s. Even the Honduran military, usually corrupt, has at times brought about reform. An alliance of the military and organized labor in the early 1970s

produced a series of reforms in response to pressure from the less advantaged sectors of the population; in 1974, the military government developed a five-year plan to integrate the rural poor into the national economy and to increase social services in the area. The state has often shown a paternalistic face rather than a brutal, repressive one. The capacity for reform led one candidate in the 1981 presidential campaign to comment: "We Hondurans are different. There is no room for violence here."

There are now many signs of change. Agrarian reform slowed after 1976, prompting a peasant-association leader to remark: "In order to maintain social peace in the countryside, the peasants' needs will have to be satisfied to avoid revolt." In 1984, the Honduran government initiated a land-titling program and issued about 1,000 titles per month to landless peasants. The government's agrarian-reform program, which is under the control of the National Agrarian Institute, has always been characterized by the carrot and the stick. While some *campesinos* ("peasants") have been granted titles to land, others have been jailed or killed. Former military and security personnel apparently murdered several indigenous minority rights leaders in 2004.

Honduran campesinos, according to *Central America Report,* "have had a long and combative history of struggling for land rights." In 1987, hundreds of peasants were jailed as "terrorists" as a result of land invasions. Occupation of privately owned lands has become increasingly common in Honduras and reflects both population pressure on and land hunger of the peasantry. Land seizures by squatters are sometimes recognized by the National Agrarian Institute. In other cases, the government has promoted the relocation of people to sparsely populated regions of the country. Unfortunately, the chosen relocation sites are in tropical rain forests, which are already endangered throughout the region. The government wishes to transform the forests into rubber and citrus plantations or into farms to raise rice, corn, and other crops.

Peasants who fail to gain access to land usually migrate to urban centers in search of a better life. What they find in cities such as the capital, Tegucigalpa, are inadequate social services, a miserable standard of living, and a municipal government without the resources to help. In 1989, Tegucigalpa was deeply in debt, mortgaged to the limit, months behind in wage payments to city workers, and plagued by garbage piling up in the streets. In 2004 the capital city was plagued by a crime wave conducted by youth gangs, drug trafficking, police implication in high-profile crimes, and the murder of street children by death squads.

FREEDOM

Former president Reina reduced the power of the military. Constitutional reforms in 1994–1995 replaced obligatory military service and the press-gang recruitment system with voluntary service. As a result, the size of the army declined.

The nation's economy as a whole fared badly in the late 1980s. But by 1992, following painful adjustments occasioned by the reforms of the government of President Rafael Callejas, the economy again showed signs of growth. Real gross domestic product reached 3.5 percent, and inflation was held in check. Still, unemployment remained a persistent problem; some agencies calculated that two thirds of the workforce lacked steady employment. A union leader warned: "Unemployment leads to desperation and becomes a time bomb that could explode at any moment."

In addition to internal problems, pressure was put on Honduras by the International Monetary Fund. According to the *Caribbean & Central America Report,* the first phase of a reform program agreed to with the IMF succeeded in stabilizing the economy through devaluation of the lempira (the Honduran currency), public spending cuts, and increased taxes. But economic growth declined, and international agencies urged a reduction in the number of state employees as well as an accelerated campaign to privatize state-owned enterprises. The government admitted that there was much room for reform, but one official complained: "As far as they [the IMF] are concerned, the Honduran state should make gigantic strides, but our position is that this country cannot turn into General Motors overnight."

Opposition to the demands of international agencies was quick to materialize. One newspaper warned that cuts in social programs would result in violence. Trade-union and Catholic Church leaders condemned the social costs of the stabilization program despite the gains recorded in the credit-worthiness of Honduras.

HUMAN AND CIVIL RIGHTS

In theory, despite the continuing violence in the region, basic freedoms in Honduras are still intact. The press is privately owned and free of government censorship. There is, however, a quietly expressed concern about offending the government, and self-censorship is considered prudent. Moreover, it is an accepted practice in Honduras for government ministries and other agencies to have journalists on their payrolls.

Honduran labor unions are free to organize and have a tradition of providing their rank-and-file certain benefits. Unions are allowed to bargain, but labor laws guard against "excessive" activity. A complex procedure of negotiation and arbitration must be followed before a legal strike can be called. If a government proves unyielding, labor will likely pass into the ranks of the opposition.

In 1992, Honduras's three major workers' confederations convinced the private sector to raise the minimum wage by 13.7 percent, the third consecutive year of increases. Nevertheless, the minimum wage, which varies by occupation and location, is not adequate to provide a decent standard of living, especially in view of inflation. One labor leader pointed out that the minimum wage will "not even buy tortillas." To compound workers' problems, the labor minister admitted that about 30 percent of the enterprises under the supervision of his office paid wages *below* the minimum. To survive, families must pool the resources of all their working members. Predictably, health and safety laws are usually ignored. As is the case in the rural sector, the government has listened to the complaints of workers—but union leaders have also on occasion been jailed.

The government is also confronted with the problem of an increasing flow of rural poor into the cities. Employment opportunities in rural areas have declined as landowners have converted cropland into pasture for beef cattle. Because livestock raising requires less labor than growing crops, the surplus rural workers seek to better their opportunities in the cities. But the new migrants have discovered that Honduras's commercial and industrial sectors are deep in recession and cannot provide adequate jobs.

HEALTH/WELFARE

Honduras remains one of the region's poorest countries. Serious shortcomings are evident in education and health care, and economic growth is essentially erased by population growth. More than half of the population live in poverty.

Fortunately, many of the 300,000 refugees from Nicaragua and El Salvador have returned home. With the election of President Violeta Chamorro in Nicaragua, most of the 20,000 rebel Contras laid down their arms and went home, thus eliminating—from the perspective of the Honduran government—a source of much violence in its border regions.

To the credit of the Honduran government, which is under strong pressure from conservative politicians and businesspeople as well as elements within the armed forces for tough policies against dissent, allegations vis-à-vis human-rights abuses are taken seriously. (In one celebrated case, the Inter-American Court of Human Rights, established in 1979, found the government culpable in at least one person's "disappearance" and ordered the payment of an indemnification to the man's family. While not accepting any premise of guilt, the government agreed to pay. More important, according to the COHA *Washington Report,* the decision sharply criticized "prolonged isolation" and "incommunicado detention" of prisoners and equated such abuses with "cruel and inhuman punishment.") Former president Carlos Roberto Reina was a strong advocate of human rights as part of his "moral revolution." In 1995, he took three steps in this direction: a special prosecutor was created to investigate human-rights violations, human-rights inquiries were taken out of the hands of the military and given to a new civilian Department of Criminal Investigation, and promises were made to follow up on cases of disappearances during previous administrations. While Honduras may no longer be characterized as "the peaceable kingdom," the government has not lost touch with its people and still acts out a traditional role of patron.

From the mid-1980s to the mid-1990s, the most serious threat to civilian government came from the military. The United States' Central American policy boosted the prestige, status, and power of the Honduran military, which grew confident in its ability to forge the nation's destiny. With the end of the Contra–Sandinista armed struggle in Nicaragua, there was a dramatic decline in military assistance from the United States. This allowed President Reina to assert civilian control over the military establishment.

ACHIEVEMENTS

The small size of Honduras, in terms of territory and population, has produced a distinctive literary style that is a combination of folklore and legend.

Economic assistance from the United States in the 1980s and 1990s had some success in addressing the needs of poverty-stricken Hondurans. But that aid was sharply cut back in the late 1990s. Recently allocated United States economic aid, much of which has been motivated by Washington's concerns about drug trafficking, terrorism, and the appearance of "unfriendly" governments in the region, has been skewed by a political agenda and not the needs of Honduras. Such targeted aid does little to alleviate basic social problems, such as poverty or underemployment. Successful Honduran programs, ironically, have languished because of inadequate funding. One program provided access to potable water and was credited with cutting the infant mortality rate by half. Other programs funded vaccinations and

primary-education projects. In the words of newspaperman and development expert Juan Ramón Martínez: "Just when you [the United States] started getting it right, you walked away."

President Reina's "moral revolution" also moved to confront the problem of endemic official corruption. In June 1995, Reina alluded to the enormity of the task when he said that if the government went after all of the guilty, "there would not be enough room for them in the prisons." In 1998, just as the Honduran economy was beginning to recover from economic setbacks occasioned by turmoil in the influential Asian financial markets, Hurricane Mitch wreaked havoc on the nation's infrastructure. Roads, bridges, schools, clinics, and homes were destroyed, and thousands of lives were lost. Freshwater wells had to be reconstructed. Banana plantations were severely damaged. Recovery from this natural disaster will be prolonged and costly.

Although the press in Honduras is legally "free," *Honduras This Week* notes that many journalists have close ties to the business community and allow these contacts "rather than impartial journalism" to determine the substance of their articles. Moreover, there is a disturbing tendency for the media to praise the government in power as a "means of gaining favor with that administration."

President Ricardo Maduro made a determined effort to crack down on a rampant crime wave. Undoubtedly his focus was sharpened by the loss of his son to criminal violence in 1998. Presidential elections in 2005 were dominated by the growing incidence of violent crime, much of it attributed to youth gangs. Both candidates stressed law and order issues. The candidate of the ruling National Party urged a hard line policy against gangs. He

Timeline: PAST

1524
Honduras is settled by Spaniards from Guatemala

1821
Independence from Spain

1822–1838
Honduras is part of the United Provinces of Central America

1838
Honduras becomes Independent as a separate country

1969
Brief border war with El Salvador

1980s
Tensions with Nicaragua grow

1990s
Hurricane Mitch causes enormous death and destruction

PRESENT

2000s
AIDS is an increasing problem

Manuel Zelaya elected president in 2005

Increasing gang-related violence

endorsed the government's "Mano Duro" (Tough Hand) Law, by which membership in a gang was made a felony, and sought reinstatement of the death penalty, which had been abolished in 1937. The victor in the elections, the Liberal Party's Manuel Zelaya, is opposed the death penalty as well as the tough anti-gang legislation. Crime, he argues, in part springs from basic social problems. Poverty and unemployment drive youth into gangs, he asserted. The close results of the election indicate that Hondurans are badly divided over issues of crime and poverty.

Nicaragua (Republic of Nicaragua)

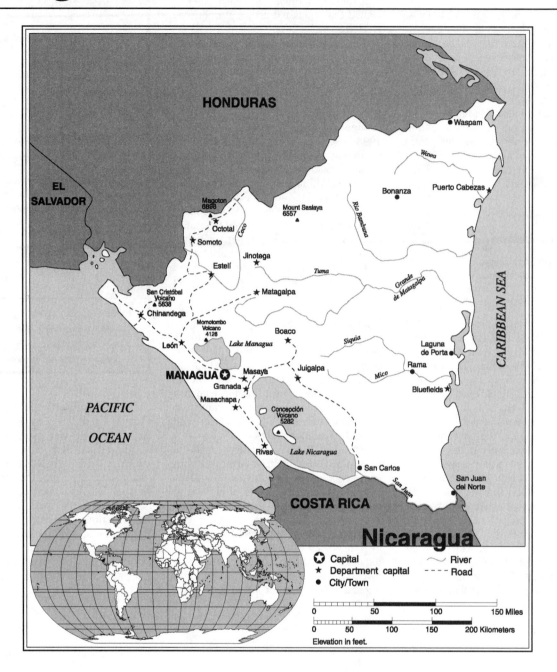

Nicaragua Statistics

GEOGRAPHY

Area in Square Miles (Kilometers):
49,985 (129,494) (about the size of
New York)
Capital (Population): Managua
1,680,000
Environmental Concerns: deforestation;
soil erosion; water pollution
Geographical Features: extensive Atlantic
coastal plains rising to central interior

mountains; narrow Pacific coastal plain
interrupted by volcanoes
Climate: tropical, but varies with elevation
(temperate highlands)

PEOPLE
Population

Total: 5,675,356 (2007 est.)
Annual Growth Rate: 1.85%
Rural/Urban Population Ratio: 37/63

Ethnic Makeup: 69% Mestizo; 17% white;
9% black; 5% Amerindian
Major Language: Spanish
Religions: 73% Roman Catholic;
15% Evangelical Protestant

Health

Life Expectancy at Birth: Male: 63 years
Female: 73
Infant Mortality Rate (Ratio): 27.14/1,000
Physicians Available (Ratio): 1/1,566

44

Education

Adult Literacy Rate: 67.5%
Compulsory (Ages): 7–13; free

COMMUNICATION

Telephones: 247,900 main lines
Daily Newspaper Circulation: 31 per 1,000 people
Cell Phones: 1,830,000
Internet Users: 155,000

TRANSPORTATION

Roadways in Kilometers (miles): 19,036 (11,828)
Railroads in Miles (Kilometers): none
Usable Airfields: 163

GOVERNMENT

Type: republic
Independence Date: September 15, 1821 (from Spain)

Head of State/Government: President Daniel Ortega is both head of state and head of government
Political Parties: Liberal Constitutionalist Party; Nicaraguan Liberal Alliance; Sandinista Renovation Movement; Alliance for the Republic; Conservative Party; Sandinista National Liberation Front; many others
Suffrage: universal at 16

MILITARY

Military Expenditures (% of GDP): 1.2%
Current Disputes: territorial or boundary disputes with Colombia, Honduras, and El Salvador

ECONOMY

Currency ($U.S. Equivalent): 19 córdobas oros = $1
Per Capita Income/GDP: $3,200/ $5,134 billion

GDP Growth Rate: 2.9%
Inflation Rate: 9.8%
Unemployment Rate: 5.6%
  Underemployment: 46.5%
Labor Force: 2,262,000
Natural Resources: gold; silver; copper; tungsten; lead; zinc; timber; fish
Agriculture: coffee; bananas; sugarcane; cotton; rice; corn; tobacco; soya; beans; livestock
Industry: food processing; chemicals; machinery; metals products; textiles and clothing; petroleum; beverages; footwear; wood
Exports: $2.235 billion (f.o.b.) (primary partners United States, Germany, El Salvador)
Imports: $3.647 billion (f.o.b.) billion (primary partners United States, Costa Rica, Guatemala)

SUGGESTED WEB SITE

http://www.cia.gov/cia/publications/factbook/index.html

Nicaragua Country Report

NICARAGUA: A NATION IN RECOVERY

Nicaraguan society, culture, and history have been molded to a great extent by the country's geography. A land of volcanoes and earthquakes, the frequency of natural disasters in Nicaragua has profoundly influenced its peoples' perceptions of life, death, and fate. What historian Ralph Woodward has written about Central America is particularly apt for Nicaraguans: Fatalism may be said to be a "part of their national mentality, tempering their attitudes toward the future. Death and tragedy always seem close in Central America. The primitive states of communication, transportation, and production, and the insecurity of human life, have been the major determinants in the region's history . . . ."

Nicaragua is a divided land, with distinct geographic, cultural, racial, ethnic, and religious zones. The west-coast region, which contains about 90 percent of the total population, is overwhelmingly white or Mestizo (mixed blood), Catholic, and Hispanic. The east coast is a sharp contrast, with its scattered population and multiplicity of Indian, Creole (in Nicaragua, native-born blacks), and Hispanic ethnic groups.

The east coast's geography, economy, and isolation from Managua, the nation's capital city, have created a distinct identity among its people. Many east-coast citizens think of themselves as *costeños* ("coast dwellers")

DEVELOPMENT

The possibility of the construction of a "dry canal" across Nicaragua has raised the hopes of thousands for a better future. A group of Asian investors is investigating the construction of a 234-mile-long rail link between the oceans to carry container cargo.

rather than Nicaraguans. Religion reinforces this common identity. About 70 percent of the east-coast population, regardless of ethnic group, are members of the Protestant Moravian Church. After a century and a half of missionary work, the Moravian Church has become "native," with locally recruited clergy. Among the Miskito Indians, Moravian pastors commonly replace tribal elders as community leaders. The Creoles speak English and originally arrived either as shipwrecked or escaped slaves or as slave labor introduced by the British to work in the lumber camps and plantations in the seventeenth century. Many Creoles and Miskitos feel a greater sense of allegiance to the British than to Nicaraguans from the west coast, who are regarded as foreigners.

SANDINISTA POLICIES

Before the successful 1979 Revolution that drove the dictator Anastasio Somoza from power, Nicaraguan governments generally

ignored the east coast. Revolutionary Sandinistas—who took their name from a guerrilla, Augusto César Sandino, who fought against occupying U.S. forces in the late 1920s and early 1930s—adopted a new policy toward the neglected region. The Sandinistas were concerned with the east coast's history of rebelliousness and separatism, and they were attracted by the economic potential of the region (palm oil and rubber). Accordingly, they hastily devised a bold campaign to unify the region with the rest of the nation. Roads, communications, health clinics, economic development, and a literacy campaign for local inhabitants were planned. The Sandinistas, in defiance of local customs, also tried to organize the local population into mass formations—that is, organizations for youth, peasants, women, wage earners, and the like. It was believed in Managua that such groups would unite the people behind the government and the Revolution and facilitate the economic, political, and social unification of the region.

In general, the attempt failed, and regional tensions within Nicaragua persist to this day. Historically, costeños were unimpressed with the exploits of the guerrilla Sandino, who raided U.S. companies along the east coast in the 1930s. When the companies left or cut back on operations, workers who lost their jobs blamed Sandino rather than the worldwide

(Courtesy of Chris and Erin Ratay/)

Known to the Spaniards as the "Gates of Hell," the craters of Volcán Masaya National Park are the most easily accessible active volcanoes in Nicaragua. Santiago crater is still active and is often seen steaming and smoking.

economic crisis of the 1930s. Consequently, there was a reluctance to accept Sandino as the national hero of the new Nicaragua. Race and class differences increased due to an influx of Sandinistas from the west. Many of the new arrivals exhibited old attitudes and looked down on the east-coast peoples as "uncivilized" or "second class."

The Miskito Question

In 1982, the government forced 10,000 Indians from their ancestral homes along the Río Coco because of concern with border security. As a result, many Indians joined the Contras, U.S.–supported guerrillas who fought against the Sandinista regime.

In an attempt to win back the Miskito and associated Indian groups, the government decided on a plan of regional autonomy. The significance of the Sandinista policy was that the government finally appreciated how crucial regional differences are in Nicaragua. Cultural and ethnic differences must be respected if Managua expects to rule its peoples effectively. The lesson learned by the Sandinistas was taken to heart by the subsequent Chamorro government, which was the first in history to appoint a Nicaraguan of Indian background to a ministerial-level position. A limited self-government granted to the east-coast region by the Sandinistas in 1987 has been

maintained; local leaders were elected to office in 1990.

A Mixed Record

The record of the Sandinista government was mixed. When the rebels seized power in 1979, they were confronted by an economy in shambles. Nineteen years of civil war had taken an estimated 50,000 lives and destroyed half a billion dollars' worth of factories, businesses, medical facilities, and dwellings. Living standards had tumbled to 1962 levels, and unemployment had reached an estimated 25 percent.

Despite such economic difficulties, the government made great strides in the areas of health and nutrition. A central goal of official policy was to provide equal access to health services. The plan had more success in urban areas than in rural ones. The government emphasized preventive, rather than curative, medicine. Preventive medicine included the provision of clean water, sanitation, immunization, nutrition, and maternal and child care. People were also taught basic preventive medical techniques. National campaigns to wipe out malaria, measles, and polio had reasonable success. But because of restricted budgets, the health system was overloaded, and there was a shortage of medical supplies. In the area of nutrition, basic foodstuffs such as grains, oil, eggs, and milk were paid for in part by the government in an effort to

improve the general nutritional level of Nicaraguans.

By 1987, the Sandinista government was experiencing severe economic problems that badly affected all social programs. In 1989, the economy, for all intents and purposes, collapsed. Hyperinflation ran well over 100 percent a month; and in June 1989, following a series of mini-devaluations, the nation's currency was devalued by an incredible 100 percent. Commerce was virtually paralyzed.

The revolutionary Sandinista government, in an attempt to explain the economic debacle, with some justice argued that the Nicaragua that it had inherited in 1979 had been savaged and looted by former dictator Somoza. The long-term costs of economic reconstruction; the restructuring of the economy to redistribute wealth; the trade embargo erected by the United States and North American diplomatic pressure, designed to discourage lending or aid from international institutions such as the International Monetary Fund; and the high cost of fighting a war against the U.S.–supported Contra rebels formed the backdrop to the crisis. Opposition leaders added to this list various Sandinista economic policies that discouraged private business.

The impact of the economic crisis on average Nicaraguans was devastating. Overnight, prices of basic consumer goods such as meat, rice, beans, milk, sugar, and cooking oil were increased 40 to 80 percent. Gasoline prices doubled. School-teachers engaged in work stoppages in an effort to increase their monthly wages of about $15, equal to the pay of a domestic servant. (To put the teachers' plight into perspective, note that the cost of a liter of milk absorbed fully 36 percent of a day's pay.)

FREEDOM

The creation in 2008 of Citizens Power Councils by the government concerns opposition leaders who see the councils not as an exercise in direct democracy, but as a ploy by President Ortega to control society and to bypass the wishes of the National Assembly. Councils were given power over government programs and, allegedly, could administer those programs preferentially in the interests of the Sandinista Party.

As a hedge against inflation, other Nicaraguans purchased U.S. dollars on the black market. *Regionews,* published in Managua, noted that conversion of córdobas into dollars was "seen as a better proposition than depositing them in savings accounts."

Economic travail inevitably produces dissatisfaction; opinion polls taken in July

1989 signaled political trouble for the Sandinistas. The surveys reflected an electorate with mixed feelings. While nearly 30 percent favored the Sandinistas, 57 percent indicated that they would not vote for President Daniel Ortega.

The results of the election of 1990 were not surprising, for the Sandinistas had lost control of the economy. They failed to survive a strong challenge from the opposition, led by the popular Violeta Chamorro.

Sandinista land reform, for the most part, consisted of the government's confiscation of the huge estates of the ousted Somoza family. These lands amounted to more than 2 million acres, including about 40 percent of the nation's best farmland. Some peasants were given land, but the government preferred to create cooperatives. This policy prompted the criticism that the state had simply become an old-style landowner. The Sandinistas replied that "the state is not the same state as before; it is a state of producers; we organized production and placed it at the disposal of the people." In 1990, there were several reports of violence between Sandinista security forces and peasants and former Contras who petitioned for private ownership of state land.

The Role of the Church

The Revolution created a sharp division within the Roman Catholic Church in Nicaragua. Radical priests, who believed that Christianity and Marxism share similar goals and that the Church should play a leading role in social change and revolution, were at odds with traditional priests fearful of "godless communism." Since 1979, many radical Catholics had become involved in social and political projects; several held high posts in the Sandinista government.

One priest of the theology of liberation was interviewed by *Regionews*. The interviewer stated that an "atheist could say, 'These Catholics found a just revolution opposed by the Church hierarchy. They can't renounce their religion and are searching for a more convenient theology. But it's their sense of natural justice that motivates them." The priest replied: "I think that's evident and that Jesus was also an 'atheist,' an atheist of the religion as practiced in his time. He didn't believe in the God of the priests in the temples who were allied with Caesar. Jesus told of a new life. And the 'atheist' that exists in our people doesn't believe in the God that the hierarchy often offers us. He believes in life, in man, in development. God manifests Himself there. A person who believes in life and justice in favor of the poor is not an atheist." The movement, he noted,

would continue "with or without approval from the hierarchy."

The Drift to the Left

As has historically been the case in revolutions, after a brief period of unity and excitement, the victors begin to disagree over policies and power. For a while in Nicaragua, there was a perceptible drift to the left, and the Revolution lost its image of moderation. While radicalization was a dynamic inherent in the Revolution, it was also pushed in a leftward direction by a hostile U.S. foreign policy that attempted to bring down the Sandinista regime through its support of the Contras. In 1987, however, following the peace initiatives of Latin American governments, the Sandinista government made significant efforts to project a more moderate image. *La Prensa,* the main opposition newspaper, which the Sandinistas had shut down in 1986, was again allowed to publish. Radio Católica, another source of opposition to the government, was given permission to broadcast after its closure the year before. And antigovernment demonstrations were permitted in the streets of Managua.

Significantly, President Ortega proposed reforms in the country's election laws in April 1989, to take effect before the national elections in 1990. The new Nicaraguan legislation was based on Costa Rican and Venezuelan models, and in some instances was even more forward-looking.

An important result of the laws was the enhancement of political pluralism, which allowed for the National Opposition Union (UNO) victory in 1990. Rules for organizing political parties, once stringent, were loosened; opposition parties were granted access to the media; foreign funding of political parties was allowed; the system of proportional representation permitted minority parties to maintain a presence; and the opposition was allowed to monitor the elections closely.

HEALTH/WELFARE

Nicaragua's deep debt and the austerity demands of the IMF have had a strongly negative effect on citizens' health. As people have been driven from the health service by sharp cuts in government spending, the incidence of malnutrition in children has risen. Reported deaths from diarrhea and respiratory problems are also on the increase.

The Sandinistas realized that to survive, they had to make compromises. In need of breathing space, the government embraced

the Central American Peace Plan designed by Costa Rican president Óscar Arias and designed moderate policies to isolate the United States.

On the battlefield, the cease-fire unilaterally declared by the Sandinistas was eventually embraced by the Contras as well, and both sides moved toward a political solution of their differences. Armed conflict formally ended on June 27, 1990, although sporadic violence continued in rural areas.

A PEACEFUL TRANSITION

It was the critical state of the Nicaraguan economy that in large measure brought the Sandinistas down in the elections of 1990. Even though the government of Violeta Chamorro made great progress in the demilitarization of the country and national reconciliation, the economy remained a time bomb.

ACHIEVEMENTS

The Nicaraguan poet Rubén Dario was the most influential representative of the Modernist Movement, which swept Latin America in the late nineteenth century. Dario was strongly critical of injustice and oppression.

The continuing economic crisis and disagreements over policy directions destroyed the original base of Chamorro's political support. Battles between the legislative and executive branches of government virtually paralyzed the country. At the end of 1992, President Chamorro closed the Assembly building and called for new elections. But by July 1995, an accord had been reached between the two contending branches of government. Congress passed a "framework law" that created the language necessary to implement changes in the Sandinista Constitution of 1987. The Legislative Assembly, together with the executive branch, are pledged to the passage of laws on matters such as property rights, agrarian reform, consumer protection, and taxation. The July agreement also provided for the election of the five-member Consejo Supremo Electoral (Supreme Electoral Council), which oversaw the presidential elections in November 1996.

The election marked something of a watershed in Nicaraguan political history. Outgoing president Chamorro told reporters at the inauguration of Arnoldo Alemán Lâcayo: "For the first time in more than 100 years . . . one civilian, democratically elected president will hand over power to another." But the election did not mask the fact that Nicaragua was still deeply polarized and that the Sandinistas only grudgingly accepted their defeat.

President Alemán sought a dialogue with the Sandinistas, and both sides agreed to participate in discussions to study poverty, property disputes occasioned by the Sandinista policy of confiscation, and the need to attract foreign investment.

The Alemán administration confronted a host of difficult problems. In the Western Hemisphere, only Haiti is poorer. Perhaps 80 percent of the population were unemployed or underemployed, and an equal percentage lived below the poverty line. Just as the economy began to show some signs of recovery from years of war, Hurricane Mitch devastated the country in 1998 and profoundly set back development efforts, as all available resources had to be husbanded to reconstruct much of Nicaragua's infrastructure.

Economic malaise compounded by allegations of corruption and illegal enrichment undermined the credibility of the Alemán government. Dissatisfaction among voters was registered at the polls, resulting in Sandinista victories in Managua and nine of 17 provincial capitals in municipal elections in November 2000. A contributing factor was the emergence of the Conservative Party, which split the anti-Sandinista vote. Interestingly, the Sandinista victor in Managua, Herty Lewites, has styled himself as a "revolutionary businessman and defender of social justice"—that is, a popular pragmatist.

Organized labor has shown a similar pragmatic dimension in Nicaragua. Labor leaders have quietly supported both globalization and the policies of the World Trade Organization because of the jobs that would be created. Another effect of globalization, not only in Nicaragua but also throughout the region, has been the further erosion of the *siesta* (nap) tradition. In the words

of a Nicaraguan-government official, the emerging world economy demands that "we stay open all day."

The administration of President Enrique Bolaño Geyer, elected in 2002, saw some improvement. There was some economic growth in 2003, private investment increased, and exports rose. For the foreseeable future, however, Nicaragua will remain poor.

President Bolaños became politically isolated, however. His campaign against government corruption, which ensnared former President Alemán, led to his abandonment by his own conservative Constitutionalist Liberal Party. Remarkably, the conservatives allied with Daniel Ortega's Sandinista Party with the object, in the words of the *New York Times,* "to regain power without holding an election that neither man could win." The state electoral commission, under Ortega's direction, "lowered the threshold for averting a run-off election to 35 percent of the vote from 45 percent." Ortega won the 2006 contest, a sign that many Nicaraguans wanted more rapid change. To implement change, however, the Nicaraguan government needs an infusion of aid. Some of that aid has been provided by Venezuela in the form of 10 million barrels of petroleum a year, which is sufficient to meet the country's energy needs. Under the deal, Nicaragua is able to purchase the oil at half the market price and has 23 years to pay off the rest at two percent interest. "The deal," according to the *New York Times,* "hands Nicaragua what amounts to a large low-interest loan every month for infrastructure projects and social programs." Critics charge that the loans are not part of the national budget. Roberto Courtney, the Executive Director of the Nicaraguan Ethics and Transparency lobby that supports openness in government, stated: "It's off the books—no

institutions, no controls." Such secrecy opens the door to possible corruption and misuse of the monies, which the Nicaraguan people will not tolerate. If Ortega is to enjoy a successful presidency he must govern for all Nicaraguans and not just the party faithful.

Timeline: PAST

1522
Nicaragua is explored by Gil González

1821
Independence from Spain

1823
Nicaragua joins the United Provinces of Central America

1838
Nicaragua becomes independent as a separate state

1855
William Walker and filibusters (U.S. insurgents) invade Nicaragua

1928–1934
Augusto César Sandino leads guerrillas against occupying U.S. forces

1934–1979
Domination of Nicaragua by the Somoza family

1979
Sandinista guerrillas oust the Somoza family

1990s
A cease-fire allows an opening for political dialogue; Hurricane Mitch devastates the country

PRESENT

2000s
Sandinistas win municipal elections in November 2000

2006
Daniel Ortega again elected president

Panama (Republic of Panama)

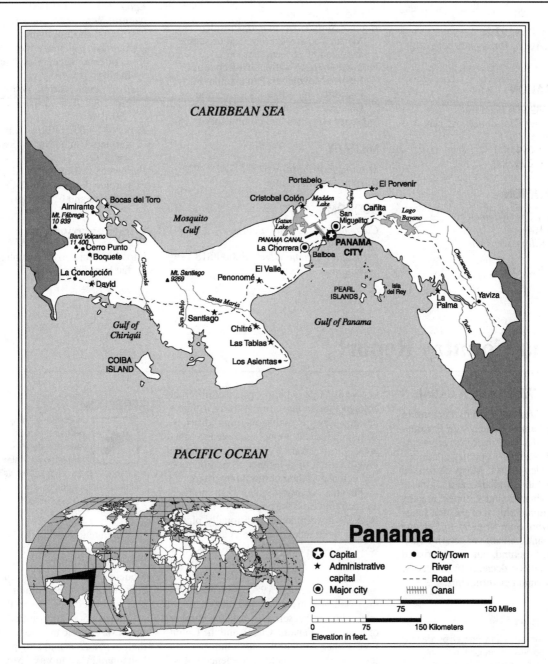

Panama

- ⊛ Capital
- ★ Administrative capital
- ◉ Major city
- ● City/Town
- ∿ River
- --- Road
- ⊬⊬⊬⊬ Canal

0 — 75 — 150 Miles
0 — 75 — 150 Kilometers
Elevation in feet.

Panama Statistics

GEOGRAPHY

Area in Square Miles (Kilometers):
30,185 (78,200) (about the size of South Carolina)
Capital (Population): Panama City (708,738)
Environmental Concerns: water pollution; deforestation; land degradation; soil erosion
Geographical Features: interior mostly steep, rugged mountains and dissected upland plains; coastal areas largely plains and rolling hills
Climate: tropical marine

PEOPLE

Population

Total: 3,242,173 (2007 est.)
Annual Growth Rate: 1.5%
Rural/Urban Population Ratio: 44/56
Major Languages: Spanish; English
Ethnic Makeup: 70% Mestizo; 14% West Indian; 10% white; 6% Indian and others
Religions: 85% Roman Catholic; 15% Protestant and others

Health

Life Expectancy at Birth: 73 years (male); 78 years (female)

49

GLOBAL STUDIES

Infant Mortality Rate (Ratio):
    15.96/1,000
Physicians Available (Ratio): 1/856

Education

Adult Literacy Rate: 92%
Compulsory (Ages): for 6 years between
    6–15; free

COMMUNICATION

Telephones: 432,900 main lines
Daily Newspaper Circulation: 62 per
    1,000 people
Cell Phones: 1,694,000
Internet Users: 220,000

TRANSPORTATION

Roadways in Miles (Kilometers):
    6,893 (11,100)
Railroads in Kilometers (Miles):
    355 (208)
Usable Airfields: 116

GOVERNMENT

Type: constitutional democracy
Independence Date: November 3, 1903
    (from Colombia)
Head of State/Government: President
    Martín Torrijos is both head of state
    and head of government
Political Parties: Nationalist Republican
    Liberal Movement; Panamanian Party;
    Patriotic Union Party; Democratic
    Change; Popular Party; others
Suffrage: universal and compulsory at 18

MILITARY

Military Expenditures (% of GDP): 1%
Current Disputes: none

ECONOMY

Currency ($U.S. Equivalent):
    1.00 balboa = $1
Per Capita Income/GDP: $9,000/$18.17
    billion

GDP Growth Rate: 7.8%
Inflation Rate: 5.1%
Unemployment Rate: 7.2%
Labor Force: 1,471,000
Natural Resources: copper; mahogany
    forests; shrimp; hydropower
Agriculture: bananas; rice; corn; coffee;
    sugarcane; vegetables; livestock;
    fishing
Industry: construction; petroleum;
    brewing; sugar; canal traffic
    /tourism
Exports: $9.662 billion(f.o.b.) (primary
    partners United States, Sweden, Costa
    Rica)
Imports: $12.1 billion (f.o.b.) (primary
    partners United States, Central
    America and Caribbean)

SUGGESTED WEB SITE

http://www.cia.gov/cia/publications/
    factbook/index.html

Panama Country Report

PANAMA: A NATION AND A CANAL

The Panama Canal, opened to shipping in 1914, has had a sharp impact on Panamanian political life, foreign policy, economy, and society. Panama is a country of minorities and includes blacks, Mestizos (mixed Indian and white), Indians, and Chinese. Many of the blacks and Chinese are the children or grandchildren of the thousands of workers who were brought to Panama to build the canal. Unable to return home, they remained behind, an impoverished people, ignored for decades by a succession of Panamanian governments.

DEVELOPMENT

Because many new ships are too large to transit the Canal, the Panamanian government unveiled plans in 2006 to expand it. Work began in 2007 and should be completed by 2014. Such a massive effort requires billions of dollars in new investment, but it is critical to the nation's economy.

The government has usually been dominated by whites, although all of the country's minorities are politically active. In areas where Indians comprise a majority of the population, they play significant roles in provincial political life. Some, such as the San Blas islanders—famous for the art form

known as Mola, which consists of different colored fabrics that are cut away to make designs—live in self-governing districts. Although Indians are not restricted to tribal areas, most remain by choice, reflecting a long tradition of resistance to assimilation and defense of their cultural integrity.

Panama's economy has both profited and suffered from the presence of the canal. Because governments traditionally placed too much reliance on the direct and indirect revenues generated by the canal tolls, they tended to ignore other types of national development. Much of Panama's economic success in the 1980s, however, was the result of a strong service sector associated with the presence of a large number of banks, the Panama Canal, and the Colón Free Zone. Agriculture and industry, on the other hand, usually experienced slow growth rates.

Because of U.S. control of the canal and the Canal Zone, this path between the seas continuously stoked the fires of Panamanian nationalism. The high standard of living and the privileges enjoyed by U.S. citizens residing in the Canal Zone contrasted sharply with the poverty of Panamanians. President Omar Torrijos became a national hero in 1977 when he signed the Panama Canal Treaties with U.S. president Jimmy Carter. The treaties provided for full Panamanian control over the canal and its revenues by 1999.

FREEDOM

In 2005 the Torrijos government repealed restrictive media laws that punished journalists and radio and television personalities for alleged "insults" against state officials. Panama's media is now free to present news and commentary.

Panamanian officials spoke optimistically of their plans for the bases they would soon inherit, citing universities, modern container ports, luxury resorts, and retirement communities. But there was much concern over the loss of an estimated $500 million that tens of thousands of American troops, civilians, and their dependents had long pumped into the Panamanian economy. Moreover, while all agreed that the canal itself would be well run, because Panamanians had been phased into its operation, there was pessimism about the lack of planning for ancillary facilities.

In 1995, more than 300 poor, landless people a day were moving into the Zone and were clearing forest for crops. The rain forest in the Canal Basin supplies not only the water essential to the canal but also the drinking water for about 40 percent of Panama's population. Loss of the rain forest could prove catastrophic. One official noted: "If we lose the Canal Basin we do

(Courtesy Dr. Paul Goodwin)

The Panama Canal has been of continuing importance to the country since it opened in 1914. Full control of the canal was turned over to Panama in 1999, marking the end of U.S. involvement and representing a source of Panamanian nationalism.

not lose only our water supply, it will also be the end of the Canal itself."

A RETURN TO CIVILIAN GOVERNMENT

President Torrijos, who died in a suspicious plane crash in 1981, left behind a legacy that included much more than the treaties. He elevated the National Guard to a position of supreme power in the state and ruled through a National Assembly of community representatives.

The 1984 elections appeared to bring to fruition the process of political liberalization initiated in 1978. But even though civilian rule was officially restored, the armed forces remained the real power behind the throne. Indeed, spectacular revelations in 1987 strongly suggested that Defense Forces chief general Manuel Antonio Noriega had rigged the 1984 elections. He was also accused of drug trafficking, gun running, and money laundering.

In February 1988, Noriega was indicted by two U.S. grand juries and charged with using his position to turn Panama into a center for the money-laundering activities of the Medellín, Colombia, drug cartel and providing protection for cartel members living temporarily in Panama.

Attempts by Panamanian president Eric Arturo Delvalle to oust the military strongman failed, and Delvalle himself was forced into hiding. Concerted efforts by the United States to remove Noriega from power—including an economic boycott, plans to kidnap the general and have the

CIA engineer a coup, and saber-rattling by the dispatch of thousands of U.S. troops to the Canal Zone—proved fruitless.

The fraud and violence that accompanied an election called by Noriega in 1989 to legitimize his government and the failure of a coup attempt in October ultimately resulted in the invasion of Panama by U.S. troops in December. Noriega was arrested, brought to the United States for trial, and eventually was convicted on drug-trafficking charges.

HEALTH/WELFARE

The Care Group, which is affiliated with Harvard Medical School, Beth Israel Hospital, and Panama's excellent Hospital Nacionál, reached agreement to create the region's first teaching hospital in the area of emergency care. Physicians from all of Latin America would be welcomed to the facility.

The U.S. economic sanctions succeeded in harming the wrong people. Noriega and his cronies were shielded from the economic crisis by their profits from money laundering. But many other Panamanians were devastated by the U.S. policy.

Nearly a decade after the invasion by U.S. troops to restore democracy and halt drug trafficking, the situation in Panama remains problematic. The country is characterized by extremes of wealth and poverty, and corruption is pervasive. The economy

is still closely tied to drug-money laundering, which has reached levels higher than during the Noriega years.

Elections in 1994 reflected the depth of popular dissatisfaction. Three quarters of the voters supported political movements that had risen in opposition to the policies and politics imposed on Panama by the U.S. invasion. The new president, Ernesto Pérez Balladares, a 48-year-old economist and businessman and a former supporter of Noriega, promised "to close the Noriega chapter" in Panama's history. During his term, he pushed ahead with privatization, the development of the Panama Canal Zone, a restructuring of the foreign debt, and initiatives designed to enhance tourism.

Unfortunately, Pérez seemed to have inherited some of the personalist tendencies of his predecessors. In 1998, he pushed for a constitutional change that would have allowed him to run for reelection in 1999. When put to a referendum in August 1998, Panamanians resoundingly defeated the ambitions of the president.

The 1999 elections, without the participation of Pérez, produced a close campaign between Martín Torrijos, the son of Omar, and Mireya Moscoso, the widow of the president who had been ousted by Omar Torrijos. Moscoso emerged as a winner, with 44 percent of the vote, and became Panama's first woman president.

Moscoso opposed many of Pérez's free-market policies and was especially critical of any further plans to privatize state-owned industries. Moscoso identified her administration with the inauguration of a "new era" for Panama's poor. Her social policies stood in direct contrast to the more economically pragmatic approach of her predecessors. Continued domination of the Legislature by the opposition render social reform difficult, but the president felt that she had to intercede on behalf of the poor, who constitute one-third of the population. Diversification of the economy remains a need, as Panama is still overly dependent on canal revenues and traditional agricultural exports. As supplement to the income produced by the canal, the Panama Canal Railway has been refurbished so that it will be able to transport container cargo in less time than it takes for a ship to transit the canal.

SOCIAL POLICIES

As is the case in most Latin American nations, Panama's Constitution authorizes the state to direct, regulate, replace, or create economic activities designed to increase the nation's wealth and to distribute the benefits of the economy to the greatest number of people. The harsh reality is that the income of one-third of Panama's population frequently fails to provide for families' basic needs.

Women, who won the right to vote in the 1940s, are accorded equal political rights under the law and hold a number of important government positions, including the presidency. But as in all of Latin America, women do not enjoy the same opportunities for advancement as men. There are also profound domestic constraints to their freedom. Panamanian law, for example, does not recognize community property; divorced or deserted women have no protection and can be left destitute, if that is the will of their former spouses. Many female heads-of-household from poor areas are obliged to work for the government, often as street cleaners, in order to receive support funds from the authorities.

ACHIEVEMENTS

The Panama Canal, which passed wholly to Panamanian control in 1999, is one of the greatest engineering achievements of the twentieth century. A maze of locks and gates, it cuts through 50 miles of the most difficult terrain on Earth.

With respect to human rights, Panama's record is mixed. The press and electronic media, while theoretically free, have experienced some harassment. In 1983, the Supreme Court ruled that journalists need not be licensed by the government. Nevertheless, both reporters and editors still exercise a calculated self-censorship, and press conduct in general is regulated by an official "Morality and Ethics Commission," whose powers are broad and vague. In 2001, some journalists complained that the Moscoso government used criminal antidefamation laws to intimidate the press in general, and its critics in particular.

In May 2004 Martín Torrijos was elected president with about 47 percent of the vote. Although he is the flag bearer of a political party built by military strongmen, including his father and Noriega, he has promised change. Cloaking himself in the garb of a populist, Torrijos has presented an image in both the cities and the countryside as the defender of the poor. He has inherited a government widely accused of corruption and a national pension system close to collapse because of overspending. His economic policies embrace a significant reconstruction of the Panama Canal to allow the passage of larger ships. The need for huge amounts of private investment will tend to temper his populism. Panama's problems are daunting, and one Panamanian university professor told the *New York Times:* "There is no way

[Torrijos] is going to be able to live up to people's expectations. He is going to have a short honeymoon."

Timeline: PAST

1518
Panama City is established

1821–1903
Panama is a department of Colombia

1903
Independence from Colombia

1977
The signing of the Panama Canal Treaties

1980s
The death of President Omar Torrijos creates a political vacuum; American troops invade Panama; Manuel Noriega surrenders to face drug charges in the United States

1990s
Mireya Moscoso is elected as Panama's first woman president; the last U.S. troops leave Panama; the Panama Canal passes to wholly local control

PRESENT

2000s
Climatic changes have been accelerated by deforestation

Martín Torrijos elected president in 2004

South America

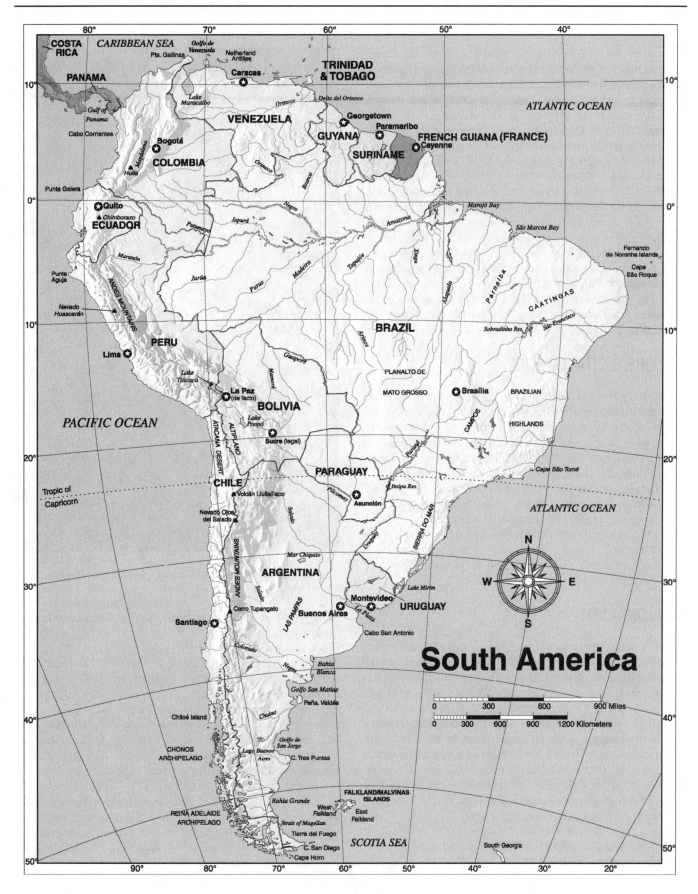

South America   An Imperfect Prism

Any overview of South America must first address the incredible geographic and climatic diversity of the region. Equatorial rain forests are found in Brazil, Ecuador, Colombia, Venezuela, and other countries; and the coastal deserts in Peru and northern Chile are among the driest and most forbidding in the world (naturalist Charles Darwin described the area as "a complete and utter desert"). More hospitable are the undulating pampas and plains of Argentina, Uruguay, central Venezuela, eastern Colombia, and southeastern Brazil. The spine of the continent is formed by the Andes Mountains, majestic and snowcapped. Because of its topography and the many degrees of latitude in which it lies, South America has extremes of temperature, ranging from desert heat to the steaming humidity of the tropics to the cold gales of Tierra del Fuego, which lies close to the Antarctic Circle. To add further to the perils of generalization, wide-ranging differences often occur within a country. Geography has played a critical role in the evolution of each of the nations of South America; it has been one of several major influences in their histories and their cultures.

NATURE'S CHALLENGE

Nature has presented the inhabitants of South America with an unrelenting challenge. On the west coast, most of the major cities are located in geologically active zones. All too frequently, earthquakes, tidal waves, volcanic activity, and landslides have taken a staggering toll of human life. And throughout the region, floods and droughts make agriculture a risky business. Periodically, for example, the appearance of a warm current off the coasts of Peru and Ecuador, a phenomenon known as *El Niño,* produces significant atmospheric events worldwide. For Peru and Ecuador, *El Niño* brings devastating floods with heavy loss of life and extensive damage to the area's infrastructure. Further economic damage results from the profound disruption of the fishing industry.

REGIONALISM

South America's diverse topography has also helped to foster a deep-seated regionalism that has spawned innumerable civil wars and made national integration an extremely difficult task. In Colombia, for instance, the Andes fan out into three distinct ranges, separated by deep valleys. Each of the nation's three major cities—Bogotá, Medellín, and Cali—dominates a valley and is effectively isolated from the others by the mountains. The broad plains to the east have remained largely undeveloped because of the difficulty of access from the centers of population. Troubling to Colombian governments is the fact that, in terms of topography, the eastern plains are tied to Venezuela and not to the Colombian cities to the west.

Similarly, mountains divide Ecuador, Peru, Bolivia, and Venezuela. In all of these nations, there is a permanent tension between the capital cities and the hinterlands. As is the case in

Courtesy of Paul Goodwin

The majestic Andes run along the entire spine of South America. These are in Chile.

those republics that have large Indian populations, the tension often is as much cultural as it is a matter of geography. But in the entire region, physical geography interacts with culture, society, politics, and economics. Regionalism has been a persistent theme in the history of Ecuador, where there has been an often bitter rivalry between the capital city of Quito, located high in the central mountains, and the port city of Guayaquil. Commonly, port cities, with their window on the world outside, tend to be more cosmopolitan, liberal, and dynamic than cities that are more isolated. Such is the case with freewheeling Guayaquil, which stands in marked contrast to conservative, traditional, deeply Catholic Quito.

Venezuela boasts six distinct geographical regions, which include mountains and valleys, plains and deserts, rivers and jungles, and a coastline. Historian John Lombardi observes that each of these regions has had an important role in identifying and defining the character of Venezuela's past and present: "Over

(Courtesy of Chris & Erin Ratay)

The cultures of the countries of the southern Cone—Argentina, Uruguay, Paraguay, and Chile—have been profoundly influenced by the geography of their vast, fertile plains. These latter-day gauchos are packing their bags for a trekking journey.

the centuries the geographical focus has shifted from one region to another in response to internal arrangements and external demands."

THE SOUTHERN CONE

The cultures of the countries of the so-called Southern Cone—Argentina, Uruguay, Paraguay, and Chile—have also been shaped by the geographical environment. Argentina, Uruguay, and Brazil's southern state of Rio Grande do Sul developed subcultures that reflected life on the vast, fertile plains, where cattle grazed by the millions. The *gaucho* ("cowboy") became symbolic of the "civilization of leather." Fierce, independent, a law unto himself, the gaucho was mythologized by the end of the nineteenth century. At a time when millions of European immigrants were flooding into the region, the gaucho emerged as a nationalist symbol of Argentina and Uruguay, standing firm in the face of whatever natives viewed as "foreign."

Landlocked Paraguay, surrounded by powerful neighbors, has for most of its history been an introspective nation, little known to the outside world. Because of its geography, most of Paraguay's population is concentrated near the capital city of Asunción. A third of the nation is tropical and swampy—not suitable for settlement. To the west, the desolate Chaco region, with its lack of adequate sources of drinkable water, is virtually uninhabitable.

Chile, with a coastline 2,600 miles long, is a country of topographic and climatic extremes. If superimposed on a map of North America, Chile would stretch from Mexico's Baja California to the Yukon in Alaska. It is on Chile's border with Argentina that the Andes soar to their greatest heights. Several peaks, including Aconcagua, reach to nearly 23,000 feet in elevation. That mountain barrier has historically isolated Chile from eastern South America and from Europe. The central valley of Chile is the political, industrial, social, and cultural heart of the nation. With the capital city of Santiago and the large port of Valparaíso, the valley holds about 70 percent of Chile's population. The valley's Mediterranean climate and fertile soil have long acted as a magnet for Chileans from other, less hospitable, parts of the country.

BRAZIL

Historian Rollie Poppino has noted that the "major miracle of Brazil is its existence as a single nation." What he implies is that Brazil embraces regions that are so distinct that they could well be separate countries. "There are actually many Brazils within the broad expanse of the national territory, and the implication of uniformity conveyed by their common flag and language is often deceptive." In Brazil, there exists a tremendous range of geographical, racial, cultural, and economic contrasts. But part of the Brazilian "miracle" lies in the ability of its people to accept the diversity as normal. Many Brazilians were unaware of the great differences within their country for years, until the improvement of internal transportation and communications as well as the impact of the mass media informed them not only of their common heritage but also of their profound regional differences.

DIVERSE PEOPLES

In many respects, the peoples of South America are as diverse as its geography. While the populations of Argentina and Uruguay are essentially European, with virtually no Indian intermixture, Chilean society is descended from Spanish conquerors and the Indians they dominated. The Indian presence is strongest in the Andean republics of Bolivia, Peru, and Ecuador—the heart of the ancient Inca civilization. Bolivia is the most Indian, with well over half its population classified as such. Mestizos (mixed white and Indian) constitute about a quarter of the population, and whites make up only about one-tenth.

Three ethnic groups are found among the populations of Colombia and Venezuela: Spanish and Indian predominate, and there are small black minorities. About 60 percent of the populations of both countries are of Mestizo or pardo (mixed blood) origin. One of Brazil's distinctive features is the rich racial mixture of its population. Peoples of Indian, European, African, and Japanese heritage live in an atmosphere largely free of racial enmity, if not degrees of prejudice.

Taken as a whole, the predominant culture is Iberian (that is, Spanish or Portuguese), although many mountain areas are overwhelmingly Indian in terms of ethnic makeup. With the conquest and colonization of South America in the sixteenth century, Spain and Portugal attempted to fasten their cultures, languages, and institutions on the land and its peoples. Spanish cities in South America—laid out in the familiar grid pattern consisting of a large central plaza bordered by a Catholic church, government buildings, and the dwellings of the ruling elite—represented the conscious intention of the conquerors to impose their will, not only on the defeated Indian civilizations but also on nature itself.

By way of contrast, the Brazilian cities that were laid out by early Portuguese settlers tended to be less formally structured, suggesting that their planners and builders were more flexible and adaptable to the new world around them. Roman Catholicism, however, was imposed on all citizens by the central authority. Government, conforming to Hispanic political culture, was authoritarian in the colonial period and continues to be so today. The conquerors created a stratified society of essentially two sectors: a ruling white elite and a ruled majority. But Spain and Portugal also introduced institutions that knit society together. Paternalistic patron–client relationships that bound the weak to the strong were common; they continue to be so today.

INDIAN CULTURE

Among the isolated Indian groups of Ecuador, Peru, and Bolivia, Spanish cultural forms were strongly and, for the most part, successfully resisted. Suspicious and occasionally hostile, the Indians refused integration into the white world outside their highland villages. By avoiding integration, in the words of historian Frederick Pike, "they maintain the freedom to live almost exclusively in the domain of their own language, social habits, dress and eating styles, beliefs, prejudices, and myths."

Only the Catholic religion was able to make some inroads, and that was (and still is) imperfect. The Catholicism practiced by Quechua- and Aymara-speaking Indians is a blend of Catholic teachings and ancient folk religion. For example, in an isolated region in Peru where eight journalists were massacred by Indians, a writer who investigated the incident reported in *The New York Times* that while Catholicism was "deeply rooted" among the Indians, "it has not displaced old beliefs like the worship of the *Apus,* or god mountains." When threatened, the Indians are "zealous defenders of their customs and mores." The societies' two cultures have had a profound impact on the literature of Ecuador, Peru, and Bolivia. The plight of the Indian, social injustice, and economic exploitation are favorite themes of these nations' authors.

Other Indian groups more vulnerable to the steady encroachment of "progress" did not survive. In the late nineteenth century, pampas Indians were virtually destroyed by Argentine cavalry armed with repeating rifles. Across the Andes, in Chile, the Araucanian Indians met a similar fate in the 1880s. Unfortunately, relations between the "civilized" world and the "primitive" peoples clinging to existence in the rain forests of Brazil, Peru, Bolivia, and Venezuela have generally improved little. But beginning in the early 1990s events in Bolivia, Brazil, Ecuador, and Venezuela signaled a marked shift toward greater Indian rights. Bolivians elected an Aymara Indian leader and activist as president in 2006. Indigenous peoples throughout the Amazon Basin, however, are still under almost daily assault from settlers hungry for land, road builders, developers, miners, loggers, and speculators—most of whom care little about the cultures they are annihilating.

AFRICAN AMERICAN CULTURE

In those South American countries where slavery was widespread, the presence of a large black population has contributed yet another dimension to Hispanic culture (or, in the case of Guyana and Suriname, English and Dutch culture). Slaves, brutally uprooted from their cultures in Africa, developed new cultural forms that were often a combination of Christian and

(PhotoLink/Getty Images)

South America's Indian cultures and modern development have never really mixed. The native cultures persist in many areas, as exemplified at a market in Ecuador.

other beliefs. To insulate themselves against the rigors of forced labor and to forge some kind of common identity, slaves embraced folk religions that were heavily oriented toward magic. Magic helped blacks to face an uncertain destiny, and folk religions built bridges between peoples facing a similar, horrible fate. Folk religions not only survived the emancipation of slaves but have remained a common point of focus for millions of Brazilian blacks.

This phenomenon had become so widespread that in the 1970s, the Roman Catholic Church made a concerted effort to win Afro-Brazilians to a religion that was more Christian and less pagan. This effort was partly negated by the development of close relations between Brazil and Africa, which occurred at the same time as the Church's campaign. Brazilian blacks became more acutely aware of their African origins and began a movement of "re-Africanization." So pervasive had the folk religions become that one authority stated that Umbada (one of the folk religions) was now the religion of Brazil. The festival of *Carnaval* ("Carnival") in Rio de Janeiro, Brazil, is perhaps the best-known example of the blending of Christianity with spiritism. Even the samba, a dance form that is central to the Carnaval celebration, had its origins in black folk religions.

IMMIGRATION AND CULTURE

Italians, Eastern and Northern Europeans, Chinese, and Japanese have also contributed to the cultural, social, and economic development of several South American nations. The great outpouring of Europe's peoples that brought millions of immigrants to the shores of the United States also brought millions to South America. From the mid-1800s to the outbreak of World War I in 1914, great numbers of Italians and Spaniards, and much smaller numbers of Germans, Russians, Welsh, Scots, Irish, and English boarded ships that would carry them to South America.

Many were successful in the "New World." Indeed, immigrants were largely responsible for the social restructuring of Argentina, Uruguay, and southern Brazil, as they created a large and dynamic middle class where none had existed before.

Italians

Many of the new arrivals came from urban areas, were literate, and possessed a broad range of skills. Argentina received the greatest proportion of immigrants. So great was the influx that an Argentine political scientist labeled the years 1890–1914 the "alluvial era" (flood). His analogy was apt, for by 1914, half the population of the capital city of Buenos Aires were foreign-born. Indeed, 30 percent of the total Argentine population were of foreign extraction. Hundreds of thousands of immigrants also flocked into Uruguay.

In both countries, they were able to move quickly into middle-class occupations in business and commerce. Others found work on the docks or on the railroads that carried the produce of the countryside to the ports for export to foreign markets. Some settled in the interior of Argentina, where they usually became sharecroppers or tenant farmers, although a sizable number were able to purchase land in the northern province of Santa Fe or became truck farmers in the immediate vicinity of Buenos Aires. Argentina's wine industry underwent a rapid transformation and expansion with the arrival of Italians in the western provinces of Mendoza and San Juan. In the major cities of Argentina, Uruguay, Chile, Peru, and Brazil, Italians built hospitals and established newspapers; they formed mutual aid societies and helped to found the first labor unions. Their presence is still strong today, and Italian words have entered into everyday discourse in Argentina and Uruguay.

Other Groups

Other immigrant groups also made their contributions to the formation of South America's societies and cultures. Germans colonized much of southern Chile and were instrumental in creating the nation's dairy industry. In the wilds of Patagonia, Welsh settlers established sheep ranches and planted apple, pear, and cherry trees in the Río Negro Valley.

In Buenos Aires, despite the 1982 conflict over the Falkland Islands, there remains a distinct British imprint. Harrod's is the largest department store in the city, and one can board a train on a railroad built with English capital and journey to suburbs with names such as Hurlingham, Temperley, and Thames. In both Brazil and Argentina, soccer was introduced by the English, and two Argentine teams still bear the names "Newell's Old Boys" and "River Plate." Collectively, the immigrants who flooded into South America in the late nineteenth and early twentieth centuries introduced a host of new ideas, methods, and skills. They were especially important in stimulating and shaping the modernization of Argentina, Uruguay, Chile, and southern Brazil.

In other countries that were bypassed earlier in the century, immigration has become a new phenomenon. Venezuela—torn by political warfare, its best lands long appropriated by the elite, and its economy developing only slowly—was far less attractive than the lands of opportunity to its north (the United States) and south (Argentina, Uruguay, and Brazil). In the early 1950s, however, Venezuela embarked on a broadscale development program that included an attempt to attract European immigrants. Thousands of Spaniards, Portuguese, and Italians responded to the economic opportunity. Most of the immigrants settled in the capital city of Caracas, where some eventually became important in the construction business, retail trade, and the transportation industry.

INTERNAL MIGRATION

Paralleling the movement of peoples from across the oceans to parts of South America has been the movement of populations from rural areas to urban centers. In every nation, cities have been gaining in population for years. What prompts people to leave their homes and strike out for the unknown? In the cases of Bolivia and Peru, the very real prospect of famine has driven people out of the highlands and into the larger cities. Frequently, families will plan the move carefully. Vacant lands around the larger cities will be scouted in advance, and suddenly, in the middle of the night, the new "settlers" will move in and erect a shantytown. With time, the seizure of the land is usually recognized by city officials and the new neighborhood is provided with urban services. Where the land seizure is resisted, however, violence and loss of life are common.

Factors other than famine also force people to leave their ancestral homes. Population pressure and division of the land into parcels too small to sustain families compel people to migrate. Others move to the cities in search of economic opportunities or chances for social advancement that do not exist in rural regions. Tens of thousands of Colombians illegally crossed into Venezuela in the 1970s and 1980s in search of employment. As is the case with Mexicans who enter the United States, Colombians experienced discrimination and remained on the margins of urban society, mired in low-paying, unskilled jobs. Those who succeeded in finding work in industry were a source of anger and frustration to Venezuelan labor-union members, who resented Colombians who accepted low rates of pay. Other migrants sought employment in the agricultural sector on coffee plantations or the hundreds of cattle ranches that dot the *llanos,* or plains. In summary, a combination of push-and-pull factors are involved in a person's decision to begin a new life.

Since World War II, indigenous migration in South America has rapidly increased urban populations and has forced cities to reorganize. Rural people have been exposed to a broad range of

Colombia, as is the case with many other Latin American nations, has experienced rapid urbanization. Large numbers of migrants from rural areas have spread into slums on the outskirts of cities, as exemplified by this picture of a section of Colombia's capital, Bogotá. Most of the migrants are poorly paid, and the struggle to meet basic needs precludes political activism.

push–pull pressures to move to the cities. Land hunger, extreme poverty, and rural violence might be included among the push factors; while hope for a better job, upward social mobility, and a more satisfying life help to explain the attraction of a city. The phenomenon can be infinitely complex.

In Lima, Peru, there has been a twofold movement of people. While the unskilled and illiterate, the desperately poor and unemployed, the newly arrived migrant, and the delinquent have moved to or remained in inner-city slums, former slum dwellers have in turn moved to the city's perimeter. Although less centrally located, they have settled in more spacious and socially desirable shantytowns. In this way, some 16,000 families created a squatter settlement practically overnight in the south of Lima. Author Hernando DeSoto, in his groundbreaking and controversial book *The Other Path,* captures the essence of the shantytowns: "Modest homes cramped together on city perimeters, a myriad of workshops in their midst, armies of vendors hawking their wares on the street, and countless minibus lines crisscrossing them—all seem to have sprung from nowhere, pushing the city's boundaries ever outward."

Significantly, DeSoto notes, collective effort has increasingly been replaced by individual effort, upward mobility exists even for the inner-city slum dwellers, and urban culture and patterns of consumption have been transformed. Opera, theater, and *zarzuela* (comic opera) have gradually been replaced by movies, soccer, folk festivals, and television. Beer, rice, and table salt are now within the reach of much of the population;

consumption of more expensive items, however, such as wine and meat, has declined.

On the outskirts of Buenos Aires there exists a *villa miseria* (slum) built on the bottom and sides of an old clay pit. Appropriately, the *barrio,* or neighborhood, is called La Cava (literally "The Digging"). The people of La Cava are very poor; most have moved there from rural Argentina or from Paraguay. Shacks seem to be thrown together from whatever is available—scraps of wood, packing crates, sheets of tin, and cardboard. There is no source of potable water, garbage litters the narrow alleyways, and there are no sewers. Because of the concave character of the barrio, the heat is unbearable in the summer. Rats and flies are legion. At times, the smells are repulsive. The visitor to La Cava experiences an assault on the senses; this is Latin America at its worst.

But there is another side to the slums of Buenos Aires, Lima, Santiago, and Rio de Janeiro. A closer look at La Cava, for example, reveals a community in transition. Some of the housing is more substantial, with adobe replacing the scraps of wood and tin; other homes double as places of business and sell general merchandise, food, and bottled drinks. One advertises itself as a food store, bar, and butcher shop. Another sells watches and repairs radios. Several promote their merchandise or services in a weekly newspaper that circulates in La Cava and two other *barrios de emergencia* ("emergency"—that is, temporary—neighborhoods). The newspaper addresses items of concern to the inhabitants. There are articles on hygiene and infant diarrhea; letters and editorials plead with people not to throw their garbage in the streets; births and deaths are recorded. The newspaper is a chronicle of progress as well as frustration: people are working together to create a viable neighborhood; drainage ditches are constructed with donated time and equipment; collections and raffles are held to provide materials to build sewers and, in some cases, to provide minimal street lighting; and men and women who have contributed their labor are singled out for special praise.

The newspaper also reproduces municipal decrees that affect the lives of the residents. The land on which the barrio sits was illegally occupied, the stores that service the neighborhood were opened without the necessary authorization, and the housing was built without regard to municipal codes, so city ordinances such as the following aimed at the barrios de emergencia are usually restrictive: "The sale, renting or transfer of *casillas* [homes] within the boundaries of the barrio de emergencia is prohibited; casillas can not be inhabited by single men, women or children; the opening of businesses within the barrio is strictly prohibited, unless authorized by the Municipality; dances and festivals may not be held without the express authorization of the Municipality." But there are also signs of accommodation: "The Municipality is studying the problem of refuse removal." For migrants, authority and the legal system typically are not helpful; instead, they are hindrances.

Hernando DeSoto found this situation to be true also of Peru, where "the greatest hostility the migrants encountered was from the legal system." Until the end of World War II, the system had either absorbed or ignored the migrants "because the small groups who came were hardly likely to upset the status quo." But when the rural-to-urban flow became a flood, the system could no longer remain disinterested. Housing and education were barred to them, businesses would not hire them. The migrants discovered over time that they would have to fight for every right and every service from an unwilling establishment. Thus, to survive, they became part of the informal sector, otherwise known as the underground or parallel economy.

On occasion, however, municipal laws can work to the advantage of newly arrived migrants. In the sprawling new communities that sprang up between Lima and its port city of Callao, there are thousands of what appear to be unfinished homes. In almost every instance, a second floor was begun but, curiously, construction ceased. The reason for the incomplete projects relates to taxes—they are not assessed until a building is finished.

These circumstances are true not only of the squatter settlements on the fringes of South America's great cities but also of the inner-city slums. Slum dwellers have been able to improve their market opportunities and have been able to acquire better housing and some urban services, because they have organized on their own, outside formal political channels. In the words of sociologist Susan Eckstein, "They refused to allow dominant class and state interests to determine and restrict their fate. Defiance and resistance won them concessions which quiescence would not."

DeSoto found this to be the case with Lima: Migrants, "if they were to live, trade, manufacture, or even consume . . . had to do so illegally. Such illegality was not antisocial in intent, like trafficking in drugs, theft, or abduction, but was designed to achieve such essentially legal objectives as building a house, providing a service, or developing a business."

This is also the story of Buenos Aires's La Cava. To open a shop in the barrio with municipal approval, an aspiring businessperson must be a paragon of patience. Various levels of bureaucracy, with their plethora of paperwork and fees, insensitive municipal officials, inefficiency, and interminable waiting, drive people outside the system where the laws do not seem to conform to social need.

Disturbing, however, is the destruction of the social fabric of some of these "illegal" communities in the environs of Rio de Janeiro. In the *favelas* of this Brazilian city a drug and gang culture has taken root. The accompanying violence has torn families apart and resulted in the deaths of many people who stood in the way drug lords who have appropriated the *favelas* as a base of operations.

AN ECCLESIASTICAL REVOLUTION

During the past few decades, there have been important changes in the religious habits of many South Americans. Virtually everywhere, Roman Catholicism, long identified with the traditional order, has been challenged by newer movements such as Evangelical Protestantism and the Charismatics. Within the Catholic Church, the theology of liberation once gained ground. The creation of Christian communities in the barrios, people who bond together to discuss their beliefs and act as agents of change, has become a common phenomenon throughout the region. Base communities from the Catholic perspective instill Christian values in the lives of ordinary people. But it is an active form of religion that pushes for change and social justice. Hundreds of these communities exist in Peru, thousands in Brazil.

NATIONAL MYTHOLOGIES

In the midst of geographical and cultural diversity, the nations of South America have created national mythologies designed to unite people behind their rulers. Part of that mythology is rooted in the wars of independence that tore through much of the region between 1810 and 1830. Liberation from European colonialism imparted to South Americans a sense of their own national histories, replete with military heroes such as José de San Martín, Simón Bolívar, Bernardo O'Higgins, and Antonio José de Sucre, as well as a host of revolutionary myths. This coming to nationhood paralleled what the United States experienced when it won its independence from Britain. South Americans, at least those with a stake in the new society, began to think of themselves as Venezuelans, Chileans, Peruvians, or Brazilians. The architects of Chilean national mythology proclaimed the emergence of a new and superior being who was the result of the symbolic and physical union of Spaniards and the tough, heroic Araucanian Indians. The legacy of Simón Bolívar lives on in particular in Venezuela, his homeland; even today, the nation's foreign policymakers speak in Bolivarian terms about Venezuela's rightful role as a leader in Latin American affairs. In some instances, the mythology generated by the wars for independence became a shield against foreign ideas and customs and was used to force immigrants to become "Argentines" or "Chileans." It was an attempt to bring national unity out of diversity.

Argentines have never solved the question of their identity. Many consider themselves European and hold much of the rest of Latin America in contempt. Following Argentina's loss in the Falklands War with Britain, one scholar suggested that perhaps Argentines should no longer consider themselves as "a forlorn corner of Europe" but should wake up to the reality that they are Latin Americans. Much of Argentine literature reflects this uncertain identity and may help to explain author Jorge Luis Borges's affinity for English gardens and Icelandic sagas. It was also an Argentine military government that invoked Western Catholic civilization in its fight against a "foreign" and "godless" communism in the 1970s.

National mythologies also tend artificially to homogenize a country's history and often ignore large segments of the population and their cultures that differ from the "official" version. Recent events in Bolivia have laid bare long-existing cleavages. The non-Indian elite is clearly concerned by the election of an Aymara as president and his vision of the nation's history and future. The "white" inhabitants of Santa Cruz in eastern Bolivia have loudly proclaimed their cultural, ethnic, and social differences with the indigenous population of the highlands and have talked of secession.

THE ARTIST AND SOCIETY

There is a strongly cultured and humane side of South America. Jeane Franco, an authority on Latin American cultural movements, observes that to "declare oneself an artist in Latin America has frequently involved conflict with society." The art and literature of South America in particular and Latin America in general represent a distinct tradition within the panorama of Western civilization.

The art of South America has as its focus social questions and ideals. It expresses love for one's fellow human beings and "has kept alive the vision of a more just and humane form of society." It rises above purely personal relationships and addresses humanity.

Much change is also evident at the level of popular culture. Andean folk music, for example, is being replaced by the more urban and upbeat chicha music in Peru; and in Argentina, the traditional tango has lost much of its early appeal. Radio and television programs are more and more in the form of soap operas, adventure programs, or popular entertainment, once considered vulgar by cosmopolitan city dwellers. South America is rather like a prism. It can be treated as a single object or region. Yet when exposed to a shaft of sunlight of understanding, it throws off a brilliant spectrum of colors that exposes the diversity of its lands and peoples.

Argentina (Argentine Republic)

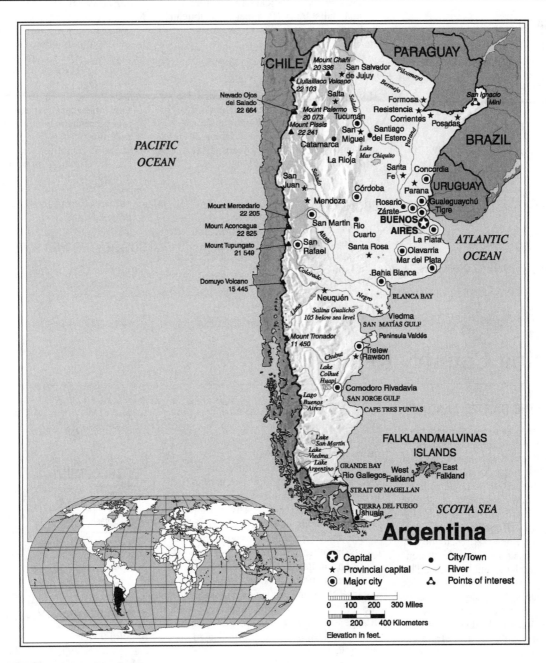

Argentina Statistics

GEOGRAPHY

Area in Square Miles (Kilometers):
1,100,000 (2,771,300) (about 4 times
the size of Texas)
Capital (Population): Buenos Aires
(12,400,000)
Environmental Concerns: soil erosion and
degradation; air and water pollution;
desertification.
Geographical Features: rich plains of the
Pampas in the north; the flat to rolling

plateau of Patagonia in the south; the
rugged Andes along western border
Climate: varied; mostly temperate;
subantarctic in southwest

PEOPLE

Population

Total: 40,301,927 (2007 est.)
Annual Growth Rate: .94%
Rural/Urban Population Ratio: 12/88

Major Languages: Spanish; Italian;
English; Ethnic Makeup: 97% white;
3% Mestizo, Indian, and others
Religions: 90% Roman Catholic (fewer
than 20% practicing); 2% Protestant;
2% Jewish; 6% others

Health

Life Expectancy at Birth: 73 years (male);
80 years (female)
Infant Mortality Rate (Ratio): 14.29/1,000
Physicians Available (Ratio): 1/376

Education

Adult Literacy Rate: 97.2%
Compulsory (Ages): 6–14; free

COMMUNICATION

Telephones: 9,460,000 main lines
Daily Newspaper Circulation: 138 per 1,000 people
Cell Phones: 31,510,000
Internet Users: 8,184,000

TRANSPORTATION

Roadways in Kilometers (miles): 229,144 (142,384)
Railroads in Kilometers (Miles): 31,902 (19,823)
Usable Airfields: 1,272

GOVERNMENT

Type: republic
Independence Date: July 9, 1816 (from Spain)

Head of State/Government: President Cristina Fernández de Kirchner is both head of state and head of government
Political Parties: Radical Civic Union; Justicialist Party (Peronist); Republican Proposal; various coalitions; others
Suffrage: universal at 18

MILITARY

Military Expenditures (% of GDP): 1.3%
Current Disputes: indefinite boundary with Chile; claims UK-administered South Georgia and South Sandwich Islands, and Falkland Islands (Islas Malvinas); territorial claim in Antarctica

ECONOMY

Currency ($U.S. Equivalent): 31 pesos = $1
Per Capita Income/GDP: $13,000/$245.6 billion
GDP Real Growth Rate: 8.5%

Inflation Rate: 8.5% (official—likely higher)
Unemployment Rate: 8.9%
Labor Force: 16,100,000
Natural Resources: fertile plains; lead; zinc; tin; copper; iron ore; manganese; petroleum; uranium
Agriculture: wheat; corn; sorghum; fruits; soybeans; tobacco; tea; livestock
Industry: food processing; motor vehicles; consumer durables; textiles; chemicals and petrochemicals; printing; metallurgy; steel
Exports: $54.6 billion (f.o.b.) (primary partners Brazil, European Union, United States)
Imports: $40.26 billion (f.o.b.) (primary partners European Union, United States, Brazil)

SUGGESTED WEB SITE

http://www.cia.gov/cia/publications/ factbook/index.html

Argentina Country Report

ARGENTINA: THE DIVIDED LAND

Writers as far back as the mid-1800s have perceived two Argentinas. Domingo F. Sarmiento, the president of Argentina in the 1860s, entitled his classic work about the country *Civilization and Barbarism.* More contemporary writers speak of Argentina as a divided land or as a city and a nation. All address the relationship of the capital city, Buenos Aires, to the rest of the country. Buenos Aires is cultured, cosmopolitan, modern, and dynamic. The rural interior is in striking contrast in terms of living standards, the pace of life, and, perhaps, expectations as well. For many years, Buenos Aires and other urban centers have drawn population away from the countryside: Today, Argentina is 88 percent urban.

There are other contrasts. The land is extremely rich and produces a large share of the world's grains and beef. Few Argentines are malnourished, and the annual per capita consumption of beef is comparable to that of the United States. Yet this land of promise, which seemed in the 1890s to have a limitless future, has slowly decayed. Its greatness is now more mythical than real. Since the Great Depression of the 1930s, the Argentine economy has, save for brief spurts, never been able to return to the sustained growth of the late nineteenth and early twentieth centuries.

In the 1990s, the Argentine economy enjoyed a brief period of stability and growth. Inefficient and costly state enterprises were privatized, with the exception of the petroleum industry, traditionally a strategic sector reserved to the state. A peso tied to the dollar brought inflation under control, and the pace of business activity, employment, and foreign investment quickened.

The nation's economy is vulnerable to events in other parts of the world, however. The collapse of the Mexican peso in the early 1990s and the economic crises in Russia and, especially, Asia in the late 1990s had profound negative effects in Argentina. The global slowdown in the new millennium further complicated the economic situation.

By the first quarter of 2002, the economy was in crisis. A foreign debt of $142 billion (which works out to $3,000 for every man, woman, and child in the country), declining export revenues, high unemployment, and the inability of the government to win International Monetary Fund support for additional loans forced a devaluation of the currency.

Argentine economic history has been typified by unrealized potential and unfulfilled promises. Much depends on the confidence of the Argentine people in the leadership and policies of their elected representatives. Five changes of government

between December 2001 and March 2002 suggest a wholesale *lack* of confidence.

DEVELOPMENT

Argentina convinced the IMF to help its economic recovery without following the strict full fiscal discipline measures usually required. Economic recovery was well underway in 2004 and in 2007 the real GDP growth rate reached 8.5%.

AUTHORITARIAN GOVERNMENT

In political terms, Argentina has revealed a curious inability to bring about the kind of stable democratic institutions that seemed assured in the 1920s. Since 1930, the military has seized power at least half a dozen times. It must be noted, however, that it has been civilians who have encouraged the generals to play an active role in politics. Historian Robert Potash writes: "The notion that Argentine political parties or other important civilian groups have consistently opposed military takeovers bears little relation to reality."

Argentina has enjoyed civilian rule since 1983, but the military is still a presence. Indeed, one right-wing faction, the *carapintadas* ("painted faces"), responsible for

(United Nations photo/P. Teuscher/UN133443)

Well known for its abundant grains and beef, Argentina also has a large fishing industry. These fishing boats are in the bay of the Plata River in Buenos Aires.

mutinies against President Raúl Alfonsín in 1987 and 1988, have organized a nationwide party and have attracted enough votes to rank as an important political force. An authoritarian tradition is very much alive in Argentina, as is the bitter legacy of the so-called Dirty War.

THE DIRTY WAR

What made the latest era of military rule different is the climate of political violence that gripped Argentina starting in the late 1960s. The most recent period of violence began with the murder of former president Pedro Aramburu by left-wing guerrillas (Montoneros) who claimed to be fighting on behalf of the popular but exiled leader Juan Perón (president from 1946 to 1955 and from 1973 to 1974). The military responded to what it saw as an armed challenge from the left with tough antisubversion laws and official violence against suspects. Guerrillas increased their activities and intensified their campaign to win popular support.

Worried by the possibility of a major popular uprising and divided over policy, the military called for national elections in 1973, hoping that a civilian government would calm passions. The generals

could then concentrate their efforts on destroying the armed left. The violence continued, however, and even the brief restoration of Juan Perón to power failed to bring peace.

In March 1976, with the nation on the verge of economic collapse and guerrilla warfare spreading, the military seized power once again and declared a state of internal war, popularly called the Dirty War. Between 1976 and 1982, between 10,000 and 30,000 Argentine citizens "disappeared." Torture, the denial of basic human rights, harsh press censorship, officially directed death squads, and widespread fear came to characterize Argentina.

The labor movement—the largest, most effective, and most politically active on the continent—was, in effect, crippled by the military. Identified as a source of leftist subversion, the union movement was destroyed as an independent entity. Collective-bargaining agreements were dismantled, pension plans were cut back, and social-security and public-health programs were eliminated. The military's intent was to destroy a labor movement capable of operating on a national level.

The press was one of the immediate victims of the 1976 coup. A law was decreed warning that anyone spreading information derived from organizations "dedicated to subversive activities or terrorism" would be subject to an indefinite sentence. To speak out against the military was punishable by a 10-year jail term. The state also directed its terrorism tactics against the media, and approximately 100 journalists disappeared. Hundreds more received death threats, were tortured and jailed, or fled into exile. Numerous newspapers and

magazines were shut down, and one, *La Opinión,* passed to government control.

The ruling junta justified these excesses by portraying the conflict as the opening battle of "World War III," in which Argentina was valiantly defending Western Christian values and cultures against hordes of Communist, "godless" subversives. It was a "holy war," with all of the unavoidable horrors of such strife.

By 1981, leftist guerrilla groups had been annihilated. Argentines slowly began to recover from the shock of internal war and talked of a return to civilian government. The military had completed its task; the nation needed to rebuild. Organized labor attempted to re-create its structure and threw the first tentative challenges at the regime's handling of the economy. The press carefully criticized both the economic policies of the government and the official silence over the fate of *los desaparecidos* ("the disappeared ones"). Human-rights groups pressured the generals with redoubled efforts.

OPPOSITION TO THE MILITARY

Against this backdrop of growing popular dissatisfaction with the regime's record, together with the approaching 150th anniversary of Great Britain's occupation of Las Islas Malvinas (the Falkland Islands), President Leopoldo Galtieri decided in 1982 to regain Argentine sovereignty and attack the Falklands. A successful assault, the military reasoned, would capture the popular imagination with its appeal to Argentine nationalism. The military's tarnished image would regain its luster. Forgiven would be the excesses of the Dirty War. But the attack ultimately failed.

In the wake of the fiasco, which cost thousands of Argentine and British lives, the military lost its grip on labor, the press, and the general population. Military and national humiliation, the continuing economic crisis made even worse by war costs, and the swelling chorus of discontent lessened the military's control over the flow of information and ideas. Previously forbidden subjects—such as the responsibility for the disappearances during the Dirty War—were raised in the newspapers.

The labor movement made a rapid and striking recovery and is now in the forefront of renewed political activity. Even though the movement is bitterly divided into moderate and militant wings, it is a force that cannot be ignored by political parties on the rebound.

The Falklands War may well prove to be a watershed in recent Argentine history. A respected Argentine observer, Torcuato DiTella, argues that the Falklands crisis

FREEDOM

Evidence was presented in Argentina's courts in 2007 implicating Roman Catholic priests with the excesses of the Dirty War, a struggle that was framed by the military as a "holy war." The case is seen as a victory by human rights advocates.

was a "godsend," for it allowed Argentines to break with "foreign" economic models that had failed in Argentina. Disappointed with the United States and Europe over their support of Great Britain, he concludes: "We belong in Latin America and it is better to be a part of this strife-torn continent than a forlorn province of Europe."

Popularly elected in 1983, President Raúl Alfonsín's economic policies initially struck in bold new directions. He forced the International Monetary Fund to renegotiate Argentina's huge multi-billion-dollar debt in a context more favorable to Argentina, and he was determined to bring order out of chaos.

One of his most difficult problems centered on the trials for human-rights abuses against the nation's former military rulers. According to *Latin American Regional Reports,* Alfonsín chose to "distinguish degrees of responsibility" in taking court action against those who conducted the Dirty War. Impressively, Alfonsín put on trial the highest authorities, to be followed by action against those identified as responsible for major excesses.

Almost immediately, however, extreme right-wing nationalist officers in the armed forces opposed the trials and engineered a series of mutinies that undermined the stability of the administration. In 1987, during the Easter holiday, a rebellion of dissident soldiers made its point, and the Argentine Congress passed legislation that limited the prosecution of officers who killed civilians during the Dirty War to those only at the highest levels. Mini-mutinies in 1988 resulted in further concessions to the mutineers by the Alfonsín government, including reorganization of the army high command and higher wages.

Carlos Menem was supported by the military in the presidential election of May 1989, with perhaps 80 percent of the officer corps casting their votes for the Peronist Party. Menem adopted a policy of rapprochement with the military, which included the 1990 pardon of former junta members convicted of human-rights abuses. Historian Peter Calvert argues that Menem chose the path of amnesty because elements in the armed forces "would not be content until they got it." Rebellious middle-rank officers were well disposed toward Peronists,

and Menem's pardon was "a positive gain in terms of the acceptance of the Peronists among the military themselves." In essence, then, Menem's military policy was consistent with other policies in terms of its pragmatic core. And the military seems to have been contained; military spending has been halved, the army has been reduced from 100,000 to 20,000 soldiers, military enterprises have been divested, and mandatory service has been abandoned in favor of a professional force.

Significant progress has been made with regard to "disappeared" people. In 1992, President Menem agreed to create a commission to deal with the problem of children of the disappeared who were adopted by other families. Many have had their true identities established as a result of the patient work of "The Grandmothers of the Plaza de Mayo" and by the technique of cross-generational genetic analysis. (In 1998, former junta chief Admiral Emilio Massera was arrested on charges of kidnapping—that is, the distribution to families of babies born to victims of the regime.) In 1995, the names of an additional 1,000 people were added to the official list of the missing. Also, a retired military officer revealed his part in pushing drugged prisoners out of planes over the South Atlantic Ocean.

ECONOMIC TRAVAIL

The Argentine economy under President Alfonsín was virtually out of control. Inflation soared. The sorry state of the economy and spreading dissatisfaction among the electorate forced the president to hand over power to Carlos Menem six months early.

Menem's new government worked a bit of an economic miracle, despite an administration nagged by corruption and early policy indecision, which witnessed the appointment of 21 ministers to nine cabinet positions during his first 18 months in office. In Menem's favor, he was not an ideologue but, rather, an adept politician whose acceptance by the average voter was equaled by his ability to do business with almost anyone. He quickly identified the source of much of Argentina's chronic inflation: the state-owned enterprises. From

the time of Perón, these industries were regarded as wellsprings of employment and cronyism rather than as instruments for the production of goods or the delivery of services such as electric power and telephone service. "Ironically," says Luigi Manzetti, writing in *North-South FOCUS,* "it took a Peronist like Menem to dismantle Perón's legacy." While Menem's presidential campaign stressed "traditional Peronist themes like social justice and government investments" to revive the depressed economy, once he was in power, "having inherited a bankrupt state and under pressure from foreign banks and domestic business circles to enact a stiff adjustment program, Menem reversed his stand." He embraced the market-oriented policies of his political adversaries, "only in a much harsher fashion." State-owned enterprises were sold off in rapid-fire order. Argentina thus underwent a rapid transformation, from one of the world's most closed economies to one of the most open.

Economic growth began again in 1991, but the social costs were high. Thousands of public-sector workers lost their jobs; a third of Argentina's population lived below the poverty line, and the gap between the rich and poor tended to increase. But both inflation and the debt were eventually contained, foreign investment increased, and confidence began to return to Argentina.

In November 1993, former president Alfonsín supported a constitutional reform that allowed Menem to serve another term. Menem accepted some checks on executive power, including reshuffling the Supreme Court, placing members of the political opposition in charge of certain state offices, creating a post similar to that of prime minister, awarding a third senator to each province, and shortening the presidential term from six to four years. With these reforms in place, Menem easily won another term in 1995.

Convinced that his mandate should not end with the conclusion of his second term, Menem lobbied hard in 1998 for yet another constitutional reform to allow him to run again. This was not supported by the Supreme Court.

The Radical Party won the elections in 1999. Almost immediately President Fernando de la Rua confronted an economy mired in a deepening recession. Rising unemployment, a foreign debt that stood at 50 percent of gross domestic product, and fears of a debt default prompted the government to announce tax increases and spending cuts to meet IMF debt targets. At the end of 2001, the economic crisis triggered rioting in the streets and brought down the de la Rua administration and three others that followed in rapid succession.

By the end of 2002 the economy was in such shambles that some provinces began to issue their own currencies, farmers resorted to barter—exchanging soy beans for agricultural equipment—and many Argentines seriously considered emigration. Crime rates rose and people lost faith in governments that seemed incapable of positive policies and all-to-susceptible to corruption.

This dismal picture began to change with the election of Néstor Kirchner in May 2003. During his first year in office he called on Congress to begin impeachment proceedings against the widely hated Supreme Court. The justices were accused of producing verdicts that reflected payoffs and political favors. Kirchner also laid siege to Argentina's security forces: he ordered more than 50 admirals and generals into early retirement and dismissed 80 percent of the high command of the notoriously corrupt Federal Police.

Finally, after years of severe malaise, the economy began to turn around in 2003. Kirchner noted that the IMF had abandoned Argentina in 2001 as its economy spiraled downward. Consequently the Argentine president, in the words of *New York Times* reporter Tony Smith, "felt justified in resolutely refusing to make a series of concessions that negotiators for the monetary fund wanted in exchange for refinancing $21.6 billion in debt that Argentina owes to multilateral institutions . . ." In March 2005, President Kirchner announced a debt settlement that paid the nation's creditors as little as 30 cents on the dollar. Argentina, in effect, worked out a deal in accord with Argentine economic realities.

FOREIGN POLICY

The Argentine government's foreign policy has usually been determined by realistic appraisals of the nation's best interests. From 1946, the country moved between the two poles of pro-West and nonaligned. President Menem firmly supported the foreign-policy initiatives of the United States and the UN. Argentine participation in the Persian Gulf War and the presence of Argentine troops under United Nations command in Croatia, Somalia, and other trouble spots paid dividends: Washington agreed to supply Argentina with military supplies for the first time since the Falklands War in 1982. President Kirchner has assumed an independent posture. The U.S. invasion of Iraq was cast as a violation of international law and Argentina has moved closer to Latin American regimes not in the good graces of Washington, that is, Bolivia, Brazil, Venezuela, and Cuba.

President Kirchner, having stood up to the demands of the IMF, has now moved steadily away from Washington's free trade agenda. He has also moved closer to Hugo Chávez of Venezuela and signed a series of economic agreements. By identifying with populist leaders in South America Kirchner established Argentina's independence from the United States.

WOMEN AND ARGENTINA'S POLITICAL FUTURE

In 1991, Argentina was the first Latin American country to implement a gender quota law in its lower legislative house, the Chamber of Deputies. The law was extended to the Senate in 2001. Every third name on all party ballots must be a woman. In 2006, 39 percent of the legislature was female and in 2007 Argentina elected its first woman president, Cristina Fernández de Kirchner. This development, which is not confined to Argentina, may be partially explained by the fact that women are seen by voters as one way to replace traditional politicians who have promised much but delivered little.

Kirchner's first months in office have been difficult, in large part because inflation has once again reached double digits. Her economic policy will largely determine success or failure. In Kirchner's favor is a political opposition that is hopelessly fractured.

Timeline: PAST

1536
Pedro de Mendoza establishes the first settlement at Buenos Aires

1816
Independence of Spain

1865–1870
War with Paraguay

1912
Electoral reform: Compulsory male suffrage

1946–1955 and 1973–1974
Juan Perón is in power

1976–1982
The Dirty War

1980s
War with Great Britain over the Falkland Islands; military mutinies and economic chaos

1990s
Economic crises in Mexico, Russia, and Asia slow the economy

PRESENT

2003
Economic recovery well underway

2007
Cristina Fernández de Kirchner elected Argentina's first woman president

Bolivia (Republic of Bolivia)

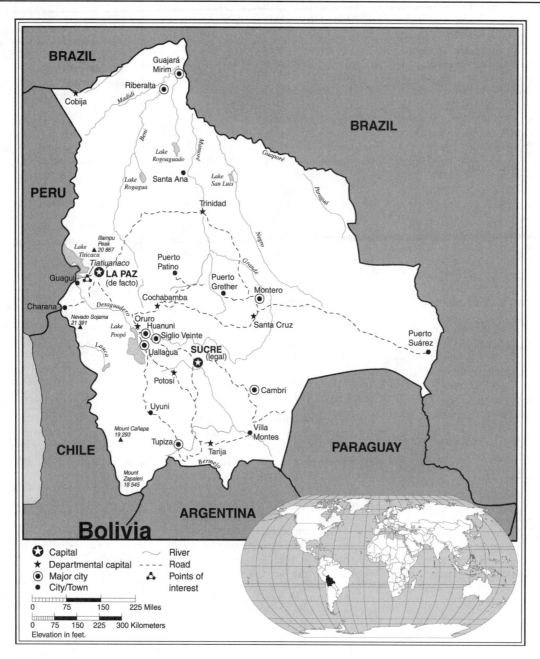

Bolivia Statistics

GEOGRAPHY

Area in Square Miles (Kilometers):
424,162 (1,098,160) (about 3 times the size of Montana)
Capital (Population): La Paz (de facto) (1,000,000); Sucre (legal)
Environmental Concerns: deforestation; soil erosion; desertification; loss of biodiversity; water pollution
Geographical Features: rugged Andes Mountains with a highland plateau (Altiplano), hills, lowland plains of the Amazon Basin
Climate: varies with altitude; from humid and tropical to semiarid and cold

PEOPLE

Population

Total: 9,119,152 (2007 est.)
Annual Growth Rate: 1.42%
Rural/Urban Population Ratio: 39/61

Major Languages: Spanish; Quechua; Aymara
Ethnic Makeup: 30% Quechua; 25% Aymara; 30% Mestizo; 15% white
Religions: 95% Roman Catholic; Protestant

Health

Life Expectancy at Birth: Male: 63 years Female: 69 years
Infant Mortality Rate (Ratio): 50.43/1,000
Physicians Available (Ratio): 1/3,663

Education

Adult Literacy Rate: 86.7%
Compulsory (Ages): 6–14; free

COMMUNICATION

Telephones: 646,300 main lines
Daily Newspaper Circulation: 69 per 1,000 people
Cell Phones: 2,421,000
Internet Users: 580,000

TRANSPORTATION

Roadways in Kilometers (miles): 62,479 (38,823)
Railroads in Kilometers (Miles): 3,504 (2,177)
Usable Airfields: 1,061

GOVERNMENT

Type: republic
Independence Date: August 6, 1825 (from Spain)

Head of State/Government: President Evo Morales is both head of state and head of government
Political Parties: Movement Toward Socialism; Free Bolivia Movement; Movement without Fear; Nationalist Revolutionary Movement; National Unity; National Democratic Power; Social Alliance; many others
Suffrage: universal and compulsory at 18 if married, at 21 if single

MILITARY

Military Expenditures (% of GDP): 1.9%
Current Disputes: dispute with Chile over water rights; seeks sovereign corridor to the South Pacific Ocean

ECONOMY

Currency ($U.S. Equivalent): 7.54 bolivares = $1
Per Capita Income/GDP: $4,400/$12.8 billion

GDP Growth Rate: 4%
Inflation Rate: 12%
Unemployment Rate: 8%; underemployment
Labor Force: 4,793,000
Natural Resources: tin; natural gas; petroleum; zinc; tungsten; antimony; silver; iron; lead; gold; timber; hydropower
Agriculture: soybeans; coffee; coca; cotton; corn; sugarcane; rice; potatoes; timber
Industry: mining; smelting, petroleum; food and beverages; tobacco; handicrafts; clothing
Exports: $4.259 billion (f.o.b.) (primary partners United Kingdom, United States, Peru)
Imports: $3.107 billion (f.o.b.) (primary partners United States, Japan, Brazil)

SUGGESTED WEB SITE

http://www.cia.gov/cia/publications/factbook/geos/bl.html

Bolivia Country Report

BOLIVIA: AN INDIAN NATION

Until recently, the images of Bolivia captured by the world's press were uniformly negative. Human-rights abuses were rampant, a corrupt and brutal military government was deeply involved in cocaine trafficking, and the nation was approaching bankruptcy.

Other images might include Bolivia's complex society. So intermixed has this multiethnic culture become that one's race is defined by one's social status. So-called whites, who look very much like the Indians with whom their ancestors intermarried, form the upper classes only because of their economic, social, and cultural positions—that is, the degree to which they have embraced European culture.

DEVELOPMENT

Although nationalistic policies have stifled private investment, the government now enjoys a fiscal surplus, after years of deficits, because of greatly increased revenues as a result of higher taxes on mining and hydrocarbon exports. Inflation reached double digits in 2007.

Another enduring image fixed in the literature is Bolivia's political instability. The actual number of governments over the past 200 years is about 80, however, and not the 200 commonly noted. Indeed,

elected governments have been in power for the past two decades. What outsiders perceive as typical Latin American political behavior clouds what is unusual and positive about Bolivia.

One nineteenth-century leader, Manuel Belzu, played an extremely complex role that combined the forces of populism, nationalism, and revolution. Belzu encouraged the organization of the first trade unions, abolished slavery, promoted land reform, and praised Bolivia's Indian past.

In 1952, a middle-class–led and popularly supported revolution swept the country. The ensuing social, economic, and political reforms, while not erasing an essentially dual society of "whites" and Indians, did significantly ease the level of exploitation. Most of the export industries, including those involved with natural resources, were nationalized. Bolivia's evolution—at times progressive, at times regressive—continues to reflect the impulse for change.

THE SOCIETY: POSITIVE AND NEGATIVE ASPECTS

Bolivia, despite the rapid and startling changes that have occurred in the recent past, remains an extremely poor society. In terms of poverty, life expectancy, death rates, and per capita income, the country ranks among the worst in the Western Hemisphere.

Rights for women have made slow progress, even in urban areas. In 1975, a woman was appointed to the Bolivian Supreme Court; and in 1979, the Bolivian Congress elected Lidia Gueiler Tejada, leader of the lower house, as president. Long a supporter of women's rights, Tejada had drafted and pushed through Congress a bill that created a government ministry to provide social benefits for women and children. That remarkably advanced legislation has not guaranteed that women enjoy a social status equal to that of men, however. Furthermore, many women are likely unaware of their rights under the law.

Bolivia's press is reasonably free, although many journalists are reportedly paid by politicians, drug traffickers, and officials to increase their exposure or suppress negative stories. A few journalists who experienced repression under previous governments still practice self-censorship.

URBANIZATION

Santa Cruz has been transformed in the last 50 years from an isolated backwater into a modern city with links to the other parts of the country and to the rest of South America. From a population of 42,000 in 1950, the number of inhabitants quickly rose to half a million in the mid-1980s and is now growing at the rate of

(Courtesy of Jorge Tutor)

Bolivia has a complex society, tremendously affected by the continued interplay of multiethnic cultures. The influence of indigenous peoples on Bolivia remains strong.

about 8 percent a year. Bolivia's second largest city, its population now exceeds that of the de facto capital, La Paz.

Most of the city's population growth has been the result of rural-to-urban migration, a phenomenon closely studied by geographer Gil Green. On paper, Santa Cruz is a planned city, but, since the 1950s, there has been a running battle between city planners and new settlers wanting land. "Due to the very high demand for cheap land and the large amount of flat, empty, nonvaluable land surrounding it, the city has tended to expand by a process of land invasion and squatting. Such invasions are generally overtly or covertly organized by political parties seeking electoral support of the low-income population." In the wake of a successful "invasion," the land is divided into plots that are allocated to the squatters, who then build houses from whatever materials are at hand. Then begins the lengthy process of settlement consolidation and regularization of land tenure. Once again the new land is subdivided and sold cheaply to the low-income population.

FREEDOM

A corrupt judicial system, overcrowded prisons, and violence and discrimination against women and indigenous peoples are perennial problems in Bolivia, despite protective legislation.

Perhaps the pace of urbanization as a result of internal migration is most pronounced in El Alto, which hardly existed on maps 30 years ago. It is now a "city" of 700,000 and overlooks La Paz. The rapid growth actually reflects a profound crisis in Bolivia. Tens of thousands of Aymara and Quechua-speaking miners and peasant farmers have been driven to El Alto by their inability to make a living in rural areas. Over the past five years it has become, in the works of a local newspaper editor, "the capital of social protest in Bolivia." In fact, a rebellion centered in El Alto succeeded in driving President Gonzalo Sánchez from power in 2003 and threatened to do the same to his successor, Carlos Mesa.

The character of what has been termed the "Ideology of Fury" is complex and springs from a broad range of contexts. Perhaps most important, Bolivia's indigenous majority has suffered centuries of neglect and abuse. President Mesa noted as much when he explained the uprising as an "eruption of deeply held positions, over many centuries, that have been accumulating." There appear to have been two more immediate catalysts: U.S. insistence on the eradication of coca and the government's proposal to export natural gas to the United States through the construction of a pipeline to Chile.

With respect to coca cultivation, Bolivian politicians for years have promised to put an end to the trade and substitute other crops such as pineapples, coffee, black pepper, oregano, and passion fruit. Unfortunately most of the government's efforts were put on eradication and not alternative development. The United States, according to economist Jeffrey Sachs, "has constantly made demands on an impoverished country without any sense of reality or an economic framework and strategy to help them in development." The net result was the impoverishment of thousands of peasant farmers, who have since migrated to El Alto and become the taproot of the "Ideology of Fury." What was not appreciated by Washington and Bolivian politicians who were fearful of losing U.S. aid money, was that coca is central to indigenous culture. Certainly much is exported in the form of coca paste or cocaine. In the 1990s it was calculated that illegal exports contributed the equivalent of 13 to 15 percent of Bolivia's gross domestic product and that coca by-products accounted for as much as 40 percent of total exports, both legal and illicit. Today, about 400,000 Bolivians are estimated to live off coca and cocaine production. U.S. wishes run afoul of the multifaceted heritage of coca, the sacred plant of the Incas. There is virtually no activity in domestic, social, or religious life in which coca does not play a role; thus, attempts to limit its cultivation have had profound repercussions among the peasantry.

HEALTH/WELFARE

Provisions against child labor in Bolivia are frequently ignored; many children may be found shining shoes, selling lottery tickets, and as street vendors.

Indigenous resistance to coca eradication now centers on Evo Morales, the head of the coca growers' federation, who emerged victorious in the presidential elections of 2005. Morales's new party, the Movement Toward Socialism, has undertaken the modification of the laws against coca cultivation, regardless of the wishes of the United States. "There has to be a change, to a policy that is truly Bolivian, not one that is imposed by foreigners with the pretext that eradication will put an end to narcotics trafficking," said a member of Congress and an ally of Morales. The

ACHIEVEMENTS

The Bolivian author Armando Chirveches, in his political novel *La Candidatura de Rojas* (1909), produced one of the best examples of this genre in all of Latin America. The book captures the politics of the late nineteenth century extraordinarily well.

president himself coined the phrase: "Yes to coca, no to cocaine."

The second catalyst involved the proposed gas pipeline. While there are good historical reasons for Bolivian antipathy towards Chile (Chile deprived Bolivia its access to the Pacific as a result of territorial adjustments following the War of the Pacific in 1879–1880), resistance to the pipeline also has a social dimension. As reported in *The New York Times*, a Chilean pollster noted: "Part of the democratic process is assuring that people are going to get a piece of the cake, and that has been lacking in Bolivia. Bolivians are suspicious of whoever is making the deal because they think the "elite always puts money in its own pockets, and we are left on the streets with nothing to eat." Regionalism also plays a role in the controversy. Gas-producing regions, those with large deposits of lithium, and even farmers in Santa Cruz who have experienced a boom in soybean exports, now demand a significant voice in the distribution of the wealth they produce as well as a degree of autonomy from La Paz.

Regional tensions reached a boiling point in May 2008 when Santa Cruz voted on a statute to seek more autonomy from the La Paz government. One provincial legislator who helped draft the statute told a *New York Times* reporter: "We do not want the creation of another republic. But we do want control over our own destiny and our own resources." The statute, if implemented, would accord Santa Cruz the right to elect its own legislature, create its own police force, and raise taxes for public works. It would also allow the province to negotiate royalty rights with energy companies. Part of the drive for autonomy springs from provincial fears that the Morales government plans to break up large rural estates and redistribute land to migrants who have flooded into Santa Cruz from the impoverished highlands.

What is unfolding in Bolivia is the latest manifestation of a problem that has been brewing since the 1950s. Santa Cruz is the economic engine that drives the country and it is in this province that most of the nation's wealth is concentrated. La Paz and the highlands want a greater distribution of that wealth.

The success of the indigenous majority in Bolivia in toppling one government and then winning the presidency has both emboldened their leaders, who relish their new found power, and awakened a sense

Timeline: PAST

1538
Spanish settle the altiplano (high plain)

1825
Bolivian declaration of independence of Spain

1879–1880
The War of the Pacific with Chile; Bolivia loses access to the sea

1932–1935
The Chaco War with Paraguay

1952–1964
Reforms: nationalization of mines, land reform, universal suffrage, creation of labor federation

1990s
Privatization of the economy accelerates; labor unrest grips the mining sector Bolivia's indigenous people achieve a new political voice

PRESENT

2000s
President Sánchez de Lozada forced to resign

Bolivia's indigenous majority demands economic, political, and social reform

Aymara leader Evo Morales elected president in 2005

of racial pride among the Aymara and Quechua. As one unemployed carpenter told reporter Larry Rohter: "They may still say that we are only Indians, but now we can see what is happening and what the Aymara nation can do when it is united."

President Morales will now have to put his rhetoric into action if he is to mollify the demands of an awakened and angry indigenous population. It will be impossible for Bolivia to develop its extensive natural resources in the face of an indigenous and regional resistance that does not take into account their needs. If the government can link development to the creation of jobs, if it finally begins to deliver on years of unfulfilled promises with regard to health care and education, and if it can pursue a coca policy that respects the culture of the majority of the population and stems from Bolivian reality and not Washington's wishes, then perhaps a modus vivendi can be reached. If not, the future will bring further economic malaise and political upheaval.

Brazil (Federative Republic of Brazil)

Brazil Statistics

GEOGRAPHY

Area in Square Miles (Kilometers):
3,285,670 (8,512,100) (slightly smaller than the United States)
Capital (Population): Brasília (2,455,903)
Environmental Concerns: deforestation; water and air pollution; land degradation
Geographical Features: mostly flat to rolling lowlands in the north; some plains, hills, mountains, and a narrow coastal belt
Climate: mostly tropical or semitropical; temperate zone in the south

PEOPLE*

Population

Total: 190,010,647 (2007 est.)
Annual Growth Rate: 1.01%
Rural/Urban Population Ratio: 21/79
Ethnic Makeup: 55% white; 38% mixed; 6% black; 1% others
Major Languages: Portuguese; Spanish; English; French
Religions: 70% nominal Roman Catholic; 30% others

Health

Life Expectancy at Birth: 68 years (male); 76 years (female)

70

Infant Mortality Rate (Ratio): 27.62/1,000
Physicians Available (Ratio): 1/681

Education

Adult Literacy Rate: 88%
Compulsory (Ages): 7–14; free

COMMUNICATION

Telephones: 38,800,000 main lines
Daily Newspaper Circulation: 47 per
  1,000 people
Cell Phones: 99,919,000
Internet Users: 42,600,000

TRANSPORTATION

Roadways in Kilometers (miles):
  1,751,868 (1,088,560)
Railroads in Kilometers (miles): 29,295
  (18,203)
Usable Airfields: 4,263

GOVERNMENT

Type: federal republic
Independence Date: September 7, 1822
  (from Portugal)

Head of State/Government: President Luiz
  Inacio "Lula" Da Silva is both head of
  state and head of government
Political Parties: Brazilian Democratic
  Movement Party; Liberal Front
  Party; Workers' Party; Brazilian
  Workers' Party; Democratic
  Labor Party; Popular Socialist Party;
  others
Suffrage: voluntary at 16; compulsory
  between 19 and 70; voluntary over 70

MILITARY

*Military Expenditures (% of
  GDP):* 2.6%
Current Disputes: boundary disputes with
  Uruguay

ECONOMY

Currency ($U.S. Equivalent): 1.754
  reals = $1
Per Capita Income/GDP: $9,700/$1.269
  trillion
GDP Growth Rate: 4.9%
Inflation Rate: 4.1%
Unemployment Rate: 9.8%

Labor Force: 99,470,000
Natural Resources: bauxite; gold; iron
  ore; manganese; nickel; phosphates;
  platinum; tin; uranium; petroleum;
  hydropower; timber
Agriculture: coffee; rice; corn;
  sugarcane; soybeans; cotton; manioc;
  oranges
Industry: textiles; shoes; chemicals;
  cement; lumber; iron ore; tin;
  steel; aircraft; motor vehicles
  and parts; other machinery and
  equipment
Exports: $159.2 billion (f.o.b.) (primary
  partners United States, Argentina,
  Germany)
Imports: $115.6 billion (f.o.b.) (primary
  partners United States, Argentina,
  Germany)

SUGGESTED WEB SITE

http://www.cia.gov/cia/publications/
  factbook/geos/br.html

*Note: Estimates explicitly take into account the
effects of excess mortality due to AIDS.

Brazil Country Report

BRAZIL: A TROUBLED GIANT

In 1977, Brazilian president Ernesto Geisel stated that progress was based on "an integrated process of political, social, and economic development." Democracy, he argued, was the first necessity in the political arena. But democracy could only be achieved "if we also further social development . . . , if we raise the standard of living of Brazilians." The standard of living, he continued, "can only be raised through economic development."

It was clear from his remarks that the three broad objectives of democratization, social progress, and economic development were interconnected. He could not conceive of democracy in a poor country or in a country where there were "gaps, defects, and inadequacies in the social realm."

CONCEPTS OF PROGRESS

Geisel's comments offer a framework within which to consider not only the current situation in Brazil but also historical trends that reach back to the late nineteenth century—and, in some instances, to Portugal. Historically, most Brazilians have believed that progress would take place within the context of a strong, authoritarian state. In the nineteenth century, for example,

a reform-minded elite adapted European theories of modernization that called for government-sponsored changes. The masses would receive benefits from the state; in this way, the elite reasoned, pressure for change from the poorer sectors of society would be eliminated. There would be progress with order. *Ordem e Progresso* ("Order and Progress") is the motto that graces the Brazilian flag; the motto is as appropriate today as it was in 1889, when the flag first flew over the new republic.

The tension among modernization, social equity, and order and liberty was first obvious in the early 1920s, when politically isolated middle-class groups united with junior military officers (*tenentes*) to challenge an entrenched ruling class of coffee-plantation owners. By the mid-1920s, the tenentes, bent on far-reaching reforms, conceived a new role for themselves. With a faith that bordered at times on the mystical and a philosophy that embraced change in the vaguest of terms, they felt that only the military could shake Brazil from its lethargy and force it to modernize. Their program demanded the ouster of conservative, tradition-minded politicians; an economic transformation of the nation; and, eventually, a return to strong, centralized constitutional rule. The tenentes also proposed

labor reforms that included official recognition of trade unions, a minimum wage and maximum workweek, restraints on child labor, land reform, nationalization of natural resources, and a radical expansion of educational facilities. Although the tenentes were frustrated in their attempts to mold policy, many of their reforms were taken up by Getulio Vargas, who seized power in 1930 and imposed a strong, authoritarian state on Brazil.

THE 1964 REVOLUTION

In some respects, the goals of the tenentes were echoed in 1964, when a broad coalition of civilians—frustrated by an economy that seemed to be disintegrating, concerned with the "leftist" slant of the government of João Goulart, and worried about a social revolution that might well challenge the status and prestige of the wealthy and the middle classes—called on the military to impose order on the country.

The military leaders did not see their intervention as just another coup but, rather, as a revolution. They foresaw change but believed that it would be dictated from above. Government was highly centralized, the traditional parties were virtually frozen out of the political process, and the military

Certain areas of Brazil attract enormous numbers of visitors from all over the world. This beach in Rio de Janeiro has one of the most famous skylines in South America.

and police ruthlessly purged Brazil of elements considered "leftist" or "subversive." (The terms were used interchangeably.) Order and authority triumphed over liberty and freedom. The press was muzzled, and human-rights abuses were rampant.

Brazil's economic recovery eventually began to receive attention. The military gave economic growth and national security priority over social programs and political liberalization. Until the effects of the oil crisis generated by the Organization of Petroleum Exporting Countries (OPEC) in 1973 began to be felt, the recovery of the Brazilian economy was dubbed a "miracle," with growth rates averaging 10 percent a year.

The benefits of that growth went primarily to the upper and middle classes, who enjoyed the development of industries based largely on consumer goods. Moreover, Brazil's industrialization was flawed. It was heavily dependent on foreign investment, foreign technology, and foreign markets. It required large investments in machinery and equipment but needed little labor, and it damaged the environment through pollution of the rivers and air around industrial centers. Agriculture was neglected to the point that even basic foodstuffs had to be imported.

THE IMPACT OF RURAL-TO-URBAN MIGRATION

The stress on industrialization tremendously increased rural-to-urban migration and complicated the government's ability to keep up with the expanded need for public health and social services. In 1970, nearly 56 percent of the population were concentrated in urban areas; by the late 1990s, 79 percent of the population were so classified. These figures also illustrate the inadequacies of an agrarian program based essentially on a "moving frontier." Peasants evicted from their plots have run out of new lands to exploit, unless they move to the inhospitable Amazon region. As a result, many have been attracted by the cities.

The pressure of the poor on the cities, severe shortages of staple foods, and growing tension in rural areas over access to the land forced the government to act. In 1985, the civilian government of José Sarney announced an agrarian-reform plan to distribute millions of acres of unused private land to peasants. Implementation of the reform was not easy, and confrontations between peasants and landowners occurred.

MILITARY RULE IS CHALLENGED

Nineteen seventy-four was a crucial year for the military government of Brazil. The virtual elimination of the urban-guerrilla threat challenged the argument that democratic institutions could not be restored because of national security concerns.

Pressure grew from other quarters as well. Many middle- and upper-class Brazilians were frightened by the huge state-controlled sector in the economy that had been carved out by the generals. The military's determination to promote the rapid development of the nation's resources, to control all industries deemed vital to the nation's security, and to compete with multinational corporations concerned Brazilian

© Photodisc/PunchStock

By the late 1980s, agrarian reforms that were designed to establish peasants in plots of workable land had caused the depletion of Brazilian jungle and, as space and opportunities diminished, there was a large movement of these people to the cities. The profound urban crowding in Brazil is illustrated by this photo of a section of Rio de Janeiro.

of hundreds of political exiles; the Party Reform Bill in essence reconstructed Brazilian politics. Under the provisions of the Party Reform Bill, new political parties could be established—provided they were represented in nine states and in 20 percent of the counties of those states. The new parties were granted the freedom to formulate political platforms, as long as they were not ideological and did not favor any single economic class. The Communist Party was outlawed, and the creation of a workers' party was expressly forbidden. (Communist parties were legalized again in 1985.)

DEVELOPMENT

Sound economic policies, including a floating exchange rate, attention to inflationary pressures, and conservative fiscal practices produced record trade surpluses between 2003 and 2007. The government seeks to combine strong growth with a reduction of the debt burden.

The law against the establishment of a workers' party reflected the regime's concern that labor, increasingly anxious about the state of the economy, might withdraw its traditional support for the state. Organized labor had willingly cooperated with the state since the populist regime of Getulio Vargas (1937–1945). For Brazilian workers in the 1930s, the state was their "patron," the source of benefits. This dependence on the government, deeply rooted in Portuguese political culture, replaced the formation of a more independent labor movement and minimized industrial conflict. The state played the role of mediator between workers and management. President Vargas led the workers to believe that the state was the best protector of their interests. (Polls have indicated that Brazilian workers still cling to that belief.)

If workers expect benefits from the state, however, the state must then honor those expectations and allocate sufficient resources to assure labor's loyalty. A deep economic crisis, such as those that occurred in the early 1960s, in the early 1990s, and again between 2001 and 2003 endangers the state's control of labor. In 1964, organized labor supported the coup, because workers felt that the civilian regime had failed to perform its protective function. This phenomenon also reveals the extremely shallow soil in which Brazilian democracy has taken root.

Organized labor tends not to measure Brazilian governments in political terms, but within the context of the state's ability to address labor's needs. For the rank-and-file

businesspeople, who saw their role in the economy decreasing.

Challenges to the military regime also came from the Roman Catholic Church, which attacked the government for its brutal violations of human rights and constantly called for economic and social justice. One Brazilian bishop publicly called the government "sinful" and in "opposition to the plans of God" and noted that it was

the Church's moral and religious obligation to fight it. After 1974, as Brazil's economic difficulties mounted, the chorus of complaints grew insistent.

THE RETURN OF DEMOCRACY

The relaxation of political repression was heralded by two laws passed in 1979. The Amnesty Bill allowed for the return worker, it is a question not of democracy or military authoritarianism, but of bread and butter. President Sarney, in an effort to keep labor loyal to the government, sought the support of union leaders for a proposal to create a national pact with businesspeople, workers, and his government. But pervasive corruption, inefficient government, and a continuing economic crisis eventually eroded the legitimacy of the elites and favored nontraditional parties in the 1989 election. The candidacy of Luís Inácio da Silva, popularly known as Lula and leader of the Workers' Party, "was stunning evidence of the Brazilian electorate's dissatisfaction with the conduct of the country's transition to democracy and with the political class in general." He lost the election by a very narrow margin. In 2002, he won the election and promised to "end hunger."

Workers continue to regard the state as the source of benefits, as do other Brazilians. Many social reformers, upset with the generals for their neglect of social welfare, believe that social reform should be dispensed from above by a strong and paternalistic state. Change is possible, even welcome—but it must be the result of compromise and conciliation, not confrontation or nonnegotiable demands.

THE NEW CONSTITUTION

The *abertura* (political liberalization) of Brazil climaxed in January 1985 with the election of President Sarney, a civilian, following 21 years of military rule. Importantly, the Brazilian military promised to respect the Constitution and promised a policy of nonintervention in the political process. In 1987, however, with the draft of a new constitution under discussion, the military strongly protested language that removed its responsibility for internal law and order and restricted the military's role to that of defense of the nation against external threats. According to *Latin American Regional Reports: Brazil,* the military characterized the draft constitution as "confused, inappropriate, at best a parody of a constitution, just as Frankenstein was a gross and deformed imitation of a human being."

Military posturing aside, the new Constitution went into effect in October 1988. It reflects the input of a wide range of interests: The Constituent Assembly—which also served as Brazil's Congress—heard testimony and suggestions from Amazonian Indians, peasants, and urban poor as well as from rich landowners and the military. The 1988 Constitution is a document that captures the byzantine character of Brazilian politics and influence peddling and reveals compromises made by conservative and liberal vested interests.

The military's fears about its role in internal security were removed when the Constituent Assembly voted constitutional provisions to grant the right of the military independently to ensure law and order, a responsibility it historically has claimed. But Congress also arrogated to itself the responsibility for appropriating federal monies. This is important, because it gives Congress a powerful check on both the military and the executive office.

FREEDOM

Violence against street children, indigenous peoples, homosexuals, and common criminals at the hands of the police, landowners, vigilante groups, gangs, and hired thugs is commonplace. Homicide committed by police is the third-leading cause of death among children and adolescents. Investigation of such crimes is lax and prosecution of the perpetrators sporadic. Indians continue to clash with miners and landowners.

Nationalists won several key victories. The Constituent Assembly created the concept of "a Brazilian company of national capital" that can prevent foreigners from engaging in mining, oil-exploration risk contracts, and biotechnology. Brazilian-controlled companies were also given preference in the supply of goods and services to local, state, and national governments. Legislation reaffirmed and strengthened the principle of government intervention in the economy should national security or the collective interest be at issue.

Conservative congressional representatives were able to prevail in matters of land reform. They defeated a proposal that would have allowed the compulsory appropriation of property for land reform. Although a clause that addressed the "social function" of land was included in the Constitution, it was clear that powerful landowners and agricultural interests had triumphed over Brazil's landless peasantry.

In other areas, however, the Constitution is remarkably progressive on social and economic issues. The workweek was reduced to a maximum of 44 hours, profit sharing was established for all employees, time-and-a-half was promised for overtime work, and paid vacations were to include a bonus of 30 percent of one's monthly salary. Day-care facilities were to be established for all children under age six, maternity leave of four months and paternity leave of five days were envisaged, and workers were protected against "arbitrary dismissal." The Constitution also introduced a series of innovations that would increase

significantly the ability of Brazilians to claim their guaranteed rights before the nation's courts and ensure the protection of human rights, particularly the rights of Indians and peasants involved in land disputes.

Despite the ratification of the 1988 Constitution, a functioning Congress, and an independent judiciary, the focus of power in Brazil is still the president. A legislative majority in the hands of the opposition in no way erodes the executive's ability to govern as he or she chooses. Any measure introduced by the president automatically becomes law after 40 days, even without congressional action. Foreign observers perceive "weaknesses" in the new parties, which in actuality are but further examples of well-established political practices. The parties are based on personalities rather than issues, platforms are vague, goals are so broad that they are almost illusions, and party organization conforms to traditional alliances and the "rules" of patronage. Democratic *forms* are in place in Brazil; the *substance* remains to be realized.

The election of President Fernando Collor de Mello, who assumed office in March 1990, proves the point. As political scientist Margaret Keck explains, Collor fit well into a "traditional conception of elite politics, characterized by fluid party identifications, the predominance of personal relations, a distrust of political institutions, and reliance on charismatic and populist appeals to *o povo*, the people." Unfortunately, such a system is open to abuse; revelations of widespread corruption that reached all the way to the presidency brought down Collor's government in 1992 and gave Brazilian democracy its most difficult challenge to date. Populist President Lula da Silva's government has also been increasingly dogged by charges of corruption. In September 2005 thousands of protesters, including workers, students, and businessmen took to the streets and accused the ruling Workers Party of bribing lawmakers and complicity in illicit campaign funding. Such scandals bring to light a range of strengths and weaknesses that presents insights into the Brazilian political system.

THE PRESS AND THE PRESIDENCY

Brazil's press was severely censored and harassed from the time of the military coup of 1964 until 1982. Not until passage of the Constitution of 1988 was the right of free speech and a free press guaranteed. It was the press, and in particular the news magazine *Veja,* that opened the door to President Collor's impeachment. In the words of *World Press Review,* "Despite government pressure to ease off, the magazine continued to uncover the president's malfeasance, tugging hard at the threads of Collor's unraveling administration. As others in the media followed suit, Congress was forced to begin an investigation and, in the end, indict Collor." The importance of the event to Brazil's press, according to *Veja* editor Mario Sergio Conti, is that "It will emerge with fewer illusions about power and be more rigorous. Reporting has been elevated to a higher plane. . . ."

While the failure of Brazil's first directly elected president in 29 years was tragic, it should not be interpreted as the demise of Brazilian democracy. Importantly, according to Brazilian journalist Carlos Eduardo Lins da Silva, writing in *Current History,* many "Brazilians and outside observers saw the workings of the impeachment process as a sign of the renewed strength of democratic values in Brazilian society. They were also seen as a healthy indicator of growing intolerance to corruption in public officials."

The military, despite persistent rumors of a possible coup, has to date allowed the constitutional process to dictate events. For the first time, most civilians do not see the generals as part of the solution to political shortcomings. But many Brazilians still assume that most politicians are "crooked."

THE RIGHTS OF WOMEN AND CHILDREN

Major changes in Brazilian households have occurred over the last decade as the number of women in the workforce has dramatically increased. In 1990, just over 35 percent of women were in the workforce, and the number was expected to grow. As a result, many women are limiting the size of their families. More than 20 percent use birth-control pills, and Brazil is second only to China in the percentage of women who have been sterilized. The traditional family of 5.0 or more children has shrunk to an average of 3.4. With two wage earners, the standard of living has risen slightly for some families. Many homes now have electricity and running water. Television sales increased by more than 1,000 percent in the last decade.

HEALTH/WELFARE

The quality of education in Brazil varies greatly from state to state, in part because there is no system of national priorities. The uneven character of education has been a major factor in the maintenance of a society that is profoundly unequal. The provision of basic health needs remains poor, and land reform is a perennial issue.

In relatively affluent, economically and politically dynamic urban areas, women are more evident in the professions, education, industry, the arts, media, and political life. In rural areas, however, especially in the northeast, traditional cultural attitudes, which call upon women to be submissive, are still well entrenched.

Women are routinely subjected to physical abuse in Brazil. Americas Watch, an international human-rights group, reports that more than 70 percent of assault, rape, and murder cases take place in the home and that many incidents are unreported. Even though Brazil's Supreme Court struck down the outmoded concept of a man's "defense of honor," local courts routinely acquit men who kill unfaithful wives. Brazil, for all intents and purposes, is still a patriarchy.

Children are also in many cases denied basic rights. According to official statistics, almost 18 percent of children between the ages of 10 and 14 are in the labor force, and they often work in unhealthy or dangerous environments. Violence against urban street children has reached frightening proportions. Between January and June 1992, 167 minors were killed in Rio de Janeiro; 306 were murdered in São Paulo over the first seven months of the year. In July 1993, the massacre in a single night of seven street children in Rio de Janeiro resulted, for a time, in cries for an investigation of the matter. In February 1997, however, five children were murdered on the streets of Rio.

THE STATUS OF BLACKS

Scholars continue to debate the actual status of blacks in Brazil. Not long ago, an elected black member of Brazil's federal Congress blasted Brazilians for their racism. However, argues historian Bradford Burns, Brazil probably has less racial tension and prejudice than other multiracial societies.

A more formidable barrier, Burns says, may well be class. "Class membership depends on a wide variety of factors and their combination: income, family history and/or connections, education, social behavior, tastes in housing, food and dress, as well as appearance, personality and talent." But, he notes, "The upper class traditionally has been and still remains mainly white, the lower class principally colored." Upward mobility exists and barriers can be breached. But if such advancement depends upon a symbolic "whitening out," does not racism still exist?

This point is underscored by the 1988 celebration of the centennial of the abolition of slavery in Brazil. In sharp contrast to the government and Church emphasis on racial harmony and equality were the public protests by militant black groups claiming that Brazil's much-heralded "racial democracy" was a myth. In 1990, blacks earned 40 percent less than whites in the same professions.

THE INDIAN QUESTION

Brazil's estimated 200,000 Indians have suffered greatly in recent decades from the gradual encroachment of migrants from the heavily populated coastal regions and from government efforts to open the Amazon region to economic development. Highways have penetrated Indian lands, diseases for which the Indians have little or no immunity have killed thousands, and additional thousands have experienced a profound culture shock. Government efforts to protect the Indians have been largely ineffectual.

The two poles in the debate over the Indians are captured in the following excerpts from *Latin American Regional Reports: Brazil.* A Brazilian Army officer observed that the "United States solved the problem with its army. They killed a lot of Indians. Today everything is quiet there, and the country is respected throughout the world." And in the words of a Kaingang Indian woman: "Today my people see their lands invaded, their forests destroyed, their animals exterminated and their hearts lacerated by this brutal weapon that is civilization."

Sadly, the assault against Brazil's Indian peoples has accelerated, and disputes over land have become more violent. One case speaks for itself. In the aftermath of a shooting incident in which several Yanomamö Indians were killed by prospectors, the Brazilian federal government declared that all outsiders would be removed from Yanomamö lands, ostensibly to protect the Indians. Those expelled by the government included anthropologists, missionaries, doctors, and nurses. A large number of prospectors remained behind. By the end of 1988, while medical personnel had not been allowed back in, the number of prospectors had swelled to 50,000 in an area peopled by 9,000 Yanomamö. The Indians have been devastated by diseases, particularly malaria, and by mercury poisoning as a result of prospecting activities upriver from Yanomamö settlements. In 1991, cholera began to spread among indigenous Amazon peoples, due to medical waste dumped into rivers in cholera-ridden Peru and Ecuador.

The new Constitution devotes an entire chapter to the rights of Indians. For the first time in the country's history, Indians have the authority to bring suits in court to defend their rights and interests. In all such cases, they will be assisted by a public prosecutor. Even though the government established a large protected zone for Brazil's Yanomamö

(World Bank/Julio Pantoja/JPBR-1512-3-B)

A family makes its way down a mud-filled road in Vila Da Canpas in the Amazon region of Brazil, near Manaus. For many, the only transportation available is by foot.

Indians in 1991, reports of confrontations between Indians and prospectors have persisted. There are also Brazilian nationalists who insist that a 150-mile-wide strip along the border with Venezuela be excluded from the reserve as a matter of national security. The Yanomamö cultural area extends well into Venezuela; such a security zone would bisect Yanomamö lands.

THE BURNING OF BRAZIL

Closely related to the destruction of Brazil's Indians is the destruction of the tropical rain forests. The burning of the forests by peasants clearing land in the traditional slash-and-burn method, or by developers and landowners constructing dams or converting forest to pasture, has become a source of worldwide concern and controversy.

Ecologists are horrified by the mass extinction of species of plants, animals, and insects, most of which have not even been catalogued. The massive annual burning (equivalent in one recent year to the size of Kansas) also fuels the debate on the greenhouse effect and global warming. The problem of the burning of Brazil is indeed global, because we are all linked to the tropics by climate and the migratory patterns of birds and animals.

ACHIEVEMENTS

Brazil's cultural contributions to the world are many. Authors such as Joaquim Maria Machado de Assis, Jorge Amado, and Graciliano Ramos are evidence of Brazil's high rank in terms of important literary works. Brazilian music has won millions of devotees throughout the world, and Brazil's *Cinema Novo* (New Cinema) has won many awards.

World condemnation of the destruction of the Amazon basin has produced a strong xenophobic reaction in Brazil. Foreign Ministry Secretary-General Paulo Tarso Flecha de Lima informed a 24-nation conference on the protection of the environment that the "international community cannot try to strangle the development of Brazil in the name of false ecological theories." He further noted that foreign criticism of his government in this regard was "arrogant, presumptuous and aggressive." The Brazilian military, according to Latin American Regional Reports: Brazil, has adopted a high-profile posture on the issue. The military sees the Amazon as "a kind of strategic reserve vital to national security interests." Any talk of transforming the rain

forests into an international nature reserve is rejected out of hand.

Over the next decade, however, Brazilian and foreign investors will create a 2.5 million-acre "green belt" in an already devastated area of the Amazon rain forest. Fifty million seedlings have been planted in a combination of natural and commercial zones. It is hoped that responsible forestry will generate jobs to maintain and study the native forest and to log the commercial zones. Steady employment would help to stem the flow of migrants to cities and to untouched portions of the rain forest. On the other hand, to compound the problem, landless peasants in 16 of Brazil's states launched violent protests in May 2000 to pressure the government to provide land for 100,000 families, as well as to grant millions of dollars in credits for poor rural workers.

FOREIGN POLICY

If Brazil's Indian and environmental policies leave much to be desired, its foreign policy has won it respect throughout much of Latin America and the developing world. Cuba, Central America, Angola, and Mozambique seemed far less threatening during the Cold War to the Brazilian government than they did to Washington. Brazil is more concerned about its energy needs, capital requirements, and trade opportunities.

President Lula da Silva's foreign policy has been characterized by the United States as "leftward" leaning, especially since it has moved closer to other populist governments in the region, such as Venezuela (Hugo Chavez), or Bolivia (Evo Morales). Closer relations have also been established with Castro's Cuba. Lula continues to attack the United States' invasion of Iraq and is distrustful of Washington's free-trade agenda. It must be understood that Brazil's current foreign policy, both in terms of its economic and political contexts, has another dimension. Standing up to the United States plays well at home and in the region and may be used to balance domestic policies that fall short of the radical solutions many of his followers expected. Lula himself disdains political labels such as "leftist" and, as he told a *New York Times* reporter, the class struggle was about results for the people and he didn't care if it was called "Socialism or Christianity or simply ethics." Brazil's foreign policy likewise should not be labeled but seen as one of pragmatism.

ECONOMIC POLICY

In mid-1993, Finance Minister Fernando Henrique Cardoso announced a plan to restore life to an economy in shambles. The so-called Real Plan, which pegged the new Brazilian currency (the real) to the dollar, brought an end to hyperinflation and won Cardoso enough popularity to carry him to the presidency. Inflation, which had raged at a rate of 45 percent per month in July 1994, was only 2 percent per month in February 1995. His two-to-one victory in elections in October 1994 was the most one-sided win since 1945.

President Cardoso transformed the economy through carefully conceived and brilliantly executed constitutional reforms. A renovated tax system, an overhauled social-security program, and extensive privatization of state-owned enterprises were supported by a new generation of legislators pledged to support broad-based reform.

But, as was the case in much of Latin America in 1995, Mexico's financial crisis spread quickly to affect Brazil's economy, in large measure because foreign investors were unable to distinguish between Mexico and other Latin American nations. A similar problem occurred in 1998 with the collapse of Asian financial markets. Again, foreign investors shied away from Brazil's economy, and President Cardoso was forced to back away from a promise not to devalue the real. With devaluation in 1999 and signs of recovery in Asian markets, Brazil's economic

Timeline: PAST

1500
Pedro Alvares Cabral discovers and claims Brazil for Portugal

1822
Declaration of Brazil's independence

1888
The Golden Law abolishes slavery

1889
The republic is proclaimed

1944
The Brazilian Expeditionary Force participates in the Italian campaign

1964
The military seizes power

1980s–1990s
Economic, social, and ecological crises

1990s
President Fernando Collor de Mello is convicted; the Asian financial crisis plunges Brazil into deep recession

PRESENT

2000s
Brazil wins praise for its handling of its HIV/AIDS problem

Luis Inacio da Silva, "Lula," elected president in 2002; Brazil pursues independent foreign and economic policies

2006
"Lula" re-elected president

prospects brightened considerably. Exports rose, and Brazil was able to finance its foreign debt through bond issues. In 2000 and 2001, however, the economy slowed, and concerns were expressed about energy supplies and costs, and the default of Brazil's major trading partner, Argentina, on its foreign debt. Economic uncertainty emboldened Congress to initiate a probe against corruption in government. Life for average Brazilians remained difficult. Cardoso's loss of popularity opened the door to the political opposition who were able to capitalize on presidential elections in 2002, when Luis Inacio da Silva, or "Lula" as he is popularly known, won a resounding triumph at the polls.

Lula, who worried many foreign observers because of his "leftist" ideology attacked Brazil's myriad problems in a pragmatic fashion. Labor unions, who supported his presidency and expected all of the benefits of political patronage, have been somewhat disillusioned. Lula, in attempt to bring the nation's spending under control, significantly called the public workforce. With regard to the economy, his policies have not been "leftist" but have more closely adhered to classical economic approaches. This has calmed the fears of foreign investors.

Cardoso's laudable economic reforms did not succeed in transforming the quality of Brazilian democracy.

The lament of Brazilian journalist Lins da Silva is still accurate: "Brazilian elites have once again shown how capable they are of solving political crises in a creative and peaceful manner but also how unwilling to promote change in inequitable social structures." The wealth of the nation still remains in the hands of a few, and the educational system has failed to absorb and train as many citizens as it should. Police continue routinely to abuse their power. Lula, who's own family roots lie in the favelas, is deeply sensitive to the needs of Brazil's poor and disadvantaged. He has made a point of visiting the slums, of listening to the complaints and needs of people, of behaving, in short, like the classic "patron."

On a positive note, Brazil's progress in the struggle against AIDS, a disease that contributed to the deaths of 9,600 people in Brazil in 1996, is among the best in the world. In simple terms, the government uses language in the Paris Convention of 1883 to produce low-cost generic drugs similar to costlier medications manufactured abroad. Everyone in Brazil infected with the HIV virus is provided with a "cocktail" of drugs, and with training in how to take them effectively. More than 100,000 Brazilians are on the drug regimen, at an annual cost of $163 million. In 2000, AIDS–related deaths declined to 1,200, and the rate of transmission was sharply reduced.

At a broader level, Brazil has prospered from its membership in Mercosur, a regional trade organization that consists of Argentina, Brazil, Paraguay, and Uruguay. The success of Mercosur has expanded relations with other countries, especially Chile, which became an "associate" member in 1997. Lula, like Cardoso before him, is opposed to Washington's efforts to forge a Free Trade Area of the Americas (FTAA), in part because Mercosur and Brazil consider Europe a more important market and do not send a high percentage of their exports to the United States. Brazil has kept the pressure on other South American governments to convince them to join with Mercosur, not only in a "South American Free Trade Agreement," but in closer ties with the European Union. This independent policy has provided Brazil with leverage in the era of globalization.

Brazil has also become a leader in the use of ethanol as a fuel. Derived from cane sugar, it is used by approximately 80 percent of all vehicles. On the negative side, the use of land to produce fuel has resulted in higher food prices, a fact not lost on tens of thousands of Brazilians who live in poverty.

Chile (Republic of Chile)

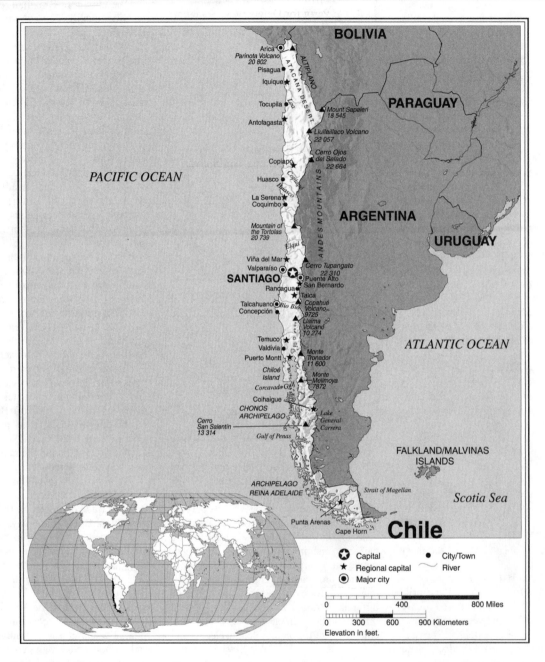

Chile Statistics

GEOGRAPHY

Area in Square Miles (Kilometers):
292,280 (756,945) (about twice the
size of Montana)
Capital (Population): Santiago 5,428,590
(urban)
Environmental Concerns: air and water
pollution; deforestation; loss of
biodiversity; soil erosion; desertification
Geographical Features: low coastal
mountains; a fertile central

valley; rugged Andes Mountains
in the east
Climate: temperate; desert in the north;
Mediterranean in the center; cool and
damp in the south

PEOPLE

Population

Total: 16,284,741 (2007 est.)
Annual Growth Rate: 0.92%

Rural/Urban Population Ratio: 16/84
Major Language: Spanish
Ethnic Makeup: 95% European and
Mestizo; 3% Indian; 2% others
Religions: 70% Roman Catholic;
15% Evangelical; 8.3% none

Health

Life Expectancy at Birth: 74 years (male);
80 years (female)
Infant Mortality Rate (Ratio): 8.36/1,000
Physicians Available (Ratio): 1/875

78

Education

Adult Literacy Rate: 95.7%
Compulsory (Ages): for 8 years; free

COMMUNICATION

Telephones: 3,326,000 main lines
Daily Newspaper Circulation: 101 per 1,000 people
Cell Phones: 12,451,000
Internet Users: 4,156,000

TRANSPORTATION

Roadways in Kilometers (miles): 79,606 (49,464)
Railroads in Kilometers (miles): 6,585 (4,092)
Usable Airfields: 358

GOVERNMENT

Type: republic
Independence Date: September 18, 1810 (from Spain)

Head of State/Government: President Michelle Bachelet is both head of state and head of government
Political Parties: Christian Democratic Party; Party for Democracy; Socialist Party; National Renewal; Independent Democratic Union; Radical Social Democratic; Alliance for Chile; others
Suffrage: universal and compulsory at 18

MILITARY

Military Expenditures (% of GDP): 2.6%
Current Disputes: boundary or territorial disputes with Argentina, and Bolivia; territorial claim in Antarctica

ECONOMY

Currency ($U.S. Equivalent): 465 pesos = $1
Per Capita Income/GDP: $14,400/$107.7 billion
GDP Growth Rate: 5.2%

Inflation Rate: 6.5%
Unemployment Rate: 7%
Labor Force: 6,970,000
Natural Resources: copper; timber; iron ore; nitrates; precious metals; molybdenum; fish; hydropower
Agriculture: wheat; corn; grapes; beans; sugar beets; potatoes; fruit; beef; poultry; wool; timber; fish
Industry: copper and other minerals; foodstuffs; fish processing; iron and steel; wood and wood products; transport equipment; cement; textiles
Exports: $66.43 billion (f.o.b.) (primary partners, European Union, United States, Japan)
Imports: $41.8 billion (f.o.b.) (primary partners United States, European Union, Argentina)

SUGGESTED WEB SITE

http://www.cia.gov/cia/publications/factbook/geos.ci.html

Chile Country Report

CHILE: A NATION ON THE REBOUND

In September 1973, the Chilean military, with the secret support of the U.S. Central Intelligence Agency (CIA), seized power from the constitutionally elected government of President Salvador Allende. Chile, with its long-standing traditions of free and honest elections, respect for human rights, and freedom of the press, was quickly transformed into a brutal dictatorship that arrested, tortured, and killed thousands of its own citizens. In the larger sweep of Chilean history, however, the coup seemed to be the most recent and severe manifestation of a lengthy conflict between social justice, on the one hand, and the requirements of order dictated by the nation's ruling elite, on the other. This was true in the colonial period, when there was conflict between the Roman Catholic Church and landowners over Indian rights. It was also apparent in later confrontations among Marxists, reformers, and conservatives.

FORM, NOT SUBSTANCE

Form, as opposed to substance, had characterized the rule of the Christian Democrats in the 1960s, when they created many separate rural unions, supposedly to address the needs of *campesinos* ("peasants"). A divided union movement in effect became a form of government control that prevented the emergence of a single powerful rural organization.

DEVELOPMENT

Chile, with an average gross domestic product growth of 6 percent over the last decade, has become a model for other Latin American nations. Bilateral trade agreements have continued with Mexico, Venezuela, and Bolivia. Trade agreements were also signed with the United States and the European Union.

In the early 1970s, President Allende—despite his talk of socialism and his genuine attempt to destroy the institutions and values of an old social order—used as his weapon of transformation, a centralized bureaucracy that would have been recognized by sixteenth-century viceroys and nineteenth-century presidents. Allende's attempts to institute far-reaching social change led to a strong reaction from powerful sectors of Chilean society who felt threatened.

THE 1973 COUP D'ETAT

When the military ousted Allende, it had the support of many Chileans, including the majority of the middle class, who had been hurt by the government's economic policies, troubled by continuous political turmoil, and infuriated by official mismanagement. The military, led by General Augusto Pinochet, began a new experiment with another form of centrist rule: military authoritarianism. The generals made it clear that they had not restored order merely to return it to the "discredited" constitutional practices of the past. They spoke of regeneration, of a new Chile, and of an end to the immorality, corruption, and incompetence of all civilian politics. The military announced in 1974 that, "guided by the inspiration of [Diego] Portales"—one of nineteenth-century Chile's greatest civilian leaders—"the government of Chile will energetically apply the principle of authority and drastically punish any outburst of disorder and anarchy."

The political, economic, and social reforms proposed by the military aimed at restructuring Chile to such an extent that there would no longer be a need for traditional political parties. Economic policy favored free and open competition as the main regulator of economic and social life. The Chilean state rid itself of hundreds of state-owned corporations, struck down tariffs designed to protect Chilean industry from foreign competition, and opened the economy to widespread foreign investment. The changes struck deeply at the structure of the Chilean economy and produced a temporary but sharp recession, high unemployment, and hundreds of bankruptcies.

(Department of Defense photo by R. D. Ward)

President Michelle Bachelet is both head of state and head of government.

A steep decline in the standard of living for most Chileans was the result of the government's anti-inflation policy.

FREEDOM

Chile's first woman president, Michelle Bachelet, who was elected in 2006, was arrested, tortured, and exiled by the Pinochet dictatorship. Her father died while in prison. She said that she "was a victim of hatred, and I have dedicated my life to reversing that hatred."

Social-welfare programs were reduced to a minimum. The private sector was encouraged to assume many functions and services once provided by the state. Pensions were moved entirely to the private sector as all state programs were phased out. In this instance, the state calculated that workers tied through pensions and other benefits to the success of private enterprise would be less likely to be attracted to "non-Chilean" ideologies such as Marxism, socialism, and even Christian democracy. State-sponsored health programs were also cut to the bone, and many of the poor now paid for services once provided by the government.

THE DEFEAT OF A DICTATOR

To attain a measure of legitimacy, Chileans expected the military government to produce economic achievement. By 1987,

and continuing into 1989, the regime's economic policies seemed successful; the economic growth rate for 1988 was an impressive 7.4 percent. However, it masked critical weaknesses in the Chilean economy. For example, much of the growth was overdependent on exports of raw materials—notably, copper, pulp, timber, and fishmeal.

Modest economic success and an inflation rate of less than 20 percent convinced General Pinochet that he could take his political scenario for Chile's future to the voters for their ratification. But in the October 5, 1988, plebiscite, Chile's voters upset the general's plans and decisively denied him an additional eight-year term. (He did, however, continue in office until the next presidential election determined his successor.) The military regime (albeit reluctantly) accepted defeat at the polls, which signified the reemergence of a deep-rooted civic culture and long democratic tradition.

Where had Pinochet miscalculated? Public-opinion surveys on the eve of the election showed a sharply divided electorate. Some political scientists even spoke of the existence of "two Chiles." In the words of government professor Arturo Valenzuela and Boston Globe correspondent Pamela Constable, one Chile "embraced those who had benefited from the competitive economic policies and welfare subsidies instituted by the regime and who had been persuaded that power was best entrusted to the armed forces." The second Chile "consisted of those who had been victimized by the regime, who did not identify with Pinochet's anti-Communist cause, and who had quietly nurtured a belief in democracy." Polling data from the respected Center for Public Policy Studies showed that 72 percent of those who voted against the regime were motivated by economic factors. These were people who had lost skilled jobs or who had suffered a decrease in real wages. While Pinochet's economic reforms had helped some, it had also created a disgruntled mass of downwardly mobile wage earners.

Valenzuela and Constable explain how a dictator allowed himself to be voted out of power. "To a large extent Pinochet had been trapped by his own mythology. He was convinced that he would be able to win and was anxious to prove that his regime was not a pariah but a legitimate government. He and other officials came to believe their own propaganda about the dynamic new Chile they had created." The closed character of the regime, with all lines of authority flowing to the hands of one man, made it "impossible for them to

accept the possibility that they could lose." And when the impossible occurred and the dictator lost an election played by his own rules, neither civilians on the right nor the military were willing to override the constitutional contract they had forged with the Chilean people.

HEALTH/WELFARE

Since 1981, all new members of Chile's labor force have been required to contribute 10 percent of their monthly gross earnings to private-pension-fund accounts, which they own. Unfortunately, in 2006 new retirees discovered that their pensions fell far below the guaranteed threshold. One reason was that expenses for managing the funds consumed as much as 33 percent of workers' contributions.

In March 1990, Chile returned to civilian rule for the first time in almost 17 years, with the assumption of the presidency by Patricio Aylwin. His years in power revealed that tensions still existed between civilian politicians and the military. In 1993, for example, General Pinochet mobilized elements of the army in Santiago—a move that, in the words of the independent newspaper La Época, "marked the crystallization of long-standing hostility" between the Aylwin government and the army. The military had reacted both to investigations into human-rights abuses during the Pinochet dictatorship and proposed legislation that would have subordinated the military to civilian control. On the other hand, the commanders of the navy and air force as well as the two right-wing political parties refused to sanction the actions of the army.

President Aylwin regained the initiative when he publicly chastised General Pinochet. Congress, in a separate action, affirmed its supremacy over the judiciary in 1993, when it successfully impeached a Supreme Court justice for "notable dereliction of duty." The court system had been notorious for transferring human-rights cases from civil to military courts, where they were quickly dismissed. The impeachment augured well for further reform of the judicial branch.

Further resistance to the legacy of General Pinochet was expressed by the people when, on December 11, 1993, the center-left coalition candidate Eduardo Frei Ruiz-Tagle won the Chilean presidential election, with 58 percent of the vote. As part of his platform, Frei had promised to bring the military under civilian rule. The parliamentary vote, however, did not give him the two-thirds majority needed to push through such

Courtesy of Paul Goodwin

Chilean Vineyard. Wine has become a major export.

a reform. The trend toward civilian government, though, seemed to be continuing.

Perhaps the final chapter in Pinochet's career began in November 1998, while the former dictator was in London for medical treatment. At that time, the British government received formal extradition requests from the governments of Spain, Switzerland, and France. The charges against Pinochet included attempted murder, conspiracy to murder, torture, conspiracy to torture, hostage taking, conspiracy to take hostages, and genocide, based on Pinochet's alleged actions while in power.

British courts ruled that the general was too ill to stand trial, and Pinochet returned to Chile. In May 2004 a Chilean appeals court revoked Pinochet's immunity from prosecution. Still, in November 2005 Pinochet was arrested on charges of tax fraud and passport forgery in connection with secret bank accounts he maintained under false names in other countries. Almost simultaneously a Chilean judge indicted him on human-rights abuses. Previously, the army had accepted blame for human-rights abuses during the Pinochet era. As the army commander wrote in a Santiago newspaper: "The Chilean Army Chile has taken the difficult but irreversible decision to assume responsibility for all punishable and morally unacceptable acts in the past attributed to it as an institution. . . . Never and for no one can there be any ethical justification for violations of human rights." Importantly, the army's admissions is reassuring to those who wish to pursue human-rights issues but were fearful of the military's possible

reaction. Pinochet's death in 2006, before he could be brought to trial, only partially closed this sad chapter in Chile's history.

THE ECONOMY

By 1998, the Chilean economy had experienced 13 consecutive years of strong growth. But the Asian financial crisis of that year hit Chile hard, in part because 33 percent of the nation's exports in 1997 went to Asian markets. Copper prices tumbled; and because the largest copper mine is government-owned, state revenues contracted sharply. Following a sharp recession in 1999, the economy once again began to grow. However, domestic recovery has been slow. Unemployment remained high at 9 percent of the workforce, and a growth rate of 5.5 percent did not produce sufficient revenue to finance President Lagos's planned social programs and education initiatives. The sluggish global economy in 2001 was partly to blame, as prices fell for copper, Chile's number-one export.

Although there is still a large gap between the rich and poor in Chile, those living in poverty has been reduced from 40 percent to 20 percent over the course of the last decade. The irony is that Chile's economic success story is built on the economic model imposed by the Pinochet regime. "Underlying the current prosperity", writes *New York Times* reporter Larry Rohter, "is a long trail of blood and suffering that makes the thought of reversing course too difficult to contemplate." Many Chileans want to bury the past and move on—but the persistence of memory will not

allow closure at this time. Chile has chosen to follow its own course with respect to economic policy. While many of its neighbors in the Southern Cone—notably Argentina, Brazil, Bolivia, Peru, Ecuador, and Venezuela—have moved away from free trade and open markets, Chile remains firmly wed to both.

Newly elected President Michelle Bachelet, Chile's first woman president, who served in the outgoing Lagos government first as minister of health and then as minister of defense, remains committed to close ties to the United States and to free trade. As a Socialist she will strive to meet the needs of women and the poor—but she will also keep in place economic policies that have made the Chilean economy one of the most dynamic in the region. Unemployment continues to fall, standing at 7.8 percent in 2006 and 7 percent at the end of 2007. Bachelet has also amassed a $20 billion Economic and Social Stabilization Fund to provide for social spending. A portion of the high revenues generated by the state-owned copper industry provides money for the fund.

Not all Chileans are pleased with Bachelet's policies. Some are opposed to social change and others feel that change has not occurred as quickly as they expected. Gender has certainly been an issue both during her campaign for the presidency and in the first year of her administration. In an interview with journalist David Rieff she stated that "women say that my election represents a cultural break with the past—a past of sexism, of misogyny." That past exists in the present as Bachelet's male critics complain about her apparent "indecisiveness."

Peruvian novelist and politician Mario Vargas Llosa observes that while Chile "is not paradise," it does have a "stability and economic dynamism unparalleled in Latin America." Indeed, "Chile is moving closer to Spain and Australia and farther from Peru or Haiti." He suggests that there has been a shift in Chile's political culture. "The ideas of economic liberty, a free market open to the world, and private initiative as the motor of progress have become embedded in the people of Chile."

ACHIEVEMENTS

Chile's great literary figures, such as Gabriela Mistrál and Pablo Neruda, have a great sympathy for the poor and oppressed. Other major Chilean writers, such as Isabel Allende and Ariel Dorfman, have won worldwide acclaim.

Chilean novelist Ariel Dorfman has a different perspective: "Obviously it is better to be dull and virtuous than bloody and Pinochetista, but Chile has been a very gray country for many years now. Modernization doesn't always have to come with a lack of soul, but I think there is a degree of that happening."

SIGNS OF CHANGE

Although the Chilean Constitution was essentially imposed on the nation by the military in 1980, there are signs of change. The term for president was reduced from eight to six years in 1993; and in 1997, the Chamber of Deputies, the lower house of the Legislature, approved legislation to further reduce the term of a president to four years, with a prohibition on reelection. Military courts, which have broader peacetime jurisdiction than most other countries in the Western Hemisphere, have also come under scrutiny by politicians. According to the *Revista Hoy*, as summarized by *CHIP News*, military justice reaches far beyond the ranks. If, for example, several people are involved in the commission of a crime and one of the perpetrators happens to be a member of the military, all are tried in

a military court. Another abuse noted by politicians is that the military routinely uses the charge of sedition against civilians who criticize it. A group of Christian Democrats wants to limit the jurisdiction of the military to military crimes committed by military personnel; eliminate the participation of the army prosecutor in the Supreme Court, where he sits on the bench in cases related to the military; grant civilian courts the authority to investigate military premises; and accord civilian courts jurisdiction over military personnel accused of civilian-related crimes. The military itself, in 2004, in an effort to improve its tarnished image has worked in the background to hold accountable those officers involved in human-rights abuses in the past.

Another healthy sign of change is a concerted effort by the Chilean and Argentine governments to discuss issues that have been a historical source of friction between the two nations. Arms escalation, mining exploration and exploitation in border areas, and trade and investment concerns were on the agenda. The Chilean foreign relations minister and the defense minister sat down with their Argentine counterparts in the first meeting of its kind in the history of Argentine–Chilean relations.

Timeline: PAST

1541
The founding of Santiago de Chile

1818
Independence of Spain is proclaimed

1964–1970
Revolution in Liberty dramatically alters Chilean society

1973
A military coup ousts President Salvador Allende; General Augusto Pinochet becomes president

1988
Pinochet is voted out—and goes

1990s
Asian financial woes cut into Chilean economic growth

PRESENT

2000s
Ricardo Lagos, a moderate Socialist, wins the presidency in December 1999–January 2000 elections

Lagos government accelerates prosecution of human-rights abusers

2006
Chile elects its first woman president, Verónica Michelle Bachelet Jeria

Colombia (Republic of Colombia)

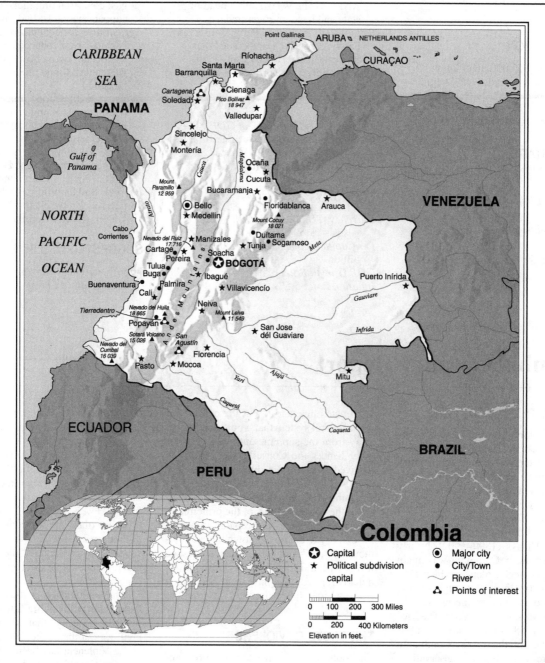

Colombia Statistics

GEOGRAPHY

Area in Square Miles (Kilometers):
440,000 (1,139,600) (about 3 times the
size of Montana)
Capital (Population): Bogotá 7,033,914
(urban)
Environmental Concerns: deforestation;
soil damage; air pollution
Geographical Features: flat coastal
lowlands; central highlands; high Andes
Mountains; eastern lowland plains

Climate: tropical on coast and
eastern plains; cooler in
highlands

PEOPLE

Population

Total: 44,379,598 (2007 est.)
Annual Growth Rate: 1.43%
Rural/Urban Population Ratio: 27/73
Major Language: Spanish

Ethnic Makeup: 58% Mestizo; 20% white;
14% mulatto; 4% African; 3% African
Indian; 1% Indian
Religions: 90% Roman Catholic; 10% other

Health

Life Expectancy at Birth: 68 years (Male);
76 years (Female)
Infant Mortality Rate (Ratio): 20.1/1,000;
Indians 233/1,000
Physicians Available (Ratio): 1/1,078

83

Education

Adult Literacy Rate: 92.8%
Compulsory (Ages): for 5 years between 6 and 12; free

COMMUNICATION

Telephones: 37,865,000 main lines
Daily Newspaper Circulation: 55 per 1,000 people
Cell Phones: 29,763,000
Internet Users: 6,705,000

TRANSPORTATION

Roadways in Kilometers (miles): 112,998 (70,207)
Railroads in Kilometers (miles): 3,304 (2,053)
Usable Airfields: 934

GOVERNMENT

Type: republic

Independence Date: July 10, 1810 (from Spain)
Head of State/Government: President Alvaro Uribe Velez is both head of state and head of government
Political Parties: Liberal Party; Conservative Party; Alternative Democratic Pole; Radical Change; Social Unity Party
Suffrage: universal at 18

MILITARY

Military Expenditures (% of GDP): 3.4%
Current Disputes: civil war; maritime boundary dispute with Venezuela; territorial disputes with Nicaragua

ECONOMY

Currency ($U.S. Equivalent): 1905 pesos = $1
Per Capita Income/GDP: $7,200/$116.4 billion
GDP Growth Rate: 6.5%
Inflation Rate: 5.5%

Unemployment Rate: 10.6%
Labor Force: 20,650,000
Natural Resources: petroleum; natural gas; coal; iron ore; nickel; gold; copper; emeralds; hydropower
Agriculture: coffee; cut flowers; bananas; rice; tobacco; corn; sugarcane; cocoa beans; oilseed; vegetables; forest products; shrimp farming
Industry: textiles; food processing; petroleum; clothing and footwear; beverages; chemicals; cement; gold; coal; emeralds
Exports: $28.39 billion (f.o.b.) primary partners United States, European Union, Andean Community)
Imports: $30.83 billion (f.o.b.) (primary partners United States, European Union, Andean Community)

SUGGESTED WEB SITE

http://www.cia.gov/cia/publications/ factbook/index.html

Colombia Country Report

COLOMBIA: THE VIOLENT LAND

Colombia has long been noted for its violent political history. The division of political beliefs in the mid-nineteenth century into conservative and liberal factions produced not only debate but also civil war. To the winner went the presidency and the spoils of office. That competition for office came to a head during the savage War of the Thousand Days (1899–1902). Nearly half a century later, Colombia was again plagued by political violence, which took perhaps 200,000 lives. Although on the surface it is distinct from the nineteenth-century civil wars, *La Violencia* ("The Violence," 1946–1958) offers striking parallels to the violence of the 1800s. Competing factions were again led by conservatives and liberals, and the presidency was the prize. Explanations for this phenomenon have tended to be at once simple and powerful. Colombian writers blame a Spanish heritage and its legacy of lust for political power.

Gabriel García Márquez, in his classic novel *One Hundred Years of Solitude,* spoofed the differences between liberals and conservatives. "The Liberals," said Aureliano Buendia's father-in-law, "were Freemasons, bad people, wanting to hang priests, to institute civil marriage and divorce, to recognize the rights of illegitimate children as equal to those of

legitimate ones, and to cut the country up into a federal system that would take power away from the supreme authority." On the other hand, "the Conservatives, who had received their power directly from God, proposed the establishment of public order and family morality. They were the defenders of the faith of Christ, of the principle of authority, and were not prepared to permit the country to be broken down into autonomous entities." Aureliano, when later asked if he was a Liberal or a Conservative, quickly replied: "If I have to be something I'll be a Liberal, because the Conservatives are tricky."

THE ROOTS OF VIOLENCE

The roots of the violence are far more complex than a simple quest for spoils caused by a flaw in national character. Historian Charles Bergquist has shown that "divisions within the upper class and the systematic philosophical and programmatic positions that define them are not merely political manifestations of cultural traits; they reflect diverging economic interests within the upper class." These opposing interests developed in both the nineteenth and twentieth centuries. Moreover, to see Colombian politics solely as a violent quest for office ignores long periods of relative peace (1902–1935). But whatever the underlying causes of the violence, it

has profoundly influenced contemporary Colombians.

La Violencia was the largest armed conflict in the Western Hemisphere since the Mexican Revolution (1910–1917). It was a civil war of ferocious intensity that cut through class lines and mobilized people from all levels of society behind the banner of either liberalism or conservatism. That elite-led parties were able to win popular support was evidence of their strong organization rather than their opponents' political weakness.

These multiclass parties still dominate Colombian political life, although the fierce interparty rivalry that characterized the civil wars of the nineteenth century as well as La Violencia has been stilled. In 1957, Colombia's social elite decided to bury partisan differences and devised a plan to end the widespread strife. Under this National Front agreement, the two parties agreed to divide legislative and bureaucratic positions equally and to alternate the presidency every four years from 1958 to 1974. This form of coalition government proved a highly successful means of elite compromise.

THE IMPACT OF LA VIOLENCIA

The violence has left its imprint on the people of Colombia in other ways. Some scholars have suggested that peasants now shun political action because of fear of renewed violence. Refugees from La Violencia generally experienced confusion and a loss of values. Usually, rising literacy rates, improved transportation and communications, and integration into the nation's life produce an upsurge of activism as people clamor for more rapid change. This has not been the case in rural Colombia. Despite guerrilla activity in the countryside—some of which is a spin-off from La Violencia, some of which until recently had a Marxist orientation, and some of which is banditry—the guerrillas have not been able to win significant rural support.

La Violencia also led to the professionalization and enlargement of the Colombian armed forces in the late 1950s and early 1960s. Never a serious participant in the nation's civil wars, the military acquired a new prestige and status unusual for Colombia. It must be considered an important factor in any discussion of Colombian politics today.

DEVELOPMENT

Drug-related crime has become the most common cause of death after cancer and has also contributed to a wave of kidnappings. This, together with continuing political violence, has had a damping effect on the nation's economy and deterred both tourists and investors. For example, petroleum exports have become significant for Colombia, but pipelines are vulnerable to sabotage by guerrillas.

A standoff between guerrillas and the military prompted the government of Virgilio Barco to engage reluctantly in a dialogue with the insurgents, with the ultimate goal of peace. In 1988, he announced a three-phase peace plan to end the violence, to talk about needed reforms, and ultimately to reincorporate guerrillas into society. This effort came to fruition in 1991, when the guerrilla movement M-19 laid down its arms after 16 years of fighting and engaged in political dialogue. Other guerrilla groups, notably the long-lived (since 1961) Colombian Revolutionary Armed Forces (FARC) and the National Liberation Army (ELN), led by a Spanish priest, chose to remain in the field.

Numbering perhaps 10,000, the guerrillas claim that their armed insurgency is about social change; but as *The Economist* has observed, lines between revolution and crime are increasingly blurred. Guerrillas ambush army units, attack oil pipelines, engage in blackmail, and kidnap rich ranchers and foreign oil

executives for ransom. Some guerrillas are also apparently in the pay of the drug traffickers and collect a bounty for each helicopter they shoot down in the government's campaign to eradicate coca-leaf and poppy fields.

DRUGS AND DEATH

The guerrillas have a different perspective. One FARC leader asserted in an interview with the Colombian news weekly *Semana* that the guerrillas had both political and social objectives. Peace would come only if the government demilitarized large portions of the country and took action against the paramilitary organizations, some of them private and some of them supported by elements within the government. President Andrés Pastrana, who feared losing control of the country as well the credibility of his government, began to press for peace talks in January 1999 and, as a precondition to peace, agreed to demilitarize—that is, to withdraw government soldiers from a number of municipalities in southern Colombia. The United States objected that any policy of demilitarization would result in looser counter-narcotics efforts and urged a broader program to eradicate coca crops through aerial spraying. Critics of the policy claim that crop eradication plays into the hands of the guerrillas, who come to the support of the peasants who grow the coca. There is substance in the criticism, for by late 1999 FARC guerrillas controlled about 40 percent of the countryside.

FARC leaders, contrary to reports of foreign news media, disingenuously claim not to be involved in drug trafficking and have offered their own plan to counter the drug problem. It would begin with a government development plan for the peasants. In the words of a FARC leader: "Thousands of peasants need to produce and grow drugs to live, because they are not protected by the state." Eradication can succeed only if alternative crops can take the place of coca. Rice, corn, cacao, or cotton might be substituted. "Shooting the people, dropping bombs on them, dusting their sown land, killing birds and leaving their land sterile" is not the solution.

The peace talks scheduled between the government and the guerrillas in 1999 stalled and then failed, in large measure because of distrust on the part of FARC. Although a large portion of southern Colombia was demilitarized, the activities of paramilitary organizations were not curbed, and the United States sought to intensify its eradication policy. In the meantime, the Colombian Civil War entered its fourth decade.

In addition to the deaths attributed to guerrilla warfare, literally hundreds of politicians, journalists, judges, and police officers have been murdered in Colombia. It has been estimated that 10 percent of the nation's homicides are politically motivated. Murder is the major cause of death for men between ages 15 and 45. The violence resulted in 250,000 deaths in the 1990s; 300,000 people have left the country; and, since the late 1980s, 1½ million have been internally displaced or become refugees. While paramilitary violence accounts for many deaths, drug trafficking and the unraveling of Colombia's fabric of law are responsible for most. As political scientist John D. Martz writes: "Whatever the responsibility of the military or the rhetoric of government, the penetration of Colombia's social and economic life by the drug industry [is] proving progressively destructive of law, security and the integrity of the political system." Colombian political scientist Juan Gabriel Tokatlian echoed these sentiments in 2001 when he wrote: "The state is losing sovereignty and legitimacy. The left-wing guerrillas and the right-wing paramilitaries control more territory than the government."

Drug traffickers, according to *Latin American Update,* "represent a new economic class in Colombia; since 1981 'narcodollars' have been invested in real estate and large cattle ranches." The newsmagazine *Semana* noted that drug cartels had purchased 2.5 million acres of land since 1984 and now own one-twelfth of the nation's productive farmland in the Magdalena River Basin. More than 100,000 acres of forest have been cut down to grow marijuana, coca, and opium poppies. Of particular concern to environmentalists is the fact that opium poppies are usually planted in the forests of the Andes at elevations above 6,000 feet. "These forests," according to Semana, "do not have great commercial value, but their tree cover is vital to the conservation of the sources of the water supply." The cartels also bought up factories, newspapers, radio stations, shopping centers, soccer teams, and bullfighters. The emergence of Medellín as a modern city of gleaming skyscrapers and expensive cars also reflects the enormous profits of the drug business.

Political scientist Francisco Leal Buitrago argues that while trafficking in narcotics in the 1970s was economically motivated, it had evolved into a social phenomenon by the 1980s. "The traffickers represent a new social force that wants to participate like other groups—new urban groups, guerrillas and peasant movements. Like the guerrillas, they have not been able to participate politically. . . ."

HEALTH/WELFARE

Rape and other acts of violence against women are pervasive but seldom prosecuted. Spousal abuse was not considered a crime until 1996. Law 294 on family violence identifies as crimes violent acts committed within families, including spousal rape. Although the Constitution of 1991 prohibits it, discrimination against women persists in terms of access to employment and equal pay for equal work.

Domestic drug consumption has also emerged as a serious problem in Colombia's cities. *Latin American Regional Reports* notes that the increase in consumption of the Colombian form of crack, known as *bazuko,* "has prompted the growth of gangs of youths in slum areas running the bazuko business for small distributors." In Bogotá, police reported that more than 1,500 gangs operated from the city's slums.

URBANIZATION

As is the case in other Andean nations, urbanization has been rapid in Colombia. But the constantly spreading slums on the outskirts of the larger cities have not produced significant urban unrest or activism. Most of the migrants to the cities are first generation and are less frustrated and demanding than the general urban population. The new migrants perceive an improvement in their status and opportunities simply because they have moved into a more hopeful urban environment. Also, since most of the migrants are poorly paid, their focus tends to be on daily survival, not political activism.

Migrants make a significant contribution to the parallel Colombian economy. As is the case in Peru and other South American countries, the informal sector amounts to approximately 30 percent of gross domestic product.

The Roman Catholic Church in Colombia has also tended to take advantage of rapid urbanization. Depending on the

individual beliefs of local bishops, the Church has to a greater or lesser extent embraced the migrants, brought them into the Church, and created or instilled a sense of community where none existed before. The Church has generally identified with the expansion and change taking place and has played an active social role.

Marginalized city dwellers are often the targets of violence. Hired killers, called *sicarios,* have murdered hundreds of petty thieves, beggars, prostitutes, indigents, and street children. Such "clean-up" campaigns are reminiscent of the activities of the Brazilian death squads since the 1960s. An overloaded judicial system and interminable delays have contributed to Colombia's high homicide rate. According to government reports, lawbreakers have not been brought to justice in 97 to 99 percent of *reported* crimes. (Perhaps three-quarters of all crimes remain unreported to the authorities.) Increasingly, violence and murder have replaced the law as a way to settle disputes; private "justice" is now commonly resorted to for a variety of disputes.

SOCIAL CHANGE

Government has responded to calls for social change and reform. President Virgilio Barco sincerely believed that the eradication of poverty would help to eliminate guerrilla warfare and reduce the scale of violence in the countryside. Unfortunately, his policies lacked substance, and he was widely criticized for his indecisiveness.

President César Gaviria felt that political reform must precede social and economic change and was confident that Colombia's new Constitution would set the process of national reconciliation in motion. The constitutional debate generated some optimism about the future of liberal democracy in Colombia. As Christopher Abel writes, it afforded a forum for groups ordinarily denied a voice in policy formulation—"to civic and community movements in the 40 and more intermediate cities angry at the poor quality of basic public services; to indigenous movements . . . ; and to cooperatives, blacks, women, pensioners, small businesses, consumer and sports groups."

ACHIEVEMENTS

Colombia has a long tradition in the arts and humanities and has produced international figures such as the Nobel Prize–winning author Gabriel García Márquez; the painters and sculptors Alejandro Obregón, Fernando Botero, and Edgar Negret; the poet León de Greiff; and many others well known in music, art, and literature.

Violence and unrest have thwarted all of these efforts. Since the mid-1980s, according to a former Minister of Defence writing in 2000, 200 car bombs had exploded in Colombian cities, an entire democratic left of center party (the Unión Patriotica) had been eliminated by right-wing paramilitaries, and 4 presidential candidates, 200 judges and investigators, half of the supreme court justices, 1,200 police, 151 journalists, and 300,000 ordinary Colombians had been murdered.

While some scholars have described Colombia as a "failed state" others perceptively note that the focus should be on what holds the nation together in the face of unprecedented assaults. In the words of political scientist Malcolm Deas, Colombia is more united than fragmented, ethnically and religiously homogeneous, and its regional differences, while real, are not especially divisive. President Alvaro Uribe, a tough-minded pragmatist, has worked hard to restore the rule of law to Colombia. His first year in office resulted in a significant reduction in murder and kidnapping and attacks by guerrillas, as well acreage devoted to coca cultivation. Economic recovery was underway, as is indicated by the increased amount of highway traffic. Colombians, for the first time in years, felt more secure and, in 2004, 80 percent of the voting population supported Uribe. A reflection of both his popularity and success was the decision of Colombia's Congress to pass an amendment to the Constitution that would allow Uribe to run for reelection in 2006. As of March 2006 polls indicated that Uribe maintained a high approval rate of 70 percent and success at the polls was expected.

ECONOMIC POLICIES

Colombia has a mixed economy. While state enterprises control domestic participation in the coal and oil industries and play a commanding role in the provision of electricity and communications, most of the economy is dominated by private business. At this point, Colombia is a moderate oil producer. A third of the nation's legal exports comes from the coffee industry, while exports of coal, cut flowers, seafood, and other nontraditional exports have experienced significant growth. In that Colombia is not saddled with an onerous foreign debt, its economy is relatively prosperous.

Contributing to economic success is the large informal sector. Also of tremendous importance are the profits from the illegal-drug industry. *The Economist* estimated that Colombia grossed perhaps $1.5 billion in drug sales in 1987, as compared to official export earnings of

$5.5 billion. Indeed, over the past 20 years, profits from drug trafficking have grown to encompass between 25 and 35 percent of Colombia's legal exports. Perhaps half the profits are repatriated—that is, converted from dollars into local currency. An unfortunate side effect of the inflow of cash is an increase in the inflation rate.

FOREIGN POLICY

In the foreign-policy arena, President Barco's policies were attacked as low-profile, shallow, and too closely aligned to the policies of the United States. While Presidents Gaviria and Samper tried to adopt more independent foreign policy lines, especially in terms of the drug trade, Presidents Pastrana and Uribe have welcomed United States aid against drug trafficking and its attendant evils.

With an uneasy peace reigning in Central America, Colombia's focus has turned increasingly toward its neighbors and a festering territorial dispute with Venezuela over waters adjacent to the Guajira Peninsula. Colombia has proposed a multilateral solution to the problem, perhaps under the auspices of the International Court of Justice. Venezuela continues to reject a multilateral approach and seeks to limit any talks to the two countries concerned. It is likely that a sustained deterioration of internal conditions in either Venezuela or Colombia will keep the territorial dispute in the forefront. A further detriment to better relations with Venezuela is the justified Venezuelan fear that Colombian violence as a result of guerrilla activity, military sweeps, and drugs will cross the border. As it is, thousands of Colombians have fled to Venezuela to escape their violent homeland. Venezuela's president recently infuriated Colombia's

government when he independently opened negotiations with guerrillas and implied that they had more power than did President Uribe. Tensions between the two countries intensified briefly in 2008 when Colombia, following a raid into Ecuador to root out a guerrilla camp, discovered evidence that Venezuela's President Chavez apparently funded FARC.

THE CLOUDED FUTURE

Francisco Leal Buitrago, a respected Colombian academic, argues forcefully that his nation's crisis is, above all, "political": "It is the lack of public confidence in the political regime. It is not a crisis of the state itself . . . , but in the way in which the state sets the norms—the rules for participation—for the representation of public opinion. . . ."

Constitutional reforms have taken place in Colombia, but changes in theory must reflect the country's tumultuous realities. Many of those in opposition have looked for a political opening but in the meantime continue to wage an armed insurgency against the government. Other problems, besides drugs, that dog the government include corruption, violence, slow growth, high unemployment, a weak currency, inflation, and the need for major reforms in banking. To get the economy on track, the International Monetary Fund has recommended that Colombia broaden its tax base, enhance municipal tax collections, get tough on tax evasion, and reduce spending.

Endemic violence and lawlessness, the continued operation of guerrilla groups, the emergence of mini-cartels in the wake of the eclipse of drug kingpins, and the attitude of the military toward conditions in Colombia all threaten any kind of

progress. The hard-line antidrug trafficking policy of the United States adds another complicated, and possibly counterproductive, dimension to the difficult task of governing Colombia.

Timeline: PAST

1525
The first Spanish settlement at Santa Marta

1810
Independence from Spain

1822
The creation of Gran Colombia (including Venezuela, Panama, and Ecuador)

1830
Independence as a separate country

1899–1902
War of the Thousand Days

1946–1958
La Violencia; nearly 200,000 lose their lives

1957
Women's suffrage

1980s
The drug trade becomes big business

1990s
Violence hampers progress; an earthquake kills or injures thousands in central Colombia

PRESENT

2000s
Colombia's violence threatens to involve its neighbors

2006
President Uribe re-elected president

2008
Growing tensions with neighboring Venezuela and Ecuador

Ecuador (Republic of Ecuador)

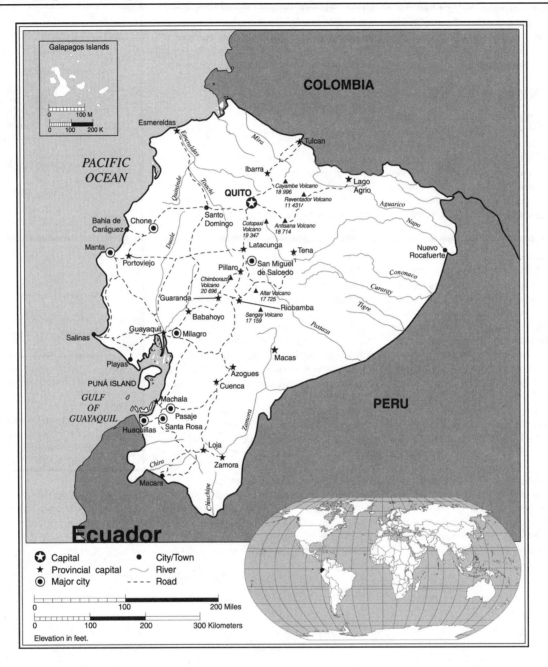

Ecuador Statistics

GEOGRAPHY

Area in Square Miles (Kilometers):
109,454 (283,560) (about the size of
Nevada)

Capital (Population): Quito (2,100,000)

Environmental Concerns: deforestation;
soil erosion; desertification; water
pollution; pollution from petroleum
wastes

Geographical Features: coastal
plain; inter-Andean central
highlands; flat to rolling eastern
jungle

Climate: varied; tropical on the coast and
in the inland jungle; cooler inland at
higher elevations

PEOPLE

Population

Total: 13,755,680 (2007 est.)

Annual Growth Rate: 1.55%

Rural/Urban Population Ratio: 40/60

Major Languages: Spanish; Quechua and
other Amerindian languages

Ethnic Makeup: 65% Mestizo;
25% Indian; 10% Spanish, black,
and others

Religions: 95% Roman Catholic;
5% indigenous and others

Health

Life Expectancy at Birth: 74 years (male);
80 years (female)

Infant Mortality Rate (Ratio):
 22.1/1,000
Physicians Available (Ratio):
 1/904

Education

Adult Literacy Rate: 91%
Compulsory (Ages): for 6 years between 6
 and 14; free

COMMUNICATION

Telephones: 1,754,000 main lines
Daily Newspaper Circulation: 72 per
 1,000 people
Cell Phones: 8,485,000
Internet Users: 1,549,000

TRANSPORTATION

Roadways in Kilometers (miles):
 43,197 (26,841)
Railroads in Kilometers (miles):
 966 (600)
Usable Airfields: 406

GOVERNMENT

Type: republic
Independence Date: May 24, 1822 (from
 Spain)
Head of State/Government: President
 Rafael Correa is both head of state and
 head of government
Political Parties: Democratic Left; Social
 Christian Party; Pachakutik; Popular
 Democratic Movement; Alianza PAIS
 Movement; Christian Democratic
 Union; Concentration of Popular
 Forces; National Action Institutional;
 Renewal Party; Rodolsist Party; others
Suffrage: universal and compulsory for
 literate people ages 18–65; optional for
 other eligible voters

MILITARY

Military Expenditures (% of GDP): 2.8%

ECONOMY

Currency ($U.S. Equivalent): 1.00
 dollar = $1

Per Capita Income/GDP: $7,100/$43.76
 billion
GDP Growth Rate: 1.8%
Inflation Rate: 2.2%
Unemployment Rate: 9.8%; significant
 underemployment
Labor Force: 4,550,000
Natural Resources: petroleum; fish;
 timber; hydropower
Agriculture: bananas; coffee; cocoa;
 rice; potatoes; manioc; plantains;
 sugarcane; livestock; balsa wood;
 fish; shrimp
Industry: petroleum; food processing;
 textiles; metalwork; paper products;
 wood products; chemicals; plastics;
 fishing; lumber
Exports: $13.3 billion (f.o.b.) (primary
 partners United States, Colombia, Italy)
Imports: $13 billion (f.o.b.) (primary
 partners United States, Colombia,
 Japan)

SUGGESTED WEB SITE

http://www.cia.gov/cia/publications/
 factbook/geos.ec.html

Ecuador Country Report

ECUADOR: A LAND OF CONTRASTS

Several of Ecuador's great novelists have had as the focus of their works the exploitation of the Indians. Jorge Icaza's classic *Huasipungo* (1934) describes the actions of a brutal landowner who first forces Indians to work on a road so that the region might be "developed" and then forces them, violently, from their plots of land so that a foreign company's operations will not be impeded by a troublesome Indian population.

That scenario, while possible in some isolated regions, is for the most part unlikely in today's Ecuador. In recent years, despite some political and economic dislocation, Ecuador has made progress in health care, literacy, human rights, freedom of the press, and representative government. Indigenous peoples have been particularly active and over the past decade have demanded cultural rights. An indigenous political party, Pachakutik, has identified with Ecuador's nonindigenous poor and won several seats in Congress. In protest against an economic program of austerity and reflecting ethnic and social conflict, several of these groups in league with midlevel army officers moved to topple President Jamil Mahuad from power in January 2000. It was South America's first successful coup in a quarter of a century. In April 2005 President Lucio Gutierrez, who was behind the coup, was himself ousted from the executive office.

He lost the support of indigenous leaders, middle-class homemakers, and students who were angry both over his inability to deliver on promises made and widespread corruption. Austerity policies have hurt the indigenous poor and Ecuador's large public debt has hamstrung social programs.

Although Ecuador is still a conservative, traditional society, it has shown an increasing concern for the plight of its rural inhabitants, including the various endangered Indian groups inhabiting the Amazonian region. The new attention showered on rural Ecuador—traditionally neglected by policymakers in Quito, the capital city—reflects in part the government's concern with patterns of internal migration. Even though rural regions have won more attention from the state, social programs continue to be implemented only sporadically.

DEVELOPMENT

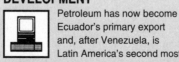

Petroleum has now become Ecuador's primary export and, after Venezuela, is Latin America's second most important supplier of oil to the United States. Throughout 2005 and 2006 oil protestors disrupted both production and delivery and demanded that oil companies invest more in the poor Amazonian communities where they operate.

Two types of migration are currently taking place: the move from the highlands to the coastal lowlands and the move from the countryside to the cities. In the early 1960s, most of Ecuador's population was concentrated in the mountainous central highlands. Today, the population is about equally divided between that area and the coast, with more than half the nation's people crowded into the cities. So striking and rapid has the population shift been that the director of the National Institute of Statistics commented that it had assumed "alarming proportions" and that the government had to develop appropriate policies if spreading urban slums were not to develop into "potential focal points for insurgency." What has emerged is a rough political parity between regions that has led to parliamentary paralysis and political crisis.

The large-scale movement of people has not rendered the population more homogenous but, because of political parity, has instead fractured the nation. Political rivalry has always characterized relations between Quito, in the sierras, and cosmopolitan Guayaquíl, on the coast. The presidential election of 1988 illustrated the distinctive styles of the country. Rodrigo Borja's victory was regionally based, in that he won wide support in Ecuador's interior provinces. Usually conservative in its politics, the interior voted for the

(United Nations photo/UN155089)

The migration of the poor to the urban areas of Ecuador has been very rapid and of great concern to the government. The increase in inner-city population can easily lead to political unrest. The graffiti in the photo says, "We don't want a dictatorship."

candidate of the Democratic Left, in part because of the extreme populist campaign waged by a former mayor of Guayaquíl, Abdalá Bucaram. Bucaram claimed to be a man of the people who was persecuted by the oligarchy. He spoke of his lower-class followers as the "humble ones," or, borrowing a phrase from former Argentine president Juan Perón, *los descamisados* ("the shirtless ones"). Bucaram, in the words of political scientist Catherine M. Conaghan, "honed a political style in the classic tradition of coastal populism. He combined promises of concrete benefits to the urban poor with a colorful anti-oligarchic style." Bucaram's style finally triumphed in 1996, when he won election to the presidency.

A similar style and message propelled the country's current president, the charismatic Rafael Correa, to power. He, like Bucaram, addressed the plight of marginalized elements of society and embraced the rhetoric of populism in his campaign. Correa conceived of himself as "morally superior" and said he was "God's envoy." While he has promised a "citizen's revolution," Correa also seeks to rewrite Ecuador's constitution with an eye to strengthening the executive office. Venezuela's Hugo Chávez and his professed "Bolivarian Revolution" are admired by Correa, although he is careful to chart an independent course for Ecuador.

EDUCATION AND HEALTH

Central to the government's policy of development is education. Twenty-nine percent of the national budget was set aside for education in the early 1980s, with increases proposed for the following years. Adult literacy improved from 74 percent in 1974 to 87 percent by 1995. In the central highlands, however, illiteracy rates of more than 35 percent are still common, largely because Quechua is the preferred language among the Indian peasants.

FREEDOM

Ecuador's media, with the exception of two government-owned radio stations, are in private hands and represent a broad range of opinion. They are often critical of government policies, but they practice a degree of self-censorship because of defamation laws whose violation carry a three-year prison term.

The government has approached this problem with an unusual sensitivity to indigenous culture. Local Quechua speakers have been enlisted to teach reading and writing in both Quechua and Spanish. This approach has won the support of Indian leaders who are closely involved

in planning local literacy programs built around indigenous values.

Health care has also shown steady improvement, but the total statistics hide sharp regional variations. Infant mortality and malnutrition are still severe problems in rural areas. In this sense, Ecuador suffers from a duality found in other Latin American nations with large Indian populations: Social and racial differences persist between the elite-dominated capitals and the Indian hinterlands. Income, services, and resources tend to be concentrated in the capital cities. Ecuador, at least, is attempting to correct the imbalance.

The profound differences between Ecuador's highland Indian and its European cultures is illustrated by the story of an Indian peasant who, when brought to a clinic, claimed that he was dying as the result of a spell. He told the doctor, trained in Western medicine, that, while traveling a path from his highland village down to a valley, he passed by a sacred place, where a witch cast a spell on him. The man began to deteriorate, convinced that this had happened. The doctor, upon examination of the patient, could find no physical reason for the man's condition. Medicine produced no improvements. The doctor finally managed to save his patient, but only after a good deal of compromise with Indian culture. "Yes," he told the peasant, "a witch has apparently cast a spell on you and you are indeed dying." And then the doctor announced: "Here is a potion that will remove the spell." The patient's recovery was rapid and complete. Thus, though modern medicine can work miracles, health-care workers must also be sensitive to cultural differences.

THE ECONOMY

Between 1998 and 2000, the Ecuadoran economy was hit hard by two crises. Falling petroleum prices in combination with the ravages of the El Niño phenomenon transformed a $598 million surplus in 1997 into a troubling $830 million deficit in 1998. Petroleum revenues fell to third place, behind exports of bananas and shrimp, which themselves were devastated

HEALTH/WELFARE

Educational and economic opportunities in Ecuador are often not made available to women, blacks, and indigenous peoples. Most of the nation's peasantry, overwhelmingly Indian or Mestizo, are poor. Infant mortality, malnutrition, and epidemic disease are common among these people.

by bad weather (in the case of shrimp, due to the dramatic warming of waters in the eastern Pacific as a result of El Niño).

President Jamil Mahuad was confronted from the outset of his administration with some daunting policy decisions. A projected growth rate for 1998 of only 1 percent and an inflation rate that soared to 40 percent resulted in budget austerity and an emergency request to Congress to cut spending and prepare legislation for the privatization of Ecuador's telecommunications and electrical industries. The privatization plans raised the ire of nationalists. In the mid-1990s, the government privatized more than 160 state-owned enterprises and, in an effort to modernize and streamline the economy, cut the number of public employees from 400,000 to 260,000.

The sharp economic downturn resulted in severe belt-tightening by the Mahuad government, threw people out of work, produced social and political upheaval, and led to a coup. The military quickly handed over power to the civilian vice president, Gustavo Noboa, to finish out Mahuad's term. Noboa took steps to restore Ecuador's economic viability and adopted some of Mahuad's unpopular policies, including "dollarization" of the economy and continued privatization of state enterprises.

Chronic political instability, which saw the removal of three presidents between 1997 and 2005, has had a negative impact on the government's ability to formulate policies and deliver needed programs on a consistent basis. One result is a continuous drumbeat of opposition from a broad range of Ecuadorans, from the indigenous peoples of the Amazon to the slums around large cities to a large sector of the middle class. The climate for foreign investment has become troublesome and attacks on oil fields and facilities have tended to negate any benefits that might have accrued from rising petroleum prices. President Correa's tighter controls on the private oil industry have put a damper on foreign investment and slowed the economy, which had grown at a rate of 5.5 percent between 2002 and 2006.

BITTER NEIGHBORS

A long legacy of boundary disputes that reached back to the wars for independence created a strained relationship between Ecuador and Peru, which erupted in violence in July 1941. Ecuador initiated an undeclared war against Peru in an attempt to win territory along its southeastern border, in the Marañón River region, and, in the southwest, around the town of Zaramilla. In the 1942 Pact of Peace, Amity, and Limits, which followed a stunning Peruvian victory, Ecuador lost about 120,000 square miles of territory. The peace accord was guaranteed by Argentina, Brazil, Chile, and the United States. In January 1995, the usual tensions that grew each year as the anniversary of the conflict approached were given foundation when fighting again broke out between Peru and Ecuador; Peruvian soldiers patrolling the region had stumbled upon well-prepared and waiting Ecuadoran soldiers. Three weeks later, with the intervention of the guarantors of the original pact, the conflict ended. The Peruvian armed forces were shaken from their smug sense of superiority over the Ecuadorans, and the Ecuadoran defense minister used the fight to support his political pretensions.

ACHIEVEMENTS

Ecuadoran poets have often made their poetry an expression of social criticism. The so-called Tzántzicos group has combined avant-garde techniques with social commitment and has won a measure of attention from literary circles.

The border war sent waves of alarm through the rest of Latin America, in that it reminded more than a dozen nations of boundary problems with their neighbors. Of particular concern were revelations made in 1998 and 1999 that individuals within the Argentine government and the military had sold arms to the Ecuadoran military during the conflict. Argentina was embarrassed because it was one of the original guarantors of the 1942 Pact of Peace.

On October 16, 1998, the Legislatures of Ecuador and Peru supported an agreement worked out by other governments in the region to end the border dispute. Under the terms of the agreement, Peru's sovereignty of the vast majority of the contested territory was affirmed. Ecuador won a major concession when it was granted navigation rights on the Amazon River and its tributaries within Peru and the right to establish trading centers on the river. In that both parties benefited from the negotiation, it is hoped that a lasting peace will have been effected.

Relation between Ecuador and Colombia deteriorated in 2008. Colombian troops crossed the border and attacked a guerrilla camp used by FARC (Colombian guerrillas). More broadly, Ecuador has demanded that the United States close its large airbase at Manta, which is used for drug surveillance flights.

Timeline: PAST

1528
First Spanish contact

1822
Ecuador is part of Gran Colombia (with Panama, Venezuela, and Colombia); independence as a separate state

1929
Women's suffrage

1941
A border war with Peru

1990s
Modernization laws aim to speed the privatization of the economy
Popular dissatisfaction with the government's handling of the economy rises

PRESENT

2000s
El Niño devastates the coastal economy; refugees and drug activity spill into Ecuador from Colombia

2006
Rafael Correa elected president

2007
Constituent Assembly begins to re-write Ecuador's constitution

Guyana (Cooperative Republic of Guyana)

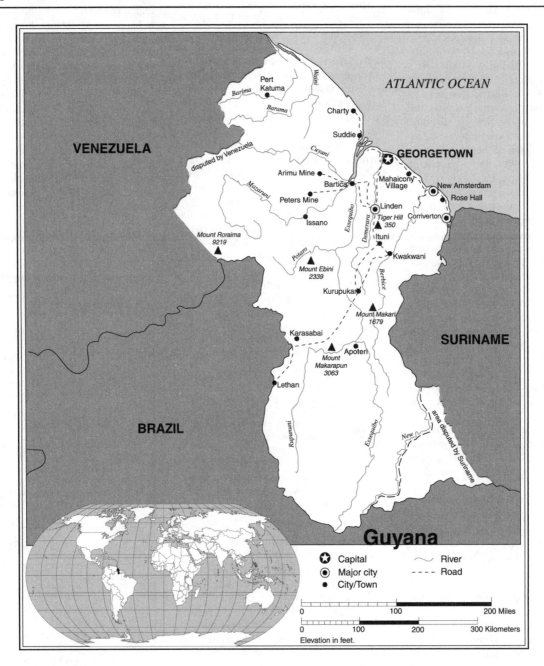

Guyana Statistics

GEOGRAPHY

Area in Square Miles (Kilometers): 82,990
(215,000) (about the size of Idaho)
Capital (Population): Georgetown
(250,000)
Environmental Concerns: water pollution;
deforestation
Geographical Features: mostly rolling
highlands; low coastal plain; savannah
in the south
Climate: tropical

PEOPLE*

Population

Total: 769,095 (2007 est.)
Annual Growth Rate: 0.23%
Rural/Urban Population Ratio:
74/36
Major Languages: English; indigenous
dialects; Creole; Hindi; Urdu
Ethnic Makeup: 51% East Indian, 30%
black; 14% mixed; 4% Amerindian;
2% white and Chinese

Religions: 50% Christian; 33% Hindu;
9% Muslim; 8% others

Health

Life Expectancy at Birth: 63 years (male);
69 years (female)
Infant Mortality Rate (Ratio): 31.35/1,000
Physicians Available (Ratio): 1/3,000

Education

Adult Literacy Rate: 98.9%
Compulsory (Ages): 6–14; free

92

COMMUNICATION

Telephones: 110,000 main lines
Daily Newspaper Circulation: 97 per
 1,000 people
Cell Phones: 281,400
Internet Users: 160,000

TRANSPORTATION

Roadways in Kilometers (miles): 4,949
 (7,970)
Usable Airfields: 93

GOVERNMENT

Type: republic
Independence Date: May 26, 1966 (from
 the United Kingdom)
Head of State/Government: President
 Bharrat Jagdeo; Prime Minister
 Samuel Hinds

Political Parties: People's National
 Congress; People's Progressive Party;
 Alliance for Change; others
Suffrage: universal at 18

MILITARY

Military Expenditures (% of GDP): 1.8%
Current Disputes: territorial disputes with
 Venezuela and Suriname

ECONOMY

Currency ($U.S. Equivalent): 203.7
 Guyanese dollars = $1
Per Capita Income/GDP: $5,300/$896.8
 million
GDP Growth Rate: 4.5%
Inflation Rate: 10.4%
Unemployment Rate: 9% (Official-likely
 higher)

Natural Resources: bauxite; gold;
 diamonds; hardwood timber; shrimp;
 fish
Agriculture: sugar; rice; wheat; vegetable
 oils; livestock; potential for fishing and
 forestry
Industry: bauxite; sugar; rice milling;
 timber; fishing; textiles; gold mining
Exports: $499.4 million (f.o.b.) (primary
 partners United States, Canada, United
 Kingdom)
Imports: $835.8 million (f.o.b.) (primary
 partners United States, Trinidad and
 Tobago, Netherland Antilles)

SUGGESTED WEB SITE

http://www.cia.gov/cia/publications/
 factbook/geos/gy.html

---

*Note: Estimates explicitly take into account the
effects of excess mortality due to AIDS.

Guyana Country Report

GUYANA: RACIAL AND ETHNIC TENSIONS

Christopher Columbus, who cruised along what are now Guyana's shores in 1498, named the region *Guiana*. The first European settlers were the Dutch, who settled in Guyana late in the sixteenth century, after they had been ousted from Brazil by a resurgent Portuguese Crown. Dutch control ended in 1796, when the British gained control of the area. In 1815, as part of the treaty arrangements that brought the Napoleonic Wars to a close, the Dutch colonies of Essequibo, Demerera, and Berbice were officially ceded to the British. In 1831, the former Dutch colonies were consolidated as the Crown Colony of British Guiana.

DEVELOPMENT

Moderate economic growth continued into 2007. In 2007, the Inter-American Development Bank canceled Guyana's $470 million debt, an amount equivalent to 48 percent of GDP. Development is hindered by a shortage of skilled labor and a woefully inadequate infrastructure. Trade negotiations were continued with China on an accelerated basis.

Guyana is a society deeply divided along racial and ethnic lines. East Indians make up the majority of the population. They predominate in rural areas, constituting the bulk of the labor force on the sugar

plantations, and they comprise nearly all of the rice-growing peasantry. They also dominate local businesses and are prominent in the professions. Blacks are concentrated in urban areas, where they are employed in clerical and secretarial positions in the public bureaucracy, in teaching, and in semiprofessional jobs. A black elite dominates the state bureaucratic structure.

Before Guyana's independence in 1966, plantation owners, large merchants, and British colonial administrators consciously favored some ethnic groups over others, providing them with a variety of economic and political advantages. The regime of President Forbes Burnham revived old patterns of discrimination for political gain.

Burnham, after ousting the old elite when he nationalized the sugar plantations and the bauxite mines, built a new regime that simultaneously catered to lower-class blacks and discriminated against East Indians. In an attempt to address the blacks' basic human needs, the Burnham

FREEDOM

One of the priorities of the Jagan governments was the elimination of all forms of ethnic and racial discrimination, a difficult task in a country where political parties are organized along racial lines. It was hoped that Guyana's indigenous peoples would be offered accelerated development programs to enhance their health and welfare.

government greatly expanded the number of blacks holding positions in public administration. To demonstrate his largely contrived black-power ideology, Burnham spoke out strongly in support of African liberation movements. The government played to the fear of communal strife in order to justify its increasingly authoritarian rule.

In the mid-1970s, a faltering economy and political mismanagement generated an increasing opposition to Burnham that cut across ethnic lines. The government increased the size of the military, packed Parliament through rigged elections, and amended the Constitution so that the president held virtually imperial power.

There has been some improvement since Burnham's death in 1985. The appearance of newspapers other than the government-controlled *Guyana Chronicle* and the public's dramatically increased access to television have served to curtail official control of the media. In politics, the election of Indo-Guyanese leader

HEALTH/WELFARE

The government has initiated policies designed to lower the cost of living for Guyanese. Prices for essentials have been cut. Money has been allocated for school lunch programs and for a "food-for-work" plan. Pensions have been raised for the first time in years. The minimum wage, however, will not sustain an average family.

Cheddi Jagan to the presidency reflected deep-seated disfavor with the behavior and economic policies of the previous government of Desmond Hoyte. President Jagan identified the nation's foreign debt of $2 billion as a "colossally big problem, because the debt overhang impedes human development."

While president, Hoyte once pledged to continue the socialist policies of the late Forbes Burnham; but in the same breath, he talked about the need for privatization of the crucial sugar and bauxite industries. Jagan's economic policies, according to *Latin American Regional Reports,* outlined an uncertain course. During his campaign, Jagan stated that government should not be involved in sectors of the economy where private or cooperative ownership would be more efficient. In 1993, however, he backed away from the sale of the Guyana Electric Company and had some doubts about selling off the sugar industry. In Jagan's words:

ACHIEVEMENTS

The American Historical Association selected Walter Rodney for the 1982 Beveridge Award for his study of the Guyanese working people. The award is for the best book in English on the history of the United States, Canada, or Latin America. Rodney, the leader of the Working People's Alliance, was assassinated in 1980.

"Privatization and divestment must be approached with due care. I was not elected president to preside over the liquidation of Guyana. I was mandated by the Guyanese people to rebuild the national economy and to restore a decent standard of living." Jagan's policies stimulated rapid socio-economic progress as Guyana embarked on the road to economic recovery.

Following Jagan's death, new elections were held in December 1997, and Janet Jagan, the ex-president's 77-year-old widow, was named president. In August 1999, she stepped down due to health reasons. She named Finance Minister Bharrat Jagdeo to succeed her.

Jagdeo's presidency has pushed infrastructure development and has promoted universal primary education. A five-year plan (2003–2007) promised to bring schools to the interior where educational opportunities have been minimal or nonexistent. He has also worked towards reducing the racial and ethnic enmity that has plagued the nation. Still, the Afro-Guyanese, who represent less than half of Guyana's population, tend to support the opposition People's National Congress party, which had held power from 1964 to 1992, and have responded to their lack of power by confronting the government on its policies, sometimes violently.

In the meantime, a divided Guyana may soon be confronted by an aggressive Venezuela, whose president seems intent on reigniting its long-standing border dispute with Guyana. With respect to rival offshore

Timeline: PAST

1616
The first permanent Dutch settlements on Essequibo River

1815
The Netherlands cedes the territory to Britain

1966
Independence

1985
President Forbes Burnham dies

1990s
The government promises to end racial and ethnic discrimination

PRESENT

2000s
Territorial disputes with Suriname and Venezuela persist

Politics remains bitterly divided along ethnic lines

2006
Disastrous floods caused by high rainfall severely damage coastal agriculture

Jagdeo re-elected president

territorial claims between Guyana and Suriname, a UN tribunal has been established to settle the issue. The problem is particularly contentious because of the oil-producing potential of the disputed area.

Paraguay (Republic of Paraguay)

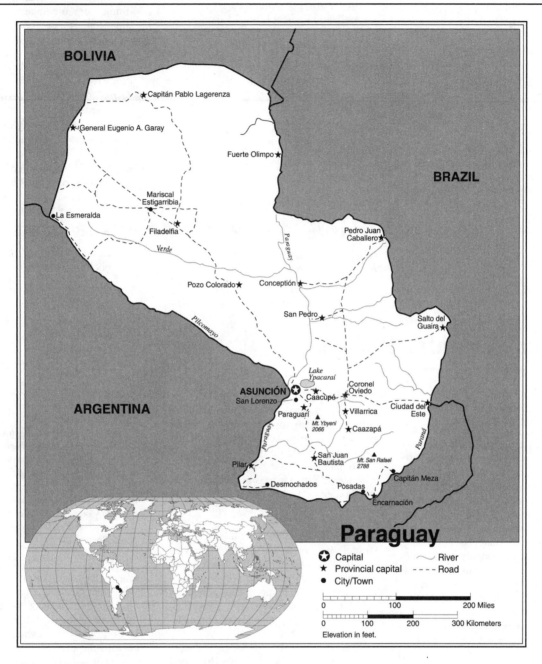

Paraguay Statistics

GEOGRAPHY

Area in Square Miles (Kilometers):
157,048 (406,752) (about the size of
California)

Capital (Population): Asunción 1,212,112

Environmental Concerns: deforestation;
water pollution; problems with waste
disposal

Geographical Features: grassy plains and
wooded hills east of Rio Paraguay;
Gran Chaco region west of the river;
mostly marshy plain near the river; dry
forest and thorny scrub elsewhere

Climate: subtropical to temperate

PEOPLE

Population

Total: 6,669,086 (2007 est.)
Annual Growth Rate: 2.42%
Rural/Urban Population Ratio: 47/53

Major Languages: Spanish; Guaraní;
Portuguese

Ethnic Makeup: 95% Mestizo; 5% white
and Indian

Religions: 90% Roman Catholic;
10% Protestant

Health

Life Expectancy at Birth: 73 years (male);
78 years (female)

Infant Mortality Rate (Ratio): 26.45/1,000

Physicians Available (Ratio): 1/1,406

Education

Adult Literacy Rate: 94%
Compulsory (Ages): 6–12

COMMUNICATION

Telephones: 331,000 main lines
Daily Newspaper Circulation: 40 per 1,000 people
Cell Phones: 3,233,000
Internet Users: 260,000

TRANSPORTATION

Highways in Kilometers (miles): 18,320 (29,500)
Railroads in Kilometers (miles): 36 (22)
Usable Airfields: 838

GOVERNMENT

Type: republic
Independence Date: May 14, 1811 (from Spain)

Head of State/Government: President Fernando Lugo is both head of state and head of government
Political Parties: Colorado Party; Authentic Radical Liberal Party; National Union Movement of Ethical Citizens; Beloved Country
Suffrage: universal and compulsory from 18 to 75

MILITARY

Military Expenditures (% of GDP): 1%
Current Disputes: none

ECONOMY

Currency ($U.S. Equivalent): 4,717 guaranis = $1
Per Capita Income/GDP: $4,000/$8.258 billion
GDP Growth Rate: 4%
Inflation Rate: 8.6%

Unemployment rate: 15.9%
Labor Force: 2,757,000
Natural Resources: hydropower; timber; iron ore; manganese; limestone
Agriculture: cotton; sugarcane; soybeans; corn; wheat; tobacco; cassava (tapioca); fruits; vegetables; livestock; timber
Industry: sugar; cement; textiles; beverages; wood products
Exports: $6.71 billion(f.o.b.) (primary partners Brazil, Argentina, European Union)
Imports: $7.56 billion (f.o.b.) (primary partners Brazil, United States, Argentina)

SUGGESTED WEB SITE

http://www.cia.gov/cia/publications/factbook/index.html

Paraguay Country Report

PARAGUAY

Paraguay is a country of paradox. Although there is little threat of foreign invasion and guerrilla activity is insignificant, a state of siege was in effect for 35 years, ending only in 1989 with the ouster of President (General) Alfredo Stroessner, who had held the reins of power since 1954. Government expenditures on health care in Paraguay are among the lowest in the Western Hemisphere, yet life expectancy is impressive, and infant mortality reportedly has fallen to levels comparable to more advanced developing countries. On the other hand, nearly a third of all reported deaths are of children under five years of age. Educational achievement, especially in rural areas, is low.

Paraguayan politics, economic development, society, and even its statistical base

are comprehensible only within the context of its geography and Indo–Hispanic culture. Its geographic isolation in the midst of powerful neighbors has encouraged Paraguay's tradition of militarism and self-reliance—of being led by strongmen who tolerate little opposition. There is no tradition of constitutional government or liberal democratic procedures upon which to draw. Social values influence politics to the extent that politics is an all-or-nothing struggle for power and its accompanying prestige and access to wealth. These political values, in combination with a population that is largely poor and politically ignorant, contribute to the type of paternalistic, personal rule characteristic of a dictator such as Stroessner.

The paradoxical behavior of the Acuerdo Nacional—a block of opposition parties under Stroessner—was understandable within the context of a quest for power, or at least a share of power. Stroessner, always eager to divide and conquer, identified the Acuerdo Nacional as a fruitful field for new alliances. Leaping at the chance for patronage positions but anxious to demonstrate to Stroessner that they were a credible political force worthy of becoming allies, Acuerdo members tried to win the support of unions and the peasantry. At the same time, the party purged its youth wing of leftist influences.

Just when it seemed certain that Stroessner would rule until his death,

Paraguayans were surprised in February 1989 when General Andrés Rodríguez—second-in-command of the armed forces, a member of the Traditionalist faction of the Colorado Party, which was in disfavor with the president, and a relative of Stroessner—seized power. Rodríguez's postcoup statements promised the democratization of Paraguay, respect for human rights, repudiation of drug trafficking, and the scheduling of presidential elections. Not surprisingly, General Rodríguez emerged as President Rodríguez. When asked about voting irregularities, Rodríguez indicated that "real" democracy would begin with elections in 1993 and that his rule was a necessary "transition."

"Real" democracy, following the 1993 victory of President Juan Carlos Wasmosy, had a distinct Paraguayan flavor. Wasmosy won the election with 40 percent of the vote; and the Colorado Party, which won most of

HEALTH/WELFARE

The Paraguayan government spends very little on human services and welfare. As a result, its population is plagued by health problems—including poor levels of nutrition, lack of drinkable water, absence of sanitation, and a prevalence of fatal childhood diseases.

the seats in Congress, was badly divided. When an opposition victory seemed possible, the military persuaded the outgoing government to push through legislation to reorganize the armed forces. In effect, they were made autonomous.

Political turmoil has continued to characterize Paraguayan politics. Assassination, an attempted coup in 2000, endemic corruption and back room deals are stock in trade. The 2003 victory of President Nicanor Duarte Frutos continued the Colorado's half-century lock on political power.

The problems he faced were serious. Corruption, counterfeiting, contraband, money laundering, and organized crime are entrenched. Despite campaign promises that "there will be no place for people who believe the party and state are there to be abused to the detriment of the country," few Paraguayans expected change. There were other issues that clouded the future. The commercialization of agriculture and high population growth led to a dramatic increase in the number of landless families who have begun to migrate to urban areas where they resettle in shanty towns. Poverty effects nearly 60 percent of the population.

The Colorados failed to resolve Paraguay's basic social problems and, for the first time in 62 years, were voted out of power in 2008. The new president, Fernando Lugo, is a former Roman Catholic bishop and a populist with socialist views. But he eschews comparisons with other populist leaders in the region. As he stated: "Chávez (president of Venezuela) is a soldier, I am a holy man. Evo (Evo Morales, president of Bolivia) is an Indian, I am not an Indian. Correa (president of Ecuador) is an intellectual, I am not an intellectual. I am simply an individual who feels for the people, feels their pain, their hopes."

ACHIEVEMENTS

Paraguay has produced several notable authors, including Gabriel Casaccia and Augusto Roa Bastos. Roa Bastos makes extensive use of religious symbolism in his novels as a means of establishing true humanity and justice.

THE ECONOMY

It is difficult to acquire accurate statistics about the Paraguayan economy, in part because of the large informal sector and in part because of large-scale smuggling and drug trafficking. It is estimated that 20 percent of the nation's economy has been driven by illicit cross-border trafficking and that almost all of Paraguay's tobacco exports are illicit, counterfeit, or both. President Lugo intends to renegotiate Paraguay's contracts for power generated by the Itaipú hydroelectric dam that straddles the border with Brazil. Although both countries equally share the electrical output, Paraguay uses only 7 percent and sells the remainder to Brazil at a fixed price that is currently 20 times less than the market rate. A better price would significantly aid Paraguay's economy. There is also concern about the "Brazilianization" of the eastern part of Paraguay, which has developed to the point at which Portuguese is heard as frequently as Spanish or Guaraní, the most common Indian language.

Timeline: PAST

1537
The Spanish found Asunción

1811
Independence is declared

1865–1870
War against the "Triple Alliance": Argentina, Brazil, and Uruguay

1954
General Alfredo Stroessner begins his rule

1961
Women win the vote

1989
Stroessner is ousted in a coup

1990s
A new Constitution is promulgated

PRESENT

2000s
Attempted coup in 2000

Peru (Republic of Peru)

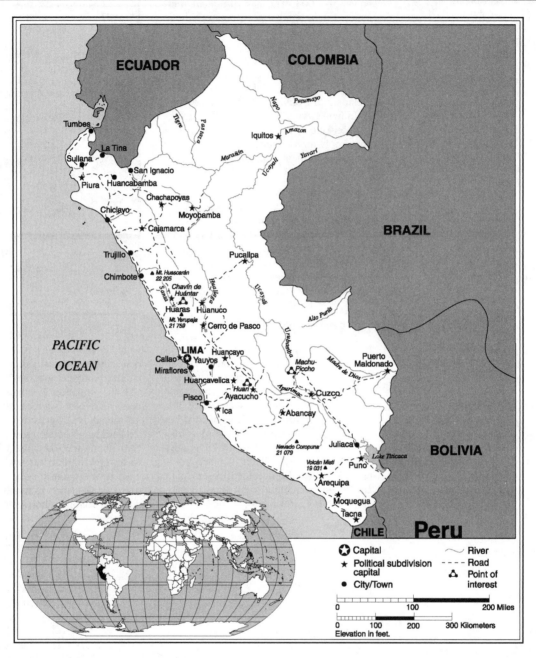

Peru Statistics

GEOGRAPHY

Area in Square Miles (Kilometers):
496,087 (1,285,200) (about the size of Alaska)
Capital (Population): Lima 7,819,436
Environmental Concerns: deforestation; overgrazing; soil erosion; desertification; air and water pollution
Geographical Features: western coastal plain; high and rugged Andes Mountains in the center; eastern lowland jungle of Amazon Basin
Climate: temperate to tropical

PEOPLE

Population

Total: 28,674,757 (2007 est.)
Annual Growth Rate: 1.29%
Rural/Urban Population Ratio: 29/71

Major Languages: Spanish; Quechua; Aymara
Ethnic Makeup: 45% Indian; 37% Mestizo; 15% white, and others
Religions: 81% Roman Catholic; 16.3% unspecified or none

Health

Life Expectancy at Birth: 68 years (male); 72 years (female)
Infant Mortality Rate (Ratio): 30/1,000
Physicians Available (Ratio): 1/1,116

98

Education

Adult Literacy Rate: 87.7%
Compulsory (Ages): 6–11; free

COMMUNICATION

Telephones: 2,332,000 main lines
Daily Newspaper Circulation: 86 per
 1,000 people
Cell Phones: 8,500,000
Internet Users: 6,100,000

TRANSPORTATION

Roadways in Kilometers (miles): 78,829
 (48,982)
Railroads in Kilometers (miles): 1989
 (1236)
Usable Airfields: 237

GOVERNMENT

Type: republic
Independence Date: July 28, 1821 (from
 Spain)

Head of State/Government: President
 Alan Garcia is both head of state and
 head of government
Political Parties: Union for Peru;
 Peruvian Aprista Party; National
 Unity (coalition); Alliance for the
 Future (coalition); Centrist Front; Peru
 Possible; Peruvian Nationalist Party;
 others
Suffrage: universal at 18

MILITARY

Military Expenditures (% of GDP): 1.5%
Current Disputes: a boundary dispute
 with Ecuador was resolved in 1999

ECONOMY

Currency ($U.S. Equivalent): 2.9 New
 Sols = $1
Per Capita Income/GDP: 7,600/$84.54
 billion
GDP Real Growth Rate: 7.5%
Inflation Rate: 3.5%

Unemployment Rate: 7.4% (Lima);
 extensive underemployment
Labor Force: 9,419,000
Natural Resources: copper; silver; gold;
 petroleum; timber; fish; iron ore; coal;
 phosphate; potash
Agriculture: coffee; sugarcane; rice;
 wheat; potatoes; plantains; coca;
 livestock; wool; fish
Industry: mining; petroleum; fishing;
 textiles and clothing; food processing;
 cement; auto assembly; steel;
 shipbuilding; metal fabrication
Exports: $27.14 billion(f.o.b.) (primary
 partners United States, Japan, China)
Imports: $18.75 billion(f.o.b.) (primary
 partners United States, Colombia,
 Venezuela)

SUGGESTED WEB SITE

http://www.cia.org/cia/publications/
 factbook/index.html

Peru Country Report

PERU: HEIR TO THE INCAS

The culture of Peru, from pre-Hispanic days to the present, has in many ways reflected the nation's variegated geography and climate. While 55 percent of the nation is covered with jungle, coastal Peru boasts one of the world's driest deserts. Despite its forbidding character, irrigation of the desert is made possible by run-offs from the Andes. This allows for the growing of a variety of crops in fertile oases that comprise about 5.5 percent of the land area.

Similarly, in the highlands, or *sierra,* there is little land available for cultivation. Because of the difficulty of the terrain, only about 7 percent of the land can produce crops. Indeed, Peru contains the lowest per capita amount of arable land in South America. The lack of fertile land has had—and continues to have—profound social and political repercussions, especially in the southern highlands near the city of Ayacucho.

THE SUPREMACY OF LIMA

Historically, coastal Peru and its capital city of Lima have attempted to dominate the sierra—politically, economically, and, at times, culturally. Long a bureaucratic and political center, in the twentieth century Lima presided over the economic expansion of the coast. Economic opportunity in

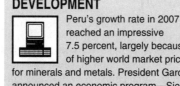

DEVELOPMENT

Peru's growth rate in 2007 reached an impressive 7.5 percent, largely because of higher world market prices for minerals and metals. President Garcia announced an economic program—Sierra Exportadora—to stimulate economic growth in Peru's central and southern highlands. Economic growth in these regions would help to stem the flow of sierra dwellers to urban areas.

combination with severe population pressure in the sierra caused Lima and its port of Callao to grow tremendously in population, if not in services.

Ironically, the capital city has one of the worst climates for dense human settlement. Thermal inversions are common; between May and September, they produce a cloud ceiling and a pervasive cool fog.

Middle- and upper-class city dwellers have always been ignorant of the people of the highlands. Very few know either Quechua or Aymara, the Indian languages spoken daily by millions of Peruvians. Yet this ignorance of the languages—and, by extension, of the cultures—has not prevented government planners or well-meaning intellectuals from trying to impose a variety of developmental models on the inhabitants of the sierra. In the late

nineteenth century, for example, modernizers known collectively in Latin America as Positivists sought in vain to transform indigenous cultures by Europeanizing them. Other reformers sought to identify with the indigenous peoples. In the 1920s, a young intellectual named Victor Raúl Haya de la Torre fashioned a political ideology called APRISMO, which embraced the idea of an alliance of Indoamerica to recover the American states for their original inhabitants. While his broader vision proved to be too idealistic, the specific reforms he recommended for Peru were put into effect by reform-minded governments in the 1960s and 1970s. Sadly, reform continued to be developed and imposed from Lima, without an understanding of the rationale behind existing agrarian systems or an appreciation of a peasant logic that was based not on production of a surplus but on attaining a satisfying level of well-being. Much of the turmoil in rural Peru today stems from the agrarian reform of 1968–1979.

AGRARIAN REFORM

From the mid-1950s, rural laborers in the central and southern highlands and on the coastal plantations demonstrated an increasingly insistent desire for agrarian reform. Peasant communities in the sierra staged a series of land invasions and challenged the domination of the large estate, or *hacienda,* from outside. Simultaneously, tenants living on the estates pressured the hacienda system from within. In both cases, peasants wanted land.

The Peruvian government responded with both the carrot and the stick. A military regime, on the one hand, tried to crush peasant insurgency in 1962 and, on the other, passed agrarian reform legislation. The laws had no practical effect, but they did give legal recognition to the problem of land reform. In the face of continued peasant unrest in the south, the military enacted more substantial land laws in 1963, confiscating some property and redistributing it to peasants. The trend toward reform continued with the election of Francisco Belaunde Terry as president of a civilian government.

FREEDOM

President Garcia has initiated a tough anti-drug trafficker program and has incarcerated two dozen members of the Tijuana drug cartel who were responsible for overseeing shipments of cocaine to the United States through Mexico. Fears of drug-related violence were intensified following the assassination of a judge who was trying people associated with the Tijuana cartel.

In the face of continued peasant militancy, Belaunde promised far-ranging reforms, but a hostile Congress refused to provide sufficient funds to implement the proposed reforms. Peasant unrest increased, and the government feared the development of widespread rural guerrilla warfare.

Against this backdrop of rural violence, the Peruvian military again seized power in 1968. To the astonishment of most observers, the military chose not to crush popular unrest but, rather, to embrace reforms. Clearly, the military had become sensitive to the political, social, and economic inequalities in Peru that had bred unrest. The military was intent on revolutionizing Peru from the top down rather than waiting for revolution from below.

In addition to land reform, the military placed new emphasis on Peru's Indian heritage. Tupac Amaru, an Incan who had rebelled against Spanish rule in 1780–1781, became a national symbol. In 1975, Quechua, the ancient language of the Inca, became Peru's second official language (along with Spanish). School curricula were revised and approached Peru's Indian heritage in a new and positive light.

NATIONALIZATION AND INTEGRATION

Behind the reforms, which were extended to industry and commerce and included the nationalization of foreign enterprises, lay the military's desire to provide for Peru a stable social and political order. The military leaders felt that they could provide better leadership in the quest for national integration and economic development than could "inefficient" civilians. Their ultimate goal was to construct a new society based on citizen participation at all levels.

As is so often the case, however, the reform model was not based on the realities of the society. It was naively assumed by planners that the Indians of the sierra were primitive socialists and wanted collectivized ownership of the land. In reality, each family's interests tended to make it competitive, rather than cooperative, with every other peasant family. Collectivization in the highlands failed because peasant communities outside the old hacienda structure clamored for the return of traditional lands that had been taken from them over the years. The Peruvian government found itself, awkwardly, attempting to defend the integrity of the newly reformed units from peasants who wanted their own land.

THE PATRON

Further difficulties were caused by the disruption of the patron–client relationship in the more traditional parts of the sierra. Hacienda owners, although members of the ruling elite, often enjoyed a tight bond with their tenants. Rather than a boss–worker relationship, the patron–client tie came close to kinship. Hacienda owners, for example, were often godparents to the children of their workers. A certain reciprocity was expected and given. But with the departure of the hacienda owners, a host of government bureaucrats arrived on the scene, most of whom had been trained on the coast and were ignorant of the customs and languages of the sierra. The peasants who benefited from the agrarian reform looked upon the administrators with a good deal of suspicion. The agrarian laws and decrees, which were all written in Spanish, proved impossible for the peasants to understand. Not surprisingly, fewer than half of the sierra peasants chose to join the collectives; and in a few places, peasants actually asked for the return of the hacienda owner, someone to whom they could relate. On the coast, the cooperatives did not benefit all agricultural workers equally, since permanent workers won the largest share of the benefits. In sum, the reforms had little impact on existing trends in

agricultural production, failed to reverse income inequalities within the peasant population, and did not ease poverty.

The shortcomings of the reforms—in combination with drought, subsequent crop failures, rising food prices, and population pressure—created very difficult and tense situations in the sierra. The infant mortality rate rose 35 percent between 1978 and 1980, and caloric intake dropped well below the recommended minimum. More than half of the children under age six suffered from some form of malnutrition. Rural unrest continued.

RETURN TO CIVILIAN RULE

Unable to solve Peru's problems and torn by divisions within its ranks, the military stepped aside in 1980, and Belaunde was again elected as Peru's constitutional president. Despite the transition to civilian government, unrest continued in the highlands, and the appearance of a left-wing guerrilla organization known as Sendero Luminoso ("Shining Path") led the government to declare repeated states of emergency and to lift civil guarantees.

In an attempt to control the situation, the Ministry of Agriculture won the power to restructure and, in some cases, to liquidate the cooperatives and collectives established by the agrarian reform. Land was divided into small individual plots and given to the peasants. Because the plots can be bought, sold, and mortgaged, some critics argue that the undoing of the reform may hasten the return of most of the land into the hands of a new landed elite.

HEALTH/WELFARE

Peru's poor and the unemployed expect President Toledo to adopt policies that will stimulate the economy in ways that will generate employment and provide the revenue necessary for health care, social programs, and education.

Civilian rule, however, has not necessarily meant democratic rule for Peru's citizens. This helps to explain the spread of Sendero Luminoso despite its radical strategy and tactics of violence. By 1992, according to Diego García-Sayán, the executive director of the Andean Commission of Jurists, the Sendero Luminoso controlled "many parts of Peruvian territory. Through its sabotage, political assassinations, and terrorist actions, Sendero Luminoso has helped to make political violence, which used to be rather infrequent, one of the main characteristics of Peruvian society."

Machu Picchu, a famous Inca ruin, stands atop a 6,750-foot mountain in the Peruvian Andes.

Violence was not confined to the guerrillas of Sendero Luminoso or of the Tupac Amaru Revolutionary Movement (MRTA). Economist Javier Iguíñiz, of the Catholic University of Lima, argued that a solution to the violence required an understanding that it flowed from disparate, autonomous, and competing sources, including guerrillas, right-wing paramilitary groups, the Peruvian military and police forces, and cocaine traffickers, "particularly the well-armed Colombians active in the Huallaga Valley." Sendero Luminoso, until recently, was also active in the Huallaga Valley and profited from taxing drug traffickers. Raúl González, of Lima's Center for Development Studies, observed that as both the drug traffickers and the guerrillas "operate[d] outside the law, there has evolved a relationship of mutual convenience in certain parts of Huallaga to combat their common enemy, the state."

President Alan García vacillated on a policy toward the Sendero Luminoso insurgency. But ultimately, he authorized the launching of a major military offensive against Sendero Luminoso bases thought to be linked to drug trafficking. Later,

determined to confront an insurgency that claimed 69,000 victims, President Alberto Fujimori armed rural farmers, known as *rondas campesinas,* to fight off guerrilla incursions. (The arming of peasants is not new to Peru; it is a practice that dates to the colonial period.) Critics correctly feared that the accelerated war against insurgents and drug traffickers would only strengthen the Peruvian military's political power.

A BUREAUCRATIC REVOLUTION?

Peruvian author Hernando DeSoto's best-selling and controversial book *The Other Path* (as opposed to Sendero Luminoso, or Shining Path), argues convincingly that both left- and right-wing governments in Latin America in general and in Peru in particular are neo-mercantile—that is, both intervene in the economy and promote the expansion of state activities. "Both strengthened the role of the government's bureaucracy until they made it the main obstacle, rather than the main incentive, to progress, and together they produced, without consulting the electorate,

almost 99 percent of the laws governing us." There are differences between left- and right-wing approaches: The left governs with an eye to redistributing wealth and well-being to the neediest groups, and the right tends to govern to serve foreign investors or national business interests. "Both, however, will do so with bad laws which explicitly benefit some and harm others. Although their aims may seem to differ, the result is that in Peru one wins or loses by political decisions. Of course, there is a big difference between a fox and a wolf but, for the rabbit, it is the similarity that counts."

DeSoto attacked the bureaucracy head-on when his private research center, the Institute for Liberty and Democracy, drafted legislation to abolish a collection of requirements built on the assumption that citizens are liars until proven otherwise. The law, which took effect in April 1989, reflected a growing rebellion against bureaucracy in Peru. Another law, which took effect in October 1989, radically simplified the process of gaining title to land. (DeSoto discovered that, to purchase a parcel of state-owned land in Peru, one had to invest 56 months of effort and 207 visits to 48 different offices). The legislation will have an important impact on the slum dwellers of Lima, for it will take much less time to regularize land titles as the result of invasions and seizures. Slum dwellers with land titles, according to DeSoto, invest in home improvements at a rate nine times greater than that of slum dwellers without titles. Slum dwellers who own property will be less inclined to turn to violent solutions to their problems.

The debureaucratization campaign has been paralleled by grassroots social movements that grew in response to a state that no longer could or would respond to the needs of its citizenry. Cataline Romero, director of the Bartolome de Las Cases Institute of Lima, said that "grass-roots social movements have blossomed into political participants that allow historically marginalized people to feel a sense of their own dignity and rights as citizens." Poor people have developed different strategies for survival as the government has failed to meet even their most basic needs. Most have entered the informal sector and have learned to work together through the formation of unions, mothers' clubs, and cooperatives. Concluded Romero: "As crisis tears institutions down, these communities are preparing the ground for building new institutions that are more responsive to the needs of the majority." DeSoto concurs and adds: "No one has ever considered that most poor Peruvians are a step ahead of the revolutionaries and are already changing the country's structures, and what politicians should be doing is guiding the change and giving it an appropriate institutional framework so that it can be properly used and governed."

By 2006 the advances made by the poor in the environs of the large cities was increasingly reflected in the sierras as well. Rolando Arellano, president of a large Peruvian marketing firm, noted: "Being called *serrano* is no longer an insult. That is a very important social change. . . . It is a vindication of the sierra tradition." Indeed, what is happening in Peru mirrors what is happening in indigenous communities in Ecuador and Bolivia. Formerly marginalized people have become a political, economic, and consumer force and now have the power to influence decisively elections at the national level.

DEMOCRACY AND THE "SELF-COUP"

In April 1992, President Fujimori, increasingly isolated and unable to effect economic and political reforms, suspended the Constitution, arrested a number of opposition leaders, shut down Congress, and openly challenged the power of the judiciary. The military, Fujimori's staunch ally, openly supported the *autogolpe,* or "self-coup," as did business leaders and about 80 percent of the Peruvian people. In the words of political scientist Cynthia McClintock, writing in *Current History,* "Fujimori emerged a new caudillo, destroying the conventional wisdom that institutions, whether civilian or military, had become more important than individual leaders in Peru and elsewhere in Latin America." In 1993, a constitutional amendment allowed Fujimori to run for a second consecutive term.

In April 1995, Fujimori won a comfortable victory, with 64 percent of the vote. This was attributable to his successful economic policies, which saw the Peruvian economy grow by 12 percent—the highest in the world for 1994—and the campaign against Sendero Luminoso.

This represented the high point of Fujimori's administration. Increasingly dictatorial behavior and a fraudulent election in 2000, coupled with a severe economic slump precipitated by the crisis in Asian financial markets and the chaos wreaked on the infrastructure, coastal agriculture, and fishing industry by the phenomenon known as El Niño, undermined Fujimori's popularity. Rampant corruption was symbolized by one woman who, according to *The Christian Science Monitor,* "became so disgusted with her country's electoral fraud and corruption . . . that she undertook a simple but memorable political protest: handwashing the Peruvian flag in a public square for months on end."

ACHIEVEMENTS

Peru has produced a number of literary giants, including José Maria Mariategui, who believed that the "socialism" of the Indians should be a model for the rest of Peru; and Mario Vargas Llosa, always concerned with the complexity of human relationships.

Fujimori's decision to run for a third term, despite a constitutional prohibition, was followed by an election in April 2000 that observers characterized as "rife with fraud." Prodemocracy forces led by Alejandro Toledo, a one-time shoeshine boy, boycotted the run-off election and helped to organize a massive national protest march against Fujimori's swearing-in ceremony in July. Violence in the streets, press censorship, and revelations of

Timeline: PAST

1500
The Inca Empire is at its height

1535
The Spanish found Lima

1821
Independence is proclaimed

1955
Women gain the right to vote

1968
A military coup: far-reaching reforms are pursued

1989
Debureaucratization campaign begins

1990s
El Niño spreads economic havoc and human misery; privatization

PRESENT

2000s
Reappearance of Sendero Luminoso in 2003

2006
Alan Garcia elected president

massive corruption by Fujimori's intelligence chief, Vladomiro Montesinos, forced Fujimori to resign from office and flee the country. Interim president Valentin Paniagua began the process of national reconstruction and created several commissions to investigate corruption and human-rights abuses.

Toledo, elected president in 2001, had a rough tenure in office. Despite solid economic growth that averaged 5 percent between 2001 and 2004 and rose to 6.7 percent in 2005, he saw his popularity tumble. Persistent corruption and scandal in government, his failure to deliver on campaign promises of jobs, prosperity, and a return to democracy hamstrung his administration. Troubling also was the reappearance of Sendero Luminoso in 2003. Although small in number they attacked security personnel, took hostages, and initiated a rural campaign to win peasant support. They are well-financed because of their ties to Colombian cocaine traffickers. Indeed, former President Fujimori, whose supporters fondly refer to him as "El Chino"—and whose detractors call him "Chinochet"—still retains a large measure of popularity despite outstanding criminal charges. Many people support Fujimori because he is perceived as strong and decisive. A confident Fujimori, who had fled to Japan to escape criminal charges, appeared in Chile late in 2005 and fully expected to run as a candidate in the 2006 presidential election. But Chilean authorities, at the request of the Peruvian government, detained him while extradition papers were prepared.

The presidential campaign became particularly contentious when Ollanta Humala, a nationalist former army officer, attended a news conference in Caracas, Venezuela, where he was praised by President Hugo Chavez for "joining the battle" against the Free Trade Area of the Americas supported by the United States. Outraged, the Peruvian government withdrew its ambassador from Venezuela for interfering with its election.

Alan Garcia, a former president whose tenure was dogged by corruption and hyperinflation, won the election. In his words: "God, in whom I firmly believe, and the Peruvian people, have given me a second chance." Garcia is, above all, a pragmatist, who has the soul of a populist, but is fiscally conservative and politically centrist. When, in May 2008, women protested against rapidly rising food prices, Garcia cut taxes on food imports and ordered the army to deliver parcels of food to Lima's poorest neighborhoods.

In terms of his economic policy he is a supporter of free trade and has invited private capital to invest in a gas-export project worth billions of dollars. Garcia's foreign policy is centrist. Although something of a populist, he has consciously set himself apart from populist regimes in Venezuela and other countries and traded insults with that country's president, Hugo Chávez. In a word, Garcia is a "chameleon" who can change his colors with seamless ease.

Suriname (Republic of Suriname)

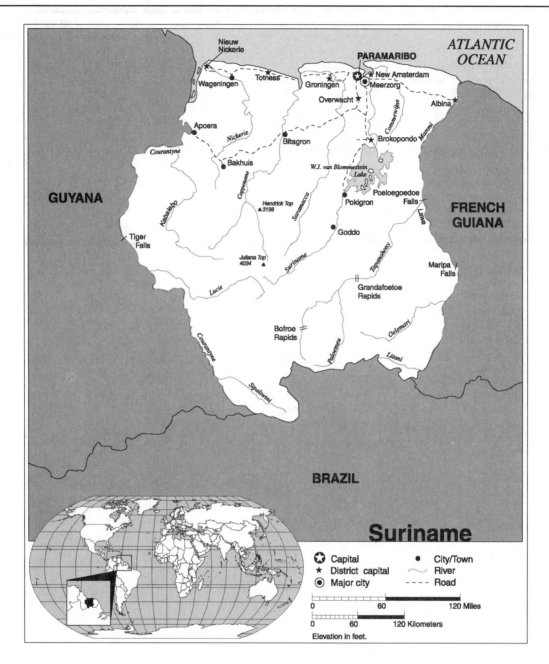

Suriname Statistics

GEOGRAPHY

Area in Square Miles (Kilometers): 63,037
(163,265) (about the size of Georgia)
Capital (Population): Paramaribo (250,000)
Environmental Concerns: deforestation;
water pollution; threatened wildlife
populations
Geographical Features: mostly rolling
hills; a narrow coastal plain with
swamps; mostly tropical rain forest
Climate: tropical

PEOPLE

Population

Total: 470,784 (2007 est.)
Annual Growth Rate: 1.1%
Rural/Urban Population Ratio: 50/50
Major Languages: Dutch;
Sranantonga; English;
Hindustani
Ethnic Makeup: 37% Hindustani (locally
called East Indian); Creole 31%;
Javanese 15%; Maroons 10%

Religions: Hindu 27.4%;
Protestant 25.2% (mostly
Moravian); Roman Catholic 22.8%;
Muslim 19.6%; other 5%

Health

Life Expectancy at Birth: 70 years (male);
76 years (female)
Infant Mortality Rate (Ratio):
20.1/1,000
Physicians Available (Ratio): 1/1,348

Education

Adult Literacy Rate: 89.6%
Compulsory (Ages): 6–16; free

COMMUNICATION

Telephones: 81,500 main lines
Daily Newspaper Circulation: 107 per 1,000 people
Cell Phones: 320,000
Internet Users: 32,000

TRANSPORTATION

Roadways in Kilometers (Miles): 2,813 (4,530)
Usable Airfields: 50

GOVERNMENT

Type: constitutional democracy
Independence Date: November 25, 1975 (from the Netherlands)

Head of State/Government: President Runaldo Ronald Venetiaan is both head of state and head of government
Political Parties: National Democratic Party; New Front for Democracy and Development; Peoples Alliance for Progress; others
Suffrage: universal at 18

MILITARY

Military Expenditures (% of GDP): 0.6%
Current Disputes: territorial disputes with Guyana and French Guiana

ECONOMY

Currency ($U.S. Equivalent): 2,780 Suriname guilders = $1
Per Capita Income/GDP: 7,800/$1.515 billion
GDP Growth Rate: 5.1%
Inflation Rate: 9.5%

Unemployment Rate: 9.5%
Labor Force: 156,700
Natural Resources: timber; hydropower; fish; kaolin; shrimp; bauxite; gold; nickel; copper; platinum; iron ore
Agriculture: paddy rice; bananas; palm kernels; coconuts; plantains; peanuts; livestock; forest products; shrimp
Industry: bauxite and gold mining; alumina and aluminum production; lumbering; food processing; fishing
Exports: $1.391 billion (f.o.b.) (primary partners Norway, Netherlands, United States)
Imports: $1.297 billion (f.o.b.) (primary partners United States, Netherlands, Trinidad and Tobago)

SUGGESTED WEB SITE

http://www.cia.gov/cia/publications/ factbook/index.html

Suriname Country Report

SURINAME: A SMALL-TOWN STATE

Settled by the British in 1651, Suriname, a small colony on the coast of Guiana, prospered with a plantation economy based on cocoa, sugar, coffee, and cotton. The colony came under Dutch control in 1667; in exchange, the British were given New Amsterdam (Manhattan, New York). The colony was often in turmoil because of Indian and slave uprisings, which took advantage of a weak Dutch power. When slavery was finally abolished, in 1863, plantation owners brought contract workers from China, India, and Java.

DEVELOPMENT

The bauxite industry, which had been in decline for 2 decades, now accounts for 15 percent of GDP and 70 percent of export earnings. Prospects for both onshore and offshore drilling for petroleum are good.

On the eve of independence from the Netherlands in 1975, Suriname was a complex, multiracial society. Although existing ethnic tensions were heightened as communal groups jockeyed for power in the new state, other factors cut across racial lines. Even though Creoles (native-born whites) were dominant in the bureaucracy as well as in the mining and industrial sectors, there was sufficient economic opportunity for all ethnic groups, so acute socioeconomic conflict was avoided.

THE POLITICAL FABRIC

Until 1980, Suriname enjoyed a parliamentary democracy that, because of the size of the nation, more closely resembled a small town or extended family in terms of its organization and operation. The various ethnic, political, and economic groups that comprised Surinamese society were united in what sociologist Rob Kroes describes as an "oligarchic web of patron–client relations" that found its expression in government. Through the interplay of the various groups, integration in the political process and accommodation of their needs were achieved. Despite the fact that most interests had access to the center of power, and despite the spirit of accommodation and cooperation, the military seized power early in 1980.

THE ROOTS OF MILITARY RULE

In Kroes's opinion, the coup originated in the army among noncommissioned officers, because they were essentially outside the established social and political system—they were denied their "rightful" place in the patronage network. The officers had a high opinion of themselves and resented what they perceived as discrimination by a wasteful and corrupt government. Their demands for reforms, including recognition of an officers' union, were ignored. In January 1980, one government official talked of disbanding the army altogether.

FREEDOM

The Venetiaan government successfully brought to an end the Maroon insurgency of 8 years' duration. Under the auspices of the Organization of American States, the rebels turned in their weapons, and an amnesty for both sides in the conflict was declared.

The coup, masterminded and led by Sergeant Desire Bouterse, had a vague, undefined ideology. It claimed to be nationalist; and it revealed itself to be puritanical, in that it lashed out at corruption and demanded that citizens embrace civic duty and a work ethic. Ideological purity was maintained by government control or censorship of a once-free media. Wavering between left-wing radicalism and middle-of-the-road moderation, the rapid shifts in Bouterse's ideological declarations suggest that this was a policy designed to keep the opposition off guard and to appease factions within the military.

The military rule of Bouterse seemed to come to an end early in 1988, when President Ramsewak Shankar was inaugurated. However, in December 1990, Bouterse masterminded another coup. The military and Bouterse remained above the rule of law, and the judiciary was not able to investigate or prosecute serious cases involving military personnel.

With regard to Suriname's economic policy, most politicians see integration

HEALTH/WELFARE

Amerindians and Maroons (the descendants of escaped African slaves) who live in the interior have suffered from the lack of educational and social services, partly from their isolation and partly from insurgency. With peace, however, it is hoped that the health, education, and general welfare of these peoples will improve.

ACHIEVEMENTS

Suriname, unlike most other developing countries, has a small foreign debt and a relatively strong repayment capacity. This is substantially due to its export industry.

Timeline: PAST

1651
British colonization efforts

1667
The Dutch receive Suriname from the British in exchange for New Amsterdam

1975
Independence of the Netherlands

1980s
A military coup

1990s
A huge drug scandal implicates high-level government officials

PRESENT

2000s
The Netherlands extends loan aid

2005
Ronald Venetiaan reelected president

into Latin American and Caribbean markets as critical. The Dutch, who suspended economic aid after the 1990 coup, restored their assistance with the election of President Ronald Venetiaan in 1991. But civilian authorities were well aware of the roots of military rule and pragmatically allowed officers a role in government befitting their self-perceived status.

In 1993, Venetiaan confronted the military when it refused to accept his choice of officers to command the army. Army reform was still high on the agenda in 1995 and was identified by President Venetiaan as one of his government's three great tasks. The others were economic reform necessary to ensure Dutch aid and establish the country's eligibility for international credit; and the need to reestablish ties with the interior to consolidate an Organization of American States–brokered peace, after almost a decade of insurgency.

A loan negotiated with the Dutch in 2001 will help Suriname to develop agriculture, bauxite, and the gold-mining industry. Unfortunately the development policy also threatens deforestation, because of timber exports, and the pollution of waterways as a result of careless mining practices. Housing and health care also ranked highly on the government's list of priorities under President Jules Wijdenbosch. The government realized that it cannot forever depend on the largesse of the Netherlands. The planning and development minister stated that aid must be sought from other countries and that Suriname must increasingly rely on its own resources.

Parliamentary elections in 2005 were hotly contested between former President Ronald Venetiaan's New Front coalition and the National Democratic Party of former dictator Desi Bouterse. Ultimately a regional assembly reelected Venetiaan as president. His government faces some difficult problems. Inflation is high, the health system is close to collapse, and the government bureaucracy is filled with officeholders who owe their positions to patronage rather than need. Venetiaan has introduced austerity measures similar to those he implemented in 1991–96 with some success at that time.

Uruguay (Oriental Republic of Uruguay)

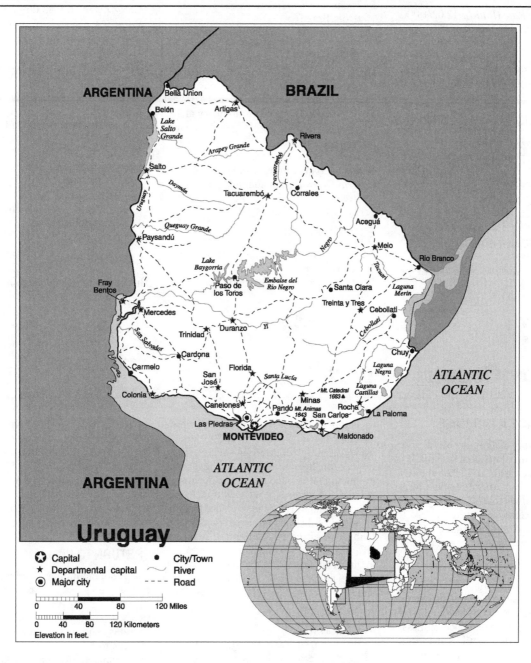

Uruguay Statistics

GEOGRAPHY

Area in Square Miles (Kilometers):
68,037 (176,215) (about the size of
Washington State)

Capital (Population): Montevideo
(1,325,968)

Environmental Concerns: transboundary
pollution from Brazilian power plant;
water pollution; waste disposal

Geographical Features: mostly rolling
plains and low hills; fertile coastal
lowland

Climate: warm temperate

PEOPLE

Population

Total: 3,460,607 (2007 est.)
Annual Growth Rate: 0.54%

Rural/Urban Population Ratio:
9/91

Major Languages: Spanish; Portunol:
Brazilero

Ethnic Makeup: 88% white; 8% Mestizo;
4% black

Religions: 66% Roman Catholic;
2% Protestant; 2% Jewish;
30% nonprofessing or
others

Health

Life Expectancy at Birth: 73 years (male);
 79 years (female)
Infant Mortality Rate (Ratio): 12.02/1,000
Physicians Available (Ratio): 1/282

Education

Adult Literacy Rate: 98%
Compulsory (Ages): for 6 years between 6
 and 14; free

COMMUNICATION

Telephones: 987,000 main lines
Daily Newspaper Circulation: 241 per
 1,000 people
Cell Phones: 2,333,000
Internet Users: 756,000

TRANSPORTATION

Roadways in Kilometers (miles):
 77,732 (48,300)
Railroads in (Kilometers) Miles: 1,243
 (2,073)
Usable Airfields: 60

GOVERNMENT

Type: republic
Independence Date: August 25, 1828
 (from Brazil)
Head of State/Government: President
 Tabaré Vázquez is both head of state
 and head of government
Political Parties: National (Blanco) Party
 factions; Colorado Party factions;
 Broad Front Coalition; others
Suffrage: universal and compulsory at 18

MILITARY

Military Expenditures (% of GDP): 1.6%
Current Disputes: boundary disputes with
 Brazil

ECONOMY

Currency ($U.S. Equivalent): 21 new
 pesos = $1
Per Capita Income/GDP: $10,700/$15.69
 billion

GDP Growth Rate: 5.7%
Inflation Rate: 8.3%
Unemployment Rate: 10.3%
Labor Force: 1,278,000
Natural Resources: arable land;
 hydropower; minor minerals;
 fisheries
Agriculture: wheat; rice; corn; sorghum;
 livestock; fish
Industry: food processing;
 textiles; chemicals; beverages;
 transportation equipment; petroleum
 products
Exports: $5.139 billion (f.o.b.) (primary
 partners Mercosur, European Union,
 United States)
Imports: $5.378 billion (f.o.b.) (primary
 partners Mercosur, European Union,
 United States)

SUGGESTED WEB SITE

http://www.cia.gov/cia/publications/
 factbook/index.html

Uruguay Country Report

URUGUAY: ONCE A PARADISE

The modern history of Uruguay begins with the administration of President José Batlle y Ordoñez. Between 1903 and 1929, Batlle's Uruguay became one of the world's foremost testing grounds for social change, and it eventually became known as the "Switzerland of Latin America." Batlle's Colorado Party supported a progressive role for organized labor and formed coalitions with the workers to challenge the traditional elite and win benefits. Other reforms included the formal separation of church and state, nationalization of key sectors of the economy, and the emergence of mass-based political parties. Batlle's masterful leadership was facilitated by a nation that was compact in size; had a small, educated, and homogeneous population; and had rich soil and a geography that facilitated easy communication and national integration.

DEVELOPMENT

In November 2007 a pulp mill began operations. Financed by foreign capital in the amount of $1.2 billion, the mill is expected to add 1.6 percent to GDP. Uruguay has experienced strong economic growth since 2004 as a result of high world market prices for its agricultural exports.

Although the spirit of Batllismo eventually faded after his death in 1929, Batlle's legacy is still reflected in many ways. Reports on income distribution reveal an evenness that is uncommon in developing countries. Extreme poverty is unusual in Uruguay, and most of the population enjoy an adequate diet and minimal standards of living. Health care is within the reach of all citizens. And women in Uruguay are granted equality before the law, are present in large numbers at the national university, and have access to professional careers.

FREEDOM

Uruguay's military is constitutionally prohibited from involvement in issues of domestic security unless ordered to do so by civilian authorities. The press is free and unrestricted, as is speech. The political process is open, and academic freedom is the norm in the national university.

But this model state fell on bad times beginning in the 1960s. Runaway inflation, declining agricultural production, a swollen bureaucracy, official corruption, and bleak prospects for the future led to the appearance of youthful middle-class urban guerrillas. Known as Tupamaros, they first attempted to jar the nation to its senses with

a Robin Hood–style approach to reform. When that failed, they turned increasingly to terrorism in an effort to destroy a state that resisted reform. The Uruguayan government was unable to quell the rising violence. It eventually called on the military, which crushed the Tupamaros and then drove the civilians from power in 1973.

RETURN TO CIVILIAN RULE

In 1980, the military held a referendum to try to gain approval for a new constitution. Despite extensive propaganda, 60 percent of Uruguay's population rejected the military's proposals and forced the armed forces to move toward a return to civilian government. Elections in 1984 returned the Colorado Party to power, with Julio Maria Sanguinetti as president.

By 1989, Uruguay was again a country of laws, and its citizens were anxious to heal the wounds of the 1970s. A test of the nation's democratic will involved the highly controversial 1986 Law of Expiration, which effectively exempted military and police personnel from prosecution for alleged human-rights abuses committed under orders during the military regime. Many Uruguayans objected and created a pro-referendum commission. They invoked a provision in the Constitution that is unique to Latin America: *Article 79* states that if

25 percent of eligible voters sign a petition, it will initiate a referendum, which, if passed, will implicitly annul the Law of Expiration. Despite official pressure, the signatures were gathered. The referendum was held on April 16, 1989. It was defeated by a margin of 57 to 43 percent.

HEALTH/WELFARE

Uruguay compares favorably with all of Latin America in terms of health and welfare. Medical care is outstanding, and the quality of public sanitation equals or exceeds that of other developing countries. Women, however, still experience discrimination in the workplace.

The winds of free-market enterprise and privatization then started to blow through the country. When Sanguinetti regained the presidency in 1994, he was expected, as the leader of the Colorado Party—the party of José Batlle—to maintain the economic status quo. But in 1995, he said that his first priority would be to reform the social-security system, which cannot pay for itself, in large part because people in Uruguay are allowed to retire years earlier than in other countries. Reform was also begun in other sectors of the economy. Government employees were laid off, tariffs were reduced, and a program to privatize state industries was inaugurated. The new policies, according to officials, would produce "a change of mentality and culture" in public administration.

In his first two years in power, Sanguinetti's successor, Jorge Batlle was unable to bring recession to an end. Low prices for agricultural exports, Argentina's economic malaise, and a public debt that stood at 45 percent of gross domestic product presented the government with difficult policy decisions. To add to these woes, the appearance of hoof-and-mouth disease in southern Brazil in mid-2001 threatened Uruguay's

Timeline: PAST

1624
Jesuits and Franciscans establish missions in the region

1828
Uruguay is established as a buffer state between Argentina and Brazil

1903–1929
The era of President José Batlle y Ordoñez; social reform

1932
Women win the right to vote

1963–1973
Tupamaro guerrillas wage war against the government

1990s
The government endorses sweeping economic and social reforms

PRESENT

2000s
President Battle struggles with the economy

Presidential elections scheduled for October 2004

2004
Tabaré Vázquez becomes president and promises a social transformation

important beef and wool industries. Once again there was talk of privatization, but a referendum held in December 2003 on the future of ANCAP, the national oil company showed that 62 percent of the electorate wanted no change. Interestingly, these same respondents also opposed monopolies. The failure of the referendum was seen by some political observers as a signal that Batlle would not win reelection in October 2004. That is exactly what happened. What was surprising was neither traditional party won the presidential election. Rather the victor, Tabaré Vázquez, headed up a broad front of political factions that ranged from Communists to Christian Democrats.

During the campaign Vázquez's rhetoric promised far-reaching changes that suggested a social transformation of the country. Uruguay's reality, however, is that it does not have the financial resources necessary to support the kinds of domestic programs that featured prominently in campaign speeches. The president has recently indicated that $100 million will be earmarked for the poor. He has also indicated that his government will reopen investigations into the disappearance of people during the years of military rule. On the foreign policy front he has reestablished relations with Cuba, raised questions about the wisdom of free-trade agreements, and moved closer to populist leaders such as Brazil's Lula and Venezuela's Chavez.

ACHIEVEMENTS

Of all the small countries in Latin America, Uruguay has been the most successful in creating a distinct culture. High levels of literacy and a large middle class have allowed Uruguay an intellectual climate that is superior to many much-larger nations.

People expect results and not rhetoric. One woman who has seen her pension drastically reduced by Uruguay's economic malaise told a *New York Times* reporter: "The front has to carry out the program it promised us. If not, the people will protest, and when it comes time to vote again, we will throw them out. We're not going to accept another neoliberal government, indifferent to people's social needs."

Be this as it may, the recovery of the Uruguayan economy, a foreign debt that is well under control, and growing investment in the country will provide the government with some of the resources it needs to finance social programs and diminish earlier criticism.

Venezuela (Bolivarian Republic of Venezuela)

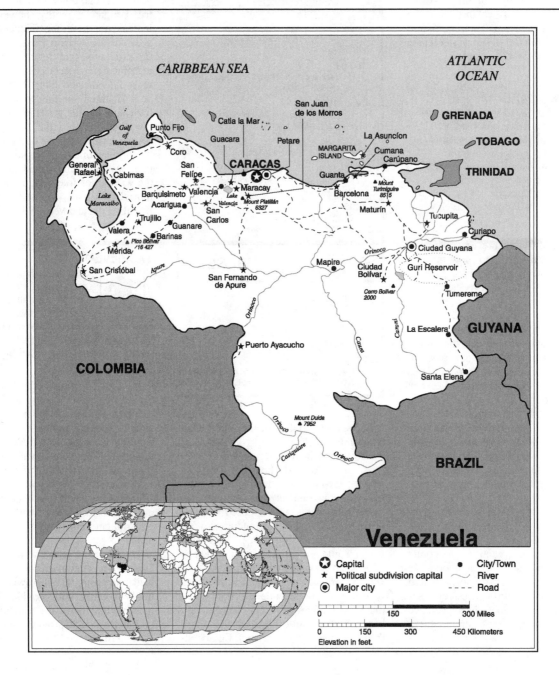

Venezuela

- ⊛ Capital
- ★ Political subdivision capital
- ◉ Major city
- • City/Town
- ∿ River
- - - - Road

0   150   300 Miles

0   150   300   450 Kilometers

Elevation in feet.

Venezuela Statistics

GEOGRAPHY

Area in Square Miles (Kilometers):
352,143 (912,050) (about twice the size of California)

Capital (Population): Caracas (3,700,000)

Environmental Concerns: water, sewage, air, oil, and urban pollution; deforestation; soil degradation

Geographical Features: a flat coastal plain and the Orinoco Delta are bordered by Andes Mountains and hills; plains (llanos) extend between the mountains and the Orinoco; Guyana Highlands and plains are south of the Orinoco

Climate: varies from tropical to temperate

PEOPLE

Population

Total: 26,023,528 (2007 est.)

Annual Growth Rate: 1.49%

Rural/Urban Population Ratio: 14/86

Major Languages: Spanish; indigenous dialects

Ethnic Makeup: 67% Mestizo; 21% white; 10% black; 2% Indian
Religions: 96% Roman Catholic; 4% Protestant and others

Health

Life Expectancy at Birth: 70 years (male); 76 years (female)
Infant Mortality Rate (Ratio): 23/1,000
Physicians Available (Ratio): 1/576

Education

Adult Literacy Rate: 93%
Compulsory (Ages): 5–15; free

COMMUNICATION

Telephones: 4,217,000 main lines
Daily Newspaper Circulation: 215 per 1,000 people
Cell Phones: 18,790,000
Internet Users: 4,140,000

TRANSPORTATION

Roadways in Kilometers (miles): 96,155 (59,748)

Railroads in Kilometers (Miles): 682 (424)
Usable Airfields: 390

GOVERNMENT

Type: republic
Independence Date: July 5, 1811 (from Spain)
Head of State/Government: President Hugo Chavez Frias is both head of state and head of government
Political Parties: Democratic Action; Movement Toward Socialism; United Socialist Party of Venezuela; Fatherland for All; We Can; Christian Democratic Party; Democratic Action
Suffrage: universal at 18

MILITARY

Military Expenditures (% of GDP): 1.2%
Current Disputes: territorial disputes with Guyana and Colombia

ECONOMY

Currency ($U.S. Equivalent): 2,146 bolivars = $1

Per Capita Income/GDP: $12,800/$166 billion
GDP Growth Rate: 8.3%
Inflation Rate: 20.7%
Unemployment Rate: 9.1%
Labor Force: 12,500,000
Natural Resources: petroleum; natural gas; iron ore; gold; bauxite; other minerals; hydropower; diamonds
Agriculture: corn; sorghum; sugarcane; rice; bananas; vegetables; coffee; livestock; fish
Industry: petroleum; mining; construction materials; food processing; textiles; steel; aluminum; motor-vehicle assembly
Exports: $65.94 billion (f.o.b.) (primary partners United States, Colombia, Brazil)
Imports: $44.38 billion (f.o.b.) (primary partners United States, Japan, Colombia)

SUGGESTED WEB SITE

http://www.cia.org/cia/publications/factbook/index.html

Venezuela Country Report

VENEZUELA: CHANGING TIMES

Venezuela is a country in transition. After decades of rule by a succession of *caudillos* (strong, authoritarian rulers), national leaders can now point to four decades of unbroken civilian rule and peaceful transfers of presidential power. Economic growth—stimulated by mining, industry, and petroleum—has, until recently, been steady and, at times, stunning. With the availability of better transportation; access to radio, television, newspapers, and material goods; and the presence of the national government in once-isolated towns, regional diversity is less striking now than a decade ago. Fresh lifestyles and perspectives, dress and music, and literacy and health care are changing the face of rural Venezuela.

THE PROBLEMS OF CHANGE

Such changes have not been without problems—significant ones. Venezuela, despite its petroleum-generated wealth, remains a nation plagued by huge imbalances, in-equalities, contradictions, and often bitter debate over the meaning and direction of national development. Some

critics note the danger of the massive rural-to-urban population shift and the influx of illegal immigrants (from Colombia and other countries), both the result of Venezuela's rapid economic development. Others warn of the excessive dependence on petroleum as the means of development and are concerned about the agricultural output at levels insufficient to satisfy domestic requirements. Venezuela, once a food exporter, periodically has had to import large amounts of basic commodities—such as milk, eggs, and meat—to feed the expanding urban populations. Years of easy, abundant money also promoted undisciplined borrowing abroad to promote industrial expansion and has saddled the nation with a serious foreign-debt problem. Government corruption was rampant and, in fact, led to the impeachment of President Carlos Andrés Pérez in 1993.

THE CHARACTER OF MODERNIZATION

The rapid changes in Venezuelan society have produced a host of generalizations as to the nature of modernization in this Andean republic. Commentators who speak

of a revolutionary break with the past—of a "new" Venezuela completely severed from its historic roots reaching back to the sixteenth century—ignore what is enduring about Venezuela's Hispanic culture.

Even before it began producing petroleum, Venezuela was not a sleepy backwater. Its Andean region was always the most prosperous area in the South American continent and was a refuge from the civil wars that swept other parts of the country. There were both opportunity and wealth in the coffee-growing trade. With the oil boom and the collapse of coffee prices in 1929, the Andean region experienced depopulation as migrants left the farms for other regions or for the growing Andean cities. In short, Venezuela's rural economy should not be seen as a static point from which change began but as a part of a dynamic process of continuing change, which now has the production of petroleum as its focus.

CULTURAL IDENTITY

Historian John Lombardi identifies language, culture, and an urban network centered on the capital city of Caracas as primary forces in the consolidation of the

(United States Dept. of the Interior, Bureau of Mines)

When oil was discovered in Venezuela, rapid economic growth caused many problems in national development. By depending on petroleum as the major source of wealth, Venezuela was at the mercy of the fickle world energy market.

nation. "Across the discontinuities of civil war and political transformation, agricultural and industrial economies, rural life styles and urban agglomerations, Venezuela has functioned through the stable network of towns and cities whose interconnections defined the patterns of control, the directions of resource distribution, and the country's identity."

One example of the country's cultural continuity can be seen by looking into one dimension of Venezuelan politics. Political parties are not organized along class lines but tend to cut across class divisions. This is not to deny the existence of class consciousness—which is certainly ubiquitous in Venezuela—but it is not a major *political* force. Surprisingly, popular support for elections and strong party affiliations are more characteristic of rural areas than of cities. The phenomenon cannot be explained as a by-product of modernization. Party membership and electoral participation are closely linked to party organization, personal ties and loyalties, and charismatic leadership. The party, in a sense, becomes a surrogate *patrón* that has power and is able to deliver benefits to the party faithful.

IMPACTS OF URBANIZATION

Another insight into Hispanic political culture can be found in the rural-to-urban shift in population that has often resulted in large-scale seizures of land in urban areas by peasants. Despite the illegality of the seizures, such actions are frequently encouraged by officials because, they argue, it provides the poor with enough land to maintain political stability and to prevent peasants from encroaching on richer neighborhoods. Pressure by the new urban dwellers at election time usually results in their receiving essential services from government officials. In other words, municipal governments channel resources in return for expected electoral support from the migrants. Here is a classic Hispanic response to challenge from below— to bend, to cooperate.

Cultural values also underlie both the phenomenon of internal migration and the difficulty of providing adequate skilled labor for Venezuela's increasingly technological economy. While the attraction of the city and its many opportunities is one reason for the movement of population out of rural areas, so too is that segment of Venezuelan culture, which belittles the peasant and rural life in general. Similarly, the shortage of skilled labor is the result not only of inadequate training but also of social values that neither reward nor dignify skilled labor.

THE SOCIETY

The rapid pace of change has contributed to a reexamination of the roles and rights of women in Venezuela. In recent years, women have occupied positions in the cabinet and in the Chamber of Deputies; several women deputies have held important posts in political parties.

Yet while educated women are becoming more prominent in the professions, there is a reluctance to employ women in traditional "men's" jobs, and blatant in-equality still blemishes the workplace. Women, for example, are paid less than men for similar work. And although modern feminist goals have become somewhat of a social and economic force, at least in urban centers, the traditional roles of wife and mother continue to hold the most prestige, and physical beauty is still often viewed as a woman's most precious asset. In addition, many men seek deference from women rather than embracing social equality. Nevertheless, the younger generations of Venezuelans are experiencing the social and cultural changes that have tended to follow women's liberation in Western industrialized nations: higher levels of education and career skills; broadened intellectualism; increasing freedom and equality for both men and women; relaxed social mores; and the accompanying personal turmoil, such as rising divorce and single-parenthood rates.

Venezuelans generally enjoy a high degree of individual liberty. Civil, personal, and political rights are protected by a strong and independent judiciary. Citizens generally enjoy a free press. There exists the potential for governmental abuse of press freedom, however. Several laws leave journalists vulnerable to criminal charges, especially in the area of libel. Journalists must be certified to work, and certification may be withdrawn by the government if journalists are perceived to stray from the "truth," misquote sources, or refuse to correct "errors." But as a rule, radio, television, and newspapers are free and are often highly critical of the government.

The civil and human rights enjoyed by most Venezuelans have not necessarily extended to the nation's Indian population in the Orinoco Basin. For years, extra-regional forces—in the form of rubber gatherers, missionaries, and developers—have to varying degrees undermined the economic self-sufficiency, demographic viability, and tribal integrity of indigenous peoples. A government policy that stressed the existence of only one Venezuelan culture posed additional problems for Indians.

In 1991, however, President Pérez signed a decree granting a permanent homeland, encompassing some 32,000 square miles in the Venezuelan Amazon forest, to the country's 14,000 Yanomamö Indians. Venezuela will permit no mining

© Kim Steele/Getty Images

Caracas, Venezuela, an ultra-modern city of 3.7 million exemplifying the extremes of poverty and wealth that exist in Latin America, sprawls for miles over mountains and valleys.

or farming in the territory and will impose controls on existing religious missions. President Pérez stated that "the primary use will be to preserve and to learn the traditional ways of the Indians." As James Brooke reported in *The New York Times,* "Venezuela's move has left anthropologists euphoric."

Race relations are outwardly tranquil in Venezuela, but there exists an underlying racism in nearly all arenas. People are commonly categorized by the color of their skin, with white being the most prized. Indeed, race, not economic level, is still a major social-level determinant. This unfortunate reality imparts a sense of frustration and a measure of hopelessness to many of Venezuela's people, in that even those who acquire a good education and career training may be discriminated against in the workplace because they are "of color." Considering that only one-fifth of the population are of white extraction, with 67 percent Mestizos and 10 percent blacks, this is indeed a widespread and debilitating problem.

President Chavez is of mixed racial ancestry and has won broad support among the disadvantaged because he has moved to remove, in the words of Benjamin Keene and Keith Haynes, "the social stigma historically attached to the terms *mulatto, mestizo,* and *black.* This new sense of dignity, not just the hope for improvement in economic status, helped to explain the fierce loyalty of these masses toward their leader." Indicative of an underlying racism among some of those opposed to Chavez are the terms of opprobrium used to describe him, including *el Mono* (the monkey) or *el Negro* (the black).

A VIGOROUS FOREIGN POLICY

Venezuela has always pursued a vigorous foreign policy. In the words of former president Luis Herrera Campins: "Effective action by Venezuela in the area of international affairs must take certain key facts into account: economics—we are a producer-exporter of oil; politics—we have a stable, consolidated democracy; and geopolitics—we are at one and the same time a Caribbean, Andean, Atlantic, and Amazonian country." Venezuela has long assumed that it should be the guardian of Simón Bolívar's ideal of creating an

independent and united Latin America. The nation's memory of its continental leadership, which developed during the Wars for Independence (1810–1826), has been rekindled in Venezuela's desire to promote the political and economic integration of both the continent and the Caribbean. Venezuela's foreign policy remains true to the Bolivarian ideal of an independent Latin America and it should come as no surprise that President Chavez has adopted the term "Bolivarian Revolution" for his movement. In the Caribbean Venezuela has invested in industry and provided cut-rate petroleum to many microstates. In South America he has established close relations with other populist governments, including those in Brazil, Bolivia, Argentina, and Uruguay. And he has openly challenged the United States with his strong stand against free-trade agreements. Chavez's enmity toward the United States extends to Latin American nations he considers tied to Washington's policies. Colombia's president, for example, is considered an imperialist lackey and recent evidence suggests that Chavez has monetarily supported Colombian guerrillas.

PROMISING PROSPECTS TURN TO DISILLUSIONMENT

The 1980s brought severe turmoil to Venezuela's economy. The boom times of the 1970s turned to hard times as world oil prices dropped. Venezuela became unable to service its massive foreign debt $45.44 billion at the (end of 2007) and to subsidize the "common good," in the form of low gas and transportation prices and other amenities. In 1983, the currency, the bolívar, which had remained stable and strong for many years at 4.3 to the U.S. dollar, was devalued, to an official rate of 14.5 bolívars to the dollar. This was a boon to foreign visitors to the country, which became known as one of the world's greatest travel bargains, but a catastrophe for Venezuelans. (In December 2007, the exchange rate was about 2,147 bolívars to the dollar on the free market.)

President Jaime Lusinchi of the Democratic Action Party, who took office early in 1984, had the unenviable job of trying to cope with the results of the preceding years of free spending, high expectations, dependence on oil, and spiraling foreign debt. Although the country's gross national product grew during his tenure (agriculture growth contributed significantly, rising from 0.4 percent of gross national product in 1983 to 6.8 percent in 1986), austerity measures were in order. The Lusinchi government was not up to the challenge. Indeed, his major legacy was a corruption scandal at the government agency Recadi, which was responsible for allocating foreign currency to importers at the official rate of 14.5 bolívars to the dollar. It was alleged that billions of dollars were skimmed, with a number of high-level government officials, including three finance ministers, implicated. Meanwhile, distraught Venezuelans watched inflation and the devalued bolívar eat up their savings; the once-blooming middle class started getting squeezed out.

HEALTH/WELFARE

A 1997 survey of children working in the informal sector revealed that 25 percent were between ages 5 and 12; that they worked more than 7 hours a day and earned about $2; and that their "jobs" included garbage collection, lotteries and gambling, and selling drugs. Fewer than half attended school. President Chavez has created 6,840 cooperatives that now employ 210,000 people, many of them who previously were unemployed or underemployed.

In the December 1988 national elections, another Democratic Action president, Carlos Andrés Pérez, was elected. Pérez, who had served as president from 1974 to 1979, was widely rumored to have stolen liberally from Venezuela's coffers during that tenure. Venezuelans joked at first that "Carlos Andrés is coming back to get what he left behind," but as the campaign wore on, some political observers were dismayed to hear the preponderance of the naive sentiment that "now he has enough and will really work for Venezuela this time."

One of Pérez's first acts upon reentering office was to raise the prices of government-subsidized gasoline and public transportation. Although he had warned that tough austerity measures would be implemented, the much-beleaguered and disgruntled urban populace took to the streets in February 1989 in the most serious rioting to have occurred in Venezuela since it became a democracy. Army tanks rolled down the major thoroughfares of Caracas, the capital; skirmishes between the residents and police and military forces were common; looting was widespread. The government announced that 287 people had been killed. Unofficial hospital sources charge that the death toll was closer to 2,000. A stunned Venezuela quickly settled down in the face of the violence, mortified that such a debacle, widely reported in the international press, should take place in this advanced and peaceable country. But tourism, a newly vigorous and promising industry as a result of favorable currency-exchange rates, subsided immediately; it has yet to recover fully.

On February 4, 1992, another ominous event highlighted Venezuela's continuing political and economic weaknesses. Rebel military paratroopers, led by Hugo Chavez, attacked the presidential palace in Caracas and government sites in several other major cities. The coup attempt, the first in Venezuela since 1962, was rapidly put down by forces loyal to President Pérez, who escaped what he described as an assassination attempt. Reaction within Venezuela was mixed, reflecting widespread discontent with Pérez's tough economic policies, government corruption, and declining living standards. A second unsuccessful coup attempt, on November 27, 1992, followed months of public demonstrations against Pérez's government.

Perhaps the low point was reached in May 1993, when Pérez was suspended from office and impeachment proceedings initiated. Allegedly the president had embezzled more than $17 million and had facilitated other irregularities. Against a backdrop of military unrest, Ramón José Velásquez was named interim president.

In December 1993, Venezuelans elected Rafael Caldera, who had been president in a more prosperous and promising era

ACHIEVEMENTS

Venezuela's great novelists, such as Rómulo Gallegos and Artúro Uslar Pietri, have been attracted by the barbarism of the backlands and the lawlessness native to rural regions. Gallegos's classic *Doña Barbara,* the story of a female regional chieftain, has become world-famous.

(1969–1974). Caldera's presidency too was fraught with problems. In his first year, he had to confront widespread corruption in official circles, the devaluation of the bolívar, drug trafficking, a banking structure in disarray, and a high rate of violent crime in Caracas. Indeed, in 1997, a relative of President Caldera was mugged and a Spanish diplomat who had traveled to Caracas to negotiate a trade agreement with Venezuela was robbed in broad daylight.

In an attempt to restore order from chaos, President Caldera inaugurated his "Agenda Venezuela" program to address the difficult

Timeline: PAST

1520
The first Spanish settlement at Cumaná

1822–1829
Venezuela is part of Gran Colombia

1829
Venezuela achieves independence as a separate country

1922
The first productive oil well

1947
Women win the right to vote

1976
Foreign oil companies are nationalized

1980s
Booming public investment fuels inflation; Venezuela seeks renegotiation of foreign debt

1990s
Social and economic crisis grips the nation; Hugo Chavez wins the presidency and sets about to redraft the Constitution; Chavez's government is challenged by massive flooding that leaves more than 30,000 people dead and many more homeless

PRESENT

2000s
A new Constitution is approved

Chavez strengthens executive power; Chavez is reelected

2006
President Chavez re-elected

2008
Growing tensions with neighboring Colombia

problems created by deep recession, financial instability, deregulation, privatization, and market reforms. The plan was showing signs of progress when it was undercut by the collapse of petroleum prices.

The stage was thus set for the emergence of a "hero" who would promise to solve all of Venezuela's ills. In the presidential election of 1998, the old parties were swept from power and a populist—the same Hugo Chavez who had attempted a coup in 1992—won with 55 percent of the popular vote. Those who expected change were not disappointed, although some of Chavez's actions have raised concerns about the future of democracy in Venezuela. A populist and a pragmatist, it is difficult to ascertain where Chavez's often contradictory policies will lead. Since taking power in February 1999, he has placed the army in control of the operation of medical clinics and has put soldiers to work on road and sewer repairs and in school and hospital construction. He has talked about the need to cut costs and uproot what he perceives as a deeply corrupt public sector—but he has refused to downsize the bureaucracy. Chavez supports privatization of the nation's pension fund and electric utilities, but he wants to maintain state control over health care and the petroleum industry.

Perhaps of greater concern is Chavez's successful bid to redraft Venezuela's Constitution, to provide "a better version." He claimed that the document had eroded democracy by allowing a political elite to rule without restraint for decades. Chavez's "democratic" vision demands special powers to revamp the economy without congressional approval. Through clever manipulation of the people by means of his own radio and television shows, and newspaper, Chavez intimidated Congress into granting him almost all the power he wanted to enact financial and economic legislation by decree. A referendum in April 1999 gave him a huge majority supporting the creation of an assembly to redraft the Constitution. A draft was completed in November. The political opposition was convinced that the new document would allow Chavez to seek a second consecutive term in office, which had been prohibited in Venezuela, and that he was doing nothing less than creating a dictatorship under the cover of democracy and the law. Their fears have been realized, as the new Constitution allows for consecutive six-year terms.

The trend towards more centralized executive authority continued in 2000 and 2001. When the new 1999 Constitution was "reprinted" in March 2000, critics noted substantial changes from the original—changes that enhanced presidential power. In the same month, a group of retired military officers called on President Chavez to halt the politicization of the armed forces. The president's response was to appoint active-duty officers to a range of important positions in the government, including the state-owned petroleum company and foreign ministry. Organized labor complained that Chavez has attempted to transform the labor movement into an appendage of the ruling political party and has ignored union leadership in direct appeals by the government to rank-and-file workers. He has alienated the Catholic hierarchy over abortion and education issues; and the media, while legally free to criticize the government, have felt the need to exercise self-censorship. Perhaps most ominously, Chavez asked for and received from a compliant Legislature permission to rule by decree on a broad spectrum of issues, from the economy to public security. The *Ley Habilitante* allows him to enact legislation without parliamentary debate or even approval.

Equally radical and unpredictable is Chavez's policy toward neighboring Colombia. Chavez opened a dialogue with Colombia's guerrillas and dismissed Colombia's protests with the statement that the guerrillas held effective power.

Chavez clearly sees himself as a major player in the region and seems to enjoy annoying the United States. He is friends with Fidel Castro, met with Saddam Hussein in Baghdad, and strengthened relations with a number of Caribbean, Central American, and South American states. Venezuela's long-standing boundary dispute with neighboring Guyana has also been resurrected.

Venezuela's future is wholly unpredictable in large measure because its current government is unpredictable. Growing dissatisfaction with Chavez's strong-arm rule precipitated street violence in early April 2002. For four days he was apparently forced from power by elements in the military, but demonstrations by Chavez's supporters resulted in his return to office. The political opposition mounted a campaign to gather the signatures necessary to force a recall vote in August 2004. Chavez emerged as the winner and announced that he would run for another six-year term in elections in 2006. Chavez's victory emboldened him to again seek constitutional changes that would essentially allow him to remain in office for as long as he wished. Unexpectedly, an electorate that is increasingly concerned by his policies voted down his proposed reforms. More to the point, many of Chavez's supporters among the poor voted against the president. Promised social programs have not been implemented and inflation eats away already meager incomes. It might be surmised that much of Chavez' fiery rhetoric on the international stage is designed to deflect attention from growing domestic difficulties.

The Caribbean

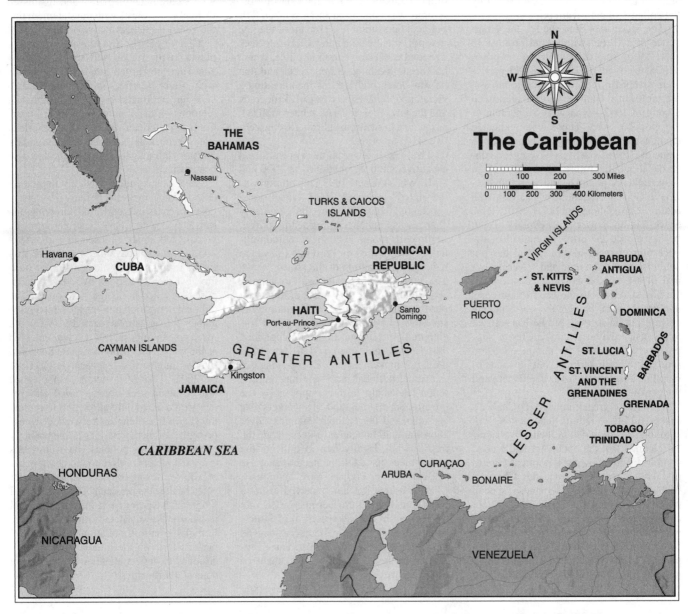

The Caribbean region consists of hundreds of islands stretching from northern South America to the southern part of Florida. Many of the islands cover just a few square miles and are dominated by a central range of mountains; only Cuba has any extensive lowlands. Almost every island has a ring of coral, making approaches very dangerous for ships. The land that can be used for agriculture is extremely fertile; but many islands grow only a single crop, making them vulnerable to fluctuations in the world market in that particular commodity.

The Caribbean   Sea·of Diversity

To construct a coherent overview of the Caribbean is an extremely difficult task because of the region's profound geographical and cultural diversity. "The history of the Caribbean is the examination of fragments, which, like looking at a broken vase, still provides clues to the form, beauty, and value of the past." So writes historian Franklin W. Knight in his study of the Caribbean. Other authors have drawn different analogies: Geographer David Lowenthal and anthropologist Lambros Comitas note that the West Indies "is a set of mirrors in which the lives of black, brown, and white, of American Indian and East Indian, and a score of other minorities continually interact."

For the geographer, the pieces fall into a different pattern, consisting of four distinct geographical regions. The first contains the Bahamas as well as the Turks and Caicos Islands. The Greater Antilles—consisting of Cuba, Hispaniola (Haiti and the Dominican Republic), Jamaica, the Cayman Islands, Puerto Rico, and the Virgin Islands—make up the second region. Comprising the third region are the Lesser Antilles—Antigua and Barbuda, Dominica, St. Lucia, St. Vincent and the Grenadines, Grenada, and St. Kitts and Nevis as well as various French departments and British and Dutch territories. The fourth group consists of islands that are part of the South American continental shelf: Trinidad and Tobago, Barbados, and the Dutch islands of Aruba, Curaçao, and Bonaire. Within these broad geographical regions, each nation is different. Yet on each island there often is a firmly rooted parochialism—a devotion to a parish or a village, a mountain valley or a coastal lowland.

CULTURAL DIVERSITY

To break down the Caribbean region into culture groups presents its own set of problems. The term "West Indian" inadequately describes the culturally Hispanic nations of Cuba and the Dominican Republic. On the other hand, "West Indian" does capture the essence of the cultures of Belize, the Caribbean coast of Central America, and Guyana, Suriname, and Cayenne (French Guiana). In Lowenthal's view: "Alike in not being Iberian [Hispanic], the West Indies are not North American either, nor indeed do they fit any ordinary regional pattern. Not so much undeveloped as overdeveloped, exotic without being traditional, they are part of the Third World yet ardent emulators of the West."

EFFORTS AT INTEGRATION

To complicate matters further, few West Indians would identify themselves as such. They are Jamaicans, or Bajans (people from Barbados), or Grenadans. Their economic, political, and social worlds are usually confined to the islands on which they live and work. In the eyes of its inhabitants, each island, no matter how small, is—or should be—sovereign. Communications by air, sea, and telephone with the rest of the world are ordinarily better than communications within the Caribbean

region itself. Trade, even between neighboring islands, has always been minimal. Economic ties with the United States or Europe, and in some cases with Venezuela, are more important.

A British attempt to create a "West Indies Federation" in 1958 was reduced to a shambles by 1962. Member states had the same historical background; spoke the same languages; had similar economies; and were interested in the same kinds of food, music, and sports. But their spirit of independence triumphed over any kind of regional federation that "threatened" their individuality. In the words of a former Bajan prime minister, "We live together very well, but we don't like to live together." A Trinidadian explanation for the failure of the federation is found in a popular calypso verse from the early 1960s:

> Plans was moving fine
> When Jamaica stab we from behind
> Federation bust wide open
> But they want Trinidad to bear the burden.

Recently, however, the Windward Islands (Dominica, Grenada, St. Lucia, and St. Vincent and the Grenadines) have discussed political union. While each jealously guards its sovereignty, leaders are nevertheless aware that some integration is necessary if they are to survive in a changing world. The division of the world into giant economic blocs points to political union and the creation of a Caribbean state with a combined population of nearly half a million. Antigua and Barbuda resist because they believe that, in the words of former prime minister Vere Bird, "political union would be a new form of colonialism and undermine sovereignty."

While political union remains problematic, the 15 members of the Caribbean Community and Common Market (CARICOM, a regional body created in 1973) began long-term negotiations with Cuba in 1995 with regard to a free-trade agreement. CARICOM leaders informed Cuba that "it needs to open up its economy more." The free-market economies of CARICOM are profoundly different from Cuba's rigid state controls. "We need to assure that trade and investment will be mutually beneficial." Caribbean leaders have pursued trade with Cuba in the face of strong opposition from the United States. In general, CARICOM countries are convinced that "constructive engagement" rather than a policy of isolation is the best way to transform Cuba.

Political problems also plague the Dutch Caribbean. Caribbean specialist Aaron Segal notes that the six-island Netherlands Antilles Federation has encountered severe internal difficulties. Aruba never had a good relationship with the larger island of Curaçao and, in 1986, became a self-governing entity, with its own flag, Parliament, and currency, but still within the Netherlands. "The other Netherlands Antillean states have few complaints about their largely autonomous relations with the Netherlands but find it hard to get along with one another."

Interestingly, islands that are still colonial possessions generally have a better relationship with their "mother" countries than

(©Iconotec.com)

The weekly open-air market in St. Lucia provides a variety of local produce.

with one another. Over the past few decades, smaller islands—populations of about 50,000 or less—have learned that there are advantages to a continued colonial connection. The extensive subsidies paid by Great Britain, France, or the Netherlands have turned dependency into an asset. Serving as tax-free offshore sites for banks and companies as well as encouraging tourism and hotel investments have led to modest economic growth.

CULTURAL IDENTIFICATION

Despite the local focus of the islanders, there do exist some broad cultural similarities. To the horror of nationalists, who are in search of a Caribbean identity that is distinct from Western civilization, most West Indians identify themselves as English or French in terms of culture. Bajans, for example, take a special pride in identifying their country as the "Little England of the Caribbean." English or French dialects are the languages spoken in common.

Nationalists argue that the islands will not be wholly free until they shatter the European connection. In the nationalists' eyes, that connection is a bitter reminder of slavery. After World War II, several Caribbean intellectuals attacked the strong European orientation of the islands and urged the islanders to be proud of their black African heritage. The shift in focus was most noticeable in the French Caribbean, although this new

ethnic consciousness was echoed in the English-speaking islands as well in the form of a black-power movement during the 1960s and 1970s. It was during those years, when the islands were in transition from colonies to associated states to independent nations, that the Caribbean's black majorities seized political power by utilizing the power of their votes.

It is interesting to note that at the height of the black-power and black-awareness movements, sugar production was actually halted on the islands of St. Vincent, Antigua, and Barbuda—not because world-market prices were low, but because sugar cultivation was associated with the slavery of the past.

African Influences

The peoples of the West Indies are predominantly black, with lesser numbers of people of "mixed blood" and small numbers of whites. Culturally, the blacks fall into a number of groups. Throughout the nineteenth century, in Haiti, blacks strove to realize an African-Caribbean identity. African influences have remained strong on the island, although they have been blended with European Christianity and French civilization. Mulattos, traditionally the elite in Haiti, have strongly identified with French culture in an obvious attempt to distance themselves from the black majority, who comprise about 95 percent of the population. African-Creoles, as blacks of the English-speaking islands prefer to be called, are manifestly less "African" than the mass of Haitians. An exception to this generalization is the Rastafarians, common in Jamaica and found in lesser numbers on some of the other islands. Convinced that they are Ethiopians, the Rastafarians hope to return to Africa.

Racial Tension

The Caribbean has for years presented an image of racial harmony to the outside world. Yet, in actuality, racial tensions are not only present but also have become sharper during the past few decades. Racial unrest broke to the surface in Jamaica in 1960 with riots in the capital city of Kingston. Tensions heightened again in 1980–1981 and in 1984, to the point that the nation's tourist industry drastically declined. A slogan of the Jamaican tourist industry, "Make It Jamaica Again," was a conscious attempt to downplay racial antagonism. The black-power movement in the 1960s on most of the islands also put to the test notions of racial harmony.

Most people of the Caribbean, however, believe in the myth of racial harmony. It is essential to the development of nationalism, which must embrace all citizens. Much racial tension is officially explained as class difference rather than racial prejudice. There is some merit to the class argument. A black politician on Barbuda, for example, enjoys much more status and prestige than a poor white "Redleg" from the island's interior. Yet if a black and a Redleg competed for the job of plantation manager, the white would likely win out over the black. In sum, race does make a difference, but so too does one's economic or political status.

East Indians

The race issue is more complex in Trinidad and Tobago, where there is a large East Indian (i.e., originally from India) minority. The East Indians, for the most part, are agricultural workers. They were originally introduced by the British between 1845 and 1916 to replace slave labor on the plantations. While numbers of East Indians have moved to the cities, they still feel that they have little in common with urban blacks. Because of their large numbers, East Indians are able to preserve a distinctive, healthy culture and community and to compete with other groups for political office and status.

East Indian culture has also adapted, but not yielded, to the West Indian world. In the words of Trinidadian-East Indian author V. S. Naipaul: "We were steadily adopting the food styles of others: The Portuguese stew of tomato and onions . . . the Negro way with yams, plantains, breadfruit, and bananas," but "everything we adopted became our own; the outside was still to be dreaded. . . ." The East Indians in Jamaica, who make up about 3 percent of the population, have made even more accommodations to the cultures around them. Most Jamaican-East Indians have become Protestant (the East Indians of Trinidad have maintained their Hindu or Islamic faith).

East Indian conformity and internalization, and their strong cultural identification, have often made them the targets of the black majority. Black stereotypes of the East Indians describe them in the following terms: "secretive," "greedy," and "stingy." And East Indian stereotypes describing blacks as "childish," "vain," "pompous," and "promiscuous" certainly do not help to ease ethnic tensions.

REVOLUTIONARY CUBA

In terms of culture, the Commonwealth Caribbean (former British possessions) has little in common with Cuba or the Dominican Republic. But Cuba has made its presence felt in other ways. The Cuban Revolution, with the social progress that it entailed for many of its people and the strong sense of nationalism that it stimulated, impressed many West Indians. For new nation-states still in search of an identity, Cuba offered some clues as to how to proceed. For a time, Jamaica experimented with Cuban models of mass mobilization and programs designed to bring social services to the majority of the population. Between 1979 and 1983, Grenada saw merit in the Cuban approach to social and economic problems. The message that Cuba seemed to represent was that a small Caribbean state could shape its own destiny and make life better for its people.

The Cuba of Fidel Castro, while revolutionary, was also traditional. Hispanic culture is largely intact. The politics are authoritarian and personality-driven, and Castro himself easily fit into the mold of the Latin American leader, or caudillo, whose charisma and benevolent paternalism won him the widespread support of his people. Castro's relationship with the Roman Catholic Church was also traditional and corresponds to notions of a dualistic culture that has its roots in the Middle Ages. In Castro's words: "The same respect that the Revolution ought to have for religious beliefs, ought also to be had by those who talk in the name of religion for the political beliefs of others. And, above all, to have present that which Christ said: 'My kingdom is not of this world.' What are those who are said to be the interpreters of Christian thought doing meddling in the problems of this world?" Castro's comments should not be interpreted as a Communist assault on religion. Rather, they express a time-honored Hispanic belief that religious life and everyday life exist in two separate spheres.

The social reforms that have been implemented in Cuba are well within the powers of all Latin American governments to enact. Those governments, in theory, are duty-bound to provide for the welfare of their peoples. Constitutionally, the state is infallible and all-powerful. Castro chose to identify with the needs of the majority of Cubans, to be a "father" to his people. Again, his actions are not so much Communistic as Hispanic.

Where Castro ran against the grain was in his assault on Cuba's middle class. In a sense, he reversed a trend that is evident in much of the rest of Latin America—the slow, steady progress of a middle class that is intent on acquiring a share of the power and prestige traditionally accorded to elites. Cuba's middle class was effectively shattered—people were deprived of much of their property; their livelihood; and, for those who fled into exile, their citizenship. Many expatriate Cubans remain bitter toward what they perceive as Castro's betrayal of the Revolution and the middle class. Fidel Castro's health problems and the subsequent designation of his brother Raúl Castro as Cuba's leader marks the passing of an era.

EMIGRATION AND MIGRATION

Throughout the Caribbean, emigration and migration are a fact of life for hundreds of thousands of people. These are not new phenomena; their roots extend to the earliest days of European

These workers in Port-de-Paix, Haiti are hand-carrying building materials up a ladder to add a second story to an existing home. Most people build with the intent of someday putting on a second story. When they get a little money they buy a few cinder/cement blocks until they have enough to build. Here they are hauling gravel to make concrete bucket by bucket. The roof is supported by many sticks that will remain there until the work is completed.

settlement. The flow of people looking for work is deeply rooted in history, in contemporary political economy, and even in Caribbean island culture. The Garifuna (black-Indian mixture) who settled in Belize and coastal parts of Mexico, Guatemala, Honduras, and Nicaragua originally came from St. Vincent. There, as escaped slaves, they intermixed with remnants of Indian tribes who had once peopled the islands, and they adopted many of their cultural traits. Most of the Garifuna (or Black Caribs, as they are also known) were deported from St. Vincent to the Caribbean coast of Central America at the end of the eighteenth century.

From the 1880s onward, patois-speaking (French dialect) Dominicans and St. Lucians migrated to Cayenne (French Guiana) to work in the gold fields. The strong identification with Europe has drawn thousands more to what many consider their cultural homes.

High birth rates and lack of economic opportunity have forced others to seek their fortunes elsewhere. Many citizens of the Dominican Republic have moved to New York, and Haitian refugees have thrown themselves on the coast of Florida by the thousands. Other Haitians seek seasonal employment in the Dominican Republic or the Bahamas. There are sizable Jamaican communities in the Dominican Republic, Haiti, the Bahamas, and Belize.

On the smaller islands, stable populations are the exception rather than the rule. The people are constantly migrating to larger places in search of higher pay and a better life. Such emigrants moved to Panama when the canal was being cut in the early 1900s or sought work on the Dutch islands of Curaçao and Aruba when oil refineries were built there in the 1920s. They provided much of the labor for the banana plantations in Central America. Further contributing to out-migration is the changing character of some island economies. Many islands can no longer compete in world markets for sugar or bananas and have been forced to diversify. In 2005 St. Kitts closed its last sugar mills, ending a 350-year relationship with what had been the island's main industry. Now hope has been placed in tourism. For agricultural workers the alternatives are retraining or emigration.

The greatest number of people by far have left the Caribbean region altogether and emigrated to the United States, Canada,

These lush mountain peaks in St. Lucia are volcanic in origin.

and Europe. Added to those who have left because of economic or population pressures are political refugees. The majority of these are Cubans, most of whom have resettled in Florida.

Some have argued that the prime mover of migration from the Caribbean lies in the *ideology* of migration—that is, the expectation that all nonelite males will migrate abroad. Sugarcane slave plantations left a legacy that included little possibility of island subsistence; and so there grew the need to migrate to survive, a reality that was absorbed into the culture of lower-class blacks. But for these blacks, there has also existed the expectation to return. (In contrast, middle- and upper-class migrants have historically departed permanently.) Historian Bonham Richardson writes: "By traveling away and returning the people have been able to cope more successfully with the vagaries of man and nature than they would have by staying at home. The small islands of the region are the most vulnerable to environmental and economic uncertainty. Time and again in the Lesser Antilles, droughts, hurricanes, and economic depressions have diminished wages, desiccated provision grounds, and destroyed livestock, and there has been no local recourse to disease or starvation." Hence, men and women of the small West Indian islands have been obliged to migrate. "And like migrants everywhere, they have usually considered their travels temporary, partly because they have never been greeted cordially in host communities."

On the smaller islands, such as St. Kitts and Nevis, family and community ceremonies traditionally reinforce and sustain the importance of emigration and return. Funerals reunite families separated by vast distances; Christmas parties and carnival celebrations are also occasions to welcome returning family and friends.

Monetary remittances from relatives in the United States, England, Canada, or the larger islands are a constant reminder of the importance of migration. According to Richardson: "Old men who have earned local prestige by migrating and returning exhort younger men to follow in their footsteps. . . . Learned cultural responses thereby maintain a migration ethos . . . that is not only valuable in coping with contemporary problems, but also provides continuity with the past."

The Haitian diaspora (dispersion) offers some significant differences. While Haitian migration is also a part of the nation's history, a return flow is noticeably absent. One of every six Haitians now lives abroad—primarily in Cuba, the Dominican Republic, Venezuela, Colombia, Mexico, and the Bahamas. In French Guiana, Haitians comprise more than 25 percent of the population. They are also found in large numbers in urban areas of the United States, Canada, and France. The typical Haitian emigrant is poor, has little education, and has few skills or job qualifications.

Scholar Christian A. Girault remarks that although "ordinary Haitian migrants are clearly less educated than the Cubans, Dominicans, Puerto Ricans and even Jamaicans, they are not Haiti's most miserable; the latter could never hope to buy an air ticket or boat passage, or to pay an agent." Those who establish new roots in host countries tend to remain, even though they experience severe discrimination and are stereotyped as "undesirable" because they are perceived as bringing with them "misery, magic and disease," particularly AIDS.

There is also some seasonal movement of the population on the island itself. Agricultural workers by the tens of thousands are found in neighboring Dominican Republic. *Madames sara,* or peddlers, buy and sell consumer goods abroad and provide "an essential provisioning function for the national market."

AN ENVIRONMENT IN DANGER

When one speaks of soil erosion and deforestation in a Caribbean context, Haiti is the example that usually springs to mind. While that image is accurate, it is also too limiting, for much of the Caribbean is threatened with ecological disaster. Part of the problem is historical, for deforestation began with the development of sugarcane cultivation in the seventeenth century. But now, soil erosion and depletion as well as the exploitation of marginal lands by growing populations perpetuate a vicious cycle between inhabitants and the land on which they live. Cultivation of sloping hillsides, or denuding the slopes in the search of wood to make charcoal, creates a situation in which erosion is constant and an ecological and human disaster likely. In 2004 days of heavy rain on the island of Hispaniola generated thousands of mudslides and killed an estimated 2,000 people in Haiti and the Dominican Republic.

A 1959 report on soil conditions in Jamaica noted that, in one district of the Blue Mountains, on the eastern end of that island, the topsoil had vanished, a victim of rapid erosion. The problem is not unique to the large islands, however. Bonham Richardson observes that ecological degradation on the smallest islands is acute. Thorn scrub and grasses have replaced native forest. "A regional drought in 1977, leading to starvation in Haiti and producing crop and livestock loss south to Trinidad, was severe only partly because of the lack of rain. Grasses and shrubs afford little protection against the sun and thus cannot help the soil to retain moisture in the face of periodic drought. Neither do they inhibit soil loss."

Migration of the islands' inhabitants has at times exacerbated the situation. In times of peak migration, a depleted labor force on some of the islands has resulted in landowners resorting to the raising of livestock, which is not labor-intensive. But livestock contribute to further ecological destruction. "Emigration itself has thus indirectly fed the ongoing devastation of island environments, and some of the changes seem irreversible. Parts of the smaller islands already resemble moonscapes. They seem simply unable to sustain their local resident populations, not to mention future generations or those working abroad who may someday be forced to return for good."

MUSIC, DANCE, FOLKLORE, AND FOOD

Travel accounts of the Caribbean tend to focus on local music, dances, and foods. Calypso, the limbo, steel bands, reggae, and African–Cuban rhythms are well known. Much of the music derives from Amerindian and African roots.

Calypso music apparently originated in Trinidad and spread to the other islands. Calypso singers improvise on any theme; they are particularly adept at poking fun at politicians and their shortcomings. Indeed, governments are as attentive to the lyrics of a politically inspired calypso tune as they are to the opposition press. On a broader scale, calypso is a mirror of Caribbean society.

Some traditional folkways, such as storytelling and other forms of oral history, are in danger of being replaced by electronic media, particularly radio, tape recorders, and jukeboxes. The new entertainment is both popular and readily available.

Scholar Laura Tanna has gathered much of Kingston, Jamaica's, oral history. Her quest for storyteller Adina Henry took her to one of the city's worst slums, the Dungle, and was reprinted in *Caribbean Review:* "We walked down the tracks to a Jewish cemetery, with gravestones dating back to the 1600s. It, too, was covered in litter, decaying amid the rubble of broken stones. Four of the tombs bear the emblem of the skull and crossbones. Popular belief has it that Spanish gold is buried in the tombs, and several of them have been desecrated by treasure seekers. We passed the East Indian shacks, and completed our tour of Majesty Pen amidst greetings of 'Love' and 'Peace' and with the fragrance of ganja [marijuana] wafting across the way. Everywhere, people were warm and friendly, shaking hands, chatting, drinking beer, or playing dominos. One of the shacks had a small bar and jukebox inside. There, in the midst of pigs grunting at one's feet in the mud and slime, in the dirt and dust, people had their own jukeboxes, tape recorders, and radios, all blaring out reggae, the voice of the ghetto." Tanna found Miss Adina, whose stories revealed the significant African contribution to West Indian folk culture.

In recent years, Caribbean foods have become more accepted, and even celebrated, within the region as well as internationally. Part of the search for an identity involves a new attention to traditional recipes. French, Spanish, and English recipes have been adapted to local foods—iguana, frogs, seafood, fruits, and vegetables. Cassava, guava, and mangos figure prominently in the islanders' diets.

The diversity of the Caribbean is awesome, with its potpourri of peoples and cultures. Its roots lie in Spain, Portugal, England, France, the Netherlands, Africa, India, China, and Japan. There has emerged no distinct West Indian culture, and the Caribbean peoples' identities are determined by the island—no matter how small—on which they live. For the Commonwealth Caribbean, nationalist stirrings are still weak and lacking in focus; while people in Cuba and the Dominican Republic have a much surer grasp on who they are. Nationalism is a strong integrating force in both of these nations. The Caribbean is a fascinating and diverse corner of the world that is far more complex than the travel posters imply.

Antigua and Barbuda

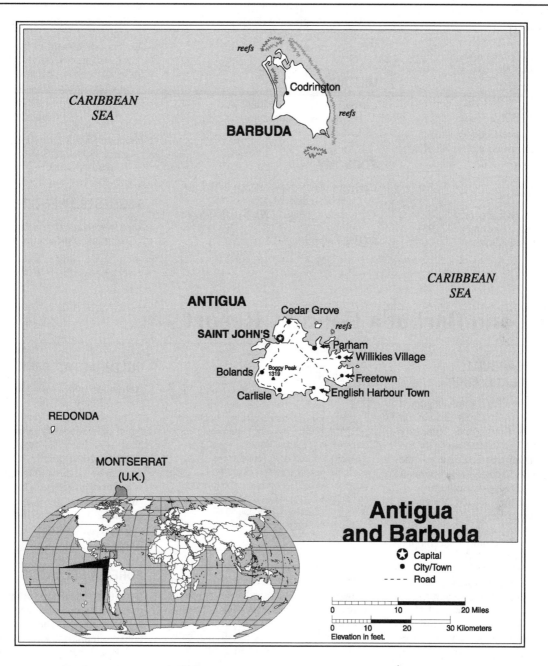

Antigua and Barbuda Statistics

GEOGRAPHY

Area in Square Miles (Kilometers):
171 (442) (about 2 1/2 times the size of Washington, D.C.)
Capital (Population): Saint John's (31,000)
Environmental Concerns: water management; clearing of trees
Geographical Features: mostly low-lying limestone and coral islands, with some higher volcanic areas

Climate: tropical marine

PEOPLE

Population

Total: 69,481 (2007 est.)
Annual Growth Rate: 0.52%
Rural/Urban Population Ratio: 64/36
Major Languages: English; Creole
Ethnic Makeup: almost entirely black African origin; some of British, Portuguese, Lebanese, or Syrian origin
Religions: 25.7% Anglican; 12.3% Seventh Day Adventist; 10.6% Pentecostal; 10.5% Moravian; 10.4% Catholic

Health

Life Expectancy at Birth: 70 years (male); 75 years (female)
Infant Mortality Rate (Ratio): 18.26/1,000
Physicians Available (Ratio): 1/1,083

Education

Adult Literacy Rate: 85.8%
Compulsory (Ages): 5–16

COMMUNICATION

Telephones: 40,000 main lines
Cell Phones: 102,000
Internet Users: 32,000

TRANSPORTATION

Roadways in Kilometers (miles): 1165 (724)
Railroads in Kilometers (miles): 48 (77)
Usable Airfields: 3

GOVERNMENT

Type: parliamentary democracy
Independence Date: November 1, 1981
 (from the United Kingdom)

Head of State/Government: Queen
 Elizabeth II; Prime Minister Baldwin
 Spencer
Political Parties: Antigua Labour Party;
 United Progressive Party; a coalition
 of opposing parties
Suffrage: universal at 18

MILITARY

Current Disputes: tensions
 between Antiguans and
 Barbudans

ECONOMY

Currency ($U.S. Equivalent): 2.75 East
 Caribbean dollars = $1
Per Capita Income/GDP: $10,900/$905
 million
GDP Growth Rate: 3.8%

Inflation Rate: 2.8%
Unemployment Rate: 11%
Labor Force: 30,000
Natural Resources: negligible;
 the pleasant climate fosters
 tourism
Agriculture: cotton; fruits; vegetables;
 sugarcane; livestock
Industry: tourism; construction; light
 manufacturing
Exports: $84.3 million (primary
 partners Caribbean, Guyana,
 United States)
Imports: $522.8 million (primary
 partners United States, United
 Kingdom, Canada)

SUGGESTED WEB SITE

http://www.cia.gov/cia/publications/
 factbook/geos/ac.html

Antigua and Barbuda Country Report

ANTIGUA AND BARBUDA: A STRAINED RELATIONSHIP

The nation of Antigua and Barbuda gained its independence from Great Britain on November 1, 1981. Both islands, tenuously linked since 1967, illustrate perfectly the degree of localism characteristic of the West Indies. Barbudans—who number approximately 1,200—culturally and politically believe that they are not Antiguans; indeed, since independence of Britain, they have been intent on secession. Barbudans view Antiguans as little more than colonial masters.

MEMORIES OF SLAVERY

Antigua was a sugar island for most of its history. This image changed radically in the 1960s, when the black-power movement then sweeping the Caribbean convinced Antiguans that work on the sugar plantations was "submissive" and carried the psychological and social stigma of historic slave labor. In response to the clamor, the government gradually phased out sugar production, which ended entirely in 1972. The decline of agriculture resulted in a strong rural-to-urban flow of people. To replace lost revenue from the earnings of sugar, the government promoted tourism.

Tourism produced the unexpected result of greater freedom for women, in that they gained access to previously unavailable

DEVELOPMENT

Land-use patterns in the islands show that 37 percent of the land is devoted to grazing, 34 percent to woodlands, 11 percent to settlements, 3 percent to tourist areas, and 3 percent to airports. Agricultural use accounts for only 8 percent of the land. Tourism, the leading source of employment, has replaced agriculture as the prime generator of revenue. Perhaps 50 percent of foreign exchange derives from tourism.

employment opportunities. Anthropologist W. Penn Handwerker has shown that a combination of jobs and education for women has resulted in a marked decline in fertility. Between 1965 and the 1980s, real wages doubled, infant mortality fell dramatically, and the proportion of women ages 20 to 24 who completed secondary school rose from 3 percent to about 50 percent. "Women were freed from dependency on their children" as well as their men and created "conditions for a revolution in gender relations." Men outmigrated as the economy shifted, and women took the new jobs in tourism. Many of the jobs demanded higher skills, which in turn resulted in more education for women, followed by even better jobs. And notes Handwerker: "Women empowered by education and good jobs are less likely to suffer abuse from partners."

CULTURAL PATTERNS

Antiguans and Barbudans are culturally similar. Many islanders still have a strong affinity for England and English culture, while others identify more with what they hold to be their African–Creole roots. On Antigua, for example, Creole, which is spoken by virtually the entire population, is believed to reflect what is genuine and "natural" about the island and its culture. Standard English, even though it is the official language, carries in the popular mind an aura of falseness.

FOREIGN RELATIONS

Despite the small size of the country, Antigua and Barbuda are actively courted by regional powers. The United States maintains a satellite-tracking station on Antigua, and Brazil has provided loans and other assistance. A small oil refinery, jointly supported by Venezuela and Mexico, began operations in 1982.

FAMILY POLITICS

From 1951 to 2004, with one interruption, Antiguan politics has been dominated by the family of Vere Bird and his Antigua Labour Party (ALP). Charges of nepotism, corruption, drug smuggling, and money laundering dogged the Vere Bird administration for years. Still, in 1994, Lester Bird

FREEDOM

The government's control of electronic media, which was strict under Prime Minister Bird's administrations, has been eased. There is now more of an air of openness and opinions divergent to those of government ministries are now regularly expressed.

managed to succeed his 84-year-old father as prime minister, and the ALP won 11 of 17 seats in elections. Lester admitted that his father had been guilty of some "misjudgments" and quickly pledged that the ALP would improve education, better the status of women, and increase the presence of young people in government.

HEALTH/WELFARE

The government has initiated programs to enhance educational opportunities for men and women and to assist in family planning. The new Directorate of Women's Affairs helps women to advance in government and in the professions. It has also sponsored educational programs for women in health, crafts, and business skills.

The younger Bird, in his State of the Nation address early in 1995, challenged Antiguans to transform their country on their own terms, rather than those dictated by the International Monetary Fund. His government would take "tough and unpopular" measures to avoid the humiliation of going "cap in hand" to foreign financial institutions. Those tough measures included increases in contributions for medical benefits, property and personal taxes, and business and motor-vehicle licenses.

ACHIEVEMENTS

Antigua has preserved its rich historical heritage, from the dockyard named for Admiral Lord Nelson to the Ebenezer Methodist Church. Built in 1839, the latter was the "mother church" for Methodism in the Caribbean.

In 2003, however, the government angered public employees, who constitute one-third of the labor force, when it failed to pay salaries on time. Tourism was stagnant and the public debt was a very high 140 percent of GDP. Economic difficulties when coupled with persistent scandal and corruption brought 90 percent of the electorate to the polls in 2004 and Bird's ALP was soundly defeated. Prime Minister Baldwin Spencer's government must now live up to the expectations of the electorate. Tourism, the earnings from which slipped from 80 percent of GDP in 1994 to only 50 percent in 2004, is a major area of concern. Internet gambling sites have emerged as a revenue supplement to tourism, but this has embroiled Antigua in a trade dispute with the United States, which places restrictions on the business. Agricultural production, consisting primarily of fruits and vegetables, concentrates on the domestic market and does not generate significant foreign exchange earnings. Spencer's administration must make some difficult choices in the near future.

Timeline: PAST

1632
The English settle Antigua

1834
Antigua abolishes slavery

1958–1962
Antigua becomes part of the West Indies Federation

1981
Independence from Great Britain

1990s
Barbuda talks of secession; Hurricane Luis devastates the islands

PRESENT

2000s
The Bird government announces a "zero tolerance" drug policy

Bird political dynasty comes to an end in 2004

The Bahamas (Commonwealth of the Bahamas)

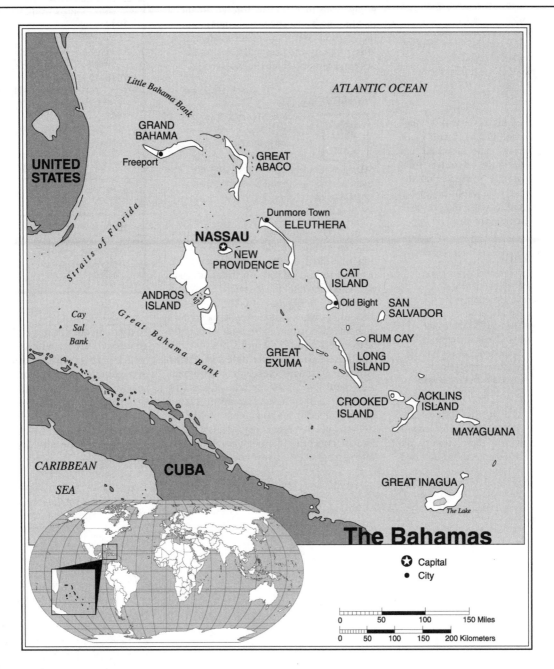

The Bahamas Statistics

GEOGRAPHY

Area in Square Miles (Kilometers):
5,380 (13,934) (about the size of
Connecticut)
Capital (Population): Nassau (210,832)
Environmental Concerns: coral-reef
decay; waste disposal
Geographical Features: long, flat coral
formations with some low, rounded hills
Climate: tropical marine

PEOPLE

Population

Total: 305,655 (2007 est.)
Annual Growth Rate: 0.6%
Rural/Urban Population Ratio: 13/87
Ethnic Makeup: 85% black; 15% white
Major Language: English
Religions: 32% Baptist; 15% Anglican;
13.5% Catholic; 8.1% Pentecostal;
22% others or not specified

Health

Life Expectancy at Birth: 62 years (male);
69 years (female)
Infant Mortality Rate (Ratio):
24.17/1,000
Physicians Available (Ratio): 1/709

Education

Adult Literacy Rate: 95.6%
Compulsory (Ages): 5–14; free

COMMUNICATION

Telephones: 133,100 main lines
Daily Newspaper Circulation: 126 per
1,000 people
Cell Phones: 227,800
Internet Users: 103,000

TRANSPORTATION

Highways in Kilometers (Miles): 1,672
(2,693)
Usable Airfields: 62

GOVERNMENT

Type: constitutional parliamentary
democracy
Independence Date: July 10, 1973 (from
the United Kingdom)

Head of State/Government: Queen
Elizabeth II; Prime Minister Hubert A.
Ingraham
Political Parties: Free National
Movement; Progressive Liberal Party
Suffrage: universal at 18

MILITARY

Military Expenditures (% of GDP): 0.5%

ECONOMY

Currency ($U.S. Equivalent): 1.00
Bahamian dollar = $1
Per Capita Income/GDP: $22,700/$6.449
billion
GDP Growth Rate: 2.8%
Inflation Rate: 2.4%
Unemployment Rate: 7.6%

Labor Force: 181,900
Natural Resources: salt; aragonite;
timber
Agriculture: citrus fruits; vegetables;
poultry
Industry: tourism; banking; cement;
oil refining and transshipment;
salt production; rum; aragonite;
pharmaceuticals; steel pipe
Exports: $674 million (primary partners
United States, Switzerland, United
Kingdom)
Imports: $2.401 billion (primary partners
United States, Italy, Japan)

SUGGESTED WEB SITE

http://www.cia.gov/cia/publications/
factbook/index.html

The Bahamas Country Report

BAHAMAS: A NATION OF ISLANDS

Christopher Columbus made his first landfall in the Bahamas in 1492, when he touched ashore on the island of San Salvador. Permanent settlements on the islands were not established by the British until 1647, when the Eleutheran Adventurers, a group of English and Bermudan religious dissidents, landed. The island was privately governed until 1717, when it became a British Crown colony. During the U.S. Civil War, Confederate blockade runners used the Bahamas as a base. The tradition continued in the years after World War I, when Prohibition rum runners used the islands as a base. Today, drug traffickers utilize the isolation of the out-islands for their illicit operations.

DEVELOPMENT

Together manufacturing and agriculture account for only 10 percent of GDP. There has been little growth in either sector. Offshore banking and tourism contribute the most toward economic growth and together account for about half of the jobs on the islands.

Although the Bahamas are made up of almost 700 islands, only 10 have populations of any significant size. Of these, New Providence and Grand Bahama contain more than 75 percent of the Bahamian population. Because most economic and cultural activities take place on the larger

islands, other islands—particularly those in the southern region—have suffered depopulation over the years as young men and women have moved to the two major centers of activity.

FREEDOM

Women participate actively in all levels of government and business. The Constitution does, however, make some distinctions between males and females with regard to citizenship and permanent-resident status.

Migrants from Haiti and Jamaica have also caused problems for the Bahamian government. There are an estimated 60,000 illegal Haitians now resident in the Bahamas—equivalent to nearly one-fifth of the total Bahamian population of 300,000. The Bahamian response was tolerance until late 1994, when the government established tough new policies that reflected a fear that the country would be "overwhelmed" by Haitian immigrants. In the words of one official, the large numbers of Haitians would "result in a very fundamental economic and social transformation that even the very naïve would understand to be undesirable." Imprisonment, marginalization, no legal right to work, and even the denial of access to schools and hospitals are now endured by the immigrants.

Bahamian problems with Jamaicans are rooted differently. The jealous isolation of

each of the island nations is reflected in the peoples' fears and suspicions of the activities of their neighbors. As a result, inter-island freedom of movement is subject to strict scrutiny.

The Bahamas were granted their independence from Great Britain in 1973 and established a constitutional parliamentary democracy governed by a freely elected prime minister and Parliament. Upon independence, there was a transfer of political power from a small white elite to the black majority, who comprise 85 percent of the population. Whites continue to play a role in the political process, however, and several hold high-level civil-service and political posts.

The country has enjoyed a marked improvement in health conditions over the past few decades. Life expectancy has risen, and infant mortality has declined. Virtually all people living in urban areas have access to good drinking water, although the age and dilapidated condition of the capital's (Nassau) water system could present problems in the near future.

HEALTH/WELFARE

Cases of child abuse and neglect in the Bahamas rose in the 1990s. The Government and Women's Crisis Centre focused on the need to fight child abuse through a public-awareness program that had as its theme: "It shouldn't hurt to be a child."

The government has begun a program to restructure education on the islands. The authorities have placed a new emphasis on technical and vocational training so that skilled jobs in the economy now held by foreigners will be performed by Bahamians. But while the literacy rate has remained high, there is a shortage of teachers, equipment, and supplies.

ACHIEVEMENTS

The natural beauty of the islands has had a lasting effect on those who have visited them. As a result of his experiences in the waters off Bimini, Ernest Hemingway wrote his classic *The Old Man and the Sea*.

The government of Prime Minister Hubert A. Ingraham and his Free National Movement won a clear mandate in 1997 over the opposition Progressive Liberal Party to continue the policies and programs it initiated in 1992. *The Miami Herald* reported that the election "marked a watershed in Bahamian politics, with many new faces on the ballot and both parties facing leadership succession struggles before the next vote is due in 2002." Ideologically, the two contending political parties were similar; thus, voters made their decisions on the basis of who they felt would provide jobs and bring crime under control. In 2002 voters decided that the Progressive Liberal Party would do a better job and elected Perry Christie as prime minister. That apparently did not happen and Hubert Ingraham was again elected prime minister in 2007.

Honest government and a history of working effectively with the private sector to improve the national economy have dramatically increased foreign investment in the Bahamas. Rapid growth in the service sector of the economy has stimulated the migration of people from fishing and farming villages to the commercial tourist centers in New Providence Island, Grand Bahama, and Great Abaco. It is estimated that tourism now accounts for 60 percent of GDP and absorbs half of the labor force. Importantly, today there are more companies owned by Bahamians than ever before.

Despite new investments, many young Bahamians out-migrate. The thousands of illegal Haitian immigrants have added pressure to the job market and still worry some Bahamians that their own sense of identity may be threatened. But in general, there is a sense of optimism in the islands.

Timeline: PAST

1492
Christopher Columbus first sights the New World at San Salvador Island

1647
The first English settlement in the Bahamas

1967
Black-power controversy

1973
Independence from Great Britain

1980s
Violent crime, drug trafficking, and narcotics addiction become serious social problems

1990s
New investments create jobs and cut the unemployment rate

PRESENT

2000s
Employment is up, and so is many Bahamians' sense of optimism

2007
Hubert Ingraham elected prime minister

Barbados

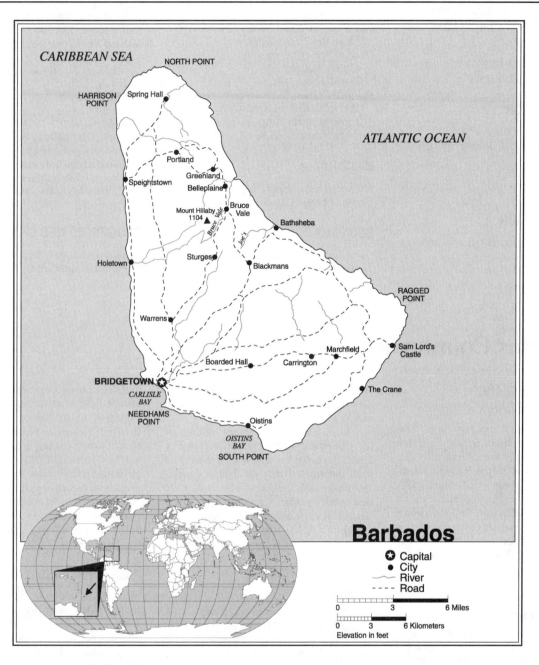

Barbados Statistics

GEOGRAPHY

Area in Square Miles (Kilometers):
166 (431) (about 2½ times the size of Washington, D.C.)

Capital (Population): Bridgetown 96,578

Environmental Concerns: pollution of coastal waters from waste disposal by ships; soil erosion; illegal solid-waste disposal

Geographical Features: relatively flat; rises gently to central highland region

Climate: tropical marine

PEOPLE

Population

Total: 280,946 (2007 est.)
Annual Growth Rate: 0.36%

Rural/Urban Population Ratio:
52/48

Major Language: English

Ethnic Makeup: 90% black; 4% White; 6% Asian and mixed

Religions: 67% Protestant (Anglican, Pentecostal, Methodist, others); 4% Roman Catholic; 17% unaffiliated; 12% others or unknown

Health

Life Expectancy at Birth: 71 years (male);
75 years (female)
Infant Mortality Rate (Ratio): 11.55/1,000
Physicians Available (Ratio): 1/842

Education

Adult Literacy Rate: 99.7%
Compulsory (Ages): 5–16

COMMUNICATION

Telephones: 134,900 main lines
Daily Newspaper Circulation: 157 per
1,000 people
Cell Phones: 206,200
Internet Users: 160,000

TRANSPORTATION

Highways in Kilometers (miles): 1,650
(1,025)
Usable Airfields: 1

GOVERNMENT

Type: parliamentary democracy;
independent sovereign state within
Commonwealth
Independence Date: November 30, 1966
(from the United Kingdom)
Head of State/Government:
Queen Elizabeth II;
David Thompson
Political Parties: Democratic Labour
Party; Barbados Labour Party; People's
Empowerment Party
Suffrage: universal at 18

MILITARY

Military Expenditures (% of GDP): 0.5%
Current Disputes: none

ECONOMY

Currency ($U.S. Equivalent): 2.02
Barbados dollars = $1

Per Capita Income/GDP: $19,700/$3.346
billion
GDP Growth Rate: 4%
Inflation Rate: 5.5%
Unemployment Rate: 10.7%
Labor Force: 128,500
Natural Resources: petroleum; fish;
natural gas
Agriculture: sugarcane; vegetables;
cotton
Industry: tourism; light
manufacturing; sugar; component
assembly
Exports: $385 million (primary partners
United Kingdom, United States,
Trinidad and Tobago)
Imports: $1.586 billion (primary partners
United States, Trinidad and Tobago,
Japan)

SUGGESTED WEB SITE

http://www.cia.gov/cia/publications/
factbook/index.html

Barbados Country Report

THE LITTLE ENGLAND OF THE CARIBBEAN

A parliamentary democracy that won its independence from Britain in 1966, Barbados boasts a House of Assembly that is the third oldest in the Western Hemisphere, after Bermuda's and Virginia's. A statement of the rights and privileges of Bajans (as Barbadians are called), known as the Charter of Barbados, was proclaimed in 1652 and has been upheld by those governing the island. The press is free, labor is strong and well organized, and human rights are respected.

DEVELOPMENT

Between 1971 and 1999, there was an approximate 30 percent decrease in the amount of land used for agriculture. Formerly agricultural land has been transformed into golf courses, residential areas, commercial developments, tourist facilities, or abandoned. Additionally, there are offshore reserves of oil and natural gas.

While the majority of the populations of the English-speaking West Indies still admire the British, this admiration is carried to extremes in Barbados. In 1969, for example, Bajan soccer teams chose English names and colors—Arsenal, Tottenham

Hotspurs, Liverpool, and Coventry City. Among the primary religions are Anglican and Methodist Protestantism.

Unlike most of the other islands of the Caribbean, European sailors initially found Barbados uninhabited. It has since been determined that the island's original inhabitants, the Arawak Indians, were destroyed by Carib Indians who overran the region and then abandoned the islands. Settled by the English, Barbados was always under British control until its independence.

FREEDOM

Barbados has maintained an excellent human-rights record. The government officially advocates strengthening the human-rights machinery of the United Nations and the Organization of American States. Women are active participants in the country's economic, political, and social life.

A DIVERSIFYING ECONOMY

In terms of wealth, as compared to other West Indian nations, Barbados is well off. One important factor is that Barbados has been able to diversify its economy; thus, the country is no longer dependent solely on sugar and its by-products rum and molasses. Manufacturing and high-technology

industries now contribute to economic growth, and tourism has overtaken agriculture as a generator of foreign exhange. Off-shore finance and information services have also become important.

The Constitution of 1966 authorized the government to promote the general welfare of the citizens of the island through equitable distribution of wealth. While governments have made a sincere effort to wipe out pockets of poverty, a great disparity in wealth still exists.

RACE AND CLASS

Barbados is a class- and race-conscious society. One authority noted that there are three classes (elite, middle class, and masses) and two colors (white/light and black). Land is highly concentrated in the hands of a few; 10 percent of the population own 95 percent of the land. Most of the nation's landed estates and businesses are owned by whites, even though they

HEALTH/WELFARE

By 2007, unemployment had dropped to 10.7 percent, from the 1993 high of 26 percent. Although prices have risen, a sound economy has given people more money to spend on consumer goods, durables, and housing.

comprise a very small percentage of the population (4 percent).

While discrimination based on color is legally prohibited, color distinctions continue to correlate with class differences and dominate most personal associations. Although whites have been displaced politically, they still comprise more than half of the group considered "influential" in the country.

ACHIEVEMENTS

Bajan George Lamming has won attention from the world's literary community for his novels, each of which explores a stage in or an aspect of the colonial experience. Through his works, he explains what it is to be simultaneously a citizen of one's island and a West Indian.

Even though Barbados's class structure is more rigid than that of other West Indian states, there is upward social mobility for all people, and the middle class has been growing steadily in size. Poor whites, known as "Redlegs," have frequently moved into managerial positions on the estates. The middle class also includes a fairly large percentage of blacks and mulattos. Bajans have long enjoyed access to public and private educational systems, which have been the object of a good deal of national pride.

Adequate medical care is available to all residents through local clinics and hospitals under a government health program. All Bajans are covered under government health insurance programs.

Timeline: PAST

1625
Barbados is occupied by the English

1647
The first sugar from Barbados is sent to England

1832
Full citizenship is granted to nonwhites

1951
Universal suffrage

1966
Independence from Great Britain

1990s
Barbados develops an offshore banking industry

PRESENT

2000s
The Arthur government continues its policy of economic diversification

2008
David Thompson elected prime minister

SEEKING A LEADERSHIP ROLE

Given the nation's relative wealth and its dynamism, Bajans have been inclined to seek a strong role in the region. In terms of Caribbean politics, economic development, and defense, Bajans feel that they have a right and a duty to lead.

The Labour Party has continued to push privatization policies. In 1993, an important step was taken toward the greater diversification of the nation's economic base with the creation of offshore financial services. By 1995, the new industry had created many new jobs for Bajans and had significantly reduced the high unemployment rate. Recent discussions on the Free Trade Area of the Americas (FTAA) has stimulated much debate among the smaller Caribbean states. While the Barbados government sees the possibilities of tying into a market of 800 million consumers, it also feels that the larger states must afford smaller nations special and differential treatment. Others are concerned about maintaining the "Bajan way of life" and worry that "the world is falling in on us." Critics charge that any new wealth would be skewed saying, it has the attributes of "fancy molasses." "Very little trickles down, the rich get richer while the poor become marginalized." Other concerns have been expressed about pollution and the possible loss, because of FTAA, of offshore financial privileges.

Cuba (Republic of Cuba)

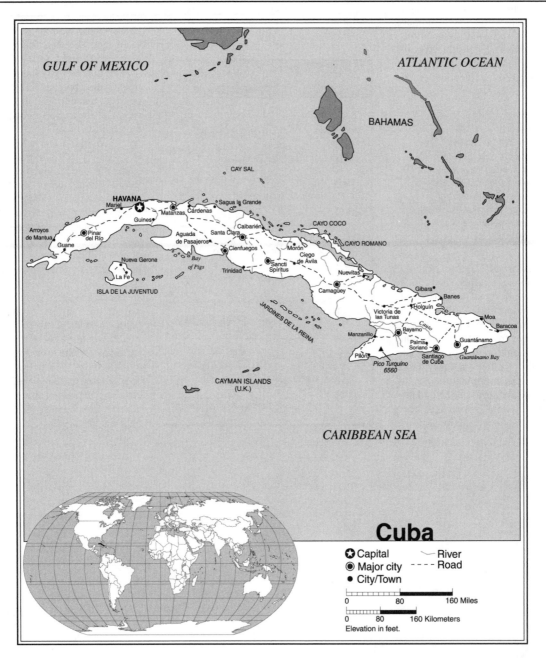

Cuba

- ✪ Capital
- ◉ Major city
- ● City/Town
- River
- - - - Road

0   80   160 Miles

0   80   160 Kilometers

Elevation in feet.

Cuba Statistics

GEOGRAPHY

Area in Square Miles (Kilometers): 44,200 (114,471) (about the size of Pennsylvania)

Capital (Population): Havana 2,600,000

Environmental Concerns: pollution of Havana Bay; threatened wildlife populations; deforestation

Geographical Features: mostly flat to rolling plains; rugged hills and mountains in the southeast

Climate: tropical

PEOPLE

Population

Total: 11,394,043 (2007 est.)

Annual Growth Rate: 0.27%

Rural/Urban Population Ratio: 24/76

Ethnic Makeup: 51% mulatto; 37% white; 11% black; 1% Chinese

Major Language: Spanish

Religion: 85% Roman Catholic before Castro assumed power

Health

Life Expectancy at Birth: 75 years (male); 79 years (female)

Infant Mortality Rate (Ratio): 6.04/1,000

Physicians Available (Ratio): 1/231

Education

Adult Literacy Rate: 99.8%
Compulsory (Ages): 6–11; free

COMMUNICATION

Telephones: 972,900 main lines
Daily Newspaper Circulation: 122 per
   1,000 people
Cell Phones: 152,700
Internet Users: 240,000

TRANSPORTATION

Roadways in Kilometers (*miles*): 60,858
   (37,815)
Railroads in Kilometers (miles): 2,985
   (4,807)
Usable Airfields: 165

GOVERNMENT

Type: Communist state
Independence Date: May 20, 1902 (from
   Spain)

Head of State/Government:
   President Raúl Castro is both
   head of state and head of
   government
Political Parties: Cuban Communist
   Party
Suffrage: universal at 16

MILITARY

Military Expenditures (% of GDP):
   3.8% (est.)
Current Disputes: U.S. Naval Base at
   Guantanamo Bay is leased to the
   United States

ECONOMY

Currency ($U.S. Equivalent):
   23.12 Cuban pesos = $1
   (official rate)
Per Capita Income/GDP: $4,500/$45.1
   billion
GDP Growth Rate: 7%
Inflation Rate: 3.6%

Unemployment Rate: 1.9%
Labor Force: 4,853,000
Natural Resources: cobalt; nickel;
   iron ore; copper; manganese; salt;
   timber; silica; petroleum; arable
   land
Agriculture: sugarcane; tobacco; citrus
   fruits; coffee; rice; potatoes; beans;
   livestock
Industry: sugar; petroleum; food; textiles;
   tobacco; chemicals; paper and wood
   products; metals; cement; fertilizers;
   consumer goods; agricultural
   machinery
Exports: $3.231 billion (f.o.b.)
   (primary partners Russia, the
   Netherlands, Canada)
Imports: $10.86 billion (f.o.b.)
   (primary partners Spain, Venezuela,
   Mexico)

SUGGESTED WEB SITE

http://www.cia.gov/cia/publications/
   factbook/index.html

Cuba Country Report

REFLECTIONS ON A REVOLUTION

Cuba, which contains about half the land area of the West Indies, has held the attention of the world since 1959. In that year, Fidel Castro led his victorious rebels into the capital city of Havana and began a revolution that has profoundly affected Cuban society. The Cuban Revolution had its roots in the struggle for independence of Spain in the late nineteenth century, in the aborted Nationalist Revolution of 1933, and in the Constitution of 1940. It grew from Cuba's history and must be understood as a Cuban phenomenon.

The Revolution in some respects represents the fulfillment of the goals of the Cuban Constitution of 1940, a radically nationalist document that was never fully implemented. It banned *latifundia* (the ownership of vast landed estates) and discouraged foreign ownership of the land. It permitted the confiscation of property in the public or social interest. The state was authorized to provide full employment for its people and to direct the course of the national economy. Finally, the Constitution of 1940 gave the Cuban state control of the sugar industry, which at the time was controlled by U.S. companies.

The current Constitution, written in 1976 and amended in 1992 and 2002, incorporates 36 percent of the articles of the 1940 Constitution. In other words, many of Castro's policies and programs are founded in Cuban history and the aspirations of the Cuban people. Revolutionary Cuba—at least in its earlier years—was very successful in solving the nation's most pressing problems of poverty. But those successes must be balanced against the loss of basic freedoms imposed by a strong authoritarian state.

ACHIEVEMENTS OF THE REVOLUTION
Education

One of the Revolution's most impressive successes has been in the area of education. In 1960, the Castro regime decided to place emphasis on raising the minimum level of education for the whole population. To accomplish this, some 200,000 Cubans were mobilized in 1961 under the slogan "Let those who know more teach those who know less." In a single year, the literacy rate rose from 76 to 96 percent. Free education was made available to all Cubans. The literacy campaign involved many Cubans in an attempt to recognize and attack the problems of rural impoverishment. It was the first taste of active public life for many women who were students or teachers and because of their

involvement, they began to redefine sex roles and attitudes.

While the literacy campaign was a resounding triumph, long-term educational policy was less satisfactory. Officials blamed the high dropout rate in elementary and junior high schools on poor school facilities and inadequate teacher training. Students also apparently lacked enthusiasm, and Castro himself acknowledged that students needed systematic, constant, daily work and discipline.

"Scholarship students and students in general," in Castro's words, "are willing to do anything, except to study hard."

Health Care

The Revolution took great strides forward in improving the health of the Cuban population, especially in rural regions. Success in this area is all the more impressive when one considers that between one-third and one-half of all doctors left the country between 1959 and 1962. Health care initially declined sharply, and the infant mortality rate rose rapidly. But with the training of new health-care professionals, the gaps were filled. The infant mortality rate in Cuba is now at a level comparable to that of developed countries.

From the outset, the government decided to concentrate on rural areas, where the

133

need was the greatest. Medical treatment was free, and newly graduated doctors had to serve in the countryside for at least two years. The Cuban health service was founded on the principle that good health for all, without discrimination, is a birthright of Cubans. All Cubans were included under a national health plan.

The first national health standards were developed between 1961 and 1965, and eight priority areas were identified: infant and maternal care, adult health care, care for the elderly, environmental health, nutrition, dentistry, school health programs, and occupational health. A program of insect spraying and immunization eradicated malaria and poliomyelitis. Cuban life expectancy became one of the highest in the world, and Cuba's leading causes of death became the same as in the United States—heart disease, cancer, and stroke.

Before the Revolution of 1959, there was very little health and safety regulation for workers. Afterward, however, important advances were made in the training of specialized inspectors and occupational physicians. In 1978, a Work Safety and Health Law was enacted, which defined the rights and responsibilities of government agencies, workplace administrators, unions, and workers.

Cuba also exported its health-care expertise. It has had medical teams in countries from Nicaragua to Yemen and more doctors overseas than the World Health Organization. From 2003 to the present Cuban medical personnel provided health care to Venezuela, which in turn provided Cuba with cheap petroleum.

Redistribution of Wealth

The third great area of change presided over by the Revolution was income redistribution. The Revolution changed the lives of rural poor and agricultural workers. They gained the most in comparison to other groups in Cuban society—especially urban groups. From 1962 to 1973, for example, agricultural workers saw their wages rise from less than 60 percent to 93 percent of the national average.

Still, Cuba's minimum wage was inadequate for most families. Many families needed two wage earners to make ends meet. All wages were enhanced by the so-called social wage, which consisted of free medical care and education, subsidized housing, and low food prices. Yet persistent shortages and tight rationing of food undermined a good portion of the social wage. Newly married couples found it necessary to live with relatives, sometimes for years, before they could obtain their own housing, which was in short supply. Food supplies, especially those provided by the informal sector, were adversely affected by a 1986 decision to eliminate independent producers because an informal private sector was deemed antithetical to "socialist morality" and promoted materialism.

Women in Cuba

From the outset of the Revolution, Fidel Castro appealed to women as active participants in the movement and redefined their political roles. Women's interests were protected by the Federation of Cuban Women, an integral part of the ruling party. The Family Code of 1975 equalized pay scales, reversed sexual discrimination against promotions, provided generous maternity leave, and gave employed women preferential access to goods and services. Although women comprised approximately 30 percent of the Cuban workforce, most were still employed in traditionally female occupations; the Third Congress of the Cuban Communist Party admitted in 1988 that both racial minorities and women were underrepresented in responsible government and party positions at all levels. Significant improvement occurred and by the end of 2007 women held about one-third of the seats in the National Assembly.

SHORTCOMINGS

Even at its best, the new Cuba had significant shortcomings. Wayne Smith, a former chief of the U.S. Interest Section in Havana who was sympathetic to the Revolution, wrote: "There is little freedom of expression and no freedom of the press at all. It is a command society, which still holds political prisoners, some of them under deplorable conditions. Further, while the Revolution has provided the basic needs of all, it has not fulfilled its promise of a higher standard of living for the society as a whole. Cuba was, after all, an urban middle-class society with a relatively high standard of living even before the Revolution. . . . The majority of Cubans are less well off materially."

Castro, to win support for his programs, did not hesitate to take his revolutionary message to the people. Indeed, the key reason why Castro enjoyed such widespread support in Cuba was because the people had the sense of being involved in a great historical process.

Alienation

Not all Cubans identified with the Revolution, and many felt a deep sense of betrayal and alienation. The elite and most of the middle class strongly resisted the changes that robbed them of influence, prestige, and property. Some were particularly bitter, for at its outset, the Revolution had been largely a middle-class movement. For them, Castro was a traitor to his class. Thousands fled Cuba, and some formed the core of an anti-Castro guerrilla movement based in South Florida.

There are many signs that the government, while still popular among many people, has lost the widespread acceptance it enjoyed in the 1960s and 1970s. While it still has the support of the older generation and those in rural areas who benefited from the social transformation of the island, limited economic growth has led to dissatisfaction among urban workers and youth, who are less interested in revolutionary heroes and more interested in economic gains.

More serious disaffection existed in the army. Journalist Georgie Anne Geyer, writing in *World Monitor,* suggests that the 1989 execution of General Arnaldo Ochoa, ostensibly for drug trafficking, was actually motivated by Castro's fears of an emerging competitor for power. "The 1930s-style show trial effectively revealed the presence of an 'Angola generation' in the Cuban military. . . . That generation, which fought in Angola between 1974

AP photo/Jorge Ray/Ap05041701478

Fidel Castro served as prime minister of Cuba from 1959 to 2008.

and 1989, is the competitor generation to Castro's own Sierra Maestra generation." The condemned officers argued that their dealings with drug traffickers were not for personal enrichment but were designed to earn desperately needed hard currency for the state. Some analysts are convinced that Castro knew about drug trafficking and condoned it; others claim that it took place without his knowledge. But the bottom line is that the regime had been shaken at the highest levels, and the purge was the most far-reaching since the 1959 Revolution.

The Economy

The state of the Cuban economy and the future of the Cuban Revolution are inextricably linked. Writing in *World Today,* James J. Guy predicted that, given the economic collapse of the former Soviet Union and its satellites, "Cuba is destined to face serious structural unemployment: its agrarian economy cannot generate the white-collar, technical jobs demanded by a swelling army of graduates. . . . The entire system is deteriorating—the simplest services take months to deliver, water and electricity are constantly interrupted . . . ," and there is widespread corruption and black-marketeering.

Oil is particularly nettlesome. For years after the collapse of the Soviet Union Cuba had no access to affordable petroleum, at great cost to the economy. That changed in 2003 when Venezuela provided Cuba with discounted oil in exchange for Cuban expertise in the areas of health and sports.

Although Castro prided Cuba on being one of the last bulwarks of untainted Marxism-Leninism, in April 1991 he said: "We are not dogmatic . . . we are realistic . . . Under the special conditions of this extraordinary period we are also aware that different forms of international cooperation may be useful." He noted that Cuba had contacted foreign capitalists about the possibility of establishing joint enterprises and remarked that more than 49 percent foreign participation in state businesses was a possibility.

In 1993, Castro called for economic realism. Using the rhetoric of the Revolution, he urged the Legislative Assembly to think seriously about the poor condition of the Cuban economy: "It is painful, but we must be sensible. . . . It is not only with decisiveness, courage and heroism that one saves the Revolution, but also with intelligence. And we have the right to invent ways to survive in these conditions without ever ceasing to be revolutionaries."

ACHIEVEMENTS

A unique cultural contribution of Cuba to the world was the Afro-Cuban movement, with its celebration of black song and dance rhythms. The work of contemporary prize-winning Cuban authors such as Alejo Carpentier and Edmundo Desnoes has been translated into many languages.

A government decree in September 1993 allowed Cubans to establish private businesses; today, Cubans in some 140 professions can work on their own for a profit. At about the same time, the use of dollars was decriminalized, the Cuban currency became convertible, and, in the agricultural sector, the government began to transform state farms into cooperatives. Farmers are now allowed to sell some of their produce in private markets and, increasingly, market forces set the prices of many consumer goods. Managers in state-owned enterprises have been given unprecedented autonomy; and foreign investment, in contrast with past practice, is now encouraged.

Still, the Cuban economy has continued its decline. Mirta Ojito, writing in *The New York Times,* sees older revolutionaries "coming to terms with the failure of their dreams." Cuba now resembles most other underdeveloped countries, with "many needy, unhappy, sad people." The Revolution was supposed to make Cuba prosperous, "not merely survive," and end the country's dependence on the U.S. dollar. By 1999, dollars in circulation in Cuba had created a parallel speculative economy.

So pervasive had the parallel dollar economy become that in October 2004 Castro decreed that dollars would no longer be accepted for commercial transactions anywhere on the island, although dollar bank accounts would still be legal. Expatriate Cubans, who remit perhaps $1 billion annually to relatives on the island, were told to send euros, British pounds, or Canadian dollars. There was certainly a pragmatic side to Castro's decision. By encouraging people to convert their dollars to what was called the "convertible peso" (after a period of grace the government would charge 10 percent to exchange dollars for pesos; there would be no exchange charge for other currencies), Castro was able to provide his government with the dollars needed to purchase critical inputs for Cuba's economy. In the words of Mexico's former ambassador to Cuba, as reported in the *New York Times,* "I don't think this is a political decision at all. It's a pragmatic move." Cuba had to buy more oil than it had planned, and so it urgently needed dollars. Castro was also responding to United States efforts to strengthen economic sanctions against Cuba by setting limits on the amount of money that people could send to relatives on the island.

With the new millennium, Cuba's infrastructure continued to crumble. In 2001, salaries averaged just $15 per month, and the weekly ration card given to each family provided one chicken, just over three pounds of rice and beans, sugar, and two pints of cooking oil. With rising prices, it is not surprising that prostitution, moonlighting, black-marketeering, and begging have rapidly increased. Castro talked with CARICOM states about the possibilities of free trade, but the stifling bureaucracy makes it much easier to export *from* rather than export *to* Cuba.

Freedom Issues

Soon after the Revolution, the government assumed total control of the media. No independent news organization is allowed, and all printed publications are censored by the government or the Communist Party. The arts are subject to strict censorship, and even sports must serve the purposes of the Revolution. As Castro noted: "Within the Revolution everything is possible. Outside it, nothing."

In many respects, there is less freedom now in Cuba than there was before the Revolution. Cuba's human-rights record is not good. There are thousands of political prisoners, and rough treatment and torture—physical and psychological—occur. The Constitution of 1976 allows the repression of all freedoms for all those who oppose the Revolution. U.S. political scientist William LeGrande, who was sympathetic to the Revolution, nevertheless noted that "Cuba is a closed society. The Cuban Communist Party does not allow dissenting views on fundamental policy. It does not allow people to challenge the basic leadership of the regime." But here, too, there are signs of change. In 1995, municipal elections were held under a new system that provides for run-offs if none of the candidates gains a clear majority. In an indication of a new competitiveness in Cuban politics, 326 out of 14,229 positions were subject to the run-off rule.

THE FUTURE

It will be difficult for the government to maintain the unquestioned support of the Cuban population. There must be continued positive accomplishments in the economy. Health and education programs are successful and will continue to be so. "Cubans get free health care, free education and free admission to sports and cultural events [and] 80 percent of all Cubans live in rent-free apartments, and those who do pay rent pay only between 6 and 10 percent of their salaries," according to James J. Guy.

But there must be a recovery of basic political and human freedoms. Criticism of the government must not be the occasion for jail terms or exile. The Revolution must be more inclusive and less exclusive.

Although Castro was never effectively challenged, there are signs of unrest on the island. The military, as noted, is a case in point. Ironically, although Castro lost a good deal of luster internationally as a result of statist economic policies, recent trends in the region away from free trade and toward more authoritarian forms of government has given Cuba strong allies in South America.

Still, many Cubans are frustrated with their lives and continue to take to the sea in an attempt to reach the United States. Thousands have been intercepted by the United States Coast Guard and have been interned.

Fidel Castro embodied the Cuban Revolution and enjoyed staying power. When presented with a gift of a Galapagos tortoise, Castro asked how long they lived. The reply, "More than a hundred years," prompted Castro to say, "How sad it is to outlive one's pets." That longevity for Castro is now at an end. Health problems forced him to hand over the reins of power to his brother, Raúl.

The smooth transition disappointed critics of the regime who hoped that Fidel Castro's passing from the political stage would produce upheaval. In January 1999 *The Economist* asked: "What will follow Fidel?" The magazine suggested that Cubans could be faced with violence and political turmoil, for there were "no plausible political heirs in sight, no credible opposition, and an exiled community eager not only for return but also for revenge." Raúl Castro is less ideological-driven than his brother and is certainly more pragmatic. He realizes that Cuba faces profound economic problems and has taken steps to increase food production. Local farm leaders will be relied on to make more decisions in an effort to stimulate agricultural production, increase the sale and distribution of food, and substitute imports. Private farmers and cooperatives have also been encouraged to bring unused government land into production. It was estimated that more than half of the arable land in Cuba was underused or fallow because of official mismanagement. The government has also decided to removed the prohibition on citizens from owning cell phones, even though their cost is prohibitive for most Cubans. Nevertheless, it signals an opening for Cubans to access information previously unavailable. Additionally, it has been made easier for state workers to gain title to homes they once rented.

Raúl Castro appreciates the need for change. But change can also produce a "revolution of rising expectations" which could be difficult to manage.

Dominica (Commonwealth of Dominica)

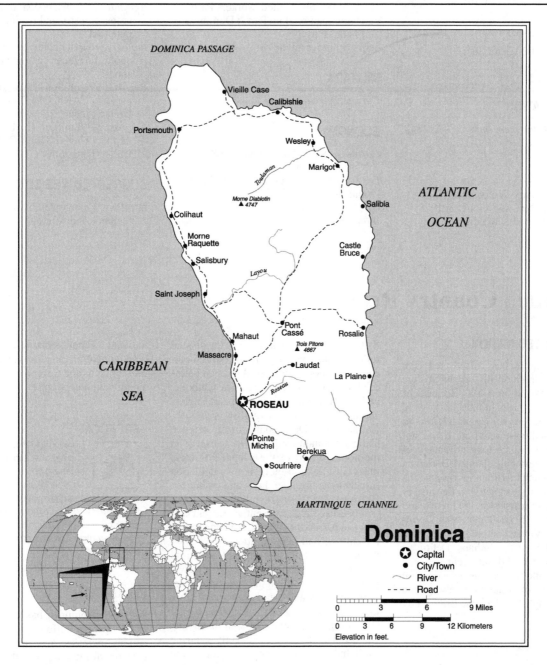

Dominica Statistics

GEOGRAPHY

Area in Square Miles (Kilometers):
289 (752) (about 4 times the size of
Washington, D.C.)
Capital (Population): Roseau (17,000)
Geographical Features: rugged mountains
of volcanic origin
Climate: tropical

PEOPLE

Population

Total: 72,386 (2007 est.)
Annual Growth Rate: 0.18%
Rural/Urban Population Ratio: 30/70
Major Languages: English; French Creole
Ethnic Makeup: mostly black; some Carib
Indians

Religions: 61.4% Roman Catholic;
28% Protestant

Health

Life Expectancy at Birth: 72 years (male);
78 years (female)
Infant Mortality Rate (Ratio):
14.61/1,000
Physicians Available (Ratio): 1/2,112

GLOBAL STUDIES

Education

Adult Literacy Rate: 94%
Compulsory (Ages): 5–15; free

COMMUNICATION

Telephones: 21,000 main lines
Cell Phones: 41,800
Internet Users: 26,000

TRANSPORTATION

Highways in Kilometers (miles): 780 (484)
Usable Airfields: 2

GOVERNMENT

Type: parliamentary democracy
Independence Date: November 3, 1978
   (from the United Kingdom)

Head of State/Government: President
   Nicholas J. O. Liverpool; Prime
   Minister Roosevelt Skerrit
Political Parties: United Workers Party;
   Dominica Freedom Party; Dominica
   Labour Party
Suffrage: universal at 18

MILITARY

Current Disputes: none

ECONOMY

Currency ($U.S. Equivalent): 2.68 East
   Caribbean dollars = $1
Per Capita Income/GDP: $3,800/$279
   million
GDP Real Growth Rate: 3.2 %
Inflation Rate: −0.1%

Unemployment Rate: 23%
Labor Force: 25,000
Natural Resources: timber
Agriculture: fruits; cocoa; root
   crops; forestry and fishing
   potential
Industry: soap; coconut oil; tourism;
   copra; furniture; cement blocks;
   shoes
Exports: $94 million (f.o.b.) (primary
   partners CARICOM, United Kingdom,
   United States)
Imports: $296 million (f.o.b.) (primary
   partners United States, CARICOM,
   United Kingdom)

SUGGESTED WEB SITE

http://www.cia.gov/cia/publications/
   factbook/index.html

Dominica Country Report

A FRAGMENTED NATION

Christopher Columbus discovered the island of Dominica on his second voyage to the New World in 1493. Because of the presence of Carib Indians, who were known for their ferocity, Spanish efforts to settle the island were rebuffed. It was not until 1635 that France took advantage of Spanish weakness and claimed Dominica as its own. French missionaries became the island's first European settlers. Because of continued Carib resistance, the French and English agreed in 1660 that both Dominica and St. Vincent should be declared neutral and left to the Indians. Definitive English settlement did not occur until the eighteenth century, and the island again became a bone of contention between the French and English. It became Britain's by treaty in 1783.

Dominica is a small and poor country that gained its independence from Great Britain in 1978. Culturally, the island reflects a number of patterns. Ninety percent of the population speak French patois (dialect), and most are Roman Catholic, while only a small minority speak English and are Protestant. Yet English is the official language. Descendants of the original Carib inhabitants still live in a reserve in the northern part of the island. For years many in the non-indigenous population saw them as drunken, lazy, and dishonest. But others see them as symbolically important because they represent an ancient culture and fit into the larger Caribbean search for cultural and national identity. In 2004 the newly elected chief of the Caribs told the *Chronicle,* a Dominican weekly newspaper, that ". . . we are the rightful owners of this country and we deserve much more than we get. . . . '[We] . . . need a bigger share of development.' " A significant step was taken in this direction in 2005 when the Carib Indians were given a cabinet position in the government of the ruling Dominica Labour Party. There is also a small number of Rastafarians who identify with their black African roots.

Today, Dominica's population is broken up into sharply differentiated regions. The early collapse of the plantation economy left pockets of settlements, which are still isolated from one another. A difficult topography and poor communications exaggerate the differences between these small communities. This contrasts with nations such as Jamaica and Trinidad and Tobago, which have a greater sense of national awareness because there are good communications and mass media that reach most citizens and foster the development of a national perception.

EMIGRATION

Although Dominica has a high birth rate and its people's life expectancy has measurably increased over the past few years, the growth rate has been dropping due to significant out-migration. Out-migration is not a new phenomenon. From the 1880s until well into the 1900s, many Dominicans sought economic opportunity in the gold fields of French Guiana. Today, most move to the neighboring French departments of Guadeloupe and Martinique.

THE ECONOMY

Dominica's chief export, bananas, has suffered for some years from natural disasters and falling prices. Hurricanes blew down the banana trees in 1979, 1980, 1989, and

HEALTH/WELFARE

With the assistance of external donors, Dominica has rebuilt many primary schools destroyed in Hurricane Hugo in 1989. A major restructuring of the public health administration has improved the quality of health care, even in the previously neglected rural areas.

ACHIEVEMENTS

Traditional handcrafts—especially intricately woven baskets, mats, and hats—have been preserved in Dominica. Schoolchildren are taught the techniques to pass on this dimension of Dominican culture.

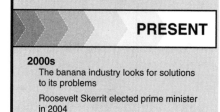

Timeline: PAST

1493
Dominica is sighted on Christopher Columbus's second voyage

1783
Dominica is deeded to the British by France

1978
Independence of Great Britain

1979–1980
Hurricanes devastate Dominica's economy

1989
Hurricane Hugo devastates the island

1990s
Dominica seeks stronger tourism revenues, especially in ecotourism

The banana industry is in crisis

PRESENT

2000s
The banana industry looks for solutions to its problems

Roosevelt Skerrit elected prime minister in 2004

1995, and banana exports fell dramatically. A drop in banana prices in 1997 prompted the opposition Dominica Freedom Party to demand that Dominica become part of a single market in order to take advantage of set prices enjoyed by the producers of Martinique and Guadeloupe. Recent talks among producers, Windward Island governments, and the European Union focused on the need for radical changes in the banana industry. The head of the Windward Islands Banana Development and Exporting Company said that the industry should be "market-led rather than production-led." He also noted that the industry was too fragmented, with 10,000 growers all over the islands. This was one reason why costs were high and yields low. With new technology, an acre should produce 20 tons of fruit instead of the four tons now harvested. Together with other banana-producing small states in the Caribbean, Dominica has increasingly turned to non-traditional crops, including root crops, cucumbers, flowers, hot peppers, tomatoes, and nonbanana tropical fruits.

Hard-pressed for revenue, the *Economist* reports that Dominica has traded on its sovereignty for cash. It has sold passports to foreigners, hosted off-shore banks, and voted with Japan in favor of commercial whaling. The "favorite local game" involves playing off China and Taiwan for economic gain.

POLITICAL FREEDOM

Despite economic difficulties and several attempted coups, Dominica still enjoys a parliamentary democracy patterned along British lines. The press is free and has not been subject to control—save for a brief state of emergency in 1981, which corresponded to a coup attempt by former prime minister Patrick John and unemployed members of the disbanded Defense Force. Political parties and trade unions are free to organize. Labor unions are small but enjoy the right to strike. Women have full rights under the law and are active in the political system; former prime minister Mary Eugenia Charles was the Caribbean's first woman to become a head of government.

Dominican Republic

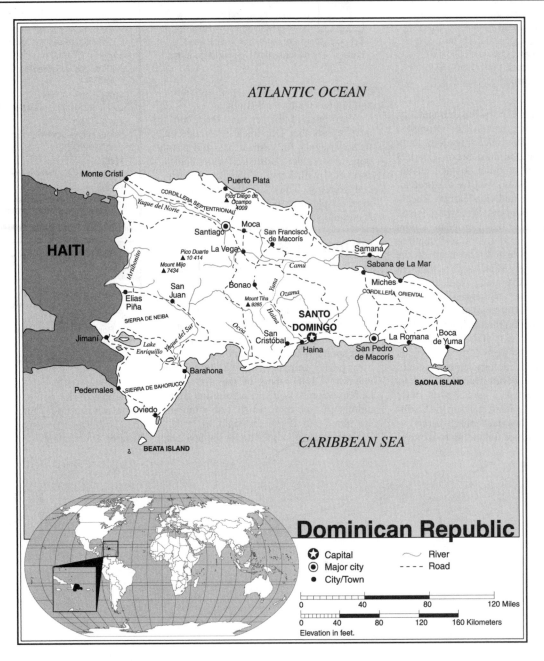

Dominican Republic Statistics

GEOGRAPHY

Area in Square Miles (Kilometers): 18,712 (48,464) (about twice the size of New Hampshire)

Capital (Population): Santo Domingo (2,253,437)

Environmental Concerns: water shortages; soil erosion; damage to coral reefs; deforestation; damage from Hurricane Georges

Geographical Features: rugged highlands and mountains with fertile valleys interspersed

Climate: tropical maritime

PEOPLE

Population

Total: 9,365,818 (2007 est.)

Annual Growth Rate: 1.5%

Rural/Urban Population Ratio: 37/63

Major Language: Spanish

Ethnic Makeup: 73% mixed; 16% white; 11% black

Religions: 95% Roman Catholic; 5% others

Health

Life Expectancy at Birth: 71 years (male); 75 years (female)

Infant Mortality Rate (Ratio): 27.94/1,000

Physicians Available (Ratio): 1/1,076

Education

Adult Literacy Rate: 87%
Compulsory (Ages): 6–14

COMMUNICATION

Telephones: 897,000 main lines
Daily Newspaper Circulation: 35 per
  1,000 people
Cell Phones: 4,606,000
Internet Users: 1,232,000

TRANSPORTATION

Highways in Kilometers (Miles): 12,600
  (7,825)
Railroads in Kilometers (Miles): 757 (470)
Usable Airfields: 34

GOVERNMENT

Type: republic
Independence Date: February 27, 1844
  (from Haiti)

Head of State/Government: President
  Leonel Fernández is both head of state
  and head of government
Political Parties: Dominican
  Revolutionary Party; Social Christian
  Reformist Party; Dominican Liberation
  Party; others
Suffrage: universal and compulsory at 18,
  or at any age if married; members
  of the armed forces or the police
  cannot vote

MILITARY

Military Expenditures (% of GDP): 0.8%
Current Disputes: none

ECONOMY

Currency ($U.S. Equivalent): 33.8
  Dominican pesos = $1
Per Capita Income/GDP: $9,200/$22.54
  billion
GDP Growth Rate: 7.2 %

Inflation Rate: 5.8%
Unemployment Rate: 15.5%
Labor Force: 3,986,000
Natural Resources: nickel; bauxite; gold;
  silver; arable land
Agriculture: sugarcane; coffee;
  cotton; cocoa; tobacco; rice;
  beans; potatoes; corn; bananas;
  livestock
Industry: tourism; sugar processing;
  ferronickel and gold mining; textiles;
  cement; tobacco
Exports: $6.881 billion (f.o.b.)
  (primary partners United States,
  Belgium, Asia)
Imports: $12.89 billion (f.o.b.)
  (primary partners United States,
  Venezuela, Mexico)

SUGGESTED WEB SITE

http://www.cia.org/cia/publications/
  factbook/index.html

Dominican Republic Country Report

DOMINICAN REPUBLIC: RACIAL STRIFE

Occupying the eastern two-thirds of the island of Hispaniola (Haiti comprises the western third), the Dominican Republic historically has feared its neighbor to the west. Much of the fear has its origins in race. From 1822 until 1844, the Dominican Republic—currently 73 percent mixed, or mulatto—was ruled by a brutal black Haitian regime. One authority noted that the Dominican Republic's freedom from Haiti has always been precarious: "Fear of reconquest by the smaller but more heavily populated (and, one might add, black) neighbor has affected Dominican psychology more than any other factor."

DEVELOPMENT

There has been impressive economic growth since 2005. The service sector, driven by tourism and free trade zones, has passed agriculture in terms of number of people employed. Fully three-fourths of exports find their way to the United States.

In the 1930s, for example, President Rafael Trujillo posed as the defender of Catholic values and European culture against the "barbarous" hordes of Haiti. Trujillo ordered the massacre of from 12,000 to 20,000 Haitians who had settled in the Dominican Republic in search of work. For years, the Dominican government had encouraged Haitian sugarcane cutters to cross the border to work on the U.S.–owned sugar plantations. But with the world economic depression in the 1930s and a fall in sugar prices and production, many Haitians did not return to their part of the island; in fact, additional thousands continued to stream across the border. The response of the Dominican government was wholesale slaughter.

Since 1952, a series of five-year agreements have been reached between the two governments to regularize the supply of Haitian cane cutters. An estimated 20,000 cross each year into the Dominican Republic legally, and an additional 60,000 enter illegally. Living and working conditions are very poor for these Haitians, and the migrants have no legal status and no rights. Planters prefer the Haitian workers because they are "cheaper and more docile" than Dominican laborers, who expect reasonable food, adequate housing, electric lights, and transportation to the fields. Today, as in the 1930s, economic troubles have gripped the Dominican Republic; the government has promised across-the-board sacrifices.

There is a subtle social discrimination against darker-skinned Dominicans, although this has not proved to be an insurmountable obstacle, as many hold elected political office. Discrimination is in part historical, in part cultural, and must be set against a backdrop of the sharp prejudice against Haitians. This prejudice is also directed against the minority in the Dominican population who are of Haitian descent. For example, during the contested presidential election of 1994, President Joaquín Balaguer Ricardo introduced the issue of race when questions were raised about his opponent's rumored Haitian origins. President Leonel Fernández has worked hard for better relations with Haitians, but the bitter memories and policies of the past undercut his efforts.

FREEDOM

Dominican politics remain volatile even as the country returns to economic stability. The media are generally free, but from time to time the government reveals a degree of intolerance against its critics.

WOMEN'S RIGHTS

Women in the Dominican Republic have enjoyed political rights since 1941. While in office, President Balaguer, in an unprecedented move, named women governors for eight of the country's 29 provinces. Sexual discrimination is prohibited by law, but women have not shared equal social or economic status or opportunity with men. Divorce, however, is easily obtainable, and women can hold property in their own names. A 1996 profile of the nation's population and health noted that 27 percent of Dominican households were headed by women. In urban areas, the percentage rose to 31 percent.

HEALTH/WELFARE

Sociologist Laura Raynolds notes that a restructuring of labor that moved thousands of women into nontraditional agriculture and manufacturing for export has reduced them to a "cheap and disciplined" workforce. Their work is undervalued to enhance profits. In that the majority of these workers are mothers, there has been a redefinition of family identity and work.

AN AIR OF CHANGE

Progress toward a political scene free of corruption and racism has been fitful. The 1994 presidential election was marred by what multinational observers called massive fraud. The opposition claimed that Balaguer not only "stole the election" but also employed racist, anti-Haitian rhetoric that "inflamed stereotypes of Haitians in the Dominican Republic." Widespread unrest in the wake of the election, together with pressure from the Roman Catholic Church, the Organization of American States, and the United States, resulted in the "Pact for Democracy," which forced Balaguer to serve

ACHIEVEMENTS

Some of the best baseball in the hemisphere is played in the Dominican Republic. Three of its citizens, pitcher Pedro Martinez and sluggers Sammy Sosa and David Ortiz, have become stars in major-league baseball in the United States. They have raised awareness of their country and have contributed to the welfare of Dominicans.

a shortened two-year term as president. New elections in 1996 returned Leonel Fernández to the presidency.

A brief economic recovery was followed by sharp recession. Inflation soared to 10 percent a month in 2003, the slowdown in the global economy cut into the tourist industry, and assembly plants in the free trade zone were forced to cut back. Many of the problems were blamed on President Hipólito Mejía's economic policies, which included a $2.4 billion bail-out of the nation's third largest commercial bank—bankrupted by massive fraud. In elections in 2004 Mejía resorted to demagoguery, distributed motorcycles at cut rates, and promised a 30 percent raise to public employees. He lost the election to former president Leonel Fernández, who pledged to cut inflation, stabilize the exchange rate, and restore investor confidence. Fernández largely succeeded and the Dominican Republic has enjoyed steady economic growth since 2005. Inflation is under control. The nation

Timeline: PAST

1496
The founding of Santo Domingo, the oldest European city in the Americas

1821
Independence from Spain is declared

1822–1844
Haitian control

1844
Independence as a separate state

1930–1961
The era of General Rafael Trujillo

1965
Civil war and U.S. intervention

1990s
Diplomatic relations are restored with Cuba

Hurricane Georges slams into the nation, killing many and causing $1.3 billion in damage

PRESENT

2000s
Leonel Fernández elected president in May 2008

still suffers from high unemployment and underemployment; there is also a skewed distribution of wealth. Ten percent of the population control 40 percent of the national income. Fernández was returned to power in 2008 and promised to continue his economic policies.

Grenada

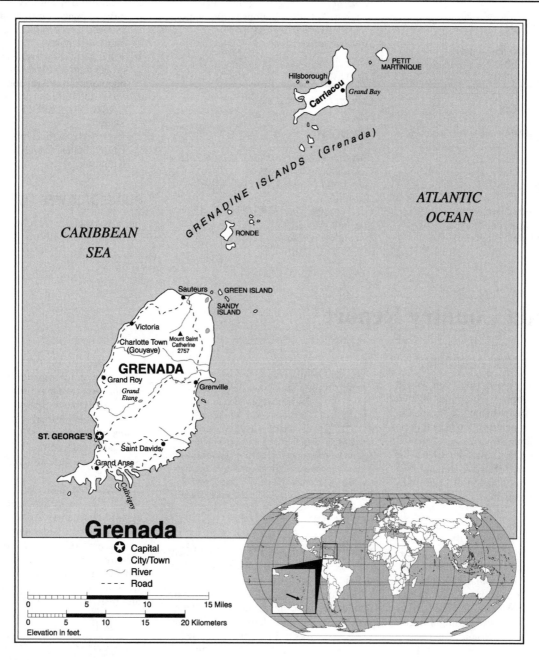

Grenada

⊗ Capital
● City/Town
〜 River
--- Road

| 0 | 5 | 10 | 15 Miles |
| 0 | 5 | 10 | 15 | 20 Kilometers |

Elevation in feet.

Grenada Statistics

GEOGRAPHY

Area in Square Miles (Kilometers):
133 (340) (about twice the size of
Washington, D.C.)
Capital (Population): St. George's
(7,500)
Geographical Features: volcanic in
origin, with central mountains
Climate: tropical

PEOPLE

Population

Total: 89,971 (2007 est.)
Annual Growth Rate: 0.33%
Rural/Urban Population Ratio: 64/36
Major Languages: English; French patois
Ethnic Makeup: 82% black;
5% East Indian

Religions: 53% Roman Catholic;
13% Anglican; 33% other Protestant

Health

Life Expectancy at Birth: 63 years (male);
67 years (female)
Infant Mortality Rate (Ratio):
13.92/1,000
Physicians Available (Ratio): 1/2,045

Education

Adult Literacy Rate: 96%
Compulsory (Ages): 5–6; free

COMMUNICATION

Telephones: 27,700 main lines
Cell Phones: 46,200
Internet Users: 19,000

TRANSPORTATION

Highways in Kilometers (Miles):
   1,040 (646)
Usable Airfields: 3

GOVERNMENT

Type: parliamentary democracy
Independence Date: February 7, 1974
   (from the United Kingdom)

Head of State/Government: Queen
   Elizabeth II; Prime Minister Keith
   Mitchell
Political Parties: New National Party;
   Grenada United Labour Party; National
   Democratic Congress
Suffrage: universal at 18

MILITARY

Current Disputes: none

ECONOMY

Currency ($U.S. Equivalent): 2.68 East
   Caribbean dollars = $1
Per Capita Income/GDP: $3,900/$454
   million
GDP Growth Rate: 0.9%
Inflation Rate: 3%
Unemployment Rate: 12.5%

Labor Force: 42,300
Natural Resources: timber; tropical fruit;
   deepwater harbors
Agriculture: bananas; cocoa;
   nutmeg; mace; citrus fruits;
   avocados; root crops; sugarcane;
   corn; vegetables
Industry: food and beverages; spice
   processing; textiles; light assembly
   operations; tourism; construction
Exports: $38 million (primary partners
   CARICOM, United Kingdom, United
   States)
Imports: $343 million (primary partners
   United States, CARICOM, United
   Kingdom)

SUGGESTED WEB SITE

http://www.cia.gov/cia/publications/
   factbook/index.html

Grenada Country Report

GRENADA: A FRESH BEGINNING

On his third voyage to the New World in 1498, Christopher Columbus sighted Grenada, which he named Concepción. The origin of the name Grenada cannot be clearly established, although it is believed that the Spanish renamed the island for the Spanish city of Granada. Because of a fierce aboriginal population of Carib Indians, the island remained uncolonized for 100 years.

Grenada, like most of the Caribbean, is ethnically mixed. Its culture draws on several traditions. The island's French past is preserved among some people who still speak patois (a French dialect). There are few whites on the island, save for a small group of Portuguese who immigrated earlier in the century. The primary cultural identification is with Great Britain, from which Grenada won its independence in 1974.

Grenada's political history has been tumultuous. The corruption and violent tactics of Grenada's first prime minister, Eric Gairy, resulted in his removal in a bloodless coup in 1979. Even though this action marked the first extra-constitutional change of government in the Commonwealth Caribbean (former British colonies), most Grenadians supported the coup, led by Maurice Bishop and his New Joint Endeavor for Welfare, Education, and Liberation (JEWEL) movement. Prime Minister Bishop, like Jamaica's Michael Manley before him, attempted to

DEVELOPMENT

Hurricanes Ivan and Emily devastated Grenada in 2004 and 2005. The costs of rebuilding have created a significant debt that acts as a drag on the economy. Nutmeg and cocoa cultivation has largely recovered from the damage. Tourism and investment in the service sector of the economy have increased substantially over the past few years.

break out of European cultural and institutional molds and mobilize Grenadians behind him.

Bishop's social policies laid the foundation for basic health care for all Grenadians. With the departure of Cuban medical doctors in 1983, however, the lack of trained personnel created a significant health-care problem. Moreover, although medical-care facilities exist, these are not always in good repair, and equipment is aging and not reliable. Methods of recording births, deaths, and diseases lack systemization in Grenada, so it is risky to rely on local statistics to estimate the health needs of the population. There has also been some erosion from Bishop's campaign to accord women equal pay, status, and treatment. Two women were elected to Parliament, but skilled employment for women tends to be concentrated in the lowest-paid sector.

On October 19, 1983, Bishop and several of his senior ministers were killed during the course of a military coup. Six days later, the United States, with the token assistance of soldiers and police from states of the Eastern Caribbean, invaded Grenada, restored the 1974 Constitution, and prepared the way for new elections (in 1984).

According to one scholar, the invasion was a "lesson in a peacemaker's role in rebuilding a nation. Although Grenada has a history of parliamentary democracy, an atmosphere of civility, fertile soil, clean drinking water, and no slums, continued aid has not appreciably raised the standard of living and the young are resentful and restless."

FREEDOM

Grenadians are guaranteed full freedom of the press and speech. Newspapers, most of which are published by political parties, freely criticize the government without penalty. The OAS reported ballot fraud in the elections of November 2003, thus giving PM Keith Mitchell yet another term.

Grenada's international airport, the focus of much controversy, has pumped new blood into the tourist industry. Moves have also been made by the Grenadian

Timeline: PAST

1498
Grenada is discovered by Christopher Columbus

1763
England acquires the island from France by treaty

1834
Slavery is abolished

1958–1962
Member of the West Indies Federation

1974
Independence from Great Britain

1979
A coup brings Maurice Bishop to power

1983
Prime Minister Bishop is assassinated; U.S. troops land

1995
Former mathematics professor Keith Mitchell is elected prime minister

PRESENT

2000s
Venezuela experiments with new shipping routes to Grenada to expand markets in both nations

government to promote private-sector business and to diminish the role of the government in the economy. Large amounts of foreign aid, especially from the United States, have helped to repair the infrastructure.

In recent years, foreign governments such as Kuwait, attracted by the power of Grenada's vote in the United Nations, have committed millions of dollars to Grenada's infrastructure. Some of these partnerships, particularly that involving Japan's access to Caribbean fish stocks, may have severe consequences for Grenadians in the future.

HEALTH/WELFARE

Grenada still lacks effective legislation for regulation of working conditions, wages, and occupational-safety and health standards. Discrimination is prohibited by law, but women are often paid less than men for the same work.

Significant problems remain. Unemployment has not significantly decreased; it remains at 12.5 percent (2007) of the workforce. Not surprisingly, the island has experienced a rising crime rate.

Prime Minister Keith Mitchell of the New National Party has promised to create more jobs in the private sector and to cut taxes to stimulate investment in small, high-technology businesses. He also stated that government would become smaller and leaner.

ACHIEVEMENTS

A series of public consultations have been held with respect to the reestablishment of local government in the villages. Some 52 village councils work with the government in an effort to set policies that are both responsive and equitable.

Just as the economy had begun to experience its first significant growth in decades, Hurricane Ivan struck the island a direct hit in 2004. It killed many people, destroyed or damaged 90 percent of the island's structures, and devastated the nutmeg crop, dealing the economy a serious blow. Privatization has continued, attracting foreign capital. As is the case in much of the Caribbean, tourism has become an important source of revenue and employment in Grenada, with a rapid expansion of the service sector. Despite the decline of agricultural exports, Grenada has maintained its position as the world's second-largest exporter of nutmeg. To protect forested areas and what remains of its agricultural base, in 2001 the government developed a "Land Bank" policy. Designed to promote the efficient use and management of all agricultural lands, the government helps those who want to engage in agricultural pursuits but lack access to land, and pressures landowners who have not maintained prime agricultural land in a productive state.

Haiti (Republic of Haiti)

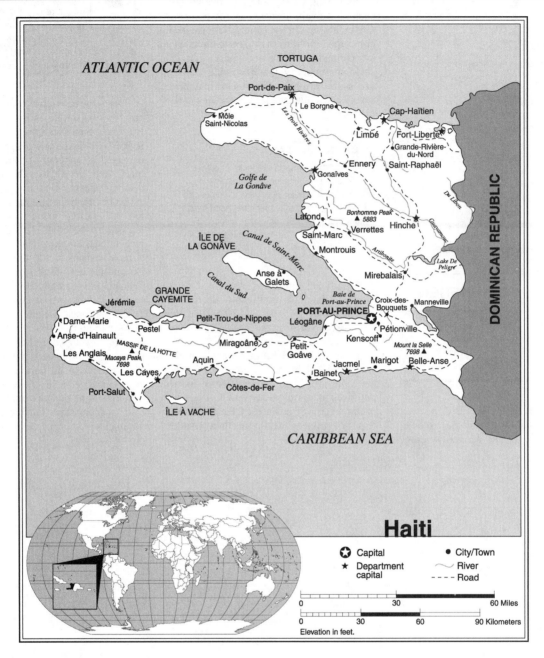

Haiti Statistics

GEOGRAPHY

Area in Square Miles (Kilometers):
10,714 (27,750) (about the size of Maryland)

Capital (Population): Port-au-Prince (1,277,000)

Environmental Concerns: extensive deforestation; soil erosion; inadequate potable water

Geographical Features: mostly rough and mountainous

Climate: tropical to semiarid

PEOPLE*

Population

Total: 8,706,497 (2007 est.)
Annual Growth Rate: 2.45%
Rural/Urban Population Ratio: 68/32

Major Languages: French; Creole

Ethnic Makeup: 95% black; 5% mulatto and white

Religions: 80% Roman Catholic (of which the majority also practice Vodun); 16% Protestant; 4% others

Health

Life Expectancy at Birth: 55 years (male); 58 years (female)

Infant Mortality Rate (Ratio): 63.8/1,000
Physicians Available (Ratio): 1/9,846

Education

Adult Literacy Rate: 52.9%

COMMUNICATION

Telephones: 145,300 main lines
Daily Newspaper Circulation: 7 per 1,000
  people
Cell Phones: 500,200
Internet Users: 650,000

TRANSPORTATION

Highways in Kilometers (miles): 4,160
  (2,588)
Usable Airfields: 13

GOVERNMENT

Type: republic
Independence Date: January 1, 1804
  (from France)

Head of State/Government: President
  René Preval
Political Parties: Front for Hope
  (coalition); Fusion (coalition Socialist
  party); National Front for the
  Reconstruction of Haiti; Struggling
  People's Organization; Democratic
  Alliance (coalition)
Suffrage: universal at 18

MILITARY

Military Expenditures (% of GDP): 0.4%
Current Disputes: claims
  U.S.–administered Navassa
  Island

ECONOMY

Currency ($U.S. Equivalent): 38.35
  gourdes = $1
Per Capita Income/GDP: $1,900/$6.331
  billion
GDP Growth Rate: 3.5%
Inflation Rate: 8.9%

Unemployment Rate: 66% have no
  formal jobs
Labor Force: 3,600,000
Natural Resources: bauxite; copper;
  calcium carbonate; gold; marble;
  hydropower
Agriculture: coffee; mangoes; sugarcane;
  rice; corn; sorghum; wood
Industry: sugar refining; flour milling;
  textiles; cement; tourism; light
  assembly based on imported parts
Exports: $554.8 million (f.o.b.) (primary
  partners United States, European
  Union)
Imports: $1.884 billion (f.o.b.) (primary
  partners United States, European
  Union)

SUGGESTED WEB SITE

http://www.cia.gov/cia/publications/
  factbook/geos/ha.html

---

*Note: Estimates explicitly take into account
the effects of excess mortality due to AIDS.

Haiti Country Report

HAITI

Haiti, which occupies the western third of the island of Hispaniola (the Dominican Republic comprises the other two-thirds), was the first nation in Latin America to win independence from its mother country—in this instance, France. It is the poorest country in the Western Hemisphere and one of the least developed in the world. Agriculture, the main employer of the population, is pressed beyond the limits of the available land; the result has been catastrophic deforestation and erosion. While only roughly 30 percent of the land is suitable for planting, 50 percent is actually under cultivation. Haitians are woefully poor, suffer from poor health and lack of education, and seldom find work. Even when employment is found, wages are miserable, and there is no significant labor movement to intercede on behalf of the workers.

A persistent theme in Haiti's history has been a bitter rivalry between a small mulatto elite, consisting of 3 to 4 percent of the population, and the black majority. When François Duvalier, a black country doctor, was president (1957–1971), his avowed aim was to create a "new equilibrium" in the country—by which he meant a major shift in power from the established, predominantly mulatto, elite to a new, black middle

class. Much of Haitian culture explicitly rejects Western civilization, which is identified with the mulattos. The Creole language of the masses and their practice of Vodun (voodoo), a combination of African spiritualism and Christianity, has not only insulated the population from the "culturally alien" regimes in power but has also given Haitians a common point of identity.

DEVELOPMENT

Haiti's agricultural sector, where the vast majority of people earn a living, continues to suffer from massive soil erosion caused by deforestation, poor farming techniques, overpopulation, and low investment.

Haitian intellectuals have raised sharp questions about the nation's culture. Modernizers would like to see the triumph of the French language over Creole and Roman Catholicism over Vodun. Others argue that significant change in Haiti can come only from within, from what is authentically Haitian. The refusal of Haitian governments to recognize Creole as the official language has only added to the determination of the mulatto elite and the black middle class to exclude the rest of

FREEDOM

Demobilized soldiers and armed political factions are responsible for much of the violence in Haiti and have come to dominate drug trafficking. The rule of law cannot be maintained in the face of judicial corruption and a dysfunctional legal system. On the positive side, parliamentary democracy was restored in form in 2006.

the population from effective participation in political life.

For most of its history, Haiti has been run by a series of harsh authoritarian regimes. The ouster in 1986 of President-for-Life Jean-Claude Duvalier promised a more democratic opening as the new ruling National Governing Council announced as

HEALTH/WELFARE

Until 30 years ago, Haiti was self-sufficient in food production. It must now import about a third of its food needs. Nevertheless, the country has a rapidly expanding population, with a doubling time of 35 years overall, far faster than the Caribbean average of 52 years.

(Courtesy of Robert Buss)

These children in Port-de-Paix are dressed in their school uniforms, a requirement, whether in public or private school. Since it is a privilege for children to attend and there is a cost, only 50 percent of children are registered for school. They have little to no materials to work with and most learning is done through memorization.

U.S. troops, was returned to power in 1994. Once an uneasy stability was restored to the country, U.S. troops left the peacekeeping to UN soldiers.

Although there was a period of public euphoria over Aristide's return, the assessment of the *Guardian,* a British newspaper, was somber: Crime rates rose precipitously,

ACHIEVEMENTS

In the late 1940s, Haitian "primitive" art created a sensation in Paris and other art centers. Although the force of the movement has now been spent, it still represents a unique, colorful, and imaginative art form.

political violence continued, and Aristide's enemies were still in Haiti—and armed. Haitians, "sensing a vacuum," took the law "into their own hands."

René Préval, who had served briefly as Aristide's prime minister, was himself elected to the presidency in 1996. According to *Caribbean Week,* Préval was caught between "a fiercely independent Parliament [and] an externally-imposed structural adjustment programme. . . ." Préval, presiding over a divided party, was unable to have his choices for cabinet posts approved by the Legislature, which left Haiti without an effective government from 1997 to 1999.

Aristide was reelected in 2000 in a vote characterized by irregularities and fraud. The result was parliamentary paralysis, as the opposition effectively boycotted Aristide's few initiatives, and a country where virtually every institution failed to function. Violent protests and equally violent government repression finally forced Aristide from power at the end of February, 2004. Meanwhile, the suffering of Haiti's people continued unabated, compounded by heavy spring rains and mudslides that killed perhaps 2,000 people.

For the next year and a half a bitterly divided nation attempted to lay the groundwork for new elections in the midst of rampant crime, gang violence, politically motivated attacks and murders, and widespread police corruption. Some 7,000 United Nations peacekeepers themselves came under assault. Political scientists began to use Haiti as an example of a "failed state." Elections were finally held in February 2006 and René Préval won with 51 percent of a contested vote. He has promised to come to the aid of Haiti's poor—but many have made that promise before. Particularly worrisome have been statements by exiled president

its primary goal the transition to a freely elected government. Political prisoners were freed; the dreaded secret police, the Tontons Macoute, were disbanded; and the press was unmuzzled.

The vacuum left by Duvalier's departure was filled by a succession of governments that were either controlled or heavily influenced by the military. Significant change was heralded in 1990 with the election to power of an outspoken Roman Catholic priest, Jean-Bertrand Aristide. By the end of 1991, he had moved against the military and had formulated a foreign policy that sought to move Haiti closer to the nations of Latin America and the Caribbean. Aristide's promotion of the "church of the poor," which combined local beliefs with standard Catholic instruction, earned him the enmity of both conservative Church leaders and Vodun priests. The radical language of his Lavalas (Floodtide) movement, which promised sweeping economic and social changes, made business leaders and rural landowners uneasy.

Perhaps not surprisingly in this coup-ridden nation, the army ousted President Aristide in 1991. It took tough economic sanctions and the threat of an imminent U.S. invasion to force the junta to relinquish power. Aristide, with the support of

Timeline: PAST

1492
The island is discovered by Christopher Columbus; named Hispaniola

1697
The western portion of Hispaniola is ceded to France

1804
Independence from France

1957–1971
The era of President François Duvalier

1971
Jean-Claude Duvalier is named president-for-life

1986
Jean-Claude Duvalier flees into exile

1991
A military coup ousts President Jean-Bertrand Aristide

PRESENT

2000s
The suffering of millions continues

Aristide ousted in February 2004

2006
René Préval elected president

2008
Food riots break out as prices rise

Jean-Bertrand Aristide that he intends to return to Haiti.

There are few signs of improvement in Haiti. More than 80 percent of the population lives in poverty and 54 percent live in extreme poverty. The economy grew by a modest 3.5 percent in 2007, in large part because of help from the International Monetary Fund. Exports of garments and automobile parts to the United States, which assessed no tariffs on these goods, have helped the economy. It is sobering that Haiti's primary source of foreign exchange is in the form of remittances sent from abroad. These monies are twice the amount earned from exports. Haiti is one of the first countries to feel the impact of rapidly rising food prices worldwide. People are desperate, many eat "cookies" composed largely of earth, and food riots have become increasingly violent.

Jamaica

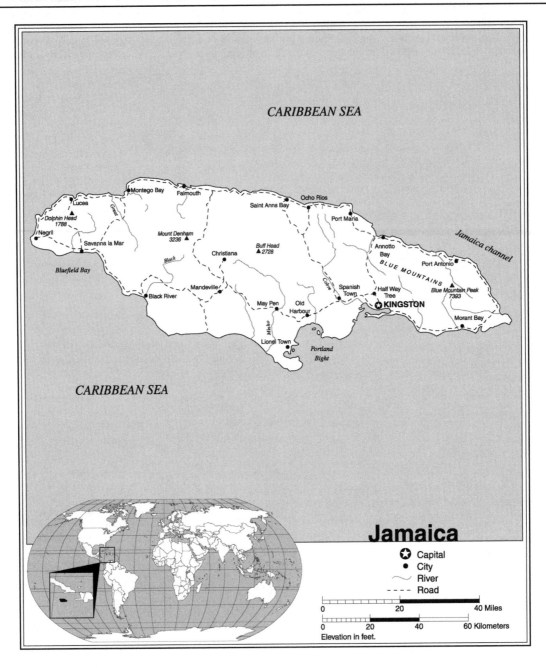

Jamaica Statistics

GEOGRAPHY

Area in Square Miles (Kilometers):
4,244 (10,991) (slightly smaller than Connecticut)
Capital (Population): Kingston (651,880) (metro)
Environmental Concerns: deforestation; damage to coral reefs; water and air pollution

Geographical Features: Mostly mountains, with a narrow, discontinuous coastal plain
Climate: tropical; temperate interior

PEOPLE

Population

Total: 2,780,132 (2007 est.)
Annual Growth Rate: 0.78%

Rural/Urban Population Ratio:
46/54
Major Languages: English; Jamaican Creole
Ethnic Makeup: 90% black; 7% mixed; 3% East Indian, white, Chinese and others
Religions: 62.5% Protestant; 2.6% Catholic; 21% none specified.

Health

Life Expectancy at Birth: 71 years (male); 75 years (female)
Infant Mortality Rate (Ratio): 15.73/1,000
Physicians Available (Ratio): 1/6,043

Education

Adult Literacy Rate: 87.9%
Compulsory (Ages): 6–12; free

COMMUNICATION

Telephones: 319,000 main lines
Daily Newspaper Circulation: 65 per 1,000 people
Cell Phones: 2,804,000
Internet Users: 1,232,000

TRANSPORTATION

Roadways in Kilometers (miles): 20,996 (13,046)
Usable Airfields: 34

GOVERNMENT

Type: constitutional parliamentary democracy
Independence Date: August 6, 1962 (from the United Kingdom)
Head of State/Government: Queen Elizabeth II; Prime Minister Bruce Golding
Political Parties: People's National Party; Jamaica Labour Party; National Democratic Movement
Suffrage: universal at 18

MILITARY

Military Expenditures (% of GDP): 0.6%
Current Disputes: none

ECONOMY

Currency ($U.S. Equivalent): 71.2 Jamaican dollars = $1
Per Capita Income/GDP: $4,800/$8.905 billion
GDP Growth Rate: 1.5%
Inflation Rate: 7.1%
Unemployment Rate: 10.2%
Labor Force: 1,255,000
Natural Resources: bauxite; gypsum; limestone
Agriculture: sugarcane; bananas; coffee; citrus fruits; potatoes; vegetables; poultry; goats; milk
Industry: tourism; bauxite; textiles; food processing; light manufacturers; rum; cement; metal
Exports: $2.229 billion (f.o.b.) (primary partners United States, European Union, Canada)
Imports: $5.709 billion (f.o.b.) (primary partners United States, CARICOM; European Union)

SUGGESTED WEB SITES

http://www.cia.gov/cia/publications/factbook/index.html

Jamaica Country Report

JAMAICA: "OUT OF MANY, ONE PEOPLE"

In 1962, Jamaica and Trinidad and Tobago were the first of the English-speaking Caribbean islands to gain their independence. A central problem since that time has been the limited ability of Jamaicans to forge a sense of nation. "Out of many, one people" is a popular slogan in Jamaica, but it belies an essential division of the population along lines of both race and class. The elite, consisting of a small white population and Creoles (Afro-Europeans), still think of themselves as "English." Local loyalties notwithstanding, Englishness permeates much of Jamaican life, from language to sports. According to former prime minister Michael Manley: "The problem in Jamaica is how do you get the Jamaican to divorce his mind from the paralysis of his history, which was all bitter colonial frustration, so that he sees his society in terms of this is what crippled me?"

Manley's first government (1975–1980) was one of the few in the Caribbean to incorporate the masses of the people into a political process. He was aware that in a country such as Jamaica—where the majority of the population were poor, ill educated, and lacked essential services—the promise to provide basic needs would win him widespread support. Programs to provide Jamaicans with basic health care

and education were expanded, as were services. Many products were subjected to price controls or were subsidized to make them available to the majority of the people. Cuban medical teams and teachers were brought to Jamaica to fill the manpower gaps until local people could be trained.

DEVELOPMENT

The Jamaican economy, already fragile, suffered a further setback in 2007 with widespread devastation caused by Hurricane Dean. High unemployment and underemployment is a perennial problem. Persistent violent crime and drug activity also have a negative impact on potential investment in the island.

However, Jamaica's fragile economy could not support Manley's policies, and he was eventually opposed by the entrenched elite and voted out of office. But Manley was returned to office in 1989, with a new image as a moderate, willing to compromise and aware of the need for foreign-capital investment. Manley retired in 1992 and was replaced as prime minister by Percival J. Patterson, who promised to accelerate Jamaica's transition to a free-market economy. The government

FREEDOM

Despite the repeal of the controversial Suppression of Crime Act of 1974, the Parliament, in the face of persistent high levels of crime, provided for emergency police powers. Some critics charge that the Parliament in essence re-created the repealed legislation in a different guise.

instituted a policy of divestment of state-owned enterprises.

The challenges remain. Crime and violence continue to be major social problems in Jamaica. The high crime rate threatens not only the lucrative tourist industry but the very foundations of Jamaican society. Prime Minister Patterson called for a moral reawakening: "All our programs and strategies for economic progress are doomed to failure unless there is a drastic change in social attitudes. . . ." A stagnant economy, persistent inflation, and unemployment and underemployment combine to lessen respect for authority and contribute to the crime problem. In 2001, Amnesty International noted that in proportion to population, more people are killed by police in Jamaica than anywhere else in the world. Many of the deaths are the result of clashes with gangs of drug dealers, who usually outgun the police. Jamaica counted 1,000 murders in 2002, more, proportionately, than in South Africa, and less than Colombia or El Salvador. It remains a violent society, and the nation continues to walk the narrow line between liberty and license.

HEALTH/WELFARE

Jamaica's "Operation Pride" was designed to combine a dynamic program of land divestment by the state with provisions to meet demands for housing. Squatter colonies would be replaced by "proud home owners."

As is the case in many developing-world countries where unemployment and disaffection are common, drug use is high in Jamaica. The government is reluctant to enforce drug control, however, for approximately 8,000 rural families depend on the cultivation of ganja (marijuana) to supplement their already marginal incomes.

Some of Jamaica's violence is politically motivated and tends to be associated with election campaigns. Both major parties have supporters who employ violence for political purposes. The legal system has been unable to contain the violence or bring the guilty to justice, because of a pervasive code of silence enforced at the local level.

The Patterson government moved deliberately in the direction of electoral reform in an attempt to reduce both violence and fraud. Reelected to fourth term in 2002, PM Patterson hoped to match Jamaica's

ACHIEVEMENTS

Marcus Garvey was posthumously declared Jamaica's first National Hero in 1964 because of his leading role in the international movement against racism. He called passionately for the recognition of the equal dignity of human beings regardless of race, religion, or national origin. Garvey died in London in 1940.

political stability with improvements in the nation's social and economic sectors. He successfully addressed inflation through tight monetary and fiscal policies and redressed Jamaica's debt by privatizing inefficient state enterprises.

On the positive side, human rights are generally respected, and Jamaica's press is basically free. Press freedom is observed in practice within the broad limits of libel laws and the State Secrets Act. Opposition parties publish newspapers and magazines that are highly critical of government policies, and foreign publications are widely available.

Jamaica's labor-union movement is strong and well organized, and it has contributed many leaders to the political process. Unions are among the strongest and best organizations in the country and are closely tied to political parties.

Long-term Prime Minister Patterson stepped down from office in 2006 and was replaced by Portia Simpson Miller, Jamaica's first woman leader. Unfortunately, Simpson Miller's choices for ministerial positions proved a liability. Several were

Timeline: PAST

1509
The first Spanish settlement

1655
Jamaica is seized by the English

1692
An earthquake destroys Port Royal

1944
Universal suffrage is proclaimed

1962
Independence from Great Britain

1990s
Violent crime and strong-armed police responses plague the island

Percival J. Patterson is elected prime minister

PRESENT

2000s
Gun battles break out in Kingston

Patterson reelected to a fourth term in 2002

2006
Portia Simpson Miller elected Jamaica's first woman prime minister

2007
Bruce Golding elected prime minister

accused of mismanagement and corruption, accusations that colored a bitter election campaign in 2007. Simpson Miller was defeated by Bruce Golding in a close and contentious vote. Jamaica's serious social and economic problems in the meantime remain daunting.

St. Kitts–Nevis (Federation of St. Kitts and Nevis)

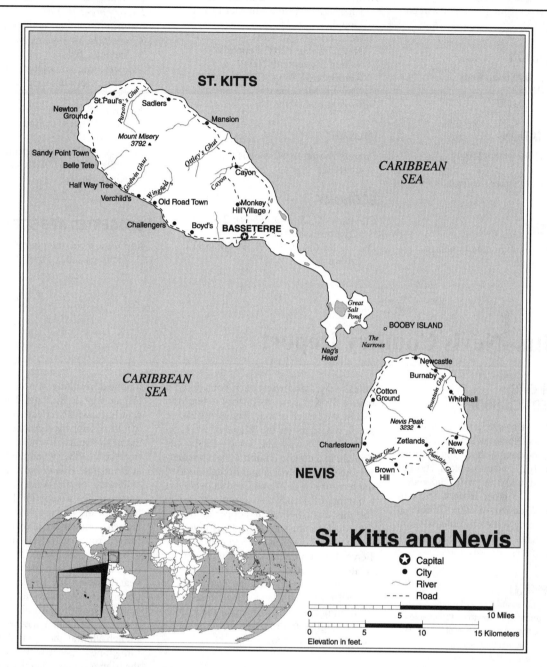

St. Kitts–Nevis Statistics

GEOGRAPHY

Area in Square Miles (Kilometers):
101 (261) (about 1½ times the size of Washington, D.C.)
Capital (Population): Basseterre (13,000)
Geographical Features: volcanic, with mountainous interiors
Climate: subtropical

PEOPLE

Population

Total: 39,349 (2007 est.)
Annual Growth Rate: 0.62%
Rural/Urban Population Ratio: 66/34
Major Language: English
Ethnic Makeup: mainly of black African descent

Religions: Anglican; other Protestant sects; Roman Catholic

Health

Life Expectancy at Birth: 70 years (male); 75 years (female)
Infant Mortality Rate (Ratio): 13.74/1,000
Physicians Available (Ratio): 1/1,057

Education

Adult Literacy Rate: 97.8%
Compulsory (Ages): for 12 years between ages 5 and 18

COMMUNICATION

Telephones: 25,000 main lines
Cell Phones: 10,000
Internet Users: 10,000

TRANSPORTATION

Highways in Kilometers (Miles): 320 (199)
Railroads in Kilometers (Miles): 58 (36)
Usable Airfields: 2

GOVERNMENT

Type: constitutional monarchy within Commonwealth

Independence Date: September 19, 1983 (from the United Kingdom)
Head of State/Government: Queen Elizabeth II; Prime Minister Denzil Douglas
Political Parties: St. Kitts and Nevis Labour Party; People's Action Movement; Nevis Reformation Party; Concerned Citizens Movement
Suffrage: universal at 18

MILITARY

Current Disputes: Nevis has threatened to secede

ECONOMY

Currency ($U.S. Equivalent): 2.68 East Caribbean dollars = $1
Per Capita Income/GDP: $8,200/$520 million

GDP Growth Rate: 6%
Inflation Rate: 8.7%
Unemployment Rate: 4.5%
Labor Force: 18,170
Natural Resources: negligible
Agriculture: rice; yams; vegetables; bananas; fish
Industry: tourism; cotton; salt; copra; clothing; footwear; beverages
Exports: $84 million (primary partners United States, United Kingdom, CARICOM)
Imports: $383 million (primary partners United States, CARICOM, United Kingdom)

SUGGESTED WEB SITES

http://www.cia.gov/cia/publications/factbook/index.html

St. Kitts–Nevis Country Report

ST. KITTS–NEVIS: ESTRANGED NEIGHBORS

On September 19, 1983, the twin-island state of St. Kitts–Nevis became an independent nation. The country had been a British colony since 1623, when Captain Thomas Warner landed with his wife and eldest son, along with 13 other settlers. The colony fared well, and soon other Caribbean islands were being settled by colonists sent out from St. Kitts (also commonly known as St. Christopher).

DEVELOPMENT

The islands' recent robust economic growth is attributable to the diversification of the agricultural side of the economy. Tourism and investment in related construction projects, the promotion of offshore banking, and export-oriented manufacturing are largely responsible for the growth.

The history of this small island nation is the story of the classic duel between the big sea powers of the period—Great Britain, France, and Spain—and the indigenous people—in this case, the Carib Indians. (Although much of the nation's history has centered around St. Kitts, the larger of the two islands, Nevis, only two miles away, has always been considered a part of St. Kitts, and its history is tied into that of the larger island.) The British were the first settlers on the island of St. Kitts but were followed that same year by the French. In a unique compromise, considering the era, the British and French divided the territory in 1627 and lived in peace for a number of decades. A significant reason for this British–French cooperation was the constant pressure from their common enemies: the aggressive Spanish and the fierce Carib Indians. The Caribs, for a while, played a role similar to that of Indians in the French and Indian War in North America a century later. They were adept at forming alliances with either the French or the English to drive one or the other or both from the region.

FREEDOM

The election in 1984 of Constance Mitcham to Parliament signaled a new role for women. She was subsequently appointed minister of women's affairs. However, despite her conspicuous success, women still occupy a very small percentage of senior civil-service positions.

With the gradual elimination of the mutual threat, Anglo–French tensions again

mounted, resulting in a sharp land battle at Frigate Bay on St. Kitts. The new round of hostilities, which reflected events in Europe, would disrupt the Caribbean for much of the next century. Events came to a climactic head in 1782, when the British garrison at Brimstone Hill, commonly known as the "Gibraltar of the West Indies," was overwhelmed by a superior French force. In honor of the bravery of the defenders, the French commander allowed the British to march from the fortress in full formation. (The expression "peace with honor" has its roots in this historic encounter.) Later in the year, however, the British again seized the upper hand. A naval battle at Frigate Bay was won by British Admiral Hood following a series of brilliant maneuvers. The defeated French admiral, the Count de Grasse, was in turn granted "peace with honor." Thereafter, the islands remained under British rule until their independence in 1983.

AGRICULTURE

Before the British colonized the island, St. Kitts was called Liamiuga ("Fertile Isle") by the Carib Indians. The name was apt, because agriculture for most of its history played a big role in the economy of the islands. Tourism and offshore banking and business facilities definitively replaced sugar has the largest generator of foreign exchange.

HEALTH/WELFARE

The demise of the sugar industry in 2005 resulted in the loss of employment for about 4 percent of the population. Effected workers will likely seek employment in other kinds of agriculture, the tourism industry, or out-migrate. Although a minimum wage exists by law, the amount is less than what a person can reasonably be expected to live on.

Because the sugar market was so unstable and because world market prices were so low, the decision was made to phase out the sugar industry altogether. The last mill closed its doors in 2005. Agricultural production will now likely be geared toward local or regional markets.

ECONOMIC CHANGE

Unlike such islands as Barbados and Antigua, St. Kitts–Nevis for years chose not to use tourism as a buffer to offset any disastrous fluctuations in sugar prices. On St. Kitts, there was an antitourism attitude that can be traced back to the repressive administration of Prime Minister Robert Bradshaw, a black nationalist who worked to discourage tourism and threatened to nationalize all land holdings.

That changed under the moderate leadership of Kennedy Simmonds and his People's Action Movement, who remained in power from 1980 until ousted in elections in July 1995. The new administration of Denzil Douglas promised to address serious problems that had developed, including drug trafficking, money laundering, and a lack of respect for law and order.

In 1997, a 50-man "army" was created to wage war against heavily armed drug traffickers operating in the region. Agriculture Minister Timothy Harris noted that the permanent defense force "was critical to the survival of the sovereignty of the nation." Simmond's promotion of tourism took root. By 2001, tourism had become a major growth industry in the islands. Major airlines refused to schedule landings in St. Kitts until there were an adequate number of hotel rooms. Accordingly, the government promoted the construction of 1,500 rooms. A positive side-effect are the jobs produced in the construction trades and service industry.

The future of St. Kitts–Nevis will depend on its ability to broaden its economic base. PM Douglas's economic policies include the promotion of export-oriented manufactures and off-shore banking. A potential problem of some magnitude looms, however: The island of Nevis, long in the shadow of the more populous and prosperous St. Kitts, nearly voted to secede in a referendum held in August 1998. The Constitution requires a two-thirds majority for secession; 61.7 percent of the population of Nevis voted "Yes." Not surprisingly, the government is working to fashion a new federalism with "appropriate power

sharing" between the islands. That has not diminished the move toward independence for Nevis' 10,000 people. Prime Minister Douglas has also said that difference between the two islands should be the subject of constitutional reform, not repeated referenda on secession.

Timeline: PAST

1493
The islands are discovered and named by Christopher Columbus

1623
The British colony is settled by Captain Thomas Warner

1689
A land battle at Frigate Bay disrupts a peaceful accord between France and England

1782
The English are expelled by French at the siege of Brimstone Hill

The French are beaten at the sea battle of Frigate Bay; the beginning of continuous British rule

1967
Self-government as an Associate State of the United Kingdom

1983
Full independence from Great Britain

1998
A referendum on Nevis secession is narrowly defeated

PRESENT

2004
Denzil Douglas reelected for a third consecutive term

St. Lucia

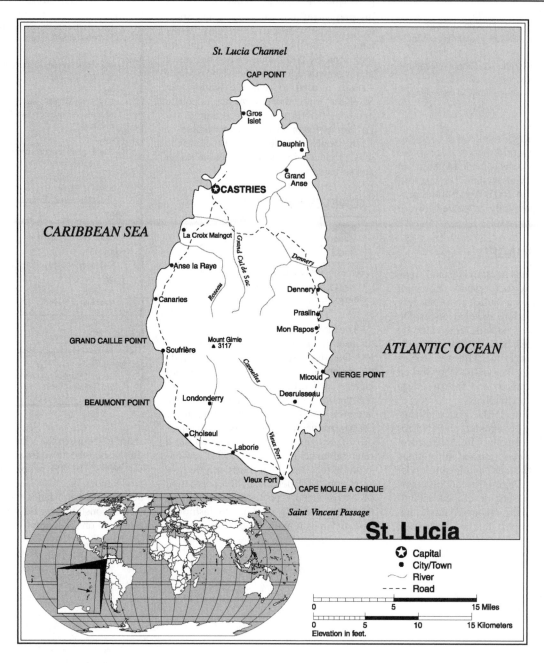

St. Lucia Statistics

GEOGRAPHY

Area in Square Miles (Kilometers):
238 (619) (about 3 times the size of
Washington, D.C.)
Capital (Population): Castries (16,800)
Environmental Concerns: deforestation;
soil erosion
Geographical Features: volcanic and
mountainous; some broad, fertile valleys
Climate: tropical maritime

PEOPLE

Population

Total: 170,649 (2007 est.)
Annual Growth Rate: 1.29%
Rural/Urban Population Ratio: 63/37
Major Languages: English; French patois
Ethnic Makeup: 82.5% black;
11.9% mixed; 2.4% East Indian
Religions: 67.5% Roman Catholic;
25% Protestant

Health

Life Expectancy at Birth: 70 years (male);
78 years (female)
Infant Mortality Rate (Ratio):
12.81/1,000
Physicians Available (Ratio): 1/2,235

Education

Adult Literacy Rate: 90.1%
Compulsory (Ages): 5–15

COMMUNICATION

Telephones: 51,100 main lines
Cell Phones: 105,700
Internet Users: 55,000

TRANSPORTATION

Highways in Kilometers (miles): 1,210 (451)
Usable Airfields: 2

GOVERNMENT

Type: constitutional monarchy within Commonwealth
Independence Date: February 22, 1979 (from the United Kingdom)
Head of State/Government: Queen Elizabeth II; Prime Minister Stephenson King

Political Parties: United Workers Party; St. Lucia Labour Party
Suffrage: universal at 18

MILITARY

Current Disputes: none

ECONOMY

Currency ($U.S. Equivalent): 2.68 East Caribbean dollars = $1
Per Capita Income/GDP: $4,800/$958 million
GDP Growth Rate: 5.1%
Inflation Rate: 2.9%
Unemployment Rate: 20%
Labor Force: 43,800
Natural Resources: forests; sandy beaches; minerals (pumice); mineral springs; geothermal potential

Agriculture: bananas; coconuts; vegetables; citrus fruits; root crops; cocoa
Industry: clothing; assembly of electronic components; beverages; corrugated cardboard boxes; tourism; lime processing; coconut processing
Exports: $288 million (primary partners United Kingdom, United States, CARICOM)
Imports: $791 million (primary partners United States, CARICOM, United Kingdom)

SUGGESTED WEB SITES

http://www.cia.gov/cia/publications/factbook/index.html

St. Lucia Country Report

ST. LUCIA: ENGLISH POLITICS, FRENCH CULTURE

The history of St. Lucia gives striking testimony to the fact that the sugar economy, together with the contrasting cultures of various colonial masters, was crucial in shaping the land, social structures, and lifestyles of its people. The island changed hands between the French and the English at least seven times, and the influences of both cultures are still evident today. Ninety percent of the population speaks French patois (dialect), while the educated and the elite prefer English. Indeed, the educated perceive patois as suitable only for proverbs and curses. On St. Lucia and the other patois-speaking islands (Dominica, Grenada), some view the common language as the true reflection of their uniqueness. English, however, is the language of status and opportunity. In terms of religion, most St. Lucians are Roman Catholic.

DEVELOPMENT

Foreign investment tied to offshore banking and tourism soared in 2006. Construction related to tourism helped boost employment opportunities. Although St. Lucia has the Eastern Caribbean's most diverse manufacturing sector, the government is also trying to revive the banana industry.

The original inhabitants of St. Lucia were Arawak Indians who had been forced off the South American mainland by the Carib Indians. Gradually, the Carib also moved onto the Caribbean islands and destroyed most of the Arawak culture. Evidence of that early civilization has been found in rich archaeological sites on St. Lucia.

FREEDOM

The St. Lucian parliament introduced controversial legislation in 2003 that calls for possible imprisonment for knowingly publishing false news that harms the public good. Media watchdogs have warned that this law threatens freedom of the press.

The date of the European "discovery" of the island is uncertain; it may have occurred in 1499 or 1504 by the navigator and mapmaker Juan de la Cosa, who explored the Windward Islands during the early years of the sixteenth century. The Dutch, French, and English all established small settlements or trading posts on the island in the seventeenth century but were resisted by the Caribs. The first successful settlement dates from 1651, when the French were able to maintain a foothold.

The island's political culture is English. Upon independence from Great Britain in 1979, St. Lucians adopted the British parliamentary system, which includes specific safeguards for the preservation of human rights. Despite several years of political disruption, caused by the jockeying for power of several political parties and affiliated interests, St. Lucian politics is essentially stable.

THE ECONOMY

St. Lucia has an economy that is as diverse as any in the Caribbean. Essentially agricultural, the country has also developed a tourism industry, manufacturing, and related construction activity. A recent "mineral inventory" has located possible gold deposits, but exploitation must await the creation of appropriate mining legislation.

HEALTH/WELFARE

The minister of agriculture has linked marginal nutrition and malnutrition in St. Lucia with economic adjustment programs in the Caribbean. He noted that the success achieved earlier in raising standards of living was being eroded by "onerous debt burdens."

U.S. promises to the region made in the 1980s failed to live up to expectations. Although textiles, clothing, and nontraditional goods exported to the United States increased as a result of the Caribbean Basin Initiative, St. Lucia remained dependent on its exports of bananas. About a third of the island's workforce were involved in banana production, which accounts for 90 percent of St. Lucia's exports.

ACHIEVEMENTS

St. Lucians have won an impressive two Nobel prizes. Sir W. Arthur Lewis won the prize in 1979 for economics, and in 1993, poet Derek Walcott won the prize for literature. When asked how the island had produced two Nobel laureates, Wolcott replied: "It's the food."

St. Lucia's crucial banana industry suffered significant production losses in 1997 and 2001 in large part because of drought. Exports were half of the normal volume, and St. Lucia fell short of filling its quota for the European Union. A 1999 European Union decision to drop its import preferences for bananas from former colonial possessions in the Caribbean together with increased competition from Latin American growers created an urgent demand to diversify St. Lucia's economy. Increased emphasis has been placed on exports of mangos and avocados. Tourism, light manufacturing, and offshore banking have also experienced growth. Despite these attempts unemployment, inflation, a high cost of living, and drug trafficking remain serious problems and have led to periodic unrest.

Timeline: PAST

638
The English take possession of St. Lucia

1794
The English regain possession of St. Lucia from France

1908
Riots

1951
Universal adult suffrage

1979
Independence from Great Britain

1990s
Banana production suffers a serious decline

PRESENT

2000s
Economic diversification becomes a critical need

2007
Stephenson King sworn in as prime minister following the death of Sir John Compton

St. Lucia, like several other islands, has also succeeded in trading on its sovereignty—a vote in the United Nations—to raise revenue. Since 1997, when banana exports reached crisis proportions, St. Lucia has supported the claims of China over the independence of Taiwan.

EDUCATION AND EMIGRATION

Education in St. Lucia has traditionally been brief and perfunctory. Few students attend secondary school, and very few (3 percent) ever attend a university. Although the government reports that 95 percent of those eligible attend elementary school, farm and related chores severely reduce attendance figures. In recent years, St. Lucia has channeled more than 20 percent of its expenditures into education and health care. Patient care in the general hospital was made free of charge in 1980.

Population growth is relatively low, but emigration off the island is a significant factor. For years, St. Lucians, together with Dominicans, traveled to French Guiana to work in the gold fields. More recently, however, they have crossed to neighboring Martinique, a French department, in search of work. St. Lucians can also be found working on many other Caribbean islands.

St. Vincent and the Grenadines

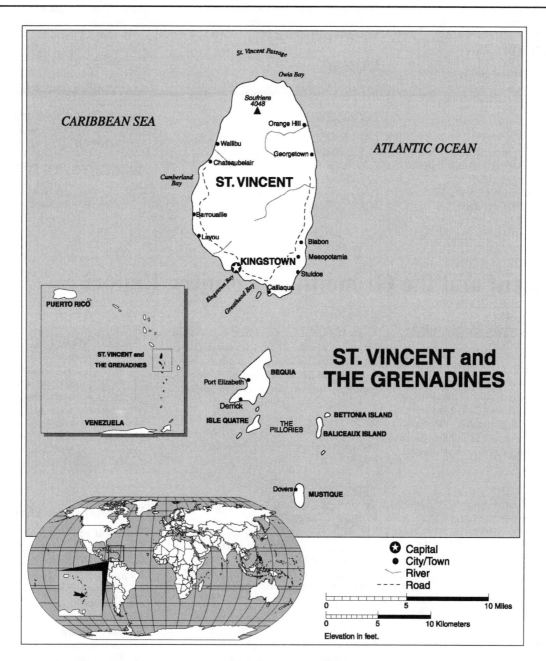

St. Vincent and the Grenadines Statistics

GEOGRAPHY

Area in Square Miles (Kilometers):
131 (340) (about twice the size of
Washington, D.C.)
Capital (Population): Kingstown (10,600)
Environmental Concerns: pollution of
coastal waters and shorelines by
discharges from pleasure boats
Geographical Features: volcanic;
mountainous
Climate: tropical

PEOPLE

Population

Total: 118,149 (2007 est.)
Annual Growth Rate: 0.259%
Rural/Urban Population Ratio: 50/50
Major Languages: English; French patois
Ethnic Makeup: 66% black; 19% mixed;
6% East Indian
Religions: 47% Anglican; 28% Methodist;
13% Roman Catholic

Health

Life Expectancy at Birth: 72 years (male);
76 years (female)
Infant Mortality Rate (Ratio):
14.01/1,000
Physicians Available (Ratio):
1/2,708

Education

Adult Literacy Rate: 96%

GLOBAL STUDIES

COMMUNICATION

Telephones: 22,600 main lines
Cell Phones: 87,600
Internet Users: 10,000

TRANSPORTATION

Highways in Kilometers (Miles): 1,040
   (646)
Usable Airfields: 6

GOVERNMENT

Type: Parliamentary democracy,
   independent sovereign state within the
   British Commonwealth
Independence Date: October 27, 1979
   (from the United Kingdom)

Head of State/Government: Queen
   Elizabeth II; Prime Minister Ralph
   Gonsalves
Political Parties: Unity Labour Party;
   New Democratic Party;
Suffrage: universal at 18

MILITARY

Current Disputes: none

ECONOMY

Currency ($U.S. Equivalent): 2.68 East
   Caribbean dollars = $1
Per Capita Income/GDP: $3,600/$528
   million
GDP Growth Rate: 4.4%
Inflation Rate: 1%

Unemployment Rate: 15%
Labor Force: 41,680
Natural Resources: negligible
Agriculture: bananas; arrowroot;
   coconuts; sweet potatoes; spices; small
   amount of livestock; fish
Industry: food processing; cement;
   furniture; clothing; starch; tourism
Exports: $193 million (primary partners
   CARICOM, United Kingdom, United
   States)
Imports: $578 million (primary partners
   United States, CARICOM, United
   Kingdom)

SUGGESTED WEB SITES

http://www.cia.gov/cia/publications/
   factbook/index.html

St. Vincent and the Grenadines Country Report

ST. VINCENT AND THE GRENADINES

Vincentians, like many other West Indians, either identify with or, as viewed from a different perspective, suffer from a deep-seated European orientation. Critics argue that it is an identification that is historical in origin, and that it is negative. For many, the European connection is nothing more than the continuing memory of a master–slave relationship.

DEVELOPMENT

Grenada's economy, which grew by a startling 10 percent in 2006, slowed somewhat in 2007. Leading the surge were the offshore and tourism industries and construction activities associated with both. Over 200,000 tourists visited the islands in 2007.

St. Vincent is unique in that it was one of the few Caribbean islands where run-away black slaves intermarried with Carib Indians and produced a distinct racial type known as the Garifuna, or black Carib. Toward the end of the eighteenth century, the Garifuna and other native peoples mounted an assault on the island's white British planters. They were assisted by the French from Martinique but were defeated in 1796. As punishment, the Garifuna were deported to what is today Belize, where they formed one of the bases of that nation's population.

In 1834, the black slaves were emancipated, which disrupted the island's economy by decreasing the labor supply. In order to fill this vacuum, Portuguese and East Indian laborers were imported to maintain the agrarian economy. This, however, was not done until later in the nineteenth century—not quickly enough to prevent a lasting blow to the island's economic base.

FREEDOM

The government took a great step forward in terms of wage scales for women by adopting a new minimum-wage law, which provided for equal pay for equal work done by men and women. Violence against women remains a significant problem.

St. Vincent, along with Dominica, is one of the poorest islands in the West Indies, although there has been some recent improvement. The current unemployment rate (2007) is estimated at 15 percent. With more than half the population under age 15, unemployment will continue to be a major problem in the foreseeable future.

Formerly one of the West Indian sugar islands, St. Vincent's main crops are now bananas and arrowroot. The sugar industry was a casualty of low world-market prices and a black-power movement in the 1960s that associated sugar production with memories of slavery. Limited sugar production has been renewed to meet local needs.

HEALTH/WELFARE

Minimum wages established in 1989 range from $3.85 *per day* in agriculture to $7.46 in industry. New minimums were presented to parliament in 2003. Clearly, the minimum is inadequate, although most workers earn significantly more than the minimum. The government's debt burden makes funding of social programs difficult.

THE POLITICS OF POVERTY

Poverty affects everyone in St. Vincent and the Grenadines, except a very few who live in comfort. In the words of one Vincentian, for most people, "life is a study in poverty." In 1969, a report identified malnutrition and gastroenteritis as being responsible for 57 percent of the deaths of children under age five. Those problems persist.

Deep-seated poverty also has an impact on the island's political life. Living on the verge of starvation, Vincentians cannot appreciate an intellectual approach to politics. They find it difficult to wait for the effects of long-term trends or coordinated development. Bread-and-butter issues are what concern them. Accordingly, parties speak little of basic economic and social change, structural shifts in the economy, or the latest economic theories. Politics is reduced to personality contests and rabble-rousing. Prime Minister Ralph Gonsalves, elected to a second term in 2005, remarked that he was tired of "perpetual warfare of a verbal kind" and has urged national reconciliation.

Despite its economic problems, St. Vincent is a free society. Newspapers are uncensored. Some reports, however, have noted that the government has on occasion granted or withheld advertising on the basis of a paper's editorial position.

ACHIEVEMENTS

A regional cultural organization was launched in 1982 in St. Vincent. Called the East Caribbean Popular Theatre Organisation, its membership extends to Dominica, Grenada, and St. Lucia.

Unions enjoy the right of collective bargaining. They represent about 11 percent of the labor force. St. Vincent, which won its independence from Great Britain in 1979, is a parliamentary, constitutional democracy. Political parties have the right to organize.

POLITICS AND ECONOMICS

While the country's political life has been calm, relative to some of the other Caribbean islands, there are signs of voter unrest. Prime Minister James Mitchell was reelected in 1999 for an unprecedented fourth five-year term, but his New Democratic Party lost some ground in the Legislature. In 2001 Ralph Gonsalves and his Unity Labour Party narrowly won election; in 2005 they gained 12 seats in the 15-seat parliament. Gonsalves, as reported by *BBC News,* is known to his followers as "Comrade Ralph" and campaigned on his government's economic record. He could point to meaningful economic growth and the completion of dozens of major projects.

Bananas once accounted for two-thirds of St. Vincent's export earnings. That figure fell to 50 percent in 2004 and to 33 percent in 2005. As is the case with other Windward Islands, St. Vincent's economy has been hurt by the 1999 European Union decision to phase out preferential treatment to banana producers from former colonial possessions. Not surprisingly drug trafficking, marijuana cultivation, and money laundering have increased as a result of the general economic malaise.

In 2001, along with other islands in the Windwards, St. Vincent entered talks with European Union officials with an eye to improving both yields and quality of bananas. There was general agreement that the entire Windward Islands banana industry needed restructuring if the industry is to survive.

Timeline: PAST

1498
Christopher Columbus discovers and names St. Vincent

1763
Ceded to the British by France

1795
The Carib War

1902
St. Vincent's La Soufrière erupts and kills 2,000 people

1979
Independence from Great Britain

1990s
A new minimum-wage law takes effect

PRESENT

2000s
The country's financial problems remain severe

2001
Ralph Gonsalves assumes the post of prime minister

2005
Gonsalves wins second term

Trinidad and Tobago (Republic of Trinidad and Tobago)

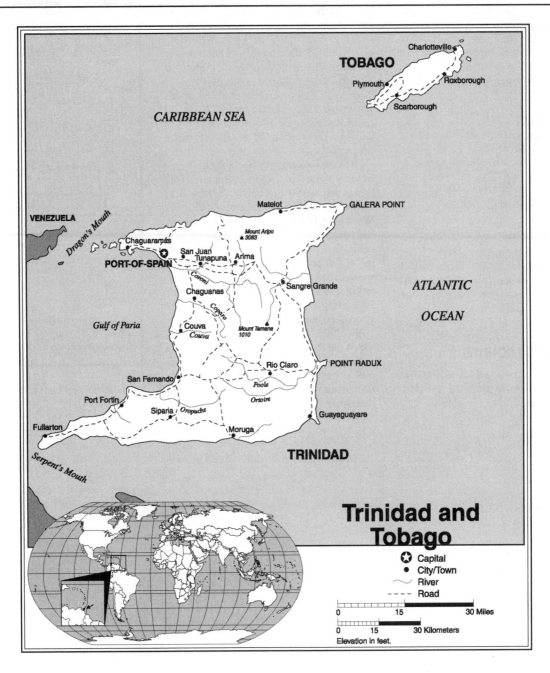

Trinidad and Tobago Statistics

GEOGRAPHY

Area in Square Miles (Kilometers):
1,980 (5,128) (about the size of Delaware)

Capital (Population): Port-of-Spain (49,031)

Environmental Concerns: water pollution; oil pollution of beaches; deforestation; soil erosion

Geographical Features: mostly plains, with some hills and low mountains

Climate: tropical

PEOPLE

Population

Total: 1,056,608 (2007 est.)
Annual Growth Rate: −0.88%
Rural/Urban Population Ratio: 28/72

Major Language: English
Ethnic Makeup: 40% East Indian; 37,5% black; 20.5% mixed
Religions: 26% Roman Catholic; 22.5% Hindi; 7.8% Anglican; 22% other Protestant; 5.8% Muslim

Health

Life Expectancy at Birth: 66 years (male); 68 years (female)

Infant Mortality Rate (Ratio):
24.33/1,000
Physicians Available (Ratio):
1/1,191

Education

Adult Literacy Rate: 98.6%
Compulsory (Ages): 5–12; free

COMMUNICATION

Telephones: 325,500 main lines
Daily Newspaper Circulation: 139 per
1,000 people
Cell Phones: 1,655,000
Internet Users: 163,000

TRANSPORTATION

Highways in Kilometers (Miles): 8,320
(5,167)
Usable Airfields: 6

GOVERNMENT

Type: parliamentary democracy
Independence Date: August 31, 1962
(from United Kingdom)
Head of State/Government: President
George Maxwell Richards; Prime
Minister Patrick Manning
Political Parties: People's National
Movement; United National Congress;
Democratic Action Congress; others
Suffrage: universal at 18

MILITARY

Current Disputes: none

ECONOMY

Currency ($U.S. Equivalent): 6.35
Trinidad/Tobago dollars = $1
Per Capita Income/GDP: $21,700/$14.15
billion

GDP Real Growth Rate: 5.5%
Inflation Rate: 7.6%
Unemployment Rate: 6%
Labor Force: 615,400
Natural Resources: petroleum; natural
gas; asphalt
Agriculture: cocoa; sugarcane; rice; citrus
fruits; coffee; vegetables; poultry
Industry: petroleum; chemicals; tourism;
food processing; cement; beverages;
textiles
Exports: $14.13 billion (f.o.b.) (primary
partners United States, CARICOM,
Latin America)
Imports: $6.477 billion (f.o.b.) (primary
partners United States, Venezuela,
European Union)

SUGGESTED WEB SITE

http://www.cia.gov/cia/publications/
factbook/index.html

Trinidad and Tobago Country Report

TRINIDAD AND TOBAGO: A MIDDLE-CLASS SOCIETY

The nation of Trinidad and Tobago, which became independent of Great Britain in 1962, differs sharply from other Caribbean countries in terms of both its wealth and its societal structure. More than one-third of its revenues derive from the production of crude oil. Much of the oil wealth has been redistributed and has created a society that is essentially middle class. Health conditions are generally good, education is widely available, and the literacy rate is a very high 98 percent.

DEVELOPMENT

The economy has experienced rapid growth thanks to vast reserves of natural gas, which has attracted investors from developed countries. The government has also promoted the use of natural gas, instituting a program to encourage consumers to switch from gasoline.

The country also enjoys an excellent human-rights record, although there is a good deal of tension between the ruling urban black majority and East Indians, who are rural. The divisions run deep and parallel the situation in Guyana. East Indians feel that they are forced to submerge their culture and conform to the majority. In the

words of one East Indian, "Where do Indians fit in when the culture of 40 percent of our people is denied its rightful place and recognition; when most of our people exist on the fringes of society and are considered as possessing nothing more than nuisance value?"

The lyrics of a black calypso artist that state the following are resented by East Indians:

If you are an East Indian
And you want to be an African
Just shave your head just like me
And nobody would guess your
nationality.

The prosperity of the nation, however, tends to mute these tensions.

Freedom of expression and freedom of the press are constitutionally guaranteed as well as respected in practice. Opposition viewpoints are freely expressed in the nation's Parliament, which is modeled along British lines. There is no political censorship. Opposition parties are usually supported by rural Hindu East Indians; while they have freely participated in elections, some East Indians feel that the government has gerrymandered electoral districts to favor the ruling party.

Violent crime and political unrest, including an attempted coup by black fundamentalist Muslim army officers in 1990, have become a way of life in the nation in

recent years. Prime Minister Basdeo Panday, elected in 1996, noted that there were still agendas, "political and otherwise," that divided Trinidadian society. "How much better it will be," he stated, "if all in our society, and particularly those in a position to shape mass consciousness, will seize every opportunity to promote and mobilise the greater strength that comes out of our diversity. . . ."

FREEDOM

Freedom of expression on the islands is guaranteed by the Constitution. The independent judiciary, pluralistic political system, and independent and privately owned print media assure that free expression exists in practice as well as in theory.

Trade-union organization is the most extensive among Caribbean nations with ties to Britain and includes about 30 percent of the workforce. In contrast to other West Indian states, unions in Trinidad and Tobago are not government-controlled, nor are they generally affiliated with a political party.

Women are well represented in Parliament, serve as ministers, and hold other high-level civil-service positions. Several groups are vocal advocates for women's rights.

HEALTH/WELFARE

Legislation passed in 1991 greatly expanded the categories of workers covered by the minimum wage. The same legislation provided for 3 months' maternity leave for household and shop assistants as well as other benefits. Citizens enjoy the highest per capita incomes in Latin America.

In an attempt to redress imbalances in the nation's agricultural structure, which is characterized by small landholdings—half of which are less than five acres each—the government has initiated a land-redistribution program using state-owned properties and estates sold to the government. The program is designed to establish more efficient medium-size family farms, of five to 20 acres, devoted to cash crops.

The islands' economic fortunes have tended to reflect the prices it can command from its exports of oil and liquefied natural gas. Petrochemicals, steel, aluminum, and plastics have contributed significantly to the nation's high growth rate. In 2001, British Petroleum began development of the Kapok gas field with a completion date of 2003. The project gives the nation one of the largest offshore gas-handling facilities in the world. Importantly, the company has indicated that the facility will conform to the most stringent environmental safeguards.

Of some concern to the government are the inroads made by Venezuela into its Caribbean market for refined petroleum.

Venezuelan foreign policy has used oil to buy influence in the region and its low prices undercut Trinidad. A possible solution was discussed in 2006 whereby Venezuelan crude would be refined in Trinidad.

ACHIEVEMENTS

Eric Williams, historian, pamphleteer, and politician, left his mark on Caribbean culture with his scholarly books and his bitterly satirical *Massa Day Done.* V. S. Naipaul is an influential author born in Trinidad. Earl Lovelace is another well-known Trinidadian author. He won the 1997 Commonwealth Writers' Prize for his novel *Salt.*

TOBAGO

Residents of Tobago have come to believe that their small island is perceived as nothing more than a dependency of Trinidad. It has been variously described as a "weekend resort," a "desert island," and a "tree house"—in contrast to "thriving," "vibrant" Trinidad. Tobagans feel that they receive less than their share of the benefits generated by economic prosperity.

In 1989, the Constitution was reviewed with an eye to introducing language that would grant Tobago the right to secede. The chair of the Tobago House of Assembly argued that, "in any union, both partners should have the right to opt out if they so desire." Others warn that such a provision would ultimately snap the ties that bind two peoples into one. Trinidadian

Timeline: PAST

1498
The island now called Trinidad is discovered by Columbus and later colonized by Spain

1797
Trinidad is captured by the British

1889
Tobago is added to Trinidad as a colonial unit

1962
Independence from Great Britain

1980s
Oil-export earnings slump

1996
Basdeo Panday is elected prime minister

PRESENT

2000s
Further development of the natural-gas industry

2005–2007
Tension between Venezuela and Trinidad over competition for petroleum markets in the Caribbean region

Patrick Manning re-elected prime minister

opposition leaders have observed that the areas that have historically supported the ruling party have more and better roads, telephones, and schools than those backing opposition parties. Partly to mollify Tobagans, the government has invested in tourism-related projects on the island.

Female Leaders On Rise In Central, South America

JACK CHANG

Buenos Aires, Argentina—Defying Latin America's long-time reputation as a bastion of machismo, women in South America are winning political power at an unprecedented rate and taking top positions in higher education and even, albeit more slowly, in business.

The election last year of Michelle Bachelet to Chile's presidency and the all-but-certain victory of Cristina Fernandez de Kirchner in Argentina's presidential balloting on Sunday are the most visible examples of the trend.

South American women also are leading important social movements and are earning, studying, and speaking out more than ever. For the first time, women are forcing their traditionally male-dominated societies to confront such issues as domestic violence and reproductive health.

"I think there's been a general change," said Elena Highton, who in 2004 became Argentina's first female Supreme Court judge appointed by a democratically elected government. She promptly headed a commission on domestic violence.

"This is the time of the woman, and people want to try something new," Highton said "Women are seen as more believable, more honest, more direct. And in this world dominated by men, we've seen lots of failures."

It's a fundamental shift in a region long ruled almost exclusively by men, where the influence of women was relegated to the home or, in public life, to supporting roles for powerful spouses.

Such perceptions changed for good, many say, with Bachelet's election last year in one of the most socially conservative countries in the hemisphere. A single mother and an atheist with no family member already in power, Bachelet, 56, won support from male and female Chileans in her historic election.

Public opinion polls in neighboring Argentina show similar widespread support for Kirchner, a longtime politician and current senator who's expected to win the contest to succeed her husband, Nestor, in this country's top job. Kirchner has frequently cited U.S. presidential candidate Sen. Hillary Clinton as an inspiration.

Women are considered possible successors to the top spot elsewhere in South America.

In Paraguay, former education minister Blanca Ovelar is a top candidate to represent the long-ruling Colorado Party in next April's presidential race. In Brazil, presidential chief of staff Dilma Rousseff has emerged as a possible front-runner for the presidency in 2010. They follow women who were elected president in Central America in the 1990s, Violeta Barrios de Chamorro in Nicaragua and Mireya Moscoso Rodriguez in Panama.

Latin American women still trail men in key measures of social well-being, according to the World Economic Forum, which ranks gender equality in 115 countries based on education, health and economic and political participation. Of Latin American countries, Colombia ranked the highest, 22nd out of 115 countries, and Guatemala, the lowest, at 95th.

But women are steadily catching up, United Nations statistics show. In many instances, the gaps are closing much faster than they are in the United States.

For example, the average wage of urban Latin American women has grown from 70 percent of men's in 1990 to 90 percent this year, and they're expected to reach parity by 2015, U.N. figures show.

For comparison, U.S. women earned 77 percent of what men earned working full-time, year-round jobs in 2006.

In the business world, women make up as much as 35 percent of the managers in private companies, also a dramatic increase from just a decade ago, according to the International Labor Organization. However, they still account for only 10 percent of company presidents and vice presidents, according to a seven-country survey by the U.S.-based think tank the Inter-American Dialogue.

Fourteen countries in Latin America, have passed quota laws requiring that as many as 40 percent of the candidates for political posts be women. Similar laws require that women fill a minimum number of union leadership posts and even executive-branch positions.

That's produced dramatic results in countries such as Argentina, the first in the region to implement quotas. Women now make up 35 percent of the lower house and 43 percent of the Senate.

Latin America's Left Turn

JORGE G. CASTAÑEDA

A Tale of Two Lefts

Just over a decade ago, Latin America seemed poised to begin a virtuous cycle of economic progress and improved democratic governance, overseen by a growing number of centrist technocratic governments. In Mexico, President Carlos Salinas de Gortari, buttressed by the passage of the North American Free Trade Agreement, was ready for his handpicked successor to win the next presidential election. Former Finance Minister Fernando Henrique Cardoso was about to beat out the radical labor leader Luiz Inácio Lula da Silva for the presidency of Brazil. Argentine President Carlos Menem had pegged the peso to the dollar and put his populist Peronist legacy behind him. And at the invitation of President Bill Clinton, Latin American leaders were preparing to gather in Miami for the Summit of the Americas, signaling an almost unprecedented convergence between the southern and northern halves of the Western Hemisphere.

What a difference ten years can make. Although the region has just enjoyed its best two years of economic growth in a long time and real threats to democratic rule are few and far between, the landscape today is transformed. Latin America is swerving left, and distinct backlashes are under way against the predominant trends of the last 15 years: free-market reforms, agreement with the United States on a number of issues, and the consolidation of representative democracy. This reaction is more politics than policy, and more nuanced than it may appear. But it is real.

Starting with Hugo Chávez's victory in Venezuela eight years ago and poised to culminate in the possible election of Andrés Manuel López Obrador in Mexico's July 2 presidential contest, a wave of leaders, parties, and movements generically labeled "leftist" have swept into power in one Latin American country after another. After Chávez, it was Lula and the Workers' Party in Brazil, then Néstor Kirchner in Argentina and Tabaré Vázquez in Uruguay, and then, earlier this year, Evo Morales in Bolivia. If the long shot Ollanta Humala wins the April presidential election in Peru and López Obrador wins in Mexico, it will seem as if a veritable left-wing tsunami has hit the region. Colombia and Central America are the only exceptions, but even in Nicaragua, the possibility of a win by Sandinista leader Daniel Ortega cannot be dismissed.

The rest of the world has begun to take note of this left-wing resurgence, with concern and often more than a little hysteria. But understanding the reasons behind these developments requires recognizing that there is not one Latin America left today; there are two. One is modern, open-minded, reformist, and internationalist, and it springs, paradoxically, from the hard-core left of the past. The other, born of the great tradition of Latin American populism, is nationalist, strident, and close-minded. The first is well aware of its past mistakes (as well as those of its erstwhile role models in Cuba and the Soviet Union) and has changed accordingly. The second, unfortunately, has not.

Utopia Redefined

The reasons for Latin America's turn to the left are not hard to discern. Along with many other commentators and public intellectuals, I started detecting those reasons nearly fifteen years ago, and I recorded them in my book *Utopia Unarmed: The Latin American Left After the Cold War*, which made several points. The first was that the fall of the Soviet Union would help the Latin American left by removing its geopolitical stigma. Washington would no longer be able to accuse any left-of-center regime in the region of being a "Soviet beachhead" (as it had every such government since it fomented the overthrow of Jacobo Arbenz's administration in Guatemala in 1954); left-wing governments would no longer have to choose between the United States and the Soviet Union, because the latter had simply disappeared.

The second point was that regardless of the success or failure of economic reforms in the 1990s and the discrediting of traditional Latin American economic policies, Latin America's extreme inequality (Latin America is the world's most unequal region), poverty, and concentration of wealth, income, power, and opportunity meant that it would have to be governed from the left of center. The combination of inequality and democracy tends to cause a movement to the left everywhere. This was true in western Europe from the end of the nineteenth century until after World War II; it is true today in Latin America. The impoverished masses vote for the type of policies that, they hope, will make them less poor.

Third, the advent of widespread democratization and the consolidation of democratic elections as the only road to power would, sooner or later, lead to victories for the left—precisely because of the social, demographic, and ethnic configuration of the region. In other words, even without the other proximate causes, Latin America would almost certainly have tilted left.

This forecast became all the more certain once it became evident that the economic, social, and political reforms implemented in Latin America starting in the mid-1980s had not delivered on their promises. With the exception of Chile, which has been governed by a left-of-center coalition since 1989, the region has had singularly unimpressive economic growth rates. They remain well below those of the glory days of the region's development (1940–80) and also well below those of other developing nations—China, of course, but also India, Malaysia, Poland, and many others. Between 1940 and 1980, Brazil and Mexico, for example, averaged six percent growth per year; from 1980 to 2000, their growth rates were less than half that. Low growth rates have meant the persistence of dismal poverty, inequality, high unemployment, a lack of competitiveness, and poor infrastructure. Democracy, although welcomed and supported by broad swaths of Latin American societies, did little to eradicate the region's secular plagues: corruption, a weak or nonexistent rule of law, ineffective governance, and the concentration of power in the hands of a few. And despite hopes that relations with the United States would improve, they are worse today than at any other time in recent memory, including the 1960s (an era defined by conflicts over Cuba) and the 1980s (defined by the Central American wars and Ronald Reagan's "contras").

But many of us who rightly foretold the return of the left were at least partly wrong about the kind of left that would emerge. We thought—perhaps naively—that the aggiornamento of the left in Latin America would rapidly and neatly follow that of socialist parties in France and Spain and of New Labour in the United Kingdom. In a few cases, this occurred—Chile certainly, Brazil tenuously. But in many others, it did not.

One reason for our mistake was that the collapse of the Soviet Union did not bring about the collapse of its Latin American equivalent, Cuba, as many expected it would. Although the links and subordination of many left-wing parties to Havana have had few domestic electoral implications (and Washington has largely stopped caring anyway), the left's close ties to and emotional dependency on Fidel Castro became an almost insurmountable obstacle to its reconstruction on many issues. But the more fundamental explanation has to do with the roots of many of the movements that are now in power. Knowing where left-wing leaders and parties come from—in particular, which of the two strands of the left in Latin American history they are a part of—is critical to understanding who they are and where they are going.

Origins of the Species

The left—defined as that current of thought, politics, and policy that stresses social improvements over macroeconomic orthodoxy, egalitarian distribution of wealth over its creation, sovereignty over international cooperation, democracy (at least when in opposition, if not necessarily once in power) over governmental effectiveness—has followed two different paths in Latin America. One left sprang up out of the Communist International and the Bolshevik Revolution and has followed a path similar to that of the left in the rest of the world. The Chilean, Uruguayan, Brazilian, Salvadoran, and, before Castro's revolution, Cuban

Communist Parties, for exam[...] the popular vote at one poin[...] front" or "national unity" [...] established a solid prese[...] significant influence in [...]

By the late 1950s [...] had lost most of the[...] ruption, submission[...] governments, and as[...] discredited them in the eye[...] the Cuban Revolution brought new[...] In time, groups descended from the old [...] with Havana-inspired guerrilla bands. There [...] some tensions. Castro accused the leader of the Bolivia[...] munist Party of betraying Che Guevara and leading him to h[...] death in Bolivia in 1967; the Uruguayan and Chilean Communist Parties (the region's strongest) never supported the local Castroist armed groups. Yet thanks to the passage of time, to Soviet and Cuban understanding, and to the sheer weight of repression generated by military coups across the hemisphere, the Castroists and Communists all came together—and they remain together today.

The origin of the other Latin American left is peculiarly Latin American. It arose out of the region's strange contribution to political science: good old-fashioned populism. Such populism has almost always been present almost everywhere in Latin America. It is frequently in power, or close to it. It claims as its founders historical icons of great mythical stature, from Peru's Víctor Raúl Haya de la Torre and Colombia's Jorge Gaitán (neither made it to office) to Mexico's Lázaro Cárdenas and Brazil's Getúlio Vargas, both foundational figures in their countries' twentieth-century history, and to Argentina's Juan Perón and Ecuador's José Velasco Ibarra. The list is not exhaustive, but it is illustrative: many of these nations' founding-father equivalents were seen in their time and are still seen now as noble benefactors of the working class. They made their mark on their nations, and their followers continue to pay tribute to them. Among many of these countries' poor and dispossessed, they inspire respect, even adulation, to this day.

These populists are representative of a very different left— often virulently anticommunist, always authoritarian in one fashion or another, and much more interested in policy as an instrument for attaining and conserving power than in power as a tool for making policy. They did do things for the poor— Perón and Vargas mainly for the urban proletariat, Cárdenas for the Mexican peasantry—but they also created the corporatist structures that have since plagued the political systems, as well as the labor and peasant movements, in their countries. They nationalized large sectors of their countries' economies, extending well beyond the so-called commanding heights, by targeting everything in sight: oil (Cárdenas in Mexico), railroads (Perón in Argentina), steel (Vargas in Brazil), tin (Victor Paz Estenssoro in Bolivia), copper (Juan Velasco Alvarado in Peru). They tended to cut sweetheart deals with the budding local business sector, creating the proverbial crony capitalism that was decried much later. Their justifications for such steps were always superficially ideological (nationalism, economic bottom pragmatic: they needed money to ... like taxes. They squared that circle by cap-...ource or monopoly rents, which allowed them ... on the *descamisados*, the "shirtless," without ... on the middle class. When everything else fails, ... went, spend money.

...akeover for the radical left is exactly ...at is needed for good governance ...n the region.

The ideological corollary to this bizarre blend of inclusion of the excluded, macroeconomic folly, and political staying power (Perón was the dominant figure in Argentine politics from 1943 through his death in 1974, the Cárdenas dynasty is more present than ever in Mexican politics) was virulent, strident nationalism. Perón was elected president in 1946 with the slogan "Braden or Perón" (Spruille Braden was then the U.S. ambassador to Buenos Aires). When Vargas committed suicide in 1954, he darkly insinuated that he was a victim of American imperialism. Such nationalism was more than rhetorical. In regimes whose domestic policy platform was strictly power-driven and pragmatic, it was the agenda.

These two subspecies of the Latin American left have always had an uneasy relationship. On occasion they have worked together, but at other times they have been at war, as when Perón returned from exile in June 1973 and promptly massacred a fair share of the Argentine radical left. In some countries, the populist left simply devoured the other one, although peacefully and rather graciously: in Mexico in the late 1980s, the tiny Communist Party disappeared, and former PRI (Institutional Revolutionary Party) members, such as Cuauhtémoc Cárdenas, Porfirio Muñoz Ledo, and the current presidential front-runner, López Obrador, took over everything from its buildings and finances to its congressional representation and relations with Cuba to form the left-wing PRD (Party of the Democratic Revolution).

More recently, something funny has happened to both kinds of leftist movements on their way back to power. The communist, socialist, and Castroist left, with a few exceptions, has been able to reconstruct itself, thanks largely to an acknowledgment of its failures and those of its erstwhile models. Meanwhile, the populist left—with an approach to power that depends on giving away money, a deep attachment to the nationalist fervor of another era, and no real domestic agenda—has remained true to itself. The latter perseveres in its cult of the past: it waxes nostalgic about the glory days of Peronism, the Mexican Revolution, and, needless to say, Castro. The former, familiar with its own mistakes, defeats, and tragedies, and keenly aware of the failures of the Soviet Union and Cuba, has changed its colors.

Castro's Unlikely Heirs

When the reformed communist left has reached office in recent years, its economic policies have been remarkably similar to those of its immediate predecessors, and its respect for democracy has proved full-fledged and sincere. Old-school anti-Americanism has been tempered by years of exile, realism, and resignation.

The best examples of the reconstructed, formerly radical left are to be found in Chile, Uruguay, and, to a slightly lesser extent, Brazil. This left emphasizes social policy—education, antipoverty programs, health care, housing—but within a more or less orthodox market framework. It usually attempts to deepen and broaden democratic institutions. On occasion, Latin America's age-old vices—corruption, a penchant for authoritarian rule—have led it astray. It disagrees with the United States frequently but rarely takes matters to the brink.

In Chile, former President Ricardo Lagos and his successor, Michelle Bachelet, both come from the old Socialist Party (Lagos from its moderate wing, Bachelet from the less temperate faction). Their left-wing party has governed for 16 consecutive years, in a fruitful alliance with the Christian Democrats. This alliance has made Chile a true model for the region. Under its stewardship, the country has enjoyed high rates of economic growth; significant reductions in poverty; equally significant improvements in education, housing, and infrastructure; a slight drop in inequality; a deepening of democracy and the dismantling of Augusto Pinochet's political legacy; a settling of accounts (although not of scores) regarding human rights violations of the past; and, last but not at all least, a strong, mature relationship with the United States, including a free-trade agreement signed by George W. Bush and ratified by the U.S. Congress and Washington's support for the Chilean candidate to head the Organization of American States. U.S.–Chilean ties have continued to prosper despite Chile's unambiguous opposition to the U.S. invasion of Iraq in the UN Security Council in 2003.

In Uruguay, Vázquez ran for president twice before finally winning a little more than a year ago. His coalition has always been the same: the old Uruguayan Communist Party, the Socialist Party, and many former Marxist Tupamaro guerrillas, who made history in the 1960s and 1970s by, among other things, kidnapping and executing CIA station chief Dan Mitrione in Montevideo in 1970 and being featured in Costa-Gavras' 1973 film *State of Siege*. There was reason to expect Vázquez to follow a radical line once elected—but history once again trumped ideology. Although Vázquez has restored Uruguay's relations with Cuba and every now and then rails against neoliberalism and Bush, he has also negotiated an investment-protection agreement with the United States, sent his finance minister to Washington to explore the possibility of forging a free-trade agreement, and stood up to the "antiglobalization, politically correct" groups in neighboring Argentina on the construction of two enormous wood-pulp mills in the Uruguay River estuary. He refused to attend Morales' inauguration as president of Bolivia and has threatened to veto a bill legalizing abortion if it gets to his desk. His government is, on substance if not on rhetoric, as economically orthodox as any other. And with good reason: a country of 3.5 million inhabitants with the lowest poverty rate and the least inequality in Latin America should not mess with its relative success.

Brazil is a different story, but not a diametrically opposed one. Even before his inauguration in 2003, Lula had indicated that he would follow most of his predecessor's macroeconomic policies and comply with the fiscal and monetary targets agreed on with the International Monetary Fund (IMF). He has done so, achieving impressive results in economic stability (Brazil continues to generate a hefty fiscal surplus every year), but GDP growth has been disappointing, as have employment levels and social indicators. Lula has tried to compensate for his macro-economic orthodoxy with innovative social initiatives (particularly his "Zero Hunger" drive and land reform). At the end of the day, however, perhaps his most important achievement on this front will be the generalization of the Bolsa Familia (Family Fund) initiative, which was copied directly from the antipoverty program of Mexican Presidents Ernesto Zedillo and Vicente Fox. This is a successful, innovative welfare program, but as neoliberal and scantly revolutionary as one can get.

On foreign policy, Brazil, like just about every Latin American country, has had its run-ins with the Bush administration, over issues including trade, UN reform, and how to deal with Bolivia, Colombia, Cuba, and Venezuela. But perhaps the best metaphor for the current state of U.S.–Brazilian relations today was the scene in Brasilia last November, when Lula welcomed Bush at his home, while across the street demonstrators from his own party burned the U.S. president in effigy.

The Workers' Party, which Lula founded in 1980 after a long metalworkers' strike in the industrial outskirts of São Paulo, has largely followed him on the road toward social democracy. Many of the more radical cadres of the party, or at least those with the most radical histories (such as José Genoino and José Dirceu), have become moderate reformist leaders, despite their pasts and their lingering emotional devotion to Cuba. (Lula shares this devotion, and yet it has not led him to subservience to Castro: when Lula visited Havana in 2004, Castro wanted to hold a mass rally at the Plaza de la Revolución; instead, Castro got a 24-hour in-and-out visit from the Brazilian president, with almost no public exposure.) Lula and many of his comrades are emblematic of the transformation of the old, radical, guerrilla-based, Castroist or communist left. Granted, the conversion is not complete: the corruption scandals that have rocked Brazil's government have more to do with a certain neglect of democratic practices than with any personal attempt at enrichment. Still, the direction in which Lula and his allies are moving is clear.

Overall, this makeover of the radical left is good for Latin America. Given the region's inequality, poverty, still-weak democratic tradition, and unfinished nation building, this left offers precisely what is needed for good governance in the region. If Chile is any example, this left's path is the way out of poverty, authoritarian rule, and, eventually, inequality. This left is also a viable, sensitive, and sensible alternative to the other left—the one that speaks loudly but carries a very small social stick.

Populism Redux

The leftist leaders who have arisen from a populist, nationalist past with few ideological underpinnings—Chávez with his military background, Kirchner with his Peronist roots, Morales with his coca-leaf growers' militancy and agitprop, López Obrador with his origins in the PRI—have proved much less responsive to modernizing influences. For them, rhetoric is more important than substance, and the fact of power is more important than its

responsible exercise. The despair of poor constituencies is a tool rather than a challenge, and taunting the United States trumps promoting their countries' real interests in the world. The difference is obvious: Chávez is not Castro; he is Perón with oil. Morales is not an indigenous Che; he is a skillful and irresponsible populist. López Obrador is neither Lula nor Chávez; he comes straight from the PRI of Luis Echeverría, Mexico's president from 1970 to 1976, from which he learned how to be a cash-dispensing, authoritarian-inclined populist. Kirchner is a true-blue Peronist, and proud of it.

For all of these leaders, economic performance, democratic values, programmatic achievements, and good relations with the United States are not imperatives but bothersome constraints that miss the real point. They are more intent on maintaining popularity at any cost, picking as many fights as possible with Washington, and getting as much control as they can over sources of revenue, including oil, gas, and suspended foreign-debt payments.

Argentina's Kirchner is a classic (although somewhat ambiguous) case. Formerly the governor of a small province at the end of the world, he was elected in the midst of a monumental economic crisis and has managed to bring his country out of it quite effectively. Inflation has been relatively controlled, growth is back, and interest rates have fallen. Kirchner also renegotiated Argentina's huge foreign debt skillfully, if perhaps a bit too boldly. He has gone further than his predecessors in settling past grievances, particularly regarding the "dirty war" that the military and his Peronist colleagues waged in the 1970s. He has become a darling of the left and seems to be on a roll, with approval ratings of over 70 percent.

But despite the left-wing company he keeps, Kirchner is at his core a die-hard Peronist, much more interested in bashing his creditors and the IMF than in devising social policy, in combating the Free Trade Agreement of the Americas (FTAA) than in strengthening Mercosur, in cuddling up to Morales, Castro, and Chavez than in lowering the cost of importing gas from Bolivia. No one knows exactly what will happen when Argentina's commodity boom busts or when the country is forced to return to capital markets for fresh funds. Nor does anyone really know what Kirchner intends to do when his economic recovery runs out of steam. But it seems certain that the Peronist chromosomes in the country's DNA will remain dominant: Kirchner will hand out money, expropriate whatever is needed and available, and lash out at the United States and the IMF on every possible occasion. At the same time, he will worry little about the number of Argentines living under the poverty line and be as chummy with Chávez as he can.

Chávez is doing much the same in Venezuela. He is leading the fight against the FTAA, which is going nowhere anyway. He is making life increasingly miserable for foreign—above all American—companies. He is supporting, one way or the other, left-wing groups and leaders in many neighboring countries. He has established a strategic alliance with Havana that includes the presence of nearly 20,000 Cuban teachers, doctors, and cadres in Venezuela. He is flirting with Iran and Argentina on nuclear-technology issues. Most of all, he is attempting, with some success, to split the hemisphere into two camps: one pro-Chavez, one pro-American.

At the same time, Chávez is driving his country into the ground. A tragicomic symbol of this was the collapse of the highway from Caracas to the Maiquetía airport a few months ago because of lack of maintenance. Venezuela's poverty figures and human development indices have deteriorated since 1999, when Chávez took office. A simple comparison with Mexico—which has not exactly thrived in recent years—shows how badly Venezuela is faring. Over the past seven years, Mexico's economy grew by 17.5 percent, while Venezuela's failed to grow at all. From 1997 to 2003, Mexico's per capita GDP rose by 9.5 percent, while Venezuela's shrank by 45 percent. From 1998 to 2005, the Mexican peso lost 16 percent of its value, while the value of the Venezuelan bolivar dropped by 292 percent. Between 1998 and 2004, the number of Mexican households living in extreme poverty decreased by 49 percent, while the number of Venezuelan households in extreme poverty rose by 4.5 percent. In 2005, Mexico's inflation rate was estimated at 3.3 percent, the lowest in years, while Venezuela's was 16 percent.

Although Chávez does very little for the poor of his own country (among whom he remains popular), he is doing much more for other countries: giving oil away to Cuba and other Caribbean states, buying Argentina's debt, allegedly financing political campaigns in Bolivia and Peru and perhaps Mexico. He also frequently picks fights with Fox and Bush and is buying arms from Spain and Russia. This is about as close to traditional Latin American populism as one can get—and as far from a modern and socially minded left as one can be.

The populist left leaders who are waiting in the wings look likely to deliver much the same. Morales in Bolivia has already made it to power. López Obrador in Mexico is close. Although Humala in Peru is still a long shot, he certainly cannot be dismissed. Such leaders will follow the footsteps of Chávez and Kirchner, because they have the same roots and share the same creed. They will all, of course, be constrained by their national realities—Morales by the fact that Bolivia is South America's poorest nation, López Obrador by a 2,000-mile border with the United States, Humala by a fragmented country and the lack of an established political party to work with.

Still, they will tread the same path. Morales and Humala have both said that they will attempt either to renationalize their countries' natural resources (gas, oil, copper, water) or renegotiate the terms under which foreign companies extract them. López Obrador has stated that he will not allow private investment in PEMEX, Mexico's state-owned oil company, or in the national electric power company. He has given away money right and left in Mexico City, financing his magnanimity with debt and federal tax revenues. Morales has deftly played on his indigenous origins to ingratiate himself with the majority of his country's population, to whom he is promising everything but giving very little. Morales and Humala have received at least rhetorical support from Chavez, and Morales' first trip abroad was to Havana, his second to Caracas. Humala, a retired lieutenant colonel in the Peruvian army, has confessed to being an admirer of the Venezuelan president. Like Chávez, he started his political career with a failed coup, in his case against Alberto Fujimori in 2000. López Obrador's deputy, certain to be the next

mayor of Mexico City, has openly declared his admiration for Chávez and Castro, despite having been a high-level official under Salinas.

What will prove most damaging is that the populist left loves power more than democracy, and it will fight to keep it at great cost. Its disregard for democracy and the rule of law is legendary. Often using democratic means, it has often sought to concentrate its power through new constitutions, take control of the media and the legislative and judicial branches of government, and perpetuate its rule by using electoral reforms, nepotism, and the suspension of constitutional guarantees. Chávez is the best example of this left, but certainly not the only one: López Obrador has already committed himself to "cleaning up" Mexico's Supreme Court and central bank and opposes any autonomy for the country's infant regulatory agencies.

This populist left has traditionally been disastrous for Latin America, and there is no reason to suppose it will stop being so in the future. As in the past, its rule will lead to inflation, greater poverty and inequality, and confrontation with Washington. It also threatens to roll back the region's most important achievement of recent years: the establishment of democratic rule and respect for human rights.

Right Left, Wrong Left

Distinguishing between these two broad left-wing currents is the best basis for serious policy, from Washington, Brussels, Mexico City, or anywhere else. There is not a tremendous amount Washington or any other government can actually do to alter the current course of events in Latin America. The Bush administration could make some difference by delivering on its promises to incumbents in the region (on matters such as immigration and trade), thereby supporting continuity without interfering in the electoral process; in South American nations where there is a strong European presence, countries such as France and Spain could help by pointing out that certain policies and attitudes have certain consequences.

But there is a much bolder course, a more statesmanlike approach, that would foster a "right left" instead of working to subvert any left's resurgence. This strategy would involve actively and substantively supporting the right left when it is in power: signing free-trade agreements with Chile, taking Brazil seriously as a trade interlocutor, engaging these nations' governments on issues involving third countries (such as Colombia, Cuba, and Venezuela), and bringing their leaders and public intellectuals into the fold. The right left should be able to show not only that there are no penalties for being what it is, but also that it can deliver concrete benefits.

The international community should also clarify what it expects from the "wrong left," given that it exists and that attempts to displace it would be not only morally unacceptable but also pragmatically ineffective. The first point to emphasize is that Latin American governments of any persuasion must abide by their countries' commitments regarding human rights and democracy. The region has built up an incipient scaffolding on these matters over recent years, and any backsliding, for whatever reason or purpose, should be met by a rebuke from the international community. The second point to stress is that all governments must continue to comply with the multilateral effort to build a new international legal order, one that addresses, among other things, the environment, indigenous people's rights, international criminal jurisdiction (despite Washington's continued rejection of the International Criminal Court and its pressure on several Latin American governments to do the same), nuclear nonproliferation, World Trade Organization rules and norms, regional agreements, and the fight against corruption, drug trafficking, and terrorism, consensually defined. Europe and the United States have enormous leverage in many of these countries. They should use it.

Finally, Washington and other governments should avoid the mistakes of the past. Some fights are simply not worth fighting: If Morales wants to squabble with Chile over access to the sea, with Argentina over the price of gas, with Peru over border issues and indigenous ancestry, stand aside. If, for whatever reason, López Obrador wants to build a bullet train from Mexico City to the U.S. border, live and let live. If Chávez really wants to acquire nuclear technology from Argentina, let him, as long as he does it under Internatio[...] vision and safeguards. Under no [...] accept the division of the hemisphere [...] United States, against the United States—b[...] split, the Americas themselves always lose out. [...] happened over Cuba in the 1960s and over Central [...] the 1980s. Now that the Cold War is over, it should nev[...] pen again. So instead of arguing over whether to welcome [...] bemoan the advent of *the* left in Latin America, it would be wiser to separate the sensible from the irresponsible and to support the former and contain the latter. If done right, this would go a long way toward helping the region finally find its bearings and, as Gabriel García Márquez might put it, end its hundreds of years of solitude.

JORGE G. CASTAÑEDA is the author of *Utopia Unarmed: The Latin American Left After the Cold War* and *Compañero: The Life and Death of Che Guevara*. Having resigned as Mexico's Foreign Minister in 2003, he is currently Global Distinguished Professor of Politics and Latin American Studies at New York University.

Corruption
...nerica

"Some lev... ...ruption is endemic to the region's states almost regardle... of their economic policies."

KURT WEYLAND

In Latin America as elsewhere, the relationship between market reforms and political corruption has been a matter of some contention. Academic economists and World Bank officials used to argue that neoliberal reforms diminish malfeasance. As economic resources are allocated by the market rather than the state, politicians and government leaders have fewer opportunities to extract bribes in exchange for channeling illicit benefits to their cronies. By contrast, political scientists have claimed that neoliberal reforms open up new avenues for collusion. The privatization of public enterprises, which involves political decisions over reallocating huge chunks of property, can be skewed by payments under the table. And as public services are contracted out to private providers, kickbacks can influence who receives favorable deals.

In the December 2005 issue of *Current History,* Colgate's Michael Johnston argued that "neoliberal reforms do not so much end corruption as privatize it." The recent Latin American experience corroborates this claim. Market reforms, especially privatization, have indeed been associated with scandalous corruption in a number of cases. The disposition of state property has allowed for enormous malfeasance.

But governments that implemented neoliberal programs have not been equally shameless in taking advantage of these opportunities for graft. Whereas the administrations of Carlos Menem in Argentina (1989–1999), Fernando Collor de Mello in Brazil (1990–1992), and Alberto Fujimori in Peru (1990–2000) were notorious for large-scale corruption, the governments of Fernando Henrique Cardoso in Brazil (1995–2002) and César Gaviria in Colombia (1990–1994) were comparatively clean— though not completely so. Indeed, Cardoso, Gaviria, and their ministers were not any more corrupt than their predecessors or successors who did not enact market reforms.

Neoliberalism as such has not significantly boosted corruption in Latin America. The cancerous growth of malfeasance has depended instead on the type of government that executed market reforms. Where neopopulist outsiders such as Menem,

Collor, and Fujimori spearheaded this great transformation, cases of graft multiplied and the amount of bribes reached unprecedented levels. However, where established party politicians such as Cardoso and Gaviria enacted privatization, existing mechanisms of political accountability kept graft in check.

The evidence is clear, moreover, that some level of corruption is endemic to the region's states almost regardless of their economic policies. Malfeasance may have reached particular brazenness in some countries, but it remains widespread throughout Latin America. Indeed, the entrenched nature of bribery has become strikingly obvious with the recent eruption of scandals in the "model democracy" of Costa Rica and the "model party" of Brazil, President Luiz Inácio Lula da Silva's Workers' Party (PT). These avowedly clean settings constituted "least likely cases" for graft; its documented occurrence offers stunning proof of the difficulty of withstanding temptations.

There is some hope for improvement, however. While market reforms have allowed for greater corruption, the outrage prompted by bribery scandals and the gradual emergence of institutional reforms are triggering efforts to rein in malfeasance. These efforts hold the promise of eventually introducing cleaner government.

Opportunity and Motive

Why does neopopulism produce an explosion of corruption? Neopopulist leaders concentrate power, skew institutional checks and balances, and zealously increase their own autonomy. They have the latitude as a result to engage in malfeasance. And given neopopulism's lack of institutionalization, leaders need massive resources to ensure loyalty from their aides and to consolidate popular support. They tend to collect these funds through kickbacks. Thus, neopopulist leaders have the opportunity and incentive to engage in high levels of corruption.

Neopopulist appeals tend to find resonance during acute crises that jeopardize popular well-being. To escape from serious hardship, many citizens eagerly support a savior who promises to turn the country around with bold, determined countermeasures. In Latin America, not surprisingly, the troubles and travails caused by the debt crisis of the 1980s and the hyperinflation that erupted in a number of countries provided fertile ground for the emergence of personalistic, plebiscitarian leaders. Where profound economic difficulties coincided with violent political challenges, such as the brutal Shining Path insurgency in Peru, complete political outsiders without any organized support could be swept into office on the back of exalted popular hopes for salvation.

To tackle these problems in a determined fashion, neopopulist leaders such as Collor, Fujimori, and Menem relentlessly concentrated power in the presidency, weakened the other branches of government, and undermined intermediary organizations in civil society. They forced the hand of parliaments through daring brinkmanship or usurped legislative functions by passing unprecedented numbers of emergency decrees. They packed the courts, appointed provisional judges and kept them dependent, and engineered the impeachment of judges who challenged them. They also neglected party building, engaging instead in divide-and-rule tactics against existing parties and outmaneuvering and splitting societal organizations. In all these ways, they undermined competing power centers and boosted their own independence and predominance.

Neopopulist presidents depicted this political centralization as indispensable for breaking resistance from "special interests," for pushing through rescue measures, and for restoring economic and political stability. They stressed the need for a forceful attack on pressing problems, even at the risk of disrespecting some formal rules. But their enhanced authority and autonomy undermined institutional checks and balances and weakened democratic mechanisms of accountability. Governing the nation as they saw fit, they claimed unlimited discretion. This opened up opportunities to use political decisions for personal enrichment.

In fact, neopopulist leaders had strong political incentives to resort to corruption. The absence of institutionalization makes personalistic, plebiscitarian rule precarious. Lacking a firm support organization, neopopulist presidents often govern with heterogeneous teams. They cannot count on the loyalty and discipline of the top aides whom they appoint, including ministers and heads of the armed forces. To cement support from these close collaborators, neopopulist leaders offer a share of the spoils. Complicity in corruption ensures continued cooperation and offers the leader a disciplining device; if an aide proves recalcitrant, damaging evidence can always be leaked. Shared graft thus serves as a functional equivalent for the internal cohesion and discipline that a party organization guarantees to established politicians.

Corruption—if undetected—can also help the leader stabilize and augment his mass support. Neopopulists base their government on majoritarian backing by the people, as expressed in elections and referenda, which these leaders like to call. But campaigns for these contests are expensive in contemporary Latin America. In the absence of an established party apparatus that could marshal support through grassroots mechanisms, neopopulist leaders need to build up their own campaign staff and apply costly tactics such as television advertising. Funding these activities requires sizeable war chests. Bribery proceeds are crucial for filling these financial needs. Thus, while neopopulist leaders certainly use corruption to pad their private bank accounts, they also need it for renewing and retaining mass support, the most important base of their rule.

Kickbacks and Bribes

For these reasons, neopopulist leaders took advantage of the opportunities created by market reform to engage in exorbitant graft. The privatization of public enterprises proved especially susceptible to corruption. In exchange for kickbacks, presidents and their aides often agreed to excessively low sales prices and favored one bidder over competitors.

The privatization deals conducted in Carlos Menem's Argentina in the early 1990s were notorious for egregious corruption. Displaying the sense of impunity created by neopopulist leadership, the official in charge, María Julia Alsogaray—a close crony of President Menem's—was brazen enough to flaunt her ill-begotten wealth at a time when most Argentines suffered from recession and austerity. Some later transfers of state property were marred by equally scandalous irregularities. For instance, the privatization of the postal system and of airports favored a shady businessman, Alfredo Yabrán, who commanded special access to Menem. An investigative reporter who sought to shed light on these transactions was assassinated, and when the resulting public outcry put the spotlight on Yabrán, he committed suicide. Some of the privatization deals in Menem's Argentina took place in a gray zone between personal favoritism and organized crime.

Menem also used the sale of public enterprises to build political support among leading business groups. By allowing powerful industrial captains to buy huge chunks of public property on the cheap, he sought to guarantee backing for his government and his reelection project. Although it is difficult to document whether illicit payments greased the wheels of this favoritism, Menem did amass millions of dollars while in office, as the discovery of secret bank accounts in foreign countries suggests.

In Brazil, President Collor and his aides took advantage of a tough economic stabilization measure to extract voluminous bribes. To drain liquidity from the economy and thus force down hyperinflation, the new chief executive in March 1990 pushed a decree through Congress that froze all bank accounts above a level of approximately $1,100. Businesspeople suddenly lacked funds to pay their workers, buy needed materials, and service their debts. In despair, many offered side payments to regain access to their own money. Collor's former campaign treasurer, Paulo César Farias, used this bottleneck to collect bribes. He also took advantage of privatization deals and public works contracts to extract enormous commissions. As São Paulo businesspeople complained, these kickbacks—which had run at 15 to 20 percent of a transaction under Collor's predecessor—reached unprecedented levels of 30 to 40 percent under this neopopulist upstart. The effect was to sully the entire market reform program.

Neopopulist Alberto Fujimori gained special predominance in Peru's battered polity. Using his autonomy and power, he and his spymaster, Vladimiro Montesinos, built up an extensive corruption network. They skimmed off part of the foreign aid that sought to help Peruvians survive the terrible economic and sociopolitical crisis of the early 1990s, charged illicit commissions on a number of privatization deals, and evidently even accepted payments from drug traffickers in exchange for turning a blind eye to their continued operations on national territory. By one estimate, Fujimori may have stolen, through all of these maneuvers, more than $180 million.

As his most distinctive initiative, Montesinos bought off large segments of Peru's power elite. He handed cash and other benefits to businesspeople, generals, media owners, and legislative politicians—and filmed these transactions to keep the recipients vulnerable and under his control. In this way, he sought to stabilize Fujimori's neopopulist leadership, which in its lack of institutionalization remained precarious. In fact, as renewed economic difficulties and large-scale underemployment diminished the president's mass backing, the political incentive to purchase support increased. When the electorate denied Fujimori a congressional majority in the 2000 elections, Montesinos sought to persuade opposition deputies, with the help of substantial payments, to shift sides.

The Better Reformers

Exorbitant corruption has not always accompanied neoliberal programs in Latin America. Where established party politicians conducted ambitious market reforms in democratic settings, graft did not rise above normal levels. While there certainly was a good deal of malfeasance, especially in privatization deals and public works contracts, it did not become the cancerous growth that characterized Menem's Argentina, Collor's Brazil, and Fujimori's Peru.

Presidents who rose through the existing party system and who governed with the help of broad coalitions did not command the latitude and power to subordinate government decision making to their own whims and desires. They could not boost their personal leadership at the expense of other power centers and dismantle mechanisms of accountability and control. Instead, they had to govern largely inside existing institutional and political constraints, which limited their room for discretion, including malfeasance.

Where a small cabal takes over the state, corruption tends to increase because a few partners in crime have incentives to cover each other's tracks. By contrast, where a wide-ranging alliance shares government responsibility, a president who promotes excessive corruption risks having his misdeeds exposed by discontent factions. The broader and more heterogeneous the governing coalition, the less secure any pact of impunity. Moreover, an influential parliament, reasonably independent courts, and a minimally vigilant civil society will keep presidents on their toes.

For these reasons, the Cardoso government implemented market reforms in Brazil without engaging in outrageous corruption. Although it collected tens of billions of dollars through privatization deals and public bids for service provision and infrastructure projects, levels of graft did not sky-rocket. While some officials involved in these transactions appear to have skimmed off commissions, these "cuts" did not reach the exorbitant percentages that were common under the Collor government.

Also, the ignominious impeachment of the neopopulist leader on corruption charges helped induce subsequent administrations to limit malfeasance. To legitimate the resumption of market reform after Collor's ouster, Cardoso had to ensure that his own administration was reasonably clean. Privatization procedures were therefore designed to foster authentic competition.

In a similar vein, Gaviria's administration in Colombia enacted a wide-ranging and ambitious program of market reforms without boosting the levels of corruption prevailing in that country. Hailing from the long-established Liberal Party, the president had a reputation to safeguard; in fact, since party politicians seek to promote the political fortunes of their organizations, they also face the long shadow of the future, which they do not want to jeopardize for the sake of immediate payoffs. And since Gaviria could count on organized backing, he did not need to amass a huge war chest to build his own support network through side payments; instead, he could rely on traditional patronage mechanisms inside the confines of formal legality.

In its quest to make Brazilian politics less corrupt, the Workers' Party itself became more corrupt.

As a result, Colombia's privatization of public enterprises followed institutional procedures that ensured reasonably clean results. It is noteworthy that the Gaviria administration accomplished this feat in a country swimming in drug money, which severely tainted the subsequent presidential election of 1994 and undermined the legitimacy of the non-neoliberal government of Ernesto Samper (1994–1998). By contrast, no incriminating evidence against Gaviria and his leading aides has surfaced.

The experiences of the Cardoso and Gaviria administrations demonstrate that neoliberalism in Latin America does not inevitably boost corruption. While the political decisions that spearhead economic restructuring open up opportunities for extracting enormous bribes, not all governments have the incentive and capacity to take advantage of these chances for malfeasance.

Endemic Graft

But bribery continues to be entrenched in many Latin American countries, regardless of their economic policy. Only Chile and Uruguay ranked among the 50 "cleanest" countries worldwide in Transparency International's 2005 "Corruption Perceptions Index." Colombia, Brazil, Mexico, and Peru are afflicted by widespread and substantial graft, and even sophisticated Argentina suffers from more serious malfeasance. In this group of nations, petty corruption is common, with police officers regularly taking advantage of alleged traffic violations to extort bribes. Many politicians and public officials are venal, charging commissions for a variety of decisions through which they favor their cronies. Even votes on major reform bills can be for sale: the short-lived Argentine government of Fernando de la Rúa (1999–2001), which promised to restore public probity after the excesses of the Menem regime, literally bought support in the Senate to pass an important labor reform.

Venezuela traditionally has been one of the most corrupt countries in Latin America. Fabulous oil wealth has long induced politicians and government officials to engage in exorbitant theft. In times of bonanza resulting from high international petroleum prices, there was enough booty for everyone who commanded political influence and even some leftovers for broader sectors of the population. As Venezuela's economic fortunes declined in the 1980s and 1990s, however, citizen outrage at this uncontrolled looting of the public treasury grew. Fed up, a majority of voters eventually cleaned house and elected a neopopulist outsider, Hugo Chávez, president in 1998. A leftist nationalist, this personalistic plebiscitarian leader rejected neoliberalism. But Chávez's power grab and removal of political and institutional checks and balances allowed him and his aides to engage in as many shady dealings as their predecessors. Hundreds of millions of petrodollars deposited in an economic stabilization fund are unaccounted for, and corruption appears to be rife in the extensive spending programs that the new administration has introduced. While the increasingly closed nature of the Chávez government has suppressed definite proof, the available evidence suggests that neopopulism and the recent oil bonanza have sustained an orgy of graft.

Nothing demonstrates the extent of malfeasance in contemporary Latin America more strikingly than its recent appearance in settings that seemed to be immune to this problem, namely the "Switzerland" of Central America, Costa Rica, and Brazilian President Lula da Silva's Workers' Party, which had promised to clean up Brazilian politics.

The neighbor of notorious problem cases, Costa Rica has long been regarded as a well-administered country. Boasting a centrist two-party system in a consolidated democracy, Costa Rica has instituted reliable mechanisms of transparency and accountability. Moreover, technical and bureaucratic cadres inside state institutions have shown a strong esprit de corps, which tends to keep malfeasance in check. Given widespread commitment to clean government, any evidence of shady dealings could ruin a public official's career. This deterrence worked for decades.

But over the past 15 years, Costa Rica's gradual advance toward market reform has created new opportunities for extracting kickbacks. For instance, public services that the state used to discharge are now contracted out to private companies. And to forestall the "exit" of service users to more appealing private alternatives, public institutions have embarked on renewed modernization efforts, which require the purchase of equipment and the construction of new facilities. This increase in public–private cooperation encouraged private companies to offer bribes to obtain favorable treatment. Institutions that have long symbolized clean government have unexpectedly seen corruption grow in their midst.

Neopopulist leaders have the opportunity and incentive to engage in high levels of corruption.

Since top-level officials had to approve major deals and extracted kickbacks in return, two of the country's former presidents have recently been under house arrest for their involvement, and a third former chief executive has had to stay out of the country to avoid this fate. These cases have stunned and embarrassed Costa Rica. The cancer that has long afflicted so much of Latin America is now spreading to this fading model democracy as well.

The case of the Brazilian Workers' Party (Partido dos Trabalhadores—PT) offers an even more striking indication that corruption remains widespread in the region. This program-oriented, well-organized upstart organization was touted as a promising alternative to the established parties, which relied heavily on patronage and routinely engaged in shady dealings. To use their proclaimed commitment to administrative probity for electoral advantage, PT politicians routinely excoriated cases of malfeasance among their adversaries and showcased a PT "clean style of governing" (modo petista de governor) in some well-run cities with PT mayors.

But at the same time that it was winning accolades for its modern approach to administration, the PT began to use traditional means to bolster its political fortunes and defray the exorbitant costs of electoral campaigns in Brazil. Because voluntary donations from businesspeople to this socialist party remained sparse, PT mayors introduced forced collections by charging illegal commissions on public service contracts, especially municipal transport and trash collection. These locally extorted kickbacks fed the party's national campaign war chest; for instance, Lula da Silva's main marketing strategist in the 2002 presidential campaign was paid out of a slush fund.

Moreover, after the PT won the federal presidency in late 2002, it sought to ensure governability by purchasing support from fickle congressional allies. For this purpose, it instituted a system of monthly salary supplements for deputies who reliably voted with the government. Ironically, the PT felt compelled to engage in this crass vote buying because it was reluctant to apply the traditional method for sustaining coalition government in Brazil, namely by appointing as ministers opportunistic politicians who promised support in exchange for patronage. Since the PT wanted to control policy making in most issue areas, it insisted on dominating the cabinet and sought instead to forge a legislative majority by offering streams of cash to deputies.

Thus, the party that seemed to hold the greatest hope for renovating Brazil's clientelistic, patronage-infested political system eventually ceded to the temptation to apply dirty tricks that it had so loudly condemned. The fragmented nature of Brazil's party system, which forces any government to garner support from patronage-obsessed opportunists, induces even a seemingly clean newcomer to apply dishonest tactics. In its quest to make Brazilian politics less corrupt, the Worker's Party itself became more corrupt. This turn of events sharply demonstrates the difficulty of instituting clean government in Latin America. If the Workers' Party cannot accomplish this feat, who can?

Cleanup Efforts

Not all is lost, however. Although corruption continues to be widespread in Latin America, there have also been efforts to rein in malfeasance. The striking levels that bribery reached in a number of cases, such as Menem's Argentina, Collor's Brazil, and Fujimori's Peru, have provoked outcries in public opinion that have had significant political ramifications. Corruption scandals have destroyed the careers of powerful politicians and triggered institutional reforms that have ranged from greater judicial independence to freedom-of-information laws.

Interestingly, these efforts at cleaning up Latin American politics have taken some inspiration from neoliberalism. While the initial, radical phase of market reform opened up opportunities for increased corruption, later stages have placed priority on institutional reconstruction and sought to enhance transparency, accountability, and the rule of law. Domestic neoliberal experts and especially the international financial institutions have pressed for reining in executive discretion and for strengthening institutional checks and balances. They have begun to oppose the concentration of power in the presidency, which they had promoted or tolerated in the initial stage of market reform in order to facilitate a profound restructuring of the economy.

Not surprisingly, this development has cast neopopulists in a new light. Once the "destructive" phase of neoliberalism had passed and political opposition to the new development model had been broken, neopopulism turned from a functional support of the reform process into an obstacle to the institutionalization of the market system. As the main task shifted from dismantling the state-interventionist scheme to building and consolidating a new institutional framework, the autonomy and power of neopopulist leaders became increasingly problematic. Neoliberal economists and international organizations such as the World Bank have sought to professionalize public administration, strengthen the judiciary, reinforce mechanisms of accountability, and augment transparency. These efforts also have aimed to limit the opportunities for corruption and other forms of malfeasance.

Political and societal actors inspired by democratic and republican principles, which proscribe the use of public office for private enrichment and illicit partisan advantage, have strongly supported and often spearheaded these efforts to clean up Latin American politics. In earlier decades, many citizens had begrudgingly tolerated the corruption of a political leader with a certain resignation: "He steals, but he gets things done." While good performance still helps contemporary politicians to withstand charges of malfeasance, influential sectors of the population have turned ever more indignant and have come to demand punishment for public officials who engage in bribery. Given incontrovertible evidence of wrongdoing, former Presidents Collor and Fujimori have had their political rights suspended for many years. Less directly implicated, Argentina's Menem managed to run in the 2003 presidential election, but widespread belief in his involvement with misdeeds guaranteed his eventual defeat.

While the exemplary punishment and striking political failure of corruption-tainted leaders serve as a deterrent for future malfeasance, the institutional changes enacted in a number of Latin American countries offer a more reliable prospect for gradually enhancing probity in Latin American politics. For instance, in Argentina, President Néstor Kirchner's administration, which came into office in 2003, has restored greater independence to a Supreme Court that Menem had packed in the early 1990s and controlled thereafter. In Brazil, the Cardoso government managed to have Congress pass a fiscal responsibility law, which strengthened public spending oversight. And after the downfall of Fujimori, Peru enacted a freedom-of-information law designed to ensure more transparency in political decision making. Investigative journalists in all these countries eagerly reveal information about dishonest dealings, helping to hold the political class accountable. In Brazil, fierce competition among major print media fuels the exercise of this watchdog role.

Seeds of Hope

Thus, political and institutional changes have diminished the chances for bribery and other misdeeds to go undetected and unpunished. While these accountability mechanisms by no means operate in a foolproof fashion, they hold the promise of gradually forcing advances toward cleaner government. Certainly, the case of the Brazilian PT suggests there will be many setbacks. Progress is unlikely to be any faster than during the lengthy and continuing struggle against corruption in the first world. In the United States, after all, it took many decades to push back the spoils system, introduce a civil service, and dismantle local party machines.

As was the case in advanced industrialized countries, institutional change in Latin America remains reversible and subject to erosion; formal rules can be evaded, bent, and even broken, often with impunity. But recent moves toward greater transparency and accountability—often instituted in reaction to the corruption scandals perpetrated by neopopulist leaders who enacted neoliberal reforms—offer some glimpse of hope. The struggle for cleaner government will remain an uphill battle, but it may not be as hopeless as the task that the ancient gods imposed on Sisyphus.

KURT WEYLAND is a professor of government at the University of Texas at Austin. He is the author of *The Politics of Market Reform in Fragile Democracies: Argentina, Brazil, Peru, and Venezuela* (Princeton University Press, 2002) and editor of *Learning from Foreign Models in Latin American Policy Reform* (Woodrow Wilson Center Press, 2004).

Latin America's Resurgence

Region has fresh chance to entrench growth and break cycle of crisis

ANOOP SINGH AND CHARLES COLLYNS

Latin America often appears to lurch from the cusp of success to the depths of crisis, so to talk about resurgence invites skepticism. Nevertheless, much of the region has witnessed a swift and robust recovery from the successive financial crises of 2001–02. Within two years, the region's economic growth reached 5.6 percent in 2004, a 24-year high. Growth rates of about 4 percent in 2005 and 3¾ percent projected for 2006 are well above historical averages.

Since the so-called "lost decade" of the 1980s, Latin America has made progress on several fronts. Just 25 years ago, military dictatorships outnumbered civilian elected governments by two to one. Today the region is in the midst of an election cycle that will set the policy agenda and shape the continent for years to come. Destructive hyperinflation is becoming a dim memory, and Latin America is building resilience to external shocks by adopting market reforms and entrenching sound macroeconomic policies—raising the prospect that the current expansion will be more enduring than in previous cycles.

However, persistently low per capita income growth, high or rising poverty, and rates of inequality that remain among the highest in the world . . . have risked undermining popular support for reform programs launched during the 1990s that held out great promise but often yielded disappointing results—especially relative to other emerging market countries. Targeted social programs have helped meet specific needs, such as raising literacy and health standards, but interrupted reforms and growth, and recurring financial crises, meant that broader social improvements remained elusive—especially for the bulk of indigenous peoples. . . . Thus, there has been a growing sense in many countries that the benefits of global integration have been unevenly distributed, accruing primarily to those in upper-income brackets, while the costs have been borne by the less-wealthy majority. In a few countries, there has even been a growing militancy among disenfranchised groups.

Given that many Latin American countries, including the largest, are holding elections over the next year or so, . . . the central question is whether the recent resurgence can be sustained once the global environment—still relatively benign despite high oil prices—becomes less friendly. After all, sustained, and even higher growth is critical to making a decisive

impact on social and poverty indicators that remain weak with national poverty rates exceeding 40 percent of the population and secondary school enrollment averaging 62 percent. To provide perspective, this article draws on experience since the start of market-based reforms in the early 1990s to highlight policy priorities for the future.

Better Performance

Latin American economies have generally performed well in the past two years. Growth has been significantly above historical averages, particularly in commodity-rich economies that have benefited from robust global demand. . . . Mexico and South American countries have gained, in particular, from the surge in fuel, food, and metals prices, and have generally been able to exploit these opportunities by expanding production—in some cases very substantially—although most oil exporters have not been able to do so.

Inflation has stabilized in single digits, after a brief uptick. External positions have strengthened as booming exports have helped generate current account surpluses. Easy global liquidity conditions have contributed to capital inflows and rising international reserves. . . . And the recovery has also been better balanced than past episodes, with less reliance on domestic demand. . . .

This recent improvement in performance reflects policy efforts over a number of years that are now bearing fruit—with some countries, such as Brazil, Chile, and Mexico, leading the way (see box). What are the key elements? Every country is different, but there are several common factors.

Low inflation. The 1990s saw the establishment of low inflation, a striking achievement for Latin America, given its earlier record of high inflation. An important reason has been the emergence of widespread public awareness of the need to bring inflation down, leading to popular resistance to policies that would risk reigniting inflationary pressures, anchored by improved frameworks for monetary and fiscal policies.

Policy flexibility. The adoption of market-determined exchange rates by many Latin American countries has greatly improved

A Star Performer

...any in Latin America, Chile's economic perfor-
...ce in recent decades is enviable. From 1982–97,
...rate of growth averaged 6½ percent, with per capita
income more than doubling. Although growth slowed
during 1998–2003, reflecting in part the regional financial crisis, it rebounded in 2004 and has held strong in
2005. This robust growth, combined with macroeconomic stability, helped bring down poverty from about
39 percent in 1990 to 19 percent in 2003.

What is Chile's secret for success? Prudent fiscal
policies, a move to inflation targeting, a freely floating
exchange rate, and trade openness (with average tariffs
of only 2 percent) tell much of the story.

Chile's fiscal rule, in place since 2000—a cyclically-
adjusted surplus of 1 percent of GDP in the accounts of
the central government—has been instrumental in providing an effective countercyclical stimulus while bringing down public debt. It has allowed the government to
run deficits when economic growth is below trend and
to accumulate surpluses when the external environment
is favorable and economic growth strong. The fiscal
surpluses have been used to prepay government debt,
reducing debt-to-GDP ratios. This, along with ratings
upgrades and low world interest rates, has contributed
to record-low sovereign spreads, well below the average for emerging markets.

The full-fledged inflation-targeting framework—the
central bank aims to keep consumer price inflation
within a 2–4 percent target range over a 12–24 month
horizon—that has been in place since 2000 has been
successful in reducing inflation while allowing the peso
to float freely. Indeed, inflation averaged 2¾ percent a
year during 2000–04, down from about 8 percent in the
mid-1990s.

Chile has also worked hard to establish good governance and a business-friendly environment. According
to the latest *Global Competitiveness Report* published
by the World Economic Forum, Chile ranks 23rd in the
world, compared with the average ranking for emerging
markets of 64.

a major step forward—in contrast to the expansionary policies
that led to large deficits during previous periods of easy access
to international capital markets. Lower debt ratios have been
supported by buoyant economic activity, exchange rate appre-
ciations, and—in the case of Argentina—debt restructuring.

Improved external positions. The present upturn has been
driven by strong and geographically more diversified exports
and terms-of-trade gains. The resulting current account surpluses have raised reserves markedly and have significantly cut
dependence on external capital inflows. This contrasts with earlier episodes, when capital inflows and domestic demand fueled
much of the upswing, leading to wider current account deficits
and overvalued currencies.

Reduced external financing vulnerabilities. The better
fiscal and current account positions have helped Latin America
keep external issuance of bonds, equities, and loans well below
the peaks of the late 1990s. Near-term vulnerabilities have also
been reduced, as many governments in the region have taken
advantage of the current benign international financial conditions to prefinance coming debt payments ahead of a full
election calendar, and potentially less favorable global market
conditions, in 2006.

Expanded domestic capital market role. Several countries—
notably Brazil, Chile, Colombia, Mexico, and Peru—have
increased their reliance on domestic debt issuance, reducing
their vulnerability to exchange rate risk and increasing liquidity
in local currency markets. . . . Some countries, including Brazil,
Colombia, and Uruguay, have also issued external bonds in local
currency.

Institutional development. Economic institutions have become
stronger, although the experience is highly differentiated by
country and has not been uniformly sustained. The most rapid
improvement was in the early 1990s, with some regression during the financial turbulence of 2000–02. Improvements include
the evolution of more autonomous central banks . . . , stronger
fiscal management in a growing number of countries, better
management of public enterprises (including through privatization), and stronger financial regulation and supervision.

the flexibility and resilience of the macroeconomic policy frameworks. In parallel, the region has also successfully developed
a more robust basis for monetary policy by moving away from
exchange rate anchors and toward growing reliance on inflation-
targeting regimes and autonomous central banks. The success
of the region's inflation-targeting regimes and the willingness
of country authorities to tackle inflationary pressures at an early
stage have bolstered the credibility of monetary policy and contributed to prospects for a more durable recovery. . . .

Stronger fiscal positions and lower public debt. From
2002 to end-2005, the public debt-to-GDP ratio for the region
is projected to fall by about 19 percent of GDP, with declines in
virtually all the major countries. . . . The strengthening of fiscal
positions through the generation of primary surpluses has been

Perceptions: Falling Short

Yet despite the better economic conditions, Latin Americans
continue to express a high degree of frustration with results that
fall short of their expectations. Successive surveys by the opinion research group Latinobarómetro show that while there is
strong support for democratic governments over authoritarian
regimes—as well as for maintaining market economies—people
are dissatisfied with the level of economic progress, the privatization of public services, the trustworthiness of public institutions, overall governance, and the amount of corruption. Many
feel that their country has been governed for the benefit of a
few powerful interests. And well over half believe that it would
take more than 10 years to tackle corruption in the region, with
a third believing that corruption will never be eliminated.

Foreign investors are similarly frustrated with the high level of corruption. Indeed, cross-regional comparisons of the business climate generally portray Latin America in a poor light. The World Economic Forum's *Global Competitiveness Report* suggests that Latin America ranks well behind emerging Asia and Europe, and is falling further behind, especially on the quality of public institutions and technical innovation—shortcomings that reduce incentives for investment and entrepreneurship.

Setting Priorities

Going forward, it is vital to build on the foundations for higher sustained growth, not only to insure against external risks—the strong global commodity prices and demand that have partly underpinned strong export growth may not last—but also to close the gap in growth performance with other dynamic emerging market regions and reduce poverty. While the overall impact of the recent increases in oil prices on the region's growth prospects has been small thus far, a further surge in oil prices could weigh on growth in partner industrial countries, weaken robust world demand for nonfuel commodities, and reverse some of the improvements to the trade balance realized since 2002. Oil-importing countries, especially those in Central America, have already been particularly affected.

For the region as a whole, the risks related to a slowdown in growth in China are rising—even though China's share of total regional exports is still modest. Exporters of some key products (such as iron ore, soybeans, and copper) would be particularly exposed since China constitutes a significant proportion of their world consumption.

Widening risk spreads for emerging market countries would also harm fiscal and external positions in many countries. The region has benefited from the unusually low level of global interest rates, which has encouraged a "search for yield" and bid down spreads on emerging market debt. Although countries in the region have used this favorable environment to strengthen fiscal positions and debt management, debt-to-GDP ratios in many countries remain very high—generally above 50 percent of GDP—and there remains a high dependence on exchange rate-linked and short-term instruments. Thus, Latin America is vulnerable to sudden shifts in global capital market conditions.

To counter these risks, Latin American governments need to act on several fronts. **First, to reduce macroeconomic vulnerabilities, policymakers should focus on:**

Reducing public debt. Despite recent progress, debt ratios continue to exceed the average of the mid-1990s, and generally remain above levels deemed conducive to sustained growth and broader macroeconomic stability, especially for countries with a history of default and high inflation. There are grounds for optimism because of the institutional strengthening that has taken place in many countries in recent years; in this context, fiscal rules and responsibility laws have proven helpful in containing discretionary procyclical spending in a number of Latin American countries, including Brazil, Chile, Colombia, and Peru. For oil exporters such as Ecuador, Mexico, and Venezuela, today's high prices provide an exceptional opportunity to further reduce public debt. Further efforts to curb nonessential expenditures, broaden and boost revenues, and improve budget flexibility would also spur growth by making room for increased spending on productivity-enhancing and poverty-reducing physical and social infrastructure.

Keeping inflation low. Notwithstanding the remarkable progress in reducing inflation, scope exists to further entrench these gains, especially in the face of higher and more volatile oil prices. For example, sustaining the credibility of inflation-targeting frameworks that have helped anchor inflation expectations in a number of large Latin American countries will require keeping exchange rates flexible. Further steps to enhance central bank independence and policy transparency would also be helpful. Countries that pursue alternative policy approaches because of dollarization or specific trading patterns need to take special care to maintain sufficient robustness and flexibility in fiscal and structural policies.

Accelerating financial sector reforms. Latin America still lags behind other regions in financial intermediation and credit availability. Real interest rates remain high in many countries, reflecting, among other things, inefficiencies in the banking system and, in some cases, the taxation of banking transactions. Countries need to strengthen financial system regulation, build consolidated supervision, bring financial regulation up to international prudential standards, and upgrade bankruptcy laws. The continued development of local currency capital markets (including the deepening of local government and corporate bond markets, equity markets, and the introduction of derivative products, where appropriate) to manage interest rate and exchange rate risk would help improve the efficiency of financial intermediation. A strengthening of financial sectors would also help reduce the high level of dollarization that still characterizes some countries. Peru has shown that a combination of good macroeconomic policies and improved financial sector regulation can successfully reduce dollarization.

Second, to raise low saving and investment ratios, and attract investors, policymakers should focus on:

Managing natural resources efficiently. Despite having the largest proven oil reserves in the world after the Middle East, the region has been slow to take full advantage of the oil price boom. The sluggish trend in output reflects short-term factors—including sporadic work stoppages—as well as deeper, underlying constraints that have inhibited necessary investments. Among the latter have been weak public finances, the dominant position of national oil companies with generally weak governance, and an unpredictable policy environment that has limited private-sector investment. A stronger national consensus is needed in many countries on improving the climate for new investment in these sectors, as well as on ensuring that the benefits are more equitably shared.

Improving the investment climate. Latin America generally does less well than other, more rapidly growing regions in providing the key ingredients of a friendly investment climate. Heavy regulation of the entry and exit of businesses, cumbersome labor force practices, and weak contract enforcement divert domestic capital and investment overseas—often hitting hardest small- and medium-sized enterprises and those in rural areas. Business climates need to be improved to encourage private investment, particularly by improving regulatory frameworks and strengthening competition policy. Governance also needs to be better; corruption and weaknesses in the rule of law undercut investor confidence in the enforceability of contracts and property rights.

Reforming labor markets. Labor market reforms—notably absent for most Latin American countries in the 1990s—will, over time, yield broad-based benefits, including more rapid growth of employment in the formal sector. The state should provide safety nets to deal with transitional problems associated with intersectoral mobility, and invest in workers' training and skill upgrading. Such reforms assume greater significance in the context of increased trade liberalization to encourage labor to move from less productive to more productive employment sectors.

Liberalizing and diversifying trade. Notwithstanding recent gains, Latin America is still relatively closed to international trade compared with other dynamic regions, contrasting sharply with the openness in the capital account. Trade initiatives—including the Central American Free Trade Agreement . . .—may help, and a successful and ambitious conclusion to the Doha Round also could provide a significant boost. Despite the success in diversifying exports, the U.S. market accounted for over 40 percent of the increase in the region's exports between 2002 and 2004. Thus, robust growth in the United States, and continued access to U.S. markets, will be necessary to sustain healthy export performance, especially for countries with strong U.S. trade ties, such as Mexico.

Fulfilling Its Potential

Latin America's recent resurgence amid continuing favorable external conditions provides another historic opportunity for the region to catalyze its considerable natural and human capital resources into sustained and higher growth. Latin America's potential has never been in doubt—it has achieved several stretches of rapid growth in recent decades—but all too often, policy inconsistencies have precipitated debt and financial crises.

With more consistent policies, the region could have sustained growth rates in the order of those found among the more rapidly growing emerging market countries in Asia.

The crucial challenge now for the region is to build on its recent resurgence, minimize the policy swings and uncertainties that have undercut previous growth episodes, entrench the forces generating the current growth momentum, and deepen structural reforms—especially those related to institutional strengthening and the labor market—that will limit harmful discretion, reduce rigidities, and open up new avenues for private investment and entrepreneurship. Much greater macroeconomic stability would contribute to the consolidation of robust democracies, providing a suitable backdrop for the many elections that lie ahead.

References

Corporación Latinobarómetro, 2004, "A Decade of Measurements" (*Santiago, Chile: Corporación Latinobarómetro*).

Foxley, Alejandro, 2004, "Successes and Failures in Poverty Eradication: Chile," paper presented at the World Bank conference on Scaling Up Poverty Reduction: A Global Learning Process, held in Shanghai, May 25–27.

International Monetary Fund, 2004, *World Economic Outlook: A Survey by the Staff of the International Monetary Fund,* April, World Economic and Financial Surveys (Washington).

———, 2005, *World Economic Outlook: A Survey by the Staff of the International Monetary Fund,* April, World Economic and Financial Surveys (Washington).

Reinhart, Carmen, Kenneth Rogoff, and Miguel Savastano, 2003, "Debt Intolerance," Brookings Papers on Economic Activity 1 (Washington: Brookings Institution) pp. 1–74.

Singh, Anoop, and others, 2005, *Stabilization and Reform in Latin America,* IMF Occasional Paper 238 (Washington: International Monetary Fund).

World Bank Institute surveys of public officials in a number of countries: *http://worldbank.org/wbi/governance/capacity-build/d-surveys.html.*

World Economic Forum, 2005, *Global Competitiveness Report,* 2005–06 (Geneva).

ANOOP SINGH is Director of the IMF's Western Hemisphere Department and **CHARLES COLLYNS** is Deputy Director. This article draws on a longer study prepared by IMF staff (Singh and others, 2005).

Latin America's Indigenous Peoples

GILLETTE HALL AND HARRY ANTHONY PATRINOS

In December 1994, the United Nations proclaimed 1995–2004 the International Decade of the World's Indigenous Peoples. In Latin America—where indigenous peoples comprise some 10 percent of the population—the ensuing decade coincided with an upsurge of indigenous movements exercising political influence in new and increasingly powerful ways. In 1994, the Zapatista Rebellion took place in Chiapas, Mexico. In Ecuador, indigenous groups took to the streets five times, leading to negotiations with the government and, ultimately, constitutional change; similar demonstrations in Bolivia led to the fall of the Sanchez-Lozada government in 2003. In Guatemala, home to Nobel Prize winner Rigoberta Menchu—an indigenous Mayan—the country's bitter civil war ended in 1996, with the Peace Accords that included an Agreement on the Identity and Rights of Indigenous Peoples. And Peru elected its first indigenous president, Alejandro Toledo, in 2000.

But palpable change on the economic front has been slower. In 1994, a World Bank report (Psacharopoulos and Patrinos) provided the first regional assessment of living standards among indigenous peoples, finding systematic evidence of socioeconomic conditions far worse than those of the population on average. Ten years later, a major World Bank follow-up study (Hall and Patrinos, 2005) found that while programs have been launched to improve access to health care and education, indigenous peoples still consistently account for the highest and "stickiest" poverty rates in the region. This slow progress poses a major hurdle for many countries trying to reach the UN Millennium Development Goal (MDG) of halving the 1990 poverty rate by 2015.

Who are the indigenous peoples of Latin America? While there is great diversity among groups, they share certain characteristics, such as distinct language (even if many no longer speak it fluently), culture, and attachment to land—all stemming from the fact that their ancestry can be traced to the original, pre-Colombian inhabitants of the region. Estimates for the number of indigenous people vary from 28 million to 43 million. In the five countries that have the largest indigenous populations—Bolivia, Ecuador, Guatemala, Mexico, and Peru—indigenous peoples represent a significant share of the population (in Bolivia, they are the majority). There are literally hundreds of different indigenous groups. In Mexico alone, there are 56 recognized indigenous groups and 62 living languages.

Despite greater political power, indigenous peoples still lag behind.

A Yawning Gap

The World Bank's 1994 report uncovered striking evidence of low human capital (education and health) as a driving force behind the high poverty rates, coupled with evidence of social exclusion via labor market discrimination and limited access to public education and health services. What does the picture look like now?

Poverty. For the five countries with the largest indigenous populations, poverty rates for indigenous peoples remained virtually stagnant over the past decade—or where rates did fall, they fell less on average than for the rest of the population. . . . In the three cases where national poverty rates declined (Bolivia, Guatemala, and Mexico), the rate for indigenous peoples registered a smaller decline, or none at all. In Ecuador and Peru, overall poverty rates increased, but for the indigenous, there was little change. This pattern suggests that indigenous peoples may be less affected by macroeconomic trends, whether positive or negative—although evidence from Ecuador suggests that even if the negative impact of a crisis is small for indigenous households, it takes them longer to recover. The poverty gap (average difference between the incomes of the poor and the poverty line) among indigenous peoples is also deeper, and shrank more slowly over the decade, compared to the same indicators among non-indigenous populations.

Education. Education is one of the main factors that propel people out of poverty, yet indigenous peoples continue to have fewer years of education than non-indigenous ones. In Bolivia, non-indigenous children have 10 years of schooling versus 6 for indigenous; in Guatemala, the years are 6 versus 3. The good news is that in all countries the schooling gap shrank over the 1990s, following trends established in earlier decades. But the bad news is that the average increase in earnings as a result of each additional year of schooling (the private rate of return to each year of schooling) is slightly lower for the indigenous—in Bolivia, it is 9 percent for the non-indigenous and 6 percent for the indigenous. Moreover, the gap is widening at higher schooling levels. What is behind this failure? The culprit may well be the quality of education that indigenous people receive. Recent standardized tests in the region reveal that indigenous students achieve significantly lower scores—from 7 to 27 percent lower—on reading and math tests.

Health. Indigenous peoples, especially women and children, continue to have less access to basic health services. As a result, major differences in indigenous and non-indigenous health indicators persist, ranging from maternal mortality to in-hospital births and vaccination coverage. In all five countries, health insurance coverage remains relatively low, failing to surpass 50 percent of the population. In three of the five countries (Bolivia, Guatemala, and Mexico), coverage of indigenous families lags substantially behind the rest of the population. An important gap to emerge is that indigenous children continue to exhibit extremely high malnutrition rates, even in countries that have otherwise virtually eliminated this problem. In Mexico, just 6 percent of children nationwide are underweight compared with almost 20 percent of indigenous children.

Labor. Evidence that indigenous peoples face significant disadvantages in the labor market is strong across the region. In late 2004, the portion of the difference in earnings between indigenous and non-indigenous peoples that is "unexplained"—perhaps due to discrimination or other unidentified factors—represented one-quarter to over one-half of the total differential, with the average at about 42 percent. This means that while about half of the earnings differential can be influenced by improvements in human capital (education, skills, and abilities that an indigenous person brings to the labor market), another half may result from discriminatory labor market practices or other factors over which the indigenous person has little control.

Starting to Make Headway

Over the past decade, significant political and policy changes have occurred with potential bearing on poverty and human development outcomes among indigenous peoples. These changes range from constitutional mandates and greater political representation to increased social spending and a proliferation of differentiated programs, such as bilingual education. Yet while some improvements have occurred in human development outcomes, particularly in education, these changes have yet to bring about the desperately needed reductions in indigenous poverty because of poor education quality, poor health outcomes for children, and limited opportunities once today's children reach the labor market. And although political representation of indigenous groups has increased in recent decades, they still cite lack of support from and a lack of voice in government as a substantive reason for their continued poverty.

Against that background, what shape should the future policy agenda take? Our results suggest that it must be broad enough to embrace issues such as land rights, labor legislation, and access to credit. On the human development front, we would suggest the following:

First, *more and better education.* Functional bilingual education programs are needed—including schools where teachers speak the same indigenous language as the students; teachers are prepared to teach in a bilingual classroom environment; and parents and the community participate in the design of curricular materials. Well-designed, well-implemented, and rigorously evaluated programs can produce significant returns. In Guatemala, indigenous students enrolled in bilingual schools tend to have higher attendance and promotion rates, and lower repetition and dropout rates. Bilingual education, despite the higher cost associated with teacher training and materials, may lead to cost savings through lower grade repetition and hence lower unit costs and more places generated for new students. In Guatemala in 1996, the cost savings were estimated at $5 million, equal to primary education for 100,000 students. Policymakers must also step up efforts to get all children in school, with incentives such as cash transfer programs. From 1997–99, Mexico's cash transfer program—*Oportunidades* (formerly *Progresa*)—resulted in higher school attainment among indigenous peoples and a significant reduction in the skills gap between indigenous and non-indigenous children.

Second, *better health.* Efforts need to be focused on the persistently high levels of malnutrition and associated high infant mortality rates, vulnerability to disease, and low schooling outcomes. Policies should promote equal opportunities for indigenous peoples—a sort of "head start"—including programs for maternal and child health and family planning. In some cases, it may be necessary to ensure that indigenous health practices that have proved effective be made available through national health systems. Ecuador, for example, is experimenting with combined services that offer a choice between modern and traditional medicine. It may also be necessary to train skilled providers in indigenous languages and cultural sensitivity.

Third, *better social service delivery.* The substantial progress in certain human capital inputs—such as quantity of school and health services—for indigenous peoples over the 1990s may not have led to a significant impact on earnings because of an insufficient voice in service delivery. Thus, there may be a need to explore strategies to strengthen the direct influence of beneficiaries on service providers. These could include enhancing client power or leverage of parents through choice or voice directly at the school level. Putting recipients at the center of service provision could also help by enabling them to monitor providers and amplify their voice in policymaking. Already, Mexico has been putting this idea into practice: the compensatory education program gives indigenous peoples a small but significant role in school management. Impact evaluations have shown this to be effective (Shapiro and Moreno, 2004).

In addition, better analysis of the conditions and needs of indigenous peoples, based on an improved data collection effort, would be essential. At present, there is no systematic way of accurately identifying indigenous peoples in census or household surveys. Thus, a list of standardized questions for surveys in different years and countries should be developed. It could include self-identification, language (mother tongue, commonly used language, language used at home, and secondary language), dominant group in the local community, and parents' mother tongues. Statistical agencies should also include a special survey module to delve deeper into the causes of poverty and constraints faced by indigenous peoples, as well as opportunities. That module could study traditional medicine practice, religious and community activities, land ownership, and bilingual schooling.

W e hope that by building on the changes observed during the first indigenous peoples' decade, the next decade will bring them greater gains—in terms of human development, material well-being, and culturally appropriate economic and social development. The first step lies in setting realistic goals in terms of poverty reduction and human development, starting with disaggregated information on the MDG indicators. This would facilitate monitoring during the decade, coinciding with the culmination of the MDG period in 2015. Along with targets, monitoring, and evaluation, indigenous peoples—not just the leaders but community members and families as well—should participate in realizing these important goals.

In his 1934 book, *Fire on the Andes,* journalist Carleton Beals wrote "the uncut umbilical cord of South America's future is its

duality, still the secret of political turmo[...]
Until this duality is reconciled, [the region][...]
peace, can achieve no real affirmation of its [...]
fact that 70 years later a report must still be written[...]
duality signals the great depth of the inequalities, a[...]
magnitude of the task ahead.

References

Hall, Gillette, and H. A. Patrinos (eds.), 2005, *Indigenous Peoples, Poverty and Human Development in Latin America* (Palgrave Macmillan, United Kingdom).

Psacharopoulos, George, and H. A. Patrinos (eds.), 1994, *Indigenous People and Poverty in Latin America: An Empirical Analysis* (Washington: World Bank).

Shapiro, J., and J. Jorge Moreno, 2004, "Compensatory Education for Disadvantaged Mexican Students: An Impact Evaluation Using Propensity Score Matching," World Bank Policy Research Working Paper 3334 (Washington).

GILLETTE HALL AND HARRY ANTHONY PATRINOS are Economists in the World Bank's Human Development Department, Latin America and the Caribbean Region.

...merica's weight in the world has been shrinking. It is not an economic powerhouse, a security threat, or a population bomb. Even its tragedies pale in comparison to Africa's. The region will not rise until it ends its search for magic formulas. It may not make for a good sound bite, but patience is Latin America's biggest deficit of all.

MOISÉS NAÍM

Latin America has grown used to living in the backyard of the United States. For decades, it has been a region where the U.S. government meddled in local politics, fought communists, and promoted its business interests. Even if the rest of the world wasn't paying attention to Latin America, the United States occasionally was. Then came September 11, and even the United States seemed to tune out. Naturally, the world's attention centered almost exclusively on terrorism, the wars in Afghanistan, Iraq, and Lebanon, and on the nuclear ambitions of North Korea and Iran. Latin America became Atlantis—the lost continent. Almost overnight, it disappeared from the maps of investors, generals, diplomats, and journalists.

Indeed, as one commentator recently quipped, Latin America can't compete on the world stage in any aspect, even as a threat. Unlike anti-Americans elsewhere, Latin Americans are not willing to die for the sake of their geopolitical hatreds. Latin America is a nuclear-weapons free zone. Its only weapon of mass destruction is cocaine. In contrast to emerging markets like India and China, Latin America is a minor economic player whose global significance is declining. Sure, a few countries export oil and gas, but only Venezuela is in the top league of the world's energy market.

Not even Latin America's disasters seem to elicit global concern anymore. Argentina experienced a massive financial stroke in 2001, and no one abroad seemed to care. Unlike prior crashes, no government or international financial institution rushed to bail it out. Latin America doesn't have Africa's famines, genocides, an HIV/AIDS pandemic, wholesale state failures, or rock stars who routinely adopt its tragedies. Bono, Bill Gates, and Angelina Jolie worry about Botswana, not Brazil.

But just as the five-year-old war on terror pronounced the necessity of confronting threats where they linger, it also underscored the dangers of neglect. Like Afghanistan, Latin America shows how quickly and easy it is for the United States to lose its influence when Washington is distracted by other priorities.

In both places, Washington's disinterest produced a vacuum that was filled by political groups and leaders hostile to the United States.

No, Latin America is not churning out Islamic terrorists as Afghanistan was during the days of the Taliban. In Latin America, the power gap is being filled by a group of disparate leaders often lumped together under the banner of populism. On the rare occasions that Latin American countries do make international news, it's the election of a so-called populist, an apparently anti-American, anti-market leader, that raises hackles. However, Latin America's populists aren't a monolith. Some are worse for international stability than is usually reported. But some have the potential to chart a new, positive course for the region. Underlying the ascent of these new leaders are several real, stubborn threads running through Latin Americans' frustration with the status quo in their countries. Unfortunately, the United States'—and the rest of the world's—lack of interest in that region means that the forces that are shaping disparate political movements in Latin America are often glossed over, misinterpreted, or ignored. Ultimately, though, what matters most is not what the northern giant thinks or does as much as what half a billion Latin Americans think and do. And in the last couple of decades, the wild swings in their political behavior have created a highly unstable terrain where building the institutions indispensable for progress or for fighting poverty has become increasingly difficult. There is a way out. But it's not the quick fix that too many of Latin America's leaders have promised and that an impatient population demands.

The Left Turn That Wasn't

In the 1990s, politicians throughout Latin America won elections by promising economic reforms inspired by the "Washington Consensus" and closer ties to the United States. The Free Trade Area of the Americas offered hope for a better economic future for all. The United States could count on its neighbors to the south as reliable international allies. In Argentina, for example, the country's political and military links with the United States were so strong that in 1998, it was invited to become part of a select group of "major non-NATO allies." Today, however, President Néstor Kirchner nurtures a 70-percent approval rating by lobbing derision and invective against the "empire" up north. His main ally abroad is Venezuelan President Hugo Chávez, not George W. Bush. Nowadays, running for political office in Latin America openly advocating privatization, free trade, or claiming the support of the U.S. government is political suicide. Denouncing the corruption and inequality spurred by the "savage capitalism" of the 1990s, promising to help the poor and battle the rich, and disparaging the abusive international behavior of the American superpower and what is seen as its "globalization" ruse is a political platform that has acquired renewed potency throughout the region. In nearly every country, these ideas have helped new political leaders gain a national following and in Argentina, Bolivia, and Venezuela, even to win the presidency. In most other countries, notably in Mexico, Peru, Ecuador, and Nicaragua, proponents of these views enjoy wide popular support and are a fundamental factor in their countries' politics.

Latin America can't compete on the world stage in any way, not even as a threat.

So what happened? The first alarm bells sounded with the election in rapid succession of Chávez in Venezuela in 1998, Luiz Inácio "Lula" da Silva in Brazil in 2002, Kirchner in Argentina in 2003, and Tabaré Vázquez in Uruguay in 2004. All of them represented left-of-center coalitions and all promised to undo the "neoliberal excesses" of their predecessors. All of them also stressed the need to reassert their nations' independence from the United States and limit the superpower's influence.

Yet, none of these new presidents really delivered on their more extreme campaign promises, especially their plans to roll back the economic reforms of the 1990s. Brazil's Lula has followed an orthodox economic policy, anchored in painfully high interest rates and the active promotion of foreign investments. In Argentina, the only significant departure from the economic orthodoxy of the 1990s has been the adoption of widespread price controls and a disdainful attitude toward foreign investors.

In Venezuela, the rhetoric (and sometimes the deeds) are more in line with rabid anti-American, antifree trade, and anti-market postures. Chávez routinely denounces free-trade agreements with the United States: He has been known to say that "[c]apitalism will lead to the destruction of humanity," and that the United States is the "devil that represents capitalism." Chávez's anti-trade posture conveniently glosses over the reality that Venezuela enjoys a de facto free trade agreement with the United States. In fact, America is the top market for Venezuela's oil. During Chávez's tenure, Venezuela has become one of the world's fastest-growing markets for manufactured American

products. And even the capitalist devils that are the objects of Chávez's wrath aren't suffering as much as might be expected. As the *Financial Times* reported in August, "Bankers traditionally face firing squads in times of revolution. But in Venezuela, they are having a party." Local bankers close to the regime are reaping huge profits. Foreign bankers who cater to the wealthy return from trips to Caracas with long lists of newly acquired clients in need of discreet "asset management" abroad.

Although some of these populist leaders have so far failed to live up to the radical economic changes they promised on the campaign trail, the gaps between incendiary rhetoric and actual practice have been far narrower in the region's foreign policies—especially in Venezuela and its relations with the United States. President Chávez, easily the world's most vocal anti-American leader, has called President George W. Bush, among other things, a "donkey," "a drunkard," and "an assassin." Not even Osama bin Laden has spouted such vitriol. Chávez has embraced Cuban leader Fidel Castro as his mentor and comrade-in-arms, and in so doing, he has become the region's most visible leader since Che Guevara. Like Che, Chávez often seems hell-bent on sparking an armed confrontation to further his revolution; he calls Saddam Hussein a "brother," and is arming new local militias with 100,000 AK-47s to repel the "imminent" U.S. invasion. His international activism now routinely takes him around the world. In Damascus this summer, Chávez and Syrian President Bashar Assad issued a joint declaration stating that they were "firmly united against imperialist aggression and the hegemonic intentions of the U.S. Empire."

The main concern is not just that Chávez is developing close ties with prominent U.S. foes worldwide, but rather his efforts to refashion the domestic politics of his neighboring countries. His persona and his message are certainly attractive to large blocs of voters in other countries. Politicians elsewhere in Latin America who emulate him and his platforms are gaining popularity, and it's hard to imagine that Chávez is refraining from using his enormous oil wealth to support their political ascendancy. The international concern about trends in Latin America peaked in late 2005, as 12 presidential elections were scheduled for the ensuing months. In several countries—Bolivia, Costa Rica, Ecuador, Mexico, Nicaragua, and Peru—leftist candidates with Chávez-sounding platforms stood a good chance of winning.

Yet that expectation did not come to pass. So far, the only election where a Chávez ally has won is Bolivia. There, Evo Morales, the leader of the coca growers, announced that he would become "the United States' worst nightmare," and quickly proceeded to enter into a close alliance with Venezuela and Cuba. But the election of Chávez-backed candidates turned out to be more the exception than the rule. Surprisingly, running for office with too close an identification with Chávez or his policies has become an electoral kiss of death. Not even his promises of supplying cheap oil and financial aid if his candidate won were enough to compensate for the strong voter backlash against a foreign president openly trying to influence the outcome of national elections.

But the electoral defeat of candidates running on platforms perceived to be too extreme or too close to Chávez does not mean that the ideas they represent are unappealing. Latin American voters are aggrieved, impatient, and eager to vote for new candidates who offer a break with the past and who promise a way out of the dire present.

If Not Left, Then Where?

Since the late 1990s, Latin American political systems have been rocked by a wide variety of frustrations. Therefore lumping the different types of discontent under generic "leftist" or "populist" monikers is misleading. Indeed, in today's Latin America, some of the grievances are clearly anti-market, while others are rooted in dissatisfactions caused not by overreliance on the market but by governmental overreach. Curbing corruption, for example, is a strong political demand that is unlikely to be satisfied by increasing the economic activities controlled by an already overwhelmed and corrupt public sector. Other grievances unite the far left and the far right. Economic nationalists who resent the market-opening reforms that allow foreign products to displace locally made ones include both right-wing business groups who profited handsomely from the protectionism, as well as leftist labor leaders who have seen their ranks shrink as local factories went out of business, unable to compete with foreign imports.

The responses to these political demands have also been varied. Some leaders, like Chávez and Kirchner, are behaving in a traditional, populist fashion, relying on massive and often wasteful public spending, on prices kept artificially low through governmental controls, or the scapegoating of the private sector to cement their popularity. Many others, however, like Lula in Brazil, Vicente Fox in Mexico, Alvaro Uribe in Colombia, or Ricardo Lagos in Chile have been models of more responsible economic governance and have shown a willingness to absorb the costs of unpopular but necessary economic policies.

What unites almost all Latin American countries, however, are two long-standing trends that multiply and deepen the variety of the grievances that are sprouting throughout the region: prolonged mediocre economic performance, and the decay of traditional forms of political organization, and political parties in particular.

Latin America has suffered from slow economic growth for more than a quarter-century. Episodes of rapid growth have been short lived and often ended in painful financial crashes with devastating effects on the poor and the middle class. Economic growth in Latin America has been slower than it was in the 1960s and 70s, worse relative to all other emerging markets in the world, and unremittingly less than what the region itself needs to lift the poor standard of living of most of the population. This economic disappointment has become increasingly unacceptable to voters who have been promised much and gotten little and who have become better informed than ever about the standards of living of others at home and abroad. Latin Americans are fed up. Naturally, the frustrations produced by the wide gap between expectations and reality and between the living standards of the few who have so much and the many who have almost nothing create fertile ground for the fractious politics that make governing so difficult. Inevitably, political parties, and especially those in power, have suffered tremendous losses

Latin American Merchandise Exports
(as a percentage of world total)

Foreign Direct Investment into Latin America
(as a percentage of world total)

Shrinking Share. Latin America's economic clout continues to slide.

Sources for Charts, Bottom: Economic Commission for Latin America and the Caribbean; Top: World Trade Organization

in loyalty, credibility, and legitimacy. Some of this disrepute is well deserved and often self-inflicted, as most political parties have failed to modernize their thinking or replace their ineffectual leaders. Corruption, patronage, and the use of politics as the fastest route for personal wealth are also rampant.

But it is also true that governing in a region where the political attitudes of large swaths of the population are imbued with rage, revenge, and impatience, and where the machinery of the public sector is often broken, is bound to end in failure. Because the region is resource-rich, the most common explanation for poverty amid so much imagined wealth is corruption. End the corruption and the standard of living of the poor will more or less automatically improve, goes the thinking. This assumption of course ignores the fact that a nation's prosperity depends more on being rich in competent public institutions, rule of law, and a well-educated population than in exportable raw materials.

Moreover, while the widespread presence and ravaging effects of corruption are indisputable, the reality is that poverty in Latin America owes as much, if not more, to the region's inability to find ways to compete more effectively in a globalized economy than to the pervasive thievery of those in power. It is hard to argue that China or India or the fast-growing economies of East Asia are substantially less corrupt than Latin America. Yet their growth rates and their ability to lift their populations out of poverty have been better than those of Latin America. Why? The fact is that the region's democracy and activist politics make its wages too high to compete with the low-wage Asian economies. Latin America's poor educational systems and low level of technological development make it unable to compete effectively in most international markets where success is driven by know how and innovation. With its high wages and low technology, Latin America is having a hard time fitting into the hypercompetitive global economy. That fact gets far less attention than others that are more urgent, visible, or politically popular. Yet many of these problems—unemployment, poverty, slow economic growth—are manifestations of national economies that are ill-suited to prosper under the conditions prevalent in today's world.

The Waiting Game

Like all fundamental development problems, Latin America's global competitive shortcomings cannot be reduced simply or quickly. The specific reasons behind a country's disadvantageous position in the global economy vary. Alleviating them requires simultaneous efforts on many fronts by different actors over a long period. And herein lies a central difficulty besetting all attempts to create positive, sustained change in Latin America: They all take more time than voters, politicians, investors, social activists, and journalists are willing to wait before moving on to another idea or another leader.

Latin America's most important deficit is patience. Unless the patience of all influential actors is raised, efforts will continue to fail before they are fully tested or executed. Investors will continue to ignore good projects that cannot offer quick returns, governments will only pick policies that can generate rapid, visible results even if they are unsustainable or mostly cosmetic, and voters will continue to shed leaders that don't deliver soon enough.

Reducing the patience deficit is impossible without alleviating Latin America's most immediate and urgent needs. But it is a mistake to assume that sustainable improvements will only occur as a result of radical, emergency measures. Large-scale social progress will require years of sustained efforts that are not prematurely terminated and replaced by a new, "big-bang" solution. Continuous progress demands the stability created by agreement on a set of basic shared goals and ideas among major political players. In the past, this patience was either ruthlessly forced on the population by military governments or induced by the adoption of a similar ideology shared by influential social groups. Both approaches are highly problematic and not viable in the long run.

Therefore, rather than seeking ideological consensus or forcing ideological hegemony, Latin Americans should build from what exists and seems to be working, rather than dismiss what already exists just because its champions are political competitors. Only those individuals and organizations who are able to bridge ideological divides and bring together different

approaches will fix Lat[...]
And give them time.

It's not as though there's no [...]
gressive governance. Former Pre[...]
Cardoso in Brazil and Lagos in Chile [...]
logical perspectives and developed prag[...]
balance conflicting demands. Both came fr[...]
grounds and while in office made enormous a[...]
cessful efforts to fight poverty and improve social [...]
But they were also quite sensitive about the need to m[...]
economic stability—which often meant painful cuts in pu[...]
spending—and to foster an attractive business environment for [...]
investors. Although neither Cardoso nor Lagos was able to drastically overhaul his nation's poor social conditions, both easily rank among the most effective and successful presidents of the last decade—anywhere. They made far more progress in alleviating poverty in their countries than any of the more strident Latin American revolutionaries whose radical efforts on behalf of the poor so often ended up creating only more poverty and inequality.

With its high wages and low technology, Latin America is having a hard time fitting into the global economy.

It is natural for Latin American citizens and politicians to be captivated by promises that seem too good to be true. People who find themselves in dire straits naturally want extreme, quick solutions. Latin Americans have been experimenting with brutal, heavy handed swings in their political economies since the 1970s. Yet, this search for silver-bullet solutions, though understandable given the grave problems of the region, is mistaken. Latin Americans must learn that, precisely because their illnesses are so acute, the solutions must be, paradoxically, more tempered. It might seem counterintuitive to reject the promises of the men and women offering radical change for a region so used to failure and neglect, but it may be the only way to lift millions out of poverty, and in the process, get Latin America back on the map.

Moisés Naím is editor in chief of *Foreign Policy*.

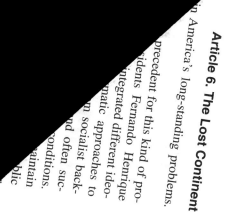

Article 6. The Lost Continent

America's long-standing problems.

...precedent for this kind of pro-
...idents Fernando Henrique
...ntegrated different ideo-
...matic approaches to
...n socialist back-
...d often suc-
...conditions.
...aintain
...blic

...sistent poverty and inequality in Latin America.

...Arias

After going through bouts of crisis or economic slow-down in the late 1990s and early 2000s, Latin America now enjoys brighter economic prospects and an ongoing recovery. But poverty and income inequality remain stubbornly high and deep-rooted. While the region overall is on track to meet the Millennium Development Goals (MDGs) relating to human development—being ahead of other regions in terms of child mortality, access to safe water, and gender equity in education—it lags behind on achieving the poverty goal (together with sub-Saharan Africa). Indeed, the World Bank estimates that Latin America is at risk of falling short (by 1 percentage point) of meeting the MDG of halving the 1990 level of poverty by 2015.

Exactly how big is the poverty problem? How come more progress has not been made? And what can be done to turn the situation around? This article explores these questions, suggesting that the key to reducing poverty in Latin America, a region of half a billion people, is to create a level playing field—providing the poor with the opportunities to improve their living standards through access to education, health, infrastructure, and financial services. Improving the access of the poor to assets and services will help them share in, and contribute to, economic growth.

A Snapshot of the Problem

Poverty measurement is a challenge for analysts and policymakers. International organizations use purchasing power parity (or PPP) figures, as these facilitate international comparisons. Using a level of $1 PPP a day, the World Bank estimates that extreme poverty in the region declined from 11.3 percent in 1990 to 9.5 percent in 2001—although, because of population growth, the number of people living on $1 a day stayed at 50 million during that period. . . . For more recent years, preliminary estimates show a slight increase in the poverty rate. But based on a benchmark of $2 PPP a day, the region has not made much of a dent in poverty. The World Bank estimates that poverty has held at around 25 percent of the population since the mid-1990s. And because of population growth, the number of poor actually increased to around 128 million in the early 2000s.

Yet analysts and regional organizations frequently quote poverty levels in Latin America and the Caribbean that are much higher. That is because countries adopt their own national poverty lines to take account of both domestic economic and social conditions and their own standard of well-being. These national lines are not strictly comparable across countries, but they do enable governments to track progress and determine the number of people who could potentially benefit from poverty alleviation policies according to country-specific living standards.

Using national poverty lines (based on data from the Socio-Economic Database for Latin America and the Caribbean), poverty affects 39 percent of Latin Americans, meaning that more than 200 million lack incomes sufficient to cover basic food and nonfood expenditures. As for extreme poverty—which attempts to measure the inability to pay for a food basket of minimum caloric intake—the rate dropped slightly from 22.5 percent in the early 1990s to 18.6 percent in the early 2000s, with the actual number of people living in extreme poverty now standing at around 96 million.

Moreover, the regional averages hide considerable differences in the levels and trends among countries. For example, according to national poverty data, the poverty rate ranges from above 60 percent in Bolivia and Honduras to below 30 percent in Chile and Uruguay. Moreover, even within countries, these rates vary significantly, especially along ethnic lines. . . . In Mexico, recent data show that 90 percent of the indigenous population live below the national poverty line compared to 47 percent for the non-indigenous population. In Guatemala, these figures are 74 percent and 38 percent, respectively. And in Brazil, poverty among the Afro-descendants is 41 percent compared to 17 percent among the whites.

Accounting for the High Poverty Rate

Why has poverty remained so high? First, economic growth has been insufficient. It is well documented that sustained poverty reduction is closely associated with economic growth, but the region achieved a lukewarm 1 percent per capita growth rate over the past 15 years. Moreover, the responsiveness of the incomes of the poor to that growth (known as poverty-growth elasticity) can vary greatly. One factor that feeds into the degree of responsiveness is the level of inequality, and in the case of Latin America, inequality of incomes is extremely high. . . . As a result, on average, each 1 percent of growth in the region translates into just 1 percentage point fall in poverty—and for the region as a whole over the past 15 years, growth has barely averaged above 1 percent annually.

Second, the growth that has occurred during this period has not generally been pro-poor . . . , [F]or many countries, such as Paraguay and Argentina, since the mid-1990s per capita income for the poorest 40 percent fell, not rose. In those countries in which per capita incomes for the poorest rose, the increase was less than for the average population as a whole. Only in a handful of cases—Chile, Nicaragua, and Peru—was the increase in the incomes of the poor significantly above the national average growth.

Third, although macroeconomic stability in the region over the past 15 years has generally improved, the succession of economic crises, particularly in the late 1990s and early 2000s, proved devastating for the poor. For example, the poverty rate shot up from 30.8 percent to 58.0 percent in Argentina between 1999 and 2002, and from 26.6 percent to 42.2 percent in the Dominican Republic between 2002 and 2004. Indeed, several studies have shown that economic crises in the region since the mid-1980s have ratcheted up poverty rates even after economic recovery from the crisis has taken hold.

Fourth, the poor lack the minimum level of assets to fully benefit from the growth process. This includes deficiencies in the level and quality of education and health, as well as in access to basic social services and infrastructure, such as paved roads, reliable electricity, clean water, and sewerage. They also face unequal opportunities in access to credit, justice, risk management, and property rights. And the poor often face lower returns to their endowments and productive activities because of their place of residence or plain discrimination.

Finally, we have more evidence now that deep poverty and inequalities of opportunity can also undercut growth, as argued in the World Bank's *World Development Report 2006* . . . and a forthcoming World Bank report on Latin America. Thus inequalities of opportunity not only prevent Latin America's poor from benefiting from growth but can also lower economic prosperity for the region's population as a whole. Inequality of opportunity matters the most for development policy because it is amenable to effective public policy intervention.

Providing Opportunities

So what can policymakers do to turn the situation around? A vital component of any poverty reduction plan will include addressing the constraints that the poor face in accessing assets and services, so that they can secure better jobs and boost productivity. A key way to do this is through concerted actions in social policy and the growth and competitiveness agendas of most countries. But additional efforts are needed to ensure that the poor benefit at least as much as the rest of the population from actions on these fronts. This is, however, a multifaceted

challenge. In some cases, the poor will benefit the most from targeted programs such as means-tested conditional cash transfers, urban development of slums, or rural infrastructure programs. In other cases, the provision of services need reform to ensure that the poor are well served (assuring similar quality of education, or promoting financial expansion). The good news is that there are a number of promising avenues under way in the region.

Building human capital with smart transfers. Human capital (encompassing the level of education, health, and nutrition of the population) is quintessential for enhancing the productivity of Latin America's poor. Recently several countries have successfully pursued a new generation of cash transfer programs. In previous decades, there was a lot of skepticism about the potential role of cash transfer programs as poverty alleviation mechanisms, because they were seen largely as short-run remedies that were difficult to target effectively and ran the risk of being appropriated for political purposes. The new wave of social assistance makes cash transfers conditional on the beneficiaries sending their children to school and receiving basic maternal and infant health care. As a result of strong positive impacts from rigorous evaluations in Brazil, Colombia, Honduras, Mexico, and Nicaragua conditional cash transfers are now regarded as important components of a long-term poverty reduction strategy. These programs are well targeted, and while their impact on primary enrollment is small where levels are already high, they have had a large impact on delaying dropout and improving transition rates and secondary enrollment (especially for girls). Overall, the average impact on the grade attained at school is up by between 0.6 to 1.4 years. . . . However, the coverage of these programs remains relatively small, and they are by no means substitutes for well-designed measures to improve overall access and the quality of educational, health care, and child nutrition services.

Access to financial services. In Latin America, many populist financial policies that were launched in the name of the poor have failed. Unfortunate examples are subsidized credit and direct state lending—policies that almost always ended up favoring the better off. Countries have also tried microcredit, but even where it has been successful, it constitutes a very small fraction of credit to the private sector. In fact, informal finance institutions such as rotating savings and credit associations are often less efficient than well-developed credit markets (Besley, Coate, and Loury, 1994). In that sense, expanding financial services to the poor requires broadening the reach of formal financial institutions by improving the banking sector's infrastructure for financial intermediation and developing approaches that encourage banks to offer affordable financial products to poor households.

Access to infrastructure. Another promising initiative—although it awaits rigorous impact evaluation—is the territorial approach to infrastructure provision, where assets and services may be provided exploiting local knowledge, local economies of scale, and complementary development projects. In urban areas, programs like the *Favela Bairro* in Brazil show that it is possible to turn urban slums around and capitalize the investments made by their inhabitants. A comprehensive program to improve physical infrastructure and public services, education, and commerce, and provide income-generating activities has helped boost both living conditions and the local economy. In rural areas, community driven development efforts facilitated the efficient delivery of basic infrastructure and services, including rural roads, electricity, and potable water, in conjunction with credit and technical assistance. The flagship example is the community-driven development projects in northeast Brazil, where communities prioritize, manage, and monitor investments through participatory municipal councils. A key element of success is having an integrated vision of subnational development based on local knowledge.

Translating Opportunities into Incomes

How can the equalization of opportunities be turned into higher incomes and eventually a higher quality of life? The key is productive employment. And for that reason, moving out of poverty in a sustainable way will require generating good jobs and enabling the poor to access them. Over the past 15 years, employment in Latin America did rise, but most of the jobs were created in the informal sector. This may be partly the result of the growing number of women participating in the labor force and a shift toward jobs in the service sector. But ultimately, the size of the informal sector reflects decisions taken by firms and workers for whom the rational choice is to operate outside the regulatory framework. Their low productivity leaves them unable to pay taxes or make social security contributions.

To reverse this is an enormous challenge for the region. Part of the solution is an increase in productivity by leveling the playing field for the poor in terms of equality of opportunities. It also requires changes in tax and labor legislation, along with more efficient public services and a better quality and more inclusive social protection system. Ultimately, workers must be able to afford health and old-age risk protection.

How will a more inclusive social policy for the poor be financed? Countries choose how much they want to tax and redistribute. In Latin America, the implicit social contract in the current structure of taxes and transfers has failed to provide equal opportunities to vast segments of the population. With exceptions, taxation is low and distortionary and social transfers go disproportionately to the rich, either through public pensions, nonpreventive health care, or public tertiary education (De Ferranti and others, 2004). In many cases, an equilibrium of low taxes and low public expenditures is maintained because the rich and the middle class opt out. Health services, education, and social protection are paid directly by the rich, who do not have any interest in exerting political pressure to improve the quality of these services when they are provided by the government. The challenge for Latin America is to modify the social contract to make it more inclusive for both taxation and expenditure. This implies ensuring that the pattern of social expenditures in general is not biased against the poor.

Defining an Effective Strategy

Since poverty is multifaceted, countries will need to adopt policy interventions on multiple fronts, subject to scarce financial and political capital. This means that they will have to find a way of coordinating these various interventions, and the hope has been that this could be done through an integrated poverty reduction strategy (PRS). In recent years, many Latin American countries have tried this route, but the results are quite mixed.

The poorest countries (Bolivia, Guyana, Honduras, and Nicaragua) started implementing PRSs in early 2000 under the Heavily Indebted Poor Countries initiative. The idea was to link sector strategies to poverty reduction in an integrated manner, while monitoring progress to assess the effectiveness of the strategy. However, continuity and policy implementation have been weak, the participatory decision-making process has not always been regular, and poverty monitoring processes still have to be strengthened. As for the middle-income countries, several of them—including Colombia, Guatemala, Mexico, Paraguay, and Peru—have crafted PRSs or national development strategies. In some cases, these have been government-crafted strategy documents; in others, participatory processes were or are being tried. In most cases, the strategies have not been effective in prioritizing how to tackle the key constraints in the economy so that growth is translated more effectively into poverty reduction.

These experiences point to three main lessons in shaping the agenda for poverty reduction:

First, *sustained growth is the cornerstone for poverty reduction, but it needs to be accompanied by integrated strategies that encompass economic and social policies to enable the poor to benefit and be part of the growth process.* Most governments in poor- and middle–income countries are paying more attention to growth and to policies that facilitate and foster job creation—not relying only on social sector policies aimed at assisting the poor. Countries should recognize and act on poverty reduction being also part of the agenda for growth and competitiveness.

Second, *any strategy must prioritize and define the appropriate and realistic set and sequence of policies, taking into account financial, administrative, and political constraints.* A strategy must distinguish between "the essential and the merely desirable" (Grindle, 2004). It must establish a roadmap, a sequence, and transitional strategies, particularly when in the short run some segments may lose from needed reforms. So far national plans have, in many cases, been a comprehensive collection of well-intentioned policies and valid objectives, reflecting the fact that poverty reduction implies making progress on a multiplicity of fronts. But prioritization, although scientifically and politically complex, is essential. It implies identifying what set of reforms, and in what sequencing, is most effective at reducing poverty, given budget constraints and what is politically feasible. The challenge for each country is to establish a strategy that takes account of both the fiscal and human resources, as well as the political capital, required to pursue policy change.

Third, *progress needs to be monitored and evaluated.* Formal poverty reduction strategies in heavily indebted poor countries have included the implementation of monitoring and evaluation systems. At the project level, there is a growing interest in impact evaluation, and several countries (Brazil, Chile, Colombia, Mexico, and Peru) have made progress in implementing various aspects of integrated monitoring and evaluation systems. Such systems allow performance and financial indicators at the program and sector level to be monitored and fed into a centralized system that can be used in the budgetary allocation process. But progress in this area is uneven, and there is a long way to go before these systems and a results-oriented culture are institutionalized. The key point is that for resources to be spent in providing opportunities to the poor, the state has to facilitate accountability and needs to establish the mechanisms for a transparent and efficient monitoring of the use of public resources.

Thus, while poverty and inequality remain entrenched, it is becoming increasingly clear how progress can be made on improving living standards in Latin America. The huge disparities between the rich and poor should be tackled by providing the poor with a fair social and productive asset base—that is, leveling the playing field. This will allow them to move out of poverty, so long as they are able to access the opportunities in the labor market that will enable them to boost their incomes. And this will in turn improve economic prospects for all Latin Americans. Several avenues are pr[...] tive. But in most cases, the biggest challenge will [...] and implementing the priorities of poverty reduction st[...] given the financial and political constraints.

References

Economic Commission for Latin America and the Caribbean, 2005, *Objetivos de Desarrollo del Milenio: una mirada desde América Latina y el Caribe* (Santiago, Chile).

Gasparini, Leonardo, 2005, *Ethnicity and the Millennium Development Goals* (Washington: World Bank).

Grindle, Merilee, 2004, "Good Enough Governance: Poverty Reduction and Reform in Developing Countries," *Governance: An International Journal of Policy, Administration, and Institutions,* Vol. 17, No. 4, pp. 525–548.

World Bank, 2005a, Global Monitoring Report (Washington: World Bank).

———, 2005b, *World Development Report 2006: Equity and Development* (Washington: World Bank).

World Bank (forthcoming), *Vicious and Virtuous Circles in Growth and Poverty Reduction, Latin America and Caribbean Region* (Washington: World Bank).

JAIME SAAVEDRA is Manager of the Poverty and Gender Unit in the Latin America and the Caribbean Region of the World Bank. OMAR S. ARIAS is a Senior Economist in the same unit.

...merica's Drug Problem

"With violence mounting in Mexico and Brazil, and a real risk of deterioration spreading across much of the region, dealing with the drug crisis clearly requires a sharper focus and more imaginative approaches."

MICHAEL SHIFTER

At a 1990 antidrug summit of Andean leaders in Cartagena, Colombia, Peruvian President Alan Garcia asked then-President George H. W. Bush a disconcerting question: "Where's the beef?" With that takeoff on a popular television commercial, Garcia exposed the limitations of a U.S. antidrug proposal that emphasized law enforcement and security and gave relatively short shrift to social development programs. García viewed development initiatives as essential to wean farmers away from coca in significant producer countries like Peru.

Today, García has returned to Peru's presidency in a remarkable political comeback and is still dealing with a President Bush—this time with George W.—and with the stubbornly vexing drug problem. Garcia is notably less antagonistic toward Washington than he was during his first term (he has enthusiastically embraced a free trade agreement with the United States) and is keen to obtain as much antidrug aid as possible (Peru received some $107 million in 2006). But the signs of continuing irritation over an issue that sharply divides the United States and Latin America are unmistakable. To highlight a point that was no doubt unwelcome for Washington, García remarked at a December 2006 press briefing that the coca leaf has multiple uses, including in salads, herbal teas, and even coca liqueur cocktails.

García's position echoes one famously advanced by Bolivia's president Evo Morales, who long headed (indeed, still heads) that country's politically active coca growers' union. Morales has frequently drawn a distinction between the myriad traditional uses of coca, which should be recognized and even celebrated, and the production and trafficking of cocaine, which should be sanctioned and punished. In fact, just hours after García's press briefing on the subject in Lima, Morales delivered a speech in Chimoré, a coca-growing town in central Bolivia, indicating that his government would accept a proposal to expand legal coca production from the current 29,700 to some 49,400 acres. U.S. officials, of course, view this distinction with considerable skepticism. From their perspective, coca production inexorably leads to cocaine trafficking.

Beyond a U.S. drug policy that appears frozen on its three essential, longstanding pillars—extradition, eradication, and interdiction—the problems associated with the consumption, production, and trafficking of drugs in Latin America and the Caribbean have become increasingly far-reaching and deleterious. Over the past decade, the drug phenomenon has become regionwide, no longer restricted to the producing Andes. Few places in the hemisphere manage to escape its baneful effects. Indeed, overwhelming evidence points to a direct relationship between drugs and the criminal violence that has skyrocketed in country after country. In Mexico and Brazil, Latin America's two largest countries, the incoming administrations of Presidents Felipe Calderón and Luiz Inácio Lula da Silva face no more daunting challenge.

Moreover, the astronomical revenues generated by the drug trade—the United Nations has estimated its total global value at $400 billion—fuel the rampant corruption that eats away at already fragile institutions. Precarious governance structures, such as the justice system, are both cause and consequence of the enormous drug problem. The negative consequences for the region's economic performance, which badly lags that of many other areas of the world, are similarly troubling.

It is by no means clear how best to stem and reverse the spreading deterioration. The coca-versus-cocaine distinction has merit, but hardly constitutes a clear-cut and comprehensive solution to such a deep-seated problem. U.S. policy has registered several undeniable short-term gains in reducing coca production, extraditing criminals, and interdicting drug traffic. New banking regulations have been imposed in an attempt to control the flow of illegal funds. Trade preferences for Andean products put in place in 1991, and extended for six months at the end of 2006, have helped provide legal employment. Still, the overall data are disappointing at best. The level of resources spent by the U.S. government to combat drug trafficking in Latin America has increased nearly tenfold over the past 25 years (amounting to more than $6.5 billion since 2000), yet drug prices have fallen and the drug market remains remarkably robust.

All Latin American governments and leaders are frustrated by the corrosive drug problem—and by Washington's response to it, which is widely criticized as unilateral, rigid, and largely ineffective. Latin Americans are particularly bitter about the perceived hypocrisy of the United States, given its notorious drug-consuming habits.

The politically motivated violence that wracked Central America in the 1980s has been replaced by burgeoning criminality.

Unfortunately, it is unrealistic to expect much change in U.S. drug policy. Washington officials, now distracted by Iraq and the war on terror, are loath to think creatively about such a politically risky issue lest they be seen as "soft on drugs." Although U.S. policy continues to produce scant progress and considerable ill will among distrustful hemispheric neighbors, a serious reevaluation seems unlikely any time soon.

Quite apart from what Washington does or does not do, however, the problem in Latin America is acute and is metastasizing in ominous ways, negatively affecting the region's outlook in a range of critical spheres. Beyond the understandable bemoaning of the shortcomings of U.S. drug policy, it is vital that the region's leadership devote the resources and political attention necessary to devise viable solutions. While there is not more urgent priority for the region's well-being, Latin America's institutional capacity to handle the drug-related crisis remains woefully inadequate.

High Anxiety in the Andes

In the popular imagination, the drug issue in Latin America is inextricably tied to the Andean region and, in particular, Colombia. Colombia produces over 90 percent of the cocaine consumed in the United States from its approximately 144,000 hectares of coca fields.

Moreover, of all the Andean countries—indeed in all of Latin America—Colombia is most in sync with the anti-narcotics approach advocated by Washington. Over the years there have been differences and disagreements on a variety of questions, particularly related to the sensitive issue of extradition. But, beginning with the administration of Andrés Pastrana (1998–2002), when the multiyear antidrug aid package known as Plan Colombia was backed by the Clinton administration and approved by the U.S. Congress, Washington and Bogotá have converged on drug policy. Since Plan Colombia was launched in 2000, the United States has provided Colombia with over $4 billion in mostly antidrug, military, and police assistance. Outside of the Middle East, Colombia is the largest recipient of U.S. security aid.

Just a few years ago the country was commonly depicted as a "failed state." Today that characterization is inapt. U.S. aid has certainly helped stem the deteriorating conditions in Colombia and enabled the government to reassert its authority. Particularly during the first years of the Alvaro Uribe administration, which

began in 2002, the reductions in killings and kidnappings were impressive by any measure, contributing to greater confidence and optimism among most Colombians. Thanks in part to more military equipment and training, the state improved its capacity to protect Colombian citizens.

At the same time, however, it is hard to make the case that Plan Colombia has succeeded in reducing the drug problem—in Colombia, the wider region, or the United States. The results are particularly dismal when viewed in relation to the huge cost invested in the antidrug effort. Even the focal point of eradication programs in the Putumayo region of southern Colombia has witnessed meager gains overall. Current policy instruments are simply unable to match the power of market forces; coca may be effectively eradicated in one area, only to pop up in another. This so-called balloon effect can be seen within Colombia and the Andean region as a whole. Even when one country registers a success, it is often offset by a neighbor's setbacks.

The Colombian experience since the early 1980s suggests that any economic benefits that might be derived from the drug trade are significantly outweighed by its negative, often devastating consequences. The human toll in terms of deaths attributable to the drug problem—at all levels of Colombian society—has been incalculable. The country's three principal armed groups, the Revolutionary Armed Forces of Colombia (FARC), the National Liberation Army (ELN), and the para-military forces, are substantially involved in the drug business—including thousands of militants who have been recently demobilized. The revelations in late 2006 of the deep infiltration by para-military groups into Colombia's political system have triggered a growing scandal and illustrate the magnitude and gravity of the problem. Corruption affecting the public sector and private organizations is profound. The gains made in enhancing state authority risk reversal unless serious steps are taken to contain the spreading crisis and to clean up Colombia's sullied politics.

No other issue affects so many Latin American citizens in so many ways.

While each of Colombia's neighbors has felt the effects of that country's battle with illegal armed groups, Ecuador has been the most vulnerable to Colombia's eradication efforts, particularly the fumigation of coca crops. The border between the two nations is extremely porous, and there have been spillover effects—refugees and violence—from the implementation of Plan Colombia. There is also a serious dispute about the health and environmental impact of the glyphosate used in spraying the coca.

Ecuador's new president, Rafael Correa, has taken a particularly adamant stand against crop fumigation, a position that has broad appeal among Ecuadorans who believe their country has been unnecessarily dragged into the Colombian conflict, with little compensation for their contribution and sacrifice. Indeed, Correa, reflecting Ecuadoran public opinion and invoking the principle of sovereignty, has made it clear that he will not renew the lease with the United States for its anti-narcotics base in the coastal town of Manta when it expires in 2009. Although its coca production is negligible, Ecuador serves as a key transit point—a record 45 metric tons of cocaine were seized at the border in 2005—and thus suffers consequences reflected in institutional corruption and associated violence.

Venezuela, too, is not a drug-producing nation, yet it is hardly immune to the wider problem. The government of Hugo Chávez denied charges made in December 2006 by the U.S. ambassador in Caracas, William Brownfield, that over the past decade drug trafficking through Venezuela has grown tenfold. Mirroring wider distrust and antagonism in the bilateral relationship, there has been virtually no cooperation between the Venezuelan and U.S. governments on the drug problem since early August 2005, when Chávez accused U.S. drug-enforcement agents of espionage. In recent years common crime has jumped considerably; Venezuela now has the highest rate of killings by guns in all of Latin America. Although the skyrocketing level of crime is not entirely drug-related, some of the violence can be traced to the widespread availability of drugs and the growing presence of organized trafficking operations.

Along with Colombia, Bolivia and Peru are the main coca-producing countries in Latin America. Both have extensive cooperation programs with the United States focused on eradication and interdiction. In Bolivia, the first year of the Morales government has seen stepped-up cocaine interdiction efforts and implementation of a cooperative coca reduction approach in the Chapare region. But the armed forces still play a front-line enforcement role criticized by some rights groups. Moreover, the successes in Chapare will be hard to repeat in other coca-growing areas. For political reasons, Morales has to move cautiously and remain sensitive to the coca growers who represent a pillar of his political base. Despite some predictable friction with the United States regarding Morales's coca-versus-cocaine distinction, an eventual accommodation on drug policy between Washington and La Paz remains a possibility.

Peru's acute and pervasive crime problem can be attributed in some measure to the production, trafficking, and consumption of illegal drugs. In 2006, Ollanta Humala, a former military official, campaigned for president on a law-and-order platform, winning the first round and garnering nearly 48 percent of the vote in the second. Sensing hardening public opinion and wanting to send a message, García in one of his first acts as president pushed for the death penalty for those convicted of terrorism. García framed his proposal as a response to the resurgence of the Shining Path movement. Although it no longer poses a strategic threat to the Peruvian state, the group continues to be active and problematic, as evidenced by its brutal ambush and murder of five police officers and three civilians in Ayacucho in December 2006—and it is buttressed by links to drug trafficking and production. The sentencing of Peru's former national security chief, Vladimiro Montesinos, to life in prison for massive corruption during the 1990s, closely tied to drug trafficking operations, underscores the corrosive impact of drugs on governance and institutions.

Huge Stakes in Mexico

Although the commonly invoked term "Colombianization" may distort more than it clarifies given the particularity of each situation, there is little question that Mexico's drug-related problems of violence and corruption have acquired greater urgency and now rank as top priorities on the country's political and public policy agendas. It is notable that, shortly after Calderón assumed the presidency on December 1, he undertook a bold offensive against drug traffickers in his home state of Michoacán. The president dispatched nearly 7,000 federal forces to deal with feuding gangs responsible for some 500 murders in 2006 alone. More than 2,000 Mexicans were killed in drug-related incidents nationwide last year, a big jump from 2005. Whether or not Calderón's move will prove effective, it was a clear measure of his decisiveness and his responsiveness to Mexico's increasingly intolerant attitudes toward unchecked drug-related violence. This approach contrasts sharply with the perceived inaction of the preceding Vicente Fox administration on this potent issue.

Most Mexican specialists who track drug-related security challenges are far from sanguine about conditions improving, at least in the short term. They point to the growing strength, proliferation, and fragmentation of the country's myriad drug traffickers, making them much harder to contain, along with the insufficient resources and instruments at the disposal of the Mexican government to deal effectively with the problem. In addition, there are serious reservations over whether Mexico's military or police forces should take the lead in combating the well-armed drug traffickers. While many argue that this is properly a police function and that mobilizing the military carries risks for abuse, others maintain that the police are thoroughly corrupt, unreliable, and ill-equipped to handle increasingly violent traffickers. In 2001, Mexico's attorney general fired more than 1,400 federal officers for their involvement in the drug trade. In either case, the state's limited capacity—in both resources and institutions—is striking. As in Colombia and elsewhere, despite the admirable and often tremendously courageous efforts of judges, prosecutors, mayors, law enforcement officials, and journalists, the drug problem tends to penetrate and debase Mexico's public and private institutions.

The connections between Mexico's drug-related difficulties and the United States are many and profound. For starters, Mexico is the transit route for roughly 70 percent to 90 percent of the illegal drugs entering the United States. Without America's strong appetite for illegal drugs it is doubtful Mexico would be forced to wage such a battle. In addition, traffickers can easily obtain weapons such as AK-47s, most of which are smuggled from the United States. Along the U.S.-Mexico border, the kidnapping trade, closely tied to the drug trade, is flourishing. Officials maintain that Americans now have the same chance of getting abducted on the U.S. side as in notoriously dangerous Mexican border towns like Nuevo Laredo. But the United States, lax in controlling the illegal arms trade, cannot afford to scold Mexico for not doing its part in addressing its public safety problem. Nor can the United States afford to adopt hard-line and symbolically offensive measures aimed at controlling immigration, such as constructing a wall along the border. Such unwarranted and counterproductive responses erode the good will and mutual confidence that are essential to tackling a grave and shared challenge.

Central America's Struggles

Perhaps even more dramatic than the Mexican case are the experiences of the Central American and Caribbean countries, many of which have weak states and are struggling to deal with severe strains that often stem from the drug trade. In Central America, the civil wars have ended, but the problem of physical insecurity—aggravated by the availability of arms—persists, and may even be more acute than before. The politically motivated violence that wracked Central America in the 1980s has been replaced by burgeoning criminality at many levels, including transnational and local, much of it a product of illegal drug trafficking.

Guatemala, Central America's largest country, reached a peace agreement with guerrillas a decade ago, but its government today is woefully ill-equipped to keep rampant criminality in check. Much of the violence reportedly derives from what are often referred to as "dark forces" or "parallel powers" that have transnational connections, are sometimes linked with the country's security services, and are often involved in the drug trade. Large cocaine and heroin deliveries enter Guatemalan ports via speedboats and fishing vessels, then are broken down into smaller shipments and sent over land to the United States via Mexico. Traffickers are often paid in drugs, which then enter the domestic market and contribute to the rise in common crime, a related but distinct phenomenon afflicting the country. Polls show that public opinion in Guatemala, as elsewhere, is decidedly in favor of tougher measures—"zero tolerance" platforms are popular—to deal severely with violent criminals.

Guatemala has some of the gangs or "maras" (the term comes from *marabunta,* a plague of ants that devours everything in its path) that are estimated to have roughly 100,000 members in Central America alone. But the influence of these groups is most pronounced and troubling in El Salvador. The homicide rate there has soared, increasing by 25 percent between 2004 and 2005 alone, making it among the highest in the world. Here, too, public security forces have been unable to deal with the spreading problem. El Salvador's gangs are heavily involved in the drug trade, acting as enforcers and dealers within established distribution networks, creating their own inroads and supply chains, and using profits and addiction to recruit new members.

Over the past decade, the drug phenomenon has become regionwide, no longer restricted to the producing Andes.

The mara problem, particularly in El Salvador, is closely tied to the immigrant experience in the United States, where young Salvadoran males first became involved with gangs and then were deported. In Honduras, too, the maras and pervasive insecurity pose one of the most difficult tests for the new government of Manuel Zelaya. In Nicaragua, Costa Rica, and Panama, the gang problem and drug-related violence are less severe, but all three countries serve as transit points for drug shipments to the United States, a fact that poses a significant threat to democratic governance.

The small states of the Caribbean are especially vulnerable to being overwhelmed by drug-related activities. Just as the "balloon effect" functions when law enforcement agencies try to eradicate coca production, traffickers frequently switch their routes to avoid authorities when interdiction efforts are concentrated in a particular area such as Central America. Given access to technology and ample financial resources, drug traffickers are remarkably mobile and adaptive, representing as such the dark side of globalization. Caribbean islands, particularly the Bahamas, Jamaica, Cuba, and Hispaniola, are often used to traffic drugs to the United States and Europe. Money laundering and the inevitable, attendant corruption are also widespread in a number of Caribbean countries, where weak governmental authorities have difficulty exercising effective control. Some Caribbean nations—Jamaica, for example—have also witnessed high levels of criminal violence, some of which is drug-related, along with considerable drug consumption.

For U.S. policy, and particularly the Miami-based U.S. Southern Command, Central America and the Caribbean's burgeoning mara problem and patterns of drug trafficking are of utmost concern. Unfortunately, few instruments and resources are available to help bolster structures of governance and repair the frayed institutional and social fabric in these countries. The emphasis, instead, is on law enforcement, with support for police and military forces. Police forces, however, typically lack professional training and are seldom capable of dealing with such potent—often well-funded, well-organized, and well-armed—illegal forces. And, in view of Central America's recent history with civil conflict and human rights violations, relying on the armed forces carries enormous risks of backsliding.

Lula's Challenge

Brazil's institutional capacity and resources far exceed those of the smaller Central American and Caribbean states. Yet, in looking ahead to Lula's second term as president, one of the most troubling factors—and a potential source of instability—is the rampant insecurity in the country's major cities, where homicide is the leading cause of death among 15- to 24-year-olds. The drug trade fuels much of this violence. In Rio de Janeiro, for example, gang warfare is the norm. Some have characterized daily life in the city's *favelas* (shantytowns), where 17 percent of Rio's citizens live, as resembling a civil war. Most of the violence, studies show, can be tied to either obtaining or using drugs. São Paulo has also witnessed high levels of violence, largely as a result of the introduction of crack and powder cocaine. Drug dealing and drug use now account for approximately 20 percent of the city's murders. The First Command of the Capital (PCC) has evolved into a particularly formidable and brutal criminal organization, in part sustained by drug trafficking, that operates out of São Paulo's prisons.

In recent years, drug consumption in Brazil has increased substantially. Brazil is currently the second-largest consumer of cocaine in the world, after the United States (together, the two countries account for roughly half of the cocaine consumed globally). Consumption patterns affect all socio-economic levels. At the same time, Brazil remains a major transit country for drugs shipped chiefly to Europe. Some 90 tons of cocaine enter Brazil each year, and approximately 40 tons—15 percent of total South American cocaine exports—are sent abroad. São Paulo has become a particularly significant export center and a hub for complex transnational drug trafficking and money-laundering networks.

Like other Latin American leaders, Lula is under enormous pressure to adopt tough measures to contain the spreading criminality. Apart from the public health dimensions of the crisis, the drain on already strapped institutions, and the corruption effect, there is a risk that deepening insecurity could dampen tourism and foreign investment rates. This, in turn, would jeopardize the prospect for economic growth and redistribution of resources, a central goal of the Lula government. In his first term Lula showed little reluctance to call on the armed forces, when necessary, to quell unrest and keep order in major urban centers. Lula's success in his second term—critical for broader, regional progress and the standing of Latin America as a whole—will hinge on his ability to get the drug problem under better control.

Even beyond Brazil, the effects of the drug trade are increasingly unmistakable in Southern Cone countries. As the market responds to shifts and pressures, for example, Argentina has started to play a more important role in the production and trans-shipment of cocaine—much of it directed to Europe, as the U.S. market becomes saturated. From 1999 to 2003, just eight laboratories were found in Argentina, whereas twelve were discovered in 2004 alone. The consumption of "paco" (cocaine base paste) in cities like Buenos Aires and Montevideo has exploded in recent years. Chile, too, has seen an increase in cocaine and marijuana consumption and has also been the source of precursor chemicals used in Peru and Bolivia. For new and fragile democratic governments like Paraguay's, the impact of the drug problem—connected to an array of other illicit activities—is of particular concern.

Between Resignation and Alarm

In assessing the drug problem with its multiple manifestations throughout Latin America, there is a temptation to conclude either that it is a fact of life one must accept or that it is bringing the region to utter chaos and collapse. Yet it is important to resist both complacency and panic in trying to fashion effective, sustainable solutions. Whatever the arguments in its favor, decriminalization or legalization is not politically feasible. Unfortunately, the policy menu is limited, particularly in view of scarce resources and often shaky institutions.

No other issue affects so many Latin American citizens in so many ways. Crime, corruption, and unemployment consistently emerge in polls as priority concerns for most in the region. None of these would be eliminated, but all could be alleviated, if the drug problem were dealt with more effectively. Local and national governments, external donors, and international institutions should tackle the issue directly, but they should also strengthen governance structures and seek to reduce social exclusion and poverty. To be sure, many initiatives of considerable merit have long been in place, and some gains—for example, in the Andes—have been registered. But with violence mounting in Mexico and Brazil, and a real risk of deterioration spreading across much of the region, dealing with the drug crisis clearly requires a sharper focus and more imaginative approaches.

A productive starting point would be to recognize that the drug question is not just a Colombian, Andean, Latin American, U.S., or European problem. It is fundamentally, and increasingly, global in character. Collective, multilateral responses must be fashioned. To its credit, the anti-drug-abuse commission of the regional Organization of American States has devised a technically sound and professional evaluation system to track the problem throughout the hemisphere. But the political will to convert this system into high-level, effective policy coordination has been notably lacking.

Hemispheric leaders need to lend a greater sense of urgency to the problem. For more than 15 years no regional summits involving heads of state have been held specifically focused on the drug question. It would be wise to heed the suggestion made in July 2006 by Alan García's foreign minister, José Antonio García Belaúnde, to once again convene such a gathering and give the issue heightened and more vigorous political attention.

MICHAEL SHIFTER, a *Current History* contributing editor, is vice president for policy at the Inter-American Dialogue and an adjunct professor at Georgetown University.

From *Current History*, February 2007, pp. 58–63. Copyright © 2007 by Current History, Inc. Reprinted by permission.

China's Latin Leap Forward

JOSHUA KURLANTZICK

I n fall 2004, the president of China, Hu Jintao, embarked upon a trip to Latin America that sometimes seemed more a coronation than a diplomatic offensive. In Brazil, Chile, Cuba, and Argentina, Hu was received with the highest honors of a state guest, while local legislators battled to hold receptions for him and for the delegation of Chinese businesses searching for new investments in the region. Latin businesspeople hosted Hu at barbeques and welcomed him into their factories. Latin leaders recognized China as a market economy, one of Beijing's major goals, and lavished praise on Hu, with the Brazilian president, Luiz Inácio Lula da Silva, announcing, "We want a partnership that integrates our economies and serves as a paradigm for South-South cooperation."

Hu also delivered concrete signs of China's growing relationship with Latin America. The Chinese leader signed $30 billion worth of new investment deals, upgraded bilateral trade ties with Brazil and announced an "all-weather strategic partnership" with the Latin giant, and signed some 400 agreements with Latin American nations on a range of topics. Shortly after Hu's trip, Chinese vice president Zeng Qinghong led his own entourage of Chinese officials and business leaders to Latin America, where they signed a new deal on oil and gas exploration with Caracas and offered Venezuela $700 million in credits.

Hu's grand tour of Latin America surprised many U.S. policymakers and opinion leaders, who have long considered the region the United States' natural sphere of influence, and who have not contended with another external competitor in the region in decades. An article published in *Foreign Affairs* wondered if Washington was "losing Latin America." A Senate aide told the *New York Times,* "They're taking advantage of it. They're taking advantage of the fact that we don't care as much as we should about Latin America." Congress convened hearings to examine China's presence in the Western Hemisphere, and the White House instituted a dialogue with China to explore the two powers' aims in the region.

Behind China's Offensive

In truth, neither the accolades for Hu nor the fears of China's presence in the Western Hemisphere accurately capture the current state of Beijing's dynamic new engagement with Latin America. China clearly has a strategy designed to increase its influence in developing regions—Southeast Asia, Central Asia, Africa, and Latin America—because Beijing believes it can wield greater influence there than in developed nations in Northeast Asia, Europe, and the United States.

China has enjoyed considerable success in achieving its initial goals in Latin America, which include revamping Beijing's global image, isolating Taiwan, and securing access to commodities, among other targets. At this point, China has made few difficult demands on countries in Latin America, so, for now, nations in the region get a free ride from China's involvement, benefiting from aid, investment, and diplomacy without having to make significant sacrifices to win Beijing's favor. Yet, as China expands its presence in Latin America, many of its policies could risk a backlash, lessening its ability to threaten U.S. interests in the region.

Until the past decade, Chinese relations with Latin America were extremely limited, and Latin America generally was a low foreign policy priority. China's history of fomenting ideological revolution in the developing world alienated conservative governments in Latin America. After 1949, Taiwan developed close links with, and established aid pipelines to, countries in the Western Hemisphere. Even Cuba, a fraternal communist country, was not close to Beijing. Though Cuba was the first Latin nation to recognize Communist China, Cuban leaders criticized Chinese policies at a public rally in 1965, and later complained about China's move towards capitalist economics, with Fidel Castro memorably describing Deng Xiaoping as a "numbskull." Havana and Beijing did not reestablish full ties until 1989.

China's leaders also felt little domestic pressure for a more outward-looking foreign policy. Still recovering from the Maoist era and focused on internal economic reforms, many Chinese questioned China's ability to become a regional power or even a global actor. A poll taken by the research organization Horizon Group in 1995 asked Chinese citizens their views of the "most prominent countries in the world;" one-third ranked the United States most prominent, with only 13 percent choosing China. Making relations tougher for China, Beijing was not a major aid donor and did not participate in Latin America's multilateral institutions. Until the late 1990s, China's economy had little need for Latin American exports, which were largely commodities. In 1975, Sino-Latin American trade totaled only $476 million; even 15 years later, total two-way trade totaled less than $3 billion.

By 2001, some of the impediments to Chinese influence in Latin America had begun to disappear. Between the late 1970s and 2001, Beijing abandoned its support for communist insurgencies, established diplomatic relations with more than ten Latin nations, and opened its economy to the point that it began to require significant commodities imports. In 2003, China became the world's second-largest importer of oil, after the United States, and the International Energy Agency estimates that China will import as many as 6.9 million barrels of oil per day by 2020, making it by far the largest consumer. Furthermore, as economic growth, state-sponsored nationalism, the initial outreach of Chinese businesses, and the spread of higher education in China created a worldlier, more confident citizenry, its population put pressure on the leadership for a more proactive foreign policy. Concurrently, China's leadership itself was becoming more engaged with the world, as the generation of leaders around Deng, many of whom had never studied outside China, passed from the scene.

In 2001, Jiang Zemin embarked upon the most ambitious Latin American trip undertaken by any Chinese leader. Jiang's trip was followed by a series of high-level visits to Latin America. Defense Minister Chi Haotian met with the Colombian and Venezuelan armed forces, and National People's Congress chairman Li Peng traveled to Uruguay, Argentina, and Cuba. At the same time, the Bush administration, which had come into office vowing to pay greater attention to Latin America, assigned the region a low priority after 9/11 and then further alienated many Latin American nations by appearing to tacitly support a 2002 coup attempt against Venezuelan president Hugo Chavez, a populist but elected leader. Perhaps unsurprisingly, one recent Zogby International poll of Latin American opinion leaders found that some 80 percent viewed President Bush unfavorably, and when Bush visited Argentina in November 2005 to attend a trade summit, tens of thousands of protesters greeted him.

China's Goals and Strategies

Since 2001, China's goals, strategies, and tools of influence in Latin America have come into clearer focus. As in its relations with developing regions like Southeast Asia, China has several obvious goals. China wants to ensure its access to the region's oil, gas, copper, iron, and other important resources. Unlike most Western energy companies, which operate independently from the state and rely on global markets to set prices, many Chinese firms retain close ties to the government, which distrusts global energy markets.

Chinese leaders fear that, in a conflict with the United States, Washington might be able to cut off international supply lanes or pressure American allies not to supply China. Consequently, Chinese firms search for equity stakes in oil overseas and try to "secure the entire supply chain in critical industries," according to one observer.[1] In other words, China wants to control the entire process, from oil field to tanker. And Latin America is the current center of China's global strategy.

China also clearly seeks to diminish Taiwan's formal and informal ties to Latin America, a region where Taiwan still retains formal links with Panama, Paraguay, and Guatemala,

among others. In addition, China wants nations that already recognize Beijing to not only adhere to the One China policy but also to prevent Taiwanese officials from participating in non-governmental regional forums like the Organization of American States. China also may wish to prevent governments from entering into bilateral free trade deals with the island.

Beijing also intends to promote itself as a benign, cooperative presence—as a different, more accommodating external power than the United States. If China is perceived as a benign actor, as a nation that does not threaten the region economically or militarily, it will be easier for Beijing to expand trade, boost its diplomatic offensive, and even broaden military-military cooperation such as selling arms, securing strategic shipping lanes, and developing joint training programs with nations like Venezuela. Ultimately, Beijing might even be able to use its engagement with the region to diminish U.S. influence in the Western Hemisphere, or at least pressure Washington to commit more resources to the hemisphere—resources that might otherwise be deployed in Beijing's backyard, Southeast and Northeast Asia.

The "Win-Win" Strategies

China has adopted several strategies. First, its leaders enunciate a doctrine of "win-win" relations, highlighting that even as China rises to great power status it will not interfere or meddle in other countries' internal affairs—a sharp contrast with the United States, which has a history of interventions in Latin America. Instead, Chinese leaders insist, Beijing will listen to other countries' needs and craft responses accordingly. During the 2004 Asia Pacific Economic Cooperation summit in Chile (APEC includes several Latin American nations), President Bush focused on counterterrorism cooperation and WMD proliferation. China focused on new investment in Latin America, generating favorable media coverage.[2]

China's win-win rhetoric also capitalizes on the fact that elites and publics in newly democratic nations in the region, like Mexico, often resent U.S. criticism of their human rights records. When these countries were ruled by authoritarian regimes, pressure on human rights resonated favorably with democrats. But today some of the same democrats resent Washington's censure, which they see as demeaning and failing to recognize their nations' progress. In Mexico, when U.S. officials criticized authorities for alleged use of torture,[3] Beijing responded by initiating a discussion on human rights, implicitly designed to portray both China and Mexico as unfair targets of American criticism.

As part of this strategy, Chinese leaders emphasize their empathetic understanding of issues confronting developing nations. In Brazil, Hu announced that China would always "stay on the side of the developing countries," and Hu then met with the leaders of Brazil, India, Mexico, and South Africa in an attempt to build a broader alliance of leading developing countries.[4] Lower-ranking officials constantly echo this message. In an address, National People's Congress vice chairman Cheng Siwei said, "both [China and Latin America] belong to the developing world and have identical or similar views on many issues." Chinese officials also have cultivated close relations with Brazil at the World Trade Organization, positioning the two countries as champions of the developing world at the 2003 WTO meeting in Cancun.

Additionally, Chinese leaders portray their own country as a model of state-directed economic development that has delivered two decades of powerful growth. This can resonate in Latin America, where the neoliberal economic model touted by international financial institutions—the model known as "The Washington Consensus—failed to deliver broad economic growth during the 1990s.

Indeed, in a poll of the region taken in 2002, a mere 35 percent of Latin Americans said the state should allow the private sector to control economic activity, suggesting the level of frustration with neoliberal economics. Populist, state-centered, often anti-American movements burst into the forward in Venezuela, Bolivia, and other countries. Another study showed that support for democracy was declining sharply, with more than 50 percent of Latin Americans agreeing with the statement, "I wouldn't mind if a non-democratic government came to power if it could solve economic problems"—sentiment that could prove consistent with China's model of an economic opening combined with political control.[5]

China's strategy also includes a focus on nations in the region whose bilateral relationships with Washington are strained. This is most obvious in Venezuela, but it is also noticeable in Ecuador, where in December 2004—after Washington cut off military assistance when Quito would not agree to exempt U.S. soldiers from prosecution at the International Criminal Court—China invited Ecuadorian officials to Beijing and offered a pledge of new military assistance.[6] Similarly, after the left-wing populist Evo Morales won the presidency in Bolivia late last year and Washington responded by proposing cuts in aid, China invited Morales to Beijing. There, he proclaimed China an "ideological ally" and asked it to help Bolivia develop its reserves of natural gas.[7]

China also has become what one observer called "a born-again multilateralist." Though its older leaders viewed multilateral organizations as limiting China's power, the generation under Jiang Zemin and Hu Jintao takes the opposite view—they see joining multilateral groups as a way to reduce fears of China. Consequently, they have enthusiastically embraced regional multilateral groups, from the Organization of American States (where China is now an observer) to the Inter-American Development Bank (where China has applied for donor status). It does not hurt that, as Washington has paid less attention to regional multilateralism, Beijing's participation has made it look better by comparison.

As China has upgraded its strategy towards Latin America, it has honed specific tools of influence as well. China's aid to Latin America, almost nonexistent ten years ago, now tops $700 million per year, according to an analysis by the National Defense University. Beijing adds to its aid by forgiving or rolling over Latin American debts, as it did with some $1 billion worth of Cuban debt. Much of this assistance goes towards infrastructure, such as railways in Jamaica and Argentina.[8] Some of this construction would benefit Chinese firms involved in extractive industries, but it also would address a critical need in a region contending with crumbling roads and ports.

China's aid also targets nations in the region where Taiwan has traditionally been an aid donor. In Dominica, formerly an ally of Taipei, the prime minister reportedly requested nearly $60 million in aid from Taiwan in 2004. When Taiwan provided Dominica with $9 million, China responded by offering the former British West Indian colony roughly twice as much, and Dominica switched recognition.[9] Taiwan may offer a new package of $250 million in aid to Latin America, but it cannot match China's largesse, especially as Beijing's currency reserves continue to grow.[10]

Along with aid, Beijing has encouraged its own companies in strategic industries to invest in Latin America. During the late 1990s and early 2000s, the Ministry of Foreign Trade and Economic Cooperation selected some 30 top Chinese companies to take the lead in overseas investment. As they look overseas, these national champions enjoy benefits that will help them compete, including low-interest funding from Chinese banks primarily controlled by the government. In 2004, for example, the consulting group Accenture reported that China Development Bank provided Chinese telecommunications giant Huawei with a $10 billion low-cost loan to help it develop internationally competitive mobile phone sales.

Beijing appears to be actively pressuring state-linked oil and gas firms to increase acquisitions overseas. In interviews with CLSA Asia Pacific Markets, a leading research company in China, state-owned resources firms acknowledged that Beijing had been pressuring them to invest abroad, though they insisted that their own management made the final decisions. Indeed, nearly 53 percent of China's investment abroad in 2004 was concentrated in extractive industries.[11] Owing to this focus on resources, commodity-rich Latin America received more Chinese investment in 2004 than any other region of the world.[12] Since overall net foreign investment in Latin America had been falling, this Chinese investment is even more important.

China's embrace of free trade also burnishes its image. Some potential deals, like one with Mercosur, the South American free-trade bloc, will not be as comprehensive as any agreements signed by the United States, but Beijing can present itself as a faster-moving trade partner than Washington. And, being first to sign trade agreements with the most developed countries in a region, like Chile, serves a useful purpose. Since Chile is already open to foreign competition, it will not be drastically impacted by an FTA, allowing China to combat the impression that a trade deal means being flooded with cheap Chinese goods.

China advertises its increased aid, investment, and trade agreements through effective public diplomacy, such as the promotion of Chinese language and cultural studies. Across Latin America, China is likely to establish Confucius Institutes, language and culture schools paid for by Beijing and set up at local universities. The results are evident: the number of Argentines studying Chinese reportedly tripled in 2005, and the new Mandarin program at the University of Buenos Aires has enrolled more than 1,000 students in two years.[13]

The new public diplomacy also includes setting up networks of informal summits and meetings, either in China or in Latin America, designed to bring together Chinese and Latin American opinion leaders. These summits allow China to subtly emphasize its role as a potential business partner and as a counterbalance to U.S. influence. These informal summits include the China-Caribbean Economic and Trade Cooperation Forum, initiated by Beijing and attended last year by nearly 1,000 officials from China and the Caribbean, the Latin America-China Friendship Societies, and other forums.[14]

China's formal diplomacy backstops this public diplomacy. For upwards of 15 years, Beijing has begun to retire older, more ideological diplomats, replacing them with a younger generation. As one recent case study found, beginning in the 1980s, Beijing began to upgrade the quality of its diplomats in the Western Hemisphere. It sent 110 young Chinese officials to a university in Mexico to learn Spanish. It improved the capacity of its own think tanks focusing on Latin America, rewarding specialists and ensuring that better research was available on the Western Hemisphere. And China kept its Latin America specialists focused on the region, so that someone like Jiang Yuande, China's ambassador to Brazil in 2006, already had a 30-year tour around the Portuguese-speaking world in countries like Angola and Cape Verde.[15]

Measuring China's Progress

For now, China's strategies and tools of influence appear to be working. Beijing has successfully decreased Taiwan's formal and informal relationships in Latin America. In addition to convincing Dominica and Grenada to switch recognition, China has opened commercial relations with Guatemala, often the first step towards switching recognition.[16] China also has opened a commercial office in Haiti, another Taiwanese ally, and kept Taiwan from obtaining observer status at the Organization of American States;[17] Haiti, Panama, and the Dominican Republic no longer support Taiwan's presence in the United Nations.[18] Within a decade, Taiwan may well have no formal allies in Latin America.

Beijing also has boosted trade ties. Trade volumes between China and the hemisphere have grown from only $200 million in 1975 to roughly $50 billion in 2005, though the United States accounts for more than 40 percent of Latin American exports.[19] The tide is turning, however: Argentina's exports to China rose by more than 40 percent between 1998 and 2004; Venezuela's exports to China over that same period grew by more than 19 percent; and Colombia's exports grew by nearly 10 percent.[20] China still lags far behind U.S. trade with the region, however— the United States normally accounts for half of total Latin American trade, while China is less than 5 percent. The United States' annual investment in Latin America ordinarily tops $30 billion; China's total investment is still less than $5 billion.[21]

Meanwhile, Chinese firms seem to be succeeding in their strategy of amassing resources. In Venezuela, the region's major oil producer, China National Petroleum Corporation has established a joint venture with Petroleos de Venezuela, the state oil company—once a relatively well-governed firm but now headed by Chavez loyalists. Ultimately, Chinese firms may operate as many as 15 oil fields in Venezuela.[22] In Peru, an arm of China National Petroleum Corporation has purchased a stake in Pluspetrol, which has oil fields along the Ecuadorian border.[23]

Chinese firms also have expressed interest in upgrading Peru's pipeline infrastructure, to better bring oil to Pacific ports.[24]

Perhaps most important, Beijing has convinced much of Latin America that it can be a benign and constructive actor, a drastic change from regional perceptions of China only 15 years ago, when it was either not on radar screens or was viewed by many as a rising threat. Limited polling suggests that most of the hemisphere enjoys a generally positive view of China. Even in Mexico, whose export sectors compete directly with China and whose press has highlighted the negative impact of China's economic growth on Mexican textiles and other industries, a comprehensive opinion survey taken in 2004 shows that Mexicans worry about Chinese economic competition but that "the development of China as a world power rank[s] at the bottom of the list of threats that Mexicans consider critical."[25]

This sentiment potentially boosts Beijing's influence. In democratic nations, leaders can move closer to China, since public sentiment supports better relations, including, potentially, closer military ties. In less democratic nations, like Venezuela, where a small circle of elites make decisions, China's appeal serves the same function, allowing them to build consensus on warmer relations with Beijing.

How Much of a Threat?

Despite China's successful engagement with Latin America, its growing presence in the region does not necessarily yet threaten U.S. interests. Thus far, there are few signs that Beijing seeks to directly challenge Washington's substantial military relationship with Latin America. On his trip to Latin America in 2004, Hu Jintao did not visit Colombia, perhaps because he did not want to be seen meddling with the closest U.S. ally in South America.

Some of China's relations in the region could benefit Washington. China's growing economic relationship with Latin America may prompt Beijing to take a stronger interest in regional security and thus share important regional burdens with the United States. Indeed, as China becomes more influential, it could help mediate conflicts, as it has done with North Korea in Northeast Asia. It also may play a larger role in peace-keeping operations, as China has already begun to do in Haiti. In addition, as China absorbs more of Latin America's resources, it will provide funds for Latin governments to pay off their external debts, reducing the possibility of further financial instability in the region, potentially diminishing the flow of Latin America's economic migrants.

Despite its initial gains, though, China could founder, as Latin Americans learn more about its strategies. Less than two years after China and Brazil's courtship, strains have developed in Beijing's relationship with the largest nation in South America as a flood of Chinese imports has not been matched by Chinese consumption of Brazilian goods. Other Latin American nations echo the same complaint. Argentina has imposed new non-tariff barriers on categories of Chinese imports.[26] Moreover, many opinion leaders perceive Beijing as an unfair competitor, due to Chinese labor practices, dumping, undervaluing its currency, and state support for certain industries.[27]

Some states, such as Ecuador, already fear that while China provides a welcome alternative to the United States, developing close links with Chinese oil and gas firms will leave them completely reliant on Chinese investment.[28] This fear of domination may be one reason why Ecuador is weighing a slowdown on approving Chinese investments in Ecuadorian petroleum.[29] Latin American companies also fear that Chinese firms will sign joint ventures and then force them to work as subcontractors and not as partners, as China National Petroleum Company allegedly has done with the Ecuadorian firm Dygoil.[30]

Eventually, Beijing could end up looking little different to Latin Americans than the old colonial powers, who mined and dug up the region, doing nothing to improve the capacity of locals. If Chinese investment focuses on extractive industries and adds little to the skills of the local workforce, the region could become trapped in a pattern of mercantilism with China, in which it sells natural resources to buy higher-value manufactured goods, without developing a cadre of local-country managers for Chinese firms.

Latin American leaders and publics also recognize that China's supposed dedication to developing nations is not always trust-worthy, and that China's economic model may prove no more effective than the neoliberal model. China's own socioeconomic inequalities have exposed some of the failings of Sino-style development. Some scholars even express concerns about the "Latin Americanization" of China—i.e. that China is becoming as economically unequal as Latin America.[31]

China's push could eventually constitute a threat to U.S. political, security, and economic interests. China's focus on energy could complicate U.S. access to resources. Global reserves of cheaply obtainable oil are decreasing rapidly, and Latin American imports—particularly from Venezuela—are among the nearest and cheapest for the United States. Since reserves in most of Latin America are projected to begin declining by the end of this decade, these imports will become even more crucial to U.S. energy needs.[32] Venezuela has not only threatened to cut off all U.S. shipments but also has said that it plans to boost exports to China from the current 140,000 barrels of crude oil per day to 500,000 barrels.[33]

Even as Venezuela increases shipments to China, U.S. demand for oil is unlikely to decrease—forecasts suggest imports could rise by as much as 60 percent in the next 20 years. Growing U.S. demand, combined with a shift in Venezuelan exports, could force Washington to become vastly more dependent on Middle Eastern oil.[34] This has obvious security consequences.[35]

Furthermore, as it has done in Asia, China could use its cooperative agreements in Latin America as building blocks for more substantial strategic partnerships that resemble formal alliances. These alliances ultimately could be used to counter U.S. regional interests. In Central Asia, China initiated the Shanghai Cooperation Organization, which was dismissed for years as a talk shop. But China used it to build closer ties with Central Asia and to promote regional support for a reduction in U.S. military bases.

Worse, if Beijing's influence undermines democratization in Latin America, it could bolster authoritarian leaders in the region. Finding another major source of economic assistance and diplomatic support might allow actors like Chavez more freedom to undermine U.S. counternarcotics and counterterrorism initiatives in, for example, Colombia.

The best way for Washington to guard against these possibilities, however, is not to inflate the Chinese threat but to re-engage with Latin America, rebuilding a comprehensive relationship with this region—not only with a few key allies like Colombia. China's success in the Western Hemisphere derives in good part from failed U.S. policies, such as an overemphasis on counterterrorism and overreliance on a small number of conservative leaders to make policy in the region.

Such a renewed relationship could begin by addressing what Latin America scholar Julia Sweig calls the "80/20 problem," in which Washington relies on elites—20 percent of the population—to understand entire countries. Interacting with the "other" 80 percent of populations, including more contacts with non-governmental organizations, political activists, advocates for the poor, and religious leaders, would foster deeper ties.

Washington also could re-emphasize core U.S. strengths. When Latin Americans perceive the United States as helping them achieve a free, rights-oriented system, America's appeal in the region surges. As Sweig writes, during the 1990s Washington often "set forth a positive agenda" in Latin America by backing civil societies recovering from years of war and promoting democracy. "Latin America welcomed the new approach . . . the message from the North was largely positive, inclusive, and respectful," Sweig notes.[36] If Washington returned to that approach, China's leap forward would surely slow down.

Notes

1. R. Evan Ellis, "US National Security Implications of Chinese Involvement in Latin America," Strategic Studies Institute Report, U.S. Army War College, June 2005, p. 5.

2. See, for example, Hu Jintao, "Advancing Win-Win Cooperation for Sustainable Development," speech to APEC CEO Summit, Santiago, Chile, November 19, 2004.

3. See, for example, Dane Schiller, "Justice Doesn't Always Translate Across Border," San Antonio Express-News, April 27, 2004.

4. "Hu Jintao Holds Talks with the Leaders of India, Brazil, South America, and Mexico," Ministry of Foreign Affairs of the People's Republic of China press release, July 7, 2005.

5. Michael Shifter, "The US and Latin America Through the Lens of Empire," Current History, vol. 103, no. 670 (February 2004).

6. Ellis, p. 22; and Letta Tayler, "Bush Administration Suspends Aid to Nations that Refuse to Shield Americans from War Crimes Court," Newsday, October 17, 2004.

7. "Bolivian Leader Meets 'Ideological Ally' China," Associated Press, January 9, 2006.

8. Arlene Martin-Watkins, "China Team Arrives this Month on Railway Revival Mission," Jamaica Observer, April 14, 2005.

9. William C. Gruben, "Beyond the Border: Yuan Diplomacy: China, Taiwan Vie in Latin American Trade Arena," Federal Reserve Bank of Dallas publications, iss. 6 (Nov./Dec. 2005).

10. Jacky Hsu, "Aid Offer Labeled Dollar Diplomacy," *South China Morning Post,* September 24, 2005.

11. Ellis, p. 5.

12. Ibid.

13. Vinod Sreeharsha, "East Meets West, with an Argentine Twist," *Christian Science Monitor,* September 30, 2005.

14. For more information, see http://cncforumenglish.mofcom .gov.cn.

15. Jorge Dominguez, "China's Relations with Latin America: Shared Gains, Asymmetric Hopes," Inter-American Dialogue working paper, June 2006.

16. "Taiwan and Latin America: Another Defection," *Latin America-Asia Review,* July 2005.

17. Melody Chen, "Divide and Conquer," *Taipei Times,* June 8, 2005.

18. Jacky Hsu, "Even Fewer Nations Vote for Taiwan in 12th Bid to Join the UN," *South China Morning Post,* September 17, 2004.

19. Dumbaugh and Sullivan, p. 2; also see "US-Latin Trade Boom," *Latin Business Chronicle,* March 2006, available online at www.latinbusinesschronicle.com/app/article.aspx?id=133.

20. For more information on Latin American trade see the United Nations Economic Commission for Latin America and the Caribbean, annual statistical yearbooks.

21. "US-Latin Trade Boom;" also see "Foreign Investment in Latin America and the Caribbean," United Nations Economic Commission for Latin America and the Caribbean, 2005.

22. Dumbaugh and Sullivan, p. 4.

23. "Overseas Gas and Oil Projects: Exploration and Production," China National Petroleum Corporation, available online at www.cnpc.com.cn/english/inter/Exploration.htm.

24. Ellis, p. 6.

25. Centro de Investigación y Docencia Económicas, "Mexico y el Mundo: Global Views 2004." Topline Report, Centro de Investigación y Docencia Económicas and Consejo Mexicano de Asuntos Internacionales, September 2004.

26. Matt Moffett and Geraldo Samor, "Brazil Regrets its China Affair," *Wall Street Journal,* October 10, 2005.

27. James Allen, "Lula Admits He Made Political Decision," *O Estado de Sao Paulo,* November 13, 2004.

28. Ellis, p. 29.

29. Joel Millman and Peter Wonacott, "For China, a Cautionary Tale," *Wall Street Journal,* January 11, 2005.

30. Ibid.

31. See, for example, Eric Heginbotham, "The Latin Americanization of China," *Current History,* vol. 103, no. 676 (September 2004).

32. "PFC Energy's Global Crude Oil and Natural Gas Liquids Supply Forecast," PFC Energy, released September 2004.

33. "China Makes Slow Progress in Latin America," *Petroleum Intelligence Weekly,* September 5, 2005; "Venezuela Exports 140,000 bdp of Oil to China," Xinhua, December 23, 2005.

34. Gal Luft, "In Search of Crude, China Goes to the Americas," *IAGS Energy Security,* January 18, 2005, available online at www.iags.org/n0118041.htm.

35. Ibid.

36. Julia Sweig, *Friendly Fire: Misadventures Abroad and the Making of Anti-America* (New York: PublicAffairs, 2006), p. 150.

JOSHUA KURLANTZICK is a visiting scholar at the Carnegie Endowment for International Peace and author of *Charm Offensive: How China's Soft Power is Transforming the World* (Yale University Press, 2007). Portions of this article are drawn from South of the Border: China's Strategic Engagement in Latin America and Its Implications for the United States (Center for Strategic and Budgetary Assessments, 2006).

An Early Harvest for Calderón

Contrary to many predictions, the president is not just governing but even achieving some reforms.

Such was the bitterness surrounding Felipe Calderón's narrow victory in last year's election that his inauguration on December 1st was a chaotic affair, marked by fisticuffs in the country's Congress and a semi-clandestine midnight ceremony at the presidential residence. Many pundits questioned whether Mr. Calderón would be able to govern at all. Just four months later, the political atmosphere in Mexico could hardly be more different: in late March, the government secured approval of a law to reform the public-sector pension system, the first important structural reform in a decade.

The change is tribute both to Mr. Calderón's political skills and to the disarray of his opponents. The new president hails from the same conservative National Action Party (PAN) as his predecessor, Vicente Fox, yet there the similarity ends. Mr. Fox, whose victory in 2000 ended seven decades of rule by the Institutional Revolutionary Party (PRI), aroused public expectation of change but failed to achieve much. Mr. Calderón has already shown himself to be a far more skillful politician.

He began with a show of presidential authority, sending the army on ostentatious anti-drug operations across the country in response to mounting alarm at criminal violence, and ordering a reform of the police. He has also shown skill in developing alliances. He has cultivated trade union leaders as well as state governors from all three of the main parties. He seems to have reached a working arrangement with the PRI, which holds the balance of power in Congress.

Santiago Creel, Mr. Fox's interior minister and now the PAN leader in the Senate, identifies a "radical change" in relations between the government and Congress. While Mr. Fox went over the head of Congress to appeal directly to Mexicans, Mr. Calderón, himself a former legislator, is working closely with Congress and his own party. Mr. Creel says the PAN has learned how to be a party of government and the PRI under a new leader, Beatriz Paredes, has become less obstructionist.

The president has been helped by the disarray into which the opposition was plunged by the antics of Andrés Manuel López Obrador, who lost the presidential election by just 0.6% of the votes. Mr. López Obrador's refusal to accept defeat extended to proclaiming himself the "legitimate" president and naming his own cabinet. But this is a hollow claim. "It is not even a shadow cabinet, it is a ghost cabinet," says Soledad Loaeza, a political scientist at the Colegio de México, a university.

Most Mexicans disapprove. So legislators from Mr. López Obrador's centre-left Party of the Democratic Revolution (PRD) have adopted a position worthy of the finest sophist in the agora: while paying public obeisance to their man's pretensions, in practice they talk to the government. For instance, on March 29th the PRD helped the government win a unanimous vote in the Senate for electoral and judicial reforms. However, the PRD not only voted as a block against pension reform, but also had a hand in protests against it.

The pension reform raises the retirement age and phases in individual savings accounts, matching a similar reform of private-sector pensions approved a decade ago. It aims to restore solvency to a system that is already in deficit, even though Mexico is still a demographically young country.

The speed of its passage—it was debated for a week in the Chamber of Deputies and just two days in the Senate—points to careful backroom preparation by Mr. Calderón's advisers. But opponents claim the law was railroaded through without attention to the fine print. "I'm in the state pension system, and I don't understand the reform," says Lorenzo Meyer, a historian also at the Colegio de México.

Mr. Calderón plays his cards close to his chest. But legislators expect the government's next measures to be reforms of tax and of Pemex, the state oil monopoly. The two are linked and are just as urgent as state pensions: Pemex supplies a third of government revenues and so invests too little, with the result that oil production is falling (it is down by 6% so far this year).

Oil aside, a tax system that Mr. Creel compares to a Swiss cheese ("more loopholes than substance") raises just 12% of GDP, low even for Latin America. But reforming it is highly contentious: Mr. Fox twice tried and failed. Consensus may be possible. Agustín Carstens, the finance minister, has ruled out levying VAT on food and medicine—the proposal that led to disaster for Mr. Fox.

Mr. Calderón's disciplined consensus-building may only take him so far. He is unlikely to be able to round up the votes from the PRI and PRD needed to change the constitutional taboo against private investment in energy, for example. From the other side, he also faces potential dissension in his own camp. That is especially so when it comes to reforming Mexico's shoddy schools. Josefina Vázquez, the education minister, wants to introduce evaluations of teachers. That will be resisted by the mighty teachers' union led by Elba Esther Gordillo, a former PRI stalwart who is a close ally of the president.

Some of the more traditional conservatives in the PAN are wary of Mr. Calderón's alliances. "Now that we are in power we run the risk of becoming like the old PRI," says Manuel Espino, the PAN party president. Mr. Calderón has been tolerant towards PRI governors accused of corruption—something that the PRD opposition ascribes to a pact between the new ruling party and the old.

Yet such a pact, if it exists, may be the only way to get things done. Mr. Fox was full of good intentions but clueless when it came to strategy. Mr. Calderón appears to have a sharp sense of priorities. He has yet to win over many of those who voted for his opponent, but he has certainly made a promising start.

From *The Economist*, April 7, 2007. Copyright © 2007 by The Economist Newspaper Ltd. Reprinted by permission via Copyright Clearance Center.

Youth, Violence, and Der

**"Repressive measures that have targeted youth
criminalized the younger generation threaten the
of both human rights and democracy."**

PAULO SÉRGIO PINHEIRO

GLOBAL STUDIES

The French sociologist Pierre Bourdieu once suggested that everyday violence is a solvent of human integrity. The levels of violence that are found today in almost every Latin American country constitute a true demonstration of this insight, testifying to the devastating effects of everyday brutality. And no one is more involved in this violence, both as perpetrators and victims, than the region's impoverished youth.

Some two decades after the fall of many dictatorships in Latin America—a phenomenon that raised so many hopes and allowed those of us who fought to establish democracy to dream—there is a bitter sense in the air. Campaigns for harsh, repressive measures against the poor and the young, disguised as justified wars against crime, find consistent and wide support among the local population. In this context, those who support human rights are confronted with considerable skepticism, if not threats and rejection, from many sectors of society.

It is not very difficult to understand why. Despite improvements in the juridical sphere, and despite the relatively calm and fair electoral processes introduced by democratization, an *unrule of law* continues to be a daily reality for millions of people across Latin America. Economic inequality has also increased, and the already fragile welfare state has shrunk to a minimum—deepening a widespread sense of insecurity. Perhaps most disturbingly, the levels of violence in Latin America are among the highest in the world, so much so that in some cases they surpass the mayhem in armed-conflict areas.

The situation faced by children and youth is especially critical. Data on homicides drawn from a World Health Organization study show that Latin American youth are the group most targeted for violence in the world. About 29 percent of homicides in Latin America are inflicted on children and youth from 10 to 19 years of age. Available figures indicate that homicide is the second-leading cause of death for this age group in 10 of the 21 countries of the region that have populations of over 1 million inhabitants. Youth homicide rates can be up to three times higher than national homicide rates. In Venezuela, for example, 95 percent of homicide victims are male and 54 percent of them are younger than 25.

Media coverage, as well as the issues that feature in the political agenda of Latin American leaders, indicates that the involvement of youth in criminal activities and gangs is a particular preoccupation among the nations of the region. An assessment of the reasons for this situation, and of the government responses that have been implemented, suggests that youth violence and the reactions to it are directly linked to the weakness of democratization in Latin America.

The Gangs of Central America

One place where youth violence has provoked great public insecurity is Central America, where youth gangs known as *maras* or *pandillas* have surged in the past decade. Concerns about maras, aired dramatically during election campaigns, have led local governments to elaborate ultra-tough anti-gang strategies that have attracted international attention, especially from human rights organizations. The phenomenon of maras, in fact, sheds an important light on the problem of youth violence in Latin America, in particular as organized and armed gangs expand, and allows us to reflect on the common problems found in state responses to these groups.

In my capacity as an Independent Expert appointed by the UN Secretary General to conduct a study of violence against children, I led a mission a year ago to El Salvador, Guatemala, and Honduras to gather information on the situation of the maras and the anti-maras plans. Before our mission, I was of course aware of violence in that region. But it is one thing to have information, to read reports, to know the statistics. It is another to meet with all the players in the tragedy—the *mareros* (gang members), their families, the police, the human rights activists, the judges, and the authorities—including then-President Ricardo Maduro of Honduras, one of the initiators of the so-called *mano dura* (hard hand) approach to youth violence.

After seeing in those countries—as well as in my own country, Brazil—the degrading and devastating effects of violence inflicted against stigmatized populations, it is difficult to talk about the young and the poor and the oppressed in an accurate

...her to cast them sim-
...them for their resistance
...other scholars, has observed,
...gendered by early and constant
...is one of the most tragic effects of
...mmunities throughout Latin America

...e other youth gangs, are formed through the
...riences of their members and, as such, constitute
...es. They also change their behavior and objectives in
...nce with the context in which they exist. The emergence
...e first maras occurred perhaps more than two decades ago,
...but the transformation of these groups into a key public security
concern is a more recent development.

The maras are formed mostly by young people between 16 and 25 years of age. They establish and enforce codes of loyalty and conduct. The majority of mara members display external symbols such as tattoos, exhibit specific body language, and wear distinctive clothing, thereby delineating clear territories of control and rivalry among different gangs. In many cases, mara members get involved in armed violence. The number of gang members and the real impact of the gangs on public security are motifs of many creative—and absolutely unreliable—governmental statistics. Indeed, in some instances during my mission to Central America, the figures quoted to us by different sources in the same ministry varied by 200 percent.

I am aware that the definition of gang membership has plagued researchers of youth violence since they began to study the phenomenon. I am also aware that the very concept of the gang is frequently convenient for those who wish to use the term in a discriminatory way. But one of the defining features that has separated benign organizations from traditional street gangs is involvement in criminal activity, often a reflection of the shared experience of the members.

When You're a Marero

Our discussions with adolescents during our visits in Central America clearly demonstrated that some factors are common to the life histories of mara members, pointing to root causes for their engagement in these sorts of groups. The majority of gang members came from the poorest sectors of the population and had no access to a proper education, having been abandoned or expelled from local schools.

The Public Opinion Institute of Central American University in El Salvador conducted a survey of 1,025 gang members in the San Salvador metropolitan area and found that 75 percent were unemployed. Among those employed, only half held stable jobs. And only 33 percent of those surveyed had finished high school. About 76 percent had dropped out of school.

Many of the adolescents we interviewed during the UN mission came from disrupted families, with some having faced domestic violence within their homes. Many had absolutely no expectations of finding any sort of employment. The majority of mareros were involved with petty crime around the communities that they dominated. They also had severe conflicts with gang rivals.

One tragic reality in Latin America is that violence is frequently directed by the dispossessed against their companions in misfortune. Youth gangs often use violence to meet their members' economic and social needs, further adding to already high levels of violence in their communities. For example, in my own country, the majority of homicides in São Paulo and Rio de Janeiro are committed among the working class. Very few of my white and elite compatriots are murdered and even fewer are the object of state violence.

This is no accident. The everyday violence exerted in families, factories, streets, offices, police stations, and prisons—including the violence committed by and against young people—is in the last analysis an effect of the inherent violence of economic structures, income concentration, and structural racism. This is manifested sooner or later in the form of crime and delinquency, drug addiction, alcoholism, and a whole host of minor and major everyday acts of violence—including gang violence.

Economic policies that aggravate the situation of the majority of families and their children are assiduously implemented by governments, including those described as leftist, immediately when they take power. James Vigil of the University of California at Irvine has written of the "multiple marginalities" that affect mareros. These certainly are aggravated by global processes like economic restructuring and democratic transitions after war and regional peace settlements. Frequently, during my conversations with mareros, I heard the background echo of violence as the reproduction of violent patterns internalized during civil war.

Central America's conflicts during the 1980s produced a mass migration from the region, mainly to the United States. The subsequent deportation of large groups of people back to Central America appears to have created a generation of youth who do not have clear ties either to North American communities (where most of them lived in very marginalized areas and were sometimes the victims of discrimination) or to their communities in El Salvador or Honduras. One result of these upheavals was the dismantling of local webs of family and community life, the terrain where daily interactions are sustained.

Out of these dynamics has emerged an inner-city culture—*una cultura callejera*—that seeks to replace these vanished bonds, whose absence is itself made worse by the lack of education, pervasive non- or under-employment, and a lack of social investment. In this context, the maras in a certain way represent a reconstruction of those elements that were lost and cannot be recovered. But this reconstruction constitutes a terrible burden for these young people, even as it requires enormous inventive capacities.

Across Latin America, the growth in gang membership has coincided with easy access to small arms. In a number of countries, past conflicts have facilitated the spread of small arms, identified by the World Health Organization as a key factor leading to the escalation of lethal violence in the region. In Brazil, homicides among youth have increased 77 percent in a decade, mainly because more violence has involved firearms.

The Resort to Repression

The Central American states' responses to the maras issue have had an important and negative impact and, at the same time, are revealing about Latin America's repressive tendency vis-á-vis youth violence. Public security has become a major political issue, with strident anti-maras policies serving as prominent leitmotifs in both administration policy making and election campaigns. In El Salvador and Honduras, new laws and changes in the penal code have created specific penalties for those who are considered to be mara members or are committing the crime of "illicit association."

These legal instruments have gone so far as to stipulate that the mere existence of indicia such as tattoos, certain clothes, or graffiti is sufficient for youngsters to be detained for long periods. Legal reforms in this area also have called into question recently established codes for children and adolescents, providing that mara members less than 18 years old can be tried in adult courts as adults. Many of these legal changes contradict existing national, regional, and international standards and guidelines, including prescriptions set forth by the Convention on the Rights of the Child.

The concrete results of these measures are also appalling. During our mission we heard frequent allegations of abusive and sometimes arbitrary detention of hundreds of suspected gang members, with the result that detention centers have rapidly filled and have become increasingly violent. In Honduras, two riots at such facilities between the end of 2003 and the beginning of 2004 resulted in 1,500 casualties. With violence reproduced behind bars as the gang members are imprisoned, the violence perpetrated by some maras appears to have increased. Certainly, violent rivalries between opponent gangs have grown in detention facilities, and the linkages between some potential members and their maras are enhanced.

Governments' aggressive responses to the maras reflect a sharp escalation in public rhetoric. In El Salvador, the first version of the state's anti-gang strategy was called Mano Dura, the second Super Mano Dura (heavy hand and super heavy hand). Anti-Maras Squads were created (mixing police and army—one of Latin America's favored approaches). And you would even hear references to the beginning of "mara hunting season." Some of these hunts included the president as the convoy leader. Opinions found daily in newspapers reproduce and reinforce public perceptions of the linkage between maras and the vast majority of crimes.

"Moral Panic"

These phenomena are not, of course, exclusive to Central Americans. Barry Feld of the University of Minnesota Law School has noted that "public frustration with crime, fear of the recent rise in youth violence in all continents, and the racial characteristics of violent young offenders fuel the desire 'to get tough' and provide political impetus to prosecute a larger number of youths as adults." In a 2002 essay titled "Moral Panic and Youth Violence," three Rutgers University researchers described similar scenarios

within Central America and outside it, in which the media and political establishment publicized "exaggerated claims of danger posed by unconventional youths; in turn, inflammatory rhetoric was used to justify enhanced police powers and greater investment in the traditional criminal apparatus."

Publics across Latin America, pandered to by politicians, are calling for and accepting increasingly repressive measures in an effort to stem youth violence.

It is relevant to acknowledge that the "moral panic" created by the maras is not sheer paranoia (even paranoids may have real enemies). The problem of youth violence touches on bona fide social ills that democratic governance must seriously address. Unfortunately, rather than directing the public toward an informed understanding of the problem, in the case of the mano dura rhetoric and in other Latin American wars against gangs, the media and the politicians instead pander to popular fear. The result is renewed hostility toward people who are easy to identify and dislike—the "torturable" classes, as Graham Greene described them.

The fragile implementation of reforms to the juvenile justice system also exhibits daily contradictions. Despite some good efforts, the "new" never quite replaces the old in Latin America. When it comes to youth in trouble, discourses of protection, restoration, punishment, responsibility, rehabilitation, welfare, retribution, and human rights continue to exist alongside each other in a perpetually uneasy and tremendously contradictory manner. Statements clouded in layers of rhetoric regarding the best interest of the child are spoken in tandem with the practice of incarcerating youth—thereby condemning some of them to abuse, torture, and sexual assaults—for their alleged education and training. The juvenile justice system implemented in many Latin American countries (including the three most affected by maras) reproduces the same problems that you might find in the adult system. These include slow responses to cases, an extremely high number of non-processed detainees, and a chaotic situation within detention centers.

In this respect, the juvenile justice system in the region is as bad as the one designed for adults, yet it is weaker in keeping offenders detained. Therefore, it is not very surprising to see broad popular support for proposals directed at reducing the age of criminal responsibility or creating exceptions that would allow children to be tried as adults, as proposed in the mano dura plans.

Forces of Resistance

It may help to understand the general situation in Latin America today, and especially the way democracy is perceived, if we consider the tragic linkage between limited democratization and the rise of youth violence. Latin America has undergone a democratization process with important achievements, restricted mostly to the institutional level. A recent report by the United Nations Development Program (UNDP) notes that, at present, established electoral mechanisms exist throughout Latin America, and the region is moving toward juridical and institutional adaptation to the principal international human rights standards.

At the same time, this progress has not been replicated in the population's social and economic situation. The entire region is marked by severe inequality. That is clearly the case of the three countries I visited. According to the UNDP, 79 percent of the Honduran population lives in poverty. In El Salvador, the underground market employs an estimated 42 percent of the workforce. In Guatemala, access to education is very difficult for the rural population—only 24 percent of schools are in the rural areas, where 60 percent of the country's school-age population is concentrated.

And despite the advances of democracy, it must be noted that legal rights and the rule of law continue to be elusive—particularly for the majority of poor Latin American young people. The region continues to struggle with seemingly intractable problems in criminal justice: abusive use of lethal force by police forces, extra-judicial killings, lynching, torture, abominable prison conditions, and persistent corruption. These phenomena abide despite numerous attempts to eradicate them by legislative reforms and institution building.

The deportation of large groups of people back to Central America appears to have created a generation of youth who do not have clear ties either to North American communities or to their communities in El Salvador or Honduras.

Most Latin American countries have ratified core human rights conventions and comply with the international and regional human rights regimes. They have designed special rights policies and introduced national human rights institutions, including police ombudsman offices. They have encouraged the organization of civil society, which has expanded extraordinarily. And yet, although at first such policies and measures flourish, within a few years each seems to lose efficacy and credibility.

Beatriz Affonso of the Center for Justice and International Law in Brazil has studied, for example, the efficiency of legislation that removed from the military police the privilege of trial by military courts in cases of homicide against civilians in São Paulo. Her research shows that impunity continues to reign because public prosecutors (with the Ministério Público) do not pressure the police forces to carry out proper investigations and in fact seem to be in collusion with the police to drop charges. In general, the forces within the state apparatus and in the political arena that resist change seem to prevail.

This trend is the opposite of what was forecast by democratic transition theories. It was expected that, as democratic political systems developed, there would be a clear reduction in human rights violations. Among human rights violations, none is more pervasive in Latin America than the violence against children and young people perpetrated or condoned by democratic governments.

This unfortunate dynamic is helping to create a perverse linkage between the adoption of modern international human rights standards and official reactions to youth violence. In Central America and throughout Latin America, there is a spreading incapacity or unwillingness on the part of governments to guarantee the right to life of their populations. On the contrary, under the pretext of carrying out wars on crime, governments are in reality undermining the rule of law and weakening their societies' support for the concept of democracy.

The Mantra of Prevention

How can we prevent conventional youth and teen groups from becoming violent without resorting to repressive measures and public rhetoric that are counterproductive and undermine democracy? How can we make violent communities safer and more stable? How can we break the cycle of violence and reintegrate back into society the young people who have decided to engage in illicit activities? What are the root causes that need to be urgently addressed to produce sustainable gains?

These are not easy questions. As everyone is aware, there are no easy and fast solutions. There are no prêt-á-porter plans that can be developed and replicated everywhere without regard for local circumstances. We are working with problems that have deep connections with communities and their recent histories.

Still, I believe that we already have some knowledge about what may work and what generally does not work well. Better enforcement of human rights standards, public health and protection plans that emphasize prevention and early intervention, and initiatives to minimize the chances and the seriousness of offending and re-offending are promising approaches.

In particular, we must repeat as a mantra that prevention is possible. Easy access to small arms and the recurrent and banal use of institutionalization are clear warning signs. Well-structured and easily accessible cultural and leisure facilities for youth, as well as improved integration of public schools with their communities, are essential. One evident problem that every government must face is the fact that appropriate measures will require time to have a durable impact.

They also will require sustained institutional reforms. In this respect, it is possible that the fragmented and frequently quite superficial preventive responses already in place in the region may produce even more adverse effects. Even in El Salvador, after the Mano Dura, the country tried to complement the plan with the so-called Mano Extendida (extended hand), a formal effort to provide assistance to former gang members who want to be rehabilitated. So far, unfortunately, this has been just a gesture of good intentions.

Since the promulgation of the preventive mantra, many fragmented programs have been developed in Latin America, sponsored by national and international, governmental and non-governmental organizations. It is of course vitally important to mobilize and empower communities and to promote human rights education. Yet, if these initiatives are not accompanied by consistent improvements in the state apparatus, if there is not a radical change in the functioning of the public security and judicial systems, then these efforts will not be successful, and they may even increase frustration and skepticism with regard to democratic institutions.

For the benefit of young people and the societies in which they live, it is imperative that Latin America's criminal justice systems be rendered not only more efficient but also more credible and accountable. Additionally, these systems need to be more accessible to the marginalized population that requires them the most—a population, including youth, that is normally distant from and fearful of the state's security and justice apparatus.

It is also crucial to develop a more reliable data bank on security issues. The absence of good information on youth violence and the efficacy of responses to it renders effective policy making more difficult and any form of evaluation impossible. And it is important to consider disproportionate media attention to youth violence as part of the information problem.

Above all, it is essential to ensure that all measures taken are viewed not only as matters of security, but also as human rights issues. Even if we are speaking about specific preventive measures, we are dealing with basic rights that have to be respected for the full development of human beings. In this respect, for example, the proper functioning of the education system is essential not only because it reduces the vulnerability of children to violence, but also because it serves a fundamental right of every child.

The Rights of Youth

Today, more than ever, it is clear that democracy and human rights are inseparable. Thus, we must assess the protection of human rights in tandem with the development of democracy. Publics across Latin America, pandered to by politicians, are calling for and accepting increasingly repressive measures in an effort to stem youth violence. But democracy demands the participation of children and adolescents and their recognition as full citizens (not as mini-human beings with mini-human rights). This means they have the right to be informed, to express opinions, and to be heard. It also means that economic, social, and cultural rights for youth are critical because, without access to health and education and a secure livelihood, young people cannot enjoy their civil and political rights in the future.

Democracy and the protection of human rights, including the rights of youth, are both works in progress, mutually reinforcing, and fragile. Born in the early stages of Latin America's democratization, repressive measures that have targeted youth gangs and criminalized the younger generation threaten the progress of both human rights and democracy. Leaders and citizens in the region must exercise their best efforts to ensure they are dismantled.

PAULO SÉRGIO PINHEIRO is a United Nations Independent Expert who led preparation of the 2006 UN Secretary General's Study on Violence Against Children. He is a research associate at the University of São Paulo's Center for the Study of Violence, which he founded in 1987, and a commissioner with the Inter-American Commission on Human Rights. He was assisted in the preparation of this essay by Marcelo Daher, a project specialist with the office of the High Commissioner for Human Rights in Geneva.

Shade Coffee & Tree Cover Loss
Lessons from El Salvador

ALLEN BLACKMAN, BEATRIZ ÁVALOS-SARTORIO, AND JEFFREY CHOW

In Central America, shade coffee has often helped to preserve tree cover, along with the ecological services it provides, in areas that are under pressure from ranchers, farmers, loggers, and developers. Over the past two decades, however, declining international coffee prices, rapid urbanization, and other factors have undermined shade coffee's ability to play this role in some countries.

To moderate temperature, humidity, and sunlight, most Central American coffee growers plant their crop under managed or natural tree cover. Unlike most human dominated landscapes, this mixed agro-forestry system provides many of the same ecological services associated with natural forests, including harboring biodiversity, preventing soil erosion, sequestering carbon, and facilitating aquifer recharge-albeit at a lower level than in natural forests. Shade coffee's biodiversity benefits have received particular attention. The crop grows in mountain ranges at altitudes where tropical and temperate climates overlap, areas that are extremely rich in biodiversity.[1]

Unfortunately, Central American shade coffee farmers are facing unprecedented market pressures. In 2001, after a decade of decline interrupted by short-term spikes, inflation-adjusted world coffee prices dropped to their lowest levels in fifty years. This phenomenon is commonly referred to as the coffee crisis, and its causes include the collapse of the international coffee cartel in the late 1980s, increased world supply (mainly due to exports from Vietnam and Brazil), and an increase in the bargaining power of coffee roasters. Because these factors are structural rather than cyclical, prices are unlikely to rebound to pre-1990 levels, at least not in the near term.[2] As coffee prices declined, tree cover in some Central American shade coffee areas was cleared to make way for more remunerative land uses such as urban development and conventional farming. Some of the resulting damages, including species loss and soil erosion, may be irreversible or nearly so. This problem is beginning to attract the attention of policymakers,[3] but it remains poorly understood. The only previous research on the topic was a study of tree cover loss in a 250,000-hectare shade coffee growing area in southern Mexico during the late 1990s. That study found that 3 percent of the area was cleared in the late 1990s, primarily by small-scale coffee growers planting subsistence crops to mitigate the impact of declining coffee prices.[4]

Although tree cover loss may be a problem in shade coffee areas in a number of Central American countries, it is particularly worrisome in El Salvador, the most densely populated country in the Americas and the most severely deforested. Less than 10 percent of the country's natural forests survive, and a significant share of the remaining tree cover is associated with shade coffee.[5] Data from satellite images, and interviews with Salvadoran stakeholders provide insight into the magnitude, characteristics, and drivers of tree cover loss in El Salvador's shade coffee areas during the 1990s.[6]

Coffee in El Salvador

The Salvadoran coffee sector suffered a series of shocks during the 1990s, due to falling prices and bad weather. After a decade of decline in the 1980s, coffee prices rebounded for three harvest years in the mid-to-late 1990s (1994–1995 through 1997–1998) but continued an overall downward slide in the 1998–1999 harvest season. Severe drought in 1997 associated with an El Niño event and Hurricane Mitch in 1998 also disrupted coffee production. The combined effects of these events were striking. Production, yields, wages, and permanent employment fell by 23–24 percent between 1991–1992 and 2000–2001, while exports and export revenue fell by approximately 20 percent. The impact of lower prices between 1991–1992 and 2003–2004 was even more dramatic. Production fell by 38 percent and yields by 36 percent. Wages and permanent employment fell by 64 percent, and exports and export revenue fell by 37 percent.[7]

Coffee in El Salvador grows in three main areas: the western region, located in the Apaneca-Ilamatapec mountain range; the central region, located in the El Balsamo and Chichontepc volcano mountain ranges; and the eastern region, located in the Tecapa Chinameca and Cachuatiqe mountain ranges. In the 2003–2004 harvest season, coffee was planted on a total of 161,000 hectares comprising about 9 percent of El Salvador's landmass. The western portion of the country contained just more than half of this acreage, the center portion about a third, and the east region, about a fifth.[8] For more information on coffee in the Salvadoran economy, see the box on page 213.

Ninety-five percent of El Salvador's coffee is shade grown.[9] The type and density of shade cover that farmers use depends partly on the altitude and local microclimate. Coffee farms in lowland areas typically have 40 percent shade cover, while those in highland areas typically have 20 percent shade cover.[10]

In general, high quality coffee grows at higher altitudes. The Salvadoran Coffee Council assigns coffee one of three quality standards depending on the altitude at which it is grown: "central standard" for coffee grown at 600–800 meters above sea level (MSL); "high grown" for coffee grown at 800–1,200 MSL; and "strictly high grown" for coffee grown above 1,200 MSL. Almost three-quarters of Salvadoran coffee exports are either high grown or strictly high grown. Although certified coffees, including "organic," "Rainforest Alliance certified," and "fair trade," have appeared in the past several years, they make up less than 1 percent of overall exports.[11] Given the drivers and characteristics of tree cover loss in El Salvador's shade coffee areas, unless combined with other policies, expanded certification alone is unlikely to stem this problem.

Tree Cover Loss during the 1990s

Satellite data on tree cover in El Salvador indicates that shade coffee's effectiveness as a bulwark against tree clearing eroded significantly during the 1990s. Table 1 below presents satellite data on tree cover in El Salvador for 1990 and 2000. A comparison of 1990 tree cover inside the coffee growing areas and outside these areas suggests that until 1990, shade coffee protected against tree cover loss. Although 51 percent of the noncoffee area had no tree cover, only 7 percent of the coffee regions had none.

Table 2 on page 212 presents satellite data on tree cover loss between 1990 and 2000. Fully 13 percent of land area in the three coffee regions was cleared during the 1990s. The percentage of land cleared was highest in the western region (17 percent) and lowest in the eastern region (7 percent).

Surprisingly, the conventional wisdom about where this clearing occurred was incorrect. Most stakeholders interviewed for this study believed that the lion's share of clearing in El Salvador's coffee areas during the 1990s occurred below 800 MSL, where coffee quality, and therefore the prices paid to growers, were relatively low. Table 3 on page 212 demonstrates that this is not true. For all three coffee regions, 46 percent of clearing occurred between 800 and 1,200 MSL, where coffee is classified as "high grown," and another 15 percent occurred above 1,200 MSL, where coffee is classified as "strictly high grown."

No hard data are available on the specific land uses that replaced shade coffee between 1990 and 2000. The satellite data are of little use in this regard because they lump all land uses that entail clearing into a single "nonforest" category. Interviews with regional managers of the Salvadoran Coffee Research Institute (Fundación Salvadoreña para Investigatciones del Café, or PROCAFE), El Salvador's parastatal coffee research and technical extension organization, shed light on this issue. Based on casual observation, the PROCAFE managers estimated that the majority of clearing between 1990 and 2000 in each of the 3 coffee regions was due to urbanization (see Table 4 on page 212). They reckoned that urbanization accounted for fully 90 percent of clearing in the western region and 68 percent of clearing in the central region. They thought

Table 1   Tree Cover in 1990 and 2000, by region

Type of land cover	All Coffee Regions		West		Center		East		Noncoffee Regions	
	Extent of cover (in hectares)	Percent of the regions	Extent of cover (in hectares)	Percent of the region	Extent of cover (in hectares)	Percent of the region	Extent of cover (in hectares)	Percent of the region	Extent of cover (in hectares)	Percent of the regions
1990										
Tree cover	182,410	92	78,970	94	61,970	91	40,470	92	888,350	49
No tree cover	14,590	7	4,870	6	6,410	9	3,320	8	927,480	51
Water/ no class	710	0	330	0	20	0	360	1	N/A	N/A
Total	197,710	100	84,170	100	68,400	100	44,150	100	1,815,830	100
2000										
Tree cover	161,680	82	66,830	79	56,240	82	38,610	87	999,210	55
No tree cover	34,320	17	17,010	20	12,130	18	5,180	12	816,610	45
Water/ no class	710	0	330	0	20	0	360	1	N/A	N/A
Total	196,710	100	84,170	100	68,390	100	44,150	100	1,815,820	100

Note: The digital land cover maps do not distinguish between shade coffee and other types of tree cover, so they were cross-referenced with land use maps from the Salvadoran Ministry of Agriculture.

Some columns do not total correctly.

Source: Calculated in ArcGIS from the National Aeronautics and Space Administration Jet Propulsion Laboratory's land cover maps for 1990 and 2000.

Table 2 Clearing from 1990 to 2000, by region

	All Coffee Regions		West		Center		East		Noncoffee Regions	
	Extent (in hectares)	Percent of the regions	Extent (in hectares)	Percent of the region	Extent (in hectares)	Percent of the region	Extent (in hectares)	Percent of the region	Extent (in hectares)	Percent of the regions
Cleared	24,700	13	14,000	17	7,500	11	3,200	7	229,100	12
Not cleared	172,100	87	70,200	83	60,900	89	41,000	93	1,742,800	88
Total	196,800	100	84,200	100	68,400	100	44,200	100	1,971,900	100

Source: Calculated in ArcGIS from the National Aeronautics and Space Administration Jet Propulsion Laboratory's land cover maps for 1990 and 2000.

Table 3 Clearing from 1990 to 2000 in all three coffee regions, by altitude range

Range	Area in Range		Cleared in 1990		Cleared in 2000		Cleared 1990–2000		
Meters above sea level	Extent (in hectares)	Percent of the region	Extent (in hectares)	Percent of the range	Extent (in hectares)	Percent of the range	Extent (in hectares)	Percent of the range	Percent of all clearing
0–800	78,200	40	8,680	11	14,890	19	9,440	12	38
801–1,200	90,000	46	3,890	4	13,690	15	11,510	13	47
1,201 and above	29,200	15	540	2	3,940	13	3,670	13	15
All	197,400	100	13,110	17	32,520	47	24,620	12	100

Some columns do not total correctly.
Source: Calculated in ArcGIS from the National Aeronautics and Space Administration Jet Propulsion Laboratory's land cover maps for 1990 and 2000.

Table 4 Activities responsible for clearing between 1990 and 2000, by region

Activity	Percentage		
	West	Center	East
Urban land uses	90	68	50
Row crops	10	5	10
Pasture for livestock	–	–	5
Lumber, firewood[a]	–	5	20
Accidental forest fires	–	2	5
Other	–	20	–
Total	100	100	100

[a]No land use substituted for coffee.
Some columns do not total correctly.
Source: Estimates provded by PROCAFE (Fundación Salvadoreña para Investigatciones del Café) regional managers in discussion with the authors, October 2005.

that felling trees for lumber or firewood accounted for 20 percent of clearing in the eastern region and that row crops played a significant, albeit minor, role in clearing in each region.

Drivers of Tree Cover Loss

Although the coffee crisis was undoubtedly a key cause of tree cover loss in El Salvador's shade coffee areas during the 1990s, it was by no means the only driver of this change. Interviews with stakeholders and a review of secondary evidence suggests that a complex web of interrelated factors contributed, including

a downward spiral of on-farm investment and yields, debt, poverty, urbanization, migration, and weak regulations regarding land use and land cover.

On-Farm Investments and Yields

The coffee crisis led to a downward spiral of on-farm investment and yields in the coffee sector. The spiral began when growers reacted to low prices by cutting back or completely eliminating farm management activities, such as pruning and the application of fertilizers and pesticides, which together account for approximately half of coffee production costs (per hectare).[12] Although such cost-cutting measures helped balance cash accounts in the short term, they also had short- and long-term negative impacts on yields. Reduced yields led to even lower profits, and lower profits led to further cutbacks in farm maintenance.[13] On average, yields fell by more than 20 percent, from more than 19 quintals per hectare in the 1991–1992 growing season to about 15 quintals per hectare in the 2000–2001 season.[14]

Farmer Debt

Coffee growers in El Salvador depend on annual infusions of working capital from large private banks, mainly channeled through cooperatives and coffee mills. On average, growers require approximately $40–$45 of credit per quintal of coffee produced to hire farm labor.[15] During the 1990s, the coffee growers borrowed an average of more than $200 million per year, far more than any other agricultural sector.[16] After the onset of the coffee crisis, growers' profits were so low that they were unable to repay their loans. Nevertheless, banks continued

El Salvador's Coffee Economy

In the 2003–2004 harvest season, El Salvador produced almost 2 million quintals (each quintal is a 100-pound or 46-kilogram sack of green coffee). This production represented about 1 percent of the world's total that season and 11 percent of Central America's total. Ninety percent of the crop was exported, generating more than $120 million in revenue. In the 2003–2004 season, the coffee sector employed more than 57,000 people permanently and paid some $14 million in wages.[1]

1.International Coffee Organization (ICO), 2006 coffee statistics, available at http://www.ico.org; and PROCAFE (Fundacion Salvadorena para Investigaciones del Cafe), Boletin Estadistico de la Caficultura Salvadorena (San Salvador, El Salvador: PROCAFE, 1998).

to extend credit for several years, knowing that farmers needed to produce enough coffee to repay their debts. As a result, debts mounted. Today, the total outstanding debt in the coffee sector is estimated at $200–$400 million, an average of $100–$210 per quintal or $1,200–$2,500 per hectare.

Debt contributed to tree cover loss during the 1990s in a number of ways. Indebted growers sometimes sold their land, in part or whole, to developers, conventional farmers, or ranchers to liquidate debt. In some cases, banks foreclosed on farms that had been used as collateral and also sold the land. In addition, as discussed below, indebted growers sometimes sold trees on their land for cash.[17]

Rural Poverty

During the 1990s, poverty was pervasive in rural areas of El Salvador, including coffee-growing areas. At the beginning of the 1990s, two-thirds of all rural households in El Salvador were classified as poor, and a third were classified as extremely poor. Although national poverty rates fell during the 1990s, most of the reductions were in urban, not rural areas.[18]

Rural poverty contributed to tree cover loss in coffee-growing areas in several ways. First, after the onset of the coffee crisis, poor, small-scale growers, unable to meet their basic subsistence needs from coffee alone, cleared portions of their farms to grow corn, beans, and other basic food crops. This phenomenon has been a common response to poverty and income variability among all types of rural households in El Salvador, and it is a leading cause of tree cover loss in other Central American shade coffee–growing regions.[19] In addition, poor rural households sold trees for lumber and firewood, both of which command a significant per unit price in El Salvador. Finally, in some cases, rural entrepreneurs harvested trees on abandoned or poorly supervised farms without obtaining permission.

Urbanization

With a 2000 population of 6.3 million inhabiting an area of just 21,000 square kilometers, El Salvador has more than 315 persons per square kilometer, making it the most densely populated country on the American continent. By comparison, Guatemala

and Honduras have 104 and 58 persons per square kilometer.[20] Not surprisingly, given this density, El Salvador is an increasingly urban country. In 2000, 55 percent of El Salvador's population lived in urban areas, up from 39 percent in 1970.[21] Land under urban uses grew from 0.8 percent of the national territory in 1965 to 5 percent in 1995.[22]

In less densely populated countries, urbanization in theory could help stem tree clearing by reducing population pressure in rural areas. In general, this is not what is occurring in El Salvador's shade coffee areas, however. Here, urban land uses are displacing shade coffee. Demand for land for housing has grown steadily over the past two decades, particularly since the signing of peace accords in El Salvador in 1992, and particularly in highland areas, including those used to grow coffee, which have a more hospitable climate than lowland areas. Over the past decade, many different types of farms, including coffee farms, have been divided into small lots and sold to construction companies or directly to homesteaders. This process is known as "lotification." Middle- and upper-class homesteaders are not the only beneficiaries of the lotification process. Rather, small lots averaging 250 square meters, with no preexisting buildings, infrastructure, or services, are sold at modest prices to low-income households.[23]

Strong demand for housing land has driven up land prices. In many areas, the price of agricultural land has risen well above the net present value of its lifetime productive value, making continued agricultural use unprofitable and creating powerful incentives for coffee growers to sell their farms.[24]

Migration and Remittances

Civil unrest and chronic poverty in rural areas have spurred massive internal and external migration in El Salvador over the past 20 years. Much of the internal migration has been from the eastern and northern parts of the country to the southwestern parts, including the greater metropolitan area of San Salvador. This phenomenon, along with population growth, has caused a dramatic shift in the geographic distribution of El Salvador's population. Between 1971 and 2000, the share of El Salvador's population living in the southwest rose from 53 percent to 67 percent. By comparison, the share of the country's population living in the southeast fell from 28 percent to 20 percent, and the share of the population living in the north fell from 19 percent to 13 percent.[25] To the extent internal migration has exacerbated population pressures in the southwest, it has contributed to clearing of coffee farms in this area for urban and agricultural uses.

Although internal migration during the 1990s was significant, it paled in comparison with external migration. In 2000, for example, three-quarters of rural migration was external and virtually all of it was to North America.[26] The Salvadoran ministry of foreign relations estimates that 2.5 million Salvadorans— roughly a fifth of the total population—now live abroad, and that 90 percent of these migrants live in the United States.[27]

Given this massive external migration, remittances have become a critical feature of El Salvador's economy. In 1999, Salvadoran migrants sent home more than $1.5 billion, an amount that represented 13 percent of El Salvador's gross domestic product, 64 percent of its export earnings, and almost

700 percent of its foreign investment.[28] Nationally, between 1992–1993 and 2000, the percentage of households receiving remittances rose 6 percentage points, from 14 to 20 percent. The increase was larger in rural areas (from 13 to 20 percent) than in urban areas (16 to 19 percent). The average amount of remittances per household also increased, from $76 to $121, the equivalent of the monthly minimum wage.[29]

External migration and associated remittances are likely to have had beneficial and detrimental effects on tree cover in shade coffee regions during the 1990s. On the one hand, external migration may have dampened urbanization. Also, remittances may have enabled coffee-growing households to continue producing (despite low prices and scarce credit) and avoid clearing trees altogether. On the other hand, however, according to stakeholder interviewees, remittances have fueled the demand for urban land uses and have financed the conversion of coffee farms to alternative land uses. In addition, stakeholders report that migration—external and internal—has created a scarcity of coffee labor in the eastern part of El Salvador, making coffee production much less profitable in the region.[30]

Land Use and Land Cover Management

Management of land use and land cover in El Salvador were weak during the 1990s. Prior to 1998, the main laws governing land use and land cover were the Forestry Law of 1973 and land use permitting laws. The forestry laws required those wishing to clear forest to obtain permits from the Ministry of Agriculture (*Ministerio de Agricultura y Ganaderia,* or MAG). In addition, land use planning laws required those wishing to construct buildings to obtain permits from city mayors or the Ministry of Housing and Public Works.[31] In practice, these requirements were frequently ignored. Even when they were heeded, the criteria for obtaining permits were rarely enforced and environmental impact assessments were not required. Prior to the passage of a new forestry law in 2002, MAG almost never rejected a request for a permit to clear forest.[32]

Environmental management in El Salvador took a major step forward in 1998 with the passage of the Environmental Law and the creation of the Ministry of the Environment and Natural Resources (*Ministerio de Medio Ambiente y Recursos Naturales,* or MARN). By law, MARN is required to issue permits for any changes in land use. According to government interviewees, however, MARN does not have the resources to conduct a detailed review of permit applications and approves the vast majority submitted.[33]

Conclusion

The case study of tree cover loss in El Salvador's shade coffee areas has several policy implications. First, a rapid policy response is needed. During the 1990s, tree cover in shade coffee areas was lost at a rapid rate, and there is ample reason to suspect that this trend has continued apace, given that coffee prices reached a 50-year low in 2001 and have remained well below pre-1990 levels since then. In heavily deforested El Salvador,

shade coffee provides important ecological services. To prevent soil erosion, flooding, biodiversity loss, and other types of environmental degradation that would result from further tree cover loss, action must be taken quickly.[34]

Second, command-and-control land cover and land use restrictions are needed to stem tree cover loss. In the central and western regions, where more than three-quarters of El Salvador's coffee is grown, urbanization and an inflow of financial capital from remittances have pushed land prices well above the net present value of future returns to coffee, thereby creating strong incentives for growers to sell their land to developers. In these areas, market-based conservation approaches, such as payments for environmental services and organic, fair trade, bird friendly, and other types of coffee certification, are not likely to be effective—at least not unless combined with other policies—because the financial incentives they provide for continuing to grow coffee are significantly smaller than those offered by the land market. Unfortunately, however, command-and-control regulation is not likely to be effective in the near term. To date, by all accounts, land use and land cover regulation in El Salvador has proven toothless. It will undoubtedly take some time to build the political will and institutional capacity to enforce these policies. An interim solution may be to create incentives for land developers to clear and build in a manner that minimizes environmental degradation by, for example, retaining as much tree cover as possible, avoiding ecologically sensitive areas, and retaining corridors between forested areas.

Finally, efforts to improve coffee quality and marketing can help stem further tree cover loss. Because they have a comparative advantage in producing high-quality coffee, many highland growers in El Salvador have responded to the coffee crisis by boosting quality and marketing to obtain higher prices. These efforts to improve coffee quality and marketing are targeting areas where most deforestation is occurring.

From an environmental standpoint, tree cover loss in El Salvador's shade coffee areas is cause for concern, if not alarm. Further research will determine whether it has abated or accelerated over the past seven years and whether similar clearing is occurring in other Central American countries.

Allen Blackman is a senior fellow at Resources for the Future (RFF), a non-profit, non-partisan environmental policy research institute in Washington, DC. His research focuses on environmental and natural resource management in Latin America, particularly tropical deforestation and innovative pollution control regulation. He can be reached via e-mail at blackman@rff.org. Beatriz Avalos-Sartorio is a senior agricultural research officer at the Consultative Group for International Agricultural Research Science Council Secretariat in Rome, Italy and a former Gilbert White Fellow at RFF. Her research interests include agricultural and trade policy analysis, the microeconomics of technology adoption, and shade coffee production systems in Latin America. She can be reached via e-mail at beatriz.avalossartorio@fao.org. Jeffrey Chow is a doctoral candidate at Yale School of Forestry and a former research associate at RFF. His research interests include forest resource management in developing countries and the impact of climate change on sustainable development. He can be reached via e-mail at chow@rff.org.

The authors are grateful to the Inter-American Development Bank (IADB) and the Tinker Foundation for financial support; Sergio Gil, Oscar Gómez, and Carlos Pleitez at PROCAFE for their multifaceted assistance; Sassan Saatchi at the National Aeronautics and Space Administration's Jet Propulsion Laboratory for providing their land cover data; Diego Arias, Silvia Oritz, and Sybille Nuenninghoff at IADB, Deborah Barry at the Center for International Forestry Research, and Jeffrey Jones at Centro Agronomico Tropical de Investigación y Ensenanza for helpful comments and logistical support; and to their many interviewees in El Salvador.

Notes

1. R. Rice, "Coffee Production in a Time of Crisis: Social and Environmental Connections," *SAIS Review* 23 no. 1 (2003): 221–245; and I. Perfecto, R. Rice, R. Greenberg, and M. E. Van der Voort, "Shade Coffee: A Disappearing Refuge for Biodiversity," *Bioscience* 46 no. 8 (1996): 98–608.

2. P. Varangis, P. Siegel, D. Giovannucci, and B. Lewin, *Dealing with the Coffee Crisis in Central America: Impacts and Strategies,* Policy Research Working Paper 2993 (Washington, DC: World Bank Development Research Group, March 2003).

3. Inter-American Development Bank (IADB), U.S. Agency for International Development (USAID), and World Bank, "Managing the Competitive Transition of the Coffee Sector in Central America," paper prepared for the Workshop on the Coffee Crisis and its Impact in Central America: Situation and Lines of Action, Antigua, Guatemala, 3–5 April 2002; Varangis, Siegel, Giovannucci, and Lewin, note 2; and International Coffee Organization (ICO), "Impact of Low Prices on Sustainability Indicators in the Coffee Economy," paper presented at 255th meeting of ICO Executive Board, London, England, 18–21 May 2004.

4. A. Blackman, H. Albers, B. Ávalos-Sartorio, and L. Crooks Murphy, *Deforestation and Shade Coffee in Oaxaca, Mexico: Key Research Findings,* RFF Discussion Paper 05–39 (Washington, DC, 2005), http://www.rff.org.

5. Food and Agriculture Organization (FAO) Forestry Department, *El Salvador: The Forests and the Forestry Sector,* http://www.fao.org/forestry/site/23747/en/slv.

6. This article is drawn from a longer, more technical report: A. Blackman, B. Ávalos-Sartorio, and J. Chow, *Tree Cover Loss in El Salvador's Shade Coffee Areas,* RFF Report, http://www.rff.org. The extent to which the study period coincides with—or predates—the "coffee crisis" is open to question; a precise definition of this term does not exist. Recent studies frequently use it to refer to the precipitous decline of prices between 1997 and 2001. See, for example, Varangis, Siegel, Giovannucci, and Lewin, note 2; and World Bank, *Shocks and Social Protection: Lessons from the Central American Coffee Crisis,* Report No. 31857-CA (Washington, DC, 2005). However, the overall downward trend in coffee prices that culminated in this steep five-year slide began decades earlier and many researchers use the 1989 collapse of the International Coffee Agreements (ICA) quota system to mark the start of the coffee crisis. See, for example, S. Ponte, *The Coffee Crisis,* Issue Paper (Copenhagen: Center for Development Research, 2002); and C. Gresser and S. Tickell, *Mugged: Poverty in Your Coffee Cup* (London: Oxfam, 2002). Hence, using the first definition, the study period

overlaps with the last three years of the coffee crisis. Using the second definition, it covers a 10-year period in the middle of the crisis. In both cases, however, the study period misses the trough in prices that occurred in 2001.

7. PROCAFE (Fundación Salvadoreña para Investigaciones del Café), *Boletín Estadístico de la Caficultura Salvadoreña,* (San Salvador, El Salvador: PROCAFE, 1998); Varangis, Siegel, Giovannucci, and Lewin, note 2; and World Bank, *El Salvador: Coffee Price Risk Management, Phase 2 Report* (Washington, DC, 2001).

8. PROCAFE, ibid.

9. Global Environmental Facility (GEF), *El Salvador: Promotion of Biodiversity Conservation Within Coffee Landscapes,* (Washington, DC: GEF, 1998).

10. O. Gómez, extension agent, PROCAFE, in discussion with the authors, San Salvador, 24–25 October 2005.

11. PROCAFE, note 7.

12. World Bank, note 7.

13. M. Batz, H. Albers, B. Ávalos-Sartorio, and A. Blackman, *Shade-Grown Coffee: Simulation and Policy Analysis for Coastal Oaxaca, Mexico,* RFF Discussion Paper 05–61 (Washington, DC, 2005), http://www.rff.org.

14. PROCAFE, note 7.

15. World Bank, note 7.

16. PROCAFE, note 7.

17. Three of the five cooperatives interviewed reported that they were heavily in debt and that all of their profits are allocated to servicing their loans, leaving no funds for investment. For example, managers of a small (85 hectare) reform cooperative in the west region stated that they pay $64,000 per year to service their debt and that their creditor has threatened to foreclose unless they are able to repay the outstanding principal. Similarly, a large (945 hectare) reform cooperative in the west region reported that they owe $1.8 million and pay $225,000 each year to service the debt.

18. N. Cuéllar, I. Gómez, S. Kandel, and H. Rosa, *Rural Poverty and the Environment in El Salvador: Lessons for Sustainable Livelihoods* (San Salvador: Programa Salvadoreña de Investigación Sobre Desarollo y Medio Ambiente (PRISMA), 2002).

19. J. Rodríguez-Meza, D. Southgate, and C. González-Vega, "Rural Poverty, Households' Responses to Shocks, and Agricultural Land Use: Panel Results for El Salvador," *Environment and Development Economics* 9, no. 2 (2004): 225–239; A. Blackman, H. J. Albers, B. Ávalos, and L. Crooks Murphy, *Land Cover in a Managed Forest Ecosystem: Mexican Shade Coffee,* RFF Discussion Paper 07–30 (Washington, DC, 2007), http://www.rff.org.

20. M. Cerrutti and R. Bertoncello, *Urbanization and Internal Migration Patterns in Latin America* (Buenos Aires: Centro de Estudios de Población, 2003).

21. Cerrutti and Bertoncello, ibid.

22. World Bank, *El Salvador Rural Development Study, Main Report, Volume I,* Report No. 16253-ES (Washington, DC, 1997).

23. World Bank, ibid.

24. World Bank, note 22.

25. Cuéllar, Gómez, Kandel, and Rosa, note 18.

26. Cuéllar, Gómez, Kandel, and Rosa, note 18.

27. Cuéllar, Gómez, Kandel, and Rosa, note 18.

28. K. Andrade-Eckhoff, "Intercambios Transnacionales a Través de las Migración en Centroamérica: Dimámicas, Impactos y Potencial (Transnational Migration and Exchange in Central America: Origins, Impacts, and Potential)," PowerPoint presentation, (San Salvador: Facultad LatinoAmericana de Ciencias Sociales, 2003).

29. Cuéllar, Gómez, Kandel, and Rosa, note 18.

30. Gómez, note 10; S. Nuenninghoff, sectoral specialist, IADB, in discussion with authors, San Salvador, 25 October 2005; L. A. Celis, co-country director, Proyector Fortalecimiento de la Gestión Ambiental en El Salvador (the Strengthening of Environmental Management in El Salvador Project), in discussion with authors, San Salvador, 28 October 2005; F. Barillas, President, Unión de Cooperativas de Cafetaleros de El Salvador (Union of El Salvador Coffee Farmer Cooperatives), in discussion with authors, San Salvador, 31 October 2005.

31. A key environmental regulatory gap in El Salvador is a system of comprehensive land use planning. Although a law has been drafted, it has yet to be passed. During the 1990s, no such law existed. As a result, there was a great deal of confusion about which regulatory authority—local mayors' offices or national ministries—had jurisdiction over permitting in land use planning. Celis, note 30.

32. Celis, note 30; Gómez, note 10; and J. A. Olano, director, Dirección General de Ordenamiento Forestal, Ministerio de Agricultura y Ganadería (Ministry of Agriculture and Livestock) in discussion with the authors 3 November 2005.

33. Celis, note 31; and Olano, ibid.

34. A recent study that also used satellite data concluded that in the country as a whole, including both shade coffee areas and non-shade coffee areas, "woody cover" actually increased during the 1990s, albeit from a relatively low level. See S. B. Hecht, S. Kandel, I. Gomes, N. Cuéllar, and H. Rosa "Globalization, Forest Resurgence, and Environmental Politics in El Salvador," *World Development* 34 no. 2 (2006): 308–323. If robust, this trend is encouraging. Nevertheless, tree cover in shade coffee areas still provides important ecological services and its loss is likely to have significant adverse local impacts.

Slaking a Thirst for Justic

A generation later, in both Argentina and Chile, are dealing with the perpetrators of past atrociti

BUENOS AIRES AND SANTIAGO

GLOBAL STUDIES

asphyxiating him with a plastic into his veins. His body, weigh then thrown into the sea fr however painful, has bro

Trials and in Argen

In Argentina 30,000) "d torship collal
Th

For the past 31 years, Viviana Díaz, a small, gentle woman now in her 50s, has devoted her life to finding out what happened to her father, Victor Díaz López, a former leader of Chile's Communist Party. Following the bloody coup against Salvador Allende's left-wing government in 1973, he became one of the military regime's most wanted men. After nearly three years in hiding, he was finally picked up by the DINA, the secret police of Chile's dictator, General Augusto Pinochet. His family never saw him again.

He was one of the many thousands who perished under the dictatorships that ruled many parts of Latin America in the final phase of the cold war in the 1970s and 1980s. A quarter of a century after the last successful military coup in Latin America, the region has moved on, with democracy for the most part firmly established. But in many countries, the past still poses some searching questions. Peace or justice? Retribution or reconciliation? Find the truth, however painful, or prefer the ease of forgetting?

Many argue for moving on rather than re-opening old wounds. Others reply that without justice there can be no healing and no guarantee of the rule of law. No group feels this more keenly than the relatives of the "disappeared"—those kidnapped by the state and taken to secret detention centres. Their tortured bodies, dumped in the sea or buried in unmarked graves, were rarely if ever found until well after the dictators departed. Unidentified remains are still turning up.

In most countries in the region where abuses occurred under authoritarian rule—Guatemala (where 200,000 died in a civil war between military dictatorships and left-wing guerrillas), Brazil, Mexico and Uruguay—the process of dealing with the crimes of the past has barely begun. To a lesser extent, that applies to El Salvador too. . . .

The process has gone furthest in Argentina and, especially, Chile. That marks a change. In Chile, some 3,000 people were killed or "disappeared" at the hands of Pinochet's regime. But the dictatorship's amnesty for its own crimes outlived it. Only recently have most families learned the fate of their loved ones.

Take Mr. Díaz's case. His family learnt of his arrest through an anonymous phone call. Then silence. After four months of

searching, Ms. Díaz and her mother, a washerwoman, met a woman recently released from Villa Grimaldi, a secret detention centre. She had a message for them from Marta Ugarte, another of the many communist leaders interned there. Ugarte's wrists had broken after she was strung up from the ceiling and her breasts were burned with a blow-lamp. She wanted them to know that neither she nor Mr. Díaz would ever get out alive.

For years, Ms. Díaz staged demonstrations, petitioned the pusillanimous courts and badgered officials. But she was met only with death threats, repeated arrest and continuing silence. When democracy returned to Chile in 1990, the government set up an independent inquiry into the "disappeared." Even then, the perpetrators could not be brought to justice. It was not until Pinochet's arrest in London in 1998 in response to an extradition request from Spain, and the British House of Lords' rulings that he lacked immunity under international law, that Chile's judges began to grow much bolder.

In a series of landmark rulings, Chile's Supreme Court removed most of the obstacles to trying the dictatorship's crimes. In 1999 it declared "disappearances" to be a continuing crime until death is proved. That meant they were not covered by the 1978 amnesty. In December 2006 it ruled that because Chile was in a situation of internal conflict after the 1973 coup, the Geneva Conventions applied. Serious violations of those conventions were war crimes and crimes against humanity, for which a statute of limitations could never be invoked, it said. Nor could they be subject to amnesty, it ruled last month.

According to Chile's Interior Ministry, 148 people, including nearly 50 military officers, have already been convicted for human-rights violations during the 17-year dictatorship. Over 400 more, nearly all from the armed forces, have been indicted or are under investigation. Pinochet was himself facing trial on several charges, including murder, torture, and tax evasion, when he died in December at the age of 91.

It was as a result of one of these investigations that Ms. Díaz finally learnt of her father's fate. Last month a man known (because of his size) as "the Elephant," who led the Lautaro brigade, a previously unknown elite unit of the DINA, tearfully confessed to murdering Victor Díaz at a barracks in Santiago in 1977 by

217

...ag, while cyanide was injected
...ed down by a railway sleeper, was
...m a military helicopter. The truth,
...ght her peace, says Ms. Díaz.

...Tribulations
...ina

..., at least 13,000 people (and perhaps as many as
...sappeared" or were killed during the military dicta-
...f 1976–83. Unlike Chile's, Argentina's military regime
...sed in confusion, following defeat in the Falklands war.
...first act of the democratic government of Raúl Alfonsín in
...983 was to annul the amnesty rushed through by the junta just
before it fell. A truth commission—the world's first—provided
the material for investigations by prosecutors, one of whom
was Luis Moreno Ocampo, now chief prosecutor of the International Criminal Court in The Hague. Nearly 500 people, including nine members of the four successive juntas, were charged.
Argentina thus became the first country to put its own military
rulers on trial. The army argued that it had been forced to act by
large-scale guerrilla violence. As in Chile, Argentina's military
government had at first enjoyed considerable civilian support.

Repeated barracks rebellions in protest against the prosecutions forced Mr. Alfonsín to buckle. He approved a "full-stop"
law halting new investigations, followed by another of "due
obedience" which exonerated those who claimed to have been
following orders—a defence dismissed in the Nuremberg trials after the second world war. His successor, Carlos Menem,
issued pardons to 277 of those already convicted or indicted,
including nearly 40 generals and several guerrilla leaders.

Argentines still argue about these pragmatic decisions. Public opinion was certainly against them, and the thirst for justice
was huge. One crime was not covered by the various amnesties
and pardons—that of taking away the babies of mothers who
gave birth in captivity, and giving them to couples in the security forces to bring up as their own. The real mothers were then
killed or "disappeared." According to the "Grandmothers of the
Plaza de Mayo," who from 1977 demonstrated on the square of
that name in Buenos Aires, some 500 babies were stolen in this
way, only 87 of whom have so far been traced.

Pinochet's London arrest emboldened judges in Argentina
too. Soon afterwards, General Jorge Videla, the junta president
of 1976–81, was put on trial on charges of appropriating babies.
For this, General Videla was sentenced to eight years imprisonment. He had already received a life sentence in 1985. His subsequent pardon was quashed by a judge last September on the
ground that he was guilty of crimes against humanity and could
never be pardoned. Because he is aged over 70, General Videla
is now under house arrest.

In 2005 Argentina's Supreme Court annulled the "full-stop"
and "due obedience" laws as being unconstitutional. That has
paved the way for the prosecution of other junta crimes. Of
the 772 people, nearly all in the military or secret police, now
facing charges or investigations, 260 are in pretrial detention
(including 71 under house arrest), 46 are on bail, 41 are on the
run, and 109 are dead, according to the Centre for Legal and
Social Studies, a human-rights group. Five people have so far
been convicted, including two on "disappearance" charges. The
government expects another half-dozen trials to take place this
year. Years of further trials lie ahead.

These prosecutions are backed both by the current Peronist
president, Néstor Kirchner, whose government includes several former followers of the Montonero guerrillas, and by
public opinion. Unlike armies in many other Latin American
countries, the army in Argentina is no longer much respected.
In opinion polls, 70% of respondents approved of the court's
annulment of the amnesty laws. No new prosecutions are being
brought against former guerrillas. The government argues, with
questionable logic, that they were not guilty of crimes against
humanity and are thus subject to the statute of limitations.

But prosecuting Isabel Perón, the third wife of Juan Perón,
the country's revered populist leader, is a step too far for many
Argentines. On Perón's death in 1975, Isabel, a former caba-
ret dancer, succeeded him. Amid growing economic chaos and
violence between the guerrillas and right-wing death-squads,
she signed decrees in 1975 authorising the eradication of all
"subversive elements." Some say that the Argentine Anti-
communist Alliance (known as the "Triple A"), a government-
backed death-squad, was responsible for at least 1,500 killings
during her 20-month presidency.

Since her release from prison by the Argentine junta in 1981,
Mrs. Perón has lived in Spain. She claims ignorance of abuses
during her rule. But in January she was arrested in Madrid at
the request of an Argentine judge investigating the "disappearance" of a Peronist militant in February 1976. Four days later,
a second warrant for her arrest was issued by another judge on
charges relating to the "Triple A" killings. Aged 75 and said by
her lawyers to be suffering from manic depression, Mrs. Perón
has been released on bail while awaiting the outcome of extradition proceedings. Few expect them to succeed.

As the experiences of Chile and Argentina show, each country has to find its own way of dealing with past atrocities in
accordance with its own particular circumstances and history.
Sometimes, it may take a whole generation for society to be
ready to learn the truth, as in Germany after the second world
war. At other times, an amnesty, which may later be unpicked
or annulled, may help to secure peace.

The rise of international human-rights law has helped those
who argue that in cases involving the worst crimes justice must
never be sacrificed to peace. Where conflict continues that
principle may be hard to apply. Its proponents say justice is
essential not just as an end in itself but to deter future tyrants.
Until recently, most could expect to get off scot-free. Increasingly, other countries may follow the road pioneered by Chile
and Argentina.

The Return of Populism

A much-touted move to the left masks something more co the rebirth of an influential Latin American political tradition.

GLOBAL STUDIES

The populist leade
following. They le
organised partie
bears Perón'
revolution'
Ms. B
or

Latin America, it is widely asserted, is moving to the left. The recent election victories of Evo Morales in Bolivia, of Chile's Michelle Bachelet, and of Ollanta Humala in the first round of Peru's presidential ballot . . . are seen as forming part of a seamless web of leftism which also envelops Hugo Chávez in Venezuela, Brazil's Luiz Inácio Lula da Silva, Argentina's Néstor Kirchner and Andrés Manuel López Obrador, the front-runner in Mexico's presidential election. But this glib formula lumps together some strange bedfellows and fails to capture what is really changing in Latin America.

Some of the region's new or newish presidents are of the moderate, social-democratic left. They include Lula, Ms. Bachelet in Chile, Óscar Arias in Costa Rica, and Tabaré Vázquez in Uruguay. Broadly speaking, they stand for prudent macroeconomic policies and the retention of the liberalising reforms of the 1990s, but combined with better social policies.

Mr. Chávez, Mr. Kirchner, Mr. López Obrador and, in Peru, both Mr. Humala and his likely rival in a run-off ballot, Alan García, belong in a second category. Albeit in different ways and to different degrees, all correspond to the Latin American tradition of populism. So, in some respects, does Mr. Morales in Bolivia. He is often portrayed as an indigenous leader. Yet as a young man he left his Andean-Indian village for the coca-growing region of the Chapare. His politics are those of a *mestizo* (mixed-race) trade-union leader.

"Populism" is a slippery, elusive concept. But it is central to understanding what is happening in the region. One of its many difficulties is that it is often used as a term of abuse. In many parts of the world, "populist" is loosely used to describe a politician who seeks popularity through means disparaged as appealing to the baser instincts of voters.

But populism does have a more precise set of meanings—though these vary from place to place. In nineteenth-century Russia, populists were middle-class intellectuals who embraced peasant communalism as an antidote to Western liberalism. In France, politicians from Pierre Poujade in the 1950s to Jean-Marie Le Pen have championed the "little man," especially farmers and small shopkeepers, against big corporations, unions, and foreigners.

In the United States, too, populism had rural roots, in the prairies of the Midwest. In the 1890s, the People's Party campaigned against what it saw as the grip of urban cartels over the economy. This cause reached its zenith in the 1896 presidential election, when the populists backed the campaign of William Jennings Bryan, a Democratic crusader against the gold standard.

Huey Long, the governor of Louisiana in 1928–32, was another populist. He campaigned against Standard Oil and other big companies, ramped up taxes and state social spending, and was accused of dictatorial tendencies for building a ruthless political machine.

But it is in Latin America where populism has had the greatest and most enduring influence. As in Russia and the United States, it began as an attempt to ameliorate the social dislocations caused by capitalism. In Latin America it became an urban movement. Its heyday was from the 1920s to the 1960s, as industrialisation and the growth of cities got under way in the region. It was the means by which the urban masses—the middle and working classes—were brought into the political system.

In Europe, that job was done by social-democratic parties. In Latin America, where trade unions were weaker, it was accomplished by the classic populist leaders. They included Getulio Vargas, who ruled Brazil in various guises in 1930–45 and 1950–54; Juan Perón in Argentina . . . and his second wife, Eva Duarte; and Victor Paz Estenssoro, the leader of Bolivia's national revolution of 1952. They differed from socialists or conservatives in forging multi-class alliances.

Give Me a Balcony

Typically, their leadership was charismatic. They were great orators or, if you prefer, demagogues ("Give me a balcony and I will become president," said José Maria Velasco, Ecuador's most prominent populist, who was five times elected president and four times overthrown by the army). Like Huey Long, Vargas and Perón used the new instrument of radio to reach the masses. Mr. Chávez's "Bolivarian revolution" relies heavily on his skills as a communicator, exercised every Sunday in his four-hour television programme.

Some of the populists, such as Victor Raúl Haya de la Torre, the founder of Peru's APRA party, and William Jennings Bryan, relied on religious imagery or techniques. ("You shall not crucify mankind on a cross of gold," Bryan preached.) A recent biography of Mr. Chávez remarks on his similarity to a televangelist.

s sought a direct bond with their mass d personal movements rather than well-... . Argentina's dominant political organisation ... name. Take Mr. Chávez out of the "Bolivarian ... and there would be nothing left. Contrast that with ...chelet, who presides over a stable four-party coalition, ...ula, whose Workers' Party has up to 800,000 dues-paying members.

The populists saw elections as the route to power, and pushed successfully to expand the franchise. But they also relied on mass mobilisation—on getting their followers out into the streets. They were often less than democratic in their exercise of power: they blurred the distinction between leader, party, government, and state. Perón, for example, packed the judiciary, put his own people in charge of trade unions, and rigged his re-election in 1950. Mr. Chávez used a constituent assembly to gain control of all the institutions of state. Both Mr. Morales and Mr. Humala have promised similar assemblies.

Not coincidentally, many of the populists have been military officers. That goes for Vargas, Perón, and Lázaro Cardenas, Mexico's president from 1934 to 1940, who nationalised foreign oil companies and handed land to peasants. Mr. Chávez and Mr. Humala are retired lieutenant-colonels. Part of their appeal is that of the military *caudillo,* or strongman, who promises to deliver justice for the "people" by firm measures against the "exploiters." Some scholars distinguish between military populists and civilians such as Haya de la Torre and Paz Estenssoro, whom they see as "national revolutionaries" closer to social democracy.

But there are many common threads. One is nationalism. The populists championed national culture against foreign influences. They harked back to forgotten figures from their country's past. In many respects, they were nation-builders.

While their preaching was often anti-capitalist, they made deals with some capitalists. They rallied their followers against two rhetorical enemies: the "oligarchy" of rural landlords and foreign "imperialists." They supported industry and a bigger role for the state in the economy, and they granted social benefits to workers. They often paid for this by printing money.

Though populists were not alone in favouring inflationary finance, they were particularly identified with it. Some commentary on populism has emphasised this aspect. In their book "The Macroeconomics of Populism," Rudiger Dornbusch and Sebastian Edwards characterise "economic populism" as involving a dash for growth and income redistribution while ignoring inflation, deficit finance, and other risks.

Such policies were pursued not just by populists of the past, but by Mr. García, Peru's president in 1985–90. In a milder form, they are being followed by Mr. Kirchner, Argentina's Peronist president. Mr. Chávez has been rescued from deficit financing only by Venezuela's oil windfall.

Populist economics was adopted, too, by Salvador Allende, Chile's Socialist president of 1970–73, and Nicaragua's Sandinistas. That has led many observers to use "populist" and "leftist" interchangeably—a mistake that led foreign investors to lose money when they panicked unduly when Lula won Brazil's election in 2002.

More Mussolini than Marx

In fact, there is nothing inherently left-wing about populism. Some populist leaders were closer to fascism: Perón lived as an exile in Franco's Spain for 18 years. Many favoured corporatism—the organisation of society by functional groups, rather than the individual rights and pluralism of liberal democracy.

Other writers have seen populism as a technique of political leadership more than an ideology. They have applied the term to such free-market conservatives as Peru's Alberto Fujimori and Argentina's Carlos Menem who, in different ways, sidestepped interest-groups and made direct appeals to the masses. It is not clear whether Mr. Humala, if elected in a run-off, would fall into this category—or try to mimic Mr. Chávez.

Populism is full of contradictions. It is above all anti-elitist, but creates new elites. It claims to favour ordinary people against oligarchs. But as Messrs. Dornbusch and Edwards pointed out, "at the end of every populist experiment real wages are lower than they were at the beginning." Populism brought mass politics to Latin America, but its relationship to democracy is ambivalent. Populists crusade against corruption, but often engender more.

In the 1960s, populism seemed to fade away in Latin America, squeezed by Marxism, Christian democracy, and military dictatorship. Its current revival shows that it is deeply rooted in the region's political culture. But it also involves some new elements. The new crop of populist leaders rely partly on the politics of ethnic identity: Mr. Chávez and Mr. Humala are both *mestizos*. Their coalitions are based on the poor, both urban and rural, and those labouring in the informal economy. They champion those discomfited by globalisation rather than industrialisation.

One big reason for populism's persistence is the extreme inequality in the region. That reduces the appeal of incremental reform and increases that of messianic leaders who promise a new world. Yet populism has done little to reduce income inequality.

A second driver of populism has been Latin America's wealth of natural resources. Many Latin Americans believe that their countries are rich, whereas in truth they are not. Populists blame poverty on corruption, on a grasping oligarchy or, nowadays, on multinational oil or mining companies. That often plays well at the ballot box. But it is a misdiagnosis. Countries develop through a mixture of the right policies and the right institutions. Whatever their past achievements, the populists are leading Latin America down a blind alley.

Venezuelan Women's Organizing

SARA YASSKY

I stand in an ocean of women, an ocean that I am accustomed to swimming in these days. Women from all over Venezuela have gathered in Caracas, proudly wearing red, the color of revolution. They join in solidarity to protest a ruling that has annulled a law designed to protect women and the family against violence. Maria León, president of the government-supported women's organization, Inamujer (National Institute of Women), offers hope to the other compañeras: "We will win because we have it in our hearts. We will have justice."

In 1999 the people and the Chávez government collaborated in writing a new constitution for the Bolivarian Republic of Venezuela. Venezuela became the first country in Latin America and the Caribbean to include a gender perspective within its constitution. Little pocket-sized constitutions and booklets of laws are sold on every corner and the majority of women I know proudly carry a copy. The people strongly believe in these rights, such as the constitution's Article 88, the Equal Opportunity Law for Women, and the Law Against Violence Towards Women and the Family. Influential governmental women's organizations, such as Inamujer and Banmujer, play an important role in women's liberation work, helping to ensure the implementation of laws and programs supporting women through groups like Madres del Barrio (Mother's of the Neighborhood).

These, among other laws and services, are great achievements in the struggle for women's rights. But when government laws and protections serve as the source for organizing among women, does this take away their assertiveness to claim/take our own power that we, as women, rightfully deserve? As a woman, I have had little faith in the laws of my country or in a constitution written by "white men" in the 1700s, which continues to be interpreted by new generations of white men. The system of government that I know is historically rooted in hierarchical/patriarchal structures. These penetrate every aspect of our lives, be it social, political, or economic.

"Women are always the ones who have to pay. This is how machismo works, but it will not always be like this. We need to work for our own respect. We have laws that protect us, people need to respect the laws and respect us," Lezly Belkys Lopez explains to me during a women's protest.

The law, passed in 1998, was written and implemented by Inamujer, which officially holds the main responsibility of "supervising and evaluating policies related to the condition and situation of women." The annulled articles prohibited the perpetrator/violator from visiting the home or workplace of the survivor. Inamujer mobilized their locally organized groups of women throughout Venezuela (Puntos de Encuentro) to protest these annulments, which were decided by five male Supreme Court judges in May 2006 and cannot be lawfully reviewed. Therefore, within the blink of an eye, the law has changed, leaving women vulnerable. This example shows us that although Inamujer and other groups fought incredibly hard to write and pass this important law, five men holding an immense amount of power were capable of completely destabilizing populations of women at risk. Here, I would suggest that the reliance on "protective laws" is not enough.

Thankfully, Venezuela has more to offer than just "protective laws." The government encourages people to create changes from the base. Banmujer, founded on International Women's Day 2001, supplies micro-credit loans to cooperatives consisting of 5–20 women to start their own business. Each woman receives 2,000,000 Bolivares ($930) with a 12 percent interest rate (6 percent if agriculturally related) to be repaid within 3 years. These services have reached approximately 50,000 women each year, supporting the economic independence of poverty stricken women throughout Venezuela. Not only is this institution helping to decrease the feminization of poverty, it is also supplying valuable empowerment skills to its users while fostering the idea of a popular economy. The users have also formed local support networks (Red Usuarias de Banmujer) to organize within the community and patronize one another's businesses. Women in Venezuela are being offered opportunities that no government in their past has given them before.

Equally impressive and empowering is Article 88 of the Constitution, which "recognizes work in the home as an economic activity that creates added value and produces social welfare and wealth." The article also states that women working at home are entitled to social security. Article 88 is not only the result of women's hard work, but also the work of women fighting for this recognition all over the world. The words alone are strong, but little had been done to implement this article until March of this year when the government initiated the Madres Del Barrio Mission. Created by the work ministry, Madres del Barrio began a 6-month trial period in which almost 200,000 women in "extreme poverty" received between 279,000–372,000 Bolivares ($120–$173) a month to help eradicate poverty.

When women apply for this assistance, they are subjected to a series of evaluations and interviews to determine the level of need among the applicants. Carolina Vecatequi, a regional Caracas coordinator for the mission explains: "The financial support is not the main benefit. But, with this support, women will be able to enroll and integrate into other missions. They will receive education from Missions Robinson, Ribas, or Sucre, enroll in a Vuelvan Caras workshop [mission that trains people in specific employment skills who form work cooperatives] or be accredited a micro loan to start a collective business." At the end of six months, the monetary assistance is terminated with the expectation that women have integrated themselves in other social programs and services that will be able to provide some income. This support is helping women in the struggle for liberation and rights. However, there are aspects of this support that have left me with questions.

For example, at the opening lecture for Madres del Barrio, the creator, Ivan Espinoso (a man), gave a PowerPoint presentation to an auditorium full of women. After he finished, verbal fights broke out among different women's groups over who was going to receive the aid first. The answer: those in "extreme poverty." Then women began arguing over which communities were the poorest. Since the mission asks women to quantify their level of oppression, they are placed in competition with one another for aid. Furthermore, in this case, a man was instituting a program to help women gain empowerment skills, but the women were not included in the formation process.

Madres del Barrio is one example of the Venezuelan government's good intentions, but it is also an example of the lack of connection that the powers-that-be can have with the people they are trying to help. I feel the government programs and protections cannot serve as the catalyst for women's organizing. Empowerment does not come from laws and government programs.

The women of Venezuela are truly the backbone of this country. They are incredible organizers and are always looking after the wellbeing of others.

I have found much of the focus within groups of women to be primarily based on women's education of their rights and the laws, and/or fighting for the protection/realization of such laws. I do not devalue this work, as I believe it is important and necessary. But the repeal of protections by the Venezuelan Supreme Court have shown us that laws alone cannot protect us from the patriarchy within our cultures. The necessity for such protections points to problems deep within our cultures, cultures that breed violence, where inequality is "normal," where women must continuously struggle in order to be respected and safe. The spaces for such discussion exist here in Venezuela, but I have not seen these spaces being used to challenge the roots of our oppressive, cultural norms.

We need to create more self-sustaining changes from the base that do not force women into situations where we must constantly fight to protect and pass laws that grant us safety. Of course, we can benefit from protections and programs, but they are not solving the real problems. We must not accept uncritically programs and protections given or approved by a power-wielding institution. We must be the creators and the implementers of these changes ourselves. We know what changes need to be made, so we must claim our power, unite ourselves, and win back the right to name and create the world we want to live in. I know that if any women are up to this challenge, they are the courageous luchadoras of Venezuela.

SARA YASSKY has lived in Caracas, Venezuela for the past six months learning and working with various women's community groups. She is currently in Mexico continuing such work.

Liberating *Pachamama*
Corporate Greed, Bolivia, and Peasant Resistance

DAPHNE EVIATAR

I n a rundown, dirt-stained building in El Alto, Bolivia, five young men sit behind a rickety linoleum-topped table on an auditorium stage. A rainbow banner—known locally as the *Wiphala,* a flag representing half a millennium of indigenous resistance—hangs on the wall behind them. *En Constante Vigor* is painted crudely above it.

It's nearly 9:00 P.M. on a chilly night in early December. The neighborhood meeting hall has filled with mostly men, small and dark, hunched over in dusty plastic garden chairs, the collars on their thin jackets pulled up around their necks to protect against the cold. Like most buildings in this fast-growing city high in the Andes, the hastily constructed brick and adobe structure has no modern plumbing or insulation. After a long day of manual labor at an altitude of thirteen thousand feet, the men are tired. Some doze in their chairs; others stay awake by chewing bitter green coca leaves.

Abraham Delgado Mancilla, a wiry twenty-eight-year-old in black jeans and glasses, stands onstage. He's called this meeting to present a new book he's written with his *compañeros,* as he calls them. The cover of the bright red paperback features two menacing-looking men in ski masks holding rifles. *"De las elecciones a la insurrection . . . Carajo!!"* ("From elections to insurrection—We Swear!") is printed in black letters above them. Although the text is mostly a summary of the policy positions of the eight candidates running for president in Bolivia's December elections, Mancilla is explaining why he believes that even the leading leftist candidate, Evo Morales, an Aymara Indian like himself, will not solve Bolivia's problems.

"MAS [Morales's party, the Movement Toward Socialism] isn't really going to change anything," he tells the audience, which grows as more and more men, and a few women, trickle in. "They want to work within the system. But this capitalist system, run by the *transnacionales,* has done nothing for us. What we need is a new system of our own," he continues, as murmurs of approval ripple around the room. "We need to pursue our own ideas"—and the reaction grows louder—"What we need is a revolution!" The audience bursts into applause.

A wizened old man stands up to concur. "Evo is part of the same capitalist system," he says, looking around the room like a father providing guidance to his sons. "But what kind of a revolution do we want? We learned in the streets that we can defeat the transnationalist companies and the Latifundios. Evo Morales wants to respect the laws, but we need to take back this country from the transnationalists. Today, democracy is in serious danger. The only way to save democracy is to create our own ideological direction. They talk in this election about progress, but what about liberty? We will continue to be slaves under this system. We need to create something new," he says, and younger men in the audience stand to echo his views.

This is my first visit to El Alto, and my head is spinning. Aside from the disorienting altitude, I'm trying to keep up with the mixture of Spanish and Aymara and to follow the succession of men who stand to cheer on the coming insurrection. The statements in this dingy auditorium reflect a growing sentiment across South America, where anger at the unfulfilled promises of the "Washington Consensus"—the neoliberal economic model imposed on much of the continent in the late 1980s and 1990s—has led to a succession of left-leaning governments, from Hugo Chávez in Venezuela to Luiz Ignácio Lula da Silva ("Lula") in Brazil, Néstor Kirchner in Argentina, and, most recently, Evo Morales in Bolivia. But for all the fanfare over Morales's election and an apparent shift to the radical left, the growing popular desire for radical change in Latin America may well be crushed before it gets off the ground. For a country like Bolivia—the poster child for privatization schemes fostered by the International Monetary Fund and the World Bank in the 1980s and 1990s—is now so entangled in the international economic system, whose rules protect private corporate investments, that the democratically expressed will of the nation may well be irrelevant. Not only is foreign aid from the United States contingent on maintaining that neoliberal economic system, but now private investors can essentially dictate Bolivian domestic law as well. Foreign corporations that invested in Bolivia under former regimes can use international law to preserve the status quo. In the process, they're stifling local ideas about how the country's natural resources could support more sustainable and politically palatable development. This investment-protective regime may actually undermine the interests of those same investors it aims to protect, for as it denies a democratic society the power to determine its own fate, it risks fueling the most radical elements of an already restive population. That could lead this notoriously unstable nation—already the record-holder for coups d'état—toward an even more volatile future.

In the verdant highlands of Cochabamba, *campesinos* eke out a living growing bananas, beans, and potatoes that they sell for pennies at the local market. Morales campaigned there last fall, promising something better. "You, the people who grow our food, deserve more respect," he told the Quechua men and women who crowded into the town square. Standing in a brightly decorated gazebo, wreaths of flowers and produce around his neck, Morales promised to help them: "We will nationalize Bolivia's natural resources. We will recuperate what is ours. We cannot give away what was given to us by *Pachamama* [Mother Earth]."

One of *Pachamama*'s greatest gifts to Bolivia has turned out to be a huge reserve of natural gas. In recent years, due to exploration by private companies beginning in the mid-1990s, the estimated size of Bolivia's natural gas reserves has grown from five trillion to fifty-four trillion cubic feet, and this energy source has become the great hope for the country's future. Who will control it—the government or the widely reviled foreign corporations—became the overarching question in the December presidential election. In one pueblo after another, Morales promised to "re-take" Bolivia from the *transnacionalistas* and "recuperate" the country's riches. Every other candidate, from left to right, made similar appeals to Bolivians across the political spectrum, all of whom feel they've been cheated out of the benefits of the country's natural resources.

Words like "nationalization" and "recuperation" echoed in the international media last winter, alarming the U.S. government and foreign investors. But as many Bolivians already know, President Morales will have a tough time following up the campaign rhetoric with decisive action. Bolivia is now so entrenched in a global economic system that there's no turning back. Its rulers were convinced years ago by the IMF, World Bank, and American-educated economists to let foreign companies invest on extremely favorable terms. Even former government officials who helped craft the deals admitted, when I met with them, that these terms have not been fair to Bolivia. But the international legal system makes it extremely difficult for a new leader to change them.

Under a series of bilateral investment treaties signed by former Bolivian leaders, foreign companies can sue the country's central government if it changes its laws in a way that they claim undermines the value of their investments. Specifically, they're entitled to sue the national government if it passes a law that a company believes is discriminatory or amounts to an expropriation—direct or indirect—of their investments. And those suits would not be brought in an international court or other public, transparent forum. Instead, they would be adjudicated behind closed doors by panels of three private, international arbitrators chosen by the parties involved—often, corporate lawyers who in another situation might be representing one of the foreign corporations. Despite the public consequences of these cases, affected citizens have no right to participate, view the evidence, or attend the hearings. And

the suits can seek compensation not just for the money the corporations have already invested, but for projected profits that they might have earned, had the tide of public opinion not turned against them.

For Bolivia, this is no idle threat. When the Bolivian government under former president Carlos Mesa raised taxes on natural gas production, almost all the major foreign oil companies—ExxonMobil, Spain's Repsol, the French company Total, British Gas, and Oklahoma-based Vintage Petroleum—formally notified Bolivia of their plans to sue. (The treaties require companies to notify the government six months before filing a claim.) Eventually, they agreed to wait and see what the new government does. But if Morales "nationalizes" the industry, in whatever form, they'll certainly make good on those threats, through costly litigation or by using their legal claims as a bargaining chip in negotiating new contracts.

The weight of those chips is undeniable, given the approximately $3.5 billion that private companies have already invested in the natural gas industry and their expected profits, which could total tens of billions of dollars. For Bolivia, whose annual revenues are only a little more than $2 billion a year, that's no small risk. And it comes on top of the various ways that the IMF, World Bank, and Inter-American Development Bank—under the influence of the United States, which holds virtual veto power in each institution—can wield their power, denying Bolivia loans and effectively destroying its reputation in the international financial community.

These rules were designed to foster confidence among international investors and economic stability in developing countries. But in a place like Bolivia, where the public has just demonstrated overwhelming support for dramatic change (Morales was the first president to win more than 50 percent of the vote in Bolivia's 180-year history), the anti-democratic impact of these treaties could backfire. Since 2003, Bolivians have forced out two presidents due to growing frustration with the government's failure to improve conditions for ordinary Bolivians.

In October 2003, activists learned that President Gonzalo Sánchez de Lozada, a wealthy mining entrepreneur who had played a key role in privatizing the gas industry, was considering yet another deal with foreign companies to export Bolivian natural gas—this time via a pipeline through Chile, Bolivia's age-old enemy. Convinced they wouldn't see the benefit, they determined to stop the deal. At the urging of local leaders like Mancilla, tens of thousands of Bolivians went on strike and blocked the main arteries of El Alto and La Paz, cutting Bolivia's largest city off from critical supplies of food and gas. President de Lozada ordered the military to break the road blockades, and soldiers soon killed more than sixty protesters. Thousands more then thronged the streets in protest until, finally, de Lozada was forced to flee.

Expectations were high that his successor, Carlos Mesa, could mediate the conflict. But in the end, Mesa couldn't stem the mounting anger at an economic system seen as fundamentally indifferent to the needs of Bolivians. To his credit, he tried: he passed a law that raised taxes on gas production in Bolivia's larger fields. But the law was too convoluted and too compromising to please anyone. On the left, many were angry that it allowed foreign corporations continued ownership and control of Bolivian natural gas, which by then was yielding record profits. So in May, Bolivians once again took to the streets. After weeks of blocked roads, burning tires, rubber bullets, and tear gas, President Mesa resigned.

To an outsider, Bolivians' reaction to the inequities of globalization may sound extreme. But to many Bolivians, mass actions seem the only means of holding their leaders accountable. And after five hundred years of foreign and elite exploitation of Bolivian resources, most Bolivians feel their government has much to account for.

In many ways, the anger that brought down the last two presidents dates back to the arrival of the Spanish conquistadors, when Bolivia was part of the Inca Empire. By the mid-1500s the Spanish had become enamored of the region's riches, particularly Cerro Rico, Bolivia's "rich mountain" of silver. Over the next four centuries, that one mountain turned silver mine, high in the Andean city of Potosí, would provide the Spanish close to seventy thousand tons of silver—enough, it is said, to build a bridge to Madrid. But the cost was steep; countless slaves died in its caverns.

Harsh working conditions continued until independence in 1825 and beyond. Bolivia's workers repeatedly rebelled, leading to a stunning succession of insurrections—averaging one per year until military rule finally gave way to democracy in 1982. But by then, the generals' looting had left the country in economic turmoil: in 1985, inflation reached 25,000 percent. Desperate, the elected leadership, following the advice of American economist Jeffrey Sachs, adopted a mix of radical reforms later called "shock therapy," which included devaluing the currency, eliminating tariffs, slashing state spending, and selling off state-owned industries. That soon stabilized the currency, but it also left tens of thousands who had been on the government payroll unemployed, particularly in the newly privatized tin mining industry. Many of those miners migrated to the countryside to grow coca—one of the few lucrative crops—or to the city slums as laborers.

Bolivians might have been content to wait for incremental improvements had the country not discovered, in the mid-1990s, that it was sitting on a large supply of natural gas, an increasingly important energy source. But like the rest of Bolivia's industries, the state-owned hydrocarbons business was being sold off. Instead of owning, extracting, and selling this increasingly lucrative resource, the government was contracting with a slew of foreign companies to do it. Convinced—in no small part by the World Bank and the IMF—that attracting foreign investment was key to developing the industry, Bolivia passed a law in 1996 that made those companies the owners of the gas, which they could now book as reserves on their balance sheets, and gave them virtually complete control over its production and sale. What's more, the companies had to pay only 18 percent royalties on gas produced and no taxes at all on production. Finally, the law required Bolivian gas to be sold at international market prices—even as the companies were cutting deals with Bolivia's neighbors, like Argentina, to sell gas there for far less.

As is typical in the industry, the companies locked in those favorable terms through contracts that last thirty and forty years.

The architects of Bolivia's privatization insist that the new policy succeeded: it attracted private companies and billions of dollars in foreign investment. And over the next decade, Bolivia's estimated natural gas reserves multiplied more than tenfold. But as the price of oil and gas skyrocketed in the international market, and energy prices at home climbed accordingly, Bolivians have recognized the value of what their government so easily gave away. And they've become increasingly angry that the vast majority of Bolivians still aren't receiving the benefits. Despite widespread privatization and two decades of fealty to IMF and World Bank dictates, Bolivia remains the poorest country in South America. Average Bolivians are now poorer than their grandparents were fifty years ago.

Hence the rise of their new leftist president. An Aymara Indian and former leader of the coca growers' union, Morales also appeals to the many *campesinos* who've lost their livelihood in recent years from coca farming, as the United States imposed and funded a radical coca eradication campaign. Although known in the United States as the base for cocaine, coca leaves in Bolivia are widely used for tea and herbal medicines, or chewed to stave off hunger or stay awake, especially by workers in the high altitudes. Coca growers, or *cocaleros,* are an important part of Morales's political base—a fact that gravely worries the United States.

Morales has not only claimed that coca should be a legitimate product, but he's expanded that appeal to encompass the growing view among Bolivia's indigenous population, that all "natural resources"—whether coca, water, gas, or precious metals—are not mere commodities but part of the earth's sacred bounty. That view is based on longstanding traditional Quechua and Aymara beliefs about the sanctity of the earth. And it's placed a growing number of Bolivians at odds with the perspective of Northern investment institutions such as the World Bank or the IMF and with the many multinational corporations already entrenched in the country.

"We don't think we are the owners of these resources," Oscar Olivera, a leading activist in Cochabamba, told me when I met him last November. A diminutive, pensive man, Olivera came to international attention in 2000, when he led a series of protests in Bolivia's third-largest city against a subsidiary of Bechtel, Inc., that had purchased the local water system and dramatically raised water rates. Beginning in February, the protests grew violent as police fired rubber bullets and tear gas and protesters responded with Molotov cocktails. By April, thousands of *Cochabambinos,* from poor farmers to middle-class professionals, had barricaded the roads, shut down the city, and taken over the town square. The government soon declared martial law. By the time the "water war" was won, six protesters had been killed and dozens injured. But the Bolivian government agreed to cancel its contract with the private water company.

That battle has inspired similar protests in other developing countries against privatization of local water systems. And it stemmed, in large part, from the same cultural perspective on natural resources that fueled the more recent uprisings over natural gas in El Alto and La Paz.

"We are the beneficiaries of these resources," says Olivera, who is Quechua. "This term 'natural resources' is a capitalist term. The indigenous people don't use that term. What we get from *Pachamama* must exist in harmony with all living beings. It has to be about how the people here live, with their customs. We want more social control, more participation of the people, where everything is clear and government is accountable."

Olivera and others are now helping communities develop cooperative water and other service delivery systems based on this view. He and his fellow activists also recently won a striking post–water war victory. After Bechtel withdrew from Cochabamba, it sued the government of Bolivia under a U.S.-Bolivia bilateral investment treaty. Although the company had only operated in Bolivia for four months, it claimed $25 million in damages. Enraged, Cochabamba activists launched a worldwide campaign to embarrass Bechtel into backing down. In January, Bechtel's subsidiary agreed to withdraw its claim—only the second time a company has agreed to drop a case filed under a bilateral investment treaty following local pressure.

Activists may have a harder time getting the oil companies invested in Bolivia to do the same. The usual justification for the current laws is that foreign investment is critical to a country's growth, and without legal protection, multinational corporations won't invest. But the law has gone so far to protect those companies that, in effect, they now have more control over domestic policy than do elected governments. And there's little evidence that these Bilateral Investment Treaties (or BITs) are actually needed. The Canada-based Institute for International Sustainable Development in a recent report noted that "the agreements may be *negatively* correlated to investment flows." According to its study, "countries like Brazil and Nigeria have seen large investments despite shying away from such treaties, while many Central African or Central American nations have seen little investment despite having entered into rafts of BITs." Countries such as China and Cuba, meanwhile, have attracted significant investment from countries with which they don't have these treaties. Even the World Bank, in a 2003 report, concluded that "the relatively strong protections in BITs do not seem to have increased flows of investment to signatory developing countries." Still, under pressure from corporate investors and their lawyers, the number of BITs—only 385 at the end of the 1980s, and more than 2,200 today—continues to grow.

These laws pose the greatest challenge for developing countries like Bolivia that are struggling to establish democratic legitimacy and prove to their people that their elected leaders do indeed represent them. U.S. president George W. Bush likes to boast of "the great democratic movement" that in recent decades has spurred "the swiftest advance of freedom in the 2,500 year story of democracy," crediting the United States with providing the shining example. Yet, as the United States pushes these investor-protective treaties on some of the world's weakest nations,

we make it impossible for emerging democratic leaders to make good on their promises.

I was struck by the force of these clashing worldviews as I walked out of a two-hour meeting at the World Bank headquarters in downtown La Paz in December. The bank's experts had just explained to me why Bolivia ought to retain its current contracts with the foreign oil companies and create a tax scheme tying taxes and royalties to international market conditions.

To me, a New Yorker educated in neoclassical economics, their proposals sounded fairly reasonable, if a bit complex. But if the suggestions seemed well grounded as an economic matter, they underscored just how wide is the gulf between the bank's technocrats and the Bolivian people. For weeks I'd heard candidates, activists, farmers, and neighborhood leaders assert the importance of Bolivians' reclaiming ownership and control of their natural resources. Apparently none of those pleas, which dominated the presidential campaign, had penetrated the well-guarded walls of the World Bank.

The bankers shake their heads at local ignorance. But Bolivians know that their leaders followed World Bank and IMF advice for decades, and 65 percent of the population is still poor—40 percent extremely so, according to the bank's own standards. It's not surprising that Bolivians put more faith in cultural and communal traditions than in the economic orthodoxies of Northern financial institutions.

"The identity of people and of communities has become a very important issue in the country," says Pablo Mamani, a sociologist who specializes in indigenous social movements. "Before, to be called indigenous or Aymara was considered an insult. Now, it's a sign of strength and pride. From this have come political projects, local leadership, strategic actions, and concrete demands for people's lives—for things like water and electricity."

Abraham Mancilla, the fiery speaker at the local meeting and a law student at El Alto's public university, is one of the leaders Mamani is speaking of. To him, the fact that political mobilization draws on ancient communal practices is critical. "Within our organizations, we're still governing ourselves the way our ancestors did," he told me, as we made our way through the crowded streets of El Alto on a December afternoon. "That's why we're so united. Everyone feels obligated to participate in the blockades and the marches, because it's their community responsibility. It's an obligation that comes from inside. These are the same norms and values brought from the provinces and still practiced here in the city."

Their "revolution," Mancilla tells me, would bring those values into government. "We want to see the majority construct their own type of power," he says. "We don't want a capitalist system or a neoliberal system. We want a communitarian system, a system from our own ancestors." Veterans of the water war say the same about the cooperative water systems they're putting in place. A natural gas industry, Mancilla says, could be run cooperatively, like many of those water systems are now. As for how they'd get the necessary money, Mancilla assures me that the Chinese government has already sent representatives to talk to community leaders about investing.

A communally-run oil and gas industry might have its pitfalls and likely won't happen in Bolivia anytime soon. But an industry controlled by an accountable, democratic, and transparent government, which contracts on fair terms with private companies, is a goal the vast majority of Bolivians would support. If, as the international financial system would have it, foreign corporations are able to steer the domestic government, then Bolivians will be denied even that sort of responsible management of their country's most prized natural resource. And it's that sort of constraint on democracy that may bring far more radical responses in Bolivia—and far sooner than those foreign investors might think.

DAPHNE EVIATAR, a Brooklyn-based writer and lawyer, was a 2005 Alicia Patterson Foundation fellow.

Latin America's New Petro-Politics

NADIA MARTINEZ

I n his 2006 State of the Union address, President Bush famously stated that "America is addicted to oil." He soon followed that proclamation with an announcement that his solution to the addiction is to diversify U.S. sources of oil—not to diversify away from oil with clean, renewable sources of energy.

That is sure to mean increased U.S. political attention to Latin America. Oil multinationals are already looking to intensify drilling operations in Latin America, because that's where the oil is. The U.S. government and oil and gas companies are likely to pressure Latin American countries like Mexico, Venezuela, Colombia and Ecuador—already major suppliers of oil to U.S. markets—to ramp up production and to exploit new oil and gas fields. And Big Oil is likely to propose new exploration and development projects in Costa Rica, Nicaragua, Panama, Bolivia, and Peru as the industry struggles to maintain a steady flow of energy resources to the North.

But the political landscape is rapidly evolving in Latin America, with traditional docility to U.S. economic and political demands giving way. As Latin American citizens express their discontent with conservative economic policies by electing more left-leaning leaders, countries are increasingly turning away from multinational energy companies and shifting their energy policies inward, nationally and regionally.

That approach is not likely to sit well with policymakers in Washington, or industry executives in Houston.

The Failure of Corporatization

Although Venezuelan President Hugo Chávez has become the Bush administration's least favorite pundit, he is one of several new leaders in Latin America who are vowing to run their countries differently than their predecessors, and becoming very popular because of it. Behind Chávez's blunt style and provocative speeches, such as the one at the United Nations when he referred to President Bush as the devil, is a discourse that is resonating with voters from Mexico to Argentina. Particularly, the poorest Latin Americans see, in leaders like Chávez, a sign of hope for improving their deteriorating conditions.

In the early 1990s, under the influence of the International Monetary Fund (IMF) and the World Bank, Latin American countries embarked on a series of free-market economic reforms. Central to the economic reform package was the privatization of a range of formerly state-owned industries, from phone companies to electric utilities to oil and gas companies.

The "Washington Consensus" policies of privatization, deregulation, reduced labor rights, opening to foreign trade and investment, and orienting economies to exports were a failure for Latin America's people. The Washington, D.C.-based Center for Economic Policy Research's "The Scorecard on Development" found that for low- and middle-income countries in the region, the last 25 years have seen sharply reduced economic growth as well as setbacks in health and education, when compared with the two decades before 1980.

But the Washington Consensus policies did benefit a narrow elite and foreign investors. Multinational companies, especially those in major industries like oil and gas, were able to acquire privatized government-owned enterprises on the cheap and secure outrageous profits.

Latin American energy markets really opened to multinationals with the privatization of Argentina's national oil company, Yacimientos Petroliferos Fiscales (YPF), in 1993. Similarly, in 1995, Venezuela began opening up parts of its petroleum sector to foreign investment, including the Orinoco Belt's heavy-oil deposits—the world's largest petroleum reserve. Brazil swiftly liberalized its oil industry through a constitutional amendment—the Brazilian constitution had prohibited foreign involvement in oil and gas—and in 1998 began offering several lease agreements to private oil companies to tap into Brazil's offshore oil reserves.

The case of Bolivia illustrates how large corporations, often foreign companies, reaped huge benefits from privatization at the expense of Latin American governments and people. Bolivia has the second largest gas reserves in South America, after Venezuela. The Bolivian Constitution declares that all hydrocarbons are property of the state, but in the mid-1990s, the IMF demanded the government permit the sale of oil and gas concessions to foreign companies. Bolivia complied. All of the country's gas transportation networks were sold to a consortium owned by Royal Dutch Shell and the now-defunct Enron. Other corporate winners included BP-Amoco, British Gas, Australia's BHP, Spain's Repsol and Petrobras, the Brazilian state-owned oil company. The deal allowed foreign corporations in the oil and gas business, gave them a majority share in previously state-owned companies and, at the same time, lowered the government's share of profits from the operation to a mere 18 percent, a steep drop from the previous 50 percent.

In October 2003, then-President Gonzalo Sanchez de Lozada fled the country amidst massive popular protests. Already disenchanted by his earlier privatization policies, Bolivians rose up to block yet another gas export deal, known as Pacific LNG. (That the project was meant to transport gas to Mexico and the United States via Bolivia's archrival, Chile, didn't help. The enmity dates back to 1884, when Chile swiped Bolivia's only coast following the War of the Pacific, leaving the nation landlocked.) The project was halted and the episode became known as the "gas war." Subsequently, calls for the government to retake control of Bolivia's resources expanded and gained strength. By the 2005 election, eventually won by Evo Morales, every single major candidate for president was offering significant reforms in the oil and gas sector.

Resource Sovereignty

After decades of dictatorship and civil war, it is no small feat that democratic elections have been held throughout Latin America in the last two decades. New, non-traditional leaders—like a coca farmer in Bolivia, a former metal worker in Brazil, a torture survivor in Chile, and socialists in Uruguay and Venezuela—have been elected president in countries throughout the region. In Bolivia, Evo Morales won the presidential election in December 2005 with a stunning 54 percent of the popular vote. No president in Bolivia's fractured electoral history had achieved even close to that support. In Venezuela, Chávez won another term in 2006 with 60 percent of the vote in an election where an impressive number of voters—nearly 75 percent—went to the polls.

These votes offered an explicit mandate for the new leaders to bring about significant change. In Bolivia, reasserting control of the oil and gas industry was one of the main issues of the election campaign. Shortly after taking office, Morales announced a decree nationalizing Bolivia's hydrocarbons. Government negotiators met an established six-month deadline to rewrite existing contracts with oil and gas companies. The new contracts will direct between 50 and 80 percent of oil profits to the government, according to Gretchen Gordon of the Democracy Center in Bolivia. The government's oil revenues will rise an estimated $1.3 billion in 2007, increasing to roughly $4 billion by 2011. "The challenge will be ensuring that those resources are used effectively to improve people's lives," Gordon concludes.

In Venezuela, the government has significantly increased royalties and cracked down on oil companies for underpayment of income taxes. During his re-election campaign, Chávez promised to expand his "socialism for the twenty-first century" program, which requires the government to take a dominant role in the economy and in the provision of social welfare programs, funded largely with oil revenues. Immediately after Chávez started his new term last year, the Venezuelan government resumed attempts to re-negotiate several oil contracts signed with a number of oil majors in the 1990s—including Exxon-Mobil, ChevronTexaco and ConocoPhillips—and to replace them with more favorable joint-venture agreements dominated by the state-owned oil company, known by its Spanish acronym PDVSA.

In July 2007, all the international companies doing business in Venezuela's Orinoco oil belt agreed to negotiate new contracts with the Venezuelan government. ChevronTexaco and ExxonMobil, however, announced that they would cease their Venezuelan operations. Both have reserved the right to seek compensation through international arbitration.

In Ecuador, calls for redistributing oil revenues are high on the agenda of newly elected President Rafael Correa. Oil revenues account for approximately one-third of Ecuador's national budget and over 40 percent of its export earnings. However, "the largest portion of the revenue from oil exports goes to servicing the country's massive debt," explains Debayani Kar of the Jubilee USA network. "This leaves few funds that can be allocated for social infrastructure and development, while creating an incentive for the country to pump more oil," she says. Correa has vowed to renegotiate contracts with foreign oil companies to ensure that a greater share of the oil wealth goes into the national treasury. He has also offered to leave some oil in the ground—to lessen global warming and protect endangered areas—if Ecuador's debt is cancelled.

Efforts like those of Chávez, Correa, and Morales to garner greater control over their countries' profitable oil businesses and to spread the industry's economic benefits have been extremely popular in resource-rich but economically poor countries throughout Latin America. High global oil prices mean that governments obtaining a sizeable chunk of oil profits will be able to fund a variety of social programs to assist the poor. The power flowing from exerting greater control of oil at a time of high prices has also emboldened leaders to openly distance themselves from Washington, and to seek to diminish the traditional U.S. dominance in the region by reaching out to other allies in the international community, and by increasing regional ties.

Regional Petro-Politics

Given the likely prospects for continued unrest in the Middle East, analysts expect Latin America to be the fastest-growing oil producing region in the world in the coming years. However, domestic demand is also likely to increase significantly. Large and rapidly growing countries like Brazil, Chile, and Argentina are already experiencing energy shortages and thus looking for ways to ensure steady supplies of resources to meet their demand. At the same time, as energy producers and exporters like Venezuela, Bolivia, and Ecuador look to diversify their markets, they are increasingly looking to regional buyers.

Governments have been moving to forge stronger regionalities. Venezuela has signed agreements with Central American and Caribbean countries to supply discounted oil and other petroleum products, often in exchange for something else. Cuba, for example, provides Venezuela with thousands of highly skilled professionals, teachers, and doctors, who work in the poorest areas of the country. After long and difficult negotiations, Bolivia and Brazil reached an agreement for Brazil to purchase Bolivian gas at rates many times higher than the discounted rates it had been paying. "Brazil's President Lula was criticized by his opponents for being too soft on Bolivia and allegedly playing ideological politics," explains Lucia Ortiz of Friends of the Earth in Brazil. "In the end, agreeing to pay the global market price for gas is only fair, but it does show that there is a level of solidarity among Latin American countries that wasn't there before."

The 12 South American countries have come together to create the South American Union (known as Unisur), in a process similar to the one that launched the European Union. Although the Unisur agenda includes myriad issues upon which its members are attempting to find common ground, energy integration is at the top of the list. One such proposal is to merge the region's oil and gas companies into one.

Led by Venezuela, the region's energy ministers in 2005 officially endorsed the concept of a strategic alliance of state-owned oil companies to manage and operate all aspects of the energy sector. According to its founding declaration, PetroAmerica, as it is called, "will integrate Latin America and the Caribbean on principles of self-sufficiency, and re-invest profits into development and social programs." This ambitious undertaking is already taking shape, particularly through its Caribbean subsidiary, PetroCaribe, which has established a formal structure that includes a board comprised of the members' energy ministers, as well as a secretariat, and is already carrying out several joint projects.

The Democracy Alternative

Although Latin Americans have generally welcomed these initiatives—and the wider regional strategy—to become less dependent on the United States and strengthen regional ties, some plans have been criticized as too reminiscent of business-as-usual.

For example, environmental and indigenous rights advocates are already sounding alarm bells about plans to build a 10,000-mile pipeline from Venezuela to Argentina through the Brazilian Amazon. "It is really worrisome that this project is being talked about as a done deal, without a comprehensive process of public debate and consultation," warns Maria Eugenia Bustamante, director of Amigransa, a citizens group for the protection of the Gran Sabana national park in Venezuela. "This project will directly impact some of the most vital ecological areas in this part of the world, including the Guyana Shield and the Amazon Rainforest."

Brazil has recently expressed reservations about going forward with the project. Venezuela's Chávez has declared that the project is currently "frozen," but that he remains committed to finding ways to make it happen.

As governments attempt to find ways to free themselves from the shackles of past economic failures and to chart a new path for the betterment of their peoples, their greatest challenge will be achieving a true transformation that also makes social and environmental concerns a central pillar. While they need revenue to carry out social welfare programs and to create jobs that will revive the economy, advocates are calling on Latin American leaders to be keenly aware of the negative impacts that often accompany an oil-based economy.

Other challenges will emerge as regional integration moves forward, threatening the oil multinationals of the United States. The Bush administration, for example, is scrambling to ensure that the United States isn't fully left out. In what some see as a move to counter Venezuela's collaboration with its neighbors, President Bush offered Brazil an energy deal for the production and trade of biofuels—a controversial alternative energy source—during a visit to Latin America in March 2007. The United States and Brazil are already the world's largest ethanol producers, and it is estimated that demand for the fuel will face a significant increase worldwide.

Throughout the developing world, oil has correlated with imperial subjugation, local authoritarianism and human rights abuses.

As Latin America's new wave of democracy consolidates, Latin Americans are seeking to disrupt this equation. If they can achieve positive change without excluding dissenting opinions from public debate, the region's countries could even become the world's most authentic democracies.

NADIA MARTINEZ is co-director of the Sustainable Energy and Economy Network (SEEN), a project of the Institute for Policy Studies in Washington, D.C.

Racial Disparities

Threaten Economic Vitality

In Brazil—and other countries—foreign companies cannot be passive about lost potential.

PETER ORTIZ

Osvaldo Nascimento's success eludes most Afro-Brazilians. The son of a tailor and housewife, Nascimento grew up poor, the way many of Brazil's black and indigenous population live today. Now Nascimento, a black executive in IBM Brasil, knows that corporations risk their own survival if they sit passively while Afro-Brazilians fail to realize their potential. His success remains a distant dream for most Afro-Brazilians.

"At the end of the day, it's a matter of competitiveness," Nascimento says. "We can't afford to put this [black] population aside . . . And if we don't [change], it will impact our growth and presence on a worldwide basis."

Blessed with abundant natural resources, fertile land and a diverse industrial and agricultural base, Brazil is one of the world's largest economies. It has weaned itself from foreign oil because of its technological innovation in extracting ethanol from sugar cane and creating cheaper alternative fuel. São Paulo, the third-largest city in the world, stands as a leading commerce and financial center in South America.

Underlying Brazil's success are huge disparities in employment and income for the largely undereducated and poverty-stricken population of Afro-Brazilians, who officially make up nearly half of the country's 187 million citizens. Brazilian favelas (slums) offer a dramatic contrast in major urban centers such as Rio de Janeiro and São Paulo.

Generations of poor, mostly Afro-Brazilians, built illegal homes of brick, wood, and tin, which crowd the mountain slopes of Rio, resembling stacked, multicolored LEGO bricks. One of the most notorious in Rio, Rochina, sits directly across from luxurious residences protected by tall concrete walls, security cameras and guards. In one São Paulo neighborhood, million-dollar condos with balconies that double as pools tower over another slum.

But a growing trend inspires cautious hope among Afro-Brazilians. A little more than a decade ago, Brazil reached a milestone when the government took legislative action reminiscent of the early achievements in the U.S. civil-rights struggle. With many no longer viewing the government as an enemy, black Brazilians are focusing on a potentially bigger and historically absent partner—business—to further empower their disenfranchised population, both as workers and consumers.

Business Spurs Change

Brazil's turning point as a global competitor started about 20 years ago. Faced with inefficiencies and a very closed market, Brazil had to change if it hoped to stay competitive with India and China, says Herbert de Magalhaes Drummond Neto, secretary of the Trade Promotion Operations Division.

"Brazilian companies were forced to adapt [as a global economy] and nowadays, we are much more competitive," Drummond Neto says.

Brazil exports have grown 68.6 percent in five years, from $70 billion to $118 billion. That figure is expected to reach $132 billion this year. The government is a regional trade leader with its South American neighbors and has started to reach out to Arab nations and African countries. President Luiz Inácio Lula da Silva has visited 17 African countries in two years and watched its bilateral trade with the continent grow 200 percent. For U.S.-based companies, such as Marriott and IBM, Brazil has evolved into a sophisticated regional hub on the cusp of realizing its potential. Both companies also understand the nation won't outlast its global competitors without embracing a diverse work force. So far, the efforts of these companies amount to baby steps compared with diversity practices in the United States, but they signify an unprecedented start in addressing racial inequality and promoting a robust climate for Brazil's global ambitions.

The Necessity of Corporate Involvement

Rahul Vir, general manager of the Renaissance São Paulo Hotel, envisions Brazil as a model for Marriott's other South American locations. Brazil is home to six of its 11 hotel chains in

231

Brazil abolished slavery in 1888, the ensuing panic a minority, white elite gave birth to a whitening program. Abdias do Nascimento, a noted Brazilian author and human-rights advocate, reminded his audience in a 2001 presentation from Durban, South Africa, that Brazil encouraged and subsidized massive immigration of Europeans, whose "superior" blood would prevail in race mixture and slowly eliminate the "inferior" black component.

"In other words, instead of separating the races and protecting their 'purity,' the elite opted to eliminate Africans by means of race mixture itself," Nascimento said at the Third World Conference Against Racism, Racial Discrimination, Xenophobia, and Related Forms of Intolerance.

Nascimento also participated in the Brazilian Black Front, a group founded in the 1930s to fight racial injustice. The military dictatorship exiled Nascimento from 1968 to 1981, quashing a cultural protest by artists who threatened to unveil the country's illusion of a racial democracy. What resulted was a Brazilian society that perfected an intelligent apartheid system—one where racism could thrive without the support of antidiscrimination laws that drew worldwide attention to racism in the United States and South Africa.

A year after enslaved Africans were pronounced free, Brazil ended its monarchy rule and became a republic. But this did nothing to discourage former slave owners who demanded reparations from the government, says Prof. J. Michael Turner, director of the Global Afro Latino & Caribbean Initiative at Hunter College in New York.

"They did not get [reparations], but what they did was equally awful," Turner says.

The country paid European immigrants to settle in the southern region and provided them with the best land while allowing the Afro-Brazilians living mostly in the northern region to languish, Turner says.

Under current President Luiz Inácio Lula da Silva, many Afro-Brazilians see a country coming to terms with its black self. When the president, popularly known as "Lula," appointed Matilde Ribeiro in 2003 to serve as minister of the Special Secretary for the Promotion of Racial Equality (SEPPIR), he sent a bold message. Ribeiro, who proudly embraces her role as a black militant and feminist, holds the only minister position in the Americas charged with addressing racism.

"Yes, I believe it is possible to revert this reality in less than a decade, but not [to eliminate it] completely," Ribeiro says. "The fact that [blacks] are more present in the universities, we are more present in politics, helps the [black] population to value itself and regard itself in high esteem and also to look for other ways of inclusion."

Until recently, business, like the government, was complicit in ignoring racial inequality or allowing it to put Brazil at a competitive disadvantage. Afro-Brazilians officially represent nearly 50 percent of the population, and the overwhelming majority are least prepared on nearly every social, educational, and economic level. In 2002, Brazil ranked fourth in the world for income inequality behind Sierra Leone, Central Africa Republic, and Swaziland.

—Peter Ortiz

---

the region and comprises a work force of 1,400, larger than the other South American locations combined.

"Our [Marriott Brazil] Business Council will eventually expand from Brazil to a South American Business Council, so these [diversity] activities will definitely grow into initiatives where we use the best practices from Brazil in the countries around us," Vir says.

IBM employs 9,000 people in Brazil, the largest employee base in all its Latin American operations. It works with Integrate, a non-governmental organization promoting supplier opportunities for businesses owned by Afro-Brazilians, indigenous groups and people with disabilities. The organization partners with IBM's global supplier-diversity program in preparing companies to service the needs of IBM and the greater market.

"A major objective of this program is to demonstrate the business case for diversity," Nascimento says. "We are trying to be very aggressive here and this partnership with Integrare is an indication of that."

Time Bomb Waiting to Explode

Many companies point to poor public elementary and high schools as the true culprit hurting blacks. The income distribution between the rich and poor in Brazil, where the wealthiest

10 percent receive almost half the income, remains among the worst in the world.

José Tadeu Alves, managing director of Merck Sharp & Dohme—a subsidiary of Merck & Co.—says despite being five centuries old, Brazil only has seen true economic growth in the last 50 years. Only recently have blacks shared in that growth, but it's very limited. The low pool of educated blacks limits Merck's ability to hire a more diverse work force, he says.

"Brazil has a few people with lots of money, none or very little in the middle, and a lot of people with almost nothing," Alves says. "As a country, it's a time bomb because if you don't solve the distribution of income, this country is not sustainable."

Merck's efforts center on supporting institutions such as Afrobras, a non-government organization that in 2003 inaugurated the first historically black college in Brazil, University Zumbi dos Palmares. Nearly 90 percent of the students and 47 percent of the professors at the business school are black. The university's historical significance also serves as a reminder of the challenges. Blacks represent less than 3 percent of university students nationwide. Laudeci Reis, cofounder of Quali-Afro, started her organization as a conduit for corporations seeking to hire blacks and other disenfranchised Brazilians. The organization prepares potential candidates for the job market. Reis' partners include a white Jewish woman and a black

Aids Lessons from Brazil

When its citizens faced a life-threatening disease in the 1990s, Brazil chose a controversial path from other nations' responses. While many governments, including the U.S. government, ignored or downplayed the AIDS crisis, Brazil listened as the United Nations forecast 1.2 million cases of HIV by 2002. Then-President Fernando Henrique Cardoso took action that might have outraged many in the United States.

Brazil's AIDS strategy, including free treatment for all citizens, has received worldwide praise and has produced results. The country's adult-HIV-prevalence rate was 0.5 percent in 2003, better than the 0.6 percent HIV-prevalence rate in the U.S.

"We decided it was better for society to blush a little bit than to watch thousands of people die," Cardoso wrote in his 2006 memoir. "So we . . . tailored our response to the Brazilian reality."

That response included handing out condoms at Brazil's famous. Carnival every year, making AIDS warnings mandatory before pornographic films and, in some schools, teaching students how to put on condoms.

Cardoso's administration worked with nongovernmental organizations to embrace high-risk groups such as prostitutes, drug users, prison inmates, and street children.

In 1996, Brazil guaranteed its citizens free access to antiretroviral AIDS treatment. It angered pharmaceutical companies, especially those based in the United States, by creating its own generic drugs and threatening to break patents unless the companies reduced their prices. And it rejected $40 million in U.S. AIDS, grants in 2005 after the Bush administration attached a moral clause prohibiting funding to countries that did not submit a written pledge opposing commercial sex work.

Brazil beat legal attacks by pharmaceutical companies and the U.S. government that argued the country was violating international property-rights laws. It reversed dire predictions and created a worldwide model for AIDS prevention and treatment. And, just as important it fostered an environment where pharmaceutical companies, such as Merck, No. 34 on The 2006 Diversity Inc. Top 50 Companies for Diversity list, continue to succeed.

Gracio A. dos Reis, hospital business unit director for Merck, credits Brazil for helping the company gain experience in testing and developing effective drugs.

"There are certain areas in the government that understand very well that intellectual property is important for people to invest," he says. "We feel the government is playing the role society expects of them and we have to negotiate better."

—Peter Ortiz

Brazil-Africa Relationship Benefits from High Oil Prices

Brazil's history with Africa initially was an ugly one, based on an economic system of slavery that benefited one side while destroying the other. More than three centuries later, Brazil is attempting to build the bridge to Africa, but this time it is based on mutual economic benefit. The high price of oil also is creating a growing market for ethanol, and Brazil is taking the lead.

The new bridge with Africa has been crossed often by Brazil's President Luiz Inácio Lula da Silva, who believes in the significance of a Brazil-Africa relationship because much of the Brazilian population is comprised of African descendants. "It's important to know the needs of each other and in Africa," says Herbert de Magalhaes Drummond Neto, secretary of Trade Promotion Operations Division of Brazil.

With the backing of Lula, Brazil's government has shown a strong support to this growing relationship. In just the first two years of Lula's administration, "bilateral trade between Brazil and African countries has grown 150 percent," he says.

Brazil is responsible for half of the ethanol used in the world's cars today (the other half is supplied by the United States), according to the Wharton School of Business at the University of Pennsylvania. However, only 2 percent of the fuel used in cars worldwide now is alcohol. As oil prices rise, ethanol gains popularity—nearly 75 percent of Brazil's new cars burn ethanol as well as gasoline.

Rogelio Golfarb, Brazil's director of governmental affairs and public relations, believes that with rising oil prices, the growth in ethanol, produced and exported by Brazil, will further strengthen economic ties to other countries interested in producing ethanol. "It is in the interest of Brazil that this happens," says Golfarb. To accelerate the economic synergy between Brazil and Africa, the Ministry of Foreign Affairs and the Ministry of Mines and Energy of Brazil already have started workshops on ethanol in South Africa. Efforts such as these have increased commerce with African countries from $5 billion to $12.6 billion in the last five years, according to Drummond Neto.

—Won Kim

"[Blacks] don't have the access to the education, but companies have to understand they are part of this process," Reis says. "They have to understand they have to hire people and help them." Reis agrees that the inferior educational opportunities are a huge obstacle. What frustrates her and others is the unwillingness or inability by many in Brazil to recognize how the social/economic disenfranchisement is rooted in racism.

Afro-Brazilians were not officially prohibited from attending school, living in certain neighborhoods, or restricted from public places as were many African Americans. Brazilian governments noted the absence of discriminatory legislation as evidence that

man, both Brazilian. She contends it is unrealistic for corporations to expect black candidates to have the academic qualifications of whites, but that doesn't mean they are incapable of doing the job.

Ignoring Race Hurts All

A decade after Luana Moraes first arrived in the United States to study at the University of California at Los Angeles, she remembers the stranger's words—"Hey, sister"—and how they made her feel welcome because of her black skin.

The biracial 33-year-old always identified as black, but she didn't feel solidarity based solely on skin color until she came to the United States.

"I didn't know how connected people could be because they are black, so that was a nice thing for me," Moraes says.

Today, Moraes represents an emboldened generation of Afro-Brazilians embracing their common struggle as black people. But she ran into a major roadblock three years ago, after a global chemical company hired her to develop a supplier-diversity program for black-owned enterprises.

Three months into her job, Moraes and her boss attended a diversity conference where Afro-Brazilian leaders bluntly told executives of the racial divide. The next day, Moraes' boss confronted her, ignored her defense of the speakers, and denounced them as "crazy." That boss fired Moraes, who started her own company, Differential, and consults companies in Brazil on diversity issues today.

"I saw that I lost him in the moment he opened himself to the subject [of racism]," Moraes says.

Moraes wrote a book explaining why diversity is vital for a company's survival in a country where nearly half the population is Afro-Brazilian. Brazilians need to understand that when a large population is poorly educated and has little buying power, everyone's future is in trouble, Moraes says.

"And that means my boss' job is in jeopardy," she says. "So when we talk about guaranteeing space to black kids at universities or investing in diverse suppliers, for example,

we are not talking about reducing the chances of my boss' kids' professional future . . . Without real diversity actions and concrete results, the companies will lose money, the white folks are going to have less job opportunities and their kids are going to be trapped in a very poor future."

Growing up half-white under the strong influence of a black mother, Moraes quickly grasped the contradictions that define her and many Afro-Brazilian's experiences. Children taunted her, calling her a monkey. White strangers and friends embraced her as "pardo" or mixed instead of black, which elevated her status in their eyes. She recalls a white girl telling her she hated black students.

"And I kept looking at her thinking, 'Am I not black? I sit by your side every day!' And then I understood," Moraes recalls. "I was there, in the same place she was, so I was not black. That part of me was deleted so that she could deal with my presence and give me some value."

Today, Moraes is confident she could convince her former boss to understand how racism undermines a company's competitiveness. In a society where blacks have little control of the wealth, it is not enough to battle racism as a moral or social cause, she says. She is part of a growing movement of black Brazilians battling racism on the economic front, urging whites to join their struggle and understand how the success of Afro-Brazilians is crucial to sustaining their own success.

"If I could go back to that time, I certainly would have not allowed the window my boss opened to close so fast," Moraes says. "I would have shown him what was in it for him. And I would have shown him how terrible things can be if people like him don't start doing something now."

—Peter Ortiz

racism wasn't a problem. But for many blacks, advancing in society often meant distancing themselves from color, and it wasn't unusual to hear wealthy or famous blacks identify as white.

For Humberto Adami, the racial disparities still are evident daily. The attorney, who has advocated on racial issues, took notice of the social dynamics one night at an outdoor restaurant on Rio's wealthy Copacabana beach. Except for a couple of security guards and a man begging for money, most of the faces were white. Blacks still remain largely absent from government institutions and companies. This exclusion not only hurts blacks but also businesses that can't rely on a huge portion of their population to be viable customers, Adami says.

"Everybody agrees that in Brazil you can find racism, but you cannot find the racist; you can never find a racist," he says in a sarcastic tone.

But Adami expresses hope that Brazil is recognizing its racist past.

"You see the situation and sometimes you just look to the side," Adami says, describing what happened years ago. "Now, not only are black people denouncing [racism], they are not looking to the other side."

Slow, Steady Change

Starting in the mid-1990s, the Brazilian government evolved its position on race. President Fernando Henrique Cardoso spoke out against racism and instituted affirmative-action programs to diversify governmental agencies. Universities implemented racial quotas for poor students.

Under current President Silva, popularly known as "Lula," the country has progressed further. Lula himself became the first president to hail from the working class, inspiring hope for many of Brazil's large underclass.

Affirmative-action programs increased dramatically, especially in education, where 16 public universities have adopted such programs and benefited more than 43,000 students in private universities. Prof. Jacques d'Adesky of the Universidade Candido Mendes in Rio says it's a good start, but he urges corporations to be diligent. While Brazilian law requires large corporations to hire at least 5 percent people with disabilities, there are no workplace requirements based on race or ethnicity.

Lula also created visible and powerful symbols of change in 2003 when he established the first position in the Americas dealing specifically with racial equality and appointed the first black person to the Supreme Court.

Minister Matilde Ribeiro of the Special Secretariat of Policies for the Promotion of Racial Equality (SEPPIR) office once fought the government she serves. Justice Joaquim Benedito Barbosa Gomes, an outspoken proponent on racial inequality, became the first Supreme Court judge acknowledged as a black Brazilian. He stresses that business needs to be proactive.

"For many centuries, Brazil did not move," Barbosa Gomes says. "It is absolutely necessary that government and powerful segments of our society take the initiative."

Barbosa Gomes garners a national audience in Brazil where court sessions are open to the public and televised. He speaks out against a criminal-justice system that is "particularly harsh towards blacks and is very liberal for those who have money," and enjoys a status usually reserved for celebrities.

"Every week, lots of students from all over the country come to the court, they ask for an autograph, they want to make pictures and they say, 'You know, someday I will be at your position,'" Barbosa Gomes says, adding: "It is inconceivable for a country to be a [big] global player without tackling such a big social issue as race."

When racism officially was declared an unbailable crime in 1988, Ribeiro was a militant engaged in the black movement's effort to denounce the government's propaganda of Brazil as a racial democracy. Now she wields her influence in shaping race relations in and outside of Brazil. She travels throughout South America and Africa to spark honest dialogue and action against the racism that people of color face worldwide.

Ribeiro's office works in conjunction with other ministries in Brazil to address racism across all facets of life. One effort with the Minister of Education aims to teach children African history and provide black and indigenous students from public schools with scholarships for private universities. Realizing that government can only do so much, Ribeiro also focuses on corporations. She is working with IBM and a Brazilian retail chain on a pilot internship program that she hopes attracts other corporations.

Nascimento, of IBM, likens Brazil's need to include Afro-Brazilians in society and the work-place as a "national crusade." He's pleased with Ribeiro's efforts and acknowledges seeing a greater presence of Afro-Brazilians at IBM.

"I'm now feeling more a part of this company," Nascimento says, echoing what young, black employees are telling him. "But we still have a long [way] to go."

Are You Driving on Blood Fuel?

**The UK and Europe's demand for carbon-saving biofuel is leaving
a trail of human and environmental devastation in its wake.**

KELLY NICHOLLS AND STELLA CAMPOS

Colombian farmer Jorge Garcia gazes at fields of African oil palm stretching to the horizon and beyond. He doesn't share the world's excitement about 'green' fuel, nor understand why his government, with the support of the U.S. government, the European Union (EU) and the World Bank, is aggressively pushing the establishment of vast 'biofuel' plantations, despite serious human rights abuses, links to terrorist groups, allegations of money laundering, and environmental damage. He recalls the days when he and his family lived in those same lands and farmed their own food. That was before the paramilitaries came, demanding that they leave or face the consequences. Jorge has already suffered the consequences. Two of his children have been killed, as have friends who fought against the illegal occupation of their land by African oil palm companies.

The African oil palm industry is booming in Colombia and there are plans to expand it, to meet the growing world demand for green fuel, naively considered a carbon-neutral, environment-friendly energy source. The Colombian government is also promoting such plantations as a way to combat the ever-spreading illicit cultivation of coca and poppies. The ostensible aim is to help the country's poor by providing an alternative means of subsistence. Conveniently forgotten is that just a fraction of the rural population is needed to work these plantations and the majority have to leave in droves. The handful that remain as employees of the palm oil corporations either get paid poor wages or are paid in credits and vouchers; they may then be forced to purchase basic goods at inflated prices from stores run by the paramilitaries.

The U.S. government is fulsome in its support for Colombia's African oil palm enthusiasm; up to 60 percent of USAID funding for the war-ravaged country has been targeted towards the cultivation of that single crop. The EU, World Bank, and the Inter-American Development Bank have also funded African oil palm projects in Colombia.

Nearly 60 years ago, in 1949, the newly-fledged World Bank sent economist Dr. Lauchlin Currie to head an economic mission to Colombia. In 1961, he published *Operación Colombia*, in which he wrote: 'Colombia's real rural problem is an excess rural population. . . . This excess should be transferred, *forcibly if need be,* [my italics] to the large cities and employed in public works in order to create increased consumer demand, which in turn would be met by increased industrialisation. Colombian agriculture would, meanwhile, be intensively mechanised and the remaining rural population would be employed by these large mechanised operations.'

More than 40 years later, Álvaro Uribe's Colombian government, with U.S. support, has clearly taken the message to heart.

Fuel to the Fire

In March 2007, President Bush visited Colombia—a brief, low-key visit that didn't even last a day. Why the visit? Bush was selling the idea of Latin America becoming the 'green fuel' centre of the world, with Brazil number one and Colombia, perhaps, South America's number two. And Presidents Lula of Brazil and Uribe of Colombia were buying into that.

Over the next decade, the United States of America hopes to have at least 20 percent of the fuel used in its vehicles derived from vegetation. The aim is not so much to combat global warming, which is the rationale of using biofuels in Europe. Instead it is to give some security of supply against a volatile Middle East and an increasingly intransigent Venezuela, with President Chávez more interested in supplying Castro's Cuba than in supporting the 'gas-guzzling' habits of a hostile country.

U.S. plans to convert corn into ethanol from the maize-lands of the Midwest are revealing themselves to be a sham, as one test after another shows a net loss of energy, when all factors—including fertilisers, herbicides, use of machinery, processing, and transportation to the point of use—are taken into account. Essentially, that means more fossil fuels are consumed than are saved, at least in the context of North American corn. But why should U.S. farmers worry? They receive subsidies of up to 90 percent for their role in giving the United States of America fuel security.

The story is different in the tropics, where biofuels derived from sugar cane, African oil palm, soya, or castor beans, give a net energy return. But of course, that equation doesn't take into account the lasting damage to soils, to climate, and to the environment, caused by monoculture plantations.

A day after Bush's visit, President Uribe reminded Colombia that he had already pinpointed several million hectares in the flat savannah plains of the Orinoco region, north of the Amazon and adjoining Venezuela, that could be suitable for biofuel plantations and, in particular, African oil palm. The first phase, covering a million hectares, was planned for the Department (province) of Vichada, with funding to be derived from European banks.

Corruption Rules

By Colombian law, unclaimed lands belong to the nation and can be allocated only to farmers who can prove that they have been using the land for a minimum of five years and are exploiting at least 80 percent of the area. . . . The amount granted per family is a subsistence plot which, in the case of the Department of Vichada, is a maximum of 1,294 hectares.

Land grants are booming. As *Semana,* the most prestigious Colombian weekly magazine, noted in April 2007, 'while in the year 2004 title was granted to 43 plots and in 2005 to 15, in the year 2006 the national institute for rural development (Incoder) granted title to 277 unclaimed plots.' But the land doesn't always go to those legally entitled to it.

Habib Merheg, Senator for the Andean Department of Risaralda—and therefore living far from Vichada, in the Colombian plains—bought the title to 2,400 hectares, despite not having met the time requirements.

That wasn't all. In 2006, people employed by him, including his secretary, his lawyer, and some of his business partners, 13 in all, were granted title in record time to 16,330 hectares of 'unclaimed' land, an area about half the size of Bogotá, with its eight million inhabitants. Soon after that, 18 other persons from Merheg's constituency received 21,805 hectares in the same Vichada region. Contrast that with local farmers who had been waiting years to receive rights to the same land, which they had been working, and who now find themselves landless.

Fellow senator Pilar Córdoba claims that Merheg has links to the paramilitary, inasmuch as the land that he and his associates now occupy was controlled for a long time by groups who processed drugs in the region.

The scandal of Merheg is nothing new for a country where paramilitaries have permeated every level of society, up to the top echelons of government.

Paramilitaries came into being more than 20 years ago to fight the guerrillas, in particular the FARC (Fuerzas Armadas Revolucionarios de Colombia) and—mafia-like—to protect private landowners, businesses and, not least, cocaine cartel bosses such as Ochoa and Escobar.

Since then they have engaged in a brutal regime of land-grabbing from local peasants as well as from indigenous and minority groups. Should anyone resist, they or members of their family might be made to disappear, like the *desaparecidos* of Argentina or Chile. Or they might be tortured and killed in front of their families and the community. Not even children and babies are immune from such atrocities and yet, too often, the government has looked the other way.

Violence and Corruption

Particularly affected have been the Afro-Colombians, who constitute about 26 percent of the total population of Colombia and 85 percent of the Pacific population in the Chocó, a region with some of the World's wettest rainforests and richest biodiversity. Community members in Tumaco, in Colombia's south-west corner, tell stories of armed actors coming to their doors and telling them they had three days to leave their land or they and their families would suffer. Sometimes they would be offered a small payment, insufficient to sustain them and their families. Often, they get nothing.

By no means are all the African oil palm companies tainted with corruption and malpractice. Yet nowhere has their hand-in-glove relationship with the paramilitaries been as overt as in Jiguamiandó and Curvaradó, in the Department of Chocó. Vicente Castaño, the leader of the area's paramilitaries (a group classed as a 'terrorist' organisation by the U.S. government), bragged that he was responsible for bringing African oil palm companies to the area and that he and his paramilitary group had become the legal owners of African oil palm plantations. Meanwhile, the people of Jiguamiandó and Curvaradó have suffered more than 110 assassinations and disappearances since 1996, as well as forced displacement and constant threats.

'On arriving, the paramilitaries decapitated the local pastor and forced members of the community to watch as they played football with his head'.

The paramilitaries' arrival in the region in May 1997 is scarred deep in people's memories. They decapitated the local pastor, then forced members of the community to watch as they played football with his head. They then advised the community to leave the area. Nearly six thousand people fled.

Four years later, after reclaiming the collective titles to the land from which they had been displaced, members of the community made the journey back to their homes. Where once had been their gardens and tropical rainforest there were vast tracts of African oil palm. And, as if the past had never been, the paramilitaries were again threatening the communities, forcing them to continue growing the palm or leave. In fact, the paras compounded the illegal clearance of the forest by the illegal extraction and selling of timber.

International and national human rights organisations, including the Inter-American Court of Human Rights, have denounced Urapalma, the principal company working in the area, on the grounds that, with the help of army Brigade XVII and armed civilians, it had illegally commandeered collectively titled land. But despite international attention and the 'demobilisation' of the paramilitaries, threats and violence continue.

A recently formed paramilitary group, the 'Aguilas Negras', collaborates with African oil palm companies in terrorising the remaining population, with the national army and police just standing by.

Unionised employees of palm oil companies have also been industry victims. Colombia remains the most dangerous place in the world to be a trade unionist or social movement leader. In 2001, 90 percent of all trade unionists killed worldwide were Colombian.

Over the past 10 years, nine prominent trade unionists in the oil palm industry have been assassinated. A unionist from Puerto Wilches, an oil palm growing town in an area now controlled by paramilitaries, says, 'The African oil palm companies constantly used illegally armed actors to threaten union members and silence resistance. They have cut workers' benefits and brought us to a point of slave labour.'

The violence against villagers and communities in Colombia continues apace, with some three million refugees forced from their homes since 1996. That number, some 10 percent of the total population, puts Colombia second to the Sudan in terms of internally displaced people. The paramilitaries have been able to take control of land that never was theirs through disputing the rights of those who own land collectively, such as indigenous communities and Afro-Colombians. In recent years, some of the worst atrocities have taken place in Colombia's north-east, south-east and in the Putumayo.

'Legitimate' Crops

Soil and climate studies show that Colombia has 3.5 million hectares that would be immediately suitable for growing African palm; the largest area, some two million hectares being in the Orinoco plains.

Another 2.5 million hectares could be made available after the land had been specially prepared. In 2005, Fedepalma, Colombia's African oil palm agency, reported that 275,000 hectares had been planted with the palm, of which 161,000 were in production and 114,000 in process of development. In 2006,185,000 hectares were up and running, yielding some 685,000 tonnes of oil—just under two percent of total world production.

Colombia has 53 plants for extracting the oil, with some 3,240,732 tonnes of fruit currently passing through the system. Currently, some 36 percent of the oil is exported, mostly as unrefined oil, which is far cheaper to refine abroad (e.g. in Rotterdam) than in Colombia (around $37 per tonne of crude, compared to $60).

The United Kingdom is the largest single importer of Colombian crude palm oil, taking up some 40 percent of the total exported to Europe. Like other importers, the UK takes little or no account of the huge social and environmental cost involved in the production of palm oil, whether from Colombia or elsewhere. On the contrary, organisations concerned with an economic model of development, such as USAID, the World Bank and the Inter-American Development Bank, see horizon-to-horizon plantations of 'legitimate' crops, such as African oil palm or sugarcane, as good options for Colombia, enabling the government to impose control over regions afflicted with violence, conflict, lack of public order, illicit crops, and confrontations with guerrilla forces.

Vanishing Forests

Tatiana Roa, head of environmental and social action organisation Censat-Agua Viva, loudly condemns the spread of oil-palm plantations. 'The history of the plantations is painful, stained in the blood and tears of black and indigenous communities,' she says. 'It is the history of disappearing forests that turn into plantations. It is the history of age-old traditional cultures transformed into palm oil plantation workforces. It is these voices that are calling for a halt to the destruction spurred on by the defenders of biodiesel.'

The Colombian government has its eye on the Orinoco region and a mega-project to reforest 6.3 million hectares (twice the size of Belgium) with African oil palm and other species, so is simply avoiding the issue of environmental impacts. One project in the area around Puerto Carreño, involving Spanish engineering company Ingemas, Agroforestal de Colombia and Spanish renewable energy company ERPASA, is already underway. It involves planting 90,000 hectares with African oil palm and establishing a biodiesel plant in the north of Spain. It so happens that the region has 156 ecosystems, most of which will be destroyed, in the name of green, renewable energy.

In the Curvaradó region, the illegal planting of African oil palm has led to the extinction of an estimated 26 forest species and the loss of 28 other species. In a report, *The Cultivation of Palm Oil in the Chocó,* written for the European Commission, the authors point out that the clearing of forest leads to considerable increases in topsoil run-off, to disturbances in stream-flow and to increased sediment loads in rivers and streams. Loss of biodiversity is therefore a major consequence of substituting oil palm plantations for rainforest.

Permanent forest destruction and ensuing soil degradation can lead to as much as 180 tonnes of carbon per hectare being lost to the atmosphere in the form of greenhouse gases. A successful African oil palm plantation would take as much as 50 years before it had regained the carbon sent up in smoke.

Quite aside from the initial destruction of the ecosystem, the production of palm oil on a large scale has longer term environmental implications. In Malaysia, in 2001, according to Rhett A. Butler of mongabay.com, the production of seven million tonnes of crude palm oil generated 9.9 million tonnes of solid oil wastes, palm fibre and shells, as well as 10 million tonnes of palm oil mill effluent that, given the chance to contaminate, can have serious impacts on aquatic life. The use of petroleum-based pesticides, herbicides, and fertilisers contributes to greenhouse gas emissions and reduces still further the potential carbon gains. In Indonesia, says Butler, palm plantations are so damaging to the soil that they are abandoned for scrubland. The scrub in turn can act as tinder for wildfires.

If the UK complied with the EU's target of 5.5 percent of its fuel derived from rapeseed by 2010, it would have to cover one-quarter of its arable land with that one crop alone. The EU, with a similar target, would need up to 18 million hectares. As a result, the European Commission plan is for half of biofuel energy to be homegrown and the rest to come from overseas.

'The UK is the largest single importer of Colombian crude palm oil, taking up some 40 percent of the total exported to Europe'.

The world's economy is currently expanding at about 4.5 percent per year, and demand for oil is rising by around half that amount. Translated into barrels, demand is growing by 1.9 million barrels a day, projected to reach 95.8 million barrels a day by 2012, according to figures released by the International Energy Agency in July 2007. With concerns over oil-peaking, the rush is on to produce biofuels. That production, according to the report, is set to reach 1.75 million barrels a day by 2012—not more than two percent of the world's needs.

The greater part of that increase in production, as both the United States of America and the EU are coming to realise, will have to come from the tropics, from Malaysia, Indonesia, Brazil, and Colombia. Not only is land—too often derived from chopping down the rainforest—dirt cheap, but labour is, too. Even more telling are the energy returns per hectare. If maize, as grown in the U.S. Midwest, gives a bare 145kg of oil per hectare, with 80 percent of the oil obtained being converted into ethanol, African oil palm gives a 30 times greater yield, with as much as 5,000kg of oil being obtained from the kernel and surrounding seed pulp, of which up to 80 percent may be converted into biodiesel.

Malaysia, the world's largest supplier of palm oil, followed by Indonesia, can produce biofuel at a price of around $54 per barrel, which is certainly competitive with crude oil at $70 per barrel Malaysia has dedicated almost half of its cultivated land to African oil palm and its exports to China alone are more than 3.5 million metric tonnes. Indonesia is gearing up to double its production by 2025 and has already cleared more than three million hectares of prime forest in East Kalimantan.

The idea that oil palm plantations in Colombia are likely to play a role in a process of peaceful economic development, is not simply naive, but is perverse in that it gives false legitimacy to acts of violence, whomever perpetrates them.

Multinational companies are increasingly being made aware of the human rights abuses and environmental degradation that is too often associated with the provenance of palm oil in their products. In part, perhaps, because of fears of a consumer backlash and legal ramifications, and in part because of the pursuit of ethical practice, a number of organisations, including Aarhus United, Golden Hope Plantations, the Malaysian Palm Oil Association (MPOA), Migros, Sainsbury's, Unilever and WWF, have gotten together to form the Roundtable on Sustainable Palm Oil (RSPO; www.rspo.org). The Roundtable has now expanded to include palm oil growers, processors and traders, manufacturers, retailers, banks and investors, and, not least, human rights and environmental organisations.

Jungle Law

President Uribe's government has aided and abetted the displacement of his people by enacting legislation against smallholders. The new Statute of Rural Reform, approved by the Senate on 13 June 2007, is a 'fast track' law to grant ownership in areas where previous owners—many of whom had ancestral ties to the land and were formerly protected by the Constitution, but without documents to prove their rights—had been displaced.

Previous property laws, such as that of 1936, said that only titles issued by the state were proof of ownership; however, were it shown that the same group or family had lived on and worked land for 20 years prior to 1936, either with no title or a false title, they would be given legal recognition. In 1994, that same law granted ownership to those who had worked the land for at least 20 years prior to 1974. A 2002 law reduced this time to 10 years, thus recognising false titles up to 1984.

But the latest Statute declares that land that has been abandoned or not used productively for five or more years is *baldío*, 'empty land', and thus can be claimed by the new occupiers, especially if they can prove that they will be productive—with an African oil palm plantation, for example.

This favours the drug barons and the paramilitaries, who have already taken possession of some of the best lands in Colombia. Now they need hang on to the land they acquired illegally for just one quarter of the time that had been demanded in the past, in order to get entitlement. And, of course, once they have cleared the land of its legitimate inhabitants, they can claim that the lands were no longer occupied.

Towards Sustainability

The human rights issues in Colombia and, in some regions the felling of irreplaceable tropical forests while expropriating land from its rightful owners, to make way for African oil palm, make it essential that subscribers to the Roundtable and governments, not least the Colombian government, condemn a process that has no place in the civilised world.

A mechanism must be put into place, akin to the Forest Stewardship Council (FSC), to prevent imports of palm oil derived from unacceptable social, legal, and environmental practice.

Consequently, the RSPO must move rapidly to create international legislation that, through certification, rewards good practice and boycotts abuses. That may add to the cost but hopefully will get a message through to those governments that currently condone malpractice elsewhere. The UK, as one of the main importers of palm oil from Colombia, could—and should—lead the way.

KELLY NICHOLLS AND STELLA CAMPOS are freelance journalists working in Colombia.

This Village Could Save the Planet

How two men plan to extend the ecological miracle that is Gaviotas, Colombia, across the rest of the Third World.

PAUL KAIHLA

W e're rumbling across eastern Colombia in a convoy of military jeeps and pickup trucks. Salsa music blasts out of speakers somewhere, and an unrelenting 100-degree sun is bleaching the bone-dry savanna. Although there's not a plane in the sky or a living thing on the ground for miles around, our convoy is armed to the teeth. Commandos in fatigues and flak jackets ride shotgun—with M-4 machine guns dangling from their shoulders and automatic pistols strapped above their right knees. One soldier is perched in a turret with a 7.72-mm machine gun. Another mans an MK-19 grenade launcher.

This rolling armada of arms and men has been seconded for a business mission from a military base near Colombia's eastern border that forms a front against the Revolutionary Armed Forces of Colombia (FARC)—the main opposition in a narco-insurgency that has made this drug-ridden country one of the most feared destinations on the planet. The base doubles as a sentry for a nearby U.S. Drug Enforcement Administration radar station that tracks smugglers flying loads of cocaine to transshipment points in Venezuela, just a few miles away.

But it's the human capital our convoy carries, not cocaine, that has brought out the big guns today: two men whom an Army general sitting near me describes as holding the future of Colombia—if not the world—in their hands. And our destination is not a Venezuelan drug drop, but the site of an economic miracle in the making called Gaviotas II.

The first Gaviotas, located 250 miles to the west, is the creation of the more senior of the two dignitaries at the center of our convoy. Paolo Lugari, 63, is a self-taught inventor who has become a folk hero in South America for founding a model community of sustainable development in the parched Colombian lowlands. His fellow traveler, Gunter Pauli, 51, has the aura of a matinee idol and the charismatic charm of a European Barack Obama. He's a globe-trotting entrepreneur and wheeler-dealer who speaks seven languages, makes his home in Tokyo, and carries a Belgian passport. The men make an odd couple, bound together by an audacious ambition to extend the Gaviotas model of green development and self-sufficiency across first Colombia and then the rest of the Third World.

Their shared vision begins with Gaviotas, the ecovillage Lugari launched in 1971. It's one of the most improbable field experiments in the annals of science and engineering: a free-wheeling center of innovation devoted to building a sustainable society in one of the globe's least hospitable climates. Built from scratch in a treeless corner of the country, this community of scientists, tinkerers, and refugees—now numbering more than 200—has created a verdant rainforest where once there was nothing but scrub grass. It has also devised and deployed dozens of inventions with a frequency and success rate that puts some of America's most storied technology companies to shame. Its products include a hydroelectric microturbine that generates 30 kilowatts and thousands of RPMs from a mere 1-meter drop in a low-fall dam; a system of solar panels, spherical boilers, and tanks that can provide hot water for housing projects as large as 30,000 units; and a remote-controlled zeppelin that uses videocameras to spot forest fires.

Unlike the startups that dot Silicon Valley, Gaviotas has done all this and more with virtually no funding, no well-endowed university backing, no incubators or venture capitalists, and no access to a national power grid, airport, or freeway system. In fact, Gaviotas lies 15 hours east of Bogotá, the nearest city of note, by a two-lane road that traverses the estates of narcotics traffickers and disappears occasionally into sloughs of mud. Gaviotas has been occupied from time to time by guerrilla bands. Lugari himself is a perennial kidnapping target who was captured once and let go only after the president of Colombia intervened and pleaded for his release.

The magic of Gaviotas is in the corporate counterculture that Lugari has fostered. It eschews formal meetings and time-management conventions, promotes jacks-of-all-trades over specialists, and conjures the kind of devotion to discovery that produced great mathematicians in the villages of ancient Greece. . . . "The surrounding region has had no law, high crime, and roving bands of paramilitary units," Lugari says. "Gaviotas is an experiment built on crisis management. You can't learn how to do this in a university."

Pauli is Lugari's younger alter ego. He first discovered Gaviotas in 1984 as an idealistic 27-year-old graduate of Insead, France's prestigious business school. "Gaviotas seemed almost biblical," Pauli recalls. "I took it on as my life's work." After a long internship as Lugari's intellectual disciple, Pauli has come into his own. A serial eco-entrepreneur who has made millions by running, and selling companies like Holland-based biodegradable-detergent maker eCover, Pauli represents a new generation of leadership for Gaviotas. Under an agreement with the Ministry of Defense, he has spent the past three years drawing up plans and enlisting support to build out the Gaviotas model across the entire northeastern quadrant of Colombia—a vast area roughly the size of England.

On today's trip in the military convoy, Pauli and Lugari are laying out their master plan for a group of government officials and business leaders, detailing how they can take this savanna—a region that experts had written off as agriculturally and economically barren—and, through aggressive planting and careful development, turn it into a clean-tech economy with a population of 5 million. If the enterprise succeeds (and Pauli has already lined up funding pledges worth hundreds of millions of dollars from investors such as JP-Morgan), this area could become one of the largest biodiverse reforestation projects on earth. At the same time, it would put a measurable dent in global climate change: Gaviotas II's carbon sequestration would offset the equivalent of the CO_2 emissions from all of Japan.

Pauli's deeper purpose is to create a living laboratory to show other developing countries how to do the same—how to end their dependence on oil imports and grow their economies by becoming exporters of biodiesel. "This is a high-risk, high-reward project," Pauli says. "You need an example of how you can make it work before big investors come in with a lot of money. That example is Gaviotas."

This stretch of eastern Colombia is known as the province of Vichada, and from the lofty vantage of a mini Hercules cargo plane on the first leg of our journey, it looks like Montana with sections of the Mississippi River running through it. There are no trees, roads, houses, or people—just reddish turf with sparse grasses and shrubs, etched by a meandering river punctuated by oxbow bends. Pauli and Lugari, who are harnessed into the plane's netting alongside the other VIPs like a row of would-be paratroopers, point through the portholes with proprietary pride as Gaviotas comes into view. Suddenly an amoeba-shaped oasis of verdant forest fills the vista below, an oasis that covers 20,000 acres.

The cargo plane lands on a dirt strip on the edge of Gaviotas's forest, and commandos quickly set up an armed perimeter for their high-ranking entourage. A tractor tows bewildered visitors in a motorless carriage fashioned out of a Bogotá city bus while Lugari explains that the forest around them was planted by hand with a single species, Honduran pine. Over three decades the evergreens spawned—without human intervention—an ecosystem that now boasts more than 200 plant and animal species.

This reconstituted forest also feeds raw materials like pine resin to a handful of businesses in the village, a value-added economy in the outback that was initially built by selling inventions like the solar-powered hot water system. (The U.S. embassy in Colombia is a customer.) Gaviotas, which is administered by a nonprofit foundation, sinks all its surplus into its primary asset: those Honduran pines. The entourage halts to watch a team of five men in peasant garb, with the help of a biodiesel-fueled Ford tractor, trench and plant two rows of 50 pine shoots in two minutes flat.

The group passes one of Gaviotas's earliest inventions, a tall wind turbine. It powers a pump that funnels deep aquifer water to a commercial bottling plant, an open-air building with mosaic tiles that sits near the village's cinder-block school and residential complexes. There a group of women in their 20s and 30s wearing white work coats shyly greet Lugari, Pauli, and their guests. They tell Lugari about minor tweaks they've made to the plant since his last visit a few weeks ago. Pauli has brokered a deal with the Juan Valdez chain—Colombia's version of Starbucks—to exclusively distribute Gaviotas water, which is packaged with a playful utopian logo. Like other bottled waters, it's a high-margin business. The production cost is about 5 cents per unit; the retail price is about $1. After transportation costs and the retailer's markup, Gaviotas enjoys a gross 30 percent profit.

Margins this generous have allowed Gaviotas to fund a free municipal water system for the village, invest in new inventions like the remote-controlled zeppelin, and position the place as eastern Colombia's equivalent of the Googleplex. People fight for the chance to work here because the minimum wage is 50 percent higher than in the rest of the region. Tree planters here, for example, make about $400 per month and receive free food and housing. Gaviotas has no mayor, no police, no laws, no priests. "People use their conscience, not rules," Lugari boasts. "That's why we have creativity."

It wasn't always like this. When Lugari first scouted the site in the late 1960s, it was a wasteland. He was a freelance ecobuccaneer in his mid-20s, born into a wealthy Colombian family populated by government officials. He drove to the region with his brother in an open-top Land Rover, at one point hiring a barge made of logs and oil drums to get across a river. At the time, Lugari was obsessed with the global population explosion and convinced that the invention of sustainable technologies was all that lay between human civilization and denuded ruins like the savannas of Vichada.

He conned and cajoled professors and students at Colombian campuses to contribute work-study semesters to the establishment of the project he dubbed Gaviotas, after a seagull he spotted when he first visited the site. "About twice a month, candidates could find Lugari in a rented house in Bogota leaping up from his desk to pump their hands to listen and nod and assure them that they could be 'pioneer technicians in a vast tropical frontier," writes Alan Weisman in *Gaviotas: A Village to Reinvent the World*. "They later learned he meant that they would get a hammock, mosquito netting, food, and a share in the cooking duties. Usually, they didn't learn this until 500 kilometers of roadless [savanna] separated them from home."

Lugari acquired the land that makes up Gaviotas's holdings through the Colombian equivalent of squatter's rights. The law stated that raw, unused land in the wilds of Vichada could be yours for the taking as long as you lived on it and worked it for two years. (The government suspended the statute last year because opportunists began to stake speculative claims as rumors spread about the Gaviotas II megaproject.)

One of Lugari's first converts was Jorge Zapp, the head of mechanical engineering at one of Bogotá's major universities. By 1975, 10 families were living in thatched cottages at Gaviotas and Zapp had quit the university to work there full-time. Like other arid parts of the developing world, the community lacked access to potable water; the water table had sunk below the reach of conventional hand pumps. So Zapp and a group of students invented a double-action pump: The piston pumped water as it moved in both directions, not just one. Then, thanks to Mother Nature, they came up with a cheap power source to operate it automatically: the wind turbine that now pumps the water for the bottling plant.

Few of Gaviotas's inventions can be attributed to a single author. The wind turbine went through 57 prototypes in two years with input from visitors and residents who drifted into and out of the project. "These inventions came out of spontaneous, collective thinking," Lugari says. "We don't like prima donnas." He also doesn't like formal brainstorming sessions. In his vision, the mad scientists of Gaviotas would turn every working day into one continuous mind-meld. "At Gaviotas," he says, "creativity is at a peak because people live and think together all the time, just like the ancients in the small towns in Greece."

Another trick of Lugari's is to eliminate organizational charts and the hierarchy of professional and academic titles. Ideas from peasant workers, or campesinos, and other nonexperts receive the same consideration as those of specialists. It was this kind of democratic, open-source thinking that led to the discovery that made possible the reforestation of Vichada's stingy soil—a discovery that will also provide the ecological cornerstone of Gaviotas II.

When the community began its first experimental plantings with Honduran pines in the early 1980s, the needles of the trees quickly turned yellow. Lugari and his colleagues eventually realized that the missing ingredient was a mycorrhiza fungus that would allow the trees to absorb nutrients through their roots. They stumbled on soil samples containing the fungus while visiting farmers in Honduras. Without the fungus, Gaviotas wouldn't exist.

This horticultural breakthrough—unknown in the finest forestry labs and universities around the world—led indirectly to a commercial bonanza, thanks to a chance observation by a Gaviotas cook. She liked to take walks among the pines, and when she saw sap seeping from their bark, she reported that the "trees were weeping." An amateur astronomer who'd taken up residence at Gaviotas chimed in that he'd read how resin could be extracted from such trees and used in commercial products. His investigation of the chemistry of resin laid the foundation for the Gaviotas factory that now refines ingredients for paint and turpentine from the pine pitch, along with industrial coatings like colofonia. A for-profit subsidiary, it enjoys double-digit

---

Father of Invention

Paolo Lugari's 7 Secrets for Creating Creativity.

1. **Ban brainstorming meetings**. Creativity is spontaneous. Formal meetings are a poor forum for creation. People choke because they show up for a limited time with a narrow agenda. Turn every workday into a continuous, open-ended brainstorming session.

2. **Practice da Vinci's code**. When your organization tackles a problem or a project, wipe the board clean of all assumptions and prior knowledge. "Leonardo da Vinci expressed it best," Lugari says. "Step one is a tabula rasa."

3. **Play nice with others.** At Gaviotas, new technologies grow out of a process of tweaks and upgrades, with a variety of contributors adding their own nuts and bolts. "These inventions came out of spontaneous, collective thinking," Lugari says. "We don't like prima donnas."

4. **Burn the corporate policy manual.** To think freely, you have to act freely. A fanatical dedication to free speech—unencumbered by top-down prohibitions—has produced a Gaviotas mind-set in which unproductive behavior melts away of its own accord.

5. **Rule out "degree-itis"**. There is no hierarchy based on titles; a peasant worker gets the same hearing as a Ph.D. One of the most important revenue streams at Gaviotas—the production of industrial coatings and resins from pine pitch—evolved from an observation made by one of the cooks.

6. **Master the art of indiscipline.** Big breakthroughs are often the result of people crossing disciplines. Mendel was a priest before he was a biologist; the fuel cell was invented by a lawyer. So rotate your specialists out of their specialties and promote generalists ahead of narrowly focused experts.

7. **Trash your Outlook calendar.** Give up time-management tricks and devote each hour of every workday to whatever task or inspiration arises spontaneously. If you keep filling your week with scheduled meetings and tasks, you'll snuff out your creative sparks before they have a chance to fly.

---

margins and provides Gaviotas with 20 percent of its annual revenue.

The factory's main customers are manufacturers in Bogotá, and its chief competitors are colofonia producers in China. But Gaviotas created efficiencies in the operation that would be the envy of any supply-chain guru. During the past decade, Lugari and his team have cut production costs by 50 percent. One trick: replacing the diesel generator that powered the facility with a biomass turbine whose fuel source is pine prunings. The diesel engine cost $3 or more per gallon to feed; the new generator, next to nothing. Another cost-cutting discovery: Colofonia can be solidified and stored in cardboard boxes rather than the metal drums found in most factories. Cardboard is two-thirds cheaper. "Others just hadn't thought of it," says one of the workers at the plant, a peasant displaced from his home by conflicts between narcotics traffickers, the Army, and FARC. "It's fun for us to compete with China."

The official name of Gaviotas II—the megaproject that is poised to put Gaviotas on the world stage—is Marandua. It's an area of Vichada about an hour east by plane from the original village. Marandua is Pauli's baby. For this project, Lugari has assumed the role of chief scientist and promotional figurehead. He's in the military convoy today to show the VIPs test plantings of his latest passion, an oil-producing shrub called jatropha.

It was Pauli who dug up the research that Rockefeller Foundation scientists had done on jatropha in Africa and who later discovered that it could flourish in Vichada. Unlike palm, currently the craze in tropical biodiesel production, jatropha doesn't need irrigation and can be planted directly into the ground without a root bag. The oil in the fruit it bears within a year is equal in BTUs to palm oil. As a global-warming bonus, each jatropha plant sequesters the equivalent of 8 kilograms of CO_2 over 30 years. "You're producing bio-fuel at the same time as you're capturing significant volumes of carbon," Pauli says.

The convoy has reached the Tomo River, the banks of which resemble the jagged outline of the Grand Canyon, just as the temperature hits 110 degrees. While commandos machete mangos from a small grove, a couple of visitors scurry to cool their feet in the water—until Pauli warns them that it may be infested with piranhas. His vision for this seemingly inhospitable habitat is in sync with Colombian government policy. For more than two decades, the nation's political leaders have dreamed of opening up Vichada the way Brazil did its Amazon basin. They didn't know how to do it until Pauli and Lugari gave them their road map.

The plan is to start by reforesting 250,000 acres with pine trees and jatropha, employing 12,000 field workers and 300 managers over five years—all the while creating spinoff businesses in the Gaviotas tradition. The forest's aquifers would feed a series of water-bottling plants, and the jatropha would supply biodiesel. Eventually, the government plans to expand the project to 15.6 million acres, a step that would require 1 million workers and create an infrastructure that the government estimates would ultimately support a population of 5 million. It would also transform Colombia into a major exporter of biodiesel.

The jet-setting Pauli was Gaviotas I's biggest champion in international business circles, and he is now Gaviotas II's principal promoter. Over the past two years, he has run political traplines from Asia to Europe to arrange funding from abroad and created a commercial company called Marandua Inc. to manage it. The company is currently owned by Zero Emissions Research and Initiatives, a foundation headed by Pauli, but its stake will be distributed among a growing number of institutional investors, including JPMorgan's emerging markets division, which committed itself to the project last summer, as well as Colombian banks, the European Union, and the governments of Japan and Spain. A deal worth as much as $327 million has been approved by Alvaro Uribe, the president of Colombia, who has to guarantee the investors a long-term lease to federally owned land, and currently awaits lawyering.

According to Pauli, the project will generate returns on top of direct sales of water and fuel in at least two ways: Improvements to the land will increase its value from $1 per hectare to $3,000 within the first five years. And the sale of carbon credits could bring in more than $200 million during the next 25 years. Pauli says he stands to gain nothing personally from the project. He rolled his earlier ecoprofits into his foundation, which he runs out of Tokyo, and he juggles 50 other green projects around the world. "I'm a catalyst," he says. "Remove the obstacles, and get it going."

Pauli has brought a parade of bankers and bureaucrats to Marandua to show off the tranquil landscape and demonstrate in person how their investments would be secure. Thanks to the presence of Gaviotas, he argues, Vichada is free of drugs and violence, making it the one part of the country uncontaminated by guerrillas and cartels. "These inventions and projects have kept Vichada free of coca cultivation," Pauli says. "There are no more kidnappings, no killings, no human rights violations."

But Gaviotas II still faces some very real hurdles, as we soon learn. Back at the military base, the cargo plane that brought us here has sprung a hydraulic leak. As we wait for repairs, Lugari waxes on about the future. He's dreaming about model cities that will be built in Vichada 50 years from now. Independent of fossil fuel imports and the national electric grid, their populations would be limited to 10,000, he says, in the fashion of the cities in ancient Greece.

But a listener is distracted when the base's acting commander and a couple of aides rush off to deal with an urgent report. The neighboring DEA radar base, it turns out, has a hit. The FARC is up to no good on the Tomo River, just 18 miles away. The base dispatches jet fighters to lead an assault. Gaviotas may be an ecological Shangri-la, but this is still Colombia.

PAUL KAIHLA (pkaihla@business2.com) is a senior writer at Business 2.0.

A 'Test-Drive' Transfer of Power?

Fidel Castro's health crisis could mark the beginning of a long-planned transition in Cuba.

KAREN DEYOUNG AND MANUEL ROIG-FRANZIA

Cuban leader Fidel Castro's appointment of his younger brother, Raúl, to take over temporarily as president and head of the Communist Party marks the beginning of a long-planned transition designed to maintain iron-fisted control of the island after Fidel Castro's eventual death, administration and intelligence officials say.

"This is their transition plan out for a test drive, a dress rehearsal," one intelligence official said of the surprise announcement July 31 that the Cuban leader had undergone surgery for intestinal bleeding and had relinquished "provisional" power to his brother.

Neither Fidel Castro, whose 80th birthday is on Aug. 13, nor Raúl, 75, made public appearances in the immediate aftermath of the announcement. Meanwhile, the government moved to quell rumors reaching Havana last week from the jubilant Cuban American community in Miami that Fidel was on the verge of death or had died. Republican Sen. Mel Martinez of Florida, who fled Cuba as a young boy after Castro took over in 1959, said last week that "it's certainly possible he's not alive now."

But White House spokesman Tony Snow said the administration had "no reason to believe" Castro was dead. In a statement that was attributed to Castro and read on Cuban state television last Tuesday, the Cuban leader said he was in "stable condition" and "as for my spirits, I feel perfectly fine."

The closest to an official statement was delivered in an unlikely forum last Wednesday when Ricardo Alarcón, the Cuban National Assembly president, told NPR's "All Things Considered" that Castro would not return to power for "some weeks."

The Cuban Government has taken a harder line against the island's small opposition movement in recent years, most notably cracking down on dissidents and jailing dozens who have spoken out against Castro or the Communist system in the past.

The U.S. Coast Guard and Navy were preparing to block any effort by exiles to storm the island as uncertainty mounted over Castro's condition, according to Martinez, who said he had been briefed on the plans. He compared the situation to that of Spain during the protracted death throes in 1975 of dictator Francisco Franco, whose demise "sort of trickled out day after day."

The Cubans seem to have given some thought to ensuring their announcement projected calm and continuity, one intelligence official says.

The statement issued over Castro's signature late Monday said that hard work "with scarcely any sleep" last month had provoked "an intestinal crisis" requiring "complicated" surgery. He indicated the surgery had taken place and said he would be "resting for several weeks."

Administration officials noted that Castro delivered a two-hour, twenty-minute speech on July 26 and speculated he had suffered a sudden flare-up of an ulcer or diverticulitis. He has been in visibly declining health for some time and suffers from Parkinson's disease, according to the CIA.

It has long been assumed in Washington and Havana that Raúl would take his brother's place. Castro himself announced in early June that his brother was his chosen successor.

"This is an opportunity for them to see how this would work," said the intelligence official, who was not authorized to speak on the record. "They're looking at [their own] streets, neighborhoods and places beyond, seeing how people, foreign governments and Cuban Americans react."

Administration officials said they did not expect a change in President Bush's hard-line position of economic sanctions and limited contact with Cuba. In the absence of firm information out of Havana, they restricted their comments to repeating standing policy calling for democratic elections. Snow cautioned against what he called "questions that are premised on the death of somebody who is not dead."

A month ago, the administration released a 40-page report by the Commission for Assistance to a Free Cuba, with recommendations to hasten the end of Castro's government and assist a future transition to democracy. This year's report from the three-year-old presidential commission, now jointly headed by Secretary of State Condoleezza Rice and Commerce Secretary Carlos M. Gutierrez, pledged $80 million in new funding to aid opposition and democratic forces, including Miami-based broadcasts of Radio Marti, but it offered no new policy initiatives.

It warned of Castro's growing alliance with the populist government of Hugo Chávez, president of oil-rich Venezuela, which it called a "Castro-led axis" designed to insulate the Cuban regime from democratic and economic pressures and subvert existing Latin American democracies.

In comments reported last Tuesday by Prensa Latina, the Cuban government news service, Alarcón, the National Assembly President, said celebrations over Castro's supposed death by "mercenaries and terrorists" in Miami "make me vomit."

Alarcón, a longtime aide to the Cuban leader, said that "imperialism ignores the magnitude of Fidel Castro" and that Castro would always fight until "the last moment." But that moment, Alarcón said, "was still far away."

In addition to avoiding panic at home or abroad, the July 31 statement by Castro appeared to be designed to head off any suggestion of a power struggle in Havana. Powerful younger figures, including Foreign Minister Felipe Pérez Roque and economic policy chief Carlos Lage Dávila were instructed to continue work on Castro's priorities of health, education, and energy under Raúl Castro's leadership.

Raúl Castro already holds a variety of government and party titles, including defense minister, and is the commanding general of the Cuban armed forces. Although less public than his older brother, he already wielded great power behind the scenes. He has overseen Cuba's military since the beginning, his influence rising as he also gained control over the police force. He has recently begun overseeing tourism one of the island's greatest revenue generators—and placed his military allies in key positions throughout the government.

"There has been a kind of Raúl-ista transition in Cuba for some time," says Mark Falcoff, author of the book "Cuba, the Morning After." "From an institutional point of view, this transition is already fairly well advanced."

Raúl lacks his brother's public flair, but he is known as a deft consensus-builder who has developed a large cadre of loyal followers during the past four decades.

"He has the loyalty of the senior officer corps," says Brian Latell, a former CIA analyst and author of the book "After Fidel." "His leadership and management style are very different from his brother's. He earns loyalty and keeps it."

Raúl Castro has a "duality of personality," Latell said, "a harsh, brutal, cruel side and a lesser-known sympathetic and compassionate side. The question is which of the two emerges."

The larger question in the minds of many observers is what will happen if both Castro brothers leave the scene. Although five years younger than his brother, Raul, too, is widely believed to be in poor health.

ROIG-FRANZIA reported from Antigua, Guatemala.

Glossary of Terms and Abbreviations

Agrarian Relating to the land; the cultivation and ownership of land.

Amerindian A general term for any Indian from America.

Andean Pact (Cartagena Agreement) Established on October 16, 1969, to end trade barriers among member nations and to create a common market. Members: Bolivia, Colombia, Ecuador, Peru, and Venezuela.

Antilles A geographical region in the Caribbean made up of the Greater Antilles: Cuba, Hispaniola (Haiti and the Dominican Republic), Jamaica, the Cayman Islands, Puerto Rico, and the Virgin Islands; and the Lesser Antilles: Antigua and Barbuda, Dominica, St. Lucia, St. Vincent and the Grenadines, St. Kitts–Nevis, as well as various French departments and Dutch territories.

Araucanians An Indian people of south-central Chile and adjacent areas of Argentina.

Arawak An Indian people originally found on certain Caribbean islands, who now live chiefly along the coast of Guyana. Also, their language.

Aymara An Indian people and language of Bolivia and Peru.

Bicameral A government made up of two legislative branches.

CACM (Central American Common Market) Established on June 3, 1961, to form a common market in Central America. Members: Costa Rica, El Salvador, Guatemala, and Nicaragua.

Campesino A Spanish word meaning "peasant."

Caudillo Literally, "man on horseback." A term that has come to mean "leader."

Carib An Indian people and their language native to several islands in the Caribbean and some countries in Central America and South America.

CARICOM (Caribbean Community and Common Market) Established on August 1, 1973, to coordinate economic and foreign policies.

CDB (Caribbean Development Bank) Established on October 18, 1969, to promote economic growth and development of member countries in the Caribbean.

The Commonwealth (Originally the British Commonwealth of Nations) An association of nations and dependencies loosely joined by the common tie of having been part of the British Empire.

Compadrazgo The Mexican word meaning "cogodparenthood" or "sponsorship."

Compadres Literally, "friends"; but in Mexico, the term includes neighbors, relatives, fellow migrants, coworkers, and employers.

Contadora Process A Latin American intiative developed by Venezuela, Colombia, Panama, and Mexico to search for a negotiated solution that would secure borders and reduce the foreign military presence in Central America.

Contras A guerrilla army opposed to the Sandinista government of Nicaragua. They were armed and supplied by the United States.

Costeños Coastal dwellers in Central America.

Creole The term has several meanings: a native-born person of European descent or a person of mixed French and black or Spanish and black descent speaking a dialect of French or Spanish.

ECCA (Eastern Caribbean Currency Authority) A regional organization that monitors the integrity of the monetary unit for the area and sets policies for revaluation and devaluation.

ECLA (Economic Commission for Latin America) Established on February 28, 1948, to develop and strengthen economic relations among Latin American countries.

FAO (Food and Agricultural Organization of the United Nations) Established on October 16, 1945, to oversee good nutrition and agricultural development.

FSLN (Frente Sandinista de Liberación Nacionál) Organized in the early 1960s with the object of ousting the Somoza family from its control of Nicaragua. After 1979 it assumed control of the government. The election of Violeta Chamorro in 1990 marked the end of the FSLN.

FTAA (Free Trade Area of the Americas) An effort to integrate the economies of the Western Hemisphere into a single free trade arrangement.

GATT (General Agreement on Tariffs and Trade) Established on January 1, 1948, to provide international trade and tariff standards.

GDP (Gross Domestic Product) The value of production attributable to the factors of production in a given country, regardless of their ownership. GDP equals GNP minus the product of a country's residents originating in the rest of the world.

GNP (Gross National Product) The sum of the values of all goods and services produced by a country's residents in any given year.

Group of 77 Established in 1964 by 77 developing countries. It functions as a caucus on economic matters for the developing countries.

Guerrilla Any member of a small force of "irregular" soldiers. Generally, guerrilla forces are made up of volunteers who make surprise raids against the incumbent military or political force.

IADB (Inter-American Defense Board) Established in 1942 at Rio de Janeiro to coordinate the efforts of all American countries in World War II. It is now an advisory defense committee on problems of military cooperation for the OAS.

IADB (Inter-American Development Bank) Established in 1959 to help accelerate economic and social development in Latin America.

IBA (International Bauxite Association) Established in 1974 to promote orderly and rational development of the bauxite industry. Membership is worldwide, with a number of Latin American members.

IBRD (International Bank for Reconstruction and Development) Established on December 27, 1945, to make loans to governments at conventional rates of interest for high-priority productive projects. There are many Latin American members.

ICAO (International Civil Aviation Organization) Established on December 7, 1944, to develop techniques of international air navigation and to ensure safe and orderly growth of international civil aviation. Membership is worldwide, with many Latin American members.

ICO (International Coffee Organization) Established in August 1963 to maintain cooperation between coffee producers and to control the world market prices. Membership is worldwide, with a number of Latin American members.

IDA (International Development Association) Established on September 24, 1960, to promote better and more flexible financing arrangements; it supplements the World Bank's activities.

ILO (International Labor Organization) Established on April 11, 1919, to improve labor conditions and living standards through international action.

IMCO (Inter-Governmental Maritime Consultative Organization) Established in 1948 to provide cooperation among governments on technical matters of international merchant shipping as well as to set safety standards. Membership is worldwide, with more than a dozen Latin American members.

IMF (International Monetary Fund) Established on December 27, 1945 to promote international monetary cooperation.

IPU (Inter-Parliamentary Union) Established on June 30, 1889, as a forum for personal contacts between members of the world parliamentary governments. Membership is worldwide, with the following Latin American members: Argentina, Brazil, Colombia, Costa Rica, Haiti, Mexico, Nicaragua, Paraguay, and Venezuela.

ISO (International Sugar Organization) Established on January 1, 1969, to administer the international sugar agreement and to compile data on the industry. Membership is worldwide, with the following Latin American members: Argentina, Brazil, Colombia, Cuba, Ecuador, Mexico, Uruguay, and Venezuela.

ITU (International Telecommunications Union) Established on May 17, 1895, to develop international regulations for telegraph, telephone, and radio services.

Junta A Spanish word meaning "assembly" or "council"; the legislative body of a country.

Ladino A Westernized Spanish-speaking Latin American, often of mixed Spanish and Indian blood.

LAFTA (Latin American Free Trade Association) Established on June 2, 1961, with headquarters in Montevideo, Uruguay.

Machismo Manliness. The male sense of honor; connotes the showy power of a "knight in shining armor."

Marianismo The feminine counterpart of machismo; the sense of strength that comes from controlling the family and the male.

Mennonite A strict Protestant denomination that derived from a sixteenth-century religious movement.

Mercosur Comprised of Argentina, Brazil, Paraguay, and Uraguay, this southern common market is the world's fourth largest integrated market. It was established in 1991.

Mestizo The offspring of a Spaniard or Portuguese and an American Indian.

Mulatto A person of mixed Caucasian and black ancestry.

Nahuatl The language of an Amerindian people of southern Mexico and Central America who are descended from the Aztec.

NAFTA (North American Free Trade Agreement) Established in 1993 between Mexico, Canada, and the United States, NAFTA went into effect January 1, 1994.

NAM (Non-Aligned Movement) A group of nations that chose not to be politically or militarily associated with either the West or the former Communist Bloc.

OAS (Organization of American States) (Formerly the Pan American Union) Established on December 31, 1951, with headquarters in Washington, DC.

ODECA (Central American Defense Organization) Established on October 14, 1951, to strengthen bonds among the Central American countries and to promote their economic, social, and cultural development through cooperation. Members: Costa Rica, El Salvador, Guatemala, Honduras, and Nicaragua.

OECS (Organization of Eastern Caribbean States) A Caribbean organization established on June 18, 1981, and headquartered in Castries, St. Lucia.

PAHO (Pan American Health Organization) Established in 1902 to promote and coordinate Western Hemisphere efforts to combat disease. All Latin American countries are members.

Patois A dialect other than the standard or literary dialect, such as some of the languages used in the Caribbean that are offshoots of French.

Peon Historically, a person forced to work off a debt or to perform penal servitude. It has come to mean a member of the working class.

PRI (Institutional Revolutionary Party) The dominant political party in Mexico.

Quechua The language of the Inca. It is still widely spoken in Peru.

Rastafarian A religious sect in the West Indies whose members believe in the deity of Haile Selassie, the deposed emperor of Ethiopia who died in 1975.

Rio Pact (Inter-American Treaty of Reciprocal Assistance) Established in 1947 at the Rio Conference to set up a policy of joint defense of Western Hemisphere countries. In case of aggression against any American state, all member countries will come to its aid.

Sandinistas The popular name for the government of Nicaragua from 1979 to 1990, following the ouster of President Anastasio Somoza. The name derives from César Augusto Sandino, a Nicaraguan guerrilla fighter of the 1920s.

SELA (Latin American Economic System) Established on October 18, 1975, as an economic forum for all Latin American countries.

Suffrage The right to vote in political matters.

UN (United Nations) Established on June 26, 1945, through official approval of the charter by delegates of 50 nations at an international conference in San Francisco. The charter went into effect on October 24, 1945.

UNESCO (United Nations Educational, Scientific, and Cultural Organization) Established on November 4, 1946, to promote international collaboration in education, science, and culture.

Unicameral A political structure with a single legislative branch.

UPU (Universal Postal Union) Established on July 1, 1875, to promote cooperation in international postal services.

World Bank A closely integrated group of international institutions providing financial and technical assistance to developing countries.

Bibliography

SOURCES FOR STATISTICAL REPORTS

U.S. State Department, *Background Notes* (2000–2001).
The World Factbook (2001).
World Statistics in Brief (2001).
World Almanac (2001).
The Statesman's Yearbook (2001).
Demographic Yearbook (2001).
Statistical Yearbook (2001).
World Bank, World Development Report (2000–2001).

GENERAL WORKS

Mark A. Burkholder and Lyman L. Johnson, *Colonial Latin America*, 5th ed. (New York: Oxford University Press, 2004).
David Bushnell and Neill Macaulay, *The Emergence of Latin America in the Nineteenth Century*, 2nd ed. (New York: Oxford University Press, 1994).
Franklin W. Knight, *Race, Ethnicity and Class: Forging the Plural Society in Latin America and the Caribbean* (Waco, TX: Baylor University Press, 1998).
Thomas E. Skidmore and Peter Smith, *Modern Latin America*, 6th ed. (New York: Oxford University Press, 2004).
Barbara A. Tenenbaum, ed., *Encyclopedia of Latin American History*, 5 vols. (New York: Charles Scribner's Sons, 1996).
Claudio Veliz, *The Centralist Tradition of Latin America* (Princeton, NJ: Princeton University Press, 1980).

NATIONAL HISTORIES

The following studies provide keen insights into the particular characteristics of individual Latin American nations.

Argentina

Leslie Bethell, *Argentina Since Independence* (New York: Cambridge University Press, 1994).
Nicholas Shumway, *The Invention of Argentina* (Berkeley, CA: University of California Press, 1991).

Bolivia

Herbert S. Klein, *A Concise History of Bolivia* (New York: Cambridge University Press, 2003).

Brazil

Thomas Skidmore, *Brazil: Five Centuries of Change,* (New York: Oxford University Press, 1999).
Robert M. Levine, *The History of Brazil* (Greenwood, 2003).

Caribbean Nations

Franklin W. Knight and Teresita Martínez-Vergue, *Contemporary Caribbean Cultures in a Global Context,* (Chapel Hill: University of North Carolina Press, 2005).
Louis A. Perez Jr., *Cuba: Between Reform and Revolution,* 2nd ed. (New York: Oxford University Press, 1995).

Central America

Ralph Lee Woodward Jr., *Central America: A Nation Divided,* ed. (New York: Oxford University Press, 1999).

Ralph Lee Woodward, Jr., *A Short History of Guatemala* (Editorial Laura Lee: 2005).

Chile

Brian Loveman, *Chile: The Legacy of Hispanic Capitalism,* 3rd ed. (New York: Oxford University Press, 2001).

Colombia

Frank Safford, Macro Palacios, *Colombia: Fragmented Land, Divided Society,* (New York: Oxford University Press, 2001).

Mexico

Michael C. Meyer and William L. Sherman, *The Course of Mexican History,* 7th ed. (New York: Oxford University Press, 2003).
Eric Wolf, *Sons of the Shaking Earth: The Peoples of Mexico and Guatemala; Their Land, History, and Culture* (Chicago: University of Chicago Press, 1970).
Ricardo Pozas Arciniega, *Juan Chamula: An Ethnological Recreation of the Life of a Mexican Indian* (Berkeley, CA: University of California Press, 1962).

Peru

Peter Klaren, *Peru: Society and Nationhood in the Andes,* (New York: Oxford University Press, 1999).
David P. Werlich, *Peru: A Short History* (Carbondale, IL: Southern Illinois University Press, 1978).

Venezuela

H. Michael Tarver and Julia C. Frederick, *The History of Venezuela* (Palgrave: 2006).

NOVELS IN TRANSLATION

The Latin American novel is perhaps one of the best windows on the cultures of the region. The following are just a few of many highly recommended novels.
Jorge Amado, *Clove and Cinnamon* (Avon, 1991).
Manlio Argueta, *One Day of Life* (Vintage, 1991).
Miguel Ángel Asturias, *The President* (Prospect Heights, Il: Waveland Press, 1997).
Mariano Azuela, *The Underdogs* (New World Library, 2004).
Alejo Carpentier, *Reasons of State* (Writers & Readers, 1981).
Carlos Fuentes, *The Death of Artemio Cruz* (FS&G, 1991).
Jorge Icaza, *Huasipungo: The Villagers* (Arcturus Books, 1973).
Gabriel García Márquez, *One Hundred Years of Solitude* (Harper, 1998).
Mario Vargas Llosa, *The Green House* (FS&G, 1985).
Victor Montejo, *Testimony: Death of a Guatemalan Village* (Curbstone Press, 1987).
Rachel de Queiroz, *The Three Marias* (University of Texas Press, 1991).
Graham Greene's novels about Latin America, such as *The Comedians* (NY: Penguin, 1966), and *The Power and the Glory* (NY: Penguin, 2003), and V. S. Naipaul's study of Trinidad, *The Loss of El Dorado: A History* (NY: Vintage, 1993), offer profound insights into the region.

Index

Index

Index

GLOBAL STUDIES

LATIN AMERICA

THIRTEENTH EDITION   **PAUL B. GOODWIN**

Global Studies: Latin America, Thirteenth Edition, is one in a unique series of volumes that provides readers with concise background information and current world press articles on the regions and countries of the world.

Included in this edition are background essays on Mexico, Central America, South America, and the Caribbean region, with concise reports and current statistics for each of the independent countries within these regions. In addition, a wide selection of carefully selected articles from newspapers and magazines from around the world are reprinted in this volume.

The complexity and interrelationship of today's global society demand an understanding of other countries and other people. *Global Studies: Latin America, Thirteenth Edition,* and other volumes in the *Global Studies* series are designed to provide a starting point for fostering this essential international understanding.

VOLUMES IN THE GLOBAL STUDIES SERIES

Global Studies: Africa
Global Studies: China
Global Studies: Europe
Global Studies: India and South Asia
Global Studies: Islam and the Muslim World
Global Studies: Japan and the Pacific Rim
Global Studies: Latin America
Global Studies: The Middle East
Global Studies: Russia, the Eurasian Republics, and
Central/Eastern Europe
Global Studies: The World at a Glance

Visit us on the Internet:
http://www.mhcls.com

ISBN 978-0-07-337982-1
MHID 0-07-337982-4

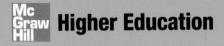

The McGraw-Hill Companies

McGraw Hill **Higher Education**

90000

9 780073 379821

www.mhhe.com